AF541791

THE JESUITS AND THE GREAT MOGUL

[*From Mr. Chester Beatty's Collection*

Frontispiece]

THE FIRST JESUIT MISSION

Arguing before Akbar, by Narsingh

(See p. 158)

THE JESUITS AND THE GREAT MOGUL

SIR EDWARD MACLAGAN

MANOHAR
2026

First published 1932
Reprinted 2021, 2023, 2025, 2026

ISBN 978-93-90729-78-4

Published by
Ajay Kumar Jain *for*
Manohar Publishers & Distributors
4753/23 Ansari Road, Daryaganj
New Delhi 110 002

Printed at
Replika Press Pvt. Ltd.

CONTENTS

INTRODUCTION

CHAPTER I

SOURCES OF INFORMATION

CONTENTS

CHAPTER II

THE FIRST MISSION TO AKBAR, 1580–1583

CHAPTER III

THE SECOND MISSION TO AKBAR, 1591

CHAPTER IV

THE THIRD MISSION TO AKBAR, 1595–1605

CHAPTER V

JAHANGIR, 1605–1627

CHAPTER VI

SHAH JAHAN, 1627–1658

CHAPTER VII

THE LATER MOGULS, 1658–1803

CHAPTER VIII

THE WORKS OF FATHER MONSERRATE, 1536–1600

CHAPTER IX

AKBAR'S CHRISTIAN WIFE

CONTENTS

CHAPTER X

THE INDIAN BOURBONS

CHAPTER XI

MIRZA ZU'LQARNAIN (1592–1656)

(A CHRISTIAN OFFICIAL IN THE MOGUL GOVERNMENT)

CHAPTER XII

DONNA JULIANA DIAZ DA COSTA (D. 1734)

(A CHRISTIAN LADY AT THE MOGUL COURT)

CONTENTS

CHAPTER XIII

CULTURE AND LANGUAGE

CHAPTER XIV

THE PERSIAN WORKS OF FATHER JEROME XAVIER

CONTENTS

CHAPTER XV

THE MISSIONS AND MOGUL PAINTING

CHAPTER XVI

THE CONGREGATIONS

CHAPTER XVII

CHURCHES AND RESIDENCES

CONTENTS

CHAPTER XVIII

CEMETERIES

CHAPTER XIX

THE TIBETAN MISSION—TSAPARANG

CONTENTS

APPENDICES

LIST OF ILLUSTRATIONS

MAPS

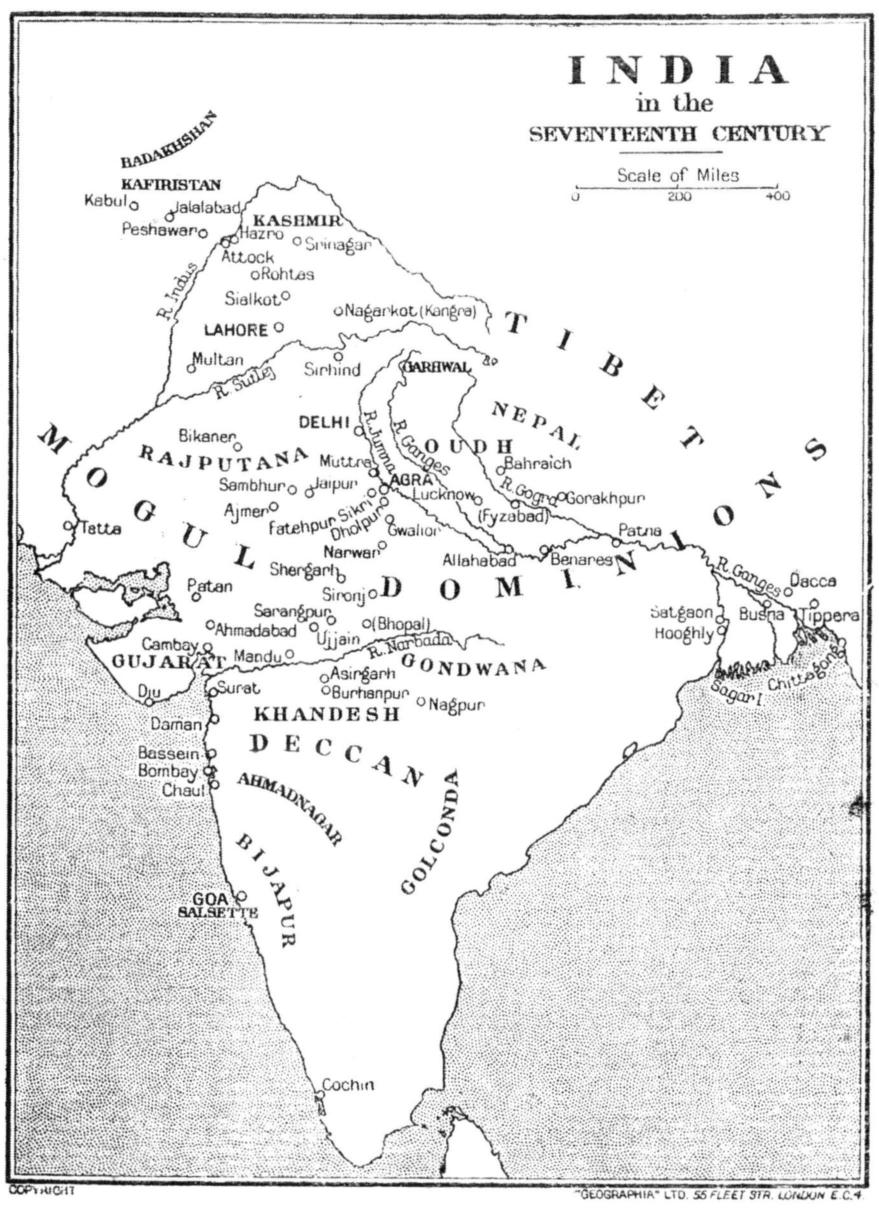
INDIA
in the
SEVENTEENTH CENTURY
Scale of Miles
0
200
400
BADAKHSHAN
KAFIRISTAN
Kabul
Jalalabad
Peshawar
KASHMIR
Hazro
Srinagar
Attock
Rohtas
R. Indus
Sialkot
Nagarkot (Kangra)
LAHORE
TIBETS
Multan
Sirhind
GARHWAL
R. Sutlej
NEPAL
DELHI
R. Jumna
R. Ganges
OUDH
Bikaner
RAJPUTANA
Muttra
Bahraich
AGRA
Sambhur
Jaipur
Lucknow
R. Gogra
Gorakhpur
Ajmer
Fatehpur Sikri
Dholpur
(Fyzabad)
Tatta
Gwalior
Patna
MOGUL DOMINIONS
Narwar
Allahabad
Benares
Shergarh
R. Ganges
Dacca
Patan
Sironj
Sarangpur
Satgaon
Busna
Tippera
Ahmadabad
(Bhopal)
Hooghly
Ujjain
Cambay
R. Narbada
GUJARAT
Mandu
GONDWANA
Asirgarh
Chittagong
Diu
Surat
Burhanpur
Nagpur
Sagar I
KHANDESH
Daman
DECCAN
Bassein
Bombay
Chaul
AHMADNAGAR
GOLCONDA
BIJAPUR
GOA
SALSETTE
Cochin
COPYRIGHT
"GEOGRAPHIA" LTD. 55 FLEET STR. LONDON E.C.4.

INTRODUCTION

DURING the first half of the sixteenth century the Indian peninsula experienced the intrusion of two vigorous foreign elements.

In 1510 the Island of Goa was occupied by the Portuguese, under Albuquerque, and in a short time the Portuguese power was established on part of the adjoining mainland and at several points upon the coast. The dominion of the Portuguese was marked by two main characteristics. They secured at an early date an almost undisputed control of the Indian seas. And they adopted a frankly proselytising policy, employing both force and persuasion to obtain the conversion of the neighbouring peoples to Christianity.

The Portuguese and the Moguls

Sixteen years after the occupation of Goa by the Portuguese, the north of India was invaded by an army from Afghānistān and Central Asia, manned by foreigners and led by the Turk, Bābur, who founded the dynasty known as that of the Moguls. The invaders, though professing the same religion as that of the dominant Muslim powers which they supplanted, differed from the bulk of the Indian population in tradition, in manners and in complexion almost as much as did the Portuguese.[1] They were not long in recognising that it was out of the question to contemplate the substitution of Islām for Hinduism throughout their dominions in Northern India, and as soon as the Mogul conquest became consolidated under the celebrated Akbar (1556–1605) a prominent problem of Mogul politics was to secure the elimination or equipoise of the racial, cultural and religious differences between the Muslims and the Hindu inhabitants of the country.

To the ordinary European of the period, the tract which we now speak of as India, so far as it lay within his purview, was reckoned as falling into two main political divisions; namely, 'India'—the seaboard tract where Portuguese influence prevailed—and 'Mogor'—the area governed by the Moguls. Several decades elapsed before the Mogul power in the north came into contact with the Portuguese authority in the south, but when the contact was established, the enquiring mind of the Mogul Ruler, distracted between Islām and Hinduism, took notice of the religion of the Portuguese, and the ardent proselytism of the Portuguese responded through the agency of the Society of Jesus.

The Society of Jesus

This Society had been established in Europe in 1539 by S. Ignatius of Loyola, and it gained its first hold on India with the arrival in 1542 of S. Francis Xavier. The Society of the Jesuits had a double mission, which comprehended on the one hand an unrelenting struggle against the forces of the Reformation in Europe and on the other an absorbing anxiety for the establishment of the true Faith in non-Christian countries. In India it was by no means the only Order interested in missionary effort, but the zeal and ability of its members, inspired by the youthful energy of its wonderful organization, soon gave it a predominant position in the field. The great adventure of evangelizing the Mogul Empire fell naturally in the first place to the Jesuits, and the story of their efforts, from their earliest mission in 1580 to their eventual disappearance in 1803, is the subject of the following pages.

Scope of this work

The authorities on which the story of the Jesuit Missions to 'Mogor' is based provide us also with much information which is of interest in connection with the general history of India. In this book, however, no effort is made to rewrite general history with the help of this information, and nothing further is attempted than to give in outline an account of the Jesuit connection with the Mogul Empire. Even in respect of the Jesuit activities, the work done by the Society in the outlying areas of the Mogul dominions, such as Bengal or Gujarāt, which were not under the control of the Jesuit Mission to Mogor, has been but lightly touched on, and the Jesuit efforts in Tibet, which, although to some extent controlled by the Mogor mission, were displayed in absolutely different surroundings, have been summarized in a separate chapter apart from the main narrative. It is recognized that even within these limits the whole field of information has not been tapped and that the account given below is necessarily subject to this and other imperfections, but it is hoped that by putting together for the first time the substance of the existing information now scattered through numerous publications, many of which are difficult of access, a basis will have been provided upon which future investigators may be able to construct a more faithful picture of the remarkable episode of the 'Mogor Mission.' Before entering on the story itself, however, it seems advisable to indicate what our existing sources of information are, and the first few pages below are accordingly devoted to this subject. These are succeeded by a brief history of the Mission from its first inception under

Akbar to its close in 1803. And then follows a series of chapters dealing with special incidents, personalities or features of the Mission, including a final chapter on the subsidiary, but fascinating, subject of the efforts of the Mission to evangelize Tibet.

An apology is perhaps due to readers of the following sketch for the frequency with which they are confronted with the authorities on which the narrative is based. This feature of the book is due to the fact that the work represents the first attempt to deal comprehensively with the episode which it commemorates; but it is also hoped that by keeping in touch with the original documents something may be gained towards realizing the spirit of the times and localities with which the narrative is concerned.

The large degree to which the book is based on the labours and the kindnesses of Father Hosten, S.J., of Darjeeling is acknowledged in the work itself and is apparent throughout its pages. I am much indebted also for expert assistance ungrudgingly given by Mr. C. J. Payne, to whose works frequent allusion is made in the book, and for kind help received from the late Sir Thomas Arnold, and from Father H. J. Thurston, S.J., Mr. A. G. Ellis, Mr. J. V. S. Wilkinson, Sir Filippo de Filippi and Sir E. Denison Ross.

[1] So much was this the case that European travellers in the seventeenth century were obsessed with the conviction that the word 'Mogul' meant 'white.' 'The word Mogoll in their language,' writes Coverte, 'is as much as to say the great white King' (A true and almost incredible report, London, 1612, p. 39), and the Sieur de la Boullaye-le-Gouz writing in 1653 says: 'Mogol est un terme des Indes qui signifie blanc' (*Voyages et Observations*, 1653, pp. 127, 132, 531). In 1611 the Englishman, Finch, speaks of the city of Lahore as occupied for the most part by Banyans or Hindu traders; 'all white men of note' (by which he apparently means Moguls and other Central Asians), 'lying in the suburbs.' Freyre, writing as late as 1678, says that the Moguls even then differed little from Europeans either in features or in complexion (Annual letter, 1670–1678).

THE JESUITS AND THE GREAT MOGUL

CHAPTER I

SOURCES OF INFORMATION

Libros, maxime autem membranas. (2 Tim. iv, 13.)

THE fact that the Jesuits maintained a mission in the Mogul Empire between 1580 and 1803 has always been known to those interested in the history of Northern India: but the amount of attention bestowed on the subject during the nineteenth century was scanty. An account of the Mission to Akbar is to be found in Hugh Murray's *Historical Account of Discoveries and Travels in Asia* which was published in Edinburgh in 1820, but it is brief and is disfigured by some unfortunate misprints of dates.[1] So also is the Rev. James Hough's *History of Christianity in India*, published in London in 1839.[2] The *Geschichte der Katholischen Missionen in Ostindien*, by Max Müllbauer, which was published at Freiburg im Breisgau in 1852, gives a wider view of the subject based largely on the earlier Jesuit histories of Indian missionary effort, but this work although a useful and careful compilation is still incomplete.[3] A further effort, directed however to a portion only of the field, was made by Prince Frederick of Schleswig-Holstein (Count von Noer), the two volumes of whose *Kaiser Akbar* were published in 1880 and 1885 respectively. His book gave an admirable account of the Mission in the time of Akbar, based on the Jesuit Chronicler du Jarric, but the account is deficient owing to his having failed to see the last volume of du Jarric's history and owing to the fact that the second volume of the Prince's work was published after his death without due recension.

Accounts published in the nineteenth century

Towards the end of the last century two further efforts were made to explore a part of the field by reference to the original authorities.

The first of the Jesuit missionaries, Father Rudolf Aquaviva, was beatified by the Church in 1893 and the attention thus drawn to him found expression in accounts of his life published in that year by Father Suau at Lille and Father Angelini at Rome.[4] These were followed in 1897 by a useful work on *The First Christian Mission to the Great Mogul*, published in Dublin by Father Francis Goldie, S.J. This book contained the results of some diligent research and copies and translations of several original documents: but so far as the Mogul Missions were concerned its scope was confined to the events of the years 1580–1583.

Meanwhile some notes on the leanings of the Mogul Emperor Akbar towards Christianity had been made by General R. Maclagan, and on his death in 1894 these notes came into my hands. With their help I explored the history of the Jesuit Missions during the reign of Akbar and in 1896 I published in the *Journal of the Asiatic Society of Bengal* a paper giving such information as was accessible to me on the subject. This paper gave a résumé of the authorities available and published translations of a certain number of original documents which had hitherto not seen the light. It dealt with the most important portion of the history of the Mission, but it did not profess to bring that history later than 1605, the date of the death of Akbar.

Since the publication of that paper much has been done not only to increase our knowledge of the period covered by it, but also to extend our information regarding the subsequent history of the Mission down to 1803. The protagonist in the exploration of these fields has been Father H. Hosten, a Belgian member of the Society of Jesus, who has worked for many years at Calcutta and Darjeeling. From the year 1907 to the present day he has devoted himself with unremitting labour to the study of every source of information connected with the history of the Jesuit Mission in Northern India. His most marked achievement was the discovery and the publication in 1914 of the lost *Commentary* of Father Monserrate, a member of the first Mission to the Court of Akbar; but this is only one among many services rendered by him towards the elucidation of this aspect of Indian history. The details of the Mission have received his attention in a large number of articles and he has put together in monographs much information regarding special features of its history. He has not

Investigations of Father Hosten, S.J.

only himself examined carefully the older printed records and traced and accumulated copies of many manuscript authorities : but has also been at pains to reproduce many of these in the original language or in English, or both, for the benefit of scholars interested in the subject. His contributions are, however, scattered through a number of periodicals which are not always easily accessible in Europe—in the *Journal*, for instance, of the Asiatic Society of Bengal,[5] in *Bengal Past and Present*, in the *Journals of the Punjab* and *United Provinces Historical Societies*, in *The Catholic Herald of India*, in *The Examiner*, Bombay, and other similar journals published in India—and have never been set forth in any connected form.[6] Father Hosten himself has other duties and is immersed also in other historical studies, so that he has not felt himself in a position to put together the results of his labours. He has, however, been good enough to give me access to a number of his scattered papers and I have, with his permission, attempted to compile from these and other sources an abstract of our existing information on the Jesuit Missions in the Mogul Empire. Although the Father is in no way responsible for the contents of this book, the chapters below, so far as they do not reproduce information already available in 1896, are very largely based on Father Hosten's various publications. The information thus made available has been supplemented by a number of transcripts of manuscripts and copies of other documents which Father Hosten has from time to time prepared with immense diligence and ungrudgingly placed at the disposal of the present writer.

And of other enquirers

It may be noted that Father Hosten has not been alone in his investigations. Certain aspects of the subject have been taken up by other Catholic priests ; by Father Felix, O.C., for instance, at Lahore, by the late Father J. B. Van Meurs, S.J., by the late Father Noti, S.J., of Bombay, and latterly by Father H. Heras, S.J., also of Bombay.[7] The contact of the Jesuit annals with the accounts of Indian historians had received attention, commencing as early as 1888, from the veteran Mr. H. Beveridge, and the immense value of the Jesuit records in supplementing the data given by the Indian histories was for the first time recognized by Mr. V. A. Smith, in his *Akbar the Great Mogul*, published in 1917.[8]

Indian sources

The purely Indian sources of information are, as might be expected, somewhat sparse, but so far as they go they are individually of considerable value. They are of three kinds.

In the first place there are the histories and other books written in the Persian language. For the period of Akbar's reign we have the advantage of possessing the works of two contemporary historians, both interested in the Jesuit activities, but each regarding them from a different point of view. On the one hand we have 'Abdul-qādir Badāonī, the trenchant champion of orthodoxy at Akbar's Court, whose Muntakhabu-t-tawārīkh carries the history of Akbar down to the year 1595,[9] and on the other hand there is Akbar's abettor and favourite minister Abu'-l-fazl, the author of the Akbarnāma, which contains a history of the same period down to 1602. For later reigns we have practically no Indian records dealing with the Missions, but in a strange work called the *Dābistān-ul-Mazāhib*, which was written about sixty years after Akbar's death, there are reproductions (how exact we cannot tell) of a discussion which is said to have taken place before Akbar between a Nazarene and a Muslim, and of another between a Nazarene and a Jew.

(i) Histories

We have also a certain number of papers which may be described as royal warrants and title-deeds issued to the Jesuits from time to time by the Mogul authorities, some of which have been preserved in the archives of the Cathedral at Agra. Fourteen of these documents, ranging in date from 1598 to 1774, were admirably reproduced and translated in a paper published by Father Felix, O.C., in 1916, in the *Journal of the Punjab Historical Society*, and they form excellent first-hand evidence of certain details in the history of the Mission. There are also some Persian documents presented to or by the Fathers which are preserved in original or in translation in the British Museum.[10]

(ii) Warrants and title-deeds

And we have, thirdly, the inscriptions on the graves of the Fathers and others who are buried in the Christian cemeteries at Agra. These inscriptions have been several times reproduced,[11] but they can best be traced in the valuable *List of Christian Tombs and Monuments of the United Provinces*, issued at Allahabad in 1911, by Mr. E. A. H. Blunt.

(iii) Inscriptions on tombs

Information from published European authorities has two main sources, namely the remarks recorded by contemporary travellers and the more systematic treatises compiled by the Jesuits themselves and other writers.

European publications.

Accounts by travellers

There is a good deal of valuable information in the records of European travellers, but as a rule it is of a scattered nature and it is, as one might expect, of varying degrees of credibility. Of those who travelled in India in the seventeenth and eighteenth centuries, few traversed the Mogul dominions, and of those who did so a certain number only were sufficiently interested in the Jesuits to make mention of them. Out of all those whose observations have come down to us, it is unnecessary to mention here more than five: an Englishman, a Portuguese, a Frenchman, an Italian and a Dutchman. We

Roe

have in the first place the Englishman Sir Thomas Roe, who was at the Mogul Court from 1615 to 1618, as ambassador for James I, and had there much intercourse, both friendly and otherwise, with the Jesuit Fathers.[12] Then there is

Manrique

Fra Sebastian Manrique, an Augustinian friar from Oporto who was deputed in 1640–1641 to intercede with the Mogul authorities on behalf of Father Antonio, one of the captives taken by the Moguls after the seizure of Hūglī in 1632, and who received attention and help from the Jesuit Fathers at Agra and Lahore.[13] Our third authority of this type

Bernier

is the admirable François Bernier, the French physician, who maintained an intimate acquaintance with the Mogul Court and dominions during the years 1659 to 1667, and has left a most interesting appreciation of the work done by the Jesuit missions in the Mogul territory.[14] A further, but less reliable and more discursive, authority is the Italian

Manucci

Manucci, who spent many of the years between 1656 and the end of the century in the Mogul country, making his living as a quack doctor and in other ways which brought him into contact with all classes from the Court downwards, including the Indian Christian population and its Jesuit

Valentyn

pastors.[15] And lastly there is the Dutch writer Valentyn who, in his *Oud- en Nieuw Oost-Indiën*, published in Amsterdam and Dordrecht in 1726, gives a History of the Great Moguls, including a reproduction of a valuable first-hand account of the reception in 1711–1712 at Lahore of a Dutch Embassy under John Joshua Ketelaar and its kind treatment by a Christian lady at Court who was a special patron of the Jesuit Fathers.[16] In one way or another these five authorities —and in a minor degree the other travellers of all nations who penetrated to the Mogul dominions—serve to give us useful outside glimpses of the Mission, checking as they do and supplementing the other information for which we are mainly dependent on the Jesuits themselves.

Jesuit histories

Of the Jesuit authorities the most systematic are the general histories compiled at various times to recount the development of the Society and of its Missions. These histories were written by learned Jesuits in

Europe who had access to first-hand authorities, and they were compiled with considerable skill and fidelity. The chief of the histories bearing on our present subject are as follows : (i) Our earliest history of the Missions is the *Historia de las Missiones que han hecho los religiosos de la compañia de Iesus para predicar el Sancto Evangelio en la India Oriental y en los Reynos de la China y Iapon*, published in two volumes at Alcala in 1601. It was written in Spanish by Father Luys de *Guzman*, S.J., Rector of the College of Toledo, and its contents are stated in the Preface to be based on (*a*) published works, (*b*) letters from the Fathers and (*c*) personal enquiries. Chapters 26–40 of Book III (pp. 240–273 of Volume I) relate to the Mogor Mission and bring the story up to the year 1599. An edition in one volume was printed at Bilbao in 1891, of which pages 140–156 reproduce the part relating to Mogor. This history constitutes an excellent authority.

Guzman

(ii) Father Fernam *Guerreiro*, S.J., of Almodovar, in Portugal, published a work which is for practical purposes a continuation of Guzman's history and which is, like that work, an authority of high importance. The first volume bears the title : *Relaçam annual das cousas que fizeram os Padres da Companhia de Jesus na India e Iapão nos annos de* 600 *e* 601 . . . *Tirada das cartas gẽraes que de lá vierão.* Guerreiro's work covered the period from 1600 to 1608 and was published in five volumes[17] which issued (with slightly differing titles) in different years, viz :

Guerreiro

(i) For 1600–1601 at Evora in 1603 (pp. 7–33 relate to Mogor).
(ii) For 1602–1603 at Lisbon in 1605 (Bk. ii, pp. 50–61, relate to Mogor and pp. 61–65 to Cathay).
(iii) For 1604–1605 at Lisbon in 1607 (pp. 98–100 relate to Bengal).
(iv) For 1606–1607 at Lisbon in 1609 (pp. 139–162 relate to Mogor and pp. 162–167 to Cathay).
(v) For 1607–1608 at Lisbon in 1611 (pp. 6–22 relate to Mogor and pp. 23–27 to Cathay).

The book is a rare one, but copies of all five volumes are in the British Museum. A copy of the volume for 1602–1603 is in the All Souls' Library at Oxford, and there are copies of some of the volumes in S. Mary's College, Kurseong, and the Goethals Library, Calcutta. A translation of the first volume in Spanish by Father Antonio Colaço, S.J., published at Valladolid in 1604, is in the British Museum and in the All Souls' Library (pp. 14–82 deal with Mogor), and a Spanish translation of the last volume by D. Suarez de Figueroa, dated 1614, is also known.[18] The last volume was published in German in 1614 as *Indianische Newe Relation.*[19] A new edition of Guerreiro's work in three volumes is being issued from the University Press at Coimbra, and the first volume containing Parts I and II of the *Relaçam* was published in 1930. Portions of the passages relating to the Mogul Empire have been published in English in Indian periodicals[20] and an excellent translation of the parts relating to the reign of Jahāngīr has recently been published (with notes) by Mr. C. H. Payne.[21]

Du Jarric

(iii) A better known and somewhat more accessible authority is Father Pierre *du Jarric* of Toulouse, who in 1608 published at Bordeaux a work entitled : *Histoire des choses plus memorables advenues tant ez Indes Orientales, que autres païs de la descouverte des Portugais, en l'establissement et progrez de la foy Chrestienne et Catholique ; et principalement de ce que les Religieux de la Compagnie de Iésus y ont faict et enduré pour la mesme fin ; depuis qu'ils y sont entrez jusques à l'an* 1600. Two further volumes appeared in 1610 and 1614, bringing the narrative up to the year 1609. In 1611 a new edition of the second volume appeared at Arras (and was reprinted in 1628) under the title *Nouvelle Histoire des choses*, etc., and this volume was also published in 1611 at Valenciennes. A Latin translation of the entire work by Martinez was published at Cologne in 1615 and entitled *Thesaurus Rerum Indicarum.* Copies of the Histoire are to be found in the British Museum, and the first volume of the Bordeaux edition is in the Bodleian Library at Oxford. Copies of the Thesaurus, though not easy to procure, are less uncommon. The Thesaurus, which is the authority ordinarily quoted, is said to be on the whole a faithful translation, but it is not free from inaccuracies.[22] Pages 492–580 of the second volume of the Thesaurus deal with the Mogul Empire down to 1600, and pages 38–226 of the third volume bring the narrative on to the year 1609. The only translation of these portions of du Jarric into English is that published with valuable notes in 1926 by Mr. C. H. Payne under the title of *Akbar and the Jesuits.* This covers the period down to the death of Akbar (1605), representing pages 429–493 of the second volume and pages 27–97 of the third volume of the original Bordeaux edition. The remaining portion of the Histoire relating to the Mogul Mission (vol. III, pp. 97–162) has never been translated.

Du Jarric's work taken as a whole is not original. He began by translating *Guzman's Historia*, and finding omissions and difficulties wrote to him but got no answer, Guzman having died about that time. He thereupon addressed Guerreiro at Lisbon, who had written some books in Portuguese on things which had happened since 1599, and received from him an obliging reply together with some books, among which were notes on Guzman's history by P. Albert Laertius, an Italian who was Provincial of India at the time. Speaking generally du Jarric's narrative up to the year 1599 is a translation of *Guzman's Historia* and from 1599 to 1609 is a translation of *Guerreiro's Relaçam*, but slight liberties have been taken with these authorities and other matter such as original letters from missionaries has also been utilized. Mr. Payne, who has carefully studied du Jarric's work, writes: ' I have compared the chapters relating to the Mogul Empire with the corresponding portions of the Historia of Guzman and the Relaçam of Guerreiro and with such others of the Jesuit writings used in their composition as I have had an opportunity of consulting; and in every case I have found that Du Jarric used his authorities with fidelity, either literally translating or carefully summarizing. Except for an occasional reflection or moral "aside," he never obtrudes himself on his readers. Errors of translation are here and there to be met with, but in a work covering close on two thousand five hundred quarto pages, compiled from materials written in at least four different languages and available in many cases only in manuscript form, our wonder is, not that Du Jarric made errors, but that he made so few.'

Bartoli

(iv) For the history of the first mission (1580–1583) a compilation of considerable value is a book published at Rome in 1663 by the voluminous Jesuit writer Father Daniel *Bartoli*—' quel terribile e stupendo Bartoli ' as one of his editors calls him—under the title *Missione al gran Mogor del P. Ridolfo Aquaviva della Compania de Gesù*; of which fresh editions issued at Milan in 1664, at Rome in 1667 (when it appeared as an ' accretion ' to the writer's *History of the Jesuits in Asia*) and at Bologna in 1672. A reprint of this work was published in 1714 by Salvioni at Rome, which has the merit of being well printed and of having at the commencement a long list of authorities on the life of Father Rudolf Aquaviva. A further reprint (of which there is a copy at the India Office) was issued at Piacenza in 1819 and is a handy book, but it does not contain the list of authorities given in the edition of 1714.

De Sousa

(v) Another authority for the earliest years of the Mission is Father Francis *de Sousa*, S.J., who in 1710 published at Lisbon an account in Portuguese of the Missions carried on in the Province of Goa between 1564 and 1585. His book is called *Oriente conquistado a Jesu Christo pelos padres da companhia de Jesus da provincia de Goa.* The work was reprinted in Bombay in 1888. Pages 146–172 (paras. 43–63) of the second volume of the original edition deal with the first Mission to Akbar (1580–1583), and a translation of these pages was published by Father Hosten in *The Examiner*, Bombay, in 1920.[23]

In the introduction to the second volume of the original Lisbon edition, the writer gives as his authorities : (*a*) a manuscript 'Chronica' of Father Sebastião Gonzalves of Ponte de Lima who was at Goa in 1593 ;[24] (*b*) the works of Daniel Bartoli mentioned above ; and (*c*) other documents of 'our secretariat at Goa, which are mentioned when referred to, that the truth may appear the better.' The narration includes information which is not in any of the previously published accounts of the Mission.

Historia Societatis

(vi) Of the general histories of the Society, the best known is probably the enormous official *Historia Societatis Jesu*, brought out at various times from 1615 to 1859 and dealing with events from 1540 to 1632. The idea of a general history of the Society started with the General Claud Aquaviva in 1598, and under his orders the heads of the Provinces of the Society were ordered to provide material. The classification of the material was commenced by Father Orlandini, and on his death in 1606 was continued by Father Sacchini who wrote the First Part of the History. After his death in 1625 it was continued first by Father Jouvency (1643–1719) and later by Father J. C. Cordara (1700–1785). The portions relating to the Mogul Mission are Pars Quinta, vol. II, pp. 449–468 (Jouvency), dealing with the years 1579 to 1610, and Pars Sexta, vol. I, pp. 59–60, 257–258, 315, and 524–529 (Cordara), bringing the story on to about the year 1621 and in the case of Tibet down to the close of the Tibet Mission.

Hazart

(vii) Another general history is the *Kerckelycke Historie van de gheheele werelt* of Father Cornelius Hazart, S.J., published in four volumes at Antwerp in 1682. Of this work Part I, pages 245–278, deals with the Mogul Mission, and takes the story down to the middle of the seventeenth century. The book has the reputation of being uncritical, and it is enlivened by some imaginative prints representing Father Rudolf Aquaviva pleading before Akbar and Father Jerome Xavier sitting beside Jahāngīr and expounding the faith.

Apart from the general histories we have two further classes of publications which help in the elucidation of this branch of Jesuit activity, namely (*a*) the recorded lists of the members of the Society attached to the various Provinces, and (*b*) the general bibliographies of Jesuit writers.

As regards the former, there are Catalogues for the Province of Goa among the Jesuit archives preserved in Europe. These catalogues, incomplete though they are and not always infallible, are useful in showing the personnel existing at different dates. A list, extracted from these catalogues, of the Fathers serving from time to time in the Mogul Mission, was prepared by the late Father J. B. Van Meurs, S.J., and was published by Father Hosten in 1911 with biographical notes.[25] From this source it has been ascertained that we have the names of eighty-one missionaries who worked in the Mission between 1580 and 1803 (omitting those who were only in Bengal or Tibet), and that in all probability the number of missionaries between these dates was not less than a hundred. These lists can be usefully supplemented with the aid of a series of books produced by Antonio Franco entitled *Imagem da virtute*, which describe the life and work of those missionaries who had gone forth from the Colleges of Evora, Coimbra and Lisbon, and with the aid of another work by the same author, published at Augsburg in 1726 and entitled *Synopsis Annalium Societatis Jesu in Lusitania, 1540–1725*, which includes (on pp. 467 *et seq.*) a catalogue of Jesuit priests proceeding each year to Indian regions, specifying the name and nationality of each.[26] A similar catalogue of the German missionaries (including Gabelsperger, Roth, Strobl and Tieffenthaler) was published, with short biographies of each, by Anton Huonder, S.J., in 1899.[27] There are also biographical calendars or Menologies by the Jesuits Guilhermy and others which although second-hand authorities may at times be useful.

Catalogues of missionaries

The bibliographies, again, constitute an authority of peculiar interest owing to the enormous literary output of the Society of Jesus. The erudition of the Jesuits has been nowhere more markedly displayed than in the bibliographies which have been prepared of the literary out-turn of the members of their Society. Among the earlier lists those of Ribadaneira (1602, 1608) and of Alegambe (1643) are the best known, but the basis of modern research is the magnificent work published in 1853–1861 (with a fresh edition in 1869–1876) by the brothers Augustus and Aloys de Backer. A valuable *Bibliographie historique de la Compagnie de Jésus* was issued by Father Carayon in 1864 and with its help an improved bibliography, on the basis of that published by the de Backers, was issued in 1890 by Father Sommervogel of Strasburg. This (with its supplements by Father Rivière) remains the standard work for reference and

Jesuit bibliographies

is of great value, including as it does notices not only of published books but also of letters and other literary productions both in print and in manuscript.

Letters and reports of the missionaries

The general histories of the Jesuits, supplemented by the lists and bibliographies above mentioned, are sources of high importance. They constitute, however, authorities of a secondary character and are based almost entirely on letters and reports written from the spot by the missionaries themselves. It is to those original letters that we must look to provide real first-hand evidence of the history of the Missions. It is on the discovery of fresh letters and on the careful study of those already known that future research regarding the Mission must mainly rely. I have accordingly, as a foundation for future study, prepared a list of such letters and reports relating to the Mogul Mission (including some concerning Tibet and Bengal) as are known to me to exist. The list will be found in Appendix I below, and it indicates that out of 174 letters and reports included in it 64 have been published, in translation or otherwise, and 110 remain in manuscript unpublished.[28]

Published letters and reports

The letters and reports which have been published have been given to the public in two different forms. Some have been printed and issued separately in book or pamphlet form, generally not long after they were written. Others were reproduced in subsequent compilations of Jesuit missionary letters from all parts of the world.

The Literae Annuae

It was the custom from an early period for each 'residence' in the Society to submit annually a report to the head of the 'Province' and for the Provincial to report annually to the General at Rome as to the progress made during the year. From these Provincial reports, abstracts (known as the *Literae Annuae*) were published with a view to keeping the various Provinces and the outside world informed as to the proceedings of the Society. This practice commenced in 1581, and for thirty-four years—that is until 1614—these 'Annual Letters' of the Society were issued continuously. There was then a break until 1650 when they again appeared for a further four years, and after 1654 the practice was discontinued.[29] The earliest volumes, till 1594, were published at Rome, and after that date they appeared at various centres—Florence, Naples, Antwerp, Douai, Mainz, Lyons, etc., according to the location of the particular Father who was deputed to undertake the compilation. As it was not always easy to get reports from all the Provinces and all the Missions, these annual abstracts were generally incomplete, and in any case the distant and comparatively unimportant Missions, such as that to Mogor, were only occasionally noticed. Of the volumes between 1581 and 1614 there are five (1588, 1590, 1591, 1596 and 1599) which I have not seen, and out of the remainder there are two only which take cognisance of events in the Mogul Empire, namely those for 1582 (pp. 111–112) and 1597 (pp. 567–573).[30] There is also an account of the Mogor Mission in the Report for 1650, but as a rule there is little information regarding Mogor to be obtained from these general abstracts.

Separate letters and reports published

On the other hand, the letters and reports written by individual missionaries and the annual reports submitted by the Provincial at Goa—especially during the early days when the Mogor Mission enjoyed the favour of Akbar and his successor Jahāngīr—were not infrequently published in Europe shortly after their submission, with a view mainly to secure publicity for the Jesuit successes in the Mission field. Among the separate publications of this character which are of use in dealing with the Mogor Mission are the following:

(*a*) A work entitled *Nouveaux Advis de l'Estat du Christianisme ès pays et royaulmes des Indes Orientales et Jappon* was published in Paris in 1582, on pages 1–4 of which is given an account of the Mogul Mission taken from the letters of Father Rudolf Aquaviva and others.

(*b*) Extracts from two letters from the Provincial at Goa, dealing with Mogor, were published in Italian by the Jesuit Father Spitilli in Rome in 1592 in his *Ragguaglio d'alcune Missioni dell' Indie Orientali e Occidentali cavato da alcuni avvisi scritti gli anni* 1590 *e* 1591. A Latin translation appeared at Antwerp in 1593 under the title of *Brevis et compendiosa Narratio Missionum quarundum Orientis et Occidentis excerpta ex quibusdam litteris a P.P. . . . datis anno* 1590 *et* 1591. A French translation followed at Lyons in 1594.

(*c*) Some further documents were published at Brescia and at Rome in 1597 in a little book by the Jesuit Father John Baptist Peruschi called *Informatione del Regno e stato del gran Rè di Mogor*. This reproduces a valuable report by the missionary Father Monserrate entitled *Relaçam do Equebar Rei dos Mogores*, prepared in 1582, and also a report of 1595 and enclosures from the Provincial at Goa. French translations appeared at Besançon and Paris in 1597 and 1598 respectively, and the book was also reproduced in 1598 at Mainz in German and in Latin. The German version was entitled *Zween kurze Bericht*, etc., and the Latin translation, which is the version most easily obtained, bears the title *Historica Relatio de potentissimi Regis Mogor, a magno Tamerlane oriundi, vita moribus et summa in Christianam Religionem propensione . . . excerpta ex variis epistolis inde acceptis anno* 1582, 91 *et* 95.[31]

(*d*) A little book of 26 pages, published at Paris in 1598 and called *Advis moderne de l'estat et grand royaume de Mogor*, by F. B. Th., gives information which is taken from, and is largely a translation of, the first part of Peruschi's book above mentioned.

(*e*) In 1601 two letters written by the Mission at Lahore in 1598 and 1599 were published at Venice and Rome under the title *Avvisi della Missione del Regno del Gran Mogor*, in an Italian compilation entitled *Copia d'una breve relatione della Christianità di Giappone*, and the same letters were also published in Latin by a Jesuit named John Oranus at Liège in a collection of papers entitled : *Japonica, Sinensia, Mogorana, hoc est De rebus apud eas Gentes a Patribus Societatis Jesu ann.* 1598 *et* 99 *gestis. A.P. Ioanne Orano in Latinam linguam versa.* Another version of the same two letters was published at Mainz in 1601 in pages 53 to 84 of a book called *Recentissima de amplissimo Regno Chinae, item de Statu rei Christianae apud magnum Regem Mogor.* The letters were again published at Leyden in 1639 as a supplement to de Dieu's *Historia S. Petri* of which mention is made in Chapter XIV.

(*f*) In 1601 the report of the Visitor, Father Pimenta, for 1599, was published, and it included quotations from two letters from Father Jerome Xavier and one from Father Pinheiro. A Latin copy appeared in Milan and an Italian version was published by Zannetti in Rome. The report was issued at Mainz in the same year under the name : *Nova Relatio Historica de Rebus in India Orientali a patribus Societatis Jesu anno* 1598 *et* 99 *gestis.* There was a Portuguese issue at Lisbon in 1602, and French versions appeared at Antwerp and at Lyons in 1601 and 1602 respectively.

(*g*) The report submitted by the Visitor from Goa in 1600 was published by Zannetti at Rome in 1602, another version appearing in Italian at Venice in the same year. A Latin version was published at Mainz in 1602 under the title : *Exemplum epistolae P. Nicolai Pimentae Provinciae Orientalis Indicae Visitatoris . . . de statu rei Christianae in India Orientali*, pages 9–25 of which relate to Mogor and pages 76–95 to Bengal. Another Latin version issued at Constance in 1603 with the designation *De felici statu et progressu rei Christianae in India Orientali epistola R.P. Nicolai Pimentae.* A German translation appeared at Constance in 1602 and a Portuguese version at Lisbon in the same year. A French translation was published at Paris in 1603 by ' L.S.D.C.' under the title : *Les miracles merveilleux advenus aux Indes Orientales.*

(*h*) A reprint of a number of Jesuit reports was published in 1605 at Antwerp by the Scotch Jesuit controversialist John Hay of Dalgetty under the title : *De Rebus Japonicis, Indicis et Peruanis epistolae recentiores . . . in librum unum coacervatae.* This book includes the whole of Peruschi's work noticed above (pp. 691–725), and Oranus' version of the Lahore letters of 1598–1599 (pp. 863–878). There is no original matter in the book, but it contains a number of first-hand authorities in a convenient form.

(*i*) A German work published at Augsburg in 1611 under the title *Drei Newe Relationes*, etc., contains (pp. 127–138) an account, compiled from Hay's book, of the general condition of the Mogul Kingdom, etc., and (pp. 139–170) a translation of a letter of 20 December, 1607, from Goa, enclosing the substance of the Mogor reports for 1606 (pp. 139–159) and 1607 (pp. 159–170).

(*j*) A collection was published by Zannetti at Rome in 1615 under the title of *Raguagli d' alcune missioni fatte . . . nell' Indie Orientali:* which relates to the years 1607–1611 and reproduces a letter of 1611 from Father Jerome Xavier of the Mogor Mission. There is a copy of this book in the Imperial Library of Calcutta.

(*k*) In 1621 the annual letters from Japan, China, Goa and Ethiopia for 1615–1619 were published in Italian at Milan and Naples and there are notices of Mogor in the Goa letter of 1619.[32]

(*l*) Similarly in 1627 were issued the Annual Reports for Ethiopia, Malabar, Brazil and India for 1620 to 1624, and among the Indian narratives for 1620, 1621 and 1624 there are notices of the Mogor Mission. These letters were published in Italian at Rome in 1627, and in the next year a French translation was published at Paris. In the Italian *Lettere Annue d'Etiopia*, etc., pp. 161–170 (1620), pp. 86–93 (1621), and pp. 336–343 (1624), and in the French *Histoire de ce qui s'est passé en Éthiopie*, etc., pp. 196–208 (1620), pp. 106–118 (1621) and pp. 439–451 (1624) deal with Mogor.

(*m*) Following these we find published at Paris in 1651 a report written by Father Maracci, Procurator of the Goa Province, and translated into French by Father Jacques de Machault under the title of *Relation de ce qui s'est passé dans les Indes Orientales*. The report was presented to the Propaganda in 1649, and pages 16–23 deal with the Mogul Mission.

(*n*) Then in 1663 a short *Relatio rerum notabilium Regni Mogor* by Father Roth was, according to Sommervogel, published at Neuburg, but I have not come across it.[33]

(*o*) From this time onwards the regular reports seem to have been no longer issued. An interesting book was however published at Trent about the year 1683 (the dedication bearing that date) entitled: *Estratto e Registro di lettere spirituali con breve narratione della Vita del Molto Reverendo Padre Antonio Ceschi di Santa Croce*. This book contains letters from the missionary Father Ceschi who died in Mogor in 1656. There is a copy in the Franciscan convent at Trent and extracts have been translated and published by Father Hosten.[34]

(*p*) So too in 1710 several letters of Father Jerome Xavier, dating from 1593 to 1617, were published by Father Bartholome Alcazar in a book called *Chrono-Historia de la Compañia de Jesus en la Provincia de Toledo*.[35] These have been translated by Father Hosten in the *Journal of the Asiatic Society of Bengal*.[36]

It will be convenient to mention, along with the above, two reports by Father Monserrate which have been published in recent years, namely the *Relaçam do Equebar Rei dos Mogores*, above referred to, which was written in 1582, and the *Mongolicae Legationis Commentarius* written in 1590. These important works were published by Father Hosten in 1912–14 and the history of their publication is a matter of such interest that it has been thought to deserve notice in a separate chapter (number VIII).

Compilations of letters

After the discontinuance of the official *Annuae Literae* of the Society and with the cessation of the practice of publishing separate letters and provincial reports, there appeared compilations published by private enterprise, and incorporating letters from missionaries which were for the most part of a private or semi-official character.

The Lettres Édifiantes et Curieuses

The best known of these compilations is the series of 'Lettres Édifiantes et Curieuses, écrites des Missions Étrangères par quelques Missionaires de la Compagnie de Jésus.' The series is comprised in 34 volumes issued in Paris between 1702 and 1741 and deals with letters ranging from 1699 to 1740. An abbreviated translation in two volumes was issued in London in 1743 by John Lockman with the title of *Travels of the Jesuits into various parts of the World*; the abbreviations being achieved by the omission of accounts of conversions and miracles, as being 'quite insipid or ridiculous to most English Readers, and indeed to all persons of Understanding and Taste.' Several fresh and supplementary editions of the 'Lettres,' without these excisions, have since been published in France and of those the best for reference is probably the Paris edition of 1780–1783 issued in twenty-six volumes by Querbœuf. It has the merit of arranging the letters in geographical order, and the information regarding India is collected in volumes X to XV of this edition. This compilation is however largely devoted to the French missionaries of whom there were few in Mogor, and the Mogul Mission is poorly represented in the *Lettres Édifiantes*, some three or four letters only having reference to that Mission.[37]

The Weltbott

Another collection of Jesuit letters—overlapping to some extent the *Lettres Édifiantes*—is the series known as Stöcklein's *Neue Weltbott*. The first 24 parts, generally bound in 3 or 6 volumes, containing letters 1 to 520, were issued by Joseph Stöcklein at Augsburg and Grätz in 1728, and after his death in 1733 other volumes appeared by other hands. There were in all 36 parts of which 32 parts only, ending with letter 640, are in the British Museum. The remaining 4 parts, ending with letter 723, are available in the Bodleian

Library at Oxford, and two further parts (37 and 38) are said by Sommervogel to be mentioned by the Jesuit writer, Eglauer. The collection contains several letters of interest regarding the Mogor Mission, three of which are also in the *Lettres Édifiantes*.[38] It is said that there are translations of the work in Spanish (1753–1757) and Italian (1825–1829), but they are apparently rare.

Unpublished manuscripts

The letters of the missionaries which are ordinarily accessible to the public in the large libraries of Europe are mainly to be found in the works above specified, that is to say in the separate publications generally issued soon after the letters were written, and in the compilations known as the *Lettres Édifiantes* and the *Neue Weltbott.* There remain a large number of letters and reports which have never yet been published or which have only appeared intermittently, either in their original language or in translation, in various learned journals or religious newspapers.[39]

(*a*) In London

Goa, as the headquarters of the Province which directed the Mogor Missions, would have been the place at which the Mission records could best be consulted, but unfortunately the bulk of the Jesuit literature at Goa was shipped off to Portugal after the banishment of the Jesuits from Portuguese territory in 1759 and there is now little or nothing in the National Library at Goa to represent the old Jesuit records.[40] By some means, however, regarding which we have no information, a number of these Jesuit manuscripts from Goa left their habitat over a century ago and were brought to England. We find accordingly that the only large collection of such manuscript letters and reports available in Europe for public inspection is that to be found in the British Museum. Ten volumes of manuscripts from the collections originally in Goa were presented to the Museum by Mr. W. Marsden in 1835 and two of these, known as Additional MSS. Nos. 9854 and 9855, deal with Portuguese Missions in the north of India between 1582 and 1693. The former of these volumes contains 25 and the latter 32 documents which are mostly letters and reports by missionaries from the Mogul Empire, but include also three Persian papers and three translations from the Persian.[41] With very few exceptions these documents remain hitherto unpublished.

The Cotton MSS. in the British Museum contain five letters of interest dating from 1615. Three of these are in original and all five of them appear in translations which were made at the time in England. These letters have been published by Father Hosten in English.[42] The Museum also contains a printed Spanish translation of a Portuguese letter of 1627 from the Tibet

Mission, and this also has been published in English by Father Hosten.[43]

There were also at one time a number of manuscript letters from Ajmīr, Agra, etc., dating from 1627 to 1668, and forming a portion of that part of Mr. W. Marsden's collection which he presented in 1835 to King's College, London, and which is now in the School of Oriental Studies. Unfortunately these particular documents, which would have have been of great interest, are now missing.[44] The collection in question, however, contains some manuscript copies of works in Persian written by the Jesuit missionaries in Mogor which are of considerable value and will be described in Chapter XIV.

Besides those above mentioned as accessible in London there are a considerable number of letters and reports from the Jesuit missionaries of Mogor in other places. Some valuable documents of which we have cognisance have temporarily at least disappeared from sight,[45] but there are others which only need further research to enable them to be made available for public use. Some valuable letters are to be found in the public libraries at Brussels, and these have been unearthed and studied, but not yet published, by Father Hosten. There are also a large number of such documents in the possession of the Society of Jesus, the location of which is known only to members of the Society. A few of them have been published of late years,[46] but there is a considerable store of such papers still to be tapped and for their future publication we must trust to members of the Society itself. In many cases when manuscripts have not been published we can rely on the printed Chronicles which were compiled from them, but as more of these unpublished documents are brought to light, we shall be less dependent than we now are on the records of the chroniclers.

(*b*) In other places

The value of the Jesuit letters and reports from the Mogul Empire for historical purposes can scarcely be overestimated. It is true that the letters are from men reporting on their own work—work to which they had devoted their lives. It is also true that the members of the Society realized the intensity of the struggle in Europe between the Jesuits and their enemies both inside and outside the Catholic Church, and the necessity for avoiding anything which might give a handle to their opponents. But the letters from Mogor, though they may at times be coloured by enthusiasm, are not open to any charge of intentional falsehood. In many instances they candidly admit failure and we may in general accept them when they tell of success. Tested by such information as we

High value of the letters and reports

possess from independent sources, Indian and European, they emerge from the examination with the greatest credit and may for historical purposes be looked on as authorities of a very high order.

The circumstances under which they were written

It is interesting to look now on these old documents where the originals have been preserved. They are written for the most part on sheets of quarto size, the lines placed close together, the writing ordinarily small and sometimes hard to decipher. Each letter is usually headed by the Cross and the invocation 'Pax Christi': often there is also prefixed the name of Jesus and sometimes the letters—M.R.A.—indicative of the Virgin Mary. At the end of some of the letters we find the Jesuit emblems of the Cross, the I H S and the three nails, and these are sometimes introduced in the form of a seal. In one respect this correspondence of the Jesuits presents a peculiarity strange to modern conceptions of official routine. It was by no means necessary that a letter should be written to the immediate Superior of the writer and it was the practice for young priests to write direct, not merely to the Superior, but also to the Provincial, the General, and even on occasions the Pope himself. In this the Jesuits were, it is true, following the custom prevalent in the secular administration of the Portuguese, but the practice is none the less remarkable in an Order so strictly disciplined as the Society of Jesus. In the contents of the letters there is a marked strain not only of sincerity and piety, but also of that culture with which the Society imbued even the most backward of its members. The letters were written in circumstances and in surroundings of a very varied character. Each letter had to be copied at least once to meet possible losses at sea, and the hands that wrote and copied them were sometimes old and feeble. 'I have no one to help me in these lands of Mogul,' wrote the aged Xavier in 1615, 'to make copies (a escribir vias) and I have not the strength which I had formerly, but my love draws strength out of my weakness.'[47] Often the letters were written in conditions of depressing solitude; such, for instance, as the letters written by Father Rudolf Aquaviva from Fatehpur Sīkrī in 1582 or that despatched by Father Andrade from the Tibetan Himalayas in 1625. The latter describes how the writer was left with no society but that of two little Tibetan boys, and adds: 'They are company enough for me, for I am not without the company of the Holy Angels.'[48] Or a letter may have been written in the face of peril, as was that despatched by Father Desideri in 1714 when about to start from Agra on the dangerous expedition to Tibet from which he might well expect never to return. After sending his heartfelt greetings to numerous friends in Europe by name, he writes to his correspondent: 'May the Lord bless you with every consolation so that we may be given the grace of meeting each other again in His holy Paradise'; and then with an unconscious echo of the death-bed letter of the Emperor Aurangzeb, written seven years before, he adds a thrice-repeated 'Farewell, Farewell, Farewell.'[49] Taken as a whole these letters bring us, as nothing else could, into touch with the personalities of the men who bore the burden of the Mission, and make us realize the devotion which inspired them in carrying out their allotted duties. Written as they were in distant localities, amid uncongenial or even inimical surroundings, in circumstances very often of discomfort, solitude, ill-health, depression and disappointment, by men who had abandoned the ordinary recreations of life, who existed in an atmosphere of study and penance, and who had little or no hope of ever seeing again the friends of their youth, they form a marvellous monument of the vitality and enthusiasm inspired by the Society to which the writers owed obedience.

NOTES

[1] Vol. II, pp. 82–96.

[2] Vol. II, pp. 260–287. His chief authority is Catrou's version of Manucci (see note 15 below).

[3] Pp. 133–149 deal with the Mission to Akbar and pp. 279–287 with subsequent activities until the middle of the eighteenth century. This work gives a useful list of authorities which includes the older Jesuit historians, Guerreiro, du Jarric, Maracci, Catrou, Stöcklein, etc., and it covers a large field, but in a condensed form. It was a thesis prepared for the Munich University and the writer appears to have been only nineteen years of age when it was written.

[4] *Les Bienheureux Martyrs de Salsette,* Lille, 1893, and *Istoria della vita e del Martirio dei Beati Rodolfo e compagni,* Rome, 1893.

[5] Apart from publishing his papers, this Society was helpful to him in many ways.

[6] A list of the chief of his publications dealing directly with the Mogul Mission which is published below as App. II has been compiled with the help of information supplied by Father Hosten himself. It represents a fraction only of his total literary output.

[7] Frequent reference will be made in subsequent notes to the work of Father Felix, a priest who, apart from his historical studies, has done a great deal of valuable work for the Catholic Christians of the Punjab. One of the Christian villages in the new Colonies in that Province has been called Khushpur (Felixtown) in recognition of his labours.

[8] The doings of the Jesuits in Mogor have also attracted the notice of more than one writer of fiction. They appear in the Dutchman Limburg-Brouwer's 'Eastern Romance' entitled *Akbar* which was published

in English in 1879. And they play a considerable part in Dr. W. W. Ireland's interesting story *Golden Bullets* which appeared in Edinburgh in 1890. The Jesuit Fathers also flit across the stage in Mrs. F. A. Steel's trilogy of *The Prince of Dreamers, A Mistress of Men* and *The Builder.*

[9] The substance of Badāonīs' information was reproduced as early as 1824 in an article in the *Quarterly Oriental Magazine* of Calcutta by the celebrated H. H. Wilson, which finds a place in Vol. II, p. 379, of his collected works (1862). And the portions of Badāonī which concern the religious history of the time are translated in Rehatsek's *The Emperor Akbar's repudiation of Esllām,* Bombay, 1866. See also Vans Kennedy, ' Notice respecting the Religion introduced into India by the Emperor Akbar ' (*Transactions Lit. Soc., Bombay,* II, 1820, p. 242).

[10] Marsden MSS. Add. 9,855, foll. 151, 153, 156, 158, 159 and 167. *J.A.S.B.*, VI, 1910, p. 452–453.

[11] See note 25, Chapter XVIII.

[12] The most recent edition of his letters and journals is the admirable volume published by Sir W. Foster, *The Embassy of Sir Thomas Roe to India,* London, 1926. The Embassy is also described by Roe's chaplain, the Rev. Edward Terry, in his *Voyage to East India* (London, 1655, reprinted in 1777). Terry's book is an expansion of information given in Purchas (MacLehose, 1905, Vol. IX) in 1625.

[13] The Itinerario of Manrique, written in Spanish, is difficult to procure, but a valuable translation with notes by the late Col. Eckford Luard, assisted by Father Hosten, has been published by the Hakluyt Society (1927–1928). Portions relating to the Mogul Empire were translated and published in the *J.P.H.S.*, I, 1912, pp. 83–106 and pp. 151–166 (concerning the Punjab), in the *J.U.P.H.S.*, I, 1918, Part II, pp. 109–121 (concerning Agra), in the *Catholic Herald of India* between January 30 and April 10, 1928 (concerning Hūglī), and September 11 to October 23, 1918 (concerning ' The Power of the Mogul ').

[14] Bernier is most accessible in Constable's edition with notes by V. A. Smith, published in London in 1914. Of the French editions that published in Amsterdam in 1724 is the edition referred to in this work.

[15] The travels of Manucci were for a long time known only by a modified abstract of them published in 1705 (and supplemented in 1708 and 1715) by the Jesuit Father Catrou at Paris. The original manuscripts of Manucci's wonderful narrative were, however, unearthed by Mr. W. Irvine in 1899, and published by him, with copious and excellent notes, under the title ' *Storia do Mogor,*' in the India Records Series in London in 1907–8.

[16] Vol. IV, Part II, pp. 161–307. *J.P.H.S.*, X, 1929 (Kuenen-Wicksteed and Vogel).

[17] The volumes as published are not numbered : but for convenience I have in referring to them given them the numbers assigned in the text above.

[18] *J.A.S.B.*, VI, 1910 (Hosten), p. 443. A copy is in the British Museum.

[19] Sommervogel, s.v. Guerreiro. I have not seen this.

[20] By Hosten, in *J.P.H.S.*, VII, 1918, pp. 50–73 (Relation of 1607–1608), and *The Examiner*, Bombay, November 22, 1919 (Relation of 1602–1603). See also *J.I.H.*, V, 1926, pp. 267–281 (J. A. d'Silva), *re* the rebellion of Khusrū.

[21] *Jahāngīr and the Jesuits*, London, 1930 (including the Travels of Benedict Goes and the Mission to Pegu). I may note that in addition to

the use which I have made of his published works, I have received a great deal of kind help from Mr. Payne, more especially in connection with the reigns of Akbar and Jahāngīr.

[22] See the detailed account of du Jarric's book (together with a reproduction of the title-page of the Bordeaux edition) in C. H. Payne's *Akbar and the Jesuits*, xxxv–xxxvii. References to du Jarric in this work will ordinarily be to the Bordeaux edition. A portion of du Jarric relating to Bengal has been translated and published by Father Saulière, S.J., in *B.P. and P.*, XIV (1917), pp. 148–158 (vol. I of du Jarric, pp. 602–612), and XIX (1919), pp. 64–80 (vol. I of du Jarric, pp. 612–628).

[23] March 13, 20 : June 12, 19 : July 3, 1920.

[24] The MS. is now in the Ajuda Library near Lisbon.

[25] *J.A.S.B.*, VI, 1910, p. 527. On pp. 538–539 *ib.*, there are alphabetical lists of the members of the Mission between 1593 and 1756. Lists of Portuguese missionaries to Bengal are separately given in *J.A.S.B.*, VII, 1911, pp. 15–35. No catalogues for Mogor are available between 1625 and 1641. (*Mem. A.S.B.*, V, 1916, p. 137.)

[26] The information regarding those who proceeded to the Mogul Mission is abstracted by Hosten in *J.A.S.B.*, VI, 1910, p. 540.

[27] *Deutsche Jesuitenmissionäre des 17 und 18 Jahrhunderts.* Ergänzungshefte zu den 'Stimmen aus Maria-Laach,' Freiburg im Breisgau, No. 74, pp. 173–180.

[28] From these 110 unpublished letters extracts, varying in length from a sentence to several pages, have been published in 24 instances. In 45 cases the letters have not been perused by anyone outside the Society.

[29] Carayon, *Bibliographie Historique,* pp. 2–5. *J.A.S.B.*, VI, 1910, p. 443 note.

[30] The letters for 1653 which I have not seen are also quoted by Müllbauer as containing references to the Mogul Mission.

[31] The first part of the title above transcribed is from the main title and the latter part from the inner title of the book. The letter of 1591 is embedded in the text and not separately distinguishable. Carayon, *Bibliographie Historique* (1864), mentions also (p. 86, no. 696) a Portuguese *Compendio* published at Lisbon in 1598 and (p. 102, no. 744) a *Nouveaux Advis* published in 1604 at Paris, which would appear to cover the same ground as Peruschi's book.

[32] The information regarding Mogor in this report is reproduced by Hosten in the *Bombay Examiner,* 3 February, 1912, and subsequent dates.

[33] One authority (Cornelius a Beughem, *Bib. Hist.*, Amsterdam, 1685, p. 285) gives the date of publication as 1668. The same title is given to the notes on Roth by Rhay taken down at Neuburg in 1664, which are mentioned in Appendix I.

[34] *The Examiner,* Bombay, 1917, July 7, 14, 21, 28, August 11, 18, September 1, 8.

[35] Part II, pp. 203–216.

[36] Vol. XXIII, 1927, pp. 109–130.

[37] For a bibliographical account of the Letters see that published by V. H. Paletits at Cleveland, Ohio, in 1910. The letters in the 1780–1783 edition relating to Mogor are : Vol. IV, p. 230 (Nādir Shah), by Saignes, 1740 ; Vol. X, p. 231, by Diusse, 28 January, 1701 ; and Vol. XII, p. 430, the well-known letter of 10 April, 1716, from Desideri at Lhāsa. In Vol. XIII, p. 390, also there is a letter from Calmette dated 24 January,

1733, which bears on the Mission to Jaipur. The information in Vols. X and XI of the *Lettres Édifiantes* relating to Missions in Bengal is reproduced by Father Hosten in *B.P. and P.*, VII, 1911, pp. 131–163.

[38] A detailed list of the letters published in this compilation down to No. 723, together with summaries of their contents, will be found in Carayon, *Bibliographie Historique*, 1864, pp. 546–570. The letters directly connected with Mogor are: No. 35, Roth, 1664; 74, Diusse, 28 Jan., 1701; 117, Koch, 1706 or 1709; 175, Desideri, 10 April, 1716; 595, Figueredo, 1735; 631, Saignes, 10 February, 1740; 643, Strobl, 6 October, 1742; 644, Strobl, 18 October, 1743; 645, Strobl, 13 October, 1743; 646, Strobl, 13 October, 1744; 647, Strobl, 27 October, 1746; 648, Strobl, 26 October, 1747; 649, Strobl, 5 Oct., 1748; 650, Strobl, 19 Sept., 1751; 651, Tieffenthaler, 22 Oct., 1750. Sommervogel and Huonder also refer to 806, Strobl, Mar., 1738, and 807, Strobl, Oct., 1740.

[39] As will be seen by a reference to the lists in Appendices I and II, Father Hosten, S.J., has been responsible for the issue of a number of letters in this way.

[40] See note on p. 517 of *Mem. A.S.B.*, III, 1914 (Hosten). There are a number of well-kept records at Lisbon dealing with the Portuguese rule in India, some of which may throw light on the Mogor Mission (Danvers, *Report on the Portuguese Records relating to the East Indies*, 1892).

[41] The documents in No. 9855 are described by W. Rees Philipps in a note reproduced by Hosten in *J.A.S.B.*, VI, 1910, pp. 448–451. Some of the documents in 9854–9855 are also described by Beveridge on pp. 452–454 of the same article.

[42] *The Examiner*, Bombay, 1919. The history of the letters of 1615 will be found in Chapter V.

[43] *J.A.S.B.*, XXI, 1925, pp. 75–81.

[44] E. Denison Ross in *Bulletin S.O.S.*, II, 1922, p. 533, Hosten in ditto, III, 1923, p. 139.

[45] e.g., The third volume of de Sousa's *Oriente Conquistado.* As to Gonsalvez, who was one of de Sousa's authorities, see *Ann. Let. Goa*, 1619, *The Examiner*, Bombay, February 10, 1912, and March 13, 1920 (Hosten), and *Mem. A.S.B.*, V, 1916 (Hosten), p. 149.

[46] Four of Jerome Xavier's letters, for instance, were published in L. J. M. Cros' *Saint François de Xavier*, Toulouse, 1894, pp. 461–467. And some other documents have been published from time to time by Hosten. Hosten gives a list of unpublished letters in *J.A.S.B.*, VI, 1910, p. 541.

[47] Letter of December 4, 1615. *J.A.S.B.*, XXIII, 1927, p. 123.

[48] Letter of September 10, 1625. *J.A.S.B.*, XXI, 1925, p. 52.

[49] Letter of August 21, 1714, published in translation by Hosten in *The Examiner*, Bombay, October 5, 1918. The original is in the Stonyhurst College Library.

To face page 23] [India Office

THE GOOD SHEPHERD

By Maskīn

(See p. 254)

CHAPTER II

THE FIRST MISSION TO AKBAR, 1580–1583

Transiens in Macedoniam adjuva nos.
(Act. Apost. xvi, 9.)

AKBAR succeeded to the Mogul throne in 1556 and was for many years occupied in consolidating his power in Northern India. In 1572, however, he turned his attention to Gujarāt, and while he was engaged in the siege of Surat, during the early part of 1573, he treated with a deputation of Portuguese from Goa, headed by one Antony Cabral. This was his first acquaintance, so far as we know, with the Portuguese and he was much struck by their valour and courtesy.[1] A few years later, in 1577, one Pedro Tavares, the commandant of Satgāon in Bengal, was at Akbar's Court with his wife, and we are told by the Chronicler Abu'-l-fazl that ' his sound sense and upright conduct won him the favour and esteem of the Emperor.'[2]

Akbar's first contact with the Portuguese

Akbar was accordingly predisposed to appreciate favourably such information as he received regarding the religion professed by the Portuguese. In writing of the year 1575 the historian Badāonī, speaking from the orthodox Muslim point of view, notices the introduction of Christian influence at the Court and describes the rationalizing tendency of Akbar's counsellors as due in part to the fact that ' Farangī priests came frequently and His Majesty enquired into the articles of their belief which are based on reason.' He adds the lines :

A Catholic priest at Akbar's Court

' Whatever imagination their intellect invents,
God laughs at the intellect of people of that creed.'[3]

As a matter of fact no priests had arrived at the Court as early as 1575, but two Jesuit priests arrived in Bengal in 1576 and attracted Akbar's favourable attention by refusing to give absolution to certain Christian merchants who had defrauded the Mogul Government of taxes due to it. Through the medium of Pedro Tavares, Akbar induced a priest called

Julian Pereira, who was in charge of Satgāon, to come to the Court at Fatehpur Sīkrī, where he arrived in March 1578.[4] Pereira occupied himself largely in exposing the errors of Islām (which Akbar had not yet publicly renounced) and Akbar was greatly interested in his teaching. We are told that when the Chief Mullā, the 'Sultān of Mecca,' defended his faith, Akbar rose up and said 'May God help me! May God help me!' as though he were not content with the Mullā's defence; and it is recorded that many fruitless discussions between the priest and the Mullās were held in his presence. He went so far as to ask the priest to teach him Portuguese, so that he might the better understand the doctrines of Christianity. The first thing he was taught was to pronounce the name of Jesus, and he took great pleasure in repeating the word many times.

Akbar's invitation to the Jesuits

In his conversations with the King, Father Pereira, who is described as a man of more virtue than learning, made mention of the Jesuit missionaries in the College of S. Paul at Goa, and said that His Majesty would gain much by hearing what they could tell him of the Christian religion, for they were more learned than himself.[5] Upon this Akbar despatched an ambassador to Goa with letters of almost identical import to the Viceroy, the Archbishop and the Jesuit Fathers.[6] The farmān to the Fathers ran as follows:

'Order of Jalāl-ud-dīn the Great, King by God appointed. Fathers of the Order of St. Paul, know that I am most kindly disposed towards you. I send 'Abdulla, my ambassador, and Dominic Pires[7] to ask you in my name to send me two learned priests who should bring with them the chief books of the Law and the Gospel, for I wish to study and learn the Law and what is best and most perfect in it. The moment my ambassadors return let them not hesitate to come with them and let them bring the books of the Law. Know also that so far as I can I shall receive most kindly and honourably the priests who will come. Their arrival will give me the greatest pleasure, and when I shall know about the Law and its perfection what I wish to know, they will be at liberty to return as soon as they like, and I shall not let them go without loading them with honours and gifts. Therefore let them not have the slightest fear to come. I take them under my protection. Fare you well.'[8]

Its acceptance

The embassy arrived at Goa in September 1579 and was received with all possible ceremony. The Viceroy feared that if missionaries were sent they would run the risk of being dealt with as hostages for the Portuguese Government, but he handed the matter over for decision to a Committee of Bishops, and this Committee decided on November 10, 1579, in favour of the despatch of a Mission.[9]

The Fathers selected for the service were Rudolf Aquaviva, Antony Monserrate, and Francis Henriquez. Of these Henriquez was a Persian by origin, a native of Ormuz and a convert from Islām, who was intended to help as interpreter to the Mission. Monserrate, a Spaniard from Catalonia, forty-three years of age, was a wise and observant man of studious habits, and to him we owe an admirable first-hand description of the Mission and of the Mogul Court, which will be noticed in a subsequent chapter.[10] Rudolf Aquaviva, the third member and the leader of the Mission, was an Italian of high social status and of outstanding sanctity. Born in 1550, the son of the Duke of Atri in the Abruzzi and nephew of Claud Aquaviva, subsequently General of the Society, he had entered the Society of Jesus against the wishes of his parents, and in spite of his delicate health entreated to be sent to bear testimony to his Saviour in the East. He arrived at Goa from Europe in the same month as that in which Akbar's embassy arrived from Fatehpur, and he at once applied to be sent to the Mogul Court. Though only thirty years of age, he was given charge of the Mission, and we shall see with what zeal he conducted it and how by his pure and austere life he endeared himself to Akbar. He had scarcely returned to Goa in 1583, after the conclusion of his Mission, when he was sent to the adjoining territory of Salsette and was there shortly afterwards murdered by a Hindu mob. In view of the circumstances of his death, the story of his life and character has been often set forth in Jesuit writings,[11] but there is no better or more intimate portrait of him than that penned by his old comrade Monserrate.

Personnel of the Jesuit Mission

'Rudolf,' says Monserrate, 'was of a very sweet disposition and so simple that he judged everyone after his own heart. Devoted to meditation and prayer above all things, he would let only the study of Persian or some other necessary occupation interfere with them. His thoughts were so assiduously fixed on God that the words "Oculi mei semper ad Dominum" (My eyes are ever toward the Lord) seemed applicable to him. To avoid fatigue he would while walking sing gently in a low voice small prayers, or ejaculations as we say. Forgetful of self he slept very often whole nights with his clothes on, just as when at work, and that either sitting, or when he happened to lie down, overcome by greater fatigue, in a position calculated to torture his body and inflict pain rather than favour rest. He wore a hair shirt, disciplined himself and very often abstained. He frequently shut himself up in silence and solitude, coming out of his room only to

Monserrate's description of Rudolf Aquaviva

say Mass. All his life he kept his virginal purity : to protect it he invoked the help of the Virgin Mother of God, to whose care he had entrusted himself and to whom he had vowed to speak in praise of her when occasion offered. In her honour he would hum to himself extempore little songs of his own invention. A careful observer of the rules and customs of the Society, especially those of poverty, he rejoiced to wear old worn-out clothes and shoes. Always abstracted in God he forgot what he was about. Very often he could not remember where he had left his hat, his spectacles, his books, etc. His face reflected his virginal modesty : whenever he spoke to the King his modesty betrayed itself in a blush. His patience was admirable and his humility most sincere.'[12]

Under the guidance of this young and enthusiastic priest the Mission started on November 17, 1579, accompanied by Akbar's ambassador and his interpreter. Of this journey the earlier chroniclers give no details, but subsequently two full descriptions of it were published. One appeared for the first time in 1710 in de Sousa's *Oriente Conquistado*, and the other, written by Monserrate himself, though known to certain writers in the eighteenth century, was not published till 1912. The two accounts without being inconsistent differ in some material respects from each other, and although we do not know the source of de Sousa's itinerary it is not impossible that it was based on information given by Father Rudolf himself.[13] The route was by Surat, Māndū, Ujjain, Sārangpur, Sironj, Narwar, Gwalior and Dholpur, and the descriptions given in both accounts of the people, the places and the state of the country are full of interest.[14] Monserrate, who had been in bad health for the greater part of the journey, was detained for some days by sickness at Narwar, but the rest of the Mission reached Fatehpur Sīkrī on February 27 or 28, 1580.[15]

Journey from Goa to Fatehpur

This Mission came to Akbar's Court at a time of great interest in the development of his religious policy, and its doings have received notice at the hands of the contemporary Indian historians, Badāonī and Abu'-l-fazl ; the former writing from the orthodox Muslim standpoint and the latter from that of Akbar's own eclecticism. We have also first-hand information recorded by the members of the Mission themselves. Some half-dozen of Father Rudolf's letters from the Court are available, in whole or in part, and Monserrate left two works of the highest value, namely the *Relaçam* (1582) which contains the best contemporary sketch of the character

Authorities regarding the Mission

and power of Akbar at the time of the Mission and the *Commentarius* (1590) which forms the best general account which we possess of the Mission itself. A short description founded on one of Father Rudolf's letters and on the *Relaçam* of Monserrate was issued by Peruschi in 1597, and a connected account of the Mission based on letters, published narratives and personal enquiries was published by Guzman in 1601. These two sources of information constitute the groundwork of the fascinating history published by du Jarric in 1608. Later compilers such as Bartoli (1667), Catrou (1708) and de Sousa (1710) appear to have had access to other sources of information, but must in the absence of due confirmation be looked on as on the whole less trustworthy authorities than the writers of the earlier documents available. In the reprint of Bartoli's narrative issued in 1714, some forty authorities are quoted, and these and other sources have been utilized in the modern monographs of Suau and Angelini (1893) and Goldie (1897) referred to on page 2 above.

Its objects, national and personal

From the above documents it may be inferred that the ultimate object of the Mission was the conversion to Christianity of the inhabitants of Mogor. But in view of the unsolicited invitation addressed to Goa and the known proclivities of Akbar, it was ardently hoped that this object might be achieved through the medium of the conversion of the King. All the efforts of the Mission were therefore at the first concentrated on the King himself. Royal converts were not unknown in the Indies: the King of the Maldives, for instance, and more than one King of Ceylon had become Christians, and a near relation of the King of Bījāpur had been baptized at Goa shortly after Father Rudolf's arrival from Europe. The baptism of a grandson of the King of Bījāpur is reported in the Annual Letters 1586–1587, and readers of Manrique's travels will remember several cases of the conversion of members of the ruling family in Arakan in the first half of the seventeenth century. There was therefore nothing impossible or fantastic in the scheme of the Mission and, as the Jesuits were admittedly the Order best fitted to deal with such cases, the Mission commenced with well-founded hopes of success.

Akbar's objects: personal

These hopes were more than justified by Akbar's own attitude. His primary concern was his personal religion. He had since boyhood been devout: he had consorted freely with Sūfīs and Darweshes; and he had only recently been found by his courtiers in a condition of religious ecstasy. Brought up as a Muslim, he came of a stock which in past generations had in more than one instance sat loosely towards

Mohammedanism. He had enquired into the tenets of his Hindu subjects and into those of the Jains and Parsis: and now he wished to extend his enquiries to the Christian religion. It was sometimes alleged in later times that his object in calling the Jesuits was merely to supply clergy for his European employees,[16] but his previous history and his treatment of the Mission point to the conclusion that he was in reality searching for a religion which would satisfy his personal needs.

At the same time—as in the case of the Fathers but on different grounds—there was probably in Akbar's mind the desire to lay hold of a religion which could be adopted by all his subjects. The predominant party in the State was Muslim and almost all the higher posts were in Muslim hands. Akbar had, it is true, with much foresight and courage, introduced a certain Hindu element, but he had to proceed with caution, and much of this new element was drawn from the feudatory princes and from families connected with himself by marriage. The appointment of Hindus to high posts sometimes met with violent opposition and there was always an undercurrent of hatred between the two communities. The Muslims used their power with little tolerance. Throughout the journey from the coast to Fatehpur, for instance, the Fathers found that the Hindu temples had been destroyed by the Mohammedans (Agarenorum diligentia omnia idolorum delubra quae plurima erant dejecta).[17] When war was in progress there was no pretence of mutual consideration; cows were freely slaughtered and infidels 'sent to hell.' Akbar realized that Islām could not be substituted for Hinduism, nor Hinduism for Islām. It was an age in which many genuine attempts had been made by sages and mystics to fuse the two religions: but without any permanent or widespread success. The only way therefore to compose the communal problem was to impose on all the people a third religion from outside. Such a solution was by no means impracticable. It was a time when an almost idolatrous reverence was shown for kingship, and Akbar had himself attained extraordinary power and had to deal with a people more than ordinarily docile. He ultimately attempted, at a date subsequent to the arrival of the Fathers, to introduce a new religion, the 'Tauhīd Ilāhī,' or Divine Monotheism: but in the meantime he was searching for other possible solutions and it is a fair conjecture that among other solutions he was considering the feasibility of experimenting with Christianity as a faith to be imposed on all his subjects.[18]

And national

However this may be, it may be observed that at the time when the Mission reached Fatehpur, Akbar while still a professing Muslim had broken away from orthodoxy. He had not yet definitely abandoned Islām nor had he promulgated the Dīn Ilāhī, but he had in June 1579 begun to recite the Khutba or Friday sermon himself and in September of the same year he obtained from the leading 'Ulamā and lawyers a pronouncement recognizing his interpretations of Islām as binding on the nation. In 1575 he had started a system of religious conferences in the 'Ibādat-khāna at Fatehpur and these, though confined at first to various phases of Islām, had since been extended so as to include representatives of Hinduism, Jainism and Zoroastrianism. On the arrival of the Jesuits he was able to include a Christian element, and scarcely were the Fathers arrived in Fatehpur than they were plunged by him into the turmoil of these disputes. To retain a true perspective of the debates it must be remembered that Akbar was pursuing with equal interest his enquiries into other forms of faith,[19] but in the Jesuit narration we naturally hear mainly of the controversies between the Christians and the Muslims. In these disputes they were generally supported by the King and his minister Abu'-l-fazl and the argument ordinarily terminated to their satisfaction.

Religious conferences at Fatehpur

Badāonī, from the Muslim standpoint, writes despondingly of these debates. 'The controversies,' he complains, 'used to pass beyond the differences of Sunnī and Shī'ah, of Hanifī and Shāf'ī, of lawyer and divine, and they would attack the very bases of belief.' The Mullās themselves were divided into two parties who 'became very Jew and Egyptian for hatred of each other.' Apart from that, 'persons of novel and whimsical opinions, in accordance with their pernicious ideas and vain doubts, coming out of ambush decked the false in the garb of the true.' He notices how Akbar 'picked and chose from anyone except a Muslim.' Brahmanism was especially favoured and 'not a day passed but a new fruit of this loathsome tree ripened into existence.' Sūfīs and Shī'ahs were also in the fray and Rājā Bīrbal 'the accursed' advocated the cause of the Pārsīs. 'Learned monks also from Europe,' he adds, 'who are called *Pādre* and have an infallible head (Mujtahid-i-kāmil) called *Pāpā* who is able to change religious ordinances as he may deem advisable for the moment and to whose authority Kings must submit, brought the Gospel, advanced proofs for the Trinity, demonstrated the title of Christianity, and made the religion of Jesus current.[20] . . . The attributes of the accursed Anti-Christ and his qualities were ascribed by these accursed

Standpoint of Badāonī

men to his Lordship The Best of the Prophets (God bless him and his family and preserve him from all Impostors).' So depressed was Badāonī that he absented himself from Court and suffered 'heartburning for the deceased religion of Islām.'

Abu'-l-fazl, on the other hand, who according to Badāonī wished to 'wander for a few days in the vale of infidelity for sport,' was favourably impressed by the attitude of the Fathers.[21] 'One night,' he says, 'the assembly in the 'Ibādat-khāna was increasing in the light of truth. Pādrī Radīf, one of the Nazarene sages, who was singular for his understanding and ability, was making points in that feast of intelligence. Some of the untruthful bigots came forward in a blundering way to answer him. Owing to the calmness of the august assembly and the increasing light of justice, it became clear that each of these was weaving a circle of old acquisitions, and was not following the highway of proof, and that the explanation of the riddle of truth was not present to their thoughts. The veil was nearly being stripped once for all from their procedure. They were ashamed and abandoned such discourse and applied themselves to perverting the words of the Gospels. But they could not silence their antagonists by such arguments.'[22] The scene is brought home to us by a contemporary picture made for the Akbarnāma as an illustration to this passage: a picture in which the Fathers sit in attitudes of intense seriousness, while the other disputants lean forward and gesticulate in eager argument.[23]

Of Abu'-l-fazl

Monserrate gives us an idea of the class of argument employed. On the night when he was first introduced to the debate, Father Rudolf, who had studied the Qur'ān in a translation,[24] followed two main lines of thought. In the first place he contended that the Gospel having been foretold in the Old Testament must be superior to the Qur'ān which was not. And secondly he argued that as Muhammad had acknowledged the divine origin of the Gospel he was inconsistent in refusing to acknowledge the divinity of Christ.[25] Later arguments dealt with the character of Muhammad's heaven, the outside witnesses to Christ's divinity, the mystery of the Incarnation and the two natures of Christ, and the inconsistency of the Qur'ān in its varying attitude towards the character of Christ's death.[26] The chronicler de Sousa adds certain other subjects of argument: the absurdity, for instance, of the imputation that the Christians had tampered with the text of the Bible, the explanation (given by Abu'-l-fazl himself, to the perfect satisfaction of the Fathers) of the doctrines of the Trinity and the Incarnation, and the personal life and views of

Attitude of the Mission to Muslim antagonists

Muhammad.[27] In the earlier stages of their Mission the Fathers were pleased to find their opponents silenced, but the vigour of their attack was such that even after their first dispute Akbar had to take them aside and warn them of the danger which they incurred. As the months passed by they realized the tenacity of their opponents and became even less tolerant of their opposition. In September 1580 Rudolf wrote to the Rector at Goa of the impossibility of getting away from the name of Muhammad. 'Nothing, Father,' he cried, 'and I say it with tears, nothing strikes the air but that diabolical name. Scarcely ever do we hear the most sweet name of Jesus. For the Moors only call him Jesus the Prophet, and say that he is not the Son of God; and I know no such Jesus nor can I say else than Jesus, Son of God. And when I say this openly and console myself by repeating "Christ Jesus, Son of God," then all the suffering and sorrow of my soul is renewed, because one of the Muhammadans cries out Stafurla (Istaghfaru'llāh)—"God forbid"; another closes his ears, a third mocks, while another blasphemes. So when I get home, I with the handful of Christians who are with us as in the Ark of Noe, nay the very walls, can repeat nothing but "Son of God, Son of God!" They seem to reply: "How can we sing the Lord's song in a strange land?"'[28]

In connection with these disputes we are told by Father Rudolf a story, which is repeated at a later stage of the Mission, of a proposed Trial by Fire, under which a Muslim and a Christian should enter a fire, each bearing his sacred book. As both Indian and European chroniclers mention it, it doubtless had some basis of fact, but the details differ in the different accounts. According to Badāonī the ordeal was proposed by a faqīr named Qutb-ud-dīn and refused by the Fathers out of cowardice. Abu'-l-fazl represents that it was the Pādrī who proposed the trial and that the liverless and blackhearted Muslims declined.[29] According to Peruschi Akbar two or three times proposed this test, but Rudolf declined to tempt God.[30] Monserrate himself declares that a similar test was suggested by Father Pereira before the Jesuits arrived and was several times put before the Jesuits.[31] It was proposed, he says, by the Muslims to Father Rudolf and was declined by him, although the King supported the proposal. Fearing that he might be accused of cowardice, Father Rudolf subsequently explained to the King that he could not expect a miracle on his particular behalf, that such trials were shown by history to be inconclusive and that they were contrary to the Law of Christ. On this the King replied that his real object in proposing the test was to get rid of a

Story of ordeal by fire

certain obnoxious Mullā by persuading him to enter the fire and that if the Fathers would help him in his scheme he would see that they came to no harm. Father Rudolf, however, declined to support this plot in any way and nothing more was heard of it.[32]

So far as the King himself was concerned, the reception accorded to the Mission was as cordial as could be desired. On arrival they were offered large sums of money, and gained much consideration by their refusal to accept more than was necessary for subsistence. They were accorded quarters in the palace and these again were changed when found unsuitable. They were given food from the royal table: and when Monserrate was ill the King proceeded to visit him and greeted him in Portuguese. In personal intercourse with the King the Fathers were treated with special courtesy. 'He never allowed them,' says Monserrate, 'to remain uncovered in his presence; both at the solemn meetings of the grandees and in private interviews, when he would take them inside for closer colloquy, he would tell them to sit near him. He would shake hands with them most familiarly and would call them apart from the body of ordinary retainers to indulge with them in private conversation. More than once, in public, he walked a short distance with Rudolf, his arm round Rudolf's neck (brachio in ejus collum extento).'[33]

Cordiality of Akbar

This familiarity encouraged the Fathers to speak to him seriously on faults in his régime or his conduct—'modeste quidem et explorato quomodo esset animo affectus,' 'modestly however and not without first examining what mood he was in.'[34] They inveighed against his encouragement of 'gladiatorii ludi' and against his toleration of Satī.[35] They upbraided him for his plurality of wives and for his negligence and tardiness in studying holy things, and bade him set apart a time for hearing the interpretation of the Divine Law. All this was received by him in a kindly spirit, and in dealing with the Fathers on religious subjects he showed befitting respect. Their sacred books and pictures were raised up and kissed by him with scrupulous reverence, and in visiting their Chapel—which he did more than once—he even took off his turban out of deference to European custom. When his sons, Salīm, Murād and Dānyāl—known to the Jesuits as Shaikh-jī, Pahārī and Dān—accompanied him, he insisted on their paying similar respect. He visited the Crib erected by the Fathers for the Christmas of 1580 and he sent his sons also

His sympathy towards Christianity

to see it. The minister, Abu'-l-fazl was appointed to instruct the Fathers in the Persian tongue and Father Monserrate was assigned to the Prince Murād (Pahārī), then about eleven years of age, to instruct him in the Portuguese language and good morals. 'His Majesty,' says Badāonī, 'ordered Prince Murād to take a few lessons in Christianity under good auspices and charged Abu'-l-fazl to translate the Gospel.' Instead of the usual *Bismillāh* (at the head of the Prince's lesson) the following line was used: 'Ai nāmī vey Gesu Christu:' that is, says Badāonī, 'O thou, whose name is merciful and very bountiful.'[36] The Jesuit version of the story is that the Prince in writing Portuguese was taught to begin with the words 'In the name of God,' and that when the King heard this he at once ordered him to add the words 'and of Jesus Christ, the true Prophet and Son of God.' Badāonī has also in another passage a somewhat obscure allusion to the King's Christian proclivities. He refers to a discussion in Akbar's presence as to the method of declining the word *Mūsā* (Moses) and expresses his satisfaction that one of those present replied: 'If I were asked how to decline '*Īsā* (Jesus), what answer should I give?'[37]

The King gave the Fathers full liberty to preach and make conversions. When a Portuguese died at the Court the Emperor allowed him to be buried with all publicity, a large procession marching through the town with crucifixes and lighted tapers. He also approved of a scheme for building a hospital and initiating what would now be termed a 'medical mission.' In matters of difficulty he bade the Fathers consult Abu'-l-fazl and confide their troubles to him as they would to himself. Abu'-l-fazl, we are told, sought instruction from them regarding the Faith, but the Fathers doubted whether he did so in order to embrace Christianity or in order to please the King and be able to give him information on the subject as occasion offered. In any case the Fathers received many favours from him and also from the King's physician.[38]

Regarding the King's attitude towards the contending faiths we are given some interesting accounts.[39] That he had no respect for Islām was evident enough, but the question was how far he was prepared to conform to Christianity. Abu'-l-fazl, it is clear, attached special importance to the influence of the 'Christian philosophers' on Akbar's mind at this time.[40] Akbar himself, however, stated quite candidly, as he had previously done to Father Pereira, that he found the doctrines of the Trinity and the Incarnation to be stumbling-blocks and that if he could accept these he would be ready to

Obstacles to his conversion

give up his kingdom, if need be, to embrace Christianity.[41] The Jesuit writings maintain that there were three other obstacles in the way. In the first place Akbar was a bad listener, and never heard an explanation to the end before starting a new subject. Secondly he was quite unable to give up the plurality of wives. And thirdly he was seeking a sign like that of the fire trial, and no sign was given him. The Fathers writing from Fatehpur are said to have described his religious position as follows:[42]

'The Emperor is not a Muhammadan, but is doubtful as to all forms of faith and holds firmly that there is no divinely accredited form of faith, because he finds in all something to offend his reason and intelligence, for he thinks that everything can be grasped by reason. Nevertheless he at times admits that no faith commends itself so much to him as that of the Gospel, and that when a man goes so far as to believe this to be the true faith and better than others, he is near to adopting it. At the Court some say he is a heathen and adores the sun. Others that he is a Christian. Others that he intends to found a new sect. Among the people there are various opinions regarding the Emperor: some holding him to be a Christian, others a heathen, others a Muhammadan. The more intelligent, however, consider him to be neither Christian nor heathen nor Muhammadan, and hold this to be the truest. Or they think him to be a Muhammadan who outwardly conforms to all religions in order to obtain popularity.'

Popular discontent regarding his attitude

Whatever the precise phase of Akbar's belief may have been at this time it is certain that these signs of free-thinking on his part were most distasteful to the Muslims, and a powerful Court party, including his mother[43] and aunt (recently returned from pilgrimage to Mecca), and backed by the whole influence of the Zanāna, did its best to thwart his supposed leanings towards Christianity. The rebellion against Akbar which broke out in Bengal early in 1580, just before the arrival of the Jesuits at Fatehpur, and the subsequent entry into the rebellion of Mīrzā Hakīm his orthodox brother at Kābul, were grounded mainly on the King's disparagement of Islām, and the Jesuit writers go so far as to speak of the rebellion as having been excited by Akbar's devotion to Christianity, Monserrate describing it as 'a war chiefly undertaken against the religion of Christ.'[44] Towards the end of the year 1580 the Kābul rebellion came to a head and the Pretender made an inroad as far as Lahore. Then Muslim opposition to the Padres became more and more marked and in order to allay suspicions Akbar ceased for a time to see the Jesuits and refused them admission to his presence.

On February 8, 1581, Akbar started to march with an immense force towards Kābul. When he was actually ready to start, the priests asked leave to accompany him, but met with a polite refusal. Next day, however, seeing Father Monserrate teaching his son Murād who was detailed for service at the front, he changed his mind and bade Monserrate join the force. We accordingly have from the pen of Father Monserrate a detailed account of Akbar's camp, his forces, the towns through which he passed, his advance beyond the Indus and his final triumphant entry into Kābul—a document which no future historian of Akbar can fail to utilize. The campaign was made in the grand style and there was much spare time for the King to enjoy himself upon the road in sport and other ways. He was able to continue his taste for religious enquiry and more than once summoned Monserrate to his presence. One day upon the bank of the Indus, the Father presented him with a written abstract of the events of Christ's Passion, and in answer to the King's enquiries explained why Christ did not come down from the Cross, why Christ allowed S. Thomas to put his fingers into his wounds and what was meant by 'sitting at the right hand of God.'[45] On the 29th of June, Akbar sent for the Father at night and asked him to point out Portugal and India in a map or book of geography (geographicae liber). He then discussed the celibacy of the clergy, the Last Judgement, the status of the Paraclete, and the relation of the Qur'ān to the Gospel. Some of his questions seemed to the Father to be shallow and trivial, and he showed that he thought the Holy Ghost to be merely another name for Christ—a mistake which the Father did not think it necessary to correct.[46] When the King had crossed the Indus he again summoned Father Monserrate and questioned him on the contents of his sacred books, the meaning of certain sacred pictures, the significance of Noah's Ark and the tenets of the Armenian and Nestorian Christians. 'The King,' says Monserrate, 'listened; but not to appear drawn to the Christian faith, he pretended sometimes to be occupied with other things. At the same time he did not fear to honour and kiss publicly the image of Christ.'[47]

The Kābul campaign. Monserrate with the army

To Father Monserrate he showed every consideration. While halting at Hazro he asked his advice as to how he should treat his rebel brother, and when the troops reached Jalālābād he insisted that the Father should halt there with his pupil Murād and recover his health. On his return from Kābul he saw him again and questioned him on the defeat of King Sebastian of Portugal in Morocco in 1578. On reaching Rohtās on his home journey he told Father Monserrate that Father Rudolf, whom he had summoned from Fatehpur, was seriously ill at Sarhind. When Father Monserrate at once entreated him for leave to go and see his companion, the King turned to those about him saying, 'See how they love each other'; and gave his assent, providing at the same time funds for the journey. Monserrate hastened to meet his friend at Lahore, but on reaching that place he himself fell ill and Father Rudolf went out alone to meet and congratulate the returning Akbar.[48] The army then moved on, and on December 1, 1581, Akbar amid great rejoicings re-entered Fatehpur Sīkrī.

Dissatisfaction, and gradual break-up of the Mission

Father Henriques had departed to Goa earlier in the year,[49] and during Akbar's absence Father Rudolf had spent the greater part of his time at Fatehpur in solitude, living the life of a recluse, devoted to prayer and penance and the study of Persian. He and his small flock had trials to endure from those around them, being at times pelted with filth and abused as Kāfirs, but he counted all this as nothing, remembering that he had not yet resisted unto blood. 'Nondum usque ad sanguinem restitimus.'[50] On the King's return Rudolf was, however, well received, and Akbar started fresh enquiries from him on subjects such as the nature of the Trinity.[51] Fresh public disputes were commenced by the King at which discussions took place regarding the attitude of the Qur'ān to unbelievers, the distinction between grace and faith, the Sonship of Christ and so forth, and the Fathers had again to be warned against excessive violence of language. The old zest for discussion was, however, gone and an attempt by Akbar to reintroduce more formal disputations had to be abandoned.[52] Christian ritual was, it is true, publicly practised, for among the innovations deplored by Badāonī we learn that 'the ringing of gongs as in use with the Christians (nawākhtan-i-nāqūs nasārī) and the showing of the figure of the Trinity (tamāshā'ī-i-sūrat-i-sālis salāsa) and the Cribs (cunabula, kanābalān) which is their time of mirth (ki khushgāhi eshān ast) and other childish playthings of theirs were daily in practice.' His chronogram to express the date was *Kufr shā'e shud,*' or 'Heresy became common'.[53] The King feeling secure after his victory, drifted definitely outside the pale of Islām and many Muslim customs were under his orders abandoned or forbidden. But this development was accompanied by the concurrent adoption by Akbar of many Hindu and Pārsi practices and by a move towards the assumption of semi-divine prerogatives. His support to the Fathers' arguments and his respect for their books began to diminish. All this was distasteful to the Fathers. They felt they were making no progress and began to think of closing their Mission. 'Giving the pearls of the Gospel to the King,' as Monserrate puts it, 'was exposing them to be trampled and trodden under foot.' The Provincial at Goa had bidden them return, but left them discretion to stay if this was found advisable. They had been troubled by the apparent duplicity of Akbar in disavowing certain hostile movements carried out by his officers against the Portuguese at Damān.[54] And a further excuse for departure presented itself in connection with a proposal made by Akbar to send an embassy to Europe to congratulate Philip II of Spain on his accession to the throne of Portugal. Akbar, however, refused to let the Fathers go, and it was only after some delay that it was decided that Father Monserrate should join the embassy and that Aquaviva should remain at Fatehpur.[55] Before the embassy started, the two Fathers had a private interview with Akbar at which he charged Monserrate with respectful messages to the Pope.[56]

Proposed embassy to the King of Spain

The embassy set forth in April 1582. It was intended to secure among other things a fresh mission of priests to Akbar's Court, and a copy of the letter which accompanied the embassy is still extant in the first 'daftar' of the Inshā-i-Abu'-l-fazl. It is addressed to the 'Ruler of the Europeans' (Farmān-riwā-i-Farang), a title appropriate to Philip II. In the course of the letter Akbar states his conviction that in comparison with the next world the present is of no account and describes his desire to learn the truth in religious matters.[57]

'Therefore,' he adds, 'we associate at convenient seasons with learned men of all religions and thus derive profit from their exquisite discourses and exalted aspirations. Our language, however, being different from yours, we hope that you will rejoice us by sending to these parts a man able to represent to us those sublime objects of research in an intelligible manner. It has been brought to our notice that the revealed books, such as the Pentateuch, the Gospels and the Psalms, have been translated into Arabic and Persian. Should these books which are profitable to all, whether translated or not, be procurable in your country, send them. Dated in the month of Rabī' u 'l-awwal in the year 990.' (March–April 1582.)

The embassy reached Surat on August 5, 1582, and from that place the ambassador, Syad Muzaffar, who had been appointed against his will, absconded to the Deccan; but Father Monserrate with the other delegate 'Abdulla Khān continued their journey by sea from Damān to Goa. As it was then too late in the season for them to be given passages to Lisbon, the journey to

Europe was postponed and ultimately 'Abdulla Khān returned to Akbar's Court without achieving the object of the embassy.

Meanwhile, even in the hour of failure, Aquaviva did not himself abandon hope. Here, for instance, is an extract from a letter which he wrote to his uncle, then General of the Society, at the very time when the embassy was leaving Fatehpur.[58]

Rudolf Aquaviva alone

'First,' he wrote, 'the Emperor is in a more hopeful state than heretofore : he desires to know our faith and attends to it with greater diligence than at first, showing much affection thereto, though impediments also are not lacking, and the love and familiarity with which he treats us leave nothing to be desired. 2. We hope to see some fruit from the Emperor's second son Pahari, a boy of 13 years of age, who is learning the Portuguese language and therewith the things relating to our faith, and who shows himself well disposed thereto and who is of great natural genius and has good inclination. Father Monserrate was his teacher and now I am. 3. We have discovered a new nation of heathen called Bottan (Tibetans) which is beyond Lahore toward the River Indus, a nation very well inclined and given to pious works. They are white men, and Mohammedans do not live among them, wherefore we hope that if two earnest Fathers are sent thither, a great harvest of other heathen may be reaped.[59] 4. There is here an old man,[60] the father of the Emperor's secretary, in whom he confides in matters of faith. He has left the world and is of great virtue and given much to contemplation of divine things, whence he appears disposed to receive the light of our faith. He is very friendly to us and listens to our faith and we have already visited him several times at his house with much consolation. 5. Where we are is the true India, and this realm is but a ladder which leads to the greater part of Asia ; and now that the Society has obtained a footing and is so favoured by so great an Emperor and by his sons, it seems not fitting to leave it before trying all possible means to commence the conversion of the continent of India ; seeing that all that has so far been done has been merely on the sea-coast.'

The case for continuing the Mission could not have been more clearly or fairly put, but the Provincial at Goa appears to have received from Father Monserrate a less hopeful report, and he again recalled Father Rudolf. The Father was, however, unable to leave, and he continued to hold his solitary outpost at the Court. His zeal was thereby only increased. Attempts on his life were suspected, but he refused to have a guard. He set himself again to study Persian so as to be able to converse freely with Akbar. He fasted rigorously and practised the most severe austerities. Many years afterwards the Prince Salīm would recall how he had found a whip covered with blood in the Father's room, and how modestly the Father tried to conceal the fact that he had been using it on himself.[61] The progress of the mission meanwhile was disappointing. Men of position who parleyed with Christianity failed to be converted, and the interpreter Domingo Pires got into some trouble of which we have not got the details. At the same time, the King maintained his affability, attended Pires' wedding, interpreted the Father's discourse to the bride, and stayed at the Father's house till nearly eight o'clock at night. He asked to see Mass celebrated and as there was no risk of irreverence his request could not be refused, but when Father Rudolf had celebrated the Divine Mystery with many tears his only comment was : 'You ate and drank, but did not invite me.'[61a] Father Rudolf remained bewildered as to the proper course to follow, and in September 1582 he wrote to the Provincial at Goa, placing the facts before him and suggesting that he should be allowed to obtain leave to go and consult the Provincial in person, as to the future of the Mission. The Provincial seems to have authorized him to obtain from the King a temporary leave of absence, if he could not obtain permission to depart altogether. Akbar who entertained a real respect for him was still loath to let him go ; but at last, in February 1583, he allowed him to proceed to Goa on the understanding that he should, if possible, return.

The following is a translation of a Portuguese version of the farmān addressed by Akbar to the Father Provincial on this occasion.[62]

Akbar's farmān permitting his departure

'God is great. Farmān of Jalāl-ud-dīn Muhammad Akbar Pādshāh Ghāzī. Lord of the sciences of all the books of the law and of the interpretations, to whom nothing pertaining to the law of Christ is hidden, but who is rather thoroughly acquainted with the divine secrets, the Father Provincial whom I greatly cherish and love, will know that the petition that he sent me was given me. It came in good condition and I saw it well, and with it friendship was increased. With regard to what he wrote to me about sending hence Father Rudolf,—since I like very much the book of the Heavenly Jesus, and desire to discover the truth of it and with the aid of his skill to find out the meanings of those who have written in the past, therefore I have much love for the Father ; and, considering that he is wise and versed in the laws, I desire to have him every hour in conversation with me, and for this reason I refused him the permission ; but as Your Paternity asked it me by letter several times, I did so, and gave him the permission ; and as my intention is that our friendship should go on increasing more and more day by day, it behoves Your Paternity to labour on your side towards preserving it, by sending Father Rudolf back to me with some other Father, and I wish this with the least possible delay ; for I desire that the Fathers of this Order be with me, because I like them much. And to the Father I said many things by word of mouth, for him to repeat them to your Paternity, which Your Paternity will consider well. Done in the moon of the month of February 1583.'

Father Rudolf Aquaviva was pressed to receive a parting present, but the only gift he would accept was the permission to take with him to Goa a family of Russian slaves who had been for a long time in Akbar's household, in the service of the Queen Mother. With this parting gift from the Great Mogul he started for Goa and arrived there in May 1583, looking, it was said, like a man who had come, not from a Court but from the penances of a novitiate.[63]

His departure from Fatehpur

While in Goa he heard of the execution of Father Campion at Tyburn and bewailed his own unworthiness for a similar fate. The end, however, was not long in coming. On the 27th July (N.S.) of the same year he was killed, with four companions, at Cuncolim in Salsette near Goa. A chapel was subsequently built at the place and several miraculous events are recorded in connection with the site.[64] Relics of the martyr were demanded in Europe. One arm was sent in 1600 to his uncle and another in 1634 to the Rector of the College at Naples. The body, with those of his companions, was buried first in Rachol and then in the Church of S. Paul at Goa. In 1862 the relics were removed to the Cathedral at Old Goa, and they were shortly afterwards deposited partly in Rome and partly in the Fort Chapel at Bombay. In 1893 Rudolf was beatified by the Church and is now known as the Blessed Rudolf Aquaviva. In Jesuit churches the post-communion prayer on July 27 is as follows :

His martyrdom

'Grant, O Lord Jesus Christ, that we who have been strengthened by participation in this salutary sacrifice, may imitate the unconquered constancy in faith and charity of Thy blessed Martyr Rudolf and his companions.'

Akbar, we are told, on hearing the news of his death was greatly grieved (graviter maeruit) and exclaimed, 'Ah me, Father! Did I not tell you not to go away? But you would not listen to me.' He loved him, says Monserrate, not because he himself wished to be a Christian, but because he recognized the Father's intense conviction of the truth of his own religion and his desire to bring others to his own way of life.[65]

NOTES

[1] And yet he made minute enquiries from these Portuguese with a view to 'civilizing this savage race' (guroh-i-wahshī), and the orders which he proceeded to issue regarding the Portuguese were couched in such language that the Portuguese hesitated to receive them (Judice Biker, *Colleccão de Tratados*, Lisbon, 1887, XIV, pp. 25–26). Akbarnāma, Elliot, *Hist. Ind.*, VI, p. 42 and translation by Beveridge (*Bib. Ind.*, 1912),

III, p. 37 and note. Monserrate *Relaçam, J.A.S.B.*, VIII, 1912 (Hosten), p. 216, *J.A.S.B.*, LXXIII, 1904 (Beveridge), pp. 52–53.

[2] Akbarnāma, Elliot, *Hist. Ind.*, VI, p. 59; Monserrate *Relaçam*, loc. cit.; Blochmann, *Ā'īn* (trans.), I, p. 440; Manrique (Luard), I, pp. 37–38; Beveridge in *J.A.S.B.*, 1888, p. 34, and 1904, p. 54. Tavares is called Partāb Bār, or Tār, or Bāz, or Bā, in various copies of the Akbarnāma and Tāb Bārrū in the Darbār-i-Akbarī. His wife is spoken of as Ulsozbā, Nashūrnā, Nasurtā, Bāsubāran or Basurbā, representations in all probability of some such name as Assunta (Beveridge in *J.A.S.B.*, 1904, p. 53, and in note in translation of Akbarnāma, *Bib. Ind.*, 1912, III, pp. 349–350).

[3] Badāonī, *Bib. Ind.* (Lowe's translation), II, p. 215.

[4] Monserrate *Relaçam, J.A.S.B.*, VIII, 1912 (Hosten), p. 218. The Christian name of the priest is variously given as Julian, Gileanes, Egidio (Giles) and Egidio Anes. He was not a Jesuit. He may have been Indian-born, for he is described by Botelho in his *Relation* as 'clerigo da terra.'

[5] Peruschi speaks of an embassy headed by Cabral 'about 1578' as having influenced Akbar (*Informatione*, p. 28, cf. *Drei Newe Relationes*, p. 134). Vincent Smith treats this embassy as historical, but there seems to be no confirmation of its having taken place, and possibly there is some confusion with the deputation of 1573 above mentioned. See Father Felix in *J.P.H.S.*, V, 1916, p. 55. Guzman and du Jarric, though giving the date 1578 for Cabral's Mission, mention it in such sequence as to lead to the supposition that 1573 was meant. See also note by Hosten in *J.A.S.B.*, VIII, 1912, p. 216.

[6] See *Annuae Literae*, 1582, p. 111.

[7] Dominic Pires was an Armenian Christian (see *Mem. A.S.B.*, V, 1916 (Hosten), p. 173).

[8] The original of the farmān is not forthcoming, but numerous translations are extant. That given in the text is Hosten's translation of Monserrate's Latin version. (Comment., fol. 6 (a).) De Sousa gives December 1578 as the date of the farmān.

[9] De Sousa, *Or. Conq.*, 1710, vol. II, p. 149, gives in full the 'Resolution of the Prelates of India concerning the Mission to the Mogol': an interesting document; see translation in *Mem. A.S.B.*, III, 1914 (Hosten), p. 545.

[10] See Chapter VIII. It is curious that the celebrated China missionary, Matthew Ricci, who was in India in 1580–1581 and describes the Mogor Mission in his letters of those years, never mentions Monserrate (*Opere Storiche*, Tacchi Venturi, Macerata, 1911, II, pp. 1–26).

[11] Bartoli's *Missione al Gran Mogor* (1714) is a Life of Rudolf, and we have in our own day Suau's *Les Bienheureux Martyrs de Salsette* (Lille, 1893), Angelini's *Istoria della Vita e del Martirio dei Beati Rodolfo e compagni* (Rome, 1893), Gruber's *Der selige Rudolf Aquaviva und seine Gefährten* (Ratisbon, 1894), and Goldie's *First Christian Mission to the Great Mogul* (Dublin, 1897). There is also an account of Rudolf in a Relation by I. Desideri to which allusion in made in Chapter XIX.

[12] Commentarius, fol. 105 (*Mem. A.S.B.*, III, 1914), translation by Hosten in the *Catholic Herald of India*, July 20, 1921, cf. Hoyland and Banerjee, *Commentary of Monserrate*, 1922, p. 192.

[13] *Oriente Conquistado*, 1710, vol. II, p. 159. See translation in *The Examiner*, Bombay (Hosten), March 13, 20; June 12, 19 and July 3,

1920; Murray's *Discoveries in Asia*, II, p. 83, and Monserrate's Commentarius (*Mem. A.S.B.*, III, 1914), fol. 17(b) to 19(a). Hosten suggests that both accounts may be by Monserrate.

[14] Maps illustrating the route will be found in Monserrate's Commentarius, in Goldie's *First Christian Mission to the Great Mogul*, 1897, p. 59, and in V. A. Smith's *Akbar the Great Mogul*, 1917, p. 172.

[15] De Sousa and Bartoli give the 27th; Guzman the 28th; du Jarric the 18th; Monserrate gives no date.

[16] Manucci; *Storia do Mogor* (Irvine), 1907, I, p. 140.

[17] Monserrate, Commentarius (*Mem. A.S.B.*, III, 1914), fol. 19(a).

[18] This view is supported by a statement by Catrou (edition of 1705, p. 96), but not so far as I am aware by other authorities, that Abu'-l-fazl recommended to Akbar that as Islām could never become the prevailing religion in India, an attempt should be made to impose Christianity. Akbar in inviting a further Mission in 1582 gave indeed as his reason that he wished to strengthen the bonds of love, harmony and union among the people (*Ind. Antiquary*, XVI, 1887, p. 136); but this falls short of Catrou's statement.

[19] This is well brought out both in Vincent Smith's book on Akbar and in Hoyland and Banerjee's introduction to their translation of Monserrate's Commentary. See also R. P. Karkaria 'Akbar and the Parsees,' *J. Bo. R.A.S.*, XIX, 1897, pp. 289–305; Jivanji Jamsedji Modi, The Parsees at the Court of Akbar,' *J. Bo. R.A.S.*, XXI, 1904, pp. 69–245, and Father Heras, S.J., 'Three Moghul Paintings on Akbar's Religious Discussions,' *J. Bo. R.A.S.*, vol. III, 1928, pp. 192–202.

[20] These quotations, except in this last sentence, are from Lowe's translation (1884), II, pp. 262–268. The original of this sentence is 'haqī'at i nasrānīat asbāt karda millat-'īsawī tarwīj dānand,' and there is some doubt whether the subject of this sentence is 'His Majesty,' or 'The Padres.' Rehatsek (in *The Emperor Akbar's Repudiation of Esllām*, 1866, p. 25), Blochmann (*Ā'īn*, I, p. 182), and Lowe assumed the former, Elliot (*Hist. Ind.*, V, p. 529) the latter.

[21] In a poem by Abu'-l-fazl and in several poems by his brother Faizī, there are sympathetic references to Christianity. See Blochmann, *Ā'īn*, I, pp. xxxii, 557 and 559; cf. also p. 581 (Nazīrī).

[22] Akbarnāma (*Bib. Ind.*, transl. by Beveridge), 1912, III, p. 368. The alternative readings for 'Radīf' are mentioned by Beveridge in his note on the passage. There can be no doubt that Rudolf Aquaviva is meant, although Abu'-l-fazl introduces this account in dealing with the year 1578–1579. See also Beveridge in *J.A.S.B.*, LXXIII, 1904, p. 51, where it is pointed out that the reference to Aquaviva in the *Bib. Ind.* edition of the Akbarnāma was presumably inserted in a recension by the author, as it does not appear in the Lucknow or Cawnpore editions.

[23] See frontispiece to this volume.

[24] As to this see Chapter XIII.

[25] Commentarius (*Mem. A.S.B.*, III, 1914), fol. 24(b).

[26] Commentarius (*Mem. A.S.B.*, III, 1914), fol. 25 (a), 35 and 36.

[27] *Or. Conq.*, vol. II, pp. 167–9, translated (Hosten) in *The Examiner*, Bombay, June 19 and July 3, 1920. In a reproduction of the disputes given in the *Dābistān* (written some sixty years after Akbar's death) the arguments for the Muslim standpoint are that the Christians had tampered with the Bible so as to omit prophetic references to Muhammad and that Muhammad's claim to be a prophet was proved by his miracle of splitting the moon. The *Dābistān* describes arguments between the

various religions ; how far they are exact we cannot tell, but they appear to be based in part on Xavier's dialogues in the Ā'īna-i-Haqq-numā to which reference is made in Chapter XIV. See Shea and Troyer's *Dābistān*, 1843, III, p. 65, and Dr. Lee's preface to Martyn's *Controversial Tracts*, 1824, p. xxxvii.

[28] Letter of Sept. 10, 1580, transld. in Goldie, *The First Christian Mission*, p. 76 ; see also Bartoli, *Missione* (Piacenza edition), p. 132.

[29] Badāonī, *Bib. Ind.*, II, p. 299 ; Lowe's translation, II, p. 308 ; Akbarnāma, Beveridge transl., III, p. 369 ; Beveridge in *J.A.S.B.*, LXXIII, 1904, p. 52.

[30] *Hist. Rel.*, p. 14 ; *Informatione*, p. 37.

[31] Commentarius (*Mem. A.S.B.*, III, 1914), fol. 21 (a) and 32 (b).

[32] Commentarius (*Mem. A.S.B.*, III, 1914), fol. 26–28. Much the same story is given in Bartoli (Piacenza edition, p. 31), and de Sousa (*Or. Conq.*, II, p. 170). The incident is treated more summarily by Guzman (*Hist.*, p. 250) and du Jarric, II, p. 449 (Payne, p. 30). Similar stories are not uncommon in the history of Christian Missions.

[33] Monserrate, Commentarius (*Mem. A.S.B.*, III, 1914), fol. 39 (a).

[34] Monserrate, Commentarius (*Mem. A.S.B.*, III, 1914), fol. 37 (a).

[35] Abu'-l-fazl has a passage illustrating both Akbar's attitude towards Satī and his recognition of the Christian attitude towards women. He tells how Akbar said to the learned Christians (the Fathers) : ' Since you reckon the reverencing of women as part of your religion and allow not more than one wife to a man, it would not be wonderful if such fidelity and life-sacrifice were found amongst your women. The extraordinary thing is that it occurs among those of the Brahman religion ' (Akbarnāma, *Bib. Ind.*, transl. by Beveridge, III, p. 372).

[36] Lowe's translation, II, p. 267. Slightly different versions are given in Blochmann, *Ā'īn*, I, p. 182, and Rehatsek, *The Emperor Akbar's Repudiation of Esllām*, p. 25. Blochmann suggested the reading ' Ai nām-i tū Jesus o Kiristo,' and says that the words are so given in the *Dābistān*, but he gives no reference to the passage where they occur. Elliot thought the words were intended to represent ' In nomine Jesu Christi.' *Hist. Ind.*, V, p. 529.

[37] Lowe's translation, II, p. 190. ' Mūsā kudām sīgha ast ? ' See Beveridge, *J.A.S.B.*, LXXIII, 1904, p. 54–55. It is just possible that the reference is to one 'Isā Khān, who was a rebel in Bengal.

[38] Hakīm 'Alī (*Ā'īn*, I, p. 466, see *J.A.S.B.*, VIII, 1912 (Hosten), p. 201. He went about this time on a mission to Bījāpur where he would be likely to meet Portuguese.

[39] The subject has been often dealt with. See the authorities quoted in note 9 to Chapter I.

[40] Akbarnāma, Beveridge's translation, *Bib. Ind.*, III, p. 398.

[41] He even went so far as to suggest that he might use the pretext of a pilgrimage to Mecca in order to go to Goa and be baptised. Monserrate, Commentarius (*Mem. A.S.B.*, III, 1914), fol. 31 (a).

[42] Peruschi, *Hist. Rel.*, p. 12 ; *Informatione*, p. 32 ; du Jarric, II, p. 448.

[43] The lady known as Mariam-makānī (dwelling with the Virgin Mary). In describing Akbar's well-known devotion to his mother, the English traveller Coryate (*Purchas' Pilgrims*, MacLehose, IV, p. 490), writes : ' He never denyed her anything but this, that she demanded of him that our Bible might be hanged about an Asses necke, and beaten about the Towne of Agra, for that the Portugals having taken a ship of

theirs at Sea, in which was found the Alcoran amongst the Moores, tyed it about the necke of a Dogge and beat the same Dogge about the Towne of Ormuz ; but hee denyed her request, saying, " That if it were ill in the Portugals to doe so to the Alcoran, it became not a King to requite ill with ill, for that the contempt of any Religion was the contempt of God, and he would not be revenged upon an innocent Booke." ' The same story is told in Bry's *Historia Indiae Orientalis*, XII, 1628, p. 32, and in *Hazart*, I, p. 268, where, however, it is attributed to Jahāngīr and Jahāngīr's mother.

[44] Commentarius (*Mem. A.S.B.*, III, 1914), fol. 42 (a).

[45] Commentarius (*Mem. A.S.B.*, III, 1914), fol. 68 (a).

[46] Commentarius (*Mem. A.S.B.*, III, 1914), fol. 71 (b)–76 (a). The mistake was doubtless due to the indeterminate application of the titles Rūhu'l-quds and Rūhu'l-lāh.

[47] Commentarius (*Mem. A.S.B.*, III, 1914), fol. 77 (a)–78 (b). According to Bartoli (*Missione*, p. 64, see Piacenza edition, pp. 39 and 43), Akbar in talking to the Fathers would sometimes fall asleep, as the result of a too copious use of spirits or *post* (opium).

[48] Commentarius (*Mem. A.S.B.*, III, 1914), fol. 70 (a), 84 (a), 87 (b), 90 (a).

[49] He died in 1597 after thirty years' work in the Society. *Annuae Literae*, 1597 (Naples, 1607).

[50] Letter quoted by Bartoli, *Missione* (Piacenza ed.), p. 60, which however dates from an earlier period. The quotation is from Heb. xii, 4.

[51] Commentarius (*Mem. A.S.B.*, III, 1914), fol. 95 (b).

[52] Commentarius (*Mem. A.S.B.*, III, 1914), fol. 98 (a) and 101 (a).

[53] Badāonī, *Bib. Ind.*, transln., II, p. 304. Blochmann, *Ā'īn*, I, p. 193. *Pros. A.S.B.*, May 1870, p. 146, and Rehatsek *The Emperor Akbar's Repudiation of Esllām* (Bombay 1866), p. 51. The conjecture ' kunābulān ' for ' bulbulān ' is Blochmann's (*Ā'īn*, I, p. 618). The date works out to A.H. 985 or A.D. 1577–1578, which is clearly too early, and from its place in the narration the passage evidently applies to A.H. 990 or A.D. 1582–1583.

[54] Father Rudolf more than once took up questions of Portuguese politics, but not, it would seem, so wholeheartedly as some of his successors.

[55] *Annuae Literae Soc. Jesu* (1582), pp. 111–112.

[56] Commentarius (*Mem. A.S.B.*, III, 1914), fol. 97 (a).

[57] The Calcutta edition of 1810, p. 42, and the Cawnpore lithographed edition of 1875, p. 37, represent the letter as addressed to the ' European scholars ' (Dānāyān-i-Farang), but there are other versions which give the reading quoted above. The vague formula ' farmānriwā-i-Farang ' may have been purposely used owing to Akbar's uncertainty as to the monarch then actually in authority at Goa. The letter has long attracted attention and full translations are given in Fraser's *Nadir Shah*, 1742, p. 12 (reproduced in Hough's *Hist. of Christianity in India*, 1839, II, p. 262, and W. C. Taylor's *History of Mohammedanism*, 1834, p. 319), and in Hanway's *Travels*, 1754, II, p. 405. Rehatsek gives the full text and a translation (from which the extract in the text is taken) in the *Indian Antiquary*, XVI, 1887, pp. 135–139. A German translation through the Latin is given by Strobl in a letter from Delhi dated 26 October, 1747 (*Weltbott*, No. 648). There the letter is represented as addressed to the King and the date is given as either A.D. 1584 or A.H. 997 (wrongly in both cases).

[58] Letter dated April 1582, Bartoli, *Missione* (Piacenza edition), p. 218.

[59] The ultimate results of this recommendation are noticed in Chapter XIX.

[60] Shaikh Mubārik, father of Abu'-l-fazl. He was then seventy-nine years old and did not die till eleven years later, in 1593. (Blochmann, *Ā'īn*, I, p. 490).

[61] Father J. Xavier's letter of 26 July, 1598; see *J.A.S.B.*, 1896, LXV, p. 75.

[61a] De Sousa, *Oriente Conquistado*, II, p. 171.

[62] Brit. Mus. Addl. MSS. 9854, fol. 4. *J.A.S.B.*, 1896, LXV, p. 59.

[63] Cf. du Jarric, II, p. 457.

[64] Pictures—all more or less imaginary—of the martyrdom are not uncommon in Europe. One of these, in the sacristy of S. Vitale at Rome, is said to date from 1603; Suau, *Les Bienheureux Martyrs de Salsette*, p. 194. A view of the chapel built at the site of the martyrdom can be seen in A. Lopes Mendes' *A India Portugueza*, Lisbon, 1886, II, p. 183.

[65] Commentarius (*Mem. A.S.B.*, III, 1914), fol. 106 (a).

CHAPTER III

THE SECOND MISSION TO AKBAR, 1591

Sic non potuistis una hora vigilare mecum ?
(Matt. xxvi, 40.)

WE hear nothing further of Akbar's relations towards Christianity till 1590, when his Court was at Lahore. In writing of the events of that year Abu'-l-fazl notes :[1]

'On the 26th Farwardīn (6th April 1590) Padre Farmaliūn came to Court from the port of Goa. Owing to His Majesty's appreciativeness, he received high honour. He possessed abundance of sense and knowledge. His Majesty made over some quick-witted and intellectual persons to be instructed by him in order that the translation of Greek books might be carried out. Varieties of knowledge were acquired. Also a large number of Farangīs and Armenians arrived and brought with them China cloths and other goods of that country.'

Leo Grimon at Lahore

The Jesuit account of the happenings of this and the following year, which are contained in two letters written in November 1590 and November 1591 respectively by the Provincial at Goa to the General of the Society at Rome,[2] tells us that in 1590 a Greek subdeacon named Leo Grimon, who is probably the Farmaliūn mentioned by Abu'-l-fazl, happened to be at the Mogul Court on his way to his native country from some place unknown,[3] and that Akbar took the opportunity of sending with him to Goa a letter for the Viceroy, together with one for the Fathers of the Society, asking for a further Mission to his Court. A translation of the warrant of safe-conduct given to Grimon has been preserved and runs as follows :[4]

Despatched to Goa

'The Command of the exalted Mahomet, great King and Lord of the Fosliere[5] to all the Captains, Viceroys, Governors, Treasurers and other officers of my realm. You are to know that I have greatly honoured and favoured Dom Leon Grimon ; and it is my will and intention that the Captains and other officers of my Kingdom should do likewise, for I hope by his means to ensure the despatch of certain other Fathers whom I have invited to come to me from Goa, and through whose holy doctrine I hope to be restored from death to life, even as their master, Jesus Christ, who came down from heaven to earth, raised many from the dead and gave them new life. On this occasion I am summoning the most learned and most virtuous of the Fathers that they may help me to a true knowledge of the Christian law and of the royal highways by which they travel to the presence of God. I therefore command, etc.'

The parwāna ordered that supplies and transport and due escort should be provided for the Fathers, and laid down their route, which was to be (so far as we can disentangle the names in their European dress) by Ahmadābād, Pātan, Bīkānīr and Multān to Lahore.

Of the two letters carried by Leo Grimon, we have a translation of that addressed to the Fathers of the Society, which runs : [6]

Akbar's letter to the Fathers at Goa

'In the Name of God. The exalted and invincible Akbar to those who are in God's grace and have tasted of his Holy Spirit and to those that are obedient to the Spirit of the Messiah and lead men to God. I say to you, learned Fathers, whose words are heeded as those of men retired from the world, who have left the pomps and honours of earth : Fathers who walk by the true way ; I would have your Reverences know that I have knowledge of all the faiths of the world both of various kinds of heathen and of the Mohammedans, save that of Jesus Christ which is from God and as such recognised and followed by many. Now in that I feel great inclination to the friendship of the Fathers I desire that I may be taught by them the Christian law. There has recently come to my Court and royal Palace one Dom Leo Grimon, a person of great merit and good discourse, whom I have questioned on sundry matters, and who has answered well to the satisfaction of myself and my doctors. He has assured me that there are in India [i.e., Portuguese India and its neighbourhood] several Fathers of great prudence and learning, and if this be so Your Reverences will be able immediately on receiving my letter, to send some of them to my Court with all confidence, so that in disputations with my doctors I may compare their several learning and character, and see the superiority of the Fathers over my doctors, whom we call Caziques,[7] and who by this means may be taught to know the truth. If they will remain in my Court, I shall build them such lodging that they may live in greater honour and favour than any Father who has up to this been in this country and when they wish to leave I shall let them depart with honour. You should therefore do as I ask of you in this letter. Written at the commencement of the moon of June.'

The Fathers at Goa were assured by Grimon that the prospects of a Mission were favourable. The King was less of a Muslim than ever. Muhammad was as hated at the Mogul's Court as in Christendom. Minarets had been destroyed and mosques were being used as stables. The King, he added, had dismissed all his wives but one[8] and had shown signs of a marked respect for Christianity. He had even celebrated the day of the Assumption of the Virgin in 1590, by bringing out and paying respect to his picture of Our Lady. Akbar's proposal was accordingly accepted with enthusiasm. Applications for appointment to the Mission were made not only by Fathers but also by students at the College. In the end two Fathers—Duarte Leitão and Christoval de Vega and a lay brother called Estevão Ribeiro[9] were selected, and left for Lahore.

Departure of a second Mission

The members of the Mission were well received and they were given a house in the palace. A school was started under their direction, which was attended by the sons of nobles as well as by the King's own son and grandson (or nephew), and the pupils were taught to read and write Portuguese.

Its speedy return

The Fathers, however, found themselves strongly opposed by a faction at the Court and soon perceived that the King had no intention of becoming a Christian. They accordingly decided to withdraw without delay. Vega left for Goa, but the Provincial wished to send him back, as he was understood to be a great favourite with Akbar; and in any case Leitão was instructed to remain where he was. The Mission, however, came shortly afterwards to an abrupt conclusion for reasons which have not come down to us and both missionaries returned to Portuguese India.[10]

NOTES

[1] Akbarnāma, *Bib. Ind.* (Beveridge's transl.), III, p. 873; Elliot, *Hist. Ind.*, VI, p. 85; Beveridge, *J.A.S.B.*, LXXIII, 1904, p. 55; Payne, *Akbar and the Jesuits*, 1926, p. 229. I am presuming that *Farmaliūn*, in Persian characters, is a mistake for *Qarmaliūn* or *Gharmaliūn* and represents Grimaleon sc. Leo Grimon, and that the reference in Abu'-l-fazl is to his visit in 1590, but as will be seen from the above references these assumptions are not free from doubt.

[2] They were published in Italian by Spitilli in 1592 and their substance is reproduced in Guzman's *Historia* of 1601 and du Jarric's *Histoire* of 1608. Fairly full extracts in English are given in *J.A.S.B.*, 1896, LXV, pp. 62–63.

[3] He returned to Lahore with the two Jesuit Fathers in 1591 and he accompanied Goes in 1603 as far as Kābul.

[4] Payne's translation of du Jarric's version.

[5] The meaning of this word has not been explained. Spitilli, in the Italian and Latin versions, reads ' Fostiera ' : see Payne, *Akbar and the Jesuits,* 1926, p. 229. Du Jarric, *Thesaurus,* has ' Follerij,' Guzman has ' Fosliera.'

[6] Slightly modified from the translations from du Jarric's French version given in *J.A.S.B.*, LXV, 1896, p. 64, and in Payne, *Akbar and the Jesuits,* p. 48 ; see du Jarric, II, p. 461.

[7] Cazique—Arabic Kashish—was the term applied by the Jesuits to the Muslim priests or mullās.

[8] See du Jarric, II, p. 458 ; Hazart, I, p. 255 ; Catrou, English edition of 1709, p. 159. In this particular no confirmation from other sources is forthcoming. The *Advis Moderne* of 1598 merely says that Akbar had seriously considered this some years previously. Cf. footnote to p. 256 of Vincent Smith, *Akbar the Great Mogul,* 1919.

[9] The name of the lay brother is recorded in a letter from Father Anthony Mendez written in 1636 (*Mem. A.S.B.*, V, 1916 (Hosten), p. 152).

[10] Leitão died in 1593 of poison. Vega became afterwards Superior of the House at Chaul and bore an excellent reputation (J. Xavier's letter of November 12, 1593, *J.A.S.B.*, XXIII, 1927, p. 114). The departure from Mogor may have been due, as indicated by Jouvency, to fear of a general revolt (*Hist. Soc. Jesu,* V, vol. II, p. 451).

CHAPTER IV

THE THIRD MISSION TO AKBAR, 1595–1605

> Bernardus colles, valles Benedictus amabat,
> Oppida Franciscus, celebres Ignatius urbes.
>
> Agra and Lahore of Great Mogul.
> (MILTON, *Paradise Lost*, XI.)

THERE was obviously some dissatisfaction at Goa, if not at Rome itself, at the hasty dissolution of the second Mission. It was still thought by many that Akbar had been on the point of becoming a Christian. 'Venerunt filii usque ad partum,' says the chronicler, 'sed virtus non est pariendi.'[1] Akbar himself was greatly dissatisfied, and in 1594 despatched another message through an Armenian Christian to the Viceroy at Goa asking for some further learned men to be sent to him. On this occasion it was the Provincial, not the Viceroy, who doubted the advisability of undertaking another Mission. After the failure of two efforts, the Provincial saw little use in a third attempt, but the Viceroy was impressed by the possibility of good results not merely of a religious but also of a political character, and the Provincial after consultation with other ecclesiastics gave his consent. For this he afterwards received the thanks of the King of Spain.[2]

Further invitation from Akbar

The selection of a priest to conduct the Mission was a matter of much importance both from the political and from the religious point of view. It was decided to appoint Father Jerome Xavier, a grand-nephew of S. Francis and at that time head of the Professed House of Goa; and with him were sent Father Emmanuel Pinheiro and Brother Benedict de Goes. They were, each in his own line, men of outstanding competence.

The third Mission. Personnel

Father Jerome Xavier was a Navarrois who belonged to the noble house of Espeleta, but in view of the fact that he was a grandson of the sister of S. Francis Xavier he himself always adopted the name of Xavier in the Society.[3] He was born in 1549 and had entered the Society in 1568 at Alcala. He had spent most of his service in India, firstly as Rector at Bassein, then at Cochin and finally at Goa. Without possessing the enthusiastic asceticism of Aquaviva, he was an earnest man of mature age who had spent most of his life in

Jerome Xavier

teaching and who had enjoyed positions of trust. For nearly twenty years he was to remain at the Mogul Court: sometimes in favour, sometimes in disgrace; working sometimes for the spiritual conversion of Emperors, and sometimes for the material advancement of the Portuguese; maintaining on the whole a prominent and honoured position, but like many who have striven with Oriental Courts finding himself little more advanced at the end than at the beginning. In the end he returned to Goa and died there in June 1617, being at the time Coadjutor-Archbishop Elect of Cranganore.[4]

Emmanuel Pinheiro

Regarding his companion Father Pinheiro we have little personal information. He was born at S. Miguel in the Azores in 1556 and embarked for India in 1592. He seems to have been the first of the Jesuits in Mogor to turn his attention seriously to the people rather than the Court and he was for many years the pastor of a considerable congregation in Lahore. He was, however, at the same time a favourite with Akbar and had much influence with him. In Jahāngīr's time he was to a large extent engaged in political work and he ultimately retired to Goa in 1615. He was anxious to return to the Mogor Mission, but within four years his health collapsed and, as the Provincial reported, 'he departed hence to a better Mission.' For some reason not explained to us—possibly on account of his complete adoption of Indian habits—he was nicknamed 'The Mogul' among his Jesuit friends.[5]

Benedict de Goes

The remaining member of the party, Brother Benedict de Goes, was like Pinheiro a native of the Azores, and though scarcely known in his lifetime bears a name which is now far more widely renowned among Orientalists and geographers than those of his two companions. As a member of the Mogul Mission he was useful but undistinguished, and he did not as a rule present himself at Court. His fame rests not on missionary successes, but on the magnificent journey which he undertook in 1603 from Lahore by way of Kābul and Yarkand to Su-cheu on the confines of China, where he died in 1607. A fuller account of him and of his travels will be given in the last chapter of this work which deals with the Tibetan Missions of the Jesuits.

Journey from Goa to Lahore

On December 3, 1594,[6] the little party, taking with them the vessels necessary for Church worship, embarked from Goa for Damān and Cambay. They had with them on their journey to Lahore a Portuguese painter and the interpreter, Domingo Pires, who had been with Father Rudolf Aquaviva. Of this journey we have an account in two separate letters from Father Pinheiro.[7] From these we learn that at Cambay the Mission met Akbar's second son, Sultān Murād, formerly Monserrate's pupil, who accorded the Fathers a brief but favourable audience in the citadel on Christmas Eve and shortly afterwards left the city. On New Year's day when he was a league distant from Cambay he sent a summons to the Fathers, which they received at 3 a.m. while they were about to celebrate the Feast of the Circumcision. Completing the service they hastened to the Camp, where they found the Prince in full darbār and were interrogated by him regarding the climate and customs of Portugal, the occupations of royalty in Europe, hunting, falconry, etc. Religion did not interest the Prince and the Father writes of him 'that he had no taste for mosques and indeed never saw them, but spent his whole time in hunting and moving about.'[8] He provided the Fathers, however, with money and transport, and they joined a large caravan containing 400 camels, 100 wagons, and 100 horses. From Cambay the party proceeded to Ahmadābād, and Father Pinheiro's letters give us interesting accounts of the Jains of Gujarāt, of the Jogīs and of a magnificent tomb near Ahmadābād, 'a work far from barbaric though in a barbarous country,' 'opus inter barbaros minime barbarum.'[9] On March 19, 1595, they left Ahmadābād, reaching Pātan on the 24th, which was Easter Eve. We are not told by what route they next proceeded, but they seem to have traversed the Rājputāna desert. The cities they passed through were utterly ruined; food ran short; the heat was intense and the mirages very irritating. The journey from Goa which should have taken two months actually occupied five, and the party was very glad when at last it was able to enter Lahore on May 5, 1595. The arrival of this large caravan from Goa, containing several 'learned Christian ascetics known by the name of Padres,' was considered an event of sufficient importance to be recorded by Abu'-l-fazl in his Akbarnāma.[10]

Authorities for the Third Mission

For the ten years from 1595 to the death of Akbar we have as our primary authorities two batches of missionary letters. One series of letters is for the period 1595–1601, and most of these were published in Europe shortly after they were written. The other series covers the years 1604–1605; these are in manuscript in the British Museum and extract translations of them were published in 1896. The Histories of Guzman and Guerreiro (from which du Jarric's history is derived) are mainly based on these letters. For the intermediate period 1600–1604, which is not covered by the letters in question, we have to rely almost entirely on Guerreiro and have not the original documents on which he based his narrative. For the whole period, 1595 to 1605, we get little or no help from Indian sources, as Badāonī's narrative ends in 1595 and the Akbarnāma of Abu'-l-fazl, which records events up to 1602, has little more to say on Akbar's contact with Christianity.

The Mission, as above noted, arrived at Akbar's Court on May 5, 1595, and Father Jerome Xavier was in attendance on Akbar for practically the whole period until Akbar's death on October 17, 1605. The history of the Mission during these ten and a half years may suitably be considered under three phases, according to the location of the Court from time to time.

Three phases of the Mission

(*a*) For some 3½ years, from May 1595 until near the end of 1598, Akbar remained (except for a summer visit to Kashmīr in 1597) at Lahore.

(*b*) Towards the end of 1598 he marched via Agra to the Deccan and returned to Agra in May 1601 some 2½ years later.

(*c*) For the remaining 4½ years, until his death in October 1605, he was almost continuously resident at Agra.

The personnel of the Mission varied somewhat during these periods.

During the stay of the Court at Lahore all the three original missionaries—Xavier, Pinheiro and Goes—remained with it: Xavier and Goes accompanying Akbar on his Kashmīr journey in 1597.

When Akbar left for Agra and the Deccan, he was accompanied by Xavier and Goes, Pinheiro being left in Lahore. An additional missionary, Father Francisco Corsi, was, however, sent from Goa to assist Pinheiro and joined the latter towards the end of 1600. After Corsi's arrival, Pinheiro travelled to the King's camp in the Deccan to consult with Xavier.

On his return from the Deccan to Agra, Akbar brought Xavier and Pinheiro with him. Goes who had been sent on an embassy to Goa in March 1601 received orders there to penetrate to Cathay, and rejoined at Agra in the summer of 1602, accompanied by a further missionary, Father Antony Machado. Pinheiro then returned to Lahore and on January 6, 1603 Goes left Agra to proceed via Lahore to Kābul and Central Asia. In June 1604 Corsi paid a visit of two months to Agra, and when Akbar died in October 1605 the Fathers at Agra were Xavier and Machado and those at Lahore, Pinheiro and Corsi.

(*a*) 1595–1598

The Mission was received at Lahore 'com muita festa'—with much pomp—and in a kindly spirit. The King in his conversations avoided the subject of religion, alleging that the subject could not be properly discussed until the Fathers had learnt Persian. He listened, however, to the accounts given to him of the progress of the Portuguese arms in India and expressed admiration at the capture by the Portuguese of a fort opposite Chaul from the Ahmadnagar troops. All this was duly reported to the King of Spain who urged his Viceroy to encourage and aid the Fathers to make progress in their Mission and to 'attain the good result expected therefrom.'[11] Meanwhile they were treated at Lahore with all due courtesy and reverence. The King when he saw them bowed his head and summoned them to sit near him, even upon the cushion reserved for himself and the Prince. He provided them with a convenient residence. He showed reverence to their pictures and came to their Chapel while they recited their Litanies, 'remaining like a Christian Prince with his knees bent and his hands clasped.' He would wear a reliquary which had the Virgin portrayed on one side and the Agnus Dei on the other.[12] He showed the Fathers his collection of European books and handed it over to them for their own use. He allowed them to start a school which was attended by the sons of some of the feudatory princes and those of the Chief of Badakhshān. Two of these pupils asked to become Christians and one even wished to be admitted to orders. The question of a site for a church at Lahore was mooted and a church was ultimately built. It was opened in 1597 while Akbar was in Kashmīr and the Governor of the City attended in person, remaining for some two hours conversing with Father Pinheiro in his house. At the following Christmas, Brother Benedict de Goes prepared a sacred Crib which was much admired. The royal princes followed Akbar's example in their attention to the Fathers and one of them went so far as to present large candles to be burnt in honour of Christ and the Virgin, accompanying his gift with liberal alms for the poor. The heir-apparent himself, Prince Salīm, became the firm friend and protector of the Mission.

Encouraging reception

Regular religious debates were no longer in vogue, but disputes occasionally took place and we hear of Akbar's setting his 'Chronologist' to dispute with Father Xavier regarding the possibilities of God having a son. So far as Islām was concerned, the King's attitude had by now

Islām abandoned by Akbar

become quite definite. He had, says the Fathers, 'utterly cast out Muhammad'—Mahometam prorsus exterminavit[13]—the Prince Salīm too scoffing at Muhammad. He had entirely overturned (omnino evertit) the Muhammadan faith. In Lahore there was no mosque (moschea nulla est) and no copy of the Qur'ān. People were condemned to death for killing cows. Whatever the King's actual faith was, it was not Islām. He was a Hindu (Gentile). He followed the tenets of the Jains (Verteas). He worshipped the Sun like the Pārsīs. He was the founder of a new sect (secta pestilens et perniciosa) and wished to obtain the name of a prophet. He had already some followers, but these were only obtained by bribery (sed auro corruptos). Nothing was further from him, at any rate, than the religion of Muhammad, and the Fathers, in spite of angry opposition from the Mullās and of well-meant warnings from their friends, were more outspoken than ever in their attacks upon Islām. On one occasion, Father Xavier was asked why more persons were possessed by devils in Christendom than among Muslims, and he did not deny the fact, but explained it—to the amusement of his hearers—by replying that the devil, having the Muslims already in his power, could afford to neglect them.

On Easter Day, 1597, an immense fire took place in the palace at Lahore[14]—a misfortune attributed by the Jesuits to the anger of Heaven at the King's irreligious presumption.

Kashmīr

To allow of the rebuilding necessitated by the fire, Akbar proceeded to Kashmīr for the summer, taking with him Father Xavier and Brother Goes: and they were absent from Lahore from May 15 to November 13. The Father was impressed by the Himalaya mountains—so much bigger, he wrote, than his own Pyrenees,—and he has left an interesting account of Kashmīr, mentioning the temperate climate, the fertility of the land, the number of streams, the vines growing on the mulberry trees, the antiquities, and much else. He describes a severe famine that took place in the valley and narrates how the mothers would put out their children in the streets to die and how the Jesuits would then collect and baptize them. In his letters from Kashmīr he shows himself an ardent advocate of a Mission to Tibet, and he seems also to have been attracted by the strange stories he heard of practices connected with the idol of Devī at Kāngra: but except for this one journey to Kashmīr we do not hear of his having spent any time in the Himalayas. It is all the more strange therefore that his name should in recent years have cropped up in connection with the wanderings of a great mystic of our own day, the Protestant Christian Sādhu Sundar Singh, in the Himalayan tracts. The Sādhu reported that in a cave in the high country round Kailās he had met in 1912 a very aged ascetic, who said that he had been born more than three hundred years previously at Alexandria and had met there a Christian saint called Yernaus (Hieronymus), the nephew of S. Francis Xavier, and that he had heard the message of the Gospel from him.[15] This report was received with some incredulity and Catholic controversialists did not fail to point out that Jerome Xavier never was at Alexandria, but the intrusion of his name in this very modern experience constitutes a strange and mysterious memorial of his personality.

Immediately on their arrival in Kashmīr both Xavier and Goes became seriously ill with a fever that lasted for two months.

Akbar evasive

Father Xavier's own prolonged illness, and afterwards that of the King, prevented any serious discussion of religious subjects, and by the time that Father Xavier had returned to Lahore, the Mission had been two and a half years at the Court, without anything in the way of success to report. The King of Spain, writing to his Viceroy at Goa in 1598, recognized that the Fathers had 'not yet produced any fruit,' but insisted none the less that the Mission should not be allowed to expire and ordered that, if the Fathers should die or have to be recalled, their places should be filled. 'The fruit,' he wrote, 'which has hitherto not shown itself, may appear whenever God pleaseth and when human hopes are perhaps the smallest.'[16] Meanwhile the attitude maintained by Akbar appeared to the Fathers as little else than one of irritating delay—'procrastinatione frustrationibusque perseverat.'[17]

(*b*) 1598–1601

Towards the end of 1598 Akbar left Lahore to invade the Deccan, taking with him Father Xavier and Brother Goes.

Progress in Lahore

Father Pinheiro, left alone in Lahore, turned his attention to evangelization and, in the troubles that inevitably followed, received reasonable support from the local Sūbadār or Viceroy.[18] Pinheiro succeeded in obtaining from him the pardon of prisoners condemned to death. Fugitives from justice took refuge in the church. The Father's intervention was constantly sought, and even great feuds between the high officials were composed by his arbitration. After the death of this Viceroy (Khwāja Shamsuddīn) and the appointment of his successor (Zain Khān Koka), efforts were made to discredit the Mission and threatening crowds assembled outside the church, but the only result was that the maligners of the Mission were imprisoned.

Father Pinheiro was indeed on one occasion drugged with *dhatūra* and his property stolen, including some valued relics, but the Viceroy and the Kotwāl gave what assistance they could to him and came in person to express their sympathy. At Christmas it was his practice to erect a Crib with representations of the Nativity and other Scriptural incidents, and these were visited by the Viceroy and other dignitaries as well as by the common people. Numbers, including the Viceroy, attended the services in Holy Week and at Easter, and the Mission was duly favoured by the authorities. Towards the end of 1600 Father Pinheiro received the assistance of Father Corsi, and after the latter had been introduced to the work, Father Pinheiro set out to visit Father Xavier at the King's camp in the Deccan.

Meanwhile Xavier after leaving Lahore at the end of 1598 had travelled with the King to Agra. While at Agra, Xavier obtained permission from the King to introduce fresh priests at Lahore and Agra, and he had also on July 15, 1599, an important conversation with him. Having obtained leave to speak privately to Akbar he informed him that he had received orders from his Superior pointing out that he must by now be sufficiently versed in Persian to be intelligible to the King and that he should forthwith obtain from the King a definite statement of his attitude. Xavier pointed out to the King the irksomeness to the Fathers of being compelled to stand idle, and asked him why he had not listened to them as he had promised to do. Akbar replied courteously, but with further procrastination. He was going, he said, towards the Deccan and would halt near Goa, where he would have more leisure to listen to them. At the same time he pointed out to Father Xavier that he had at least done this much for the Fathers that, whereas under former rulers they could not have dared to affirm the divinity of Christ, they could now do so with perfect safety. With this reply Xavier had perforce to be content.[19]

Interview with Akbar at Agra

Very soon after this interview, Akbar marched to the Deccan. His immediate object was to overcome the Sultanates of Ahmadnagar and Khāndesh, but he doubtless had also in his mind as his ultimate aim the extinction of the Portuguese settlements in India, from which he had suffered much annoyance.[20] The position of the Jesuit Fathers in his camp became accordingly a difficult one. He occupied Burhānpur and laid siege to Asīrgarh, but he found the resistance of the latter place very hard to overcome. Being in need of artillery he called on Xavier and Goes to write to the Portuguese at Chaul for guns and munitions, but Xavier refused, on the plea

The Deccan War

that such action would be contrary to the Christian faith. The chronicler du Jarric points out that Xavier must also have been influenced by the fact that the Khāndesh forces against whom Akbar was fighting were in alliance with the Portuguese.[21] In any case Xavier's refusal drew down on the Jesuits the anger of the King; and for a time—until the storm of his wrath was over—they had to withdraw from his presence.

Capture of Asīrgarh

The Jesuit chroniclers have left us a description of the capture of Asīrgarh which differs in some material respects from that recorded by the Indian historians. According to Guerreiro, the King of Khāndesh was seized by Akbar in contravention of a safe permit granted to him, the son of his Abyssinian general was killed by Akbar in cold blood, the Abyssinian himself committed suicide and the fort was ultimately bribed into surrender. The Indian historians, Abu'-l-fazl and Faizī Sarhindī, give an account more favourable to Akbar, stating for instance that the Abyssinian general's son was not murdered but committed suicide. The Jesuit account is presumed by Vincent Smith in his valuable history of Akbar to be taken direct from Father Xavier and is accepted as it stands: but certain difficulties in the way of this acceptance have been pointed out by Mr. Payne in his translation of du Jarric.[22] Whatever the truth as regards these incidents may be, the main point of interest to the Jesuits was that when the fort fell (in January 1601) seven renegade Portuguese officers who were captured among the defenders and were about to be subjected to cruel treatment, were at Father Xavier's request handed over to him and were by him reconverted to Christianity. Shortly afterwards Father Pinheiro arrived at the camp from Lahore and on his arrival he presented himself with Father Xavier before the King. Akbar received them with much kindness, laying his hands on Pinheiro's shoulder ('which he does not do save to his great captains and his special favourites') and treating with much respect the sacred pictures which the Fathers presented to him. He discussed with them the ceremony of the kissing of the Pope's foot by the Emperor and the significance attached to this form of obeisance owing to the cross worn by the Pope upon his foot.[23]

Movements of Goes

Before leaving the Deccan, Akbar despatched an embassy to Goa, and ordered Brother Goes to accompany it. The letter of March 20, 1600, accrediting the embassy is reproduced in the Jesuit Chronicles[24] and contains no repetition of the demand for spiritual assistance, but confines itself to a request for a political alliance, for the despatch of skilled craftsmen, and for facilities for the purchase of precious stones and other objects. The embassy reached Goa towards the end of May 1601 and certain captives from Asīrgarh whom Goes had brought with him, including a number of half-castes and a Portuguese Jew of over ninety years of age, were there baptized. While at Goa Brother Goes received orders to undertake the journey to Cathay which has made his name famous. Accompanied by Father Antony Machado he started from Goa in the spring of 1602 and reached Agra in the hot season of that year. Leaving Machado at Agra, he set out later for Lahore, and from that city he started in January 1603 on the adventurous journey into Central Asia from which he was never to return.[25]

(*c*) 1601–1605

Meanwhile in May 1601 Akbar had returned to Agra, taking with him Fathers Xavier and Pinheiro who were in his camp. On the arrival of Goes and Machado in the following year the Fathers formed themselves into something like a small 'College,' subject, as far as was possible, to monastic discipline and constituting indeed the largest collection of missionaries yet brought together at the Mogul headquarters. This gathering, short-lived though it was, is said to have afforded great consolation to all the Fathers; two of whom had suffered from a recent and intensely trying journey, and two from years of solitude. Pinheiro had shortly afterwards to return to Lahore, but before he went the Fathers achieved a notable success in obtaining from Akbar a written order under the royal seal, expressly permitting such of his subjects as desired to embrace Christianity to do so without let or hindrance. There was a good deal of intrigue to contend with and a good deal of obstruction, mainly on the part of one of Akbar's most prominent nobles, Mīrzā 'Azīz Koka, before the order was ultimately obtained; but as the King had hitherto evaded the issue of any but purely verbal orders, the grant of this written declaration was a valuable concession and one that proved useful on more than one occasion afterwards.[26] When this order had been secured, Pinheiro went to take leave of the King and was treated with great kindness, receiving a horse from the royal stables for his journey.

Farmān granting liberty of worship

His presence was greatly wanted in Lahore where Father Corsi had in his absence found much to contend with. A new Viceroy—Qulīj Khān—had been appointed, who had previously served in Gujarāt and had imbibed a prejudice against the Portuguese. He was moreover a staunch Muslim and was anxious to treat the Christians in Lahore as

Difficulties in Lahore

unfavourably as he dared in view of Akbar's known tolerance towards them.[27] Although he had been troublesome to Father Corsi, however, he treated Father Pinheiro with courtesy. Owing to Akbar's farmān the feasts of Christmas and Easter were celebrated with great ceremony and entire publicity. The magistrates would set prisoners free at the Fathers' request and would send them Christian delinquents to be dealt with as they saw fit. At the same time any attack by the Fathers on Muhammad would rouse the Viceroy's frenzy, and he was known to be a cruel man whose name was ' as much feared in Hindustan as were formerly those of Nero and Diocletian.' In 1604 Father Corsi was summoned by Father Xavier to proceed for a short visit to Agra, but the Viceroy fearing the effects of his reports at that place declined to let him go. Father Pinheiro having managed to arrange for his departure (in June 1604), the Viceroy called for Pinheiro, and said to him : ' Father, I am a friend to you and to the Lord Jesus : no one knows him better than I do. He had the spirit of God and neither man nor angel could speak as he spoke.' The Father, however, distrusted the Viceroy, and he tells us with what hesitation and suspicion he accepted a cup of sherbet from Qulīj Khān at his house. One of the Viceroy's sons, Mīrzā Lāhaurī, was a man of evil courses,[28] and it is strange to read how the Viceroy's daughter and granddaughter would come to the church, and how the Viceroy's wife would come also to the church, bringing an offering to Our Lady to secure her intercession for the amendment of her son. The Viceroy though afraid to seize Christians in the city was apparently ready to arrest them in the fort, and a Portuguese so arrested was induced to recite the ' Kalma.' Father Pinheiro protested, but the Viceroy swore by Murtaza 'Alī that the conversion had been voluntary. Pinheiro went away in sorrow, but on a later occasion he happened to see the man being negligently guarded, whereupon he drew nigh and taking the lost sheep upon his shoulders bore him out of the city. He was able then when confronted with the Viceroy to assure him that the Portuguese had not been to the Father's house or to his own, whereupon a ' dark cloud ' fell upon the Viceroy and his followers and nothing more was heard of the case.

The antipathy of the Viceroy was fomented by the Hindus whom Father Pinheiro had attacked for their alleged immorality and on the ground of their practising infanticide. They in their turn accused the Fathers of many crimes—that they ate human flesh, fattened up young men to be sold in Portuguese lands, and so forth. There was a long intrigue on the part of the Hindus about some houses occupied by the Fathers, and after being more than once evicted by the Viceroy the Fathers succeeded ultimately in getting orders from headquarters, through Father Xavier, under which they were permanently reinstated. The attitude of the Viceroy became more and more truculent. Christians began to flee from Lahore, and Father Pinheiro went in fear of death. The Viceroy, it was said, only abstained from killing him for fear of the King, who (he would whisper) was himself an unbelieving Kāfir like the Father. A day was indeed fixed—September 15, 1604, we are told—for the arrest of the women and children of all Christians in Lahore, but political events—a defeat on the frontier and the rumour of an advance to Lahore by Prince Salīm—deflected the intentions of the Viceroy and ultimately compelled him to depart to Agra.

In Qulīj Khān's absence, his son Chīn Qulīj, and afterwards Said Khān and Mīrzā 'Abdurrahīm, continued the administration.

Improvement in the situation at Lahore

Chīn Qulīj, though formerly hostile,[29] showed himself in a friendly light. He once spent about two hours at the church and at the Fathers' residence, ate with them and listened to their gospel stories and their discourse upon religious subjects. On a subsequent occasion the Fathers on visiting him found him in high spirits and when they asked alms he tossed up with them for the money. 'These little things,' writes Pinheiro, 'are very important here, though they may be laughed at elsewhere.'[30] So too when Said Khān was in authority his son brought young Mīrzā Ghāzī Beg of Tatta in Sind[31] with a great crowd of retainers to the church and house of the Jesuits; and even the old Qulīj Khān, on his return to Lahore, showed himself so far agreeable as to give special orders forbidding the deduction of the usual commission on a grant of a thousand rupees which the Fathers had received from Akbar.

To add to Father Pinheiro's satisfaction a just retribution overtook the chief of his Hindu opponents and he does not narrate their misfortunes without a certain gleam of pleasure. One of these Hindus was arrested by Said Khān for some act of violence and was dragged to prison by the hair of his head; his houses were destroyed and he with difficulty escaped from the town. Another lost his son who, being but a child, 'was buried near the river according to custom, but the dogs dug him up and devoured him leaving only his head.' A third, the most violent persecutor of all, who held a pargana worth over two lakhs of rupees, fled from the new Dīwān, and his son and brother were arrested and thrown into a narrow prison where 'they were obliged to pay the guards twenty or thirty rupees a day each for food, and a rupee apiece for the slightest necessity of nature; and moreover were beaten and ill-treated and called to account for three lakhs of rupees.' 'Truly,' says the Father, 'the vengeance of God is hidden. . . . May God repay them for the trouble they have given us by converting them to our Holy Faith. Amen.'

Meanwhile the Fathers in Agra though not subjected to the same dangers had their own troubles to record. At first there was little to complain of. Akbar appears to have occasionally sent for Father Xavier and to have set a mullā and a man of lukewarm religion at his side to raise objections to his arguments. The Father spoke in Persian and we have a record of his main arguments against Muhammadanism set forth under fourteen heads, this record having been delivered some years later by Father Corsi in Latin to the English clergyman Terry.[32] Akbar still refused to acknowledge the divinity of Christ and ascribed his miracles to his skill as a physician. He accepted, however, with much delight a book of Father Xavier's composition describing the life, miracles, and doctrine of Christ;[33] and an immense sensation was caused about this time both at the Court and in the town through the exhibition by the Fathers of a copy of the picture of the Madonna del Popolo at Rome.[34] When Akbar was about this period introduced for the first time to the smoking of tobacco, he called for one of the Fathers to consult him as to the advisability of his smoking.[35] At the funeral of a prominent Armenian, the ceremony was public and unimpeded; the Christians marched along carrying lighted candles, the cross uncovered was borne before them; the children saying the Creed and the Fathers reciting prayers brought up the rear. At the same time a number of half-castes, taken in the Deccan wars, were redeemed from slavery and baptized. Fifty Portuguese captives, who were held to ransom by Akbar, were, after much solicitation by the Fathers, ultimately freed and well treated. 'My lord,' said Xavier to him when the decision was given, 'you have liberated fifty captives, and in so doing have made fifty thousand Portuguese your servants.'

Position in Agra

Troubles were, however, in store at Agra as at Lahore. A discontented Portuguese circulated a rumour to the effect that the Fathers were spies and thieves and worse; indeed, as Father Jerome says, 'non erat malum in civitate which was not our doing, especially mine.' The little congregation, and more especially the Armenian part of it, began to look with suspicion on the Fathers. Xavier's efforts to see the King on the subject were unavailing and he was

Opposition of Mildenhall

in much anxiety until the Portuguese delinquent confessed the falsity of his calumnies and besought the Father by the wounds of Jesus to pardon him.[36] All these troubles were fomented, we are told, by an Englishman, John Mildenhall, then in Agra, in order to further his political aims. Mildenhall assumed the position of an ambassador from Queen Elizabeth to Akbar, and his arrival at Agra in 1603 marked the commencement of a long struggle between the English on the one side and the Portuguese, supported by the Jesuits, on the other. Mildenhall's main object was to obtain free access for English ships to the Mogul ports. When Akbar consulted the Jesuits at Agra and Lahore upon this point they are said to have shown 'exceeding great rage,' and the Jesuits who had previously been friends with Mildenhall became bitterly hostile to him. The struggle then commenced. Mildenhall accused the Jesuits of having seduced his Armenian interpreter and having given to the King's two chiefest councillors five hundred pounds sterling apiece to thwart him; and the Jesuits accused Mildenhall of having himself bribed an official whom they subsequently won over. Mildenhall after much delay obtained an audience and represented to the King in the presence of the Jesuits that whereas his Sovereign was ready to send an embassy to Akbar with valuable presents, the Jesuits during so many years had never secured an embassy or any presents for Akbar from the Portuguese Government. Father Jerome writing in September 1604 was confident that Akbar would never do a thing 'so prejudicial to the State and our Faith' as to grant the Englishman's requests, but according to Mildenhall, the King was 'very merrie,' and laughed at the Jesuits and granted the required farmān.[37]

Attitude towards Prince Salīm

During the last years of Akbar's life the position of the Heir-Apparent, Prince Salīm, gave the Jesuits much anxiety. During these years the Prince adopted an attitude approaching to open rebellion, and in August 1602 he had gone so far as to cause his father's favourite minister, Abu'-l-fazl, to be assassinated. The Fathers, without alienating the King, remained on good terms with the Prince, and at some date not specified (probably in the autumn of 1603) we find Father Xavier visiting the Prince at Fatehpur Sīkrī—then a deserted city with a few prominent buildings alone surviving among a multitude of ruins.[38] The Prince was found engaged in the curious occupation of making copper from peacocks' tails as an antidote against poison, and he received the Father with much favour and kindness. When, however, the King set out for Allahabad against his son in August 1604 (a journey which was interrupted by the death of the King's mother) he was accompanied by Father Xavier and Machado. In November 1604 the Prince returned to Agra and was ostensibly reconciled to his father. On September 21 of the following year, Akbar fell ill and on October 17 (o.s.) he died.

Death of Akbar

We have a detailed account of the circumstances attending Akbar's death in a letter of September 26, 1606, from Father Xavier, and in this he mentions the general impression that Akbar's death had been caused by poison;[39] but none of the Jesuit authorities give support to the story subsequently made current by both Indian and European writers, that Akbar had inadvertently taken poison meant by him for others.

Whether Akbar in his last moments declared himself a Muslim or not is a doubtful point. Sir Thomas Roe, writing from Ājmīr in 1616, states that he died 'in the formall profession of his sect.'[40] The Jesuits reported that when he was in his last agonies the Muslims bade him think on Muhammad (doubtless by reciting the Kalma) 'whereon he gave no sign, save that he repeated the name of God.' His son Jahāngīr in one version of his Memoirs, relates that on his death-bed Akbar repeated the confession of the Muslim faith, the Kalmat-ush-shahādat, after the Muftī, Mīrān Sadrjahān, speaking in a loud and distinct voice, and that thereafter he ordered Sadrjahān to repeat continually the appointed chapter of the Qur'ān, the Sūra Yāsīn, by his pillow, 'in order that he might be enabled to render up his soul with as little struggle as possible.'[41]

Jesuit accounts of his last days

The Jesuits themselves admit that they were unable to administer the consolations of their religion to Akbar in his last moments. The efforts which they made to see him and to speak to him during his illness are fully set forth in Father Xavier's letter of September 26, 1606, and Xavier's account is accurately summarized by Guerreiro and du Jarric in the following terms:[42]

'The Fathers, who had full information of the King's sickness, went on a Saturday to see him in the hope that he would hear the words which, after long thought and having commended the matter to God, they had prepared for this hour. But they found him amongst his Captains, and in so cheerful and merry a mood, that they deemed the time unsuitable for speaking to him of the end of this life, and decided to await another opportunity. They came away fully persuaded that he was making good progress and that rumour, as ordinarily happens when kings are sick, had exaggerated the seriousness of his malady. On the Monday following, however, it was reported on all sides that the poison which had been administered was taking effect and that His Majesty was dying. On hearing this the Fathers went to the palace; but they could find no one who could make their arrival known to the King, or dare to speak to him of them; for already such matters were more in the hands of the great nobles than of the King himself; and hence every means by which the Fathers tried to gain entrance was ineffectual.'

The French traveller, Pyrard de Laval, writing six or seven years later, tells us that Akbar 'promised and gave hope that he would become a Christian, making but one request that he should be permitted to keep all his wives, as his religion allowed: and pending solution of this question he died.'[43]

In what faith did Akbar die?

The Jesuits maintained varying traditions as to the religion in which Akbar died: some alleging that he died a Muslim, others that he was a Hindu.

On the one hand Father Anthony Botelho, who had spent several years at Agra and at Bījāpur, wrote[44] about the year 1670 that it was commonly held in Bījāpur that Akbar had died in the Christian faith. The 'Ādil Shāhī Sultān of Bījāpur, had on one occasion actually asked the Father: 'Is it true or not that the great King Akbar died a Christian?' ('Sacchehe qui barà Patxa Hacabar Christaõ muhã qui nã?') and the Father replied: 'Sire, I would to God it had been so, but he kept us deluded with such hopes and died in your sect of Muhammad.'

On the other hand, Father Xavier himself, writing in 1615, states that Akbar 'died neither as a Moor nor as a Christian, but in the Gentile sect which he had embraced.'[45] And this same tradition was prevalent in 1735 when Father Figueredo wrote that Akbar went over to Heathendom and died in idolatry.[46]

It is in any case clear that notwithstanding all the efforts and hopes of the Jesuits for his conversion Akbar did not die in the Christian faith.

NOTES

[1] The children are come to the birth and there is not strength to bring forth.—Is. xxxvii, 3. Guzman, *Historia*, I, p. 257.

[2] Guzman, *ib.*; du Jarric, II, p. 463; Da Cunha Rivara, *Archivo Portuguez Oriental,* Fasc. 3, p. 589 (Letter of Philip II to Viceroy dated January 28, 1596). Rehatsek in *Calcutta Review*, LXXXII, 1886, p. 6.

[3] A eulogy of Jerome Xavier in the *Chrono-Historia de la Compania de Jesus en la Provincia de Toledo* (Madrid 1710) is translated by Hosten in *J.A.S.B.*, XXIII, 1927, pp. 109–130.

[4] *Sommervogel*, s.v. Regarding the exact date of his death, see *J.A.S.B.*, XXIII, 1927, pp. 128–9. See also L.-J.-M. Cros, *S. François de Xavier*, Toulouse, 1894, I, p. 467.

[5] Relation by Father Botelho, translated in *Mem. A.S.B.*, V, 1916 (Hosten), p. 152. His death is reported in the Goa Annual Letter for 1619 : of which there is a summary by Hosten in *The Examiner*, Bombay, February 10, 1912.

[6] It may be noted here that in dealing with dates given by the Fathers and those given in other European accounts, we have to bear in mind the fact that the Gregorian or Reformed Calendar was introduced in Portuguese India in October 1583 (October 4 being followed immediately by October 15), while it was not in force in Protestant countries in Europe until 1752.

[7] Letters enclosed in the Provincial's report of November 1595.

[8] Peruschi, *Hist. Rel.*, p. 18 ; *Informatione*, p. 47. 'Moscheis parum addictus est, sed nec unquam vidit. Totus est in venando et spatiando.' For 'nec unquam vidit' the Italian has 'non le vede mai.'

[9] This was the tomb of Shaikh Ahmad Kattu at Sarkhej.

[10] Akbarnāma (*Bib. Ind.*, transl. Beveridge), III, p. 1027, and Beveridge in *J.A.S.B.*, 1888, p. 34. Abu'-l-fazl gives the date of arrival as the 19th of Ardibihisht or April 29, 1595 (o.s.). The difference of dates may be due partly to the use by the missionaries of the Gregorian Calendar and partly to the arrival of different parts of the caravan on different dates.

[11] Da Cunha Rivara, *Archivo Portuguez Oriental*, Fasc. 3, p. 674. Rehatsek, *Calcutta Review*, LXXXII, 1886, p. 9. The King had seen letters of the Fathers addressed to members of the Society in Portugal. His view of the position of the missionaries is exemplified by his mention of 'their services to God and to Me.' (Rivara, op. cit., p. 814.)

[12] Du Jarric, II, p. 477.

[13] In the Italian version of Peruschi this appears—'sbandito da se a fatto Mahometto' ('has utterly banished Muhammad from his thoughts'). V. A. Smith, *Akbar the Great Mogul*, 1919, p. 262.

[14] See Elliot, *Hist. Ind.*, VI, p. 132 ; Akbarnāma (*Bib. Ind.*, transl. Beveridge), III, p. 1075 ; *Annuae Literae Soc. Jesu*, 1597 (Naples, 1600), p. 570 ; Payne, *Akbar and the Jesuits*, p. 74 ; Jerome Xavier's letter of Sept. 1, 1597.

[15] Heiler's *Apostel oder Betrüger*, Munich, 1925, p. 130, and *The Gospel of Sadhu Sundar Singh*, London, 1927, p. 71, and a number of controversial letters in the *Catholic Herald of India* and *The Examiner*, Bombay, and other papers during 1923–1925. The ascetic or Mahārshi is reported to have read to the Sādhu from a roll of the Gospels written in Greek which he said had come to him from Xavier (Parker, *Sadhu Sundar Singh*, 1927, p. 77, who, however, talks of Francis Xavier).

[16] Letter of November 21, 1598. See Da Cunha Rivara, *Archivo Portuguez Oriental*, Fasc. 3, p. 919. Rehatsek, *Calcutta Review*, LXXXII, 1886.

[17] *Ann. Lit.*, 1597 (Naples, 1600), p. 568. It has been suggested (Bohlen, *Alte Indien*, 1830, I, p. 105 and Noer, *Kaiser Akbar*, I, p. 486, cf. Ritter *Erdkunde*, 1835, V, p. 627), that in his refusal to adopt Christian views Akbar was influenced by reports of the cruelties of the Inquisition at Goa, but there is nothing in the records to show that he had heard of the Inquisition.

[18] The Portuguese spoke of the Provincial Governor or Subadār as the Viceroy.

[19] Letter of August 1, 1599, quoted in Pimenta's report of December 1599. (*Nova Relatio*, 1601.)

[20] Payne's *Akbar and the Jesuits*, 1926, p. 112. Vincent Smith, *Akbar the Great Mogul*, 1919, p. 265. Akbarnāma (*Bib. Ind.*, transl. Beveridge), III, p. 409. The chief cause of trouble was the control exercised by the Portuguese over the voyages of pilgrims to Mecca.

[21] Du Jarric, III, p. 34. There were, moreover, as noted later, seven Portuguese officers among the defenders of Asīrgarh.

[22] Vincent Smith, *Akbar the Great Mogul*, 1919, pp. 276–286. Payne, *Akbar and the Jesuits*, 1926, pp. 251–258. A translation of Guerreiro's account is given with notes by Father Heras, S.J., in *Ind. Ant.*, LIII, 1924, pp. 33–41.

[23] Payne's *Akbar and the Jesuits*, pp. 110–112. Guerreiro, *Relaçam*, I, p. 10.

[24] Guerreiro, *Relaçam*, I, p. 11.

[25] See Chapter XIX.

[26] A detailed account of the proceedings connected with the grant of this farmān is given in Guerreiro, *Relaçam*, II, Part II, Chapter V, a translation of which was published by Hosten in *The Examiner*, Bombay, November 22, 1919. The Fathers had already received orders facilitating their travelling from the coast to Agra, Lahore and Cathay, and permitting them to preach in Cambay : but not a general order of this kind.

[27] Muslim writers speak of him as a pious and learned old man, with a taste for poetry. Blochmann, *Ā'īn*, I, p. 34. The Jesuits say that he was so vain of his learning that he looked down even on Aristotle.

[28] See Blochmann, *Ā'īn*, I, p. 500–1.

[29] Either he or his brother had on one occasion actually dealt Pinheiro a severe blow (huã boa pescoçada) in full darbār. Pinheiro's letter of August 12, 1605.

[30] Letter of August 12, 1605, *J.A.S.B.*, LXV, 1896, p. 104.

[31] His father had been one of the adherents of Akbar's new faith.

[32] Terry's *Voyage to East India* (edition of 1777), pp. 419–422.

[33] See Chapter XIV.

[34] See further details as to this incident in Chapter XV.

[35] The weed having come to Agra via Goa and the Deccan, see *Ind. Ant.*, I, p. 164, and Asad Beg in Elliot, *Hist. Ind.*, VI, p. 167. Akbar did not, however, take to tobacco and Jahāngīr prohibited its use (Elliot, VI, p. 351).

[36] Mem. *A.S.B.*, V, 1916 (Hosten), pp. 174–175.

[37] See Mildenhall's letter of October 3, 1606, in Purchas' *Pilgrims* (MacLehose), II, p. 299–304, and in Foster, *Early Travels in India*, 1921, p. 59. He left India after Akbar's death but returned again from Persia in 1614, and either on his return to Agra or before, he became a Roman Catholic. He is said to have taken poison which he meant for others, and died at Ajmīr ' swelled exceedingly ' in June 1614. He was buried at Agra and his tomb, which is the oldest English monument in India, was discovered by Mr. E. A. Blunt, I.C.S., in 1909. See authorities quoted in *J.P.H.S.*, I, 1911, p. 111, and Orme's *Historical Fragments* (1805), p. 341. The inscription on the tomb is ' Joa de Mendenal Ingles, moreo aos 1 . . . de Junho de 1614.' After his death there was a long controversy between the Jesuits who wished to get his estate for his relations and the East India Company who wished to obtain it for his creditors.

[38] An inscription placed by Akbar on the Buland Darwāza or High Gate of Fatehpur in 1601 to commemorate his Deccan campaign, contains the well-known sentence ' Jesus said (on Him be peace). The

world is a bridge: therefore pass over it but build not thereon.' It is not known why the saying, which has been traced to old Muslim sources, is ascribed to Jesus, and there is nothing to connect this inscription with Jesuit influence. It seems to have been suggested by an inscription on a royal tomb in Burhãnpur. See Vincent Smith in *J.U.P.H.S.*, II, ii, 1921, pp. 59–67.

[39] *Drei Newe Relationes* (Augsburg, 1611), p. 140; Guerreiro, *Relaçam*, IV, p. 145; du Jarric, II, p. 493; Payne, *Akbar and the Jesuits*, p. 203.

[40] Foster's *Roe*, p. 276.

[41] *Memoirs of the Emperor Jahangueir*, by Price, 1829 (a very second-rate authority), pp. 77–78; *J. Bo. R.A.S.*, XXII, 1908 (Karkaria), pp. 179–208; Blochmann, *Ā'īn*, I, p. 212.

[42] Guerreiro, *Relaçam*, IV, pp. 145–146; du Jarric, III, p. 93; Payne's *Akbar and the Jesuits*, 1926, p. 203.

[43] *Hakl. Soc.*, 1888, II, Part I, p. 252.

[44] British Museum, Addl. MSS. 9855, fol. 14.

[45] Letter of December 4, 1615, in *J.A.S.B.*, XXIII, 1927, p. 125.

[46] 'Sturbe in der Abgötterey,' as the *Weltbott* has it (No. 595).

To face page 69] [Courtesy of Museum of Fine Arts, Boston

THE COURT OF JAHANGIR

Including a Jesuit Priest

(See pp.242 and 258

CHAPTER V

JAHANGIR, 1605–1627

Loquebar in testimoniis tuis in conspectu regum et non confundebar. (Ps. cxviii, 46.)

Cor regis in manu Domini. (Prov. xxi, 1.)

THE Prince Salīm, who succeeded Akbar under the title of Jahāngīr, was of a more unbalanced and barbaric type than his father, but he was endowed with the same catholicity of taste, the same enquiring mind and the same religious detachment. As Prince he had shown even greater kindness to the Jesuits than Akbar himself and his confidences to Father Xavier led them to hope that 'God would one day work in him a great miracle.' He had explained to the Fathers the difficulties caused by the polygamous life which he led and his inability to be satisfied with one wife; but he listened respectfully to them and would from time to time commend himself to the Queen of Angels. His desire for Christian pictures became almost embarrassing, and he was known to have amused himself with trying how long he could stand with his arms outstretched in the form of a cross. During the later years of Akbar, when Jahāngīr was in open disagreement with his father, the missionaries had to walk warily. When he asked the authorities at Goa to send him a separate Mission, the Provincial referred him to the Mission attached to his father's Court, and when he sent the Fathers a present of a black coat, the Fathers took care to show his letter and his present to Akbar. He continued, however, to communicate with them through an Italian called Jacome Felippe, marking his letters with a cross, assuring them of his devotion to Christ, asking for their prayers, and forwarding gifts for the church and for themselves. In his conversation with the Italian he disclosed an almost Christian attitude. 'I have a very great affection,' he would say, 'for the Lord Jesus,' and he would show him a cross of gold which he wore beneath his robe. If

Favourable attitude of Jāhangīr before his accession

ever, he said, he was in danger, he would call on none but the Lord Jesus.

After his reconciliation with Akbar, his intercourse with the Fathers became more open and even more intimate. They gave him sacred images and paintings. They provided him with Father Xavier's Persian book *The Mirror of Purity*, and on the pages of the book he had paintings made of Christ and of Our Lady. And seeing the inadequacy of the church at Agra, he persuaded his father to allow another to be built, and himself subscribed a thousand crowns for the commencement of the work.[1]

Continued after his accession

It is no matter for wonder, therefore, that when he came to the throne in 1605 the hopes of the Jesuits ran high: and that they trusted, as they said, that it was he who should have redeemed Israel. For some months, indeed, after his accession and while his son Khusrū was in rebellion, he had as a matter of policy to espouse the Muslim cause, and this period was marked by a studied neglect of the Fathers and by some instances of deliberate cruelty on his part towards individual Christians. This phase, however, soon passed over and for several years thereafter the relations of the Jesuits with the new King remained cordial and encouraging. When he came to Lahore in 1606 after defeating his son Khusrū, the Fathers met him outside the city and were favourably treated.[2] In the following year when he returned from Kābul they went two leagues out of Lahore to meet him and he received them with his usual familiar gesture, placing his hand on their shoulders and asking after their welfare. When the Fathers exhibited a Crib in the Lahore church on the following Christmas he sent them several candles of fine wax; and many years later he is reported on good authority to have made a habit of attending the church on every Christmas Day.[3] When he visited the church at Agra he would be conducted thither by the Fathers under a baldachino borne by four Portuguese Christians; and a large picture of Jahāngīr was placed in the church at his own request, so that the Fathers might, as he said, remember him when they made their prayers to God.[4] The Jesuits were confirmed in possession of their house in Lahore, and provision was made for a church at Ahmadābād and later on for a cemetery at Lahore.[5] The Fathers were granted generous allowances, ten rupees a day being given to Father Xavier and smaller sums to the others.[6] The use of Christian imagery in the palaces became even more marked than in Akbar's time, and we are assured that Jahāngīr sealed the outside of his official documents with seals bearing representations of Christ and of the Virgin.[7] He would forward to the Fathers presents of wild boars which he had killed himself and he listened with interest to their explanation of the reasons why they could not accept them in Lent.[8] There was in his entourage a young Armenian called Mīrzā Zū'lqarnain, who had been cruelly maltreated by him in the first few months of his reign but had afterwards been received into favour; this youth grew up under the friendly eye of the Jesuits and was afterwards of the greatest service to them.[9] The Fathers themselves had the somewhat monotonous honour of attending daily at the King's audiences, 'going and coming to the King,' as Father Xavier put it, 'and throwing the hook into the water, hoping that the fish would bite.'[10]

His interest in Christianity

When Jahāngīr left Lahore for Agra he took two of the Fathers with him, and for some weeks at Agra, during the summer of 1608, public discussions on religion took place before him, as they had before his father Akbar. We are given long accounts of the subjects discussed and of the questions put by the King. Could a 'Prophet' like David commit sin? If the patriarchs had many wives, why should not Christians do the same? If a man had only one wife, could she be got rid of if she was blind or a leper? Have the Christians tampered with the text of the Gospels? Did the Gospels mention Muhammad? How can Muhammad be proved to be a prophet? If or when he split the moon in two, did he do it by God's help or by enchantment and illusion? How could Christians bear to see pictures of Christ suffering the disgrace of crucifixion? Was Christ called the Son of God merely as a term of respect? Did he ever claim this title for himself? What miracles did he do that others have not done? The King sometimes joined eagerly in the debates refusing to let the Fathers interrupt him. At other times he was an amused spectator and would egg on the Fathers to attack Muhammad, slapping his thighs with delight at their retorts to their opponents.[11] He even went so far as to ask the Jesuits outright what a King like himself would have to do with his wives if he became a Christian; the Fathers, though elated by the implication underlying the question, gave him the inevitable reply, and he declared that the difficulties involved were too great.[12] The Englishman, Coverte, writing as a good Protestant, reported that Jahāngīr had often said that he could find it in his heart to be a Christian 'if they had not so many Gods,'[13] and Finch, another contemporary English traveller, goes further, and states that Jahāngīr 'affirmed before all his nobles that Christianity was the soundest faith and that of Mahomet lies and fables.'[14] The more incredulous Manucci (who reached India some twenty years after Jahāngīr's death, but assures us that he had contemporary authority for his statement) informs us in his cynical way that Jahāngīr would go to the Jesuits' house in order to eat pork and drink wine, and that on ascertaining that the Christian religion alone allowed these liberties he announced that he would become a Christian.[15]

Whatever his personal intentions may have been, Jahāngīr took the extraordinary step of ordering, or allowing, certain of his nephews, sons of his deceased brother Dāniāl, to be instructed in the Christian religion by Father Corsi and then publicly baptized by Father Xavier.[16] Dāniāl had three sons, Tahmūras, Bāyasanghar and Hoshang, of whom the eldest is said by the Jesuits to have been at that time ten years of age: and we are given various versions of the motives underlying the strange incident of their baptism. Some maintained that the object was to obtain Portuguese wives of good station for the Princes and through them to introduce Portuguese women of good position into Jahāngīr's own zanāna. Others again alleged that in encouraging their baptism Jahāngīr (or the Prince Khurram prompting him) was actuated by a desire to preclude the Princes from any possibility of succeeding to the Crown. The Jesuits themselves were at first suspicious. An embassy was on the point of starting for Goa and it was surmised that this move might have been made with a view to influence the Portuguese Government. But on due consideration they decided that from their knowledge of the King they were justified in concluding that he took this step out of genuine goodwill to their Faith and as an earnest of his own future conversion.

Baptism of Jahāngīr's nephews

Whatever views may be held regarding the object which Jahāngīr had in view, the incident itself was a remarkable one. Towards midnight on July 18, 1610, Father Xavier, together with Father Pinheiro, who was then in Agra, received a summons to wait on the King. On their arrival Jahāngīr called up the sons of Dāniāl and asked the Fathers if it would be agreeable to them to take the boys over and make Christians of them. They accepted the charge with gratitude and, when the King bade them duly inform the Viceroy and the King of Portugal of the step, they replied that it was an offering which would bring joy not only to the Kings of the earth but also to the Angels in Heaven. The boys were handed over to Father Corsi for instruction and some weeks later the King urged that they should be baptized before Father Pinheiro returned to Goa. The Fathers in their enthusiasm fell on their knees and kissed his feet, while he good-humouredly patted them on the shoulders. Preparations were hurried forward and the baptisms, which took place on September 5, were made the occasion of a large public function. The Princes, clothed in Portuguese costume and wearing crosses of gold round their necks, proceeded on elephants from the palace to the church through streets packed with eager spectators. A large cortège from the Court accompanied them and some sixty Christians—including Poles, Venetians and Armenians—joined the procession on horseback. Even the Englishman, Hawkins, who was then in Agra, put aside his Protestant prepossessions for the day and rode at the head of the procession with S. George's flag carried before him 'to the honour of the English nation.'[17] At the church the Princes were received with every sign of rejoicing and the bell was rung with such violence that it broke.[18] The ceremony itself was impressive and the demeanour of the Princes brought tears to the eyes of the spectators. When baptized, they were given, as was then the practice, new names of a European complexion. The eldest, Tahmūras, was named Don Felipe after the King of Spain, Bāyasanghar became Don Carlos after the Spanish Prince of that name, and Hoshang was called Don Henrique after the last King of Portugal.[19] The conversion of these Princes was duly reported by the authorities at Goa to the King of Spain and the news was received by him with great satisfaction. The Viceroy was ordered to congratulate the Princes and the Fathers at Agra, and was instructed to give every encouragement to Jahāngīr if he showed signs of following the same course. Not only so, but a personal letter was addressed by King Philip III to Jahāngīr thanking him for his kindness to the Christians, recommending the missionaries to his goodwill and announcing that, as a sign of his appreciation, the King of Spain would treat the newly-baptized Princes as his own godchildren.[20]

Subsequent history of the Princes

For a time the attitude of the new converts seemed fairly satisfactory. Father Corsi attended them regularly for lessons, and when the King took them with him away from Agra for four months' camping in the cold weather Father Corsi went with them and continued, though on a more restricted scale, to give them their lessons. They treated their teacher with respect and affection, and the Jesuits valued these lessons chiefly as a means of counteracting the influence of the zanāna. On their return to Agra the Princes attended Mass at the church on Easter Sunday accompanied by a numerous following. At the conclusion of the service they kissed the hands of the priests, ate their Easter eggs with relish, watched the amusements provided by the Fathers[21] and returned in state on horseback accompanied by the bulk of the Christian community, including even the English. During the summer their devotions were interrupted by attacks of small-pox, but they attended church once more on the Feast of S. Ignatius (July 31, 1611).[22] In 1613 they were still receiving lessons from Father Corsi,[23] but there is then a gap in our information, and when next we hear of them they were, alas, no longer Christians. Whether this was due, as suggested by Roe and Terry, to disappointment in the expectation of securing Portuguese wives, or, as seems more likely, to the strained political relations which prevailed about this time between the Moguls and the Portuguese, the fact remains that 'they gave their crucifixes again to the Jesuits.' Writing less than five years after their baptism, Father Corsi admits that 'they learn no more to read and, that which is worst of all, they are revolted from the Faith by the order of the King by whose commission they were first made Christians. God pardon him therefore and show them how great an evil they have done.'[24] Or as another Jesuit writer says, they 'rejected the light and returned to their vomit.'[25] Their further history was a sad one; for in 1628, after the death of Jahāngīr, Hoshang and Tahmūras were seized and killed by Āsaf Khān at the instance of Shāh Jahān, and, as the Indian chronicler puts it, 'the flower-bed of existence was cleared of the weeds and rubbish of their lives.' The third Prince, Bāyasanghar, after being signally defeated in battle near Lahore, vanished into oblivion.[26]

Of all this nothing could be foreseen in 1610 and the baptism of the Princes seemed to the Jesuits at that time to be the preface to the baptism of the King himself. Jahāngīr had on one occasion sworn 'by the face of his father' that he would embrace Christianity and had explained that he was only waiting for his nobles to show him the way.[27] He had in Lahore several times promised Father Pinheiro to take this step. When Pinheiro saw him on July 16, 1610, Jahāngīr drew near to him 'so that our knees touched' and spoke earnestly to him 'as though in the confessional,' saying with emphasis that he adhered to this promise: 'sibi fixum esse Christianum fieri,' 'indubitate habeto Christo me nomen daturum.' When he handed over his nephews to the Fathers he met the comments of his courtiers by exclaiming: 'What will happen when I hand myself over?'—'Quid futurum est quando memet quoque tradidero?' The Jesuits rightly realized that if he was baptized, no small part of his Court would follow his example, and their hopes grew high.[28] It was felt that 'a great door had been opened' and the news was received with much enthusiasm at Goa. At no period had the Mission seemed to be so near to realizing its object.

In view of the extraordinary friendliness hitherto shown by Jahāngīr there were some who had already thought the time had come for a special effort to be made from Rome for the evangelization of Northern India, but the project received opposition from an unexpected quarter. The Italian traveller, Giambattista Vechiete—of whom more will be said in Chapter XIV, and who was in India during the last days of Akbar—had approached the Pope in 1608. He impressed on the Holy Father the necessity for sending an embassy to congratulate the new King, to thank him for his support and to urge him to take the final step towards conversion. He drew attention also to the overwhelming majority of the Hindus among the population of Mogor and spoke confidently of the facilities for converting them to Christianity. He drew from the Pope the exclamation: 'Oh, that the conversion could be in our time,' and the preparations for an embassy received the Pope's support. The time and place of embarkation were determined and the King of Spain's concurrence solicited. But the General of the Jesuits refused to give his consent. The Mogul, he alleged, was about to send an embassy to the Pope and it was useless in these circumstances for the Pope to make any move. The General remained impervious to all Vechiete's arguments and the scheme fell through. Three years later it was again revived, but it was again opposed by the General of the Jesuits and no such embassy was ever sent.[29]

Suggested embassy from the Pope

The Mission was accordingly continued on the existing lines. But the personnel was gradually changed. During the early years of Jahāngīr, the men who had conducted the last mission to Akbar—Fathers Jerome Xavier and Emmanuel Pinheiro—continued to influence affairs. Both were, however, getting old. Father Xavier left the Court in 1614 and died at Goa three years later, while Father Pinheiro after being absent in Gujarāt and its neighbourhood for a large part of the time subsequent to Jahāngīr's accession, left finally for Goa in 1615 'broken down with age.'[30] Meanwhile the Mission had been joined by other Fathers, of whom two at least took a prominent part in affairs during the reign of Jahāngīr, namely, Father Francis Corsi and Father Joseph de Castro.

Changes in the personnel of the Mission

Father Corsi, whose arrival has already been referred to, was a Florentine, born in 1573. He came to India in 1599 and was sent to Lahore in 1600 to work with Father Pinheiro. In 1604 he was temporarily in Agra with Father Xavier, having by then learnt the Persian and commenced learning the 'Hindustani' language. Subsequently he

Father Francis Corsi

was attached to the Court, following the King to the south, and afterwards to Kashmīr. When in the south he found himself, in spite of his Florentine nationality, in the position of an 'agent for the Portugals,' and had to support Portuguese interests against the claims of the English ambassador, Sir Thomas Roe. This he did, on the whole, with much sagacity and moderation. In 1624 he changed places with Father de Castro and for some years subsequently he was with Mīrzā Zū'lqarnain at Sāmbhar.[31] Surviving Jahāngīr by several years, he died on August 1, 1635, and is buried in the Padres Santos chapel at Agra.

He was a man of small stature, and we are told by Xavier that before Jahāngīr fully knew him he had avoided asking him questions under the impression that he might be as short in wit as in stature (curto no saber como no corpo).[32] If he is to be identified with the 'Padre Atech' of Bernier, of whom mention will be made further on, he was both small of stature and fiery in temperament, and Pinheiro speaks on one occasion of his having taken up an argument before the King 'pro solito animi ardore': but our accounts of him would lead us to conclude that his natural ardour was kept in full control. He was an enthusiast for his profession, holding that 'if there be a happy life in this world, it is that of the Religious men,' and he is described after his death as having been 'a great column of the Mission.' But he seems to have been an earnest and equable man rather than a fire-eater. Sir Thomas Roe, while dealing cautiously with him, respected him and recognized the value of his services in the cause of peace; and Roe's chaplain, Terry, described him as '(if he were indeed what he seemed to be) a man of severe life, yet of a fair and affable disposition.'[33] We have in extant Mogul miniatures a portrait of a Padre who may possibly be identified with Corsi, and if this identification is correct he was a small, thin, clean-shaven man with keen features.

Father Joseph de Castro

Father Joseph de Castro (though possibly Portuguese or Spanish by origin) was like Corsi from Italy, having been born at Turin in 1577. Unlike the Corsi of the pictures, he was a man with a beard and a corpulent figure,[34] and unlike Corsi he occupied himself more in parochial than in political duties. He first appears in the Mogor Mission in 1610 and was at Agra in 1614. He was selected in 1617 to proceed to Bombay to buy properties there as investments for the endowment of the Agra College. His subsequent career was largely in Agra, but with numerous changes to other stations. From 1619 to 1624 he seems to have been in Sāmbhar and then—changing places with Father Corsi—he was appointed to be in attendance at the Court. For the rest of Jahāngīr's reign he was, as he expressed it, 'with the King, going with him every year and running about through his kingdom.' In 1626 he was in Lahore and the grant of the cemetery there was made out in his name. In the same year he accompanied Jahāngīr to Kābul and in 1627 he went with him to Kashmīr. He then appears to have been attached to Mīrzā Zū'lqarnain in Bahraich, or its neighbourhood, and to have returned in 1632 to Agra where he suffered in the persecutions of the following year. In 1641 while again at Lahore he was able to help the Augustinian Fra Manrique by introducing him to the Wazīr Āsaf Khān, and he was executor to the Italian Veroneo who died at Lahore in that year. His headquarters from 1632 onwards were mainly at Agra, but in July 1645 he was at Sāmbhar and in the following year he was again at Lahore, where he died on December 15, 1646, at the age of seventy. He is buried, like Father Corsi, in the Padres Santos chapel at Agra and has a tombstone there, but curiously enough a duplicate tombstone mentioning the transfer of his body from Lahore was found in 1913 in the compound of the Cathedral at Agra. In the Jesuit Report for 1648–1649 it is stated that when his body was disinterred at Lahore for removal to Agra, a year after his burial, the body and the vestments were found intact.[35]

Relations with Muqarrib Khān—his baptism

The position of the Jesuits in Agra and Lahore, though favoured by the sovereign's personal proclivities, was affected also by the condition of his political relations with the Portuguese. Shortly after his arrival in Lahore from Kābul in 1607 Jahāngīr decided to send an embassy to Goa, partly with the design of establishing good relations and partly with the object of extracting those curious presents which he so much affected. For the conduct of this embassy he selected Muqarrib Khān of Pānipat, previously his personal physician and at that time in charge of Cambay. With Father Xavier's concurrence he sent Father Pinheiro to join the embassy, and shortly before the Christmas of 1607 that Father set out from Lahore, accompanied by the blessings and regrets of the Christian community of that city, to whom he had ministered for twelve years. He reached Cambay in April 1608, but as a new Viceroy was shortly expected at Goa, he and the envoy halted at Cambay. During the halt the adopted child of Muqarrib Khān fell ill, but was restored to health by Father Pinheiro's intervention, with the assistance of holy relics and the reading of the Gospel of S. Mark.[36] The child, known as Masīh-i-Kairānawī, was thereupon baptized; but he subsequently recanted and ultimately became a bigoted Muslim—going indeed so far as to wear a Qur'ān continually round his neck.[37] Early in 1609 Pinheiro proceeded himself to Goa, returning in June to Cambay to make a successful protest against the intrusion of the English at Surat and going back again to Goa in the late autumn. Muqarrib Khān having meantime been recalled to Agra and imprisoned, Pinheiro hastened also to Agra, reaching that city on July 9, 1610. By Pinheiro's intervention, Muqarrib was pardoned and reinstated and was again appointed envoy to the Portuguese Viceroy. Pinheiro left Agra on September 10, 1610, and on February 5, 1611, he duly arrived at Goa in the company of Muqarrib Khān. The trend of events in Agra—the baptism of the princes and the pronouncements of the king—had not been lost on the envoy, and the Jesuits record the astonishing fact that while Muqarrib Khān was at Goa he was baptized, receiving the Christian name of John. The incident caused much pleasure in Portuguese circles, and the King of Spain sent his congratulations. It was recognized indeed that the new convert was an 'imperfect Christian,' and the authorities at Goa treated him with some circumspection. A few years after his baptism he asked for two Christian women to be sent to his household, promising to treat them with all integrity, but the Portuguese did not trust him sufficiently to comply with his request. At the same time he maintained towards them his profession of Christianity and we have on record an official letter of his which bears the superscription of the word 'Jesu.'[38] He kept up very friendly relations with the Fathers and with the Portuguese. During his administration of Gujarāt in 1616–1618 he was the *bête noire* of the English traders and his tendency throughout was to favour his Portuguese friends, with whose help he was able to keep his insatiable master supplied with curiosities of all kinds, ranging from tapestries to guinea-fowl. In 1618 he was transferred to Bihār, and while there, in 1620, he invited the Jesuits of Hūglī to come and found a mission at Patna. He built them a church and a pleasant house on the river bank, and defended them vigorously against their opponents. He explained to them that he had been baptized and wished to live like a Christian, but would not profess his belief publicly for fear of losing his appointment. As he had several wives, he was not admitted to the sacraments, but he allowed the priest to see his principal wife and to instruct and baptize her. Father Simon Figueredo, who visited Patna in 1620, thought that Muqarrib Khān kept a priest at that place with no other object than that of attracting Portuguese trade, from which he could enrich himself.[39] However this may be,

Muqarrib Khān left Bihār in 1621 and ultimately retired to Pānipat, where he built a mausoleum for his father and died at the age of ninety without having in the meantime exhibited any further manifestations of his leanings towards the Christian faith.[40]

Inimical attitude towards William Hawkins

While Muqarrib Khān and Father Pinheiro were waiting at Cambay during the summer of 1608, there arrived at Surat a vessel displaying the flag of England for the first time in Indian waters. William Hawkins, its captain, was provided with letters from James I to the Great Mogul and claimed the right to proceed to Agra with them. The intrusion of these English rivals was strenuously resented by the Portuguese, and the attitude adopted by Muqarrib Khān towards Hawkins at the instigation of Father Pinheiro was one of obstruction and procrastination. Hawkins was impatient and suspicious. The air, to him, was thick with plots for his assassination. Pinheiro, he alleged, had bribed Muqarrib Khān to kidnap him, and when at last he was permitted to leave Surat the same evil genius inspired Muqarrib Khān to refuse him an escort. The Father, he reports, would speak of England to the officials as being a dependency of Portugal and the Englishman fell out with him over this insult in the presence of Muqarrib Khān; indeed if Hawkins could have had his will 'the Father had never spoken more.' When Hawkins reached Agra in April 1609 he still had the ubiquitous Jesuits to contend with. When King James' letter, which was in Spanish, was presented to Jahāngīr, an old Jesuit (doubtless Father Xavier) was called in to read and criticize it: and Jahāngīr had shortly afterwards the opportunity of listening to a somewhat acrimonious theological disputation between Hawkins and the Fathers on the nature of the Eucharist. The King was at first favourable to Hawkins, and every obstacle was accordingly placed in his way by the Jesuits. 'The Jesuits here,' he wrote, 'do little regard their masses and their Church matters for studying how to overthrow my affairs.' They were 'like madde dogges, labouring to work my passage out of the world,' and they had to be warned by the King that if anything happened to Hawkins they would be held responsible. When one of his Protestant following died at Agra, the Fathers, to Hawkins's great disgust, refused to let him be buried among the Christians in their cemetery. And when Hawkins himself married an Armenian lady (a step which he says that he took in order to avoid being poisoned) the Fathers declined to perform the ceremony unless he acknowledged the supremacy of the Pope—a condition which he roundly refused to accept.

Improvement of relations and departure of Hawkins

As time passed, Hawkins grew more and more exasperated at the delays of the Court, and things went less well with him. Jesuit influence gradually revived and it was further strengthened by the reappearance of Muqarrib Khān and subsequently of Father Pinheiro—described as 'an arch-knave'—in the summer of 1610. With this revival of Jesuit influence, however, the personal relations between the Jesuits and the English would seem to have improved. When a number of English were shipwrecked near Surat in September 1609, they were on the whole well treated by the Portuguese. One of them, Robert Coverte, who came to Agra and wished to return home by Persia, obtained from Father Xavier—whom he describes as being 'a man of great Credit there and greatly esteemed and well knowne in other Kingdoms'—letters of commendation to the chief rulers and the priests in the countries through which he would have to pass, together with a letter to the Englishman, John Mildenhall, who had returned from Agra to Europe some years previously.[41] Others among the shipwrecked English were assisted by Father Pinheiro to proceed from Agra to Goa and were there helped by the Jesuits (notably by their Wykehamist compatriot Father Thomas Stevens) to return by sea to Europe.[42] At Agra itself, as we have seen, Captain Hawkins had joined in the celebration of the baptism of the princes by the Jesuit Fathers. When Hawkins doubted the honesty of his subordinate, Finch, at Lahore, he went so far as to send a secret authorization to a Jesuit who was stationed there to seize Finch and his goods if he should attempt to abscond. When at last after much vacillation on the part of the King, the Jesuit policy prevailed, Hawkins was constrained to ask humbly for the good offices of the Jesuits in order that he might obtain passports for himself and his wife to allow of their proceeding through Cambay to Goa—a request with which the Fathers were glad enough to comply in order to be quit of him. On reaching Cambay at the end of 1611 he heard news of the arrival of English ships at Surat and at the same time was asked by the Jesuits to warn these ships that a strong fleet was ready to sail out against them from Goa. He suspected the intention of the request, but gave the information, hurriedly joined the English fleet himself and left India with it.[43] The whole incident was summed up by Father Xavier in a short paragraph of a letter, in which he reported the Jesuit aspect of the case, viz. that certain ultramontane heretics had attempted to disturb the happy progress of the Catholic faith in Mogor, but that the King on discovering their perfidy had banished them from the country.[44] The

Jesuits had in fact succeeded in discrediting Hawkins and his mission.

In the autumn of 1612 another English squadron arrived in Indian waters and defeated the Portuguese ships which attacked it.

Relations with Paul Canning at Agra

English prestige revived, a farmān for trade was received and an Englishman, Paul Canning, was sent to Agra to present a further letter from King James. Two incidents are related which illustrate the ensuing relations between the English and the Jesuits at the Court. We are told that one of Paul Canning's following played the cornet before the King with such success that Jahāngīr himself strove to emulate him on the instrument and ordered that he should teach one of the Court musicians how to play it. The Jesuits tried to induce the Englishman to teach the art to two of their servants, saying that this was the King's command, but he resolutely declined to meet their wishes.[45] We are further told that when an Englishman, a cousin of Paul Canning, died at Agra, the Fathers refused him burial in their cemetery, and that when Canning secured his interment there they took up the body and buried it in the highway. When Canning himself (who had been in daily dread of being poisoned by the Jesuits)[46] died shortly afterwards, both bodies were buried together on one side of the cemetery, at some distance from the other tombs, and the Jesuits made no objection to this arrangement. Indeed according to another, but less likely, version of the story the incident entailed direct intervention by the King who ordered the reinterment of the Englishmen in the cemetery and threatened the Jesuits 'not only to turn them out of his Kingdom but allsoe their dead bodies, theire countrymens, out of their graves.'[47] However this may be, the relations between the English and the Jesuits became daily more strained. The English received favours, but the Fathers—'those prattling, juggling Jesuits'—still held the King's ear and endeavoured to persuade him that England was a petty island with no resources.[48] 'The lying Jesuits,' we are told, were 'feeding the King daily with presents and strange toys,' and when the English produced their cornet player the Jesuits responded by producing a Neapolitan juggler. None of the King's nobles had 'so easy access' as the Jesuits, and the Mogul would do nothing against the Portuguese 'soe longe as that witch Savier liveth (for soe the Moores themselves terme him) which is an ould Jesuitt residinge with the Kinge whom he much affects.'[49] In spite, therefore, of the English opposition, everything at this stage pointed to the likelihood of the Fathers being able to maintain their position and influence at the Court.

At this moment, however, an entirely unexpected event took place which for a time completely overclouded the prospects of the Jesuits. In the autumn of 1613 the Portuguese, irritated at the admission of the English, seized, without any shadow of excuse, a large and valuable ship of the Moguls in which the King's mother was interested; and in view of this high-handed action it was at once decided by the Moguls to take reprisals by placing an embargo on Portuguese trade and laying siege to Damān. The missionaries suffered along with the traders. During the summer of 1614 the churches at Agra and Lahore were forcibly closed; the Fathers were deprived of their allowances; and it seemed as if all the previous hopes of the Jesuits were to end in complete disaster.[50]

The rupture between the Moguls and Portuguese, 1613–1615

Of this unfortunate time we have special information from certain letters written in 1615 by the Fathers to Europe; two by Father Corsi, one by Father Machado, and two by Father de Castro. Being unable to send these letters by sea the Fathers entrusted their despatches to a young English Protestant called Thomas who was proceeding overland to Europe by Aleppo. For some cause unknown to us the letters failed to reach their destination, but they arrived in England and were considered of sufficient interest to justify their being translated in that country. Three of the original letters and the translations of all of them are now to be found in the British Museum.[51] From these we learn that, when the outburst of repression took place in July 1614, Father Pinheiro was at Goa. Father Xavier, who according to English accounts had at first been thrown into prison,[52] was sent off from Agra to Goa 'like a banished man' to use his influence for peace;[53] and Father Corsi who accompanied the King to Ajmīr had to live there 'in a little house of straw.' Father de Castro was left alone in Agra, and he was there exposed to the first manifestations of the new policy. The Mogul officials came with arms and 'lāthīs'—cum fustibus et armis—and walled up the entrance to his church. He had to quit his residence and to store the property of the house and church in the home of a poor Christian. The allowances previously enjoyed by the Jesuits were stopped, and in order to sustain himself and his congregation Father de Castro had to sell some of the holy vessels, the gold and silver candlesticks and other articles of furniture from the house and church. The Portuguese inhabitants of Agra fled from the town.[54] The Indian Christians remained on the whole wonderfully constant, but they needed much consolation, and fresh conversions came practically

Effects on the Mission

to an end. Mass was said in a chapel in the Fathers' own residence and the women were confessed from house to house. At Lahore the blow fell even more severely. Both church and house were forcibly closed and Father Antony Machado, who was in residence at Lahore, hastened to Ājmīr to petition for the restitution of their contents. Through the mediation of Father Corsi and of Āsaf Khān, the Wazīr, they were restored to him, with the exception of the images ; but he no longer held Lahore to be safe for himself or for his congregation, and he accordingly migrated with his converts to Agra, where his arrival was a source of much comfort to Father de Castro. The Christian community at Agra was in a state of great anxiety and apprehensive of severe measures. Some outsiders showed unexpected kindness in helping them with gifts of money, but as a rule they met with contempt and abuse and felt very deeply the alteration from the position of respect and reputation which the Mission had hitherto enjoyed. In the outlying station of Ahmadābād we hear of the resident missionary—probably Father Jean de Seine—being reduced to absolute indigence and entreating the English agent for relief. Having received from him a gift of ten rupees he wrote him a thankful letter, but withal desired him to burn it, ' whereby,' as the Englishman Withington rather unfairly comments, ' I note his pride of harte, to bee willing to receave a good turne but not openlye to acknowledge that hee had neede of yt.'[55]

Resumption of peaceful relations

The storm blew over almost as suddenly as it had arisen. When Father Xavier reached Surat on his way to Goa, war had broken out and he was placed under detention by the Moguls, but he was shortly afterwards released in order to discuss terms of peace with the Portuguese Viceroy.[56] So far as the local authorities were concerned a provisional agreement was soon reached. The English and the Dutch were to be excluded from trading with the Mogul dominions, the King was to indemnify himself for the loss of his ship from the Portuguese property which he had attached, and all prisoners on either side, excluding renegades, were to be set at liberty. A copy of the draft treaty, countersigned by Father Xavier, can still be seen at Goa.[57] The treaty, however, was not acceptable to Jahāngīr, and though the Jesuits at Court pressed for its approval, the conditions, if confirmed by him, appear to have been confirmed with great reluctance. In any case, as neither side wished to continue hostilities, the parties gradually subsided into a peace, the English remaining on at Surat as before.[58] At Ahmadābād the Fathers had in September 1612 received permission to build a church, but on the outbreak of the trouble they had been dispossessed of their house to make way for the English traders. In September 1615, after the restoration of good relations, a further farmān was issued restoring the house to the Fathers and requiring the English to be accommodated elsewhere.[59]

In none of the Mission stations had there been any serious violence used during this troublous interval and the sufferings of the Christians were for the most part sufferings in reputation and means of subsistence. When the trouble was over, the Fathers were restored to their old position, the churches were released from attachment, the allowances were revived and things proceeded as before.

Things went on as before, except in one respect—the veteran Xavier was no longer with the Mission. He was now more than sixty-five years of age and weaker physically than his age warranted. He had suffered from stone and fever and other serious maladies, and his vigour had left him. He found even the writing of letters a hard task for 'an old man with little health and plenty of work.' On his arrival in Portuguese India in 1615 he was put in charge of the College of St. Paul at Goa and he found the duties there to be beyond his strength. His heart was still with the Mission which he had conducted for twenty years, and he received an invitation on behalf of the King to return to Mogor. He felt himself to be in any case near his end and he longed to return to a post where he might hope to die the death of a martyr. This was not the death decreed for him, but his end was none the less sudden and terrible. He was the victim of a conflagration in the new Goa college where he resided and he died on June 17, 1617, 'burnt and suffocated with the smoke of the fire which caught hold of his bed.'[60] In him both the Mission and the Portuguese authorities lost a valued and prudent agent.

The passing of Father Jerome Xavier

The Portuguese, in spite of the restoration of peace, had to continue their diplomatic struggle against the English, and the struggle became the more serious in view of the fact that a formal embassy of high standing from King James had now arrived in the country. This was the famous embassy of Sir Thomas Roe, who reached India in September 1615 and arrived at the King's Court at Ājmīr before Christmas. So far from accepting the expulsion of the English from India which was contemplated in Xavier's draft treaty, Roe—though he shifted his ground from time to time during his long negotiations—aimed at securing full freedom of trade for his countrymen and at bringing the English and the Moguls into

The Jesuits and Sir Thomas Roe

To face page 84] [*Victoria Memorial, Calcutta*

JAHANGIR AND HIS COURTIERS
Including a Jesuit Priest
(See p. 258)

alliance against the Portuguese. With the exception of the King himself, who counted for less than Roe supposed, the chief influences at Court—the Prince Khurram, Muqarrib Khān the Governor of Cambay, and Āsaf Khān the powerful Wazīr—were for the greater part of Roe's time in opposition to him and subject to the inspiration of the Jesuits. Roe had not been two months ashore before he found the irrepressible Jesuits 'diving deep' into his secrets[61] and belittling the value of his presents for the King.[62] To his great mortification Jahāngīr asked of Father Corsi whether the King of England were a great king that he sent presents of such small value;[63] and when he had hopes of a speedy decision on his request, Roe found objections raised at the last moment—'a Jesuiticall bone,' as he said, 'cast in over night.'[64] When the terms of the proposed settlement were argued publicly before the King, the Jesuits took up the cudgels for the Portuguese,[65] nor was it any great compensation to Roe to find that the King enjoyed hearing his Protestant interpreter, an Italian from Verona, 'rayle at the Jesuits and theyr factions.'[66] Roe insisted that the Portuguese should be excluded from Surat because he felt sure that if they were allowed ingress, their fleet would some day suddenly attack the English; and he rejected with scorn the assurance that Father Corsi guaranteed the peaceful intentions of the Portuguese—'only an Italian poore Jesuite,' he wrote, 'had enformed the Prince the Portugall would be quiett—a brave securitye!'[67] It is true that the English had twice defeated the Portuguese fleet which had been sent, as the Fathers put it, 'por castigar los hereticos Ingleses,'[68] but the Jesuits had the ear of the all-powerful Āsaf Khān and knew unfailingly how to please the Court with presents.[69] With their aid the Portuguese were able to place many obstructions in Roe's path and to protract the length of his negotiations at the Court.

Relations between Roe and Corsi

Both Roe and Corsi remained at Jahāngīr's Court on all its travels, at Ājmīr, at Māndū and at Ahmadābād; and their attitude to each other as the protagonists of their respective causes presents some features of much interest. The views held by Roe regarding the missionary efforts of the Jesuits are sufficiently indicated in a long and interesting letter which he sent in October 1616 to the Archbishop of Canterbury.[70] In this letter (to which further allusion will be made in its proper place) Roe sets himself out to recount 'how the Portugalls have crept into this kingdome and by what corners they gott in; the enterance of the Jesuits, their entertaynment, priviledges, practises, ends and the growth of their Church, whereof they sing in Europe so loud prayses and glorious successes,' and his account, valuable as it is, has an obvious Protestant bias. Apart, however, from the fact that they supported opposing interests in politics and religion, Sir Thomas Roe and Father Corsi appear on the whole to have maintained good mutual relations creditable to them both. At an early stage of their acquaintance Father Corsi suggested to Roe that they should show mutual tolerance to each other's form of faith, and that they should avoid injuring the missionary efforts of the Jesuits by exposing their differences in the face of non-Christians. 'He told him,' says Terry, the chaplain of Roe's embassy,[71] 'that they were both by profession Christians though there was a vast difference betwixt them in their professing it; and as he should not go about to reconcile the Ambassador to them, so he told him that it would be labour in vain if he should attempt to reconcile him to us. Only he desired that there might be a fair correspondence betwixt them, but no disputes. And further his desire was that those wide differences 'twixt the Church of Rome and us might not be made there to appear, that Christ might not seem by those differences to be divided amongst men professing Christianity which might be a very main obstacle and hindrance unto his great design and endeavour for which he was sent thither, to convert people to Christianity there; telling my Lord Ambassador further, that he should be ready to do for him all good offices of love and service there; and so he was.' Roe seems to have accepted this attitude. Father Corsi made a practice of visiting him once a week and informing him of such news as came to his notice; while in the case of matters in which the Jesuits would be interested Roe would send for Corsi and inform him of them. The arrangement was of value to both. Father Corsi, like others in the Society, was 'a great intelligencer,' 'knowing all news which was stirring.' Roe too would sometimes get items of news (such as the wreck and burning of a Portuguese ship in the Comoro Islands in August 1616) and would communicate them to Father Corsi.[72] When a firm in Aleppo wrote to Jerome Xavier for assistance in recovering the property of their agent who had recently died in Lahore, and the letter came into Roe's hands, he transferred it to Father Corsi for disposal and promised his own assistance at Court towards obtaining the estate.[73] Father Corsi would discuss with Roe a case in which indigo belonging to an English employee had been seized by the authorities,[74] and he provided the chaplain, Terry, with a Latin note of the arguments which had been used by Father Xavier to induce Akbar to become a Christian.[75] Father Corsi proffered his services to bring about a peace between the

English and the Portuguese, and Roe, though duly cautious in his dealings with him, accepted the view that as Christians they should accord with one another; but doubts were raised as to the authority of the Jesuit, or even of the Portuguese Viceroy, to assent to a peace on behalf of the Portuguese Government and no further progress was made. On the arrival of a pretended Spanish ambassador the King enquired of Father Corsi regarding his credentials and received from the Father a truthful reply which led to the return of the impostor and to Corsi's own discomfiture.[76] On more than one occasion Roe acknowledged the value of Father Corsi's aid by the presentation of gifts to the Father; at one time forwarding to him copies of the works of Azor and Bellarmine, and at another providing him with mementos of a more domestic character in the shape of a folding case for combs valued at £5 and a pearl-embroidered girdle.[77] Even after he had returned to England, Roe sent further presents to be delivered to Corsi by the East India Company's agents.[78]

In September 1618, the King started from Ahmadābād to return to Agra. Roe's embassy came to an end and he set out on his return journey to Europe. He and Corsi had set a good standard to govern the relations between the English and their opponents and we find several instances later on which illustrate the good feeling that not infrequently prevailed. Some years afterwards, for example, a business letter written in 1626 by Robert Young to an Englishman in Lahore, included salutations to a certain trader at that city and to 'the patherie'; meaning doubtless Father de Castro. A similar letter written by one Joseph Hopkinson, at Ahmadābād, to the English traders at the Court contained special greetings to the 'Padre' (probably again Joseph de Castro) and others, adding 'there was a great deale of love amongst us when they were here.'[79] And later on in 1638, we find the same de Castro presenting a leading English trader with a copy of Father Xavier's Persian *Lives of the Twelve Apostles*.[80] The English at Agra seem indeed to have maintained on the whole a friendly attitude towards the Jesuits, and, though they naturally enough would not join in the Corpus Christi processions, we find that they were ready to partake, to some extent, in the Christmas and Easter festivities of the Fathers.[81]

Two current stories regarding the Jesuits

The English who visited the Court of Jahāngīr looked with a certain air of detachment on the efforts of the Jesuits to bring him over to Christianity. And they retailed without incredulity, but with something of amusement, two of the current stories regarding the means adopted by the King to test the claim of the Christian religion.

One of these stories attributes to Jahāngīr the suggestion of an ordeal by fire, on lines somewhat similar to the test suggested in Akbar's time, to which allusion has already been made. The exact form of the story varies and the name of the Jesuit concerned differs in the different versions. Our best authority is that of Sir Thomas Roe, who was apparently present at the time and who described the scene in his letter of 1616 to the Archbishop of Canterbury.[82] According to him, the King called for 'the Jesuite' (the term he always applies to Father Corsi) and promised to become a Christian if a certain crucifix and picture which had survived a recent fire in Corsi's house were thrown before him into a fire and were not consumed.[83] Father Corsi, in Roe's version of the story, declined the trial in that form, but offered to go into the fire himself; and the proposal came to nothing. Terry, who tells the same story with slight variations, has recorded the reasons put forward by Father Corsi for declining the suggestion.[84] In the hands of Bernier and Manucci, who wrote many years later, the story assumes a slightly different shape. The former tells us that the King gave the name of 'Padre Atech' (Ātish, fire) to a small fiery Florentine Father at his Court—presumably Corsi—and that he called on this Father and on a Mullā to throw themselves simultaneously into a fiery furnace.[85] The latter says that a Padre whom Jahāngīr called 'Ātish' offered to sit in lighted straw with the Gospel in his hand if the Qāzī would do the same with the Qur'ān. He gives the Padre's name as Joseph da Costa—a confusion doubtless with Joseph de Castro who was at that time in Agra.[86]

The fire test

The other story of this character is that of the Sagacious Ape—a story which we should be inclined to dismiss as a romance if it were not vouched for by the trustworthy Roe. A Bengali juggler, he says, brought an ape to the King, and His Majesty 'caused in twelve several papers in Persian letters to be written the names of twelve lawgivers as Moses, Christ, Mahomett, Aly and others, and shuffling them in a bagg, bad the beast divine which was the true law; who putting in his foote tooke out that inscribed of Christ. This amazed the King, who suspecting that the ape's master could read Persian, and might assist him, wrote them anew in Court characters' (i.e. in the official cypher), 'and presented them a second time. The ape was constant, found the right, and kissed it. Whereat a principal officer grew angry, telling the King that it was some imposture, desiering that hee might have leave to make the lotts anew, and offered him selfe to punishment if the

The Sagacious Ape

ape could beguile him. He wrote the names putting only aleven into the bagg, and kept the other in his hand. The beast searchd but refused all. The King commanded to bring one ; the beast tore them in fury and made signes the true lawgivers name was not among them. The King demanded wher it was ; and hee rann to the nobleman and caught him by the hand in which was the paper inscribed with the name of Christ Jesus.' The Jesuits were amused when one of their pupils ran to them and said that the King had an ape which was a Christian. They did not deny the truth of the incident, but made light of it and declined to acknowledge that they had any hand in it. Nevertheless it was in Roe's opinion ' not unlike one of their owne games.'[87]

The story is told in a pamphlet printed in London in 1622 in which it is stated that its truth is vouched for by Sir Thomas Roe and that his chaplain, Terry, had seen the ape.[88] Terry when reproducing the tale with slight variations in his own book of Travels, denied that he had seen the incident himself, which happened a few years before his arrival in India, but he stated that he was certified of its correctness by ' divers persons who knew not one another and were differing in religion.'[89] The same tale is repeated in Bry's *India Orientalis*, printed in 1628, at Frankfurt and is illustrated in that work by an amusing woodcut, in which, among other absurdities, Jahāngīr is represented in the dress of an American Indian.[90] As a matter of fact the tale is in the main true. We have a report of the incident by Father Jerome Xavier in terms which, though less picturesque than those used by Roe, agree substantially with Roe in their purport. The trick was performed before the King between nine and ten o'clock at night on November 28, 1610, and though Father Xavier did not happen to be present himself the young sons of Prince Dāniāl saw the incident and related it to their instructor, Father Corsi. Father Xavier received confirmation of the facts from a courtier of good authority who was present and from the high judicial functionary known as the Mīr 'Adl. He himself offers no explanation of the event, beyond a hint that it was not beyond the power of God to use the brute creation, as in the case of Balaam's ass, to testify to his Name. But as regards the occurrence itself he has no doubt.[91]

The tale was reported by him more than once in his letters, and on its becoming known in Europe it immediately caught the imagination of the wonder-loving public of that time. In 1612 one Juan de Fonseca published it in Grenada in the form of a Spanish ballad. The story, as can be imagined, lost nothing of the wonderful in its ballad form, and the title of the ballad ran : ' A remarkable and marvellous report received from Father Jerome

Xavier, S.J., where an account is given of an animal or monster in Bengal which looketh into the past and future like a rational being, wanting only the power of speech; understandeth anything given to it in writing; and if given the name of Jesus treateth it with reverence, while expressing detestation of the names of false idols. It hath been put to much testing, in such wise that the King of Mogul and his whole kingdom withal have been converted to the Holy Catholic Faith, etc.'[92] A similar tale relating to the time of Akbar is said to have been preserved as a tradition among certain Christians who were transferred to Goa and Delhi many years later,[93] and the incident is also erroneously ascribed to Akbar's reign in Eusebius Nieremberg's *Life of Xavier*.[94] It seems clear, however, that the trick was performed in the early part of Jahāngīr's reign, and that the story is not apocryphal as might at first sight appear.

During the later years of Jahāngīr the Jesuit Mission was fully reinstated in the favour of the Sovereign.

Jahāngīr's later years

Writing in 1623 the Superior of the Mission speaks of his continued kindness to the Fathers and recounts several incidents indicating his reverence for the Christian Faith. We are told, for instance, how he rebuked an Armenian for not wearing a Cross, and how he upbraided a nobleman who spoke of Christ as ''Īsā' or 'Jesus' instead of using the phrase 'Hazrat 'Īsā' or 'The Lord Jesus.' The possibility of Jahāngīr's conversion was at times mooted among the Christians, but the Fathers realized that so long as the Queen, Nūr Jahān, maintained her power over him his conversion was unlikely. Her influence had weakened his interest in Christianity and the Fathers expressed their feelings in the quotation 'Avert-erunt mulieres cor ejus.'[95] They began to turn their attention to the unfortunate and intemperate Prince Parwīz, who in 1623 seemed likely to be the successor of his father Jahāngīr. When in Bengal this Prince had granted allowances to the Jesuits of Hūglī, and the Fathers were gratified when the Prince confided to them more than once that his Faith and theirs was the same: 'Dīn-i man dīn-i shumā.' 'God grant,' they wrote, 'that he may be the first Hindustani King—o primo Rei Industane—to receive baptism.' But their hopes were extinguished by the death of the Prince in 1626, a year before his father.[96]

In 1624 there seems to have been an attempt on the part of some discontented Europeans to introduce a Franciscan Mission at Agra in opposition to the Jesuits; some Religious of that Order reached the city and rumours were soon set about that they had performed miracles before the Great Mogul, even raising the dead. These rumours were, however, denied by the Franciscans themselves, who admitted that they had spoken three times only with the King and that the alms which they had received from him were obtained through the mediation of the Jesuits. The Jesuit Fathers, though no longer supplied with presents from the King on the scale prevalent in Xavier's time, remained in favour, and Father de Castro who accompanied Jahāngīr to Kashmīr in 1624 and 1627 received much attention and occasional gifts of fish and fruit from him.[97] The King and even the Queen—Nūr Jahān—would visit the Church at Lahore, and the King went so far as to express a desire to eat and drink in it.[98] There were, however, no fresh advances or incidents of note in connection with the Mission at the Imperial Court, and the chief feature of Jesuit activity in the latter years of Jahāngīr's reign was the initiation of the adventurous mission to Tsaparang in Tibet. The wonderful history of this strange mission begins with a journey over the Garhwāl passes by Father Andrade in 1624 and continues after Jahāngīr's death into the reign of his successor. It is, however, an episode in itself apart from the main current of the Mogor Mission and a separate chapter in this book has been devoted to it. So far as it affected the Mission at the Court, its consequences were unfortunate, for its claims on the time of the Superior, Father Andrade, were such that for some years the parent Mission had reason to complain of neglect.[99]

Jahāngīr's death and his alleged conversion

On October 28, 1627, Jahāngīr died of asthma on his way from Kashmīr to Lahore. Much has been written by eminent authorities on his attitude to religion, and it is generally recognized that while he sat loosely to all forms of religion and yet showed an interest in all, his interest was not of the same refined and earnest type as that of his father. Though nominally a Muslim, he had, like his father, done and said much in opposition to Islām ; and like his father, though not in so explicit a manner, had indicated a belief that he himself was on a level with Muhammad. In writing to Prince Charles (afterwards Charles I) in 1616, Sir Thomas Roe describes his attitude : 'His religione,' he says, 'is of his owne invention ; for he envyes Mahomett, and wisely sees noe reason why hee should not bee as great a prophet as hee.'[100] And Father Cabral, S.J., writing from hearsay in 1633, states that he 'was a Moor in name and dress only,' and 'more attached to Christ than to Muhammad.'[101] He doubtless from time to time gave the Jesuits to believe that he was ready to go further and to be baptized; and Austin of Bordeaux who was at his Court alleges that Jahāngīr was poisoned because he intended to become a Christian.[102] Roe, as one might expect, looked on the hopes of the Jesuits with suspicion; the King, he admitted, was very favourable to the newly planted Christian Church, often 'casting out doubtfull woords of his conversion,' but all this, he adds, was done 'to wicked purpose.'[103] De Castro tells us that when the King had a temporary illness in Kashmīr in 1627, he sent for the Father and bade him commend him to Christ, saying that if he recovered he would become a Christian; but that when he was recovered he contented himself with presenting to the Father a fine Calvary carved in amber.[104] A legend, however, grew up among the Jesuits that Jahāngīr had gone further than was commonly thought. The Report of 1649 published by Maracci spoke of a story which led one to suppose that he had been baptized in secret by Corsi,[105] but that owing to his son's antipathy to Christians he had feared to make an open confession of faith. Father Ceschi, writing in 1650, says that Jahāngīr, when at the point of death, 'ordered to call the Fathers because he would become a Christian; but his people would never call them.'[106] Bernier, writing in 1663, says that the Fathers at that date still held that when about to die Jahāngīr had asked to be made a Christian, but that his wishes had been kept hidden from them.[107] Manucci, however, writing more than sixty years after Jahāngīr's death, goes no further than to say that 'some assert that Jahāngīr was willing to become a Christian.'[108]

The tale of his secret baptism has evidently no support, nor is there any convincing evidence to show that Jahāngīr at any time—at any date during his later years—seriously contemplated conversion to Christianity.

NOTES

[1] Guerreiro, *Relaçam*, II, Part II, pp. 59–61. Payne, *Akbar and the Jesuits*, 1926, pp. 182–191, and Xavier's letters of July 26, 1598, and September 6, 1604, in *J.A.S.B.*, LXV, 1896, pp. 73–75 and 92–93.

[2] The atrocious wholesale executions which followed are described by Xavier as 'hum horrendo espectaculo,' but it is not clear whether he actually witnessed them. Letter of September 25, 1606; Payne, *Jahāngīr and the Jesuits*, 1930, p. 92.

[3] Austin of Bordeaux's letter of April 9, 1632, in *J.P.H.S.*, IV, 1916, p. 14.

[4] Undated letter of Jerome Xavier in Brit. Mus., Marsden MSS. Addl., 9854, fol. 165.

[5] *J.P.H.S.*, V, 1916 (Felix), pp. 18 and 22.

[6] Botelho's Relation in *Mem. A.S.B.*, V, 1916, p. 153. The general allowances made by Jahāngīr seem to have been 50 rupees per month

for the Mission, 50 for poor converts and 30 for church expenses; Xavier, letter of August 28, 1607; Guerreiro, IV, p. 159; and du Jarric, III, p. 115. Withington states that the allowances in Agra in 1615 were 7 rupees a month for the chief Jesuit and 3 rupees for the rest; Foster, *Early Travels in India*, 1921, p. 223. Andrade in 1623 reported that he himself had refused to take a personal allowance of 8 rupees which was twice what Xavier got at the end of his time, and took 3 rupees which was what Xavier received for the most of his time at Court; Letter of August 14, 1623. It is not easy to reconcile the various figures with each other.

[7] Guerreiro, *Relaçam*, V, p. 15. J. Xavier in Zannetti's *Raguagli*, 1615, p. 25, and in his letter of September 24, 1608.

[8] Guerreiro in *J.P.H.S.*, VII, 1918 (Hosten), p. 55. Du Jarric, III, p. 120.

[9] See more about him in Chapter XI.

[10] Letter of September 14, 1609, *J.A.S.B.*, XXIII, 1927, p. 120.

[11] Guerreiro, V, pp. 10–13; du Jarric, III, pp. 121–129. J. Xavier in Zannetti's *Raguagli*, 1615, pp. 16–24. Their chief opponent was the King's Reader, Naqīb Khān, a well-known Syad who had been responsible for the translation of Hindu classics into Persian. *Ā'īn-i-Akbarī* (Blochmann), I, pp. 447–449. The proceedings (in Persian) of these and similar debates were among the documents presented by Col Gentil to the Royal Library at Paris: see *Mémoires de litterature* (*Academie royale des Inscriptions et Belles Lettres*), Vol. XLIX (1808), p. 710 (No. 89) and p. 711 (No. 18).

[12] Xavier, letter of September 24, 1608.

[13] Coverte, *A true and almost incredible report*, 1612, p. 40. Thos. Osborne, *Collection of Voyages and Travels*, 1745, II, p. 255.

[14] Foster, *Early Travels in India*, 1921, p. 147.

[15] *Storia do Mogor*, I, p. 158.

[16] The authorities differ a good deal as to the number of Princes baptized, some speaking of two and others of three. Finch (Foster's *Early Travels in India*, 1921, pp. 147–148), and Austin of Bordeaux (*J.P.H.S.*, IV, 1916, pp. 14–15) say three: while Roe (Foster, *The Embassy of Sir Thomas Roe to India*, p. 277); Terry (*A Voyage to East India*, edition of 1777, p. 425); Tavernier (Ball and Crooke, 1925, i, p. 270); and Hazart, I, p. 267, speak of two only. Herbert (*Travels*, edition of 1677, pp. 74, 90, 94, 98) may be quoted both ways, and Hawkins (Foster's *Early Travels in India*, 1921, pp. 86 and 116) mentions no number. As a matter of fact there is no doubt from the letters of Jerome Xavier (letter in Zannetti's *Raguagli*, pp. 31–33, and letter in British Museum, Marsden MSS. Addl., No. 9854, fol. 162) that three sons of Dāniāl were baptized. There were, however, two later converts of mark mentioned by Xavier, viz. (i) a grandson of Mīrzā Muhammad Hakīm, Akbar's brother, and (ii) a grandson of a Hindu noble who had been Viceroy of Gujarāt: the former having been baptized a fortnight, and the latter two months, after the sons of Dāniāl. The names of Don Duarte and Salvador seem to have been given to these: cf. Finch (loc. cit.) and Herbert, p. 74.

[17] Foster, *Early Travels in India*, 1921, p. 148.

[18] Brit. Mus., Marsden MSS. Addl., No. 9854, fol. 164.

[19] The incident is fully related in Pinheiro's and Xavier's various letters of 1610 and is mentioned briefly in Laubegeois' letter of July 11, 1611, and January 25, 1612. See also letter dated July 10, 1612, from

Paez in Abyssinia ; Beccari, *Rerum Aeth. Scriptores*, XI, pp. 272–275.

[20] Letters of February 13 and 15, 1612, in *Collecçao de Monumentos Ineditos*, published by the Academy of Sciences at Lisbon (1884), VIII, pp. 160–163.

[21] These included the performance of a tight-rope walker and the burning of a figure of Judas, stuffed with fireworks, on the roof of the chapel.

[22] See Jerome Xavier's letters above referred to.

[23] Xavier's letter of September 23, 1613.

[24] Letter of February 26, 1615, in British Museum, Cottonian MSS., Titus, B., VIII, 231, translation published in *The Examiner*, Bombay (Hosten), August 9, 1919. The King's order was apparently due to his irritation at the conduct of the Portuguese in 1613 ; see Xavier's Letter of 1615 in *J.A.S.B.*, XXIII, 1927, p. 125.

[25] *J.A.S.B.*, VI, 1910 (Hosten), p. 530.

[26] Herbert, *Travels* (ed. 1677), p. 98. Tavernier (Ball and Crooke), I, p. 270. Peter Mundy (Hakl. Soc. Temple), II, p. 165 *note*. In Dow's *Ferishta*, 1808, III, p. 117, Bāyasanghar is said to have been strangled with his brother Hoshang : according to the Ma'āsir-ul-umarā he died in the Telingana country, and according to Austin of Bordeaux he escaped to Tartary (*J.P.H.S.*, IV, 1916, p. 15 ; cf. *J.I.H.*, II, 1922, p. 15, and VI, 1928, p. 253). The Turkish historians relate how he fled in 1632 to Turkey and 'rubbed his forehead on the Imperial Gate' at Constantinople, but evoked dislike there owing to his pride and uncouth behaviour (*Trans. R.A.S.*, 1830, pp. 462–466). An impostor raised a revolt in Kābul under his name against Shāh Jahān, but was captured and put to death. See also the Portuguese State Letter of November 6, 1632, published by J. H. da Cunha Rivara in *O Chronista de Tissuary, Nova Goa*, 1866, I, p. 97. Cf. *Calc. Rev.*, xlix, October 1869, pp. 148–150 ; and *Pros. A.S.B.*, August 1869, p. 218.

[27] Xavier in Zannetti's *Raguagli*, 1615, p. 31.

[28] See the letters quoted in note 19 above.

[29] Letter of Girolamo Vechiete in Morelli, *I Codici manoscritti volgari della Libreria Naniana*, Venice, 1776, pp. 187–8.

[30] *J.A.S.B.*, VI, 1910 (Hosten), p. 530.

[31] In his letter of January 22, 1627 (accompanying that of April 3), to the Provincial, Corsi gives a brief outline of the positions he had held. The letter is of interest as it pleads for a transfer for one year to a Novitiate Retreat at Goa on the ground of the spiritual deterioration experienced by Corsi from a continuous life of solitude. In 1627–1628 we find him writing letters from Agra, but this was owing to the fact that the Mīrzā, whose chaplain he was, happened then to be in that city. In 1631, however, he was described by the Viceroy at Goa as being in residence with the Court at Agra (Gracias, *Una dona portugueza na Corte do Grão Mogol*, 1907, p. 68).

[32] Letter of 24th Sep., 1608.

[33] Hosten, *Jesuit Missionaries in North India*, 1907, p. 10 ; Foster's *Roe*, pp. 249, 276 and 437 ; Terry (ed. 1777), p. 422 ; Maracci's *Relation*, 1651, p. 22 ; Letter of Corsi dated March 6, 1615 (British Museum, Cottonian MSS., Titus, B., VIII, 233), published in *The Examiner*, Bombay (Hosten), on August 16, 1919.

[34] Annual Report of 1648–9, *J.I.H.*, I, 1922 (Hosten), p. 247.

[35] Hosten, *Jesuit Missionaries in North India*, 1907, p. 15 ; *The*

Examiner, Bombay, August 16, 1919 (Hosten), footnote 11; *J.P.H.S.*, V, 1916, pp. 14–15; *J.A.S.B.*, XXIII, 1927 (Hosten), pp. 141–143; *Mem. A.S.B.*, V, 1916 (Hosten), p. 185; Maracci, *Relation*, 1651, p. 21; Annual Report of 1648–1649, *J.I.H.*, I, 1922 (Hosten), pp. 246–247.

[36] Guerreiro, V, p. 19.

[37] *J.P.H.S.*, V, 1916 (Felix), p. 15; Blochmann, *Ā'īn*, I, p. 543–4. Annual Letter, Cochin, 1621, *The Examiner*, Bombay (Hosten), March 23, 1912; H. R. Nevill, *Gazetteer of the Muzaffarnagar district*, Allahabad, 1903, p. 268. He was a poet and his alleged bigotry did not prevent his writing an epic on the Hindu heroine, Sītā.

[38] *Collecção de Monumentos Ineditos*, published by the Academy of Sciences, Lisbon, 1884, VI, p. 355, and 1886, VIII, p. 160. The letter is dated April 3, 1615. In 1620 one of his nephews wrote on his behalf a letter from Patna to the Superior in Bengal, which was in Portuguese and headed by 'a beautifully executed "Jesus."' Figueredo's letter December 20, 1620.

[39] *J.P.H.S.*, V, 1916 (Felix), p. 15, and *Mem. A.S.B.*, V, 1916 (Hosten), p. 122; O'Malley, *Patna Gazetteer*, 1907, p. 75. See also pp. 108–118 of the Cochin Annual Letter of 1621 in the *Histoire de ce qui s'est passé en Éthiopie*, &c., Paris, 1628, which is based on Simon Figueredo's letter of December 20, 1620.

[40] Blochmann, *Ā'īn*, I, p. 543; Wāq'āt-i-Jahāngīrī in Elliot, *Hist. Ind.*, VI, pp. 317, 320, 330; Von Poser's *Memoirs* (1675), I, p. 4; *J.P.H.S.*, VII, 1918, p. 67, the *Catholic Herald*, Calcutta, 1906, pp. 804–805, there quoted, and *The Examiner*, Bombay, 1912, pp. 117–119. A different account of Muqarrib Khān's end is given in Benī Parshād, *Hist. Jahāngīr*, p. 421.

[41] Coverte, *A true and almost incredible report*, London, 1612, p. 42; Foster, *Early Travels in India*, 1921, p. 49.

[42] The Huguenot, Pyrard de Laval (Hakl., edn. 1888, II, Part I, pp. 265–269) hints that as the English had plenty of money the assistance given by Pinheiro was not disinterested, but the fact remains that the assistance was given.

[43] For Hawkins' relations with the Jesuits, see Foster, *Early Travels in India*, 1921, pp. 64–67, 75, 77–81, 83–85, 89–90, 93 and 124, and *The Hawkins Voyages*, Hakl. Soc., pp. 394, 398, 400–405, 409 and 412. Also Guerreiro, *Relaçam*, V, p. 20, and *J.P.H.S.*, VII, 1918, pp. 63–73. Although his pass was to Goa, Hawkins had a secret understanding with the Jesuits that he might return to England: Rawlinson, *British Beginnings in India*, 1920, p. 48.

[44] Zannetti, *Raguagli*, 1615, p. 28.

[45] Calendar of State Papers, Colonial Series, East Indies (1862), 1513–1616, p. 254, No. 650; Foster, *Early Travels in India*, 1921, pp. 189–190.

[46] Orme, *Historical Fragments*, 1805, p. 333.

[47] The former account is given by Kerridge (*Letters Received*, I, p. 283) and the latter by Withington (Foster, *Early Travels in India*, 1921, p. 201). The former was in Agra about two months after Canning's death, whereas the latter (who in other respects also is a less trustworthy authority) was not there till more than a year later. After the arrival of the Dutch in Agra in 1621 the English who died there were buried in the garden of the Dutch factory, which was on the site now occupied by S. Paul's Church. Blunt, *Christian Tombs and Monuments in the United Provinces*, 1911, p. 57.

[48] *Letters Received*, I, pp. 280, 283, 284, 300.

[49] Withington, letter of November 9, 1613, quoted in Foster's *Roe*, p. 275. *Cf.* Calendar of State Papers, Colonial Series, East Indies (1862), 1513–1616, No. 659, p. 258.

[50] Foster, *Early Travels in India*, 1921, pp. 191–192; *Letters Received*, II, p. 107; Calendar of State Papers, Colonial Series, East Indies (1862), 1513–1616, p. 320, No. 767.

[51] The translations were published by Hosten in *The Examiner*, Bombay, on August 9, 16, 23, 1919.

[52] Calendar State Papers, Colonial Series, East Indies (1862), 1513–1616, p. 316, No. 763. The Jesuit authorities do not speak of any actual imprisonment and one writer when speaking of Father Busi's imprisonment in 1651 states that that was the first occasion on which any Jesuit had been imprisoned during the 70 years of the Mission's existence. Beccari, *Rer. Aethiop. Scriptores*, IX, p. 425.

[53] Before leaving Agra he had, according to Orme (*Hist. Fragments*, 1805, p. 360), made proffers and apologies, approaching the King's mother from motives of religion and his wife with expectations of presents.

[54] *Letters Received*, II, p. 143.

[55] Foster, *Early Travels in India*, 1921, p. 208.

[56] Xavier's letter of December 4, 1615, in *J.A.S.B.*, XXIII, 1927 (Hosten), p. 124. See also *Letters Received*, II, p. 150.

[57] It was discovered in the Portuguese archives by H. Heras, S.J., and was published by him with a photographic reproduction of the document in the Proceedings of the ninth meeting of the Indian Historical Records Commission, December 1926. See also Judice Biker, *Collecção de Tratados e concertos de pazes que o Estado da India Portugueza fez.*, Lisbon, 1881, I, pp. 189–193.

[58] Foster's *Roe*, p. 75.

[59] *J.P.H.S.*, V, 1916 (Felix), pp. 13–19. Thomas Kerridge in a letter of November 19, 1615, complained of the Company's investments being hindered by the coming of the Jesuits. (Shafa'at Ahmad Khān, *Sources for the History of British India*, 1926, p. 13.)

[60] *J.A.S.B.*, XXIII, 1927, pp. 119–120, 123–125, 127, 129, 131–132 and 135; de Souza, *Or. Conq.*, 1710, II, pp. 154–155. There is a connected life of Jerome Xavier in John Eusebius Nieremberg's *Claros Varones*, Madrid, 1647, IV, pp. 215–246.

[61] Foster's *Roe*, p. 77.

[62] *Ib.*, p. 78.

[63] *Ib.*, p. 99.

[64] *Ib.*, p. 102.

[65] *Ib.*, p. 131.

[66] *Ib.*, p. 124.

[67] *Ib.*, p. 124.

[68] *Ib.*, p. 105.

[69] *Ib.*, p. 236.

[70] *Ib.*, p. 271.

[71] *A Voyage to East India*, edn. of 1777, p. 423

[72] Foster's *Roe*, p. 248.

[73] *Ib.*, pp. 300 and 322.

[74] Foster, *English Factories*, 1618–1621, p. 173.

[75] Terry, *A Voyage to East India*, edn. of 1777, p. 422.

[76] Foster's *Roe*, p. 454.

[77] *Ib.*, pp. 249 and 437.

[78] Foster, *English Factories*, 1618–1621, p. 252.

[79] Foster, *English Factories*, 1624–1629, pp. 127 and 170; Calendar of State Papers, Colonial Series, East Indies (1884), 1625–1629, No. 396, p. 311. *Cf.* Hosten in *J.U.P.H.S.*, III, 1922, Part I, p. 147.

[80] See Chapter XIV.

[81] Xavier's letter of 1611 in Marsden MSS. Addl., 9854, fol. 168.

[82] Foster's *Roe*, p. 279.

[83] Their survival on the occasion of the fire in Corsi's house was looked on as a miracle. Corsi in talking to Roe disowned anything of the miraculous in the incident, but admitted that he was glad of the common opinion regarding it.

[84] *A Voyage to East India*, edn. 1777, p. 426.

[85] Constable's edition, 1914, p. 288. Amsterdam edition, 1724, II, pp. 82–83.

[86] *Storia do Mogor*, I, p. 161. See as to the whole story, Blunt, *List of Christian Tombs and Monuments in the United Provinces*, 1911, p. 34.

[87] Letter to the Archbishop of Canterbury, October 30, 1616; Foster's *Roe*, pp. 279–280.

[88] 'A True Relation of strange and admirable Accidents which lately happened in the Kingdom of the great Magor or Mogul,' printed in London by J. D. for Thomas Archer 1622: reproduced in the *Harleian Miscellany*, 1744, I, p. 251.

[89] *A Voyage to East India*, edn. of 1777, pp. 383–386.

[90] *Bry*, XII, p. 31. This volume is a translation from English and Dutch sources.

[91] British Museum, Marsden MSS. Addl., 9854, fol. 161–163. Also letter from Laubegeois of January 23, 1612.

[92] In the Ballad the opportunity was taken to add Luther and Calvin to the list of false teachers rejected by the Ape.

[93] Gentil, *Mémoires sur l'Indoustan*, 1822; introduction (written by Gentil's son), p. 22.

[94] *Claros Varones*, Madrid, 1647, IV, p. 223.

[95] III Reg., XI, 3; 'his wives turned away his heart.'

[96] Andrade, letter of August 14, 1623.

[97] *Lettere Annue*, 1620–1624, Rome, 1627, pp. 338–341; *Histoire*, Paris, 1628, pp. 439–449; Annual Letter, Cochin, 1619, in *The Examiner*, Bombay (Hosten), April 6, 1912, and Corsi's letter of June 13, 1628. These journeys with the King, especially on the Kashmīr road, were by no means pleasure-trips for the Fathers. 'The fatigues,' wrote de Castro in 1624, 'are such that only actual experience can give you an idea of them; even if you had only to load and unload daily your tent, which you have to carry on your shoulders, it would be quite enough: but besides to be called by the King, to remain near him till midnight, and then in the morning to get up very early, that is three hours after midnight, in order to say Mass, to pack your belongings, and eat once a day only, you do not imagine how tiring it is unless you have passed through it.'

[98] De Castro's letters of July 26, 1627, and August 15, 1627, *J.A.S.B.*, XXIII, 1927 (Hosten), pp. 154 and 162. 'Volse magnare [*sic*] e beuere in Chiesa delle nostre cose e da nostra mano.'

[99] See de Castro's complaints in his letter of July 26, 1627, *J.A.S.B.*, XXIII, 1927, p. 157.

[100] Foster's *Roe*, p. 270.

[101] Letter of November 14, 1633, *Catholic Herald of India* (Hosten and Besse), January 30, 1918.

[102] *J.P.H.S.*, IV, 1916, p. 15.

[103] Letter to the Archbishop of Canterbury, 1616. Foster's *Roe*, p. 276.

[104] Letters of July 26 and August 15, 1627, *J.A.S.B.*, XXIII, 1927, pp. 155 and 161.

[105] Maracci, 1651, p. 22 : 'ce qui fait penser qu'il avoit esté baptisé secrettement par le P. François Corsi, Florentin . . . son amy intime.'

[106] Letter of 1650 to his family in *The Examiner*, Bombay (Hosten), September 1, 1917, p. 348.

[107] Constable's edition, 1914, p. 288 ; Amsterdam edition, 1724, II, p. 82.

[108] *Storia do Mogor*, I, p. 160.

To face page 99] [*From the Collection of H. Vever, Paris*

SHAH JAHAN AND A COURTIER, WITH CHRISTIAN SYMBOLS

By Bichitr

(See p. 257)

CHAPTER VI

SHAH JAHAN, 1627–1658

Foris pugnae, intus timores. (2 Cor. vii, 5.)

WITH the death of Jahāngīr and the accession of Shāh Jahān the fortunes of the Jesuits entered on a new phase. The clouds began to gather—' post Phaebum nubila,' as one of the Fathers put it.[1] Free alike from the indifference of his father Jahāngīr and from the fanaticism of his son Aurangzeb, Shāh Jahān adopted the attitude of the ordinary orthodox Muslim ruler. He had no strong friendship or dislike for either Portuguese or Christians as such, but within five years of his accession the conduct of the Portuguese in Bengal had involved him in the attack and capture of their settlement at Hūglī, the internment of the captured Christians at Agra, and a short but sharp persecution of Christians generally in the Mogul dominions.

Change in the attitude of the Court

The siege and capture of Hūglī are noticed in the contemporary Indian histories, briefly in the 'Amal-i-Sālih and at greater length in the Bādshāh-nāma. The later historians Khāfī Khān and Samsām-ud-daula, author of the Ma'āsir-ul-umarā, also duly mention it. Among European accounts we have the excellent but brief description of the episode by Bernier written forty years later and a short reference to it in the *Storia do Mogor* of Manucci, who was in India in 1656 to 1717. To these somewhat exiguous sources of information have been added of late years two detailed accounts of high value which were written by European authors and have recently been made accessible to English readers : one describing the siege itself and one the time of captivity following it. The former account is given in a letter from Father John Cabral of the Society of Jesus—an eye-witness of the episode—which was written on November 14, 1633, a little more than a year after the event. Cabral was a Portuguese, born in 1599, and he had during the five years previous to the

The trouble at Hūglī in 1632. New information recently published

Hūglī incident been engaged in missionary work in Kūch Bihār and Southern Tibet. He was afterwards in Ceylon and in the Far East and died at Goa in 1669. His letter describing the siege of Hūglī which is in the possession of the Society was translated into English and published in 1918 by the Very Reverend Father L. Besse, S.J., of Trichinopoly. Our other authority—which deals mainly with events subsequent to the siege—is the *Itinerario* of Fra Manrique, to whom allusion has already been made more than once in this work. Manrique, the Spanish Augustinian, was at Chittagong shortly before the attack on Hūglī and he proceeded in 1640 to Agra and Lahore in connection with the release of one of the prisoners. An English translation of the portions of the *Itinerario* dealing with Hūglī was published by Father Hosten in 1918, together with Father Besse's translation of Cabral's letter; and since 1927 an admirable edition of the whole of Manrique's somewhat rare book by the late Colonel Luard and by Father Hosten has been made available to English readers.[2]

Origin of the trouble

The trouble at Hūglī was not due primarily to a religious quarrel. The local Governors had put no obstacles in the way of propaganda and had paid due respect to the Catholic priesthood. It is noted of the Viceroy of Dacca that he had reserved to himself the right in any particular case to forbid excommunication by the Vicar, but in other respects there had been no local interference with the Christians and the Viceroy had protected them from the attacks of Mullās and Pīrs. The hostilities undertaken by the Moguls against the Portuguese in Hūglī originated in political causes, namely the sympathy and encouragement which the Portuguese of Hūglī had given to their compatriots the Farangīs of Chittagong who were little more than pirates, ready to lend their services to the King of Arakan against the Moguls. A religious element was indeed imported into the quarrel by Shāh Jahān, probably for reasons of policy. He was regarded by the Europeans as being, at any rate at the commencement of his reign, violently anti-Christian. Father Cabral speaks of him as 'the mortal enemy of the Christian name' and Fra Manrique as 'the implacable enemy of the Portuguese and of the Christian name.'[3] He himself, in reporting the result of the siege to the Muslim Ruler of Balkh, emphasized the ill-treatment which the Muslims had received from the Portuguese and represented the issue of the siege as a triumph for Islām, 'the voice of the āzān of the Muslim' being now substituted for 'the sound of the bells of the Gabrs.'[4] For this attitude the Portuguese in Bengal and Arakan had, it is true, given some excuse. The Farangīs made slaves of large numbers of Mogul subjects, and of these slaves they made Christians—boasting, says Bernier, 'that they made more Christians in a twelve month than all the missionaries in the Indies do in ten years.'[5] The Portuguese in Hūglī not only dealt in these slaves but also maintained a rigid attitude towards all non-Christians in their own settlement. The Augustinians, and to a lesser degree the Jesuits, exercised a powerful influence there. No mendicant was allowed in the settlement; no call to prayers was permitted; and the minor heirs of deceased men of property were enslaved and baptized.[5a] The religious aspect, however, of the relations between the Moguls and the Portuguese was of subsidiary importance, and there was much apart from religion to justify the punishment of Hūglī.

The settlement at Hūglī was practically independent not only of the Mogul Court but also of the Portuguese Viceroy at Goa. It had been founded by Tavares[6] in the latter part of the sixteenth century and had flourished exceedingly as an entrepot for trade at the expense of the older Mogul port of Satgāon. The local shipping was harassed, the Farangīs and their slave trade were encouraged, and the King of Arakan was supported against the Moguls. Incidents occurred when Mogul women of note (including, according to Manucci, two slave girls of the Queen Mumtāz Mahal herself[7]) were kidnapped, and the opposition of the local Mogul governors to the settlement was fostered by fugitive Portuguese malcontents. The little oligarchy in Hūglī had exaggerated ideas of its own importance and neglected to conciliate the Mogul power. It had, rightly enough, declined to support Shāh Jahān when he was in revolt against his father, but it had also with calculated stupidity neglected to congratulate him on his accession. It is not surprising, therefore, that Shāh Jahān himself should lend his support to the local feeling against the settlement. A peremptory farmān was issued to Qāsim Khān, the Subadār at Dacca, requiring him to take immediate steps to exterminate it. Father Cabral writes that he and Father Simon Figueredo saw the farmān at Dacca and that due warning was given from other quarters to the Portuguese authorities at Hūglī, but in vain. A formidable armament both by land and by water was organized by the Subadār; its destination was concealed; and suddenly on June 26, 1632, the Mogul army appeared within a league of Hūglī supported by a Mogul fleet further down the river. According to Shāh Jahān himself the army, including followers, numbered 70,000 and the fleet was composed of 500 vessels.

Attack by the Moguls

The authorities at Hūglī were taken by surprise. The town

lay in an open plain, with no walls and only a feeble parapet of earth. The number of Portuguese defenders is put by Cabral at 300 and by Manrique at 180: and these were supported by a considerable number of Indians, consisting, however, largely of slaves. Labour was plentiful and there was a good supply of muskets. Barricades were accordingly organized, firearms were distributed and steps were taken to defend the settlement.

Siege and capture of Hūglī

Preliminary efforts at negotiation, conducted by Cabral himself, failed to secure any results. On July 2 a general assault was made and repulsed with much gallantry. The Church of Our Lady of Mercies, which was in an exposed position, was, however, stormed, and the images of the saints were in derision hung on trees. A hermit, on the other hand, with a small body of Portuguese and Indians, held bravely to the little tower of his hermitage, and caused much loss to the enemy. Further negotiations took place under the conduct of the Augustinian Antonio de Christo. The Mogul General, Bahādur Khān, insisted on the restoration of all Bengali slaves and the Jesuits as strongly deprecated the delivery of Christian souls to the Muslims. A good number, were, however, handed over and the Portuguese tendered submission; but further bickerings took place and it was resolved to hold an inner line, the area called Bali being abandoned and the monastery of St. Augustine being evacuated and burnt by the defenders. Daily fighting continued, accompanied by mutual accusations and much cruelty. Meanwhile the Mogul artillery arrived and the enemy at the same time commenced systematic mining. After further futile negotiations the Portuguese decided to cut their way out by river and on September 24 the attempt was made. The river, however, was extraordinarily low; boats got stranded; and there were the usual delays and entanglements. The enemy attacked by water and by land. 'The sharks of the sea of battle and the lions of the plains of war,' as Shāh Jahān put it, were relentless in pursuit. The settlement was occupied and burnt, and most of the Portuguese shipping was sunk or set on fire. One ship blew up just as the enemy were trying to wrest a crucifix from the arms of the Jesuit Father Fialho.[8] Brother John Rodrigues, of the same Society, fell pierced by arrows. Father Cabral himself narrowly escaped being shot when reading his breviary. Father Adrian Diaz of Cochin was decapitated by a cannon ball and Father Gregorio de los Angeles of the Augustinian Order was despatched by lances and arrows when swimming in the water. Six ships came through the ordeal but had to pass the Narrows, where the Moguls and renegade Portuguese lay in wait for them—the latter somewhat incongruously vociferating 'Santiago' as they discharged their last volleys. Three or four only of the Portuguese ships appear ultimately to have escaped, and this remnant of the garrison found a refuge in the jungles of Saugor Island.

Many of the defenders of Hūglī were taken prisoners and it is with their fate that we are chiefly concerned According to the Bādshāh-nāma 4400 prisoners were taken; according to Manucci 5000. The number of Portuguese captured is put by the Dutch authorities at 1500,[9] and the number of Farangīs taken is stated by Khāfī Khān to have been 1400. The prisoners—whether Portuguese or half-castes or Indians—were transferred bodily as slaves to Agra, and we can well imagine the hardships of this long train of captives—men, women and children—being marched from Hūglī to their destination, 900 miles distant. 'The misery of these people,' says Bernier with true feeling, 'is unparalleled in the history of modern times; it nearly resembled the grievous captivity of Babylon.' The journey occupied nine months and the prisoners arrived at Agra in chains.

The Babylonian Captivity

How many actually reached Agra we do not know. Father Corsi writing in October 1633 asserts that 4000 arrived in July of that year, and the Bādshāh-nāma states that on July 19 some 400 Farangīs were produced before Shāh Jahān.[10] 'The handsome women,' writes Bernier, 'became inmates of the seraglio: those of a more advanced age or of inferior beauty were distributed among the Omrahs: little children underwent the rite of circumcision and were made pages: and the men of adult age, allured for the most part by fair promises or terrified by the daily threat of throwing them under the feet of elephants, renounced their Christian faith.'[11] Among those who apostasized were not only half-castes but 'Portuguese of the flower of Portugal.'[12] From Bernier's account one would gather that the priests only—and not all of them—maintained their faith; but from the Indian historians it would appear that the bulk of the captives, at any rate of those that reached Agra, remained constant. The King, we are told, ordered that the principles of Islām should be explained to the prisoners and that they should be taught 'the two beautiful confessions'—'there is but one God and Muhammad is His Prophet'—and should be called upon to adopt Islām. A few 'appreciated the honour offered to them' and received allowances, but the majority rejected the proposal. These were distributed among the Amīrs for imprisonment, and many 'passed from prison to hell.'

Fate of the prisoners

As regards the priests we have a certain amount of detailed

information, mainly from Fra Manrique who came to Agra a few years later to obtain the release of Father Antonio of his Order. There were two Augustinians among the prisoners, Father Antonio de Christo and Father Francisco de la Encarnacion, together with two seculars, a Portuguese called Manoel Danhaya and an old man born in Bengal, called Manoel Garcia. These men were imprisoned, whipped, beaten and laden with chains. They were marched through the bazaars, and abused and pelted with filth. The King wished to throw them to the elephants, but he was restrained by the entreaties of his father-in-law, Āsaf Khān, and the Fathers were relegated to prison. There on August 2, 1633, Danhaya died; and Garcia died in the following March. Both are buried in the Santos Chapel at Agra, and each is described on his tombstone as having died in prison for the Faith—' morto Pelafee ' (pela fé).

Negotiations for the release of the prisoners were opened up with Goa and Father Francisco was sent to discuss terms with the Portuguese Viceroy. Meanwhile after the first outburst of persecution, permission was given to the Fathers to move freely about in Agra. Interest was exercised at Court by one Shāh Alā-ud-dīn[13] and by an Armenian (doubtless Mīrzā Zū'lqarnain), and money was provided by the Venetian Jeronimo Veroneo, by means of which many of the prisoners were released and settled in Agra.[14] The same privilege was subsequently granted to the remaining prisoners on the condition that Father Antonio returned to prison as their security until negotiations with Goa were complete. As that Father forthwith connived at the escape of the prisoners in question from Agra, he was detained in prison, and in spite of two attempts to escape he remained there for nine years until released by the efforts of Fra Manrique.

Help given to the prisoners by the Jesuits: their own sufferings

The Jesuits at Agra were at this time out of favour and were apparently unable to do much to help the captives. They had themselves suffered not a little. In the beginning of 1633 their house was invaded by soldiery and the bells removed from their church. On February 23 they were imprisoned for four days, and it was not until March 6 that they were again able to celebrate Mass. Energetic efforts were made by the Mogul officials to locate the treasure of their friend Mīrzā Zū'lqarnain. Father Corsi was ill-treated. Father de Castro who had just returned with the Mīrzā from the Eastern Provinces was so severely beaten as to become ' one sore from waist to head ' (ut a cingulo ad caput non fuerit cernere nisi unam plagam).[15] Four Fathers of the Mission were imprisoned, nor could they and the Mīrzā be released until the latter had paid down six lakhs of rupees. The Fathers were hampered by the poverty of their own converts and by the landslide towards apostacy which the events at Hūglī had occasioned. When the Christian prisoners from Hūglī arrived at Agra in the summer of 1633 the Jesuits did what they could to assist in the alleviation of their sufferings, and Father de Castro devoted himself with some success to the reconversion of renegades. The captives once again found themselves within reach of religious ministrations: and they flocked in considerable numbers to the services at the Jesuit church—at first unobtrusively but afterwards with full publicity. The Fathers, after some hesitation at the first, welcomed the arrival of these large congregations, but in doing so they presumed too much on the indulgence of the authorities, and the noisy clamour of the crowds arriving at the church gave the Muslims an excuse for drastic interference. On the last day of 1634, while Mass was being said, the King's officers rushed suddenly into the church and laid violent hands on the priests. The celebrant had just sufficient time to consume the Host, but the intruders seized and emptied the Chalice on the altar, and then marched the congregation through the streets to the Governor's tribunal. That official, having satisfied himself that the Christians were not renegades from Islām, suffered them to depart on security, on the condition that they discontinued attendance at the church. Meantime, however, the interior of the church was rudely dismantled, and the Jesuits were prohibited from proselytizing among Muslims. They were turned out of their College and took refuge in a sarai. Orders were even issued from the Court requiring their expulsion to Goa, and it was only by the intervention of Āsaf Khān that these orders were rescinded. Father de Castro followed the King's camp for five months with a petition for reinstatement, and a written farmān was ultimately secured on December 9, 1635. In compliance with this mandate the church building was utterly destroyed, but in other respects the Jesuits were restored very nearly to their former status. Among other concessions they were allowed to utilize the materials of their church for a house and were thus enabled to fit out a chapel for divine service.[16] When Fra Manrique arrived in Agra in December 1640, he spent Christmas Eve 'in a chapel belonging to the Jesuit Fathers which stood in their house.' He was recognized by the Jesuits in spite of his Mogul dress and was received by them with much kindness. He proceeded later to visit his fellow Augustinian, Father Antonio, in prison, and as he was still wearing the Mogul costume, Father Antonio, not recognizing him, asked 'in the Industan idiom' who he was. He replied in Latin, 'Tanto tempore vobiscum fui et non cognovisti me ?' (Have I been so long time with you and dost thou not know me ?) The meeting was an affectionate one and Manrique, eager to plead his friend's cause, pushed on to Lahore where Shāh Jahān then held his Court. There he was introduced by the Jesuit Father, Joseph de Castro, to the all-powerful Āsaf Khān who promptly gave orders for the release of Antonio, and at de Castro's instance Fra Manrique obtained a 'goodly alms' from Āsaf Khān to enable him to pursue his way.[17]

Apart from the Hūglī incident and its results, the history of the Mission in Mogor during the reign of Shāh Jahān was not very eventful nor are we very well documented regarding it. There are several letters of the period in the possession of the Society and brief summaries of some of them were printed by Father Hosten in 1925,[18] but the letters themselves have not been published. We have to fall back on the Annual Report for Mogor for 1648–1649, of which a translation (by the Rev. L. De Vos, S.J.) was published in 1922,[19] and on two long 'Relations' among the Marsden manuscripts, written by Father Botelho regarding the six years of his ministry at Agra (1648–1654), portions from which were published by Father Hosten in 1910 and 1916.[20] A large number of Marsden manuscripts of this period which should contain much interesting matter have unfortunately been lost, and the remainder are yet unpublished.

Information available regarding the Mission

On one subject which had much occupied the Jesuits during the previous reign—namely their controversies with the English—we hear little or nothing during the reign of Shāh Jahān. The Jesuits on the coast at Goa and elsewhere were in active negotiation with the English on commercial and other matters, and were on the whole friendly and useful. Near Agra, also, they had an opportunity which they utilized of maintaining good relations with the English: for when the Englishman Drake was shot by brigands near Dholpur in 1637, Father Joseph de Castro sent a palanquin and a surgeon from Agra, and after Drake's death sealed up the effects of the deceased, solicited Āsaf Khān to secure the punishment of the murderers, and sent information of the incident to the English at Surat.[21] Later on when the Jesuits wanted money to extend their house at Agra they received a handsome contribution from the Dutch and English residents at that place :[22] and in the time of Shāh Jahān's successor the English at Patna went so far as to allow the Jesuits to baptize converts in their factory.[23]

Good relations with the English

During the reign of Shāh Jahān, two of the more prominent of the older members of the Mission disappear, Father Corsi dying in 1635 and Father de Castro in 1645. The Mission at the beginning of the reign was under Father Francisco Leam, but in 1628 he was deposed from his post owing to his unwise participation in a local lawsuit.[24] The normal number of the staff maintained in the Mission was three, a fourth being attached to Mīrzā Zū'lqarnain ;[25] and in 1650, after the founding of the new Delhi, a Father was posted intermittently to that city.[26] We have a fairly adequate list of the Fathers who were from time to time in the Mission during this reign : but none of them seem to have been men of great distinction and there are three only of them—Fathers Ceschi, Botelho and Roth—who call for a passing notice at this stage.

Changes in the personnel of the Mission

Antonio Ceschi of Santa Croce was a man of good family who was born in 1618 at Borgo di Valsugana in the Trentino and arrived in India in 1645. Little was known of him until Father Hosten, acting on a reference in Sommervogel's *Bibliothèque*, unearthed from the Franciscan Convent at Trent a copy of a book published in that town (without date but with a dedication dated 1683) which set forth the life and correspondence of this missionary. Extracts from the book were made by Father Marco Morizzo, O.F.M., of Valsugana, and a translation of them was published by Father Hosten in 1917.[27] From them we learn that after a short stay in Salsette near Goa, Father Ceschi was nominated for service in Abyssinia, but difficulties of travel intervened and ultimately he was sent to Agra in 1648. He was subsequently invited to Srīnagar in Garhwāl by the Rājā of that place, and after more than one visit to Lahore he was in April 1652 deputed to the new capital at Delhi. The rest of his short career was devoted to the service of the congregations at that city and at Agra. So remarkable were his industry and zeal that one of the Mogul grandees facetiously suggested that he should be known not as Father Ceschi but as Father Chhah-Shakhs, meaning that he did the work of six persons. He was learned in the mathematics and found time to be interested, as few then were, in Sanskrit. He was, withal, as his old comrade Father Roth described him, 'a brave and truly apostolic man,' and he ministered with such devotion to his charge that his health gave way. He bore a trying illness with much cheerfulness and fortitude, but ultimately, after attending a dying Christian night and day for three days and accompanying the funeral to a distant cemetery through torrential rain, he

Father Antonio Ceschi

collapsed, and died (apparently in Agra)[28] on June 28, 1656. He was buried in the Church of Our Lady and his body was subsequently transferred to the Martyrs' Chapel where he now lies.[29]

Of Father Antonio Botelho we have little personal information. He was born in Portugal in 1600 and appears to have joined the Society in India. After service in Goa, Salsette, Thāna, Diū and Bāndra he made a chivalrous and adventurous journey to Suākin in 1646, and a year later he was nominated to be Visitor and Superior and Rector of the College, at Agra, where he worked from 1648 to 1654. He was made Provincial at Goa in 1667 and appears to have died there three or four years later.[30]

Father Antonio Botelho

From his letters he seems to have had a very humble opinion of his own abilities as an administrator, and he was subject to considerable mental depression as a result of distressing illness. But he is spoken of on good authority as a man of great merit and influence,[31] and he was responsible for much good and conscientious work done quietly in the Mission. His chief claim, however, to the recognition of posterity lies in the fact that after his return to Goa he prepared two valuable memoranda embodying the results of his ministry at Agra. One of these is a 'Relation of the state of Christianity which we have in the Kingdom of the Great Mogul,' an account which has been translated by Father Hosten[32] and to which a considerable number of references have been made in this book. The other is a 'Relation of the more notable things which I have observed in the Kingdom of the Great Mogul,' which gives a lengthy and detailed account of the chief features of the country and of Mogul rule.[33] The memoranda were apparently written by Father Botelho shortly before his death, some sixteen years after he left Agra,[34] and in several of his dates and facts he is clearly inaccurate. He had, moreover, no pretensions to Oriental scholarship; the word 'Akbar,' for instance, is interpreted by him to mean 'immortal,' and he is not quite clear if the words 'Shāh Jahān' are Persian or Arabic. But his descriptions are for the most part drawn from personal observation, and if his work does not betray the lucidity and charm which characterize the writings of his contemporaries Tavernier and Bernier when dealing with the same class of subjects, it constitutes a valuable supplement to the information which they provide and it contains many personal touches which give it an attractive flavour of its own. It deals for the most part with matters outside the scope of the present volume, but it includes much that leads one to regret that it has not yet been published to the world. Those who are interested in such matters will find in it many curious observations on subjects such as the heat of Agra in the summer and the cold of Lahore in the winter: the terror of dust-storms: the fish of the country, its fruits, flowers, vegetables and meat; its bird life; its betel nut, and the processes of salt manufacture. The Father gives us pictures of the Faqīrs, the observance of Ramzān, the system of postal runners, the magnificence of the royal high roads, the beauties of the province of Kashmīr, and the vicissitudes of the city of Qandahār. We learn from him about the administration of justice, the position of the Faujdār, the system of jāgīrs, the dignities of the Amīrs and the Mansabdārs, and the attitude of the feudatory Rājās. The King's palaces at Delhi and Agra are described: his throne, his zanāna, his expenses, his army, his elephants, his tents, his festivals, his chaukidārs clothed in English scarlet, and all the paraphernalia of his magnificent Court. We are given short sketches of Prince Dārā Shikoh and his brothers, but although we have also an account of the King, it is clear that the Father had little or no personal contact with Shāh Jahān himself. On the other hand, we have from Father Botelho's pen a description, which is probably unique, of Shāh Jahān's ceremonial departure from Agra in 1648 to enter into possession of the new capital at Delhi. The magnificent cavalcade issued from the fort under the eyes of Fathers Botelho and Morando who were sitting in a balcony with Mīrzā Zū'lqarnain, and the good Father occupies several pages of his narrative with a detailed account of this wonderful and memorable procession. The central figure on his caparisoned elephant, says the Father, 'had every semblance of the King he was.'

Father Henry Roth

The third of the Fathers mentioned above, Father Henry Roth or Roa, was a Bavarian, born in 1620. He joined the Mogor Mission in 1653[35] and after a term at Srīnagar in Garhwal he settled in Agra, where he became Rector of the College in 1659. While Superior of the Mission he distinguished himself by the zeal with which he helped to combat a famine which was then desolating the city. He had some knowledge of medicine and was besides a man well versed in Indian habits and literature. He appreciated the fact that the bulk of the inhabitants of India were Hindus and that in order to dispute with them it was necessary for him to learn their sacred language. He was one of the earliest among Europeans to study Sanskrit—a task at which he worked for six years under considerable difficulties—and he was probably the first to publish anything in the shape of a Sanskrit grammar. The traveller

Bernier obtained a good deal of information from him when he was at Agra and has reproduced it in his interesting letter of October 4, 1667, on 'the Superstitions, strange customs, and Doctrines of the Indous or Gentiles of Hindoustan' where he speaks of the Hindu trinity, the Hindu theory of incarnation, and other kindred subjects. While Roth was at Agra, the Jesuit Fathers Grueber and D'Orville arrived at that city on their way from Pekin to Rome, and on the death of D'Orville at Agra in 1662 Father Roth was chosen to accompany Father Grueber for the remainder of his journey. He accordingly proceeded to Europe by way of Lahore, Multān, Sind and Ispahān,[36] and reached Rome in 1664. At Rome the missionaries communicated to the erudite Father Athanasius Kircher a considerable amount of information regarding China and India which that Father reproduced in his large work *China Illustrata*, published in 1667.[37] While in Europe Father Roth visited the Trentino, and there he communicated the news of Father Ceschi's death to that Father's relations; composing at the same time a touching 'eulogium' of his old comrade, which was afterwards published with the memoirs of Ceschi to which allusion has been made above. He also visited Neuburg in Bavaria and we have a note of his conversations with the Duke of Pfalz-Neuburg, recorded by Father Theodor Rhay, the Duke's confessor.[38] He started shortly afterwards to return to India with Father Grueber, by way of Eastern Europe and Turkey, but at Constantinople his companion fell ill and he had to continue his journey alone. We have no clear information as to his movements after this, and all we can say is that he was in Agra before November 1667 and that he died there in 1668.[39] His death, unfortunately, gave occasion to a scandalous example of official intolerance. On the night on which he expired and while his body was still at the door of the Father's residence, the Kotwāl with thirty attendants made a forcible entry into the house on the pretext of ascertaining the effects left by the deceased, and it was with the greatest difficulty that the Fathers, who had secreted their church plate and pictures in the house, were able to prevent the pillage of the premises. Father Roth appears in the circumstances to have been given but maimed rites at his funeral, but his loss was greatly felt by the Mission. He was a kindly man and one whose ideals of work were high. In spite of the fact that, owing to his infirmities, his life had been one of continual suffering, he had covered more ground both in travel and in linguistic study than any of his colleagues, and they looked with admiration on his unceasing industry.[40] In describing the strenuousness of his sixteen years of hard service in the climate of Agra the chronicler employs an appropriate Latinity: 'Sexdecim totos annos impiger ibidem desudavit.'[41]

Hostile attitude of the Muslims

The bitterness of the Mogul officials against the Christians on account of the Hūglī incident gradually died down,[42] but their attitude of opposition was still maintained and from time to time there were recrudescences of ill-treatment. While the Hūglī disaster was still recent and the Bengali captives were still numerous, the disorder occurred which has above been mentioned as having entailed on the Jesuits the loss of their church. The captive Christians had celebrated Easter by hanging an effigy of Judas in the streets;[43] the incident was at once seized upon by the officials who declared that the effigy was meant to represent the Prophet, and much perturbation ensued among the Christian community. The prohibition against proselytizing among Muslims, though not rigorously enforced, impeded the actions of the Fathers and always left an opening for minor officials to interfere with them. When one of the Hūglī captives, the wife of the slave Sa'adat Khān, resorted secretly to the house of the Fathers at Agra, the Qāzī communicated his displeasure to the Jesuits and the practice had to be discontinued.[44] In 1649, Father Ceschi reported that he found the Muslims very hostile. As regards the King, though he grew kinder as he grew older, he was never as friendly as his father and the effects of the persecution of 1632–1634 were still felt.

The next trouble experienced by the Jesuits, however, was not from the Muslims or their ruler. It came from another and very unexpected quarter.

Dom Matheus

The Jesuits of Goa had in the previous generation converted a Brahman and his wife at Divar near Goa, and the Christian son of this pair, abandoning agricultural pursuits, took up some menial posts with the Franciscans. Becoming servant to a Portuguese noble, he made the journey to Portugal and thence to Rome, where he became known as Dom Matheus de Castro Melo and was ordained a priest. On a subsequent visit to Rome where he arrived with two Brahmans and many complaints, he joined the congregation of S. Filippo Neri and was, by some influence which he possessed with the College of the Propaganda, promoted in 1637 to the Bishopric of Chrysopolis *in partibus*. At the end of 1639 he returned to India in all his new dignity to flutter the ecclesiastical dovecots of Goa. The bulk of our information regarding him comes from Jesuit sources, and if these are to be trusted his future career was one of mingled truculence and eccentricity. At Goa he quarrelled with the Viceroy and the Archbishop, insisted on ordaining Brahmans and fulminated against the Franciscans and the Jesuits. After a year or two in Bījāpur, plotting against the Portuguese, he sailed for Mocha, penetrated as a pilgrim to the tomb of Muhammad, and then proceeded to Rome. In 1645 he was appointed Vicar Apostolic of Ethiopia, but got no further on his way than Cairo, where he complained of want of funds and returned to Rome. In 1648 he was again at Mocha, where he quarrelled violently with the Jesuit Parisiano and ultimately excommunicated him. By the end of 1650 he was back in India, organizing, it was said, a rebellion of Brahmans against the Goa authorities, and then, being Vicar Apostolic of 'the Kingdom of the Great Mogul, Adelkhan (Bījāpur) and Golconda,' he proceeded northward through Surat to Agra to inspect the Mogor Mission.[45]

His visit to Mogor

He reached Agra on February 1, 1651, and was received by Father Botelho who was then in charge of the Mission. From Botelho we gather incidentally that the Bishop in an outburst of patriotic or artistic discernment declared that though he had travelled in France, Spain and Rome, he had never seen anything so beautiful as the Tāj Mahal—then recently completed—at Agra.[46] He made no secret, however, of the fact that he mistrusted the Jesuits and was come to put life into the Mission. He was especially communicative to the Dutch and English residents and complained to them that the Fathers would not admit Brahmans into their schools because the Brahmans were too clever. Even with Portuguese renegades he would discuss the chances of his being able to oust 'those Paulists.'[47] From Agra he proceeded to Delhi and thence by Lahore to the King's Court in Kashmīr. At the Court he interviewed the Wazīr Sa'adulla Khān (who soon, however, got tired of him), and obtained a patron in a noble who went by the name of Mīrān Said Subhān. Here also he met a Christian doctor, Sikandar Beg, whom he is said to have shocked by his neglect of the rules of fasting. He caused embarrassment to the pious Mīrzā Zū'lqarnain who had always maintained Jesuit chaplains, and it was with some hesitation that, after consulting the Jesuit Father Busi, Zū'lqarnain gave him a present of a hundred rupees. To the Mogul officials the Bishop accused the Jesuits of being Portuguese spies, of preventing the recruitment of Dutch gunners for the King's army, and of misappropriating the estates of deceased Christians. To such a pitch were these accusations carried that ultimately Shāh Jahān ordered the arrest of Father Busi, and it was only through the bold and almost insolent intervention of Mīrzā Zū'lqarnain that orders were issued for Busi to be brought after the Royal Camp to Lahore, where, on December 3, 1651, he was ultimately set at liberty after nearly two months' imprisonment. Father Botelho, who had proceeded from Agra to Lahore in November 1651 to procure Father Busi's release, found that the Bishop was in Lahore and he had to hide in the neighbourhood until Busi was free. The Christians generally are said to have avoided Dom Matheus and he was irritated at their attitude, stating openly that they were a worthless body and too small in numbers for the notice of a man in his position. About the same time as Father Busi's arrest there was much anxiety among the Christians at Agra owing to a rumour that the officials had orders to kill the Fathers at Mass on the ensuing Sunday, and the Christians had for a time to collect together for security. These fears, however, and the harassment caused by the Bishop's visit soon passed away; and the Bishop himself—the 'aper exterminator' as the Jesuits styled him—returned to the South. The Fathers rendered thanks to God and quoted the verse: 'imperavit ventis et facta est tranquillitas magna'—'He rebuked the winds and there was a great calm.'

The Bishop's strange career was, however, not yet ended. He found it necessary before long to return to Rome to meet the charges of sedition and irregularity which had been sent to the Pope against him. We hear of him again at Marseilles and in Rome—in trouble about money and his future position—and he seems to have died, at the age of seventy-two, in 1679. His meteoric visit to Mogor had little permanent effect in itself, but the incidents connected with it indicate the uncertain footing on which the Jesuits now stood, not only with the authorities in Europe, but also with the Court of the Mogul. Shāh Jahān himself is said by Father Ceschi to have dissembled his dislike of the Jesuits 'fearing the vengeance of Christ,' but, however this may be, it is plain that his attitude remained as before unfavourable.[48]

Prince Dārā Shikoh

The time had gone by when the Jesuits might exercise a right of access to the Sovereign, and they had to be content with a certain amount of patronage from persons near the throne. The King's father-in-law Āsaf Khān had been consistently favourable to them, and the King's old playfellow Mīrzā Zū'lqarnain had been staunch throughout: but the former died in 1641 and the latter about 1656. The King himself and the bulk of his entourage being indifferent or hostile, the Jesuit activities were for some years confined to ministrations on behalf of existing Christians with occasional conversions from the middle or lower classes of society. Towards the end of the reign of Shāh Jahān, however, their old hopes revived and the establishment of influence in high places seemed once more imminent owing to the proclivities of the King's eldest son, Prince Dārā Shikoh.

The story of Dārā forms an episode which has frequently been recounted by Indian historians, but nowhere have the personality and adventures of this unfortunate Prince been more vividly portrayed than in Bernier's inimitable account of the later days of Shāh Jahān. It is there described how Dārā's younger brother Aurangzeb marched in 1658 from the South toward Agra to enforce his claim to the throne and how Aurangzeb met and defeated Dārā five leagues south of that city; how Dārā fled through Delhi to Lahore and thence by Sind to Gujarāt and Rajputāna; how he was again defeated near Ajmīr and fled to Ahmadābād; in what state of consternation and distress he was seen by Bernier near Ahmadābād; how basely he was betrayed, how cruelly he was exposed in procession through the streets of Delhi, and how atrociously he was murdered in prison by the orders of his brother.

His relations with the Jesuits

The Prince Dārā was forty-four years old when he was killed. With a certain instability of character he combined the wideness of interest, the culture and the charm which marked so many of the Princes of his House. In religious matters he had the tolerance which marked Akbar and Jahāngīr, and was well known for his patronage of mystics like Mīān Mīr and of strange ascetics like the Hebrew pantheist Sarmad, and for his curiosity regarding the philosophy of the Hindus. When Governor of Benares in 1656 he caused a Persian translation of the Upanishads to be prepared, and it was through a Latin version of this Persian translation that the Upanishads were first revealed to Europe in 1801. While maintaining the observances of Islām, Dārā imbibed extraneous views from men of other faiths and incurred the charge of infidelity which was ultimately used as the excuse for his execution. 'In private,' says Bernier, 'he was a Gentile with Gentiles and a Christian with Christians,' and there were some who insinuated that this attitude was a pretence, actuated by a desire to obtain the support of the Hindu Rājās and the assistance of European artillerymen;[49] but knowing the similar attitude of Akbar and Jahāngīr, we may impute it rather to the strain of religious eclecticism which marked their race. To the Christians Dārā was especially inclined and he was much attached to certain of the Jesuits whom he kept in his entourage. He was on good terms with Mīrzā Zū'lqarnain during the latter's lifetime, and we hear of his sending for Father Ceschi and presenting him much against his will with a dress of honour (munusculo insigni cuiusdem panni).[50] With the Jesuits he was said at times to drink wine in moderation, and like Akbar and Jahāngīr, he took pleasure in hearing them dispute with men of other religions. When the Governor of Agra was uncivil to the Fathers, Dārā furnished them with an order which secured them respectful treatment for the future.[51] The traveller Manucci, who was personally acquainted with the Prince and followed his fortunes, tells us that three of the Fathers were at Dārā's court in his time, namely the Neapolitan Stanislas Malpica, the Portuguese Pedro Juzarte, and the Fleming Henry Busi.[52] Of these by far the most distinguished was Busi, and he appears to have enjoyed a position of special intimacy with the Prince.

Father Henry Busi

Busi's original name was Henry Uwens and he was born at Nijmegen on April 23, 1618. He joined the Society in 1634 and on the death of a relation, also in the Society, named Hendrick Buys, he adopted his name in the Latin form, Busaeus, and is generally spoken of as Busi or Buseo.[53] He arrived in Goa in 1647; and early in 1648 on his way to Agra, passed through Surat, where he met the missionary Alexandre de Rhodes. He is understood to have written the Annual Report for Mogor for 1648–1649,[54] and in 1651 he was with Mīrzā Zū'lqarnain in Kashmīr where he was arrested and imprisoned as has been above related. He took his last vows at Lahore on February 23, 1653, and was afterwards for a time Superior of the Agra Mission. He died in Delhi on April 6, 1667, and was buried in the Martyrs' Chapel at Agra. Manucci tells us a strange story of the manner of his death. He says that the Father in his anxiety at the lapse of a convert became delirious and sought relief for his head by performing on himself an operation resembling that for appendicitis. The operation proved fatal, but it gave temporary relief, during which the Father had a writing drawn up and signed to the effect that he alone was responsible for his death. His decease was much lamented, not only by Christians, but also by many of the Muslim nobles, who, as Manucci observes, did not as a rule 'care a fig whether we live or die.'[55]

Dārā and Christianity

Father Busi must have been a remarkable man. He was, according to Manucci, of a fine presence, tall and portly, imposing respect by his mere appearance. He was a man of great judgement, very learned and well regulated in act and speech.[56] He was very polished, a fine mathematician and well versed in the native languages. It is to him that Bernier owed much of the information which he set forth with such lucidity and charm in his letters. Busi was popular with all classes, and at the same time upright and holy in his life. He had originally been sent to the Mission in order to meet Dārā's known interest in scientific questions and he became very intimate with the Prince, receiving from him special tokens of respect and affection.

When he first went to Delhi in 1650 it was his function to revive the intercourse between the Jesuits and the Court, which had for some years been interrupted owing to the change of capital. In addition to Prince Dārā he interviewed 'a Prince of the Blood who was Superintendent of the Nobility' and talked mathematics with him. He also had a discussion with a 'Master of the Muslims' who had a large library—'like an Arabic Escurial'—on the subject of Christ's Divinity and the abrogation of the old Law: and this discussion which lasted four hours was conducted in the most friendly spirit. With Dārā himself he had, during the visit to Delhi, two long conversations on the Christian Faith and these conversations were resumed during his later visits to the capital.[57] Father Ceschi draws us a picture of him standing near the Prince and talking familiarly with him, vested the while in the garb of poverty, while round him were five hundred nobles resplendent with gold and precious stones.[58] How far he was able to incline Dārā to an acceptance of the Christian faith it is hard to determine; Bernier implies that he had some success in this direction and Manucci wishes us to believe that Dārā died in all but name a Christian. The latter writer tells us how in Tatta, Dārā told a Carmelite monk how much he was impressed by the consistency of the views of all the Roman priests whom he had met, and how he was convinced that if there was any true faith in the world it was that of the Catholics. He tells us also how in his last hours at Delhi, Dārā begged that the doorkeepers would bring Father Busi to him and how, when this was refused, he cried out: 'Muhammad kills me and the Son of God has given me life'—'Muhammad marā mi-kushad, 'Ibn-ullah marā jān mī-bakhshad.' 'From these words,' says Manucci, 'and those which he spoke to Father Frei Pedro at the City of Tattah—namely that if any faith in the world was true, it was that taught by the European priests—and from the pains which he endured through not being able to get any priest; further from information given me by the selfsame doorkeepers, from whom I made enquiries with great eagerness and minuteness, it is to be inferred that he had a great desire to become a Christian.'[59]

How far we can give credence to a report emanating from an

authority like Manucci, even when it is as detailed and specific as the above, it would be difficult to say. But it is likely enough that Dārā was 'not far from the Kingdom.'

NOTES

[1] De Castro letter of October 8, 1633, quoted by Tanner, *Societas Jesu . . . militans*, Prague, 1675, p. 341.

[2] Hosten's and Besse's translations are in the *Catholic Herald of India*, issues between January 30 and April 10, 1918; and Cabral's account with some omissions is reproduced in Luard and Hosten's *Manrique* (Hakl. Soc., 1927), II, App. See also Bernier (Constable, 1914), pp. 174–6; Manucci, *Storia*, I, pp. 175–176 and 182–183; Elliot, *Hist. India*, VII, pp. 31–35 and 42–43 (Bādshāh-nāma), pp. 211–212 (Khāfī Khān). Hosten's translations also include extracts from the above. *Vide* also 'Padre Frey Manrique in Bengal' (Hosten), in *B.P. and P.*, XII, 1916, pp. 272–315, and XIII, 1916, pp. 1–43, and an article by H. G. Keane in *J.R.A.S.*, 1879, p. 93. The available information has been well used in J. J. Campos' detailed account of the siege in *The History of the Portuguese in Bengal*, 1919, pp. 128–140.

[3] Foster's *Roe*, pp. 88, 146, 247, 279: showing that Shāh Jahān had a similar reputation before his accession. Cf. also Foster, *English Factories*, 1634–1636, p. 241. Andrade in 1623 wrote of him as 'fino Mouro': letter of August 14, 1623.

[4] See translation of his letter to Nazar Muhammad Khān published by Hosten in the *Catholic Herald of India*, January 30–April 10, 1918.

[5] Constable's edition, 1914, p. 176. Manrique tells us how he and two others baptized 11,407 captives of the Farangīs (Hakl., I, p. 286).

[5a] Khāfī Khān in Elliot, *Hist. Ind.*, VII, pp. 211–212.

[6] The same Tavares who went to Akbar's Court in 1577 (see beginning of Chapter II). Campos, *The History of the Portuguese in Bengal*, 1919, pp. 51–54.

[7] *Storia do Mogor*, I, p. 176; Catrou, *Hist. Gén. de l'Empire du Mogol*, 1705, p. 156, goes so far as to say that two of the Queen's daughters had been converted to Christianity. It may be noted that Qāsim Khān, the Viceroy of Bengal, was married to an aunt of Mumtāz Mahal. Blochmann, *A'īn*, I, p. 499.

[8] An engraving to illustrate the death of Fialho is given in Tanner's *Soc. Jesu . . . militans*, Prague, 1675, p. 342.

[9] Dagh Register 1631–1634 quoted by Irvine in Manucci, *Storia do Mogor*, IV, p. 421. If the data provided by Cabral and Manrique are correct, these figures (for Portuguese only) must be much exaggerated.

[10] Corsi's letter of October 5, 1633; *J.A.S.B.*, VI, 1910 (Hosten), p. 458 note. Elliot, *Hist. Ind.*, VII, p. 42. Botelho in his "Relation" says he was informed by Morando, who was then in Agra, that 4000 prisoners arrived in that city, and this is the figure given by de Castro in his letter of September 5, 1635.

[11] Constable's edition, 1914, p. 177. One of the prisoners, Maria d'Ataide, became the wife of the celebrated 'Alī Mardān Khān. (Manucci, *Storia do Mogor*, III, p. 179.) Another, Thomazia Martins, was placed in charge of the King's table (*ib.*, II, p. 35).

[12] Botelho's 'Relation,' *Mem. A.S.B.*, V, 1916 (Hosten), p. 158.

[13] Hosten, *Jesuit Missionaries in Northern India*, 1907, p. 23. *J.A.S.B.*, VI, 1910 (Hosten), p. 452. He refers to these services in a petition of which there is a copy in Persian and in Portuguese in the Marsden MSS., Brit. Mus., Addl., 9855, fol. 153–156. Hosten suggests that it was he who gave security for the Christians in the beginning of 1635.

[14] Manucci, *Storia do Mogor*, I, p. 183.

[15] Tanner, *Societas Jesu . . . militans*, Prague, 1675, p. 341.

[16] The course of the persecution is not easy to follow, but appears to have been as stated in the text. See Corsi's letter of October 5, 1633; de Castro's letters of Sept. 5, 1635, Sept. 17, 1636, and April 16, 1637; *Mem. A.S.B.*, V, 1916 (Hosten), pp. 143–145, 158; *J.P.H.S.*, V, 1916 (Felix), p. 25; and Bernier, Constable's edition, 1914, p. 177. Maracci, *Relation*, 1651, p. 21.

[17] *J.P.H.S.*, I, 1912, pp. 100 and 101. Manrique, *Itin.*, 1649, pp. 343–346; (Luard), 1927, II, 152, 154, 190 and 211 (Hakl. edn.)

[18] *J.A.S.B.*, XXI, 1925, pp. 51–59.

[19] *J.I.H.*, I, 1922, pp. 236–248.

[20] *J.A.S.B.*,, VI, 1910, p. 453; *Mem. A.S.B.*, V, 1916, p. 149.

[21] Foster, *English Factories*, 1637–1641, p. 15. Blunt, *List of Christian Tombs and Monuments in the United Provinces*, 1911, p. 59.

[22] 'Relation,' *J.A.S.B.*, VI, 1910, p. 458, and *Mem. A.S.B.*, V, 1916, p. 155.

[23] Annual Report of September 7, 1686.

[24] *J.A.S.B.*, XXI, 1925 (Hosten), pp. 56–57. Details are given in Corsi's letter of June 13, 1628, and Leam's letter of October 6, 1628.

[25] *J.A.S.B.*, VI, 1910 (Hosten), p. 532.

[26] Pyrard de Laval speaks of Fathers at Delhi as early as 1611, but the presence of Fathers at Delhi at that date must have been temporary only. Hakl. edn., 1888, II, Part I, p. 252.

[27] *The Examiner*, Bombay, July 7, 14, 21, 28, August 11, 18, September 1, 8, 1917. See also Hosten, *Jesuit Missionaries in Northern India*, 1907, pp. 28–29; Felix, *J.P.H.S.*, V, 1916, pp. 97–98; Manucci, *Storia do Mogor*, I, p. 381, IV, p. 427.

[28] According to Felix, his tombstone states that he died in Agra, but this is not stated in the inscription as recorded by Blunt. Roth's letter of 1664 in *Weltbott*, No. 35, reads as though Ceschi died in Agra, and the church in Agra was, we know, a 'Church of Our Lady.'

[29] Stöcklein's *Weltbott*, No. 35, cf. *J.A.S.B.*, VI, 1910, p. 532.

[30] Hosten, *Jesuit Missionaries in Northern India*, 1907, p. 29; *Mem. A.S.B.*, V, 1916 (Hosten), p. 149; *J.A.S.B.*, VI, 1910, pp. 453 and 532; Beccari, *Rerum Aethiopicarum Scriptores*, IX, pp. 355–360.

[31] *Voyages et Missions du Père Alexandre de Rhodes*, Paris, 1854, p. 399.

[32] *Mem. A.S.B.*, V, 1916, pp. 149–165.

[33] Marsden MSS., British Museum, Addl., 9855, fols. 1–45.

[34] *J.A.S.B.*, VI, 1910 (Beveridge), p. 153.

[35] He came to India overland, and there is reason to believe that he came through Kābul, as Father Rhay of Neuburg wrote in 1664 that Roth had stated that he had met a body of Christians in that city who were obviously Christians of S. Thomas. See note 38 below; also Blunt, *List of Christian Tombs and Monuments in the United Provinces*, 1911, p. 36.

[36] According to Tavernier (who calls him 'Father Roux') he and his companion tried first to go to Persia by Attock, but failed to get a passport. Crook's *Tavernier*, 1925, I, p. 76.

[37] Kircher owed to Roth his account of the incarnations of Vishnu (*China Illustrata*, 1667, pp. 157–162 ; *La Chine Illustrée*, 1670, pp. 215–221), as well as certain travellers' tales regarding the Snake-stone (pp. 81 and 109 respectively), the snake-eating boy (pp. 82 and 111), the flying cats of Kashmīr (pp. 84 and 112), and the Bengal apes who acted as courtiers to a dog (pp. 195 and 262).

[38] In the Bibliothèque de Bourgogne, Brussels. The note is somewhat scrappy and not too accurate.

[39] Hosten and Bosk in *B.P. and P.*, XXXIX, 1930, pp. 48–52 ; Bernier (Constable's edition, 1914), p. 329 ; Wessel's *Early Jesuit Travellers in Central Asia*, 1924, p. 200.

[40] Annual Report for 1668.

[41] Beccari, *Rerum Aethiopicarum Scriptores*, IX, p. 346.

[42] The Jesuits were back in Hūglī in 1640. The Augustinians were said to have obtained a farmān permitting of their return as early as 1633. See Campos, *The History of the Portuguese in Bengal*, 1919, pp. 141–147.

[43] From Xavier's letter of 1611 (Marsden MSS. Addl., 9854, fol. 168) it appears that such effigies were sometimes filled with combustibles. See Chapter V, note 21.

[44] Manucci, *Storia do Mogor*, I, p. 202.

[45] The information is given in various documents included in Beccari's *Rerum Aethiopicarum Scriptores*, see VIII, pp. xxxi–xxxiv, IX, pp. 353, 385–388 and 401–407, and XIII, pp. 219–228, etc., and those quoted by Irvine in *Storia do Mogor*, IV, p. 423. There are also MSS. reports regarding Dom Matheus in the Bibliothèque Nationale at Paris : Catal MSS. Espagnols, 1892, p. 169, No. 553 (19 and 20). See also Müllbauer, *Geschichte der katholischen Missionen in Ostindien*, 1852, p. 350. The post of Vicar Apostolic was created in 1637 by the Propaganda and was independent of the Portuguese ecclesiastics.

[46] British Museum, Marsden MSS. Addl., 9855, fol. 5.

[47] A name given to the Jesuits in India from their College of S. Paul at Goa. See Botelho, quoted in *Mem. A.S.B.*, V, 1916 (Hosten), p. 163. Cf. *J.P.H.S.*, VII, 1918, p. 39.

[48] Beccari, *Rer. Aethiop. Script.*, VIII, pp. xxxiii–xxxiv, IX, pp. 419–425, and XIII, pp. 385–386 ; *J.P.H.S.*, V, 1916 (Felix), pp. 96–97 ; *Mem. A.S.B.*, V, 1916 (Hosten), pp. 147–148 and 163–164. Letter of Father Ceschi dated August 24, 1654, in *The Examiner*, Bombay, of September 8, 1917, p. 357. Irvine's note in Manucci, *Storia do Mogor*, IV, p. 423, and Manucci's story (I, p. 211) of the conundrum put by the Bishop to the doctors at Shāh Jahān's Court. Botelho letters of January 20 and February 1, 1652, in Marsden MSS. Addl., 9854, fol. 137–141. Dom Matheus was succeeded as Vicar Apostolic of Mogor, Bījāpur and Golconda by another Brahman protégé of the Propaganda called Custodius de Pinho, but we do not hear of the latter's having toured in the Mogul Kingdom : Müllbauer, *Geschichte der katholischen Missionen in Ostindien*, 1852, p. 350. Paulinus a J. Bartholomaeo, *India Orientalis Christiana*, Rome, 1794, p. 49.

[49] Constable's edition, 1914, pp. 6–7.

[50] Letter of August 24, 1653, *The Examiner*, Bombay, September 8, 1917, p. 357.

[51] Botelho, 'Relation.'

[52] *Storia do Mogor*, I, p. 223. Regarding Malpica and Juzarte, see Hosten, *Jesuit Missionaries in Northern India*, 1907, pp. 25–26.

[53] The confusion previously made between the two relations has been put right by Hosten and the late J. B. Van Meurs in the former's article in *The Examiner*, Bombay, October 13, 1917, p. 407. See also Irvine's Manucci, *Storia do Mogor*, IV, p. 424.

[54] *J.I.H.*, I, 1922, p. 226.

[55] *Storia do Mogor*, II, p. 155.

[56] *Ib.*, II, 154–5. A story of Botelho's gives a familiar touch. Busi, he says, was once sleeping on the roof or terrace of the College when a hailstorm came on. Being woken suddenly by the hailstones, his first impulse was to use violent ejaculations against the persons who he thought were stoning him ; his next step on seeing his mistake was to rush precipitately down with his bedding on his back—nocturnam sarcinam bajulantem—amid the laughter of his friends. British Museum, Marsden MSS. Addl., 9855, fol. 6.

[57] Annual Letter of 1650. The name of the Father deputed to Delhi in 1650 is not given in the letter, but he was almost certainly Busi.

[58] Letter of September 1, 1653, *The Examiner*, Bombay, September 8, 1917, p. 357.

[59] *Storia do Mogor*, I, pp. 324, 356. J. Campbell, a still less reliable authority, writing in 1668 informs us that Dārā ' desired to die a Xpian,' *Ind. Antiq.*, XXXV, 1906 (Temple), p. 169. Pandit Shiv Narain, however, in an interesting article in *J.P.H.S.*, II, 1913, pp. 21–38, points out that Dārā professed to have gone through the Old and New Testaments without conviction : that there is not a sign of Christianity in his written works ; and that the infidelity of which he was ultimately accused was his recognition of the Vedas, not the Bible, as the Word of God. Sir Jādunath Sarkār in his *History of Aurangzeb*, 1925, Vol. I, treats of Dārā as a true Muslim but with Sufistic tendencies. So also Blochmann in *J.A.S.B.*, XXXIX, 1870, pp. 271–9, and Mahfūz-ul-haq ' Majma'-ul-bahrain ' (*Bib. Ind.*, No. 246, 1929).

CHAPTER VII

THE LATER MOGULS, 1658–1803

Quasi absconditus vultus ejus et despectus. (Is. liii, 3.)

FROM the new King, Aurangzeb, who succeeded Shāh Jahān in 1658, the Jesuits could expect little countenance. As the enemy of Dārā and as a Muslim of the Muslims, it was unlikely that Aurangzeb would display any personal interest in Christianity. Apart from this, the change of sovereign entailed no immediate change in the position which the Jesuits occupied at Court. When Aurangzeb, for instance, went to Kashmīr soon after his accession, he desired that Father Busi should accompany him.[1] Several of the great nobles maintained friendly relations with the Jesuits. Amānat Khān, Governor of Lahore, was interested in Christianity and friendly to Christians ;[2] the celebrated Shā'ista Khān, the son of their old ally Āsaf Khān, was their well-wisher ;[3] and they had a close friend in the powerful Wazīr Ja'far Khān, who was Āsaf Khān's son-in-law. When an unfair decree was given depriving the Jesuits of the estate of a deceased Father, they were enabled by Ja'far Khān's help to obtain a reversal of the order from the King.[4] Grants of property made by Jahāngīr to the Jesuits were duly confirmed[5] and in ordinary circumstances there was no interference with their worship. There was even at one time a faint hope that Aurangzeb himself was turning his thoughts towards Christianity. The Jesuits were informed that he had said to his principal Qāzī : 'See that we are on the right path ; the Farangīs have the advantage over us in the arts and the sciences : take heed that they do not also take the palm from us in religion and in faith.' It was said that he had sent for the Persian translation of the Gospels and had only been deterred from studying it by the representations of his advisers that the book had been tampered with by the Farangī Padres and was not a book that his Majesty should read.[6] If we are to trust the dubious testimony of the British wanderer, Mr. John Campbell, Aurangzeb

Situation under Aurangzeb

took the trouble to cross-examine him about the Christian religion, and when Campbell had given him the best answers he could from his recollections of 'John Ball's Catechism,' 'the King,' he writes, 'was mighty importunate to have me instruct them in Issara san la law ('Īsā ar-rasūlu' llāh) y^{ts} y^{e} Gospell of o^{r}. $Savio^{r}$.' Original Sin and Sabbath observance were among the points which Campbell ventured to discuss, and he tells us that, when he produced the Bible as his authority, Aurangzeb treated it with all respect and kissed it.[7] Whatever truth there may have been in statements of this character the fact remains that the accession of Aurangzeb did not bring with it any sudden change in the attitude of the Court towards the Jesuits.

As time passed on however, and more especially after the death of Father Busi in 1667, the new régime with its rigid and almost fanatical adherence to Muslim principles entailed a nearly complete cessation of the proselytizing activities of the Fathers. The Jesuits had, it is true, their old farmāns from Akbar and Jahāngīr giving them free leave to preach and to convert: but the farmāns had not been confirmed by Aurangzeb and the Fathers were afraid to petition for confirmation lest the privilege should be definitely rescinded. The edict of Shāh Jahān, on the other hand, which forbade conversions from among the Muslims, remained in force, and Aurangzeb issued fresh orders which (for a time at least) forbade a Hindu to change his religion for any faith but that of Islām.[8] Conversions by the Fathers continued, but they were now on a very limited scale and were carried out with much caution and secrecy. The smallest remark in dispraise of the Prophet or the use of the words of the Kalima in talking to a friend were seized upon as excuses for bringing the delinquent before the Qāzī and for his forcible conversion to Islām. The use of statuary became an offence; the Jesuit church at Agra was searched; and although the images and pictures were successfully secreted, the Father in charge was subjected to a fine of 150 rupees. Even the collection of Christians for the celebration of Mass at the little Agra chapel became a stumbling-block to the authorities. On this point the Father in charge stood firm and declared that if there was any interference with the chapel he would put an altar in the street and celebrate Mass there: a reply which seems to have silenced the officials. But none the less it was found advisable for a time to celebrate Mass in the chapel at night. Attempts were made to intimidate the Jesuits by the erection of a Mosque alongside the College, but the Fathers decided that it was useless to enter into controversy on the incident and they were gratified to find that after a short while the Mosque was abandoned and fell into ruins.[9] At Delhi things seem to have been even more unpleasant: and though we are given no details we are told that instead of being, as in former times, less restricted at the capital than elsewhere, the Jesuits at Delhi enjoyed a lesser degree of liberty than those in other centres.[10] They had everywhere to be on their guard against misrepresentation and extortion. On one occasion a troublesome Portuguese extorted money from them by accusing them before the Qāzī at Agra of collecting copies of the Qur'ān to send to Europe to be consumed in an imaginary annual burning of the effigy of Muhammad.[11] Some of the Fathers are said to have been banished, and in the Southern Provinces of the Empire we even hear of men being beheaded for their determined adherence to Christianity.[12] Although there may have been aggravation in such cases which made them exceptional, they serve to show the increasing need for a cautious attitude on the part of the Fathers.

The most remarkable development in Aurangzeb's Muslim policy was the imposition of the Jazia or capitation tax on all unbelievers, and it is interesting to learn how the Mission was affected by this measure. The Jesuits tell us how Aurangzeb had decided that the system of providing allowances for the converts to Islām should cease, and that at the same time a poll-tax should be imposed on all male adults who did not profess that Faith. The rates varied from three and a half rupees a head per annum on the very poor to fourteen rupees for the rich, and anyone who failed to pay was forcibly compelled to become a Muslim. The Fathers themselves were placed in the highest class, but this troubled them little compared with the effects of the impost on their poverty-stricken flock. The funds of the Mission, already overburdened with the demands for the relief of destitution, were quite incapable of undertaking payment on behalf of all the poorer Christians, and in spite of efforts made to provide assistance in the more extreme cases there were large numbers of Christians who failed to pay, and who were accordingly beaten by the officials or fled from the city. The tax was introduced in 1679, and for several years the Fathers, having now no interest at Court, endured the position in silence. The sufferings of the Christians, however, and the fear of relapses to Islām, induced the Fathers after some delay to take action for redress. Interviews were sought with influential men in the city and the Jesuits supported their requests with presents of curiosities from Europe. Their efforts were so far successful that the tax at Agra, including arrears, was remitted by the local authorities, but in order to get the concession on a proper footing the Viceroy at Goa was urged to represent the matter to Aurangzeb himself. This the Viceroy agreed to do, deputing Father Magalhaens from

The Jazia

Agra to conduct an embassy on his behalf to the Mogul Court. The Court was then in the Deccan and owing to the dangers of the road it was some time before Father Magalhaens could present himself. Meanwhile the Agra subordinates again began to demand the tax and had to be pacified with bribes : but when Magalhaens presented his petition at Court in the spring of 1686, the King acceded to his request that all Christians in the Empire should be exempted from the jazia. This order was whittled down by the subordinates so as to cover the Agra Christians only ; and even this restricted rescript was not actually issued until Father Magalhaens had spent fifty more rupees in bribes. Even then all was not over, for the local officials at Agra contested the orders and were only defeated by the fact that the Fathers had been careful to keep a copy of them. The exemption was thus in the end secured for Agra and we are told that in spite of the delay in the receipt of this concession there were no defections in Agra to Islām. A separate petition was presented for the extension of the privilege to Delhi, but we do not know whether the application was successful or not.[13] The Catholic archives at Agra contain several parwānas of later date confirming exemption from the jazia, but these apply in each case to the four or five padres at Agra only and to their immediate dependents. Non-Muslims belonging to religious orders could only be exempted from the tax if they were known to be poor, and the exemption of the Fathers was given on this ground of poverty. A parwāna of 1693 specifies the names of the Fathers then exempted ; and this exemption was continued by Bahādur Shāh on his succession in 1707 in favour of the Fathers and ten dependents on the ground that the Fathers were 'faqīrs.' Similar exemption was again granted by Farrukhsiyar in 1718 and by Muhammad Shāh in 1726 on the same ground, namely that the Fathers were Christian ascetics (fuqrāe qaum 'Īsā'ī). We have no record, however, of any confirmation of the general exemption of the Christian community.[14]

In Aurangzeb's reign the Fathers had no longer the support, moral and material, that used to be afforded to them from Goa.

Diminished prestige and reduced circumstances

In view of the losses suffered by the Portuguese at the hands of the Dutch and the English it was now clear that the Portuguese power need no longer be taken into account by the Moguls, and the prestige of the Jesuits as representatives of that power had greatly diminished. Supplies of money from Goa had at the same time fallen off. Unlike some of the other Jesuit communities of that era, the Mogor Jesuits were far from wealthy, and by the middle of

Aurangzeb's reign they had begun to feel themselves in straits for subsistence; 'no one in that country,' as Tavernier says, 'leaving legacies in their favour';[15] and their letters become more and more devoted to matters of accounts and money. When the members of a French deputation to Aurangzeb were at Agra in 1668, they stayed for a time at the Jesuits' residence and expressed keen dissatisfaction at the abstemious character of the fare there presented to them by the Fathers.[16] Such conditions, however, only served to enhance the character of the Jesuits as priests. Bernier, who knew them in the earlier years of the reign, speaks of 'those excellent missionaries in this part of the world, especially Capuchins and Jesuits, who meekly impart religious instruction to all classes of men, without any mixture of indiscreet and bigoted zeal. To Christians of every denomination . . . the demeanour of these good pastors is affectionate and charitable.'[17] The Italian traveller Legrenzi bears similar testimony to 'the respect and reverence in which the Fathers at Agra were held.'[18] But most of them were men of humble outlook and moderate ability, who spent their years in ministering to the wants of the existing Christian congregation, a clientèle which included large numbers of soldiers in the Deccan, in Lahore, and even in Kābul. Of these Jesuit pastors one of the best remembered was Father Mark Antony Santucci, a saintly priest who was so held in reverence that even a century later vows were made at his tomb by Christians and non-Christians alike.[19] As a rule, however, the missionaries of those days are little more than names to us—names for the most part recorded on tombs in the cemeteries at Agra. From these we learn that Father Joseph da Costa, for instance, died at Delhi in 1685 and Father Santucci in 1689. There is a blank till 1702 when Father Antony Magalhaens died at Delhi, followed in 1706 by Father Joseph de Payva who died apparently at Peshawar, and Father Emmanuel Monteyro who died at Agra. The normal duties of these humble missionaries are recorded in one Report as being 'to convert the unbelieving, to confirm Christians in the faith, to exhort them to virtue, to administer the sacraments, to teach the young, to defend the persecuted and to comfort the dying.'[20] Much useful work was done on these lines, but it lacked the glamour attached to missionary enterprise. The traditions of the Society looked to success rather in the baptism of Kings and Princes or in striking conversions on a large scale. The Jesuits in Mogor had now no hope of progress at the Court and the tendency was to look for such openings as seemed possible for rapid and wholesale evangelization elsewhere.

It is not surprising, therefore, to find that the more earnest of the Fathers in Agra and Delhi began to seek more promising fields for evangelization in other localities. Their efforts, unfortunately, led to nothing, but it is worth while to notice briefly the circumstances connected with them.

Attempts to start fresh Mission fields

The first enterprise was of almost startling temerity, namely the conversion of the wild and almost inaccessible inhabitants of Kāfiristān. Benedict Goes when passing the borders of this country in 1603 had heard accounts of Kāfiristān which led him to believe that there might be Christians there, and this belief had been reaffirmed in Father Kircher's work, *China Illustrata*, published in 1667.[21] A few years later the Fathers in Mogor learnt from some Armenians who had come to Agra from Kābul that the inhabitants of Kāfiristān (who were not Muslim) bore a cross traced (escripta) on their heads and had probably at one time been Christians. Fired with the prospect of this new opening for their efforts, the Jesuits at Agra obtained permission to undertake a Mission to Kāfiristān, and the task was entrusted to Father Gregorio Roiz, then at Agra. Of his experiences we have no information beyond what we can gather from a meagre paragraph quoted in the Annual Report sent to Rome in 1678. In this he tells us that the people are Gentios: that they worship a stone called Mahdeu: that they bury their dead: that they are for the greater part white and well-built, and that each settlement of Kāfirs is independent of the rest. He then concludes: 'owing to their great dullness and greater barbarity I did not find dispositions in them for receiving the Faith, nor did I discover any indications that, as the Armenians had told us, they had been Christians at one time. All this obliged me to return to this College at Agra.' We have nothing to show how far (if at all) he penetrated into the country, but he speaks of mountainous ranges on his route, and the Fathers at Goa, in forwarding his report, stated that they knew from other sources 'how great were the dangers and excessive the toil which this journey had cost him.' So that we may perhaps presume that he saw something of the Kāfir country.[22] And though he became very soon convinced of the futility of missionary enterprise in that direction, the legend which connected the inhabitants of the North-West Frontier with a pre-existing Christianity still survived in another form, and a few years later we find a Jesuit Father recommending the despatch of a Mission to the country between Kābul and the mouth of the Indus on the ground that the mountaineers

Kāfiristān

of that tract were said to have crosses already branded on their bodies.[23]

There being no prospects of success in the north-west the Jesuits at Agra turned their eyes towards new fields for effort in the east. Patna, the capital of the Bihār Province, though no longer a residential Jesuit station, was employed as a *pied-à-terre* for further enterprises, and from this base attempts were made to establish missions in Eastern Bengal, in Nāgpur and in Nipāl.

Eastern Bengal

The most promising and the most audacious of the enterprises was that which dealt with the tract lying westward of Dacca, the capital of the province of Bengal.

Somewhere about the year 1670 the son of a zamīndār at Busna in this tract was captured by Portuguese pirates, and under the influence of the Augustinian friars was baptized and took the name of Don Antonio de Rozario. This young man was a small, dark, wizened figure, with slender means and little or no education, but full of the most remarkable zeal for the propagation of his Faith and endowed with an extraordinary persuasiveness of discourse. On hearing him, it was said, one had either to become a Christian or to drown oneself in the river. By his own unaided efforts he succeeded during an astonishingly short period in converting to Christianity some 20,000 of the population in the neighbourhood of his own patrimony. One would have surmised that there was something agrarian or political at the back of so extensive a movement, but the authorities did not treat it from such a standpoint. The leader of the movement, it is true, was at first arrested by the Viceroy, the renowned Shā'ista Khān, but he was subsequently released and given full scope to develop the movement, on the sole condition that he was not to extend his evangelization to the Muslim population. The charge of this immense accretion of Christian converts would naturally have fallen to the Augustinians who were established in Hūglī, Dacca, and other places in the neighbourhood, but the Augustinians were lukewarm and made little or no effort to undertake this duty. The Jesuits at Agra, on the other hand, looked with envy on this new opening and claimed an interest in Don Antonio's converts, on the ground that they lay within the Mogul Empire, in which the Jesuits had the special permission of the Mogul sovereign to preach the Gospel. In 1677, therefore, the Provincial at Goa deputed Father Anthony Magalhaens, the Rector of the College at Agra, to visit and report on this new field.

After touring through the tract the Father reported most

favourably of Don Antonio, but had also to speak of the obstructions raised by the Augustinians. He estimated the number of Christians as being between 25,000 and 30,000, but at the same time stated that beyond the receipt of baptism these converts had little or nothing of real Christianity, and were unacquainted with Confession, Communion, or the Mass.

He recommended that, with the consent of the Augustinians, a Jesuit Mission should be established in this area, and efforts were accordingly made, both locally and at Goa, to come to an understanding with the authorities of the Augustinian Order, but without success. In 1679 Father Santucci was sent from the Mogor Mission to substantiate the Jesuit claim at Busna, and in 1680 the Provincial at Goa issued orders establishing the Mission and denouncing the attitude of the Augustinians. Two Jesuits were sent to carry on the work in the villages, and the superintendence of the Mission was entrusted to Father Santucci.

The inauspicious intrusion of the Jesuits in this new field was succeeded by increasing disillusion and disappointment. Fear of the Muslims and of the Augustinians prevented their establishing themselves in Dacca and they occupied second-rate quarters in villages like Busna, Loricul and Noluacot at a distance from civilization. Their converts were scattered over a large area and were mostly of very low caste. No instruction and no persuasion could prevent them from maintaining their old Hindu customs; they sacrificed to idols and their marriages and funerals were conducted by Brahmans. Although the Provincial had warned the Fathers that they were there to enrich the souls, not the purses, of the converts, many of the Christians had accepted baptism in the hope of getting sustenance. Don Antonio, himself, whose influence was so essential for the success of the Mission, lost all his nobility of character under the pressure of debt and drink. His land-revenue was in arrears and his creditors secured his arrest and imprisonment. The Jesuits began by assisting him, but as his debts increased they had perforce to cease doing so, and within some three years of their arrival he definitely abandoned them and attached himself to the Augustinians. The Fathers worked on, securing occasional conversions, and they were loath to give up the work, but their surroundings were depressing. Their houses were miserable and their journeys painful; in the rains they were surrounded by water; communications were poor; their supplies ran short; they were plagued with mosquitoes, and they endured months of solitude accompanied by long attacks of fever, dysentery and gout. Their efforts to introduce Christian ethics and Christian observances became more and more disappointing. The Augustinians opposed them in every way and ultimately their own converts turned against them. At one time there seemed to be a possible outlet on the small Kingdom of Tipperah as the people there were less trying than in Bengal, and the Rājā had invited the Jesuits to come and discuss Christianity with him: but before long it was discovered that the Rājā was a drunkard and that his main object was to secure help against the Mogul officials, so that this alternative also had to be rejected. The Fathers after a brave struggle had at last to counsel the abandonment of their Mission, and in 1685 orders were issued for their withdrawal.[24]

The Mission of the Jesuits to Nāgpur was of a more legitimate character, but it was on a much smaller scale and also failed to bear fruit. From such scanty information as we have regarding this Mission, it would appear that in the year 1679 a Father Philippe da Faria was dispatched from Patna to Nāgpur, the residence of the Gond Chief of Deoghar who was a tributary of the Moguls. Here the Father got into touch with the local Rājā who is described as an intelligent man and a composer of poetry; and was kindly received by him. Without embracing Christianity, the Rājā admitted the falseness of his own gods, and allowed the Father to dispute with Brahmans in the bazaar. A certain number of converts were made—apparently some fifty-five in all—and the Father started, with such funds as he had, to arrange for the building of a church. To this object he devoted part of his own allowances, living in the severest poverty and clothing himself in the garb of a Sannyāsī: but by the end of 1683 his health was so affected as to necessitate his temporary return to Agra. He was a man of intense zeal and full of hope for the success of his Mission. But his superiors at Patna were less sanguine and held that the good Father was deceived in his estimate of the situation. The King, they thought, desired support against the Moguls rather than Christian doctrine. The people were obstinately wedded to caste and it was not clear how far the converts had thrown off their old religion. The officials were suspicious on account of the proximity of the diamond mines.[25] The country was very isolated; communications were difficult and the neighbourhood disturbed.[26] In spite of these drawbacks Father João Leytam proceeded from Agra to Patna with a view to visiting the devoted Faria at Nāgpur. For three months he was detained by a Hindu rebellion which was in progress south of Patna, but as his funds were running short and the monsoon was approaching he at last made an effort to proceed. Having received a permit from the Governor of Patna he left

Nāgpur

the city in the attire of a Sannyāsī, but was at once arrested as a spy and brought back to Patna. The Governor repudiated his permit, fined the Father 300 rupees and placed him for two days in prison. By this time the monsoon had set in and while the Father was still waiting in Patna orders were received from Goa for the abandonment of the Mission.[27]

The Jesuits do not give us the name of the Rājā whom Father Faria met at Nāgpur, but there can be no doubt that he was the chief known to history as Bakht Buland, whose varied career still forms a prominent landmark in the annals of the Gond Kingdom of Deoghar. In 1686, within a few months of the withdrawal of the Mission, the same Rājā proceeded to Delhi and there obtained the support of Aurangzeb against his rivals by consenting to adopt the creed of Islām.[28]

Nipāl

Regarding the further effort of the Jesuits, that which was directed to Nipāl, we have little more information than we have about Nāgpur. The Englishman, John Marshall, who was at Patna in 1670–1672, refers in a vague way to Jesuits who had travelled from Tibet to India by the Nipāl route,[29] and we have record of two occasions on which this was done. In 1628 Father Cabral who had travelled to Shigatze from Bengal returned to India through Nipāl—that being an easier route than by way of Kūch Bihār, but his extant letters tell us nothing of the country beyond the fact that he was well received by the 'King of Nipāl.'[30] Later on, in 1661–1662, the country was traversed by Father Grueber and Father D'Orville on their long journey from Pekin to Rome, and it was a result of the passage of these two Fathers from Lhāsa to the plains of India that the Jesuits first thought seriously of the evangelization of Nipāl. That country, previous to the Gurkha domination, was governed by three Rājās of the Malla tribe, and the ruler of Kātmandū at the time of Father Grueber's visit was Pratāpa Malla, a man of remarkable character. He is described by Father Grueber as a 'pagan but not an opponent of the Gospel of Christ,' and local history reveals him as a pious sovereign of mystical leanings, favourable to all creeds. He was much interested in the telescope and other scientific instruments of the Jesuits, and promised that if the Fathers would return to his Kingdom he would provide them with a house and would give them full leave to preach the Christian Faith.[31] The accounts given by Father Grueber suggested to the authorities the institution of a Mission in Nipāl. There is extant a letter dated February 23, 1667, from the Viceroy at Goa to the King of Nipāl commending to his care certain unnamed Fathers who were then proceeding to his

Kingdom :[32] and we know that in 1667 it was intended to send Father Roth to that country. It seems not unlikely that he made an exploratory journey thither before he died in 1668, but we have no record of such an expedition. Twelve years later, in 1679, Father Santucci from Patna—pending a decision regarding the opening of the Bengal Mission—did actually go to Nipāl. He had been informed by an Armenian who had travelled through that country that the Rājā (probably the Pratāpa Malla above mentioned) had often spoken to him on religious subjects and was ready to give up his own superstitions. The people of Nipāl were known to be less wedded to caste than those of India, and this fact contributed an additional inducement to attempt the conversion of the country. Father Santucci, however, remained only a few months in Nipāl, and we have no record of his experiences there beyond a statement that when he returned to Patna in the autumn of 1680 he was recovering from sickness. All we know is that when all hopes of success in Bengal had passed away, Santucci—writing in December 1684—advocated a diversion of the Jesuit efforts from that province to Nipāl: but whether anything further was done in that direction is uncertain.[33]

Nipāl, together with Patna and Tibet, passed in the early part of the eighteenth century to the jurisdiction of the Capuchins, and there was for a time a Capuchin Mission there; but, except for passing visits by the Fathers from Lhāsa, we hear nothing further of Jesuit activities in that country.

The detachment of the Jesuits from the Mogul Court, though now nearly, was not yet entirely, complete. There was a Portuguese lady connected with the Court, called Donna Juliana Diaz da Costa, with whom the Jesuits were on good terms and through whom influence could be exercised on Aurangzeb's son, the Prince Bahādur Shāh. Further details will be given in a subsequent chapter to illustrate the personality of Donna Juliana, and it will suffice here to note that Bahādur Shāh, to whose suite she was attached, was looked on as a special friend by the Fathers at Agra. When he was at Kābul in 1700–1701, he summoned Father Magalhaens thither to take charge of the Christians in his entourage and ordered the provision of all necessary facilities for his journey.[34] The Fathers at Agra who were already exempted from the poll-tax on the ground of poverty were on more than one occasion confirmed in this exemption through the direct intervention of Donna Juliana. After the accession of Bahādur Shāh to the throne as Shāh 'Ālam—a prince who though a good Muslim was not an orthodox Sunnī and was interested in religions outside Islām—her authority

Donna Juliana

increased and she was of service both to the Portuguese and to the Dutch. How far she actually influenced the religious opinions of Bahādur Shāh it is difficult to say. Father Desideri, who was in Delhi two years after Bahādur Shāh's death, alludes to a current rumour that he had received baptism. Without giving credit to this rumour, the Father was satisfied that short of actual baptism Bahādur Shāh had in many respects conformed to Christian ways. In battle he had invoked the help of the souls in purgatory and on obtaining victory had provided many masses for them. Having seen a dangerous fire extinguished by Juliana with the help of a palm branch which had been blessed by the priests on Palm Sunday, he sent every year for one of these branches and preserved it with great respect. He frequently gave valuable gifts to the churches in honour of Christ, Our Lady and the Saints, and he always said his private prayers after the Christian manner before a large picture of Christ in Gethsemane.[35]

After the death of Bahādur Shāh in 1712 the influence of Donna Juliana was maintained, though less markedly, under his successors, Jahāndār Shāh, Farrukh-siyar and Muhammad Shāh. We are informed that the mother of the last-named, having obtained her son through the intercession of S. John the Baptist, gave him the name of 'Yahya' (John) and looked on the Baptist as in some ways his patron Saint,[36] special services being held at her instance in the Christian churches on S. John's day. A strange story was afterwards current to the effect that the King at the instance of Juliana transferred his devotion from 'Yahya' to 'Yuhanna,' that is to say, from John the Baptist under his Arabic, to S. John the Baptist under his Christian appellation; and that when his cause was successful he fulfilled his vows to the Saint under the Christian terminology.[37] Apart from this there was little in Muhammad Shāh's life to connect him with Christianity, and it is with some surprise that we read how during the King's last illness he asked the Fathers for a Persian copy of a prayer to S. John, and how the Fathers being unable to get access to him despatched it to him secretly by a safe hand. Father Strobl, who was in Delhi between 1746 and 1749, had conversations with the King on religious subjects. He explained to him the meaning of the pictures in devotional books; he spoke to him of David and of Christ and he showed him a picture of the Saint of Prague (S. John of Nepomuk). The King would, indeed, on such occasions defend the use of pictures in argument against his Muslim advisers; but there seems to have been no serious inclination on his part towards the Christian faith. He was described as 'extraordinarily kind'—ungemein gütig—to the Fathers, and a great friend of the Christians—'ein grosser Freund der Christen': but we have nothing to indicate that he was in closer contact with Christianity than this.[38]

The Mission in the middle of the eighteenth century

With the death of Juliana in 1734 all intimate connection between the Jesuits and the Mogul Court disappears, and although a staff of priests continued to be maintained at Delhi, their duties lay mainly in the service of the local congregation. Father Figueredo, who was Superior of the Mission at Agra, has left a letter of the year 1735 in which he describes the Mogor Mission of his day as extending to Ahmadābād, Delhi, Mārwār, Amber, Udaipur and Lahore.[39] The Christian community of Lahore consisted mainly of soldiers in the army. The bulk of the Christian artillerymen were, however, deported by Ahmad Shāh Abdālī in 1752 to Kābul and there was no resident priest to minister to those left at Lahore: but a Father went there twice in the year, and extended his journeys to Multān, Bhakkar, Kābul and even Qandahār.[40] Four years after Figueredo wrote, the army of Nādir Shāh of Persia burst upon Northern India; Delhi was sacked and a large portion of its inhabitants massacred. The priests who were then in the capital were Matthew Rodrigues and Francis da Cruz, and they only escaped from the general massacre by hiding in the corner of a poor deserted house.[41] From this time forward the Mission of the Jesuits in Delhi may be looked on as moribund. For signs of life in their expiring enterprise we must advert for a moment to the vassal State of Jaipur.

The Mission to Jaipur

Amid the depressing annals of the decline of the Mogul Empire, it is a relief to turn to the activities of the Rājput Chief of Jaipur, the Rājā Jai Singh Sawāī. This Chief ruled his State from 1699 to 1743 and is the royal astronomer to whom India owes the famous observatories of Jaipur, Delhi, Muttra, Ujjain and Benares. The Rājā had for many years made great progress in his astronomical investigations with the aid of his Brahmin experts, but the time came when he desired to test and extend his observations with the help of European science. 'Maps and globes of the Farangīs' were obtained from Surat and a translation was made of the Logarithms of 'Don Juan Napier.' The Rājā applied for aid to Father Emmanuel de Figueredo, the Superior of the Mogor Mission, and Figueredo referred him to the latest results achieved by European investigators. He possibly also suggested to the Rājā that he should obtain experts from Europe, for we find the Rājā shortly afterwards arranging for the deputation of Father

Figueredo as the head of a mission to the Court of Portugal. About the end of 1728 or the beginning of 1729, Figueredo returned bringing with him not only the second edition of La Hire's famous astronomical Tables, but also a medical man well versed in astronomy, called Don Xavier or Pedro de Silva. De Silva remained for a long period of years in a high position in the State and his descendants are still to be found there and elsewhere.[42] But his help was not sufficient, and an examination of the Tables of La Hire led to further enquiries by the Rājā. The position of the moon as ascertained by the observations of his astronomers differed slightly from that given in the Tables. This was possibly due to a misprint, and if so the misprint was so far fortunate that it induced the Rājā to forward a document containing five interrogatories to the Jesuit Fathers Pons and Boudier in Chandernagore, and ultimately to his asking for the despatch of the Fathers to Jaipur. His request had a favourable reception. It happened that these Fathers were in difficulties with the Chandernagore authorities[43] and a new Mission at Jaipur was also looked on as a means of completing the religious 'blockade' of the Mogul dominions.[44] The Rājā moreover had shown himself most friendly to the Christians in his State, had commenced building a church for them and had himself presented offerings at Mass, so that his wishes could not lightly be refused. On January 6, 1734, accordingly, the two missionaries set out from Chandernagore to Jaipur. On their arrival they seem unfortunately to have wasted much time in disputing with the local Brahmins as to the extent to which Indian astronomy was indebted to the ancient Greeks, and we have no knowledge of the scientific results of their visit.[45] They set out in due time to see the observatory at Delhi, and from that place they returned, probably owing to continued ill-health, to Chandernagore.

The Rājā's next step was to apply to the headquarters in Rome for further assistance from the Jesuits, and in 1737 two Bavarian Fathers, Gabelsperger and Strobl, were deputed at the Rājā's expense for service in Jaipur. There was some delay before they could leave Goa and further delay at Surat owing to the disturbed conditions in Northern India, consequent on the invasion of Nādir Shāh. When, however, news arrived of the departure of Nādir's army, they were permitted to proceed, and on March 4, 1740, they reached Jaipur. There they were well received. They were given a house for their residence and they noted the consideration of the Rājā in ordering that they should be provided with chairs to enable them to sit in the European fashion. When Gabelsperger fell ill the Rājā would send messengers to enquire after his health. The Rājā would attend the Christian Mass with all reverence and would treat the pictures of Christ with due respect. When he came to Mass he left substantial gifts upon the altar and he provided the Fathers with allowances of five rupees a day with five rupees weekly for Church expenses. In order that they should not be without meat, he allowed them the use of goats' flesh and sent them meat of this description from his own kitchen. When the Mogul Emperor sent for Father Strobl to come to Delhi, the Rājā more than once found excuses for delay, and indeed appears to have intended to send Strobl as a delegate to the Pope and to the Kaiser. This was prevented by the occurrence of local disturbances in Jaipur; and in 1741, Father Gabelsperger died.[46] Two years later the Rājā himself passed away—'Three of his wives and several concubines ascended his funeral pyre on which science expired with him'[47]—and astronomy ceased thenceforward to interest the Jaipur Darbār. Not only was Rājā Jai Singh's immediate successor markedly adverse to the Brahmins, but within sixty years of Jai Singh's death there was a dissipated ruler on the *gadī* who was ready to replenish his depleted resources by selling the valuable astronomical records by weight as packing paper and breaking up for sale the copper instruments of the observatories.[48]

For a short time after Jai Singh's decease, Father Strobl still had good hopes of his successor, and continued to receive support for himself and for his church. The Christian doctor at the Court (doubtless the de Silva above mentioned) who had been a great protector of the Jesuits was, however, shortly afterwards degraded and Strobl's position became less easy. Within three years of Jai Singh's death he had obtained leave to proceed to Delhi, and there he remained for three years, in the expectation (which does not seem to have been fulfilled) of an allowance of Rs. 100 per month from the Great Mogul. In 1749 he was transferred to Narwar, but he appears after a few years to have left that place for Delhi and Agra. He died at Agra in 1758 and is buried in the Martyrs' Chapel.[49]

The Missionaries at Narwar

It has been mentioned how part of Father Strobl's ministry was spent at Narwar: and the foundation of the Church at this little town in Central India forms an interesting feature of the latter days of the Mogor Mission. The Ruler of the State was a Hindu, but after the sack of Delhi by Nādir Shāh, a Christian magnate of some importance obtained considerable influence in his darbār. The Jesuit letters are somewhat mysterious regarding the identity of this magnate, but tradition speaks of him as one of the family of Indian Bourbons which forms the subject of a subsequent chapter of this work.

Under his auspices a church was built, and the Rājā supplied money for the maintenance of a resident priest and for the support of the poorer Christians. The Jesuits stationed a missionary at Narwar from about the year 1742, but there was no question of conversions, and the congregation consisted of the retainers of the Christian nobleman. These were for the most part of low position, but they were sufficiently well off to afford from time to time a contribution for the needs of their still poorer fellow-Christians in Agra. The little congregation, however, gradually dwindled away and in 1765 the priest in charge, being apparently no longer supported by the State, found it necessary to abandon the station.[50]

The expulsion of the Jesuits from Portuguese territory, 1759

By the middle of the eighteenth century the Society had five churches only in Mogor proper; one at Narwar, one at Jaipur, one at Agra and two at Delhi. The resources of the Fathers were quickly disappearing. Indian rulers no longer maintained the subventions supplied in former times. The Agra College which had supported so many missionaries had lost its endowment. The finances of the Goa Province could not now afford to help the outlying Residences in Mogul territory, and there was no longer any hope of widespread conversions or of royal proselytes by which money could be drawn from the Church in the West. The Society was indeed passing through a time of much tribulation in Europe which had its reactions in India. In 1759 a decree was issued by the King of Portugal banishing all Jesuits from the Portuguese dominions. The Provincial centre of the Jesuits at Goa consequently disappeared, and with its disappearance the Mogor Mission as a Jesuit enterprise may be said to have come to an end. As a modern writer has observed, 'a mission founded by a heathen Emperor was thus exterminated by a Christian King.'[51]

In 1764 the Jesuits in France were similarly superseded by Louis XV and their French Missions entrusted to the 'Missions Étrangères' of Paris. In 1778 the Capuchins took over the Jesuit Mission in Chandernagore and three ex-Jesuits, priests at that station, joined the 'Missions Étrangères' and migrated to Madras and Pondicherry.[52]

The suppression of the Society by the Pope in 1773

In 1773 the Pope Clement XIV by his Brief 'Dominus ac Redemptor' suppressed the Society altogether, and the missionaries left in Mogor ceased to bear the name of Jesuits. Their activities were at first entrusted to the discalced Carmelites of Bombay and a member of that Order was appointed 'Administrator and Vicar General of the Great Mogul.' In 1781 two Carmelites, Father Angelino di San Giuseppe and Father Gregorio della Presentazione, were sent to Agra, and when they had taken charge of the Mission Father Angelino returned to Bombay. The Capuchins in Patna had authority to furnish missionaries for Agra if this were found necessary and the Mission came ultimately into their hands.[53] But in the meantime the Carmelite Father Gregorio represented the Church in Delhi and a grant of land in Pālam near Delhi was made in his name in 1801. He survived until September 29, 1807, and was then buried in the D'Eremao cemetery outside Delhi.[54]

A survival—Father Joseph Tieffenthaler

A marvellous and somewhat pathetic figure which survived the official extinction of the Mogor Mission is that of Father Joseph Tieffenthaler.[55] He was born about the year 1715 at Bolzano in the old Austrian Tyrol, and after spending two years of his early service in the Society in Spain he sailed for India in 1743 by way of the Philippines. He spent the rest of his long life in India and was constantly on the move, gathering geographical data and making astronomical observations. He was apparently intended originally for the Jaipur Observatory, but the death of the Rājā Jai Singh in 1743 and the cessation of work at the Observatory rendered this form of employment impossible. He was accordingly sent from Goa to Agra to work in the College, and shortly afterwards he began his wanderings—to Muttra, Delhi, Narwar, Goa, Surat, Jodhpur, Ajmīr, Sāmbhar, Jaipur, Gwalior and innumerable other places. In 1747, while still a comparatively young man—a 'wackerer und eiffervoller Missionarius,' as Father Strobl described him—he commenced service as a priest to the Bourbon Colony at Narwar, and continued at this task for the greater part of eighteen years. In consequence, however, of the increasing hostility to the Jesuits in Portuguese territory and the dwindling character of his Narwar congregation, he ultimately in 1765 found himself in such financial straits that he decided to appeal for pecuniary help to the 'famous English nation so well known for their humanity, liberality and charity to the poor.' This resolve started him on a new set of journeyings, by Jhānsī, Allahabad, Lucknow, Benares, Patna and Hūglī to Calcutta. Returning from Calcutta he made Lucknow his headquarters, and carried out a succession of journeys between 1766 and 1771 through the length and breadth of Oudh. He was in Agra in 1778, and even then is described as old and failing, 'vecchio cadente.'[56] While not yet seventy he was more than once described by strangers as an octogenarian, but in spite of his feeble appearance he was robust and vivacious and was able still to preach and to administer the Sacraments. It was he whose fate it was in 1781 to hand over to outsiders the Agra Mission which had been for some 200 years in the hands of the Jesuits, and it was a task which he carried out with great reluctance. The Carmelites who came to take charge of the Mission found him selling some of the Church property with the alleged object of raising funds to enable him to travel to Oudh, but while they contemplated his proceedings with a deferential amusement, they more than suspected that he hoped by further impoverishing the Mission to embarrass his successors. Whatever his object, he found it impossible to live any longer at Agra, and again resorted to the more economical amenities of Oudh.[57] Lucknow appears to have remained his chief place of residence until his death in 1785. He was buried in the Padritolla Cemetery at Agra, but tablets were erected to his memory at Lucknow and at Muttra. The latter tablet is still extant in the house of the Catholic chaplain, and the experts are puzzled as to the reason why Muttra should have been selected as the location for this memorial.[58]

Tieffen-thaler as astronomer

Of Tieffenthaler as an astronomer a very interesting account has been written by the late Father Noti, S.J., in articles published in the Journal *East and West* in 1906, and in his monograph on Jai Singh II of Jaipur.[59] Tieffenthaler had to make his calculations with instruments far less accurate than those of to-day, but his enthusiasm in ascertaining astronomical data was unbounded, and wherever he journeyed he worked out latitudes and longitudes which were on the whole surprisingly accurate. His record of work, moreover, is rigidly scientific and is not marred by anything in the way of personal reminiscences or irrelevant gossip.

His literary interests

But Father Tieffenthaler was not merely an astronomer. He was a mathematician, a geographer and a historian. He had a good knowledge of German, Italian, Spanish, French, Latin and Persian. We hear of his communicating extracts from the writings of the traveller, Otter, to the indefatigable Colonel Wilford at Benares, and it is interesting to find that these two omnivorous Orientalists met at Lucknow in 1784—'one year,' says Wilford, 'before the old man's death.' We learn also on Colonel Wilford's authority that our old Jesuit student was a 'man of austere manners and incapable of deceit.'[60]

While still in Narwar in 1759, Father Tieffenthaler was in communication with a weird pioneer of Oriental scholarship, Anquetil Duperron, who was then at Surat. Tieffenthaler's letter to Duperron, which is published by Bernoulli,[61] speaks of his experiences in India and his enthusiasm for geographical research. 'Next to the salvation of souls,' he writes, 'and their conquest for God, nothing has afforded me greater pleasure than the study of the geographical position of places, the variation of winds, the nature of the soil and the character and manners of the regions through which I am travelling. . . . It has been my endeavour to investigate and commit to writing whatsoever fell under my notice. I have spared no trouble, and undergone great hardships to disclose the mysteries of nature; thereby to acquire a greater knowledge of the Creator and fix my mind on things heavenly.'

Account of his literary publications

Then in 1776, after an interval of seventeen years, Duperron, who was by that time settled in Paris, suddenly received from the old geographer, who was then at Faizābād, a packet of maps and some loose papers. No letter accompanied the strange consignment, but merely a note giving a list of certain works which had been sent by Tieffenthaler some years previously to Copenhagen. Anquetil Duperron eagerly studied the maps which he had received—they were maps of the course of the Ganges and the Ghogra, and that of the Ganges alone was fifteen feet in length. He published a treatise on these maps in the *Journal des Savants* in 1776 with appreciative comments, and referred in his treatise to the existence of the further documents in Copenhagen, expressing a hope that they would in time be published. There the matter rested for five years.[62]

The works sent by Tieffenthaler to Copenhagen were consigned by him to a Professor named Kratzenstein, through the agency of a Dutch doctor, whom Tieffenthaler had met in India. They had reached Copenhagen in 1772 or 1773,[63] but it is not clear what instructions, if any, accompanied them. They were of a voluminous character and a wonderful monument to the industry and versatility of their author. The chief items were (i) a long geographical account of India in Latin, entitled 'Descriptio Indiae,' (ii) a treatise on the Brahmanical religion, and (iii) a Natural History of India: and there were also a number of smaller works, some of which were of considerable interest. The scholastic authorities of Copenhagen were apparently unable or indisposed to cope with the publication of these productions, and for some eight or nine years nothing was done in respect of them. We do not know what happened to the second and third of the major works mentioned above, and they seem to have disappeared. But in 1781, the first of these works, the *Descriptio Indiae*, came into the hands of the indefatigable astronomer and mathematician, Joseph Bernoulli (1744–1807), who was at that time a professor in Berlin, and Bernoulli, recognizing its merits, at once decided to translate and publish it himself. He communicated with Anquetil Duperron regarding the maps of the Ganges and the Ghogra which the latter had received from Father Tieffenthaler, and arranged with him for the publication in one series of (*a*) Tieffenthaler's *Descriptio Indiae*, (*b*) an expanded edition of Duperron's treatise on the Maps and (*c*) a copy of the *Memoir on the Map of Hindustan* composed by the English geographer Rennell : the whole accompanied with copious notes, introductions, dissertations, appendices, etc., by both Duperron and Bernoulli. The work was published in Berlin in German in three volumes which issued in 1785–1787 under the title of *Des Pater Joseph Tieffenthalers . . . historisch-geographische Beschreibung von Hindustan* : and also in French in three volumes which issued in 1786–1789, and again in 1791, under the title *Description historique et géographique de l'Inde.* The two French editions differ little from each other, but the German edition differs from both in certain respects, more especially in the contents of the second volume. In all three editions the first volume is occupied by Tieffenthaler's *Descriptio Indiae* ;[64] and the second Part of the second volume of the German edition contains three interesting papers by Tieffenthaler, namely (*a*) a translation by Tieffenthaler into Latin of an account of Nādir Shāh's invasion of India written in Persian by a Christian born at Delhi, the son of a Portuguese called Diogo Mendes who was an eye-witness of the invasion,[65] (pp. 38–63), (*b*) an account of Ahmad Shāh Abdālī's invasions written in Latin by Tieffenthaler in 1762 under the title *Brevis ac succincta narratio expeditionum bellicarum quas Afghanes seu Pattanes in Indiam susceperunt* (pp. 172–180), and (*c*) a treatise of less value on the origin of the Persian language (pp. 181–183). Tieffenthaler had in addition to these written a number of lesser works, some forty in number, of which details are given by him in the list sent in 1776 to Anquetil Duperron. These included *The Praises of the Virgin and Other Saints*, 'persicanis versibus ligatas' ; a translation into Persian of the Song of the Three Children ; an examination of the question whether Christianity existed in India at the time of the arrival of the Portuguese in that country ; and a number of geographical papers on the course of the Ganges. It is not known what happened to these lesser works.[66]

His services to Indian history and geography

The above account of his labours gives an indication of the versatile and diffuse character of Father Tieffenthaler's learning. Bernoulli, when telling us of the loss of the treatises on the Brahman religion and on the Natural History of India, states that they could be spared better than the *Descriptio Indiae*, as Father Tieffenthaler was not a Sanskrit scholar or a naturalist.[67] A perusal of his *Descriptio*, moreover, will confirm the criticism, which has been sometimes made, that Tieffenthaler's historical work suffers from the fact that he almost always fails to quote his authorities, and while, for instance, he acknowledges his obligation to Persian sources, he omits to mention what the sources in each case were. In spite, however, of his diffuseness and the uncritical character of his data, his industry and research achieved results of great value, and he has preserved much information which has helped to build up in its earlier stages our knowledge of Indian history and geography.[68]

It is sad to turn to the last scene of all. There is little enough of romance or adventure in it.

Another survival—Father Francis Xavier Wendel

After the suppression of the Society in 1773, the only remnants of the old Mogor Mission were Father Tieffenthaler and Father Wendel. The two were for many years closely associated. As early as 1759 we find Wendel providing Tieffenthaler with scientific data regarding his experiences of the heat of moonbeams,[69] and throughout their joint lives they to a large extent shared their respective pursuits. On the death of the aged Tieffenthaler in 1785 the solitary representative of the Mission was Father Wendel, who lingered on for another eighteen years.

Father Francis Xavier Wendel, a Belgian or German by origin, had come to India in 1751 and was in 1756 at the College of Diū. By 1763 he was in Lucknow. In 1769 he was sent to Agra and an inscription of that date in the Agra church shows that he was responsible for the restoration and extension of that building at the expense of Walter Reinhardt, the celebrated Sumrū. Wendel seems to have resided in Agra and Lucknow for the greater part of his life. Although he was always in precarious health,[70] his life was a long one and did not come to an end till March 20, 1803. He died in Lucknow and was, like Tieffenthaler, buried in the Padritolla Cemetery at Agra.

His career was not one of outstanding interest and we have no connected account of it, but we catch glimpses of him from time to time in the history of that period and are thus enabled to get at some idea of his personality.

Glimpses of his career

We find him, for instance, journeying in 1766 with a cavalry escort from Agra to Phaphund to solemnize the marriage of the French adventurer, René Madec with Marianne Barbette; and later on, in 1773, signing certificates of the marriage and of the baptism of the bride.[71] We find him again in his capacity as head of the Mission at Agra receiving documents from the Mogul authorities confirming the title of the Mission to lands possessed by them. According to Father Noti there are 'about five farmāns in the Catholic Mission archives which were granted to that missionary by the Great Mogul';[72] and two of these dating from 1774 and 1775 have been published, one of which confirms him in certain villages in the Agra Province and the other confirms his possession of the Lashkarpur Cemetery in Agra itself.[73]

We find something also of political leanings and political activities on the part of Father Wendel. Though many of his flock were French, his tendencies in the politics of the day were pro-British. In 1763, after the Patna massacre and the subsequent repulse of Mīr Qāsim's forces by Major Adams, he is found in correspondence with the British Army. He writes from Lucknow in November 1763 to congratulate the victorious Major Adams and to inveigh against 'the monster Sumroo,' 'the barbarous homicide,' who six years later was to provide him with funds for the restoration of the church at Agra.[74] In 1768 he was selected by the Rājā of Bhartpur to negotiate at Calcutta on his behalf, but the intervention of some local disturbances prevented the despatch of the Rājā's proposed mission.[75] Father Wendel seems, however, to have proceeded later to Calcutta, for there is extant a deed of mortgage of certain property in Calcutta, which was executed in 1781, in favour of 'the Rev. Francis Windel, late of Calcutta, at present of Lucknow.'[76] All this intercourse with the British rendered him suspect to the Commandant at Chandernagore and that officer writing to the Minister at Paris frankly accused Father Wendel of being a British agent. Whether this actually represents his position or not, the fact did not prevent him corresponding also on political subjects with the family of the Frenchman René Madec, and we have a letter written by him from Agra on March 10, 1788, to the widow of Madec, which describes graphically the political situation then prevailing in Northern India and the progress of the 'famous'—no longer 'infamous'—Sombre.[77]

His political interests

Father Wendel, moreover, though not a writer like Father Tieffenthaler, had also something of the geographer in him. A Russian named Czernichef had travelled in 1780 from Bukhārā through Kashmīr to Lucknow and Father Wendel interested himself in his experiences, communicating the diary of his travels to the learned Colonel Wilford at Benares.[78] He himself, in 1764, prepared and sent

His geographical work

to the erudite Anquetil Duperron a map showing the strategical position of the Mogul and British armies at the time of the Battle of Buxar, and the curious may still study that map among those published by Bernoulli in 1788.[79] He was also the author of a map and a memoir on the land of the Rajputs and other provinces to the south and south-west of Agra, which he drew up in 1779 and which were afterwards presented by Colonel Popham to the famous geographer Major Rennell. These labours of Father Wendel were stated by Rennell to have been most useful to him in the preparation of his own great map of Hindustan.[80]

These few brief notices constitute nearly all that we know of this shadowy figure, which flits like a ghost round the death-bed of the great enterprize commemorated in these pages.

The end

When this feeble old man expired in 1803, the last of the ex-Jesuits disappeared from the scene of the labours of the Mogor Mission.

The year 1803 saw also the capture of Delhi by the English and the final end of Mogul sovereignty. When the resuscitated Society of Jesus again established itself in the field of its former activities, thirty more years had elapsed and the Mogul Empire had passed out of history.

NOTES

[1] Manucci, *Storia do Mogor*, II, p. 154.

[2] *Ib.*, I, p. 159.

[3] *Ib.*, II, p. 322.

[4] It is open to us to disbelieve the strange story told by the adventurer Mr. J. Campbell (*Ind. Antiq.*, XXXV, 1906, pp. 137–142) that Ja'far Khān was secretly baptized in 1668 by the Protestants at Delhi, a Mr. White acting as his godfather. When his enemies, says Campbell, accused Ja'far Khān before Aurangzeb of being a Christian ' they sent to ye Padrees, imponed them, thretned some, others had Strips to Confesse, but they knew nothinge of it, noe more they did,' with the result that the King closed the proceedings by saying—Bira Jahannum ' Goe and be hanged.'

[5] See e.g., parwāna of 1671 confirming a grant of land for a cemetery in Lahore, *J.P.H.S.*, V, 1916 (Felix), p. 24.

[6] Annual Report of 1670–1678, December 27, 1678.

[7] *Ind. Antiq.*, XXXV, 1906, pp. 205–206.

[8] So says the Report of September 7, 1685, but that for 1688–1693 definitely states that the prohibition of conversions did not extend to Hindus.

[9] Annual Letter of September 7, 1686, cf. Manucci, *Storia do Mogor*, II, pp. 154–155 and 225.

[10] Legrenzi, *Il Pellegrino nell' Asia*, 1705, II, p. 243.

[11] Manucci, *Storia do Mogor*, II, p. 229.

[12] *Ib.*, II, p. 160, and IV, p. 120, which tell of the fates of a renegade friar and of a young man from Siālkot.

[13] The story of the efforts for exemption is given in the Annual Report of September 7, 1686, and we have among the Marsden MSS. two copies of a translation of the Fathers' petition to Aurangzeb which was forwarded to the Viceroy on July 10, 1684.

[14] These parwānas were published by Felix in *J.P.H.S.*, V, 1916, pp. 30–36. The five names given in the orders of 1693 are Rator, Mikal, Jān Amānūm, 'Anās and Diūk. Of these the first three may represent the Rector (Port. Reitor), Magalhaens and João Leitam and the last may be Diusse; but the identifications are uncertain. There are, according to Felix (*Agra Diocesan Calendar*, 1907, p. 246), three other rescripts in the Agra records which deal with the *jazia*, but these have not been published.

[15] *Recueil de plusieurs relations*, 1679, Pt. II, p. 67.

[16] *Ibid.*, p. 68.

[17] Constable's edition, 1914, p. 289.

[18] *Il Pellegrino nell' Asia*, II, p. 239.

[19] Bernoulli, *Description de l'Inde*, 1781, I, p. 162.

[20] Report of December 27, 1678.

[21] *China Illustrata*, 1667, p. 91. *La Chine Illustrée*, 1670, p. 122.

[22] Annual Report of December 27, 1678.

[23] Letter from Father Diusse, S.J., dated January 28, 1701, in *Lettres Édifiantes et Curieuses*, Paris, 1780, X, p. 231. The word used for the 'mouth' of the Indus is 'embouchure,' and it may possibly refer to the place where the Indus emerges from the hills, viz., the neighbourhood of Attock.

[24] The story is told in some detail in Josson, *La Mission du Bengale Occidental*, 1921, pp. 88–96. A number of documents in the Marsden MSS., British Museum, Addl., 9855, deal with this episode. See also Hosten, 'Glimpses into the Conversion of the First Dacca Christians,' *Catholic Herald of India*, August 29, etc., 1917. A note of such of the original letters as are available is given in Appendix I (b) below.

[25] It is not clear what mines are referred to: Faria alleges that the Rājā at Nāgpur had a considerable income in diamonds, and the nearest mines seem to have been those at Wairāgarh in the Chānda district (Crooke's *Tavernier*, 1925, II, p. 351).

[26] There are scattered references to Nāgpur in the correspondence about the Mission to Eastern Bengal: and there are, besides, three interesting letters in the Marsden collection dealing with the Mission, viz., one dated March 20, 1681, from Faria from Chapra to the Provincial describing his experiences, and two dated September 8 and 15, 1682, from Leytam, the Superior at Patna, to Faria, containing a series of interrogations and the replies thereto. (British Museum, Addl., 9855, fol. 135 and 145.)

[27] Annual Report of September 7, 1686.

[28] See Sarkar, *History of Aurangzeb*, 1924, V, p. 406; C. U. Wills, *The Rāj Gond Mahārājās of the Sātpura Hills*, Nāgpur, 1923, pp. 159–167; and Chatterton, *The Story of Gondwana*, 1916, p. 44.

[29] *John Marshall in India*, by Shafa'at Ahmad Khān, 1927, p. 162.

[30] Letter of June 17, 1628; Wessels, *Early Jesuit Travellers in Central Asia*, 1924, pp. 157 and 336.

[31] Sylvain Lévi, *Le Népal*, 1892, I, pp. 81–90 ; Landon, *Nepal*, 1928, I, pp. 46–47 and II, p. 232 ; Kircher, *China Illustrata*, 1667, pp. 76–77 ; *La Chine Illustrée*, 1670, pp. 103–104. There is an extraordinary Nepalese inscription of 1654 reproduced in Lévi's and Landon's books which includes French and English words in European characters and serves to indicate the outlook of the Rājā Pratāpa.

[32] Judice Biker, *Collecção de Tratados*, Lisbon, 1884, IV, pp. 135–136.

[33] See Santucci's letters of August 29, 1679, November 26, 1680, and December 20, 1684, in Marsden MSS., British Museum, Addl., 9855.

[34] Letter by Diusse, dated January 28, 1701 ; *Lettres Édif.*, Paris, 1780, X, pp. 234–235.

[35] Quoted in *O Oriente Portuguez*, Nova Goa, 1910, VII, pp. 74–75.

[36] Desideri, *Relazione*, in Filippi's translation.

[37] The story is given, though with differences of detail, by both Brouet and Gentil ; regarding whom see Chapter XII.

[38] Strobl's letters of October 27, 1746, October 26, 1747, and October 5, 1748, in *Weltbott*, Nos. 647–649.

[39] *Weltbott*, No. 595. ' Marwar ' may be a mistake for Narwar. As to Udaipur we have no other notice of a Mission in that State.

[40] *Weltbott*, No. 595, Bernoulli, *Beschreibung von Hindustan*, II, Part II, p. 174.

[41] Bernoulli, *Beschreibung von Hindustan*, II, Part II, p. 57 ; de Saignes in *Lettres Édif.*, 1780, IV, p. 260. Rodrigues died in 1748 at Narwar, and da Cruz in 1742 at Delhi : both are buried in the Martyrs' Chapel at Agra.

[42] Cf. Blunt, *List of Christian Tombs and Inscriptions in the United Provinces*, 1911, p. 48. He is spoken of in this list as Don José. Tod, *Rajast'han*, 1832, II, p. 357 (Crooke's edition, 1920, III, p. 1343), calls him Xavier. A picture of Aqlmand Khān, alias Don Pedro de Silva, is to be seen in the British Museum, *Indian Drawings*, No. XXIII, 1920–9–17, 088(2). It is a completely Orientalized portrait and represents him smoking a huqqa. Don Pedro (known also as Padre Don Pedro) was afterwards vakīl of the Rājā of Bhartpur and is several times mentioned in the *Calendar of Persian Correspondence*, published by the Government of India.

[43] *B.P. and P.*, II, 1908, p. 345.

[44] Calmette in *Lettres Édif.*, Paris, 1780, XIII, p. 393.

[45] The geographical and astronomical observations of their journey from Chandernagore to Jaipur were published in *Lettres Édif.*, Paris, 1780, XV, pp. 337–360.

[46] He died at Jaipur but was buried in the Martyrs' Chapel at Agra.

[47] Tod's *Annals and Antiquities of Rajast'han*, 1832, II, 368. (Crooke's edition, 1920, III, p. 1356.)

[48] Noti, *Land und Volk des königlichen Astronomen Dschaisingh*, II, Berlin, 1911, pp. 91–104. Stöcklein, *Weltbott*, No. 595 (letter from Figueredo) and 641–650 (letters from Strobl). *Lettres Édifiantes et curieuses*, Paris, 1780, XV, pp. 337–360. The Rājā's various observatories were visited later by Father Tieffenthaler in 1744–1765, and are briefly described in his *Descriptio Indiae*. A full account of the observatories and of the Jesuit astronomers in Jaipur is given in G. R. Kaye's valuable book, *A Guide to the Old Observatories at Delhi ; Jaipur ; Ujjain ; Benares ;* Calcutta, 1920. See also Hunter in *Asiatick Researches*, V, 1798, p. 177, and the other authorities quoted in the Bibliography attached to Kaye's book.

[49] Sommervogel s.v. Strobl. *Weltbott*, No. 647; Anton Huonder, *Deutsche Jesuiten-missionäre des 17 und 18 Jahrhunderts*, 1899, s.v. Strobl. *The Examiner*, Bombay, April 20, 1918. Barbé, *Le Nabab René Madec*, Paris, 1894, p. 39, quotes a certificate of a baptism performed at Delhi in August 1753, by Andreas Thobet, S.J., a mistake probably for Andreas Strobl. The year of his death is given as 1758 on his tomb (Blunt, *List of Christian Tombs and Monuments in the United Provinces*, 1911, p. 37), but Huonder and Sommervogel place it as late as about 1770.

[50] Strobl's letter of September 19, 1751, and Tieffenthaler's of October 22, 1750, in *Weltbott*, Nos. 650 and 651.

[51] *Recueil des decrets . . . du Roi de Portugal*, Amsterdam, 1761, II, p. 180. Blunt, *List of Christian Tombs and Monuments in the United Provinces*, 1911, p. 29.

[52] *J.A.S.B.*, VI, 1910 (Hosten), p. 537.

[53] Letter of Friar Clemente, O.D.C., dated April 12, 1782 (Propaganda Archives Indie Orientali e Cina dal 1782 al 1784 *Scritture riferite nei Congressi*, Vol. No. 37). Paulinus a S. Bartholomaeo, *India Orientalis Christiana*, Rome, 1794, p. 48; Wolff, *Researches and Missionary Labours*, 1835, p. 310.

[54] Felix in *J.P.H.S.*, V, 1916, p. 37. The name is given as ' Crecour ' in Irving, *List of Inscriptions on Christian Tombs and Monuments in the Punjab*, 1910, p. 6.

[55] He himself spelt the name as Tieffentaller.

[56] *J.A.S.B.*, VI, 1910, p. 537.

[57] Letters of Father Clemente, April 12, 1782, and of Father Angelico, 1785.

[58] Tieffenthaler gives a detailed account of his own journeyings up to 1772 in the Preface to his *Descriptio Indiae* (Bernoulli, *Description de l'Inde*, 1786, Vol. I). See also Blunt, *Christian Tombs and Monuments in the United Provinces*, 1911, pp. 51–2. Also an interesting abstract by Father Noti in *East and West* (Bombay), 1906, pp. 142–152, 269–277 and 400–413.

[59] *East and West*, 1906, loc. cit. *Land und Volk des königlichen Astronomen Dschaisingh II*, Berlin, 1911.

[60] *J.A.S.B.*, XX, 1851, p. 240. *Asiatick Researches*, IX, 1807, p. 212.

[61] *Description de l'Inde*, 1786, II, Part II, pp. 419–421.

[62] Bernoulli, *Description de l'Inde*, 1786, II, Part II, pp. 418–421. *Journal des Sçavans*, 1776, pp. 804–829.

[63] Bernoulli, *op. cit.*, I, Preface de l'Éditeur, p. x.

[64] A sketch of the plan of this work is given by Noti in *East and West*, 1906, pp. 404–405.

[65] Possibly the nephew of Donna Juliana. See Chapter XII.

[66] The list of works sent to Copenhagen is given at pp. 421–4 of Vol. III of Bernoulli's *Description* (1786–1789) and in Sommervogel s.v. Tieffenthaler. The treatise on the existence of Christianity in India before the Portuguese may be that incorporated in pp. 40–43 of Vol. I, which describes (*a*) certain mistaken identifications of Hindu deities with the Trinity and the Blessed Virgin, and (*b*) the legends of S. Bartholomew and S. Thomas.

[67] And yet he had among his other works written a Persian-Sanskrit dictionary.

[68] Blunt, *List of Christian Tombs and Monuments in the United Provinces*, 1911, p. 51. Tieffenthaler is freely quoted as an authority in the

latest Gazetteer of India : and his maps were held by Duperron to be the result of a ' travail immense ' (*Journal des Sçavans*, 1776, pp. 804–828). The ecclesiastical records of Lucknow, before being destroyed in the Mutiny, were examined by Col. A. S. Allen, who found the registers of Tieffenthaler's time written up in his own hand, generally in Latin, and sometimes in German, but was unable to discover any of the literary works above referred to ; *A.S.B. Proc.*, 1872, p. 59.

[69] Tieffenthaler's letter of 1759 in Bernoulli's *Description de l'Inde*, 1786, II, Part II, 419–421.

[70] *J.A.S.B.*, VI, 1910 (Hosten), p. 537.

[71] Emile Barbé, *Le Nabab René Madec*, Paris, 1894, pp. 39–41 ; *The Examiner*, Bombay (Hosten), April 20, 1918.

[72] *East and West*, Bombay, VI, 1906.

[73] *J.P.H.S.*, V, 1916 (Felix), pp. 46 and 48 ; *Agra Diocesan Calendar*, 1907 (Felix), p. 208.

[74] Calendar of Persian Correspondence, Imperial Record Department, Calcutta, I, pp. 258, 262–264, quoted in *The Examiner*, Bombay (Hosten), May 4, 1918. See also I, pp. 274 and 289.

[75] *Ib.*, II, pp. 241–242. His colleague in this Mission was to have been the Don Pedro de Silva mentioned in note 42 above.

[76] *B.P. and P.*, XV, 1917, p. 6.

[77] *The Examiner*, Bombay (Hosten), April 20, 1918. Emile Barbé, *Le Nabab René Madec*, Paris, 1894, pp. 40, 249.

[78] *Asiatick Researches*, VIII, 1805, pp. 319–320.

[79] *Description de l'Inde*, 1786, III, Part II, p. 238. The map is in the *Description* (Plate N), and it is also reproduced in Noti's *Das Fürstenthum Sardhana*, Freiburg, 1906, p. 25.

[80] *Description historique et géographique de l'Indostan*, Paris, 1800, I, pp. XXI–XXII, 198–199, and II, p. 242. *Jesuit Missionaries in Northern India*, 1907 (Hosten), p. 42. *Mem. A.S.B.*, III, 1914, p. 527.

CHAPTER VIII

THE WORKS OF FATHER MONSERRATE

Dixit autem Helcias pontifex ad Saphan scribam: Librum Legis reperi in domo Domini: deditque Helcias volumen Saphan qui et legit illud. (Reg. iv, 22, 8.)

THE moving spirit of the first Mission was Father Rudolf Aquaviva, but his chief colleague, Antonio Monserrate, was also a man of mark and culture, and to him we are indebted for the best account written by any European of the Court and character of Akbar.

Monserrate, his career

Father Monserrate was born at Vic de Ozona in Catalonia in 1536 and was admitted to the Society in 1558. He became Prefect of Studies at Lisbon, and during the great plague of 1569 showed the utmost zeal in helping the sick and collecting the waifs and orphans left destitute in the streets. In 1574 he embarked for India and four years later was selected, as we have seen, to accompany Father Aquaviva to Agra.

He soon earned the esteem and affection of Akbar. Monserrate is characterized by one of his biographers as a man of marked humility and in close touch with God—' homem de muita humilidade . . . homem de muito trato com Deos.'[1] He was offered (as has been already stated), and with some hesitation accepted, the post of tutor to the King's son, Prince Murād. Later on, when Akbar's brother, Mīrzā Hakīm, rebelled in Kābul, the Fathers offered to accompany Akbar on his expedition against the rebel army. From what has been written in Chapter II, it will be remembered that Akbar at first declined the offer. On the next day, however, seeing Father Monserrate in the classroom with his son, he said: ' Father, get ready for the journey, you are coming with me.' Monserrate accordingly accompanied the army of the Emperor from Agra as far as Jalālābād. His health was indifferent and under the orders of Akbar he did not proceed beyond Jalālābād. He accompanied the army, however, on its return march to Fatehpur Sīkrī, and he remained for some months with Father Aquaviva in that town. When Akbar, in 1582, sent to Goa an embassy for the King of Spain and Portugal, Father Monserrate accompanied the ambassadors on their journey. The embassy was, however, as we have seen, postponed and ultimately abandoned, and after six years' further work in Goa Monserrate received orders in February 1589 to proceed to Abyssinia. While coasting round Arabia from Maskat to Zailah he and his companion, Father Peter Paez, were seized by Arabs near Dhafār. They were kept in custody by the Arabs for some time at Ainad and afterwards by the Turks at San'a. From letters and reports written by Paez we learn that Monserrate was always in poor health, and that when the two Fathers were afterwards sent to the galleys in Mocha he nearly died. There is extant a letter written by Monserrate from San'a on July 22, 1593, to the General of the Society indicating how best he and his companion could be freed from captivity. The Fathers were ultimately redeemed from the Turks through the agency of some Indian merchants from Goa, and we find Monserrate on December 7, 1596, writing a short letter from Goa to the General announcing their liberation.[2] He was then sixty years of age and was soon afterwards posted to Salsette in the neighbourhood of Goa as to a place of rest—' tanquam in asylum quietis causa.' But it ' pleased God to call him shortly to the real place of rest ' and he died on March 5, 1600.

Such, very briefly, was the personal history of Father Antony Monserrate.[3] But his chief interest to us lies less in his personality than in the written accounts which he has left of the Mogul Empire of Akbar and of the first Jesuit Mission to Akbar's Court.

The *Relaçam do Equebar*

When he proceeded with Father Aquaviva at the end of 1579 to the Court of Akbar he received instructions from the Provincial at Goa to keep a diary of his experiences, and he carried out these instructions faithfully, writing up his experiences every evening for two and half years. On his return to Goa in 1582 an abstract was made—probably by himself—of those parts of the diary which indicated the character of Akbar and the main features of his rule. Several copies of the abstract were made in manuscript and sent to Europe, but only one of these is known to be now in existence, and it is in the possession of the Society. Although the manuscript is unsigned, and is not in Monserrate's handwriting, a comparison with his other work shows that it was undoubtedly taken from his material. Father Hosten published in 1912 a transcript of the manuscript in Portuguese, together with a translation into English ;[4] it is entitled : *Relaçam do*

Equebar Rei dos Mogores, and contains a valuable account of Akbar himself and of his Empire. We are given a description of his personal appearance, his clothing, his character, his occupations, his amusements. Then we are told of his palaces, his guards, his officials, his methods of transacting business, and we are informed of the names of his sons. The abstract goes on to mention the chief towns, rivers, mountains, and ports of the realm and to state that there were once Christian Kings in India who were destroyed by the Pathāns. The advent of the Moguls in India, the forces of Akbar, his cavalry and his elephants are then described: his system of jāgīrs, his revenues, and his treasures. This is followed by a brief account of Father Aquaviva's Mission and its effect upon the King, and the abstract ends with a description of the Tibetans, followed by the words: 'Here I stop this relation. I have made it as short as was consistent with the truth. And that this truth may be better known I beg of the reader to pray to Our Lord for the Fathers occupied in the ministry. From S. Paul's College of the Society of Jesus, Goa, in these parts of India, the 16th of November, 1582.' The date, it will be seen, though subsequent to Father Monserrate's return from Mogor to Goa, is prior to the close of Father Aquaviva's Mission.

A copy of the *Relaçam*, somewhat similar to that published in 1912 by Father Hosten, had been to a large extent reproduced in Peruschi's *Informatione* which appeared in 1597, and extracts are also made from a Portuguese or Spanish copy in Guzman's *Historia* of 1601. The work is also utilized at second-hand by du Jarric and Purchas. The *Relaçam* was available in the Spanish archives some fifty years ago, but has since been lost, as has also a copy made from it which was at one time deposited with the Royal Asiatic Society in London. A copy, moreover, which like that published by Father Hosten was anonymous, and was dated November 26, 1582, was obtained from the Spanish archives and utilized by the Count von Noer in his *Kaiser Akbar* of which the first volume was published in 1880, but this also has since disappeared.[5]

Monserrate's greatest and most valuable work, however, is a detailed and carefully prepared account of Akbar and the Mission of 1580–1582, entitled *Mongolicae Legationis Commentarius*. Not only is this work of itself of exceptional value, but the history of its preparation, of its long hibernation, and of its wonderful rediscovery in recent years is one of quite extraordinary interest.

The *Commentarius*; its preparation

Father Monserrate on his return to Goa from Agra in 1582

busied himself with the preparation of a connected narration based on his diary of 1580–1582, and when he was ordered to Abyssinia in 1589 he took his material with him. During his captivity in Arabia he revised his work, and while at Ainad he finished the book—which he called his *Commentarius*—on the feast of S. Antony of Padua, June 13, 1590. He was then marched off to San'a and on the way was robbed of his papers. They were, however, recovered by the Turkish Governor and a fair copy of his book was completed by Father Monserrate on December 11, 1590. On January 7, 1591, Monserrate added a preface dedicating the result of his labours to the General of the Order, Claudius Aquaviva, the uncle of his old companion.

From a subsequent note of his we know that he also wrote two books on his later experiences: one describing his own departure for Abyssinia and the other the Natural History of Arabia. Of these two books we have no trace and no further information. The *Commentarius* relating to Mogor dealt similarly with two distinct subjects, namely, the experiences of the Mission on the one hand and the Geography and Natural History of Northern India on the other.

Scheme of re-arrangement

It was Father Monserrate's first intention to remove from the book itself the passages dealing with the latter subjects and to reproduce them in an appendix, but ultimately he found it advisable to deal with the two groups of subjects in two separate books. The two books thus produced have disappeared from our ken, but they seem to have been in existence until a comparatively recent date. Colonel Francis Wilford, of the Bengal Engineers, who lived in Benares from 1788 to 1822 and was a voluminous contributor to the *Asiatick Researches* of Calcutta, quotes several times from Father Monserrate, and on more than one occasion states that the manuscript of Monserrate's book of travels was in his possession.[6] We know that an autograph *Commentaries of Padre Monserrate*, in two volumes, was presented by Colonel Wilford to the Library of the Asiatic Society in Calcutta shortly before his death,[7] but the book is not now to be found in that Library.

Discovery and publication of the work

The *Commentarius*, as written at San'a, on the other hand, has by a strange piece of fortune been preserved to us. Where and in whose possession it remained during the seventeenth and eighteenth centuries we do not know, but before 1818 the manuscript had found a place in the Library of the College of Fort William which was established by Lord Wellesley at Calcutta in 1800. In 1836 it was transferred from the College to the Metcalfe

Hall Collection or Calcutta Public Library, and when this library was in 1903 merged in the present Imperial Library the manuscript was transferred to the Library of S. Paul's, the Anglican Cathedral of Calcutta. There is nothing to show that during all this period it had attracted any special attention. It was only in 1909 that its real value was realized. In 1908 it had been discovered in a heap of decayed and mostly useless books in the Library of S. Paul's by the Rev. W. K. Firminger, a gentleman well known for his indefatigable researches in the domain of Anglo-Indian history ;[8] and in the following year it was seen and its value recognized by Father Hosten of the Society of Jesus. Every facility was given to Father Hosten for the study of its contents, and in 1914 he produced in the *Memoirs of the Asiatic Society of Bengal* a scholarly edition of the Latin text, with a valuable introduction. Father Hosten has done much for the cause of historical research in India, but this edition of the *Commentarius* of Monserrate is in many ways the most remarkable monument of his industry and scholarship.

Translations

A translation of the *Commentarius* with notes was brought out by Father Hosten himself with the help of Father J. Gense, S.J., of S. Mary's College, Kurseong, in successive numbers of the *Catholic Herald of India*, Calcutta, between August 11, 1920 and November 30, 1921, but this translation has never been published in book form.[9] Another useful translation with notes was published in a handy volume in 1922, by Mr. J. S. Hoyland of the Hislop College, Nāgpur, and Professor S. N. Banerjee of the Mahindra College, Patiāla.[10]

Wilford's manuscript

The *Commentarius* discovered in 1908 does not represent the manuscript referred to by Colonel Wilford. The quotations he makes do not tally with the manuscript of 1908 and the pagination he gives is different. The *Commentarius* of 1908 contains a number of passages in brackets which were doubtless intended to be transferred, in modified form, to Monserrate's contemplated 'second book,' and it does not contain certain descriptions of places which are quoted by Wilford from his manuscript. There are indications in it that in several instances the writer had not made up his mind as to the manner in which the subject-matter should be distributed between the two contemplated volumes. The manuscript possessed by Wilford was apparently entitled *De Legatione Mongolica* and was in two books, but its precise relation to the *Commentarius* which has survived is obscure. Father Hosten suggests that it represented the earliest version of the *Commentarius*, namely that completed on June 13, 1590, but the point cannot be said to have been fully elucidated. Whether Wilford possessed the surviving copy of the *Commentarius* is uncertain—there are indeed pencil marks and comments on it which have been made by an English scholar with all the tastes and learning of Wilford, but there are no means of comparing those pencil notes with any known specimen of Wilford's handwriting.

The *Commentarius*, as we have it, is the manuscript actually completed by Monserrate at San'a in 1590, but it contains certain subsequent additions made at various times and distinguishable by the various kinds of ink and pens used, some prior to and some later than Monserrate's return to India. We have, for instance, a reference to Father Xavier's Mission to Akbar which did not leave Goa till December 1594 and a possible allusion to the death of 'Abdulla Khān, King of Samarkand and Bukhāra, who died in 1598. Some of the passages of the book are very extensively modified in the manuscript and a specimen page which has been reproduced as it stands in Father Hosten's edition of 1912 shows an extraordinary number of 'author's alterations.'

Modifications made in extant versions after Dec. 11, 1590

The first page of Monserrate's narrative is missing, but its contents have been ingeniously reconstructed by Father Hosten, with the help of Monserrate's own index and of the accounts given in the recognized Jesuit histories. The missing portion deals with the earliest stage of Akbar's contact with Christianity, and the narrative, as it stands, begins with the invitation issued by Akbar to Goa in 1578. We are then told of the journey of the missionaries from Goa to Fatehpur Sīkrī and of all they saw on their way, at Surat, Māndu, Gwalior and elsewhere. They are then received by Akbar at the Court, and a description is given of Fatehpur and of the King's character and amusements. Among these latter is polo: 'lignea pila, malleis quoque ligneis pulsa, ex equis luditur.' We are told of the progress of the Mission, the disputes with the Muslims, the favours bestowed by Akbar, and the attitude of the Fathers towards him. The narrative then takes up the rebellion of Akbar's brother, Mīrzā Hakīm, Governor of Kābul, and the advance of Akbar's army towards the rebels. Monserrate, who accompanied the army, records much that is of interest, both regarding the constitution and practices of the army, and also regarding the various places visited during the journey. He tells of Muttra and Delhi; and when the army halts on the Biās he speaks of Akbar's little expedition to Kāngra and of the information received from travellers about the Tibetans. He then proceeds by Jogī Tila, Rohtās, Manikyāla and the Indus through

Summary of contents

the country of the Gakkhars and the Dilazāks. The Jats he holds to be Getae and the Kashmīrīs are clearly Jews, for their features and dress and traditions are undoubtedly Jewish and—in Lahore at least—they make money by dealing in old clothes, scraps of iron, iron bars, horseshoes, arm-rings, padlocks and other articles of the sort. The Pathāns, 'whom the Mongols call Aufgun,' speak a language which 'sounds like Spanish and, more curious still, it has even some words in common,' and their singing is 'sweet, free and high-pitched, and like that of Europeans and not the low deep howling (vox inclinata et ululans) of Asiatics.' The narration includes a description of Peshawar and its Gorkhatrī, of 'Alī Masjid, the Khaibar and Landīkhāna. At Jalālābād Monserrate is left behind on the score of illness while Akbar proceeds to Kābul. On the return journey the Father encounters some danger from fanatics in the Khaibar Pass, but all goes well. At Rohtās he hears that Father Aquaviva is ill at Sarhind and goes to meet him. The two Fathers are at Lahore when Akbar reaches that city, and at Lahore Father Monserrate himself falls ill. When the King had returned to Fatehpur the question of an embassy to Europe was taken up and the proposed closure of the Jesuit Mission to Mogor considered, and ultimately Monserrate returned to Goa, leaving Father Rudolf with the King. An account is given of Monserrate's return journey and this is followed by a description of Rudolf's recall to Goa and his martyrdom.

The narrative ends here, and the rest of the book is taken up by a description of Akbar, his palaces, revenue, administration of justice, provinces, etc., much of which had already appeared in the *Relaçam* above referred to. Monserrate then proceeds to give a semi-historical account of the Mogul invasion of India under Bābur, and the reigns and conquests of Bābur's predecessors, Chingis Khān and Tamerlane, and their successors, ending up with a discourse on the Scythians.

Index, map, authorities and style

In addition to the narrative above summarized the manuscript contains an index prepared by Monserrate himself, a list of authorities utilized, a long table of latitudes and longitudes, and a map of extraordinary interest which is reproduced in Father Hosten's edition of the *Commentarius*.[11] The list of authorities is such as we might expect from a writer of the period, and includes such names as those of Josephus, Ptolemy, Jerome, Diodorus Siculus, Aeneas Sylvius and Paulus Jovius.[12] Monserrate in his work makes considerable use of names culled from classical geography, such as Parapomisus, Arachosia, Gedrosia, Scythia, Sogdiana and the like. Almost all his Oriental names are put into Latin forms: Jalāluddīn Akbar, for instance, is Zelaldinus, Mīrzā Hakīm is Mirsachimus, Rājā Bīrbal is Billiballus, the god Maheshvara is Maessuris, Peshāwar is Pirxaurum, and Fatehpur is explained to be Nicopolis. Quotations are made from authors such as Lucan and Statius, and words such as ' diaeresis ' and ' syntagma ' are applied to the Qur'ān. The few attempts which Monserrate, after the fashion of the time, makes to use Greek words—he speaks, for instance, of ὑπερβοληκῶς and ἠκωνομαστικες,—show that he was inadequately grounded in that language, but the Latin in which the book is written, though at times crabbed, appears on the whole to be a reasonable specimen of the Latin of the day.

Importance of the publication

His book constitutes an extraordinarily valuable addition to our authorities for the period to which it relates. It is the main source of all our knowledge of the first Jesuit Mission to Akbar. It forms a useful check and supplement to contemporary narrations such as that given in the Akbarnāma regarding the rebellion of Mīrzā Hakīm. And it is an admirable first-hand authority for our knowledge of Akbar himself and his immediate surroundings. Its publication in 1914 enabled the late Mr. Vincent Smith to make good use of it in his valuable book *Akbar the Great Mogul*, published in 1919, and it will always remain an indispensable source of information for historians of the period. Its rescue from oblivion is one of the romances of research, and its scholarly publication by Father Hosten constitutes a landmark in Indian historical study.

NOTES

[1] Franco, *Imagem* (of Lisbon), 1717, p. 300 ; Paez, in his *History of Ethiopia*, says, that Monserrate was nominated to be head of the Mission of 1580, but preferred to serve under Aquaviva. (Beccari, *Rerum Aethiopicarum Scriptores*, Rome, 1910, III, p. 152.)

[2] Beccari, *Rerum Aethiopicarum Scriptores*, Rome, 1910, III, pp. 149–199, and X, pp. 371 and 394. Some earlier letters of Monserrate, written previous to his departure for India, are also mentioned by Sommervogel. There is also a letter written by him from Cochin on January 12, 1579, and a long Spanish treatise in his handwriting called *Informacion de los X'pianos de S. Thome*—in the possession of the Society—from which interesting extracts were published by Fr. Hosten, *J.A.S.B.*, XVIII, 1922, pp. 349–369.

[3] A fairly full account of the incidents in Arabia is given in Father Paez's *History of Aethiopia*, in Vols. II and III of Beccari, op. cit., and a sketch of Monserrate's life is given in Almeida's *History of Aethiopia*, V, cap. 6, op. cit., Vol. VI, pp. 30–33.

[4] *J.A.S.B.*, VIII, 1912, pp. 185–221.

[5] See the authorities quoted by Father Hosten in his article in *J.A.S.B.*, VIII, 1912, pp. 185–189. Noer's *Kaiser Akbar* (1880), I, p. 489, note, and Mrs. Beveridge's translation (1890), p. 331, note.

[6] A very useful reproduction of Colonel Wilford's various references to Monserrate is given on pp. 691–702 of Fr. Hosten's edition of the *Commentarius*, and supplementary information is given in *J.A.S.B.*, XVIII, 1922, pp. 371–374.

[7] *Asiatick Researches*, XIV, 1822, App. II. They are no longer in the possession of the Bengal Asiatic Society: see *J.A.S.B.*, XXIII, 1927, p. 81.

[8] He referred to this discovery in the *Englishman* newspaper of February 6, 1912.

[9] A few paragraphs comprising Monserrate's description of Delhi were published by Hosten with annotations in 1911 (*J.A.S.B.*, VII, 1911, pp. 99–108), and some notes on the *Commentarius* by H. Beveridge and Hosten were published in 1915 (*J.A.S.B.*, VI, 1915, pp. 187–204).

[10] *The Commentary of Father Monserrate, S.J.* (Oxford University Press).

[11] See Sven Hedin's comment on this map in *Southern Tibet*, 1922, VII, pp. 19–33.

[12] See also Chapter XIII.

CHAPTER IX

AKBAR'S CHRISTIAN WIFE

Fama est obscurior annis.
(Virg., *Aen.*, vii, 205.)

IN the latter part of 1916 there was a considerable amount of correspondence in certain of the English newspapers in India on the question whether Akbar had a Christian wife.[1] The evidence on this point has been carefully collected by Father Hosten, but no final decision has been published by him on the very confusing data available.

Discussion of 1916

It is stated in Blochmann's notes on the *Ā'īn-i-Akbarī*[2] that Akbar had an Armenian wife, but the passage in the Tūzuk-i-Jahāngīrī, which he gives as his authority, merely states that the daughter of an Armenian, who was in the service of Akbar's harem, was given in marriage to Sikandar, the father of the Armenian Christian official, Zū'lqarnain. Father Corsi writing on October 15, 1626, describes Zū'lqarnain (who lost his own mother in early youth) as having been 'brought up in the Royal House at King Akbar's order by one of the queens whom he called Mother, and King Akbar he called Father'; but this passage again does not necessarily imply either that Akbar was Zū'lqarnain's father or that one of the queens was a Christian. Although, therefore, it is not impossible that Akbar had an Armenian Christian wife there is no certain evidence of the fact.

Possible Armenian wife

There is, however, an obstinate legend which goes beyond this and declares that Akbar had a wife who was a Portuguese Christian and to whom the name of Mary is usually assigned.

Tradition of a Portuguese wife

The legend was strenuously supported in a book published by a Mr. Frederic Fanthome of Agra in 1894, called *Reminiscences of Agra*, and a number of authorities, mostly modern, were quoted by him in favour of his contention.[3] According to Mr. Fanthome, Mary, the queen of Akbar, was the daughter of one

Martindell or Martingall who was in the Imperial service, but no authority is quoted for this statement.

The tradition of the Christian wife received further and more valid support in 1907 from Mr. Ismael Gracias in a book published at Nova Goa called *Una dona portugueza na Corte do Grão Mogol*, and from Mr. C. A. Kincaid in *The Tale of the Tulsi Plant*, published at Bombay in 1908. It was stated by these authorities that a girl from a Lisbon orphanage, called Maria Mascarenhas, was shipped with other orphans to the East to help to provide wives for the Portuguese officials, and that after being captured by the Dutch and brought to Surat she was sold to the Moguls and became one of Akbar's queens. For this again, however, no adequate authority is given, and if we accept the further tradition mentioned below, which implies that Mary was married before 1581, it is impossible that she should have been captured by the Dutch, who had not then appeared in Indian waters.

We are further informed in Campbell's *Bombay Gazetteer* that in 1583 war between the Moguls and the Portuguese in Bassain and Damān was terminated by the intervention of a Portuguese lady who was an inmate of Akbar's household.[4] The origin of this story is, however, unknown, and it is curious that in Father Monserrate's detailed contemporary account of the proceedings of the period no mention should be made of such an episode.[5]

As against this vague tradition we have the fact that, so far as is known, no reference is made to any Christian wife of Akbar, either in the vernacular histories of the time, or in the Portuguese official correspondence from Goa, or in the letters of the Jesuit missionaries. It seems especially unlikely that if Akbar had had a Christian wife of Portuguese origin no mention should have been made of her by the Jesuit Fathers.[6]

The story has probably taken its origin from several sources. It was doubtless in some way suggested by the titles of Akbar's mother and of the wife of Akbar who was Jahāngīr's mother. Akbar's mother, Hamīda Begam, had the title of 'Maryam Makānī' or 'Dweller with the Virgin Mary'; and Jahāngīr's mother, a Hindu princess, had the posthumous title of 'Maryam-uz-zamānī' or 'the Mary of the Age.' Both of these are titles suitable for a Mahommedan Court, and they do not imply that the possessors of the titles bore the name of Mary or were Christians.

Probable origins of the tradition

The error encouraged by these titles has been further strengthened by the existence near Agra of two buildings, traditionally connected with the name of Mary. One of these is the ' Maryam Kī Kothī ' or ' Sonahra Makān ' at Fatehpur; and another is the tomb of Maryam at Sikandra.[7] The origin of the name attached to the building at Fatehpur is not known. From the fact that it contains the remains of a picture which may have represented the Annunciation it is possible that the name has reference to the Virgin Mary, but it is mere conjecture to connect it with the name of any of Akbar's queens. As regards the ' Roza Maryam ' at Sikandra, this building was used as a tomb for Akbar's queen, Maryam-uz-zamānī, and in view of the Catholic tradition connecting it with a Christian queen Mr. Edmund Smith, of the Archaeological Survey of India, had the crypt opened some years ago, but found no sign of a cross or other Christian symbol upon the grave.[8]

Then again the name of Mary occurs in certain official documents connected with the Jesuits which are preserved in the Agra Mission Archives. These are a paper of A.D. 1647 and a parwāna of the time of Shāh 'Ālam. The former is a written statement by one Maria Piārī, to the effect that the house in which she is living is not hers, but belongs to the Padre. The latter refers to a cemetery at Agra in possession of the Jesuits, which had been ' granted by Maryam.' But we have no information as to the identity of the Maria Piārī and the Maryam of the Agra records. Father Felix has, moreover, shown that in the later document the words under consideration should probably be read as ' az qadīm '—' from of old '—rather than as ' az Maryam '—' from Mary.'[9]

There are, therefore, some fairly intelligible explanations of the tradition that Akbar had a Christian wife called Mary, but the tradition does not, so far as evidence at present goes, rest on any basis of fact.[10]

The interest excited in the question in 1916 was, however, intensified in a curious way by the discovery of two pictures which seemed to support the theory that Akbar had a Christian wife. Lāla Bulāqi Dās, proprietor of the Muir Press in Delhi, had a large collection of Indian pictures, and among those who interested themselves in his collection had been Nawāb Mīrzā Akbar 'Alī, Prime Minister of Karauli, who lived in Delhi, and who died about the year 1910. In 1902 the Mīrzā presented to his granddaughter, the wife of Prince Bakhtiyār Shāh at Calcutta, a picture representing Akbar sitting with his arm round the neck of a lady, who might be Armenian or Portuguese, and who certainly was intended to represent a Christian as she wore a cross on her necklace. The

L. Bulāqī Dās' picture

picture was subsequently bought from the Prince's estate by Mr. A. Stephen, of Camac Street, Calcutta, and came to the notice of Father Hosten in 1916. It bore a Persian superscription —' Jalāluddīn Akbar wa Mariam Zamānī Begam,' and in September 1916 Father Hosten published an account of it in the newspapers.[11] Shortly afterwards, a further picture on the same subject, differing only in small detail from the other, but without the Persian superscription, was found in Delhi in the possession of L. Bulāqī Dās.[12] Enquiries regarding the Calcutta picture had been started by the late Mr. Ignatius Bowring, an officer of the Punjab Police, who was interested in such matters, and L. Bulāqī Dās then produced a pencil sketch of the same subject which he declared to have been bought by him twenty-five years previously. The pictures are both of a late Lucknow or semi-European style of painting, and their historical value depends entirely on the genuineness or otherwise of the pencil sketch and of the date to which it should be assigned. A photograph of the sketch was made for Father Hosten by the Survey of India, but there are circumstances connected with the production of the sketch which cast doubt upon its genuineness. L. Bulāqī Dās had published a small Urdu book on Akbar's Queens,[13] and he had exhibited other pictures at Delhi, along with sketches purporting to be the original foundation of the picture and to have been prepared by well-known artists of the past. The pictures under discussion were, moreover, curious in that they represented Akbar as smoking a ' huqqa '—a feature not impossible, but somewhat unlikely, in any portrait dating from Akbar's time, or shortly after, in view of the fact that Akbar is known to have disliked tobacco. On the data available, therefore, the pictures brought to notice in 1916 cannot be held to give any substantial support to the legend that Akbar had a Christian wife.

NOTES

[1] The *Englishman*, August 19 and 23, September 16 and 22, October 20, November 4, 15–20, 1916. The *Statesman*, September 16, 20, 24, 30, October 10, 1916. The *Indian Daily News*, September 22, 1916; the *Catholic Herald* (Calcutta), August 23, September 27, 1916 ; cf. the *Vakil* (Amritsar), September 6, 9, 13, 1916, and the *Examiner* (Bombay), 1916, p. 372. See also Hosten in *Mem. A.S.B.*, V, 1916, pp. 175–177. The whole question is discussed by Hosten again in some detail in an article : ' Akbar's Queen Mary,' in *B.P. and P.*, XXXIV, 1927, pp. 97–105.

[2] Blochmann, *A'īn*, I, p. 618 ; Syad Ahmad, *Tūzuk* (1864), p. 324;

Rogers and Beveridge, *Tūzuk*, I, p. 194. The quotation from Corsi is supplied by Father Hosten from unpublished records.

[3] His authorities are examined in detail by H. Heras, S.J., in the *Journal of Indian History* (Allahabad), September 1924, Vol. III, pp. 218–221, and easily demolished. Fanthome's book is described by Heras as 'a work as full of good will and piety as it is devoid of historical criticism.' The legend is made the basis of some highly conjectural romance in Talboys Wheeler's *Tales from Indian History*, 1881, pp. 52–58.

[4] *Bombay Gazetteer*, 1882, Vol. XIII (Thana), p. 453.

[5] Blunt, *Christian Tombs and Monuments of the United Provinces*, 1911, pp. 49–50.

[6] *J.A.S.B.*, 1896, LXV, p. 53.

[7] De Laet, *India Vera* (1631), p. 44, gives Maryam Makānī as the name of Akbar's wife, but he is wrong. Blochmann, *A'īn*, I, pp. 309, 619. Fanthome insists on identifying Maryam-uz-zamānī with the Christian wife. He also states that the captives taken away by Aquaviva in 1583 at the end of his Mission belonged to the Christian queen, but the Jesuit authorities show that they belonged to the Queen Mother, that is, to Hamīda Begam.

[8] E. Smith, *Moghul Architecture of Fathpur-Sikri*, Vol. III ; (*Arch. Survey of India*, Vol. XVIII, 1895), Part I, p. 31–38, and the same author's *Akbar's Tomb, Sikandarah* ; (*Arch. Survey of India*, Vol. XXXV, 1909), p. 1. The Roza was granted by the Government about the time of the Mutiny to the Church Missionary Society, and was used as a printing press and as an orphanage and industrial school. Cf. Latīf, *Agra* (Calcutta, 1896), p. 195. An account of the Tomb, with plans and views, was given by Gordon Sanderson in the *Ann. Report of the Arch. Survey of India for* 1910–1911, p. 94.

[9] *Catholic Calendar and Directory for the Archbishopric of Agra for the year* 1907 (Felix), p. 208 ; *Mem. As. Soc., Bengal*, V, 1916, p. 177 ; *J.P.H.S.*, V, 1916 (Felix), pp. 45, 47.

[10] This view has also the authority of K. S. Zafar Hasan. See Record of the 8th Meeting of the India Historical Records Commission, 1926, p. 167.

[11] This picture was exhibited by Mr. Stephen at the 5th Meeting of the Indian Historical Records Commission in 1923, *Record of Meeting*, p. 158.

[12] A copy of the picture is said to be in the Library of L. Srī Rām of Delhi (*J.I.H.*, I, 1922, p. 346). An anonymous correspondent in the *Statesman* newspaper of September 20, 1916, stated that there was another painting of Akbar's Christian wife in Nānā Fadnavīs' Wada at Menauli in the Satāra district, but this has not been traced. A reproduction of the two pictures referred to in the text was published in the *Statesman* of November 14, 1916.

[13] The book was seen by Father Hosten in 1916 and pronounced by him (so far as the alleged Maryam is concerned) to be a tissue of absurdities. It quotes Jalāluddīn Shirwānī, and a Tārīkh-i-Hind as its authorities, and copies from *Tales from Indian History* (London, 1881), by Talboys Wheeler, which, as above noted, is largely a work of imagination with little historical value.

CHAPTER X

THE INDIAN BOURBONS

Et Turno si prima domus repetatur origo
Inachus Acrisiusque patres mediaeque Mycenae.

(Virg., *Aen.*, vii, 371–372.)

CONNECTED with the tradition of Akbar's Christian wife is the tradition of the Indian Bourbons.

There are in certain parts of India, chiefly in the Bhopal State, a number of persons who claim descent from the marriage of a member of the Bourbon family of France with a sister of the Christian wife of Akbar.

The Bourbons of Bhopal

Shortly after the sack of Delhi by Nādir Shāh in 1737, we find a considerable number of persons bearing the name of Bourbon settled on a family jāgīr at Shergarh, near Narwar in Central India. We learn from a letter of Father Strobl, S.J., that a church with a resident priest was opened in Narwar in 1743, and Father Tieffenthaler, S.J., was for thirteen years resident chaplain to this family at Narwar. In 1778 the bulk of the Bourbons at Shergarh were massacred by the Rājā of Narwar. Those who escaped fled to Gwalior, and one Salvador Bourbon, who was then the chief representative of the family, shortly afterwards proceeded to Bhopal, where most of the Bourbons have since resided. The family for a long time held a large part of the tahsīl of Ichāwar in 'jāgīr,' and they are recorded as having 'given a succession of shrewd councillors and valiant soldiers to the State.' Balthazar or Shāhzād Masīh, the son of Salvador, married in 1821 a remarkable lady known as Madame Dulhin (The Bride), or Elisabeth de Bourbon, who remained constantly about the Court in the service of the Begams of Bhopal. Since the death of Madame Dulhin in 1882 the Bourbons have fallen in status. Most of them have for long been entirely Indian in their ways, secluding their women and in many cases bearing Mohammedan names. There are Bourbon tombs at Bhopal, and at least three of the family were buried in the Agra cemetery.[1]

According to an account given by Balthasar Bourbon to Sir

John Malcolm, and published by him in his *Central India*[2] in 1832, the founder of the family was a Frenchman called John Bourboun who came from Pari or Bevi in the time of Akbar, and nothing was said of his connection with the French royal family. It was further stated by Balthasar that the family had intermarried with only two other non-Indian families—one French and the other Armenian Roman Catholic.

Accounts of their origin: Sir J. Malcolm

When the French traveller, Louis Rousselet, was at Bhopal in 1867, he saw Madame Dulhin, and a picture of this lady is represented in his *L'Inde des Rajahs*, published in 1875.[3] In this book he gives the tradition, as communicated to him at Bhopal, that the original founder of the family, Jean de Bourbon, was made prisoner by pirates in the Mediterranean and taken to Egypt, where he rose to distinction in the Army. From Egypt he proceeded by way of Broach to Agra, where he married and had two sons. One of them, Sikandar, was granted the hereditary charge of the palace of the Begams and the fief of Shirgarh or Sirgarh. Jean de Bourbon, says Rousselet, was made by Akbar 'Seigneur de Barri et Mergarh,' places which he considers to be reminiscent of Berry and Mercœur, two of the French fiefs of the house of Bourbon. This family, he says, preserved in Bhopal an escutcheon of the founder, adorned with fleurs-de-lis. From Rousselet comes the suggestion, apparently made for the first time, that the founder of the family may have been an illegitimate son of the famous Connétable de Bourbon, who was killed at Rome in 1527. Upon this conjecture Rousselet based a romance, entitled *Le Fils du Connétable*, which he published in Paris in 1882. The book professed to be founded on statements made to the author by Madame Dulhin, but the whole work is obviously pure romance.[4]

M. Rousselet

After the death of Madame Dulhin in 1882, there was a special investigation by the political authorities into the circumstances and history of the family. There was said to have been a family history compiled in the eighteenth century and carried by a priest to Goa for safety towards the end of that century. In the investigation 'the records were found to be few and the traditions obscure,' but the general results, so far as the history of the family are concerned, were set forth in a very interesting paper by Colonel W. Kincaid in the *Asiatic Quarterly Review* of January to April 1887. The tradition had, by this time, considerably developed. It was alleged that in 1560 John Philip Bourbon, a member of the younger branch of the family of Henri IV, having killed a relation in a duel, emigrated

Col. Kincaid

from France to India. He proceeded by Madras and Bengal to Agra, where he was well received by Akbar, and was married to Julianā, the sister of Akbar's Christian wife. He was given the title of Nawāb and placed in charge of the zanāna, an office which remained with his descendants till the sack of Delhi by Nādir Shāh. Colonel Kincaid appended to his article a detailed genealogy of the family based on the above tradition.[5]

The question subsequently excited the special interest of the late Father Noti, S.J., who was at one time resident in Bombay. He obtained from the family a document purporting to be an Urdu translation of a Persian statement presented to Jahāngīr about 1605 or 1606, by Jean Philippe (who must then have been very old). In this document Jean Philippe states that he was the son of the famous Charles Connétable de Bourbon, and that his mother died shortly after his birth. He adds that he escaped from Rome after the Constable's death by arranging a mock funeral of himself, and after adventures among the Turks came on to India. Father Noti also had documents stating that John Philip's wife was an Abyssinian princess of the name of Magdalen; that Akbar had made him Rājā of Shirgarh; that he was still alive in 1606, and that he had two sons: Alexander, born about 1550, and Saveil (Charles), born about 1560. The results of Father Noti's investigations, however, have not hitherto been published.[6]

Father Noti

There is also a memorandum in the Agra episcopal archives (it is not known at what date or on what authority it was written) to the effect that 'the old church (at Agra) was built by Philip Bourbon of the house of Navarre and his wife Juliana, an Armenian lady who was in medical charge of the Emperor's harem. They are both buried in the church itself; probably the epitaphs are in Armenian.' There is, however, no trace of their tombs.[7]

Agra archives

Such, in brief, are the data on which the legend rests. In the form now prevalent, it traces the Indian Bourbon family to a John Philip of Bourbon of the House of Navarre, and to a Lady Juliana, the sister of a Christian wife of Akbar. There is strong tradition on both points, but it lacks sufficient outside support to allow us to accept it as it stands.

Evidence as regards:

Evidence exists, no doubt, that a polyglot Bible, said to be that given by the Jesuits to Akbar, was, shortly before the Mutiny of 1857, in the hands of a branch of the Bourbon family at Lucknow, and subsequently in those of a Father Adeodatus of Lucknow; and this, so far as it goes, connects the family with the immediate entourage of the Emperor Akbar.[8]

John Philip de Bourbon

On the other hand, the name 'Bourbon' is nowhere mentioned by the Jesuits, nor has any allusion been found in the contemporary Jesuit writings to anyone corresponding to the traditional John Philip; and this is the more remarkable in view of the fact that Father Jerome Xavier, who was at the Court at the time, came himself from Henri IV's country of Navarre. One Jacome Felippe is no doubt mentioned as an agent of the Jesuits with the Prince Salīm, but his name does not tally with that of John Philip and he is described as an Italian who had come from Goa with the Fathers.[9] We are told also in the Jesuit letters of 1608–1609 of an unnamed Frenchman, captured by the Turks in the Mediterranean, who was compelled to become a Muslim, and who afterwards came to Lahore with his wife and children, was known to Father Xavier, and died confessing Christianity.[10] But there is no indication that the man was identified in any way with the House of Navarre or with the Indian Bourbons. Indeed, in describing the family in Narwar which went by the name of Bourbon, the Jesuit documents tend to trace their origin to an Armenian rather than to a European ancestry.[11] No mention of John Philip has been discovered in any Indian history or memoir, and in spite of efforts which have been made by M. A. Lehuraux of Chandarnagore and others, no trace can be found in European records regarding the Bourbon family of any individual answering to the traditional ancestor of the Indian Bourbons.[12]

His wife, Juliana

So too as regards the alleged wife, Juliana. We know of two authentic ladies of this name, viz., one who was the wife of the Armenian Sikandar and mother of Mīrzā Zū'lqarnain, a lady who died before 1598; and another, known as Lady Juliana Dias da Costa, who died in 1734. Attempts have been made, but without real success, to identify the former with the wife of Jean Philippe de Bourbon. It is no doubt possible that there was at Akbar's Court another Juliana, of Portuguese origin, with medical proclivities. The existence of such a person may be indicated by a letter written in 1832 by the Bishop and Vicar Apostolic of Agra to the traveller Dr. Wolff, which says, that the Jesuits first gained Akbar's favour: 'per impegno di una certa Signora Giuliana di Goa che come Dottoressa si trovava nel Serraglio del suddetto Imperatore.'[13] But this tradition is late, and on our present information it appears unlikely that a second Juliana existed at Akbar's Court unmentioned by the Jesuits, and the probability is that her name has crept into the story by a confusion with the other two ladies of the same name mentioned above. And if there was no such Juliana as the Bourbon tradition postulates, then that tradition ceases to give support to the tradition of a Christian wife of Akbar.

The D'Eremao family

Apart, however, from the Bhopal Bourbons, there is another body of persons who claim Bourbon descent—namely, a small group connected with a family called D'Eremao. There is a Christian cemetery outside Delhi, known as the D'Eremao cemetery, in which several of this family were buried, and the former habitat of the family was Delhi and its neighbourhood.[14] The best known of the D'Eremaos were Captain Manuel D'Eremao and Lieutenant Domingo D'Eremao, who are both buried in the Delhi cemetery. Captain Manuel held high posts under the Mahrattas, and was instrumental in the cession of Hānsī to the British in 1806. He died at the age of eighty-six in 1829, and his son Domingo followed him to the grave in 1852. The family held property in the neighbourhood of Delhi, and there was litigation about this among the children of Domingo between 1882 and 1887, in the course of which interesting statements regarding the family were recorded by Paul D'Eremao, one of Domingo's sons, and by Father Keegan, the Catholic chaplain. One of Domingo's sons, the Rev. Joseph Patrick Val D'Eremao, D.D., born in 1841, was buried at Woking in 1896 after a career of some distinction as a writer and linguist.[15] Another son, Emanuel, born about 1838, was an engineer, who afterwards became a missionary, and the traditions of the family, retailed orally by him to Mrs. Pratt, a granddaughter of Lieutenant Domingo, recently resident at Simla, were communicated by the latter to Father Hosten in 1917.[16] The family, as a whole, is now in poor circumstances.

The tradition of the family is that the D'Eremaos were Bourbons and adopted the name of D'Eremao from the title of Dur-i-Yaman or Dur-i-'Amān (Pearl of the Yemen or of Oman) conferred by the Emperor Bahādur Shāh on their ancestress. The story is that Captain D'Eremao's father, Nicolas Valle de Bourbon, was killed in an affray in trying to save the life of the Emperor 'Ālamgīr II, who was assassinated in 1759: and that Nicolas's father, Sebastian, was the son of the founder of the family. The tradition has some strange resemblances to that put forward by the Bourbons of Bhopal.

Traditional descent from Gaston de Bourbon

The original founder, however, according to this story, was not a contemporary of Akbar, otherwise unknown, but a well-known historical character of a century later than Akbar, namely, Jean Baptiste Gaston de Bourbon, Duke of Orleans, the second son of Henri IV, who, towards the end of his turbulent and inglorious career, was relegated by Louis XIV to Blois. Gaston is said by the histories to have died at Blois on February 2, 1660, his body being buried at S. Denis and his heart in the Jesuit chapel at Blois.[17] But, according to the D'Eremao legend, he escaped from his internment at Blois, and came to India where he attained high position at the Mogul Court. As in the case of the Bhopal tale, we are then introduced to a Lady Juliana: but there are different versions as to her place in the story. According to the tradition handed on by Mr. Emanuel D'Eremao, Juliana was the sister of Mariam, a wife of the Mogul grandee, Mīr Jumla, who died in 1663,[18] and Juliana, after being cured from illness by a physician, was married to Gaston de Bourbon. According to a statement by Paul D'Eremao, recorded in 1885, Juliana was herself a physician and cured the mother of the king, Bahādur Shāh, of a disease in the breast; and her sister Isabel, who was brought out to India at the expense of the Emperor, married a D'Eremao. According to Emanuel D'Eremao there was a further Juliana, a granddaughter of Aurangzeb, who cured Bahādur Shāh's mother and married Sebastian Valle, the son of Gaston de Bourbon. In the will of Lieutenant Domingo D'Eremao reference is made to Juliana as his paternal grandmother, and the reference must apparently relate to this second Juliana. But the whole story is a confused one, and there are elements in it which point to artificial embellishment.

Connection of the D'Eremaos with Juliana Diaz da Costa

Taking it as a whole, this form of the Bourbon legend points to a distinct connection between the D'Eremao family and the historic character, Juliana Diaz da Costa. In the D'Eremao litigation of 1882–1887 a number of sanads were produced of which copies are still available among the Government records. The sanads are of the later years of Aurangzeb and of the time of his successor, Bahādur Shāh, and show that the lands in dispute which lay at Bhūpānī, Juliana Sarai, and other places near Delhi, were granted in the reigns of Aurangzeb and Bahādur Shāh to Musammāt Juliana and her sons. As Juliana Diaz da Costa lived in that period and is known to have had lands in the same tract, it may fairly be assumed that the D'Eremaos were connected with that lady.[19]

But their claim to descent from a Bourbon prince is another matter. There is no mention of the Bourbons, either in our historical accounts of Juliana Diaz da Costa, or in the litigation of 1882–1887, and there can be little doubt that this element in the story needs further investigation.

The following is a rough indication of the D'Eremao claim :

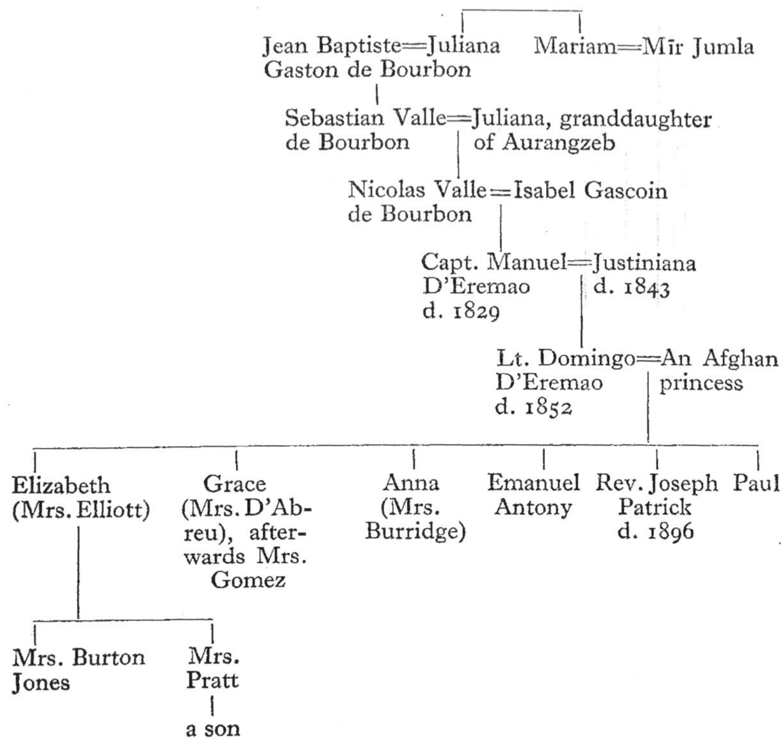

The data vary in different accounts, but the above seems to represent the prevailing tradition.

NOTES

[1] Simi Bibi Anna, wife of Pedro, d. 1832 ; Pedro d. 1833 ; Antonia d. (aged 100) 1855. Blunt's *Christian Tombs and Monuments in the United Provinces*, 1911, pp. 49, 50. Hosten in *Mem. A.S.B.*, V, 1916, pp. 179–180.

[2] Vol. I, p. 420. See also an article by ' Hyderabad ' in the *Statesman* newspaper of April 17, 1931.

[3] Page 537.

[4] The book was translated and published in London in 1892 as *The Son of the Constable of France, or The Adventures of Jean de Bourbon*.

[5] Cf. also the account of the family given by Col. Luard in the *Bhopal State Gazetteer* (1908), pp. 106–108.

[6] From certain notes recorded by Hosten, it appears that Noti had also seen a translation into Persian or Urdū of Rousselet's romance.

[7] Felix, O.C., in *Agra Diocesan Calendar*, 1907, p. 204. See also *Mem. A.S.B.*, V, 1916 (Hosten), p. 173.

[8] *Agra Diocesan Calendar*, 1907, p. 192.

[9] *J.A.S.B.*, LXV, 1896, p. 88 ; *Mem. A.S.B.*, V, 1916 (Hosten), p. 179.

[10] *Mem. A.S.B.*, 1916, p. 178.

[11] *Ibid.*, p. 180 ; cf. Bernoulli, *Description Historique et Géographique de l'Inde* (1791), I, p. 176 (*Beschreibung*, I, p. 126).

[12] Anselme's monumental work, *Histoire Générale de la Maison de France* (1726), ascribes to the Constable three children, and, although his work deals faithfully with such matters, does not credit him with any illegitimate son. (Vol. I, p. 317.) Coiffier Demoret, in his *Histoire du Bourbonnais et des Bourbons* (Paris, 1816), I, p. 423, refers to a legend that the Constable, after the death of his first wife, married secretly a Spanish lady, who had a child by him, but gives no credence to it.

[13] Wolff, *Researches and Missionary Labours*, 1835, p. 304.

[14] Irving, *List of Inscriptions on Christian Tombs or Monuments in the Punjab*, 1910, pp. 5–9.

[15] Some interesting letters written by Dr. D'Eremao to Mr. Irvine in 1895 were published in *J.R.A.S.*, 1903, pp. 355–358.

[16] See also letter from Mrs. Pratt in the *Pioneer* newspaper, December 16, 1912.

[17] Anselme, op. cit., p. 147.

[18] There may be an allusion to the wife of Mīr Jumla in the Jesuit Annual Letter from Mogor of 1648–1649 ; see translation by Hosten in *J.I.H.*, I, 1922, pp. 235, 248.

[19] It may be noted that the Valles, Vals or Velhos appear in the genealogies both of Juliana Diaz da Costa and of the D'Eremaos (*J.P.H.S.*, VII, 1918, pp. 41–2).

CHAPTER XI

MIRZA ZU'LQARNAIN (1592–1656)

(A CHRISTIAN OFFICIAL OF THE MOGUL GOVERNMENT)

In lege Domini voluntas ejus.
(Ps. i, 2.)

IT has been noticed above how during the reigns of Jahāngīr and Shāh Jahān the Jesuits received considerable support from a Christian called Mīrzā Zū'lqarnain, who occupied a fairly high rank among the Court officials of the day.

The history of Mīrzā Zū'lqarnain is of extraordinary interest, but no connected account of his life was placed before English readers until 1914. In that year Sir R. C. Temple, with the assistance of Father Hosten, published an outline of the known facts regarding Mīrzā Zū'lqarnain as an Appendix to the Hakluyt Society's edition of the *Travels of Peter Mundy*.[1] Two years later, in 1916, Father Hosten himself put together in greater detail all the recorded information on the subject of Mīrzā Zū'lqarnain and published the result in an admirable Memoir of the Asiatic Society of Bengal.[2] There is little or nothing to be added to Father Hosten's Memoir, and the following sketch is in the main an abstract of the information gathered by him.

Father Hosten's Memoir of 1916

Our original authorities regarding Zū'lqarnain are of four kinds. In the first place, we have a few notices of him in the Indian chronicles such as the *Tūzuk-i-Jahāngīrī*, the *'Amal-i-Sālih*, and the *Bādshāh-nāma*. Secondly, we have an interesting but not altogether accurate account of him in an appendix of the second volume of a *History of India* in Armenian by Thomas Khojamal, which dates from 1768, and was published in 1849 by Mesrovb David Thaliatin.[3] Thirdly, we have sundry references to him in the records of European travellers and merchants, such as Terry, Coryate, Mundy, Drake, Bernier, Manucci and Tavernier: some of these being contemporaries of the Mīrzā and some subsequent to his time. Our fourth source of information—the fullest and most reliable—is the series of letters and reports left by the Jesuit missionaries. Of Zū'lqarnain's father we hear in a letter of 1598

The original authorities

from Father Jerome Xavier, and of Zū'lqarnain himself in a letter from Father Xavier, dated September 6, 1604. We have notices also in the Annual Letters of 1619, 1620 and 1624 from Goa; in the report of April 1649 by Father John Maracci, and in several letters from Fathers Corsi, de Castro, Andrade, Ceschi and others. We have also two very important special reports: one by Father Corsi written in May 1628 on the foundation of the Agra College by Mīrzā Zū'lqarnain, a document in the possession of the Society of Jesus and published for the first time in Father Hosten's Memoir: the other by Father Antony Botelho on the history and condition of Christianity in Mogor in 1648–1654, a considerable part of which relates to Mīrzā Zū'lqarnain. The British Museum possesses the original of this latter report as well as a full Latin abstract; and translations from these also are published in the Memoir by Father Hosten. All these various sources of information—some of which had not before been made public—are fully placed before us in Father Hosten's Memoir, and they reveal to us the career of a very unusual and fascinating personality.

Sikandar the father of Zū'lqarnain

Zū'lqarnain was the son of a merchant from Aleppo who had settled in India. The name of the merchant appears to have been Hakūb or Yāqūb, but he was ordinarily known as Mīrzā Sikandar. He was usually spoken of as an Armenian, but the term was in those times loosely applied to all Eastern Christians, and a near relative of his is spoken of by the Jesuits as a 'Chaldaean.'[4] Whatever his nationality, he soon acquired great favour at Court. His wife was a Christian named Juliana and on her death, probably shortly before 1598, he was incited by Akbar to marry her sister. This proposal horrified the Fathers who were at the Court, and they protested with great boldness and persistence in the presence of Akbar himself. We are informed that with some difficulty Akbar was induced to support a request to the Pope for a dispensation; this was received in due course, but in the meantime the marriage was duly carried out, and during Akbar's reign Sikandar maintained his high position.[5] In 1596 we find an influential Christian at Court, probably Sikandar, supplying precious cloths to ornament the chapel of the Fathers at Lahore,[6] and in 1604 we hear of his having relieved the wants of released Portuguese prisoners on their way to Cambay.[7] Jahāngīr, after his succession in 1605, attempted without success to make him a Muslim, and we thenceforward hear little or nothing of him until shortly before his death in 1613. He had by that time received his dispensation, and both he and his wife were admitted in 1611 to the Sacraments. He was much with the Jesuits in these later days and large sums were dispensed by him in charity and for the support of the church. When he died he was buried with much ceremony in the Christian cemetery at Agra, and in the ensuing cold weather his body was removed to a burial-place which he had reserved for himself in Lahore. The King waived his privilege of attaching the whole property of the deceased, and his widow and children were well provided for subject to the conditions of his will.[8] We have full and interesting details regarding the will, which included, among other items, the bequest of Rs. 2000 for the church and Christians of Lahore, of Rs. 4000 for the church and Christians of Agra, and of Rs. 3000 for a grave for himself with a chapel.[9]

Sikandar had two sons by his wife Juliana: Mīrzā Zū'lqarnain and Mīrzā Sikandar, born probably in 1592 and 1595 respectively.

Zu'lqarnain's career

The Armenian historian tells us that when Zū'lqarnain was a small child Akbar saw him in Kashmīr, and being much pleased with the child's appearance he adopted him, with his father's consent, on the understanding that there would be no interference with his religion.[10] Others have gone so far as to allege that Zū'lqarnain was Akbar's own son.[11] However this may be, the boy was at an early age an inmate of the zanāna and was brought up by one of Akbar's queens with the young princes.[12] He was kindly treated by the King in public and had free access both to the palace and to the Fathers.[13] All went well until the death of Akbar, but there was temporary trouble in 1606 after the accession of Jahāngīr, who, for the first few months of his reign, adopted a strong pro-Muslim policy. That King, in one of his savage moods, insisted on the conversion of the two boys, then aged fourteen and eleven respectively, and we are given by the Fathers a harrowing account of the pathetic resistance of the boys, of their being cruelly beaten, and of their ultimate submission to circumcision and the repetition of the Kalma, or confession of Islām. When all was over, however, they still professed Christianity and the fickle Jahāngīr praised them for doing so.[14] Not only so, but he soon advanced the elder son, Zū'lqarnain, to posts of dignity. There can be little doubt that Zū'lqarnain was early made collector of the salt revenues of Sāmbhar in Rājputāna (probably in succession to his father), and that he was the 'noble and generous Christian of the Armenian race' who gave twenty rupees to the eccentric English traveller Coryate at Ajmīr in 1616.[15] He is mentioned by the Fathers in 1619 as governor of 'a certain province,' doubtless Sāmbhar, with more than 200 Christians in his service and with two Fathers in constant residence as chaplains.[16] From the Persian Memoirs of Jahāngīr he appears to have been at first in charge of the salt works at Sāmbhar and subsequently (about the year 1621) to have been put in civil and criminal charge of the Sarkār or District of that name.[17] In 1623 he applied to be transferred to Ajmīr, apparently in the same capacity (namely as Faujdār of the Sarkār), but although he spent 80,000 rupees at Court in pressing his claims he failed to get the appointment. When, however, the rebel army of Prince Khurram advanced on Sāmbhar, the Mīrzā remained strictly loyal and withdrew with a considerable force to the camp of Jahāngīr, who rewarded him with additional rank and salary.[18] Four years later, Prince Khurram succeeded to the throne as Shāh Jahān and the Mīrzā's fortunes seem, naturally enough, to have declined. Either in 1627 or shortly before, he appears to have been transferred to Bahraich, or possibly Gorakhpur, or both, whence he was recalled in 1632 to Agra.[19] He was still at Agra in November 1633 and at Lahore with the King in 1634.[20] He suffered severely during Shāh Jahān's anti-Christian outburst of 1633–1635, but was shortly afterwards restored to his old position; and in June 1636 we hear of his being with the Army at Aurangābād in the Deccan.[21] By 1640 he was again in some degree of favour, and in January 1642 he left Agra to serve with Sultān Shujā' in Bengal. In 1648 he was again in Agra and with Father Botelho watched from a balcony the spectacular progress which Shāh Jahān made towards his new capital at Delhi.[22] He held at this time the rank of 500 with 300 horse, and is described shortly afterwards as Governor of Lahore. He followed the King at one time or another to Bengal, Kābul, Lahore and Multān. In 1649 he was restored to his old post at Sāmbhar, but he resigned the service two years later and lived the rest of his life in retirement.[23]

His piety

His career, as above described, is on lines very similar to those of many officials of the Mogul Empire of the day; but it is of interest to find a career of this kind available to one who was both of foreign origin and an open professor of Christianity. From an early period in life he had attached himself to the Roman Catholic form of faith, and he generally had one or two of the Fathers appointed to his suite; so much so, that we find Sāmbhar looked on as a Jesuit 'Residence' along with Agra and Lahore. Among those who were thus with him at various times were Fathers Corsi, de Castro, Ceschi and Morando: the last-named, indeed, being his chaplain and tutor to his children for as long as twenty-two years, of which sixteen years were at a stretch.[24] Zū'lqarnain was regular in his attendance at Mass, and when travelling with the King heard Mass daily in his tent. Every day, we are told, he recited Our Lady's Rosary ; he was strict in the observance of Lent, he took the discipline on Fridays and he went frequently to confession.[25] He had a most punctilious conscience and kept with him a note-book in which he entered up his sins as they occurred.[26] When his infant child died he showed pious resignation, and when his wife was in the pains of childbirth he recovered her from imminent peril by hanging round her neck a cross studded with relics.[27] He was a student of such portions of the Scripture as were available for him in Persian, such as the Gospels and the Psalms : and he is known to have made a copy of the Gospels in Persian with his own hand for his personal use.[28] He started with great zeal a lay association or Sodality of Our Lady which under his auspices was well supported, and he encouraged by prizes the instruction of children in the Catechism.[29] In every way he presented a pattern life, and in the eyes of the Jesuits he was the ideal of a Christian in high places.

His charities

His position did not exempt him from the ill-treatment to which officials in those days were exposed, and his religion accentuated the difficulties of his position. He was apparently much pressed from time to time to become a Muslim.[30] In the troubles of 1633, following the capture of Hūglī, he was summoned to the palace at Agra, and was imprisoned until he had paid six lakhs of rupees. Even after this his house and garden were minutely searched for treasure, and he had to pay, so we are told, a further two lakhs of rupees before he and the Fathers were left alone. This payment reduced him temporarily to poverty, and the Fathers were constrained to help him by returning to him a golden chalice which he had presented to their church.[31] Throughout his career he remained in close alliance with the Fathers, and indeed he had a baptismal name of 'Belchior,' or 'Don Gonçalo,' and he was spoken of by the Fathers as 'our brother.' He showed them the greatest respect, sending escorts to meet them when they visited his territory. When Father Matthew de Payva was buried in Agra in November 1633 he helped to carry the coffin. When anxiety was caused in 1651 by the eccentricities of the Bishop of Chrysopolis, Zū'lqarnain was much distressed and made personal and violent protests (we are told that he was 'naturally irritable') to the King to protect Father Busi from persecution.[32] The Fathers who lived with him, and sometimes others also, were maintained by him at his own cost. His charity was conducted on a sumptuous scale.

When there was trouble in 1614 between the Portuguese and the Mogul authorities and the Fathers ceased for a time to obtain subventions from the King, Zū'lqarnain stepped into the breach and not only supported the Fathers but supplied alms for numerous poor Christians.[33] He was constantly maintaining needy Christians and sending alms to the Fathers for distribution among them. When two Portuguese arrived at Sāmbhar in 1623 on a journey from Bengal to Jerusalem he provided them with an escort and two horses and two hundred rupees apiece.[34] When a hurricane in 1616 devastated the Bombay coast, he sent 6000 rupees to repair a church. On the occasion of a famine about 1620, he supported numbers of starving people, and much of his help was given anonymously through others.[35] In one day he is said to have given 5000 rupees for the release of certain captives, and when the Portuguese were brought in captivity from Hūglī to Agra in 1633 he was instrumental in obtaining the liberation of many of them. Under his father's will he paid considerable sums to beneficiaries in Jerusalem, Aleppo, Goa, Agra and Lahore, amounting to some 25,000 rupees in all; he had also paid 200 per mensem to the mission for many years; he had given 20,000 for the endowment of the College; and in addition to this it was calculated in 1628 that he had given over 40,000 rupees, in cash or kind, to the purposes of the Jesuit Mission. He fully earned the title which was commonly applied to him of 'Father of the Christians of Mogor.'[36]

The endowment of the Agra College

Of his charities the most prominent was the foundation of the College or 'Collegium inchoatum' at Agra: an institution which was only slightly educational in its character and which served mainly as the chief 'residentia' or centre of the Mogor Mission.[37] To meet the expenses of the Fathers in a manner which would not subject them to the caprices of the Mogul sovereign, he was persuaded by Father Corsi in 1619 to provide an endowment from villages in Portuguese territory. With the money provided—27,000 rupees—Father Joseph de Castro negotiated the purchase of two such villages in Bombay, apparently Vadala and Parel. We have varying information as to the income thus derived, but it is clear that the villages provided a substantial sum for the maintenance of the Fathers and of the poorer Christians in Agra. Efforts had been made to obtain from the General of the Society a formal diploma recognizing Zū'lqarnain as the 'Founder' of the College, and though there was some confusion in the correspondence owing to the loss of some ships at sea, and we do not hear of the actual receipt of any such diploma, the Jesuits were satisfied that the application had been approved. On the failure of the Tibet Mission, about 1640, the revenue of the Agra College was apparently increased by the addition of another similar endowment which had been made by Zū'lqarnain for the Tibet Mission, and the endowments thus amalgamated were found of great value to the Fathers. Neither Zū'lqarnain nor the Fathers could, however, foresee that Parel, with the rest of Bombay, would be made over to the English in 1661. The Jesuits had a considerable amount of property in the Island, and after constant friction between them and the English authorities their possessions were in 1720 finally confiscated to the British Crown. The chapel and residence which had been built in Parel became the nucleus of the British Government House and are now used as a Bacteriological Laboratory. The income from Parel was under suspension from 1665 and the loss of this assistance had a serious effect on the Agra Mission, but if it had not been for the unexpected transfer of Bombay to the British Crown the prescience of Mīrzā Zū'lqarnain and Father Corsi would have secured a substantial revenue to the College for a considerable number of years.[38]

Zū'lqarnain as poet and musician

It is interesting to learn that in addition to his characteristics of piety and liberality, Zū'lqarnain had also a reputation for skill in poetry and music—a form of talent which was always held in special honour among the Moguls. Father Botelho even speaks of him as having 'among the Moors the same reputation as a poet as Camoens has here with us.' He tells us too how on one occasion, when the King had arrived from Lahore, the Prince Dārā Shikoh called out to the Mīrzā: 'Mere bhay (my brother), Mere bhay, my father has just come from Lahore; make a Torpet' (Dhurpad, i.e., a poetic composition)—'in his honour.' 'If your father were to become a Christian,' replied the Mīrzā, 'I should make a very fine hymn in his honour.'[39] We hear from the Indian historians of his composing poems on the name of Shāh Jahān;[40] and the Jesuits attributed the release of Father Busi by that Emperor to the soothing effect of a poem by the Mīrzā.[41] We are also told by Father Ceschi a curious tale, how 'a certain Christian,' whom we know to have been Zū'lqarnain, when disputing with the Moors, called on them to acknowledge his faith if a bird should repeat a song which he sang, and how a bird at that moment appeared to repeat his song. 'He is,' say the Memoirs of Jahāngīr in speaking of Zū'lqarnain, 'an accomplished composer of Hindī songs. His method in this art was correct, and his compositions were frequently brought to my notice and approval.' The '*Amal-i-Sālih* also speaks of his 'rare knowledge of Hindustānī music and melody.'[42]

We do not know the date of Zū'lqarnain's death, but he appears to have died about 1656, when he would have been sixty-four years of age. Nor do we know where he died, or in what Christian cemetery he was buried.[43]

His death

His mother, Juliana (who died in Lahore in or before 1598), is said by Bernier to have been taken into the harem of Jahāngīr, but this statement lacks support. She may, however, have been identical with a Juliana who was in medical charge of Akbar's harem, and to whom we have allusions in the Agra archives and in the Travels of Dr. Wolff.[44] She was the daughter of one 'Abdulhayy, who is described in Jahāngīr's Memoirs as ''Abdulhayy the Armenian who was in the service of the royal harem.'[45] Father Hosten and others identify this 'Abdulhayy with a Mīr, or Khwāja 'Abdulhayy, who is noted in the Persian histories as having been Mīr Adl, or Chief Justice, under Akbar, but doubts have been thrown on the possibility of an Armenian, even under Akbar, having ever been placed in such an office or receiving the appellation of 'Mīr.' Zū'lqarnain's stepmother, the sister of Juliana, together with her two sons apostatized during the troubles of 1632–1633. His brother, however, had a son George, a Christian, of whom we hear as coming from Aleppo to Mogor, and there preparing for a journey to Rome.[46]

The mother of Zū'lqarnain

Zū'lqarnain's wife is spoken of by the Fathers as Helena or Ilena. She died in 1638 and was buried in Lahore in a fine tomb in a garden owned by Zū'lqarnain.[47] The Mīrzā had, in addition to a son who died in infancy, three sons and a daughter, all of whom were married in his lifetime. The daughter was called Clara and we find her some twenty years after Zū'lqarnain's death in the position of a widow dependent for subsistence on a pittance provided by the Agra College.[48] The sons, according to the custom of the time, bore both vernacular and European names: the eldest was Mīrzā Observam or John Baptist; the second, Mīrzā Īrij or Gaspar; and the third, Mīrzā Dāniāl or Michael. We know little of them except that the first two sons died during their father's lifetime. Of the third, who was at times ill-balanced in mind, we are told a curious tale. He had fallen away to Mohammedanism but, recognizing his error, 'he felt intensely grieved and making a very big cross he took it upon his shoulder and, with a rope round his neck, dragged it about the streets of the

His wife and children

City of Delhi, confessing his sin aloud and begging God's mercy.' An arresting and pathetic picture.[49]

Possible descendants

Of further descendants of Zū'lqarnain we know very little. In a field some four miles from Agra on the Pūya Ghāt road is a group of six gravestones, one of which records the death at Delhi on March 12, 1736, of 'Bibi Anna Dessa (de Sa) the great-granddaughter (bizneta) of Mīrzā Gulcarnen.' These graves are mentioned in a paper in the Agra Cathedral Archives dating probably from 1848: they were brought to the notice of the Agra Archæological Society in 1876 and they were visited by Father Hosten in 1912. Three of the gravestones have legible inscriptions, and there are two further inscriptions in the neighbourhood, all of the period 1730–1768, recording three family names, viz. da Cruz, Cardozo and de Sa, and commemorating deaths at Bharatpur, Delhi and Agra. There is in the Padre Santos cemetery another inscription of 1775, in the French language, which may possibly be read as commemorating an Alexander de Sa who died at Agra. How far all these represent descendants of Zū'lqarnain is a matter of conjecture.[50]

NOTES

[1] Vol. II, App. E. The information given there must be looked on as superseded by Father Hosten's later work.

[2] Vol. V, No. 4, pp. 115–194 (quoted in the notes to this chapter as Hosten's Memoir). An article on the subject was presented by Father Hosten to the Asiatic Society of Bengal on July 2, 1913, and appeared in the Calcutta *Statesman* of July 6, 1913.

[3] A translation of the relevant parts of this work is given in Hosten's Memoir, pp. 191–193.

[4] Botelho's *Relation*; Hosten's Memoir, p. 159. The term was not infrequently applied to the Nestorian Christians.

[5] Letter of 1598 from Jerome Xavier (*J.A.S.B.*, LXV, 1896, p. 78). Report by Corsi, 1628: pp. 115 and 133 of Hosten's Memoir. According to Xavier, Sikandar joined the King's religion, the Dīn Ilāhī. See also note on p. 246 of Payne's *Akbar and the Jesuits*.

[6] Letter from J. Xavier of September 8, 1596; Hosten's Memoir, p. 174.

[7] Letter from J. Xavier of September 6, 1604; Hosten's Memoir, p. 116.

[8] See Xavier's letters of 1611 (in the Marsden MSS.) and of September 23, 1613.

[9] Corsi's note of 1628; Hosten's Memoir, pp. 134–135.

[10] Appendix E to Hosten's Memoir.

[11] All Xavier says on this subject is that 'this is known to God.' Letter of September 8, 1596.

[12] Corsi letter of October 15, 1626; *B.P. and P.*, XXXIV, 1927, p. 97.

[13] Letter from J. Xavier of September 8, 1596; Hosten's Memoir, p. 174.

[14] J. Xavier's letter of September 25, 1606, and Corsi's note of 1628.

The story is also given in Guerreiro (IV, p. 152), du Jarric, and Hazart. See Hosten's Memoir, pp. 118–119, 133, and Payne, *Jahangir and the Jesuits*, 1930, pp. 15–23.

[15] Purchas (MacLehose), IV, p. 487 ; Foster, *Early Travels in India*, 1921, p. 267.

[16] Annual Letter of 1619 from Goa ; Hosten's Memoir, p. 124 ; Lualdi, *L'India Orientale soggettata al Vangelo* ; Rome, 1653, pp. 362–363.

[17] Rogers and Beveridge, *Tūzuk-i-Jahāngīrī*, 1914, II, p. 194 ; Hosten's Memoir, p. 130.

[18] Andrade's letter of August 14, 1623.

[19] Letter of Azevedo of 1632 (Wessels, p. 283) and letter of de Castro, November 24, 1632. Hosten's Memoir, pp. 141–143.

[20] 'Amal-i-Sālih (Ind. Off. ed.), I, p. 178 ; Bādshāh-nāma (*Bib. Ind.*), I, p. 446 ; Hosten's Memoir, p. 142, which quotes from H. Beveridge.

[21] Foster, *English Factories in India* (1634–1636), 1911, p. 262.

[22] Letters of de Castro of January 1, 1642, and July 20, 1645 ; Hosten's Memoir, p. 146.

[23] Bādshāh-nāma (*Bib. Ind.*), II, p. 748 ; Botelho's *Relation*, see Hosten's Memoir, pp. 147, 159, 161.

[24] Maracci, *Relation*, 1651, p. 23.

[25] Annual Letter from Goa for 1619 ; Hosten's Memoir, p. 124 ; Maracci, *Relation*, p. 23.

[26] Andrade's letter of August 14, 1623.

[27] Annual Letter from Goa for 1619 ; Hosten's Memoir, pp. 125–126.

[28] Botelho's *Relation*, and Corsi's letter of October 28, 1619.

[29] Annual Letters from Goa for 1619 and 1620 ; Hosten's Memoir, pp. 124 and 126–127.

[30] Cf. Terry, *A Voyage to East India* (1777), pp. 424–425 ; Hosten's Memoir, p. 121.

[31] Botelho's *Relation ;* Hosten's Memoir, p. 161 ; *ib.*, pp. 143–144 ; Letter from Corsi, October 5, 1633, and a letter from de Castro of October 8, 1633 ; cf. *The Travels of Peter Mundy* (Hakluyt ed.), II, pp. 240–241.

[32] Botelho's *Relation ;* Hosten's Memoir, pp. 127, 159, 163–164 ; Annual Letter from Goa for 1620. The story is that in his rage he shook the pillars of the King's litter : and it is told in a different context by Figueredo in his letter of 1735. (*Weltbott*, No. 595). The Mīrzā was in his later days afflicted by gout.

[33] Corsi's note of May 1628 ; Hosten's Memoir, p. 135.

[34] Andrade's letter of August 14, 1623.

[35] Annual Letters from Goa, 1619 and 1620 ; Hosten's Memoir, pp. 125, 128.

[36] Corsi's note of May 1628 ; Hosten's Memoir, pp. 134, 140.

[37] Every ' residence ' in those days had to be affiliated to a College.

[38] See Corsi's note of 1628 ; Hosten's Memoir, pp. 132–141 ; *ib.*, pp. 131, 137. In addition to the revenue received by them from Parel the Jesuits seem to have been allowed to retain 1773 xeraphins, a large part of the revenue of Mahim, as a contribution from the Portuguese Government to provide for the Fathers in Agra. It was one of the charges against Humphry Cooke, the first English Governor of Bombay, that he corruptly allowed this deduction to be continued under English rule. Foster, *English Factories*, 1665–1667, pp. 70–74 ; 1661–1664, pp. 131, 216. See also the detailed statements in the Portuguese Manifesto of 1722 and the Viceroy's letter of January 18, 1727 (Judice Biker,

Collecção de Tratados, Lisbon, 1883, III, pp. 231–234, 330–336 and 343–348).

[39] Botelho's *Relation*. Hosten's Memoir, pp. 161–162. The story is told in a slightly different form in the Annual Report for 1650.

[40] Continuation of Bādshāh-nāma by Wāris. (Brit. Mus.), p. 392, *vide* p. 142 of Hosten's Memoir. He seems to have given some offence in a poem on Delhi in which he gave more praise to God than to his Sovereign. Annual Letter for 1648–1649 ; *J.I.H.*, I, 1922, p. 238 ; cf. *J.I.H.*, VIII, 1929 (Qānūngo), p. 52.

[41] Botelho, letter of January 20, 1652.

[42] See Father Ceschi's letter of September 5, 1651 (Bombay *Examiner*, September 8, 1917, p. 357) ; Rogers and Beveridge, *Tūzuk-i-Jahāngīrī*, 1914, II, 194 ; 'Amal-i-Sālih (Ind. Off. MS.), I, 178 ; Hosten's Memoir, pp. 141, 148, 160–161, 193.

[43] Hosten's Memoir, p. 167.

[44] Bernier's *Travels* (Constable), p. 287, Amsterdam ed., II, p. 81. Her possible relations with a Christian wife of Akbar and with the Bourbon family have been described in Chapter X ; see also Hosten's Memoir, p. 172–173.

[45] Rogers and Beveridge, *Tūzuk-i-Jahāngīrī*, 1914, II, p. 194 ; Hosten's Memoir, p. 130. He is mentioned in one of the MSS. of the Akbarnāma (*Bib. Ind.* translation, III, p. 372) as ''Abdul Hai Faringī.'

[46] Hosten's Memoir, pp. 168, 170–172. The use of the title ' Mīrzā ' for a Christian like Zū'lqarnain is also considered by Mr. Beveridge to be curious, but it seems well authenticated. Zū'lqarnain is also spoken of by the Jesuits as ' Zū'lqarnain Cururim,' but the meaning of the affix is unknown.

[47] Noti is quoted by Blunt (*List of Christian Tombs and Monuments in the United Provinces*, p. 41) as saying that she was an ' Alleman ' : that is probably a German, or a relation of one Joã Aleman, buried at Agra in 1619 ; cf. Hosten's Memoir, p. 180.

[48] Letter of Gregorio Roiz dated 5 July, 1675.

[49] Letter of de Castro of September 1, 1640, and Botelho's *Relation* ; see Hosten's Memoir, pp. 145–146, 161, 164–166. The genealogy (*ib.*, p. 182) is as follows :

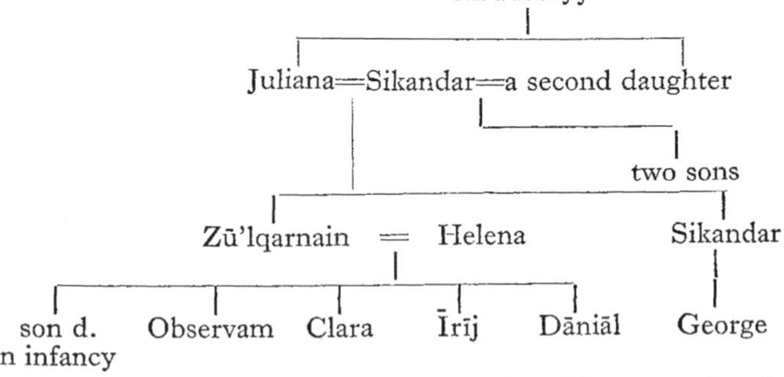

[50] Hosten's Memoir, p. 168 and App. B. The appendix gives a very thorough and interesting account of the various inscriptions. See also pp. 31 and 262 of Blunt's *Christian Tombs and Monuments in the United Provinces* (1911). A Christian called Nūrulla, resident in Delhi, is mentioned in the Jesuit Annual Report of 1678 as a relation of Zū'lqarnain.

CHAPTER XII

DONNA JULIANA DIAZ DA COSTA (D. 1734)

(A CHRISTIAN LADY AT THE MOGUL COURT)

Si inveni gratiam in oculis tuis, o rex, et si tibi placet, dona mihi animam meam pro qua rogo et populum meum pro quo obsecro.

(Esther vii, 3.)

AMONG the personages attached to the Mogul Court in the era following the death of Aurangzeb, one of the most remarkable was a Christian lady known as Juliana Diaz da Costa. Throughout a long life, ending in 1734, she represented the cause of the Christian subjects of the Emperor and maintained a friendly attitude towards the Jesuit Missions.

Sources of our information regarding Juliana Diaz da Costa

For such knowledge as we can obtain of her life we have four main classes of information available:

(i) There are notices of her in the vernacular histories, but these have yet to be explored. According to Mr. Beveridge such notices are very slight, and refer only to the date of her death and the fact that she founded a sarai near Delhi.

(ii) Another source of information is a contemporary account of her life, which is given by Father Ippolito Desideri in a part of his work on Tibet. The bulk of this work was published by Puini in his *Il Tibet* (Rome, 1904), but unfortunately he omitted the account of Juliana, along with all the other portions of the narrative which have no direct bearing on Tibet. This omission has now been rectified by Sir Filippo de Filippi in his translation of Desideri's work.[1]

(iii) We have a certain amount of information regarding her in the description of the Dutchman Ketelaar's Mission to Lahore in 1711–1712, which is given by François Valentyn in his *Oud-en Nieuw Oost-Indiën* (Amsterdam, 1726). A summary of the chief events relating to the Mission and to Juliana's connection with it is given by Father Hosten in the Punjab Historical Society's Journal for 1918, and a detailed account of the Mission (translated by Mrs. Kuenen-Wicksteed and annotated by Dr. Vogel), partly from Valentyn's book and partly from a copy of the official journal of the Mission, will be found in the same Society's Journal for 1929. Similarly, in connection with Juliana's relations with the Portuguese Government between 1710 and 1719, we have an interesting collection of correspondence, published by Mr. Ismael Gracias at Goa in 1907. And there are scattered references to her in the diaries and letters of the English Mission which was at the Mogul Court in 1717.[2]

(iv) Lastly, there are copies in the British Museum and in the Pott Collection of the Library at King's College, Cambridge (bought in 1778 from Colonel Polier, the friend of Warren Hastings), of a Persian manuscript entitled *Ahwāl-i-Bībī Juliana* which was written by one Gaston Brouet (who is probably to be identified with a certain Augustin Bravette)[3] for Colonel J. B. J. Gentil, a French gentleman who held a post of distinction in the Court of the Nawāb of Oudh between 1764 and 1775. And in Gentil's own work, entitled *Mémoire sur l'Indoustan* (Paris, 1822), there is a chapter giving a biography of Juliana. Brouet's memoir is a windy production and Gentil seems to have made little or no use of it in his own book. Indeed, it is not improbable that he never saw it, as it was written not earlier than 1774 and Gentil left Oudh in February 1775. Gentil was himself connected by marriage with the descendants of Juliana and is a respectable authority.[4]

Her father

The father of Juliana was a certain Agostino Dias da Costa. Father Hosten identifies him with a renegade mentioned by Father Botelho as having been brought as a prisoner from Hūglī to Agra in 1633, and with an Agostino Dias who met the adventurer Manucci in Multān shortly before 1659.[5] He appears to have come originally from Cochin and to have entered Mogor by way of Goa and Bengal. He became medical attendant to Prince Muazzam Bahādur Shāh, and died at Golconda not very long before the imprisonment of that prince in March 1686.

Date and place of her birth

There is some difference among the authorities as to the date and place of his daughter Juliana's birth; some saying that she was born in Cochin in 1645, and others that she was born in Bengal after 1663; others that she was born in Agra about 1657. The last of these opinions is supported by data provided by Colonel Gentil and by Father Emmanuel de Figueredo, S.J., and it appears to be approximately correct. Her parents were captured in Hūglī in 1633 and brought to Agra, and the probability is that she was born there.[6]

The historical uncertainties regarding the birth of Juliana

attend also the facts of her early life. Her mother is said by Brouet to have been a slave to a Begam at Agra, but to have been emancipated on her mistress's death and to have died shortly afterwards in the house of the Jesuit Father Antony Magalhaens. Juliana herself was married in her youth, but we have little information as to her husband. The Viceroy of Goa, writing January 11, 1711, to the King of Portugal, speaks of her husband having been sent with her by a previous Viceroy, the Conde de Alvor (1681–1686), to be surgeon to Aurangzeb;[7] while Brouet tells us that Father Antony Magalhaens at Delhi married her to a Frank who was afterwards killed in battle. In any case, we hear no more of her husband. She seems to have soon joined the service of Aurangzeb's wife, the mother of Muazzam Bahādur Shāh, and to have been entrusted with the education of several of the Princes. When Bahādur Shāh and his mother fell into disgrace in 1687, Juliana showed great devotion to their cause, and Brouet tells us wonderful tales of her secretly conveying jewels to and from their residence. It is somewhat strange that Manucci, who was for some years in the entourage of Bahādur Shāh and had access to his zanāna, makes no mention of Juliana, but there seems no doubt that when Bahādur Shāh after several years was restored to favour in 1694, she received appropriate rewards from him. When Aurangzeb died in 1707, and Bahādur Shāh contested the throne against his brother, she supported him with her advice and even attended him to battle, so we are told, on the same elephant. On his succession to the throne in 1707, Bahādur Shāh showered rewards upon her. She was given the 'rank of 4000': she obtained 1000 rupees per month and was able to bestow a lakh of rupees on the Jesuit Mission at Delhi. She was given the house of Dārā Shikoh in that city, and the revenue of four villages in the neighbourhood. She had a following of five to six thousand people and two elephants carrying two standards with white crosses on a red ground.[8] She was also given special titles which are variously recorded as 'Khānum,' 'Bībī,' and 'Fidwī Du'āgo Juliana.' In spite of this good fortune, we are assured by Gentil that she remained simple and frugal in her life; that she took no presents, and that she protected the Christian community and even brought numbers of them from Goa to Delhi.[9]

Her career

Of her interpositions in favour of the Christians we are told by Father Figueredo, who wrote in 1735 to Queen Anna Maria of Portugal that Juliana had by her powerful mediation persuaded the Emperor (Aurangzeb) to exempt the Christians from taxes to which

Her assistance to the Jesuits

even the Mohammedans were subject. So far as the jazia, or tax on non-Moslims, is concerned, we have documentary evidence of her activities in certain parwānas published by Father Felix, O.C., in 1916. Exemption had been given to certain Padres in Agra by parwānas of Aurangzeb and Shāh 'Ālam (Bahādur Shāh), and we find that in subsequent reigns Juliana had directly interposed by drawing the attention of the authorities to those old parwānas and calling for their renewal. In a parwāna of the sixth year of Farukhsiyar (1718) it is said that—' according to the statement submitted by Jalīna (ba mūjib fard guzrānīda-i Jalīna)' the Padres, ' darveshes of the Christian sect who dwell at Akbarābād and in the imperial city ' had been exempted from jazia, and that she hopes (ummedwār ast) that the exemption will be continued, and that they accordingly will be still exempted. In another, of the seventh year of Muhammad Shāh (1726), the same formula is used and the same exemption granted at the desire of ' Jalīna.'[10] Apart from procuring exemptions of this character she also herself gave 50,000 xerafins (say 75,000 rupees) to the Jesuits for the endowment of their mission after the loss of Parel.[11] She also provided large sums for the poor in Tibet and lent money to Desideri's party for their expenses on their journey to that country in 1714.[12]

During her ascendancy there was considerable negotiation between the Moguls and the Portuguese, and as might be expected she gave strong support to the Portuguese interests. Some interesting correspondence was published by Mr. Gracias in 1907, which shows the prominent part which she took in the Portuguese relations with the Mogul Court between 1710 and 1719. There are in the correspondence letters from the Viceroy at Goa to Donna Juliana, and there is even a letter from Juliana to the King of Portugal. She is described by the Viceroy as ' boa Christã ' and ' virtuozissima,' and much is said of her influence with the Mogul and her assistance to the Portuguese interests, and especially to the Portuguese Embassy which was sent to the Mogul Court under Father José da Silva. Reference is also made to the help given by her son-in-law or nephew, Diogo Mendes, and her grandson, Joseph Borges da Costa, as well as to the mediation of João de Abreu of the Society of Jesus.[13]

To the Portuguese

Her patronage was not, however, confined to Catholic nations, and when the Dutch Mission under Johan Josua Ketelaar came in 1711 to the Court of Bahādur Shāh she was equally gracious to the Dutch. On arriving at Khānkhānān Sarāi near Lahore on December 10, 1711, the Mission

To the Dutch

received a present of fruit from the Lady Juliana, and when they drove into Lahore with an Armenian bishop and some Jesuit fathers, they met a closed carriage containing Juliana, 'the Governess of the Emperor's seraglio,' and four chief wives of the Emperor, who had come to see the procession. In the subsequent negotiations Juliana was constantly in communication with the Mission. She came to visit them in their garden, entertained them to breakfast, organized receptions for them, and gave them current information and advice regarding the progress of their business. In the midst of all these proceedings, however, Bahādur Shāh suddenly died—'departed this life,' as the chronicler says, 'to hasten to a corner in the mansions of Eternal Mercy'—and after a period of turmoil, Jahāndār Shāh secured possession of the throne. Ketelaar paid his respects to the new King and attended on his favourite, Lāl Kanwar, who was accompanied by the Lady Juliana. We are told that Juliana, who was then fifty-five years of age, wished to retire to a convent at Goa, but this was not permitted and she remained with the Court, retaining, as the writer Valentyn says, the authority and influence of another Madame de Maintenon.[14]

Under Farukhsiyar and Muhammad Shāh

She seems to have temporarily lost her influence in the early days of Jahāndār's successor, Farukhsiyar (1713–1719), but when that Emperor became ill he was placed in her charge, and she is said by Gentil to have cured him after calling together a number of experts from among the Christians. Whether this implies that she was in any way responsible for the historic cure of the Emperor in 1715 by the Englishman William Hamilton, is entirely a matter of speculation. Though she is mentioned several times in the papers connected with the English Mission to which Hamilton was attached, it is chiefly in connection with the influence she exercised in favour of the Portuguese and Dutch, and there is nothing in these papers to show that she was specially instrumental in employing Hamilton or helping the English Mission.[15]

After the death of Farukhsiyar in 1719, Juliana was in attendance on Qudsia Begam, the mother of the new King, Muhammad Shāh. Under the new regime she was confirmed in the name 'Juliana' as a hereditary title of honour, and it was her duty, we are told, as the bearer of that title, to place the crown on the head of the new King.

Of the outward appearance of Donna Juliana we have no clear record. In Valentyn's book there is a print representing her as wearing a cross on her necklace and crosses on her ear-rings. The picture bears the conventional characteristics of European engravings of the period and need not be taken too seriously as a portrait. She is represented in the picture as a well-nourished lady of about forty years of age, clothed in semi-Oriental vestments, and standing with one arm outstretched before a background of palm trees.[16]

Her appearance

In July or August 1734 she died at Delhi and, according to Gentil, was buried in the Christian church at Agra: but we have no trace of her tomb.[17] The house of Dārā Shikoh, which she occupied, seems to have suffered much damage during the massacre by Nādir Shāh in 1739,[18] and Gentil tells us that it was sold in the reign of Ahmad Shāh to Nawāb Safdar Jang. The villages assigned to Juliana near Okla in the neighbourhood of Delhi, appear to have passed into the hands of the family of D'Eremao, to which allusion has been made in Chapter X. We are told that they were bequeathed some fifty years ago to the Franciscan Mission at Agra by an old couple (probably of the same family) who claimed to be descendants from the Lady Juliana, and the Mission have now a church and settlement (called Masīhgarh) in the vicinity of certain ruins which are thought to represent a house once occupied by Juliana. There was also in the same neighbourhood a sarai called after Juliana, of which portions are—or till lately were—still visible.[19]

Her properties

Although Juliana was married, we know little or nothing of her direct descendants. That she had sons is shown by the terms of the deeds by which she held her lands near Delhi, which are there recorded as having been granted to 'Juliana and her sons'; but we know nothing of them. We hear, too, of her having seven grandchildren (netos), but it is doubtful if the term refers to direct descendants. One so-called grandson, called Joseph Borges da Costa, was honoured by the King of Portugal in 1715 with the exceptional distinction of 'the habit of Christ,' but we know nothing more of him. He had a brother-in-law (or near relation) called Mendes, a name which we meet several times in the accounts of the sixteenth and seventeenth centuries in Northern India: and his own name of Borges suggests a connection with the Venetian lapidary, Hortensio Bronzoni, who married the widow of a Borges and who is buried at Agra alongside of several members of the Borges family.[20] Donna Juliana is also credited with a granddaughter (neta) who married one Joseph Tavares: who may possibly have been connected with

Her descendants and connections

Pedro Tavares who founded Hūglī in 1580 and with Lucretia Tavares, who was buried at Agra in 1660.[21]

Juliana had a sister, Angelique, married to a Dom Velho de Castro, who held a high position at Court; and when their daughter Isabella married Dom Diogo Mendes de Castro, to whom allusion has been made in an earlier part of this chapter, Bahādur Shāh himself crowned the bridegroom with a nuptial ornament. Lucia, one of Isabella's daughters, married Sebastian Velho, who was killed by the soldiers of Ahmad Shāh Abdālī in 1761, and on his death the family migrated to Faizābād. In 1772 Theresa, the daughter of Lucia, married Colonel Gentil, the biographer of Juliana, and when Colonel Gentil returned to France both Lucia and Theresa went with him. Theresa died at Bagnols in 1778, leaving a son, and Lucia died at Versailles as late as January 2, 1806.[22]

NOTES

[1] Published 1932 in the Broadway Travellers' Series.

[2] See *J.P.H.S.*, VII, 1918, pp. 45–49, and X, 1929, pp. 1–94; Gracias, *Una dona portugueza na Corte do Grão Mogol* (Nova Goa, 1907), pp. 109-172; and C. R. Wilson, *Early Annals of the English in India*, Vol. II, Part II.

[3] See Émile Barbé, *Le Nabab René Madec* (Paris, 1844), p. 38; and Hosten, "European Art at the Mogul Court," *J.U.P.H.S.*, III, May 1922, Part I, pp. 119–123. Brouet's manuscript, translated by Professor E. H. Palmer, was published in Maltebrun, *Nouvelles Annales de Voyage*, sixième série, Vol. 186 (1865), pp. 161–184.

[4] Gentil's information about Juliana is abstracted in Sir E. Cotton's article on 'The Memoirs of Col. Gentil' in *B.P. and P.*, October-December 1927, pp. 78–81. An article on the story of Juliana was published by C. R. Wilson in the *Church Quarterly Review* for October 1900, and a very useful sketch of her life was read before the Royal Asiatic Society in 1903 by H. Beveridge and afterwards published by him in *East and West* (Bombay), in June 1903. Juliana is the main subject of Gracias' book *Una dona portugueza*, above cited, which was published at Goa in 1907; and of a valuable pamphlet by Father Noti, S.J., entitled *Donna Juliana*, published in 1919 by the Xaverius-Verlag at Aachen. She is also dealt with in an article by Prof. Soares, entitled 'A Catholic Princess at the Mogul Court,' in the *S. Xavier's College Magazine*, Bombay, February 1922; and in another by Father Heras, S.J., in the *Bombay Samāchār*, October 1925, entitled 'A Portuguese Lady at the Mogul Court'; as well as in a note by the same author in the *Bombay Historical Society's Journal*, March 1928, p. 93.

[5] *Storia do Mogor*, I, pp. lxxix, 363–365; *Mem. As. Soc., Bengal*, 1916 (Hosten), pp. 163 and 189; *J.P.H.S.*, 1918, VII (Hosten), p. 39.

Heras in *Bombay Samāchār*, October 17, 1925, disputes the identification of Juliana's father with Botelho's renegade and considers that the husband of Juliana, but not her father, received a medical appointment at the Court. See also de Filippi's *Desideri*, p. 64.

[6] The 1645 date is supported by a letter published in Gracias' book, p. 163; and the date after 1663 would follow from one of Valentyn's statements. Hosten decides in favour of 1657: see *J.P.H.S.*, VII, 1918, pp. 39–40. Figueredo's remarks are given in Stöcklein, *Weltbott*, No. 595.

[7] Gracias, op. cit., p. 127.

[8] These standards are described on p. 374 and portrayed on p. 367 of Gentil's *Mémoire*. Angelo Legrenzi in describing the march from Burhānpur to Delhi with Shāh Muazzam reverses the colouring of the flags: he says, 'Noi Europei come arrollati sotto lo standardo di Christo inalborammo l'insegne della Croce roseggiante in bianca tella.' (*Il Pellegrino nell' Asia*, 1705, II, p. 230.)

[9] These imported Christians, according to Gentil (*Mémoire*, I, p. 21), preserved some interesting traditions regarding the relations between the Jesuits and Akbar.

[10] *J.P.H.S.*, V, 1916 (Felix), pp. 33–36; Figueredo, in *Weltbott*, No. 595.

[11] *Mem. A.S.B.*, V, 1916, p. 137; Judice Biker, *Collecção de Tratados*, Lisbon, 1886, XII, p. 223.

[12] Letters from Desideri, dated December 30, 1713, and August 21, 1714.

[13] Gracias, *Una dona portugueza na Corte do Grão Mogol*, Nova Goa, 1907, pp. 109–172; Judice Biker, *Collecção de Tratados*, Lisbon, 1884, V, pp. 310, 314–316; cf. *J.P.H.S.*, 1918, Vol. VII (Hosten), p. 42. Diogo Mendes may be the man of that name who provided Father Tieffenthaler (see Chapter VII) with an account of the invasion of Nādir Shāh.

[14] See abstract from Valentyn in *J.P.H.S.*, 1918, Vol. VII (Hosten), pp. 45–49, and *J.P.H.S.*, X, 1929; Irvine, *Late Moguls*, I, pp. 147–156. Jahāndār Shāh was considered by some to have owed his success in battle to the prayers of the Christians (see letter of January 14, 1714, from the Portuguese Viceroy; Gracias, *Una dona portugueza*, 1907, p. 125).

[15] C. R. Wilson, *Early Annals of the English in Bengal*, Vol. III, Part I, pp. 178, 195, 217, 291. In Mr. Beveridge's paper, however, of which an abstract is given in *J.R.A.S.*, 1903, January, p. 244, and in *J.P.H.S.*, V, 1916 (Felix), p. 30, it is stated that Donna Juliana was instrumental in the employment of Hamilton.

[16] The portrait is reproduced in *Bombay Hist. Society's Journal*, 1928, p. 96, and in Noti's pamphlet of 1919, and in de Filippi's *Desideri* (1932).

[17] The date given by the Indian historian is Rabī' I, 1147 A.H. (July 31–August 29, A.D. 1734); cf. *J.P.H.S.*, 1916 (Felix), p. 30. Gentil gives 1732 as the date of death.

[18] *Lettres édifiantes et curieuses*, Vol. IV, Paris, 1780, p. 260. The house is described as 'the house of a Christian Lady, celebrated by her piety and much esteemed by the Emperor and the Court.' The reference seems to be to Juliana (then dead) or to her niece. See Hosten, *Jesuit Missionaries in Northern India*, 1907, p. 40.

[19] See 'Franciscan Annals of India,' Agra, quoted by Hosten in *J.U.P.H.S.*, 1922, Vol. III, Part I, p. 121; see also Chapter X above.

[20] 'European Art in the Mogul Court,' by Hosten, *J.U.P.H.S.*, III, May 1922, Part I, pp. 117–118.

[21] Cf. Annual Letter for 1648–1649, translated by Hosten, *J.I.H.*, 1922, pp. 235, 248.

[22] The bewildering subject of the ascertained or possible relations of Juliana is attacked in considerable detail by Hosten in *J.P.H.S.*, VII, 1918, pp. 39–49. See also his 'European Art at the Mogul Court,' *J.U.P.H.S.*, III, 1922, pp. 115–119, *re* the Borges, and pp. 123–125 *re* the Mendes. See also Beveridge in *East and West* (Bombay), June 1907.

CHAPTER XIII

CULTURE AND LANGUAGE

Dominus dedit mihi linguam eruditam.
(Is. l, 4.)

AMONG the religious orders the Jesuits had the reputation of being the most advanced in secular learning. They devoted special attention to the education of the young and they were themselves subjected to a severe course of theological and general training in the Colleges of the Society. Their standard as disputants was high and we find the English community at Surat in 1615 complaining of the incompetence of their Protestant chaplains to 'defend God's cause against these cunning Jesuits.'[1] There were no doubt men of inferior education in the Indian Mission field, but the bulk of the Jesuits in Mogor were persons whose proficiency in the learning of the day was above the average, and we find in their writings not a few traces of the influence of classical and contemporary literature. Most of them, whatever their nationality, so far adapted themselves to their surroundings as to write when occasion required in the Portuguese language; we have letters in Portuguese, for instance, from Spaniards like Father Jerome Xavier and from Italians like Fathers Aquaviva and Corsi. They were, of course, in all cases able to read and speak the Latin language; but they were probably not well grounded in Greek; the incursions at any rate which Father Monserrate makes into that tongue in his *Commentarius* do not display more than a rudimentary knowledge of it. As regards the extent of their reading in the classical languages it would be difficult to generalize, but it is interesting to note in the case of Father Monserrate the names of the authors whom he claims to have consulted in writing his book. These include, in addition to the Bible and its commentaries, such ancient writers as Josephus, S. Jerome, Strabo, Ptolemy, Pliny, Trogus Pompeius, Apollodorus, Solinus and Lucan. Of mediæval and renaissance writers he specifies Vincent of Beauvais (1190–1264), the author of the *Speculum Historiale*; S. Antonino of Forciglione, Archbishop

European literature utilized by the Jesuits

of Florence (1389–1459), the writer of a *Summa Historiarum*; Pope Pius II (Æneas Sylvius Piccolomini, 1405–1464), who wrote Commentaries of his own times; Marcus Antonius Cocceius Sabellicus (1436–1506), the historian of Venice; Raphael Volaterraneus or Maffeius (1451–1552), known for his histories; Paolo Giovio (1483–1522), who among many other histories wrote a History of the Turks; and Juan de Barros (1496–1570), the historian of the Portuguese in Asia. He also acknowledges the assistance of other works 'of lesser note,' including the *Sylva* of Pedro Mexia (1496–1552), which contains information taken from Giovanni Battista Egnazio's book on the origin of the Turks (1473–1553); the *Collectanea* of Fulgosus, the *Geography* of Pius II, the *Life of Boniface IX* by Platina, otherwise known as Barthelemy de' Sacchi (1421–1481); the *Chronicles* of Palmieri (1405–1475), and the Turkish history of the Florentine Cambini published in 1538—and in addition the account of Tamerlane (printed in 1582) by Ruy Gonzalez de Clavijo, who travelled in Central Asia in 1403–1406.

European books in possession of the Jesuits

When the Jesuit Fathers first visited Akbar in 1580, their earliest present to him was a huge and sumptuous copy of the Bible in four languages, well bound and gilt—molto ben legata ed indorata[2]—in seven volumes. This was the Royal Polyglot (in Hebrew, Chaldee, Latin and Greek) then recently published, which was edited by Montanus and printed at Antwerp by Plantyn in 1569–1572 for King Philip II.[3] This work was subsequently returned by Akbar to the Fathers and it had a curious history, being said to have been in the hands of Catholics in Lucknow until the time of the Mutiny of 1857.[4] In one way or another a fair number of European books came into Akbar's possession, and in 1595 he not only showed them all to the members of the Third Mission, but also handed over to them for their own use such of these books as they desired.[5] The books thus taken over included the Royal Bible above mentioned, together with other Bibles and Concordances, the *Summa* and other works of S. Thomas Aquinas, the works of the scholastic writer Domingo de Soto, of S. Antonino of Forciglione,[6] of Pope Sylvester (d. 1003) and Cardinal Cajetan (1470–1534), the *Chronica of S. Francis*, the *History of the Popes*, the *Laws of Portugal*, the *Commentaries of Alfonso Albuquerque*, the writings of the Brazil missionary Juan Espeleta of Navarre (a relative of Jerome Xavier, who died in 1555), the *Exercitia Spiritualia* of S. Ignatius, the Constitutions of the Society, and a Latin Grammar written by the Jesuit Emmanuel

Alvarez (1526–1582).[7] Of several of these Akbar had duplicates.

European books met with in India

The books detailed by Father Monserrate as his authorities in the *Commentarius* were doubtless consulted by him for the most part at Goa. How far the Jesuits in Mogor were able to keep up an adequate library of European books it is impossible to say. They seem, however, to have been looked on as the natural repository of such books as were left by Europeans dying in the country, and we read of a Milanese gunner who died in Lahore in 1597 leaving all his books to the Fathers, including some technical works on the founding of cannon and on siege operations—'artis fusoriae praecepta artemque diversorum operum ad bellicos usus continentes, in quibus erat et illud, quibus artibus Mogori Diensem Armuzianamque arcem traderet.'[8] We hear of the Jesuits at Lahore exhibiting their books to the Governor of that place in 1604 or 1605,[9] and we know that in course of time they possessed a handsome library at Agra.[10] It is interesting to note that when Sir Thomas Roe in 1616 wished to give an acceptable memento to Father Corsi he presented him with copies of the works of the Spanish Jesuit Azor (1532–1603) and of the celebrated Italian Cardinal Bellarmine (1542–1621).[11] European books were also sometimes met with in the hands of persons outside the Mission. Paolo Zamān, for instance, the Persian Christian who was in India in the middle of the seventeenth century, possessed several Latin books.[12] This same Paolo Zamān was shown by Father Busi at Delhi a copy of the Jesuit Father Ricci's Account of China (the *De Christiana expeditione apud Sinas*), and on the strength of the information contained in this work Paolo Zamān himself wrote in Persian a *Tārīkh-i-Chīn* or History of China.[13] Stray copies of European books would also find their way into the hands of Indians by whom they were kept as curiosities or used for strange purposes. In 1648, for example, we are told of a Rājā who kept with great care a small Portuguese book which he asked the Fathers to explain to him, hoping to find that it contained the rules of alchemy ; and of his great disappointment when it turned out to be a manual of devotion ; 'no doubt,' says the chronicler, 'it was a golden little book which promised great treasures to the King if he abided by its precepts, but he rendered himself unworthy of the heavenly treasure of the Gospel.'[14] And similarly we hear of a Brahmin fortune-teller who used for his incantations a book in Roman characters which he could not read and which turned out on examination to be a copy of the Office of the Blessed Virgin.[15]

As mentioned above, the Fathers had at Agra a good library and it is described as containing a number of books written in Oriental languages by the fathers themselves. During the persecutions in the time of Shāh Jahān orders were issued that the books in the Agra College should be burnt, but the orders were only partially carried out, and the Fathers were able to rescue a number of their books.[16] It may be to this incident that Father Figueredo refers when he writes in 1735 that the first and original documents of the Library had been looted by the Muslims at some time previous to his writing.[17] There must have been a library at Delhi also, for Tieffenthaler tells us that in 1759 the Afghans of Ahmad Shāh Abdālī looted the Fathers' property with the exception of the books—exceptis libris Persicis, Arabicis et Europeis.[18] Apart from their own title-deeds—some of which have survived in Agra to the present day—the Fathers seem to have taken what opportunities they had to acquire Oriental documents of a religious character. It will be noticed in the following chapter how on the death of a Nestorian Archbishop on his way from Persia to Lahore, Father Pinhero possessed himself of his books, including a Persian translation of the Gospels; and how the Fathers in Agra in 1604 received Persian translations of various portions of the Holy Scriptures from the learned Florentine, Giambattista Vechiete. In the later days of the Mission, too, some curious Oriental books would from time to time come to the notice of the Fathers. In 1746, for example, Qāzī showed Father Strobl a copy of a book called *The History of the Prophets*—'full of absurd fables.'[19] In 1747 a faqīr brought to the same Father a Persian book by Farīd on the practice of austerities—'it had some good things in it, but also a number of silly ones.'[20] And in 1748 a Sūfī came to him with a small Persian book which Strobl describes as 'the Alcoran of the Sūfīs.'[21] To what extent the Fathers admitted books of this type into their libraries we do not know, but it is something to find that they had the curiosity to interest themselves in them.

Oriental books seen by the Jesuit missionaries

It was recognized that a missionary in Mogor should if possible acquire a knowledge of three languages, 'Hindustani,' Arabic and Persian.[22]

Knowledge of Oriental languages

By 'Hindustani' was meant the spoken language of the mass of the people. 'Their vulgar speech,' we are told, 'is called Indostan.'[23] The term probably included the form of speech known as Urdū,[24] but it was ordinarily employed to designate the group of languages spoken of as Hindī and the English chaplain, Terry, in describing it states that it is written (as Hindī is written) from left to right.[25] The Jesuits in speaking of 'Hindustani' had in their minds the language or languages spoken outside official circles, and as the higher officials were almost exclusively Muslims the word was used with the implication that the speaker of 'Hindustani' would ordinarily be a Hindu. We find Father Rudolf Aquaviva, for instance, suggesting in 1582 the foundation of a School in Goa to teach converts, the Muslims in Persian and the Hindus in 'Hindustani.'[26] The earlier missionaries, though chiefly occupied with Persian, did not neglect to learn the vernacular, and we hear of Father Corsi shortly after his arrival in Mogor studying 'the Hindustani language.'[27] Even in the earliest days of the Mission the Fathers introduced 'Hindustani' as well as Persian sentences in the morality plays which they staged at Christmas-time.[28] Their knowledge of the language was doubtless incomplete, and as might be expected it was not always adequate for conversation with Indian women. We are at any rate informed that when Father Aquaviva was celebrating the marriage of his interpreter Domingo Pires with an Indian woman, he had to speak in Persian and to allow Akbar who was present to interpret his meaning to the bride.[29] As the hopes of the Jesuits to influence official circles began to wane, their study of the vernacular became more pronounced, and as early as 1615 we find that the Fathers at Agra, though preaching in Persian, confessed the Christians in 'the Industan language.'[30] We not infrequently come across records of the proficiency of certain of the Fathers in the vernacular tongue. A list of missionaries in Bengal in 1632, for instance, contains a note against the name of Father Simon Figueredo to the effect that he knew the Hindustani tongue—'callet linguam Industanam.'[31] In the middle of the seventeenth century we find Father Ceschi reporting that he had learnt the difficult Industana language,[32] and we read of Father Morando as a great scholar in the Industani language,[33] and of Father Roth as having learnt the Indostana language wonderfully rapidly.[34]

The vernacular: 'Hindustani'

Even in tracts where the Hindī vernacular was not prevalent, a knowledge of the language was useful as a means of utilizing interpreters who knew it; Father Desideri, for instance, lays down that 'for any one going to Tibet it is necessary to learn the Hindustanic tongue, the language current in Mogul, and by means of it one can acquire next in Tibet the language of that country.'[35]

Fathers Ceschi and Roth went further and endeavoured to get at the thoughts of the Hindu population by acquainting themselves with the Brahmanic or Sanskrit language. Father Ceschi indeed does not seem to have got far in his studies. Shortly after his arrival in India he sent to Father Athanasius Kircher at Rome the transcript of a Sanskrit inscription which he saw near Bassein, but neither he nor Kircher could make much of the inscription.[36] Roth, on the other hand, employed the services of a Brahmin who was well inclined to Christianity and after six years' study became adequately proficient in the language. He introduced the Sanskrit character to the notice of the literati of Europe, and the curious can still see a copy of the Pater Noster and of the Ave Maria transliterated into Sanskrit by Father Roth in the *China Illustrata*, published by Father Kircher at Amsterdam in 1667.[37] Roth has been described as 'the first European Sanskritist' and his Sanskrit grammar as a most accurate work, 'exactissimum opus.'[38] In later days, a century afterwards, the erudite Father Tieffenthaler also acquired a certain knowledge of Sanskrit, in addition to his knowledge of many Eastern and Western tongues, but doubt has been cast on the profundity of his acquaintance with this particular language.[39]

Arabic

As regards Arabic, this tongue does not seem to have been much studied by the Jesuits. Father Corsi contemplated learning it,[40] but we do not know if he carried out his intention, and we cannot point to any Jesuit in Mogor who mastered Arabic. The object of learning it was solely to be able to refute the Muslim doctors from the original of the Qur'ān. We have it on the authority of Father Monserrate that the members of the First Mission knew the Qur'ān as thoroughly as Akbar's own doctors, because they had a Latin translation, which they owed to the diligence and accuracy of S. Bernard,[41] and if the chronicler du Jarric is to be trusted they had also a Portuguese translation.[42] Later Jesuit writers inform us that Aquaviva had a good knowledge of the Qur'ān, having marked for controversial purposes the passages which contradicted each other,[43] and that the Portuguese translation in the hands of the Fathers was well annotated (bem cotado).[44] The Third Mission had neither the Latin nor the Portuguese translation, and we find Father Xavier writing in 1598 to a Father Ituren in Spain for a translation in Latin or the vulgar tongue, because in Lahore he could only get the Arabic original which he could not understand. Eleven years later he was apparently offered by the same correspondent a Qur'ān in some language unspecified, but with some hesitation as to the propriety of transmitting so unholy a book.

In reply he says that he had already had a copy translated into Persian and from Persian into Portuguese, but would be glad to have an old Qur'ān, and as regards his correspondent's scruples he expressed his amusement, as 'we here are dealing from morning to night with these Moors about their things, so much so that even the bread we eat seems to have been kneaded with the water of Mahomet's Alcoran.' After all, however, his wishes were misunderstood: the Qur'ān which he ultimately received from Europe was in Arabic and he expressed his disappointment 'since we have no end of them here.'[45] It seems strange that in view of existing Muslim prejudices Xavier should have had the Qur'ān translated into Persian,[46] and still more strange that he or one of his Fathers should have undertaken the stupendous task of translating the book into Portuguese; and it is possible that his assertion refers to selected passages only. In any case the Jesuits appear as a rule to have been incapable of dealing with the original Arabic and they were to some extent impeded in their propaganda by this disability.[47]

Even translations of the Gospels into Arabic can have been of little use to them. When the Italian Vechiete presented them with a copy of the Gospels in Arabic printed in Rome in 1591, they brought the book as a specimen of the printing of Oriental characters to Jahāngīr, but that monarch, like themselves, preferred to have a translation into Persian.[48] It is a strange circumstance, therefore, that a copy of the same Arabic book should later on have been in the possession of the Fathers in Garhwāl—a Hindū district where Arabic could have been of no value to the missionaries.[49]

Persian—the First Mission

The language of the Court, of the Government, of the Muslims and of the ruling class generally in the Mogul dominions was Persian, and it was to this language the Jesuits in Mogor paid most of their attention. It was not prevalent in Portuguese India and had to be specially learnt by any missionary proceeding to Mogor. When the Fathers of the First Mission were delayed at Surat in 1580 they utilized their time by diligently studying Persian.[50] Immediately on their arrival at Fatehpur they were plunged into public controversies conducted in the Persian tongue, and in these they had at first to rely on their interpreters Father Henriquez and Domingo Pires. 'Accordingly they asked the King to provide them with a teacher who would instruct them in the Persian tongue, for that language, which is better adapted for polemical discussions, is spoken by the King, the Captains and many of the soldiers.' This duty was entrusted by Akbar to his minister Abu'-l-fazl, and we are told that Father Aquaviva made such progress under his tuition 'in the polite Persian literature which is used in scientific studies and commonly spoken by the learned, that he could hold forth in public, if not with refinedness of diction and copiousness of language, at least in such a way as to make himself understood by his hearers.' His progress excited astonishment and some even went so far as to admire his foreign accent (ipso peregrino vocis sono mirifice delectabantur). As was to be expected, however, the Fathers found themselves able to venture with greater boldness in dealing with the written than with the spoken language. They soon prepared in Persian a summary of the Gospel narratives, together with a discussion of disputed points, and submitted it to the King.[51] Later on Father Monserrate also prepared for the King a summary of the events of Christ's Passion and presented it to him when he was encamped upon the Indus in 1581.[52] The interpreters were not altogether satisfactory, and we learn that Father Henriquez, a Persian by birth, had almost forgotten his native tongue and had to learn it anew. After the departure of Henriquez to Goa, Father Aquaviva applied himself with fresh devotion to the language in order that he might be able to converse freely with the King.[53] But it is doubtful how far either he or the interpreters were efficient speakers in Persian, and it is noticeable that even before Father Aquaviva's departure, Akbar wrote to the Spanish King, pointing out the language difficulty, and stating his wish to obtain from him 'a man able to represent to us those sublime objects of research in an intelligible manner'—implying possibly that the missionaries already sent had been deficient in this respect.[54] It is interesting to note that in the same letter Akbar stated that he had heard that the Pentateuch, the Gospels and the Psalms had been translated into Persian and Arabic,[55] and asked for copies of these books 'whether translated or not.'

Persian—subsequent to the First Mission

The Mission of 1595, like that of 1580, realized fully the importance of mastering Persian. Akbar more than once impressed on them the necessity for acquiring the language and explained that if they knew Persian they would 'loose a great knot that now held him bound.' Three months after their arrival in Lahore, Father Xavier wrote, 'We are entirely occupied now in learning the Persian language and our progress leads us to believe that by God's grace we shall have mastered it within a year, and then we shall be able to say that we are at Lahore, for hitherto we have been, as it were, dumb statues.' (Et tunc dicere poterimus nos esse in Lahor: hactenus enim sumus velut statuae mutae.)[56]

Three years later Xavier confesses that the Fathers still spoke the language indifferently (mediocremente).[57] He himself soon became proficient in the language and by 1600 we are told that 'the Persians themselves take pleasure in hearing him talk and all but (tantum non) admire the propriety of his vocabulary and the choiceness of his diction.[58] He devoted himself, with the help of the ablest scholars available, to the translation of religious books into Persian and the issue of Christian propaganda in that language, producing in the course of his service a considerable volume of work, the details of which will be noticed in the following chapter. His assistants also and the subsequent members of the Mission maintained the practice of acquiring Persian. His colleague Father Pinheiro 'knew Persian so perfectly that he astonished the Mogorese.'[59] Father Corsi in 1600 studied Persian on his way north from Goa and by 1604 he was reported to have learnt the language.[60] In 1649 Father Morando was described as 'a great scholar in the Parthian language,'[61] and in 1654 Father Roth was applying himself to Persian, but it is significant that in his case the language was learnt after, and not as was usual before, the vernacular.[62] As time went on the acquisition of Persian was considered less obligatory, but the language prevailed all over Northern India for official purposes until a very late date and a knowledge of Persian was found to be useful even at a distance from the Court. Desideri, for instance, when halting at Delhi and Agra in 1714 on his way to Tibet armed himself for his journey by studying Persian,[63] and Strobl in 1743 was studying Persian in Jaipur. The latter missionary was in 1747 sufficiently acquainted with the language to be able to translate Akbar's letter of 1582 into Latin and German.[64] And the comprehensive Tieffenthaler in the late days of the Mission added a knowledge of Persian to his numerous other accomplishments.

Xavier's writings in Persian

As noted above it was in the Persian language and by the hands of Father Jerome Xavier that the bulk of the literary work of the Jesuits in Mogor was produced. Akbar himself was anxious for translations of the Scriptures and at an early stage he charged his minister Abu'lfazl to translate the Gospel.[65] Later on, when Father Xavier spoke to him of S. Ignatius, he bade him write in Persian an account of the Saint 'for the good of the whole kingdom.'[66] Whether either of these injunctions was carried out we do not know, but we have information regarding a considerable number of Persian works published by Father Xavier. The two most important of them are a Life of Christ and a Dialogue on Christian Doctrine,

The former, entitled *Mirāt-ul-Quds*, or 'Mirror of Holiness' (spoken of by the Jesuits as the 'Mirror of Purity'), described the life, miracles, death and doctrine of Christ, and was also called the *Dāstān-i-Masīh*; finished in 1602, it was read to Akbar and perused 'from end to end' by Prince Salīm.[67] The Dialogue was written in Portuguese during the Deccan War of 1601, Akbar himself being introduced as one of the speakers in the character of a philosopher in search of the Truth. Father Xavier gave to this work the title of the *Fountain of Life* and set himself to translate it into Persian,[68] but it was not issued till 1609 and the work in its Persian form was given the title of *Ā'īna-i-haqq-numā*, or 'The Truth-showing Mirror.' In the translation Xavier was assisted by persons learned in the language, but his own progress is said to have been such that the Persians themselves confessed that they had learnt from him many new phrases and figures of speech. In addition to these major works, he wrote Lives of S. Peter and the other Apostles, a translation of the Psalter, a book called *Guide of Kings* and a *History of the Martyrs.* There are also several vocabularies and grammars that have been ascribed to him, and it is clear that his literary activities covered a wide field. In 1623 the traveller Pietro della Valle sent more than one request to the Fathers at Agra for a correct copy of the Persian works written by them at the Mogul Court. His intention was to have them printed at Rome, but he does not appear to have received the copies for which he asked; for we have a list of the Persian works which della Valle brought home with him from India and these do not appear in the list.[69] A collection of Xavier's Persian works was, however, kept in the Jesuits' library at Agra as well as in the secretariat at Goa,[70] and later on, in 1649, Father Francis Morando, himself a good Persian scholar, was deputed to arrange for the copying of Xavier's works and their collection into one volume.[71] We have no information as to the results of his deputation; but some at any rate of the Persian works of Father Xavier were available at Delhi for perusal by Desideri in 1722.[72] Copies of many of Xavier's individual works are still extant, and an attempt is made in the following chapter to embody in a concise form such information as we have regarding these.

NOTES

1 *Letters Received,* III, p. 92; cf. *English Factories,* 1646–1650, p. 92.
2 Peruschi, *Informatione,* 1597, p. 33.

[3] Monserrate, *Commentarius*, fol. 24(a) ; Guzman, I, p. 246 ; du Jarric, II, p. 441 ; *J.A.S.B.*, LXV, 1896, p. 50 ; Goldie, *The First Christian Mission to the Great Mogul*, 1897, p. 63 ; Payne, *Akbar and the Jesuits*, 1926, pp. 19 and 221. The book is in eight volumes, but for some reason only seven are mentioned as having been presented to Akbar.

[4] Felix in *Agra Diocesan Calendar*, 1907, p. 192 ; *The Examiner*, Bombay, June 19, 1920, footnote 37 ; *J.P.H.S.*, V, 1916, p. 59. Persons alive in 1894 had actually seen the book. See also Chapter X, p. 164.

[5] Pinheiro's letter of September 3, 1595 ; *J.A.S.B.*, LXV, 1896, p. 68.

[6] The *History* of S. Antoninus and the *Theatrum Mundi* are quoted by Xavier in his letter of 1598 as authorities on the subject of Cathay.

[7] This corresponds to the list given by the Fathers so far as the items therein can be identified. The original lists will be found in *J.A.S.B.*, LXV, 1896, pp. 68–69 ; Payne's *Akbar and the Jesuits*, 1926, p. 63 ; and du Jarric, II, p. 471.

[8] *Literae Annuae* for 1597, p. 572.

[9] Pinheiro's letter of August 12, 1605, *J.A.S.B.*, LXV, 1896, p. 104.

[10] Strobl's letter of October 13, 1743, in *Weltbott*, No. 645.

[11] Foster's *Roe*, p. 249.

[12] Manucci, *Storia do Mogor*, II, p. 18.

[13] A copy of this History is in the Library of the Asiatic Society of Bengal. Ivanow, Catal, Curzon Collection, 1926, p. 96, No. 93 ; *Catholic Herald of India* (Hosten), November 19, 1924, pp. 737–738.

[14] Annual Report for 1648–1649 ; *J.I.H.*, February 1922, p. 231. In 1822 the traveller Moorcroft saw at Pushkyum in Ladāk a copy of the Latin Bible which was printed at Rome in 1598. It was bound in morocco and stamped with an I H S, and a cross on either side (*Travels*, 1841, II, p. 22). There was nothing to show when it had come into Ladāk, but it probably had belonged to one of the Jesuits in Mogor.

[15] Annual Report for 1648–1649 ; *J.I.H.*, February 1922, p. 232.

[16] Annual Letter of September 7, 1686.

[17] *Weltbott*, No. 595 ; *Mem. A.S.B.*, III, 1914 (Hosten), p. 528.

[18] *Beschreibung von Hindustan*, II, Part II, p. 179.

[19] *Weltbott*, No. 647.

[20] *Ibid.*, No. 648.

[21] *Ibid.*, No. 649.

[22] Figueredo in *Weltbott*, No. 595 (1735). The Father also mentions Turkish, but we hear little or nothing of this language in the accounts of the Mission. It was the hereditary language of the Mogul family, and William Hawkins tells us how, when he was at Agra in 1609, he had the advantage over the Jesuits in that he could talk Turkish with the King while they could not.

[23] *Harleian Miscellany*, I, p. 254 (date 1622).

[24] A sentence quoted by Father Botelho in the middle of the seventeenth century as having been spoken by the ruler of Bījāpur is singularly like the standard Urdū. See end of Chapter IV, and *J.A.S.B.*, LXV, 1896, p. 107.

[25] Foster, *Early Travels in India*, 1921, p. 309.

[26] Letter of September 27, 1582, *J.A.S.B.*, LXV, 1896, p. 58.

[27] Xavier's letter of September 6, 1604 ; *J.A.S.B.*, LXV, 1896, p. 96.

[28] *J.A.S.B.*, LXV, 1896, p. 72 ; du Jarric, II, p. 482.

[29] Letter of September 27, 1582 ; *J.A.S.B.*, LXV, 1896, p. 57.

[30] Letter from de Castro to Baudo, April 10, 1615.

[31] *J.A.S.B.*, VII, 1911, p. 22.

[32] Letter of 1650 to his family; *The Examiner*, Bombay (Hosten), September 1, 1917, p. 348.

[33] Maracci, *Relation*, 1649, p. 23. The Catalogue of 1647 says of him: 'Sabe perfeitamente as linguas Industana e Parçia'; Wessels, *Early Jesuit Travellers in Central Asia*, 1924, p. 80.

[34] Letter of Ceschi, August 24, 1654; *The Examiner*, Bombay (Hosten), September 8, 1917. He is described by Kircher as 'trium linguarum, Parsicae, Indostanicae et Brahmanicae instructissimus.'

[35] Puini, *Il Tibet*, p. 82 (*Memorie della Società Geografica Italiana*, Vol. X).

[36] Kircher, *China Illustrata*, 1667, p. 163; *La Chine Illustrée*, 1670, p. 222.

[37] Page 163. Max Müller in his *Lectures of the Science of Language* (1885), I, p. 175, alludes to Roth's services to Sanskrit learning. A critical account of his work by Prof. Theodor Zachariae will be found in the *Vienna Oriental Journal*, Vol. XV, Vienna, 1901, pp. 313–320.

[38] Dahlmann, *Indische Fahrten*, 1908, quoted in Dr. A. de Jong's Introduction to P. Baldaeus' *Afgoderye der Oost-indische Heydenen*, p. lxii (ed. of 1917).

[39] See Chapter VII, p. 140.

[40] Xavier's letter of September 6, 1604; *J.A.S.B.*, LXV, 1896, p. 96.

[41] *Commentarius*, fol. 25 (a). The translation in question was made in A.D. 1143 at the instigation of Peter the Venerable (1092–1156), Abbot of Cluny, the contemporary and friend of St. Bernard, by Robert of Ratine or Katine, an Englishman, and it was printed at Basle in 1543. An Italian translation of this version was published in 1547, but we do not hear of its use by the Jesuits.

[42] Du Jarric, II, p. 442; Payne, *Akbar and the Jesuits*, 1926, p. 21. Guzman (I, p. 246) says they had a translation, but does not say in what language it was. So also Nieremberg, *Claros Varones*, Madrid, 1643, II, p. 422.

[43] Tanner, *Societas Jesu . . . militans*, Prague, 1675, p. 245.

[44] De Sousa, *Oriente Conquistado*, 1710, II, p. 170; *The Examiner*, Bombay (Hosten), July 3, 1920.

[45] Letters of August 2, 1598, September 14, 1609, and December 4, 1615; *J.A.S.B.*, XXIII, 1927, pp. 119–120 and 125. The difficulty of obtaining the Latin translation may have been partly due to the fact that the first edition had a preface by Luther and the second a preface by Melancthon. Hough, *History of Christianity in India* (II, p. 283), mentions Xavier's translation of the Qur'ān into Portuguese, and his authority is La Croze, *Histoire du Christianisme des Indes* (edition of 1757, II, p. 78; edition of 1724, p. 333), but in the passage referred to the Protestant La Croze is merely referring sarcastically to Xavier's *Life of Christ* as 'une espèce d'Alcoran.'

[46] Even Jahāngīr when ordering a translation of the Holy Book into Persian had to insist that it should be word for word and should not add one letter to the exact purport of the Book. *Tūzuk* (Rogers and Beveridge), II, pp. 34–35.

[47] Monserrate, *Commentarius*, fol. 99(a).

[48] Guerreiro, *Relaçam*, IV, p. 157; Xavier's letter of September 25, 1606.

[49] See *The Examiner*, Bombay, April 15, 1922 (Hosten), and Chapter XIX, p. 354, below.

[50] Monserrate, *Commentarius*, fol. 9 (a).

[51] Monserrate, *Commentarius*, fol. 31 (b) and 32 (a).

[52] Monserrate, *Commentarius*, fol. 67 (b).

[53] *J.A.S.B.*, LXV, 1896, p. 56.

[54] See his letter of 1582 (Chapter II), and Rehatsek's comment thereon; *Ind. Antiquary*, XVI, 1887, pp. 135–9.

[55] A Polyglot edition of the Psalms, printed at Cologne in 1518, contained an Arabic version. The other translations referred to, if they existed, must apparently have been in manuscript.

[56] Letter of August 20, 1595; *J.A.S.B.*, LXV, 1896, pp. 66–67.

[57] Unpublished letter of August 1, 1598, quoted in *J.A.S.B.*, X, 1914, p. 68

[58] Letter from Pimenta of December 1, 1600; *J.A.S.B.*, XXIII, 1927, p. 70; cf. Payne, *Akbar and the Jesuits*, 1926, pp. 97 and 248.

[59] Annual Letter for 1619 quoted on p. 152 of *Mem. A.S.B.*, V, 1916 (Hosten); see *Examiner*, Bombay, February 10, 1912. As has been noted in Chapter IV, Pinheiro had among the Jesuits the sobriquet of 'The Mogul.'

[60] *J.A.S.B.*, LXV, 1896, pp. 83 and 96.

[61] Maracci, *Relation*, 1649 (Paris, 1651), p. 23. In Portuguese India it was not unusual for the vernacular languages to be written, or even printed, in Roman characters, and in 1623 we find Andrade (who was new to Mogor) receiving a Persian letter from Mīrzā Zū'lqarnain 'in Portuguese characters' and relying on Corsi for a translation of it. Andrade, letter of August 14, 1623.

[62] Ceschi's letter August 24, 1654, *The Examiner*, Bombay (Hosten), September 8, 1917, p. 358.

[63] Letter of August 21, 1714. In his *Relation*, however, he regrets the time spent by him on Persian, 'as Hindustani would have been far more useful' (de Filippi, p. 70).

[64] *Weltbott*, Nos. 645 and 648.

[65] Badāonī, *Bib. Ind.* (Lowe's translation), II, p. 267. The text (p. 260) is vague and the 'Anjīl' which was to be translated probably included the Christian scriptures generally.

[66] Xavier's letter of 1598; *J.A.S.B.*, LXV, 1896, p. 76.

[67] *J.A.S.B.*, LXV, 1896, p. 89.

[68] Payne, *Akbar and the Jesuits*, 1926, p. 97, and *J.A.S.B.*, XXIII, 1927, p. 129.

[69] *De' Viaggi di Pietro della Valle*, Rome, 1663, Vol. IV; Letter dated March 22, 1623, pp. 89–90. Pietro della Valle's *Travels in India*, Hakl. edition, 1892, I, p. 117. *J.A.S.B.*, X, 1914 (Hosten), p. 69.

[70] Botelho, 'Relation'; *Mem. A.S.B.*, V, 1916 (Hosten), p. 152.

[71] Maracci, *Relation*, 1649, p. 23.

[72] Puini, *Il Tibet*, 1904, p. xliv (*Memorie della Società Geografica Italiana*, Vol. X). Desideri intimates that he used to read Xavier's books aloud to his visitors in Delhi (de Filippi, p. 328).

To face page 203] [*From the Collection of Mr. A. P. Charles*

THE INN AT BETHLEHEM

An illustration to Xavier's *Life of Christ*

(See p. 252)

CHAPTER XIV

THE PERSIAN WORKS OF FATHER JEROME XAVIER

Audivimus eos loquentes nostris linguis magnalia Dei.
(Act. Apost. ii, 11.)

OUR information regarding Father Jerome Xavier's Persian works is incomplete and somewhat confused. The following is an abstract of our existing knowledge of these works, so far as I have been able to ascertain it.

Our information incomplete

The Jesuit bibliographies have lists of the works ascribed to him and there is also an anonymous manuscript list of unknown origin in the copy of *The Guide of Kings* in the Library of the School of Oriental Studies; but the lists are not identical and many points regarding the origin and history of the various books mentioned below are still obscure.

The Life of Christ

(I) *Mirāt-ul-Quds* (The Mirror of Holiness) or *Dāstān-i-Masīh* (Life of Christ)

Manuscripts known

Manuscripts of this work are fairly common. There is one in the Museum at Lahore dated 1602 which is incomplete and in bad condition, but bears Akbar's seal and is interleaved with eleven pictures.[1] In the Oriental Public Library at Patna there is a good and complete copy dating from 1627, besides an incomplete copy which is probably of a much later date.[2] The Asiatic Society of Bengal at Calcutta has two copies, one of which dates from 1604 and bears the seal of Akbar.[3] There is one in the School of Oriental Studies in London, on the first page of which is written in Xavier's own handwriting 'Espelho sto e puro em q̃ se trata da Vida e maravilhosa doct[a] de Jesu x[o] n[o] s[r].'[4] In the British Museum there are two copies, one dating from 1618 and one apparently from the eighteenth century: of which the former seems to have been brought from Aleppo before 1686 and the latter to have belonged to Claude Martin of Lucknow.[5] The Bodleian Library at Oxford has a copy which bears an illuminated cross on the first page and is alleged to be the original copy presented to Akbar.[6] Another copy is in the Lindsey Collection in the John Rylands Library at Manchester[7] and another, which belonged to Richard Johnson, the banker of Warren Hastings, is in the India Office.[8] The Bibliothèque Nationale at Paris has another, the Casanatense Library at Rome another,[9] and there is one in the Gotha Library which is enriched with autograph notes written by Jerome Xavier himself.[10]

In his Preface to the work, Father Xavier says that he compared his Persian version with the Latin books (ba kitābhāi Latīn), but he is doubtless referring here to his authorities and he does not imply that the work itself was first written in Latin. There seems little doubt that the original of the work was written in Portuguese and subsequently translated into Persian.[11] The Persian of the translation, according to a good authority, is easy and flowing; there are very few passages, if any, that sound outlandish.[12] For the Persian translation, Father Xavier was largely indebted to a prominent literary man of the day called 'Abdu-s-sattār ibn Qāsim of Lahore,[13] who according to the concluding note in the work itself translated the work conjointly with Xavier (ba ittifāq-i-īn banda)—a phrase which, although vague, probably implies a larger share by Xavier in the work of translation than mere supervision or consent, interpretations which have been at times applied to it.[14] Father Xavier's collaborator was a man of some mark and is more than once mentioned in Jahāngīr's Memoirs as the recipient of royal rewards for literary work.[15] He was commissioned by Akbar to study the language of the Farangīs in order to translate books into Persian on the subject of their religion and history and he prosecuted his studies under the guidance of Father Xavier (whom he calls Savīr Namūshwīr). He produced thereafter a work entitled *The Fruit of Philosophy* (Samrat-ul-filāsafa) or *The History of Europe* (Ahwāl-i-Farangistān) which gave an account of Greece and Rome and of the Lives of the Philosophers.[16] He is said by the Jesuits to have been 'as poor as Irus' when they first knew him and to have received official rank through the influence of Father Xavier; but this did not prevent him from arguing afterwards against the Christian faith or from maintaining, much to Jahāngīr's disgust, that the Hindu religion was better than that of the Jesuits.[17]

The co-operation of 'Abdu-s-Sattār

The preface of Xavier's book is dated Urdibihisht 15, 1602,[18] and commences with a curious conceit regarding the example of Akbar Bādshāh-i-Idīsha, that is to say Abgarus King of Edessa, who sent to make enquiries regarding Jesus and received in return a picture of Christ's likeness.[19] So too, under the orders of His

The contents of the book

Majesty, King Akbar, this work had been written by Jerome Xavier, who having known the subject for forty years and having studied Persian for seven or eight years had ventured to undertake the duty. Then follows the book itself, divided into four *bābs* or parts, viz. (I) the Nativity and Infancy of Christ; (II) His Miracles and Teaching; (III) His Death and Suffering; and (IV) His Resurrection and Ascension. The book was to a large extent a translation from the Gospels and it contained little in the way of doctrine or moralizing that was not to be found in the New Testament. But the story itself was expanded and many legends were included which though prevalent in Europe had been rejected by the Protestant opinion of the day: such as the stories of Joachim and Anna, the transference of the bodies of the Magi to Cologne, the portents at Rome and elsewhere at the time of the Nativity and the Crucifixion, the tale of Longinus, the prophecies of the Sibyl, and so forth.

Publication in Europe under Protestant auspices

It was for this reason a work not likely to commend itself to contemporary Protestant sentiment. Accordingly when a manuscript of the work was brought to Europe by a merchant from Persia and passed into the hands of the Arabic scholar Golius and thence into those of the Dutch Protestant writer de Dieu, it appeared to de Dieu to afford a good mark for Protestant criticism. He thereupon published it in print at Leyden in 1638 with a Latin translation and notes under the title of *Dāstān-i-Masīh Historia Christi Persice conscripta simulque multis modis contaminata a P. Hieronymo Xavier, Soc. Jesu. Latine reddita et animadversionibus notata a Ludovico de Dieu.* De Dieu's publication formed a book of 636 pages and each page of the Persian text was headed with the words 'Dāstān-i-Masīh āmmā ālūda.' The text of the manuscript (which dated from 1627) was maintained, with slight modifications to provide for verbal errors and confusion in wording, but the text was not a good one and the traveller Pietro della Valle was able later on to provide himself with a more accurate copy.[20] De Dieu's translation was stated by Alcazar to be defective in places, but was acknowledged by Alegambe to be a good one (non infideliter textum interpretatus est).[21] The 'animadversions' of de Dieu are, however, strongly adverse to the substance of the work and are permeated by the vituperative phraseology characteristic of learned controversialists in his day. 'Xaverius noster' comes in for a good deal of castigation for his inept perversions of and divagations from the plain Scripture narrative. At one place the editor exclaims, 'Quid non audet Xaverius?' 'The audacity of Xavier knows no bounds.' At another: 'Quid moratur Xaverius verum dicat an falsum modo credant Mogoriani?' 'What concern is it to Xavier whether he lies or tells the truth so long as he gets the Mogorians to believe in what he says?': and so forth. The animadversions were considered by Alegambe (1676) to deserve being burnt (rogo dignae), and the book had indeed in 1660–1661 already earned its place upon the Index. It has since formed the basis of a good deal of unsympathetic criticism of Xavier from the Protestant side,[22] but as Mr. Beveridge has remarked we owe de Dieu a debt of gratitude for having preserved by his publication a knowledge of Father Xavier's interesting work.[23]

(II) *Ā'īna-i Haqq Numā* (The Truth-showing Mirror).

The Truth-showing Mirror. Copies extant

Copies of this work are to be found in manuscript only[24] and are comparatively rare, but there is a copy in the British Museum once owned by the poet Alexander Pope which dates from the year 1610,[25] another copy in the Academy at Leningrad,[26] another in the Library of Queen's College, Cambridge,[27] another in the Casanatense Library at Rome, and another in the Edinburgh University Library.[28]

About the year 1828 a work described as the *Speculum Veritatis*, which was presumably a copy of the *Ā'īna-i Haqq Numā*, was found by a 'Rev. Mr. W.' in an obscure spot in a corner of the Kanāwar Mountains in the Himalaya of the Upper Sutlej, and this copy was sent to the scholar Csoma de Körös who was then at Kānam for elucidation, but we have no further information regarding it. Dr. Gerard who reported the discovery in 1829 surmised, with some probability, that it found its way to this obscure region from the Jesuit Mission at Tsaparang.[29]

Its composition

In the *Mirāt-ul-Quds* which issued in 1602 Father Xavier noted that he had written the greater part of a book called *Ā'īna-i-Haqq Numā* and hoped to finish it shortly.[30] The work was written out first in Portuguese. It is spoken of in Latin as 'Speculum veritatem monstrans,' and is apparently the same book as that referred to in a contemporary letter as *Fons Vitae* or *Lignum Vitae*. It is mentioned under the latter title by Father Pimenta, the Visitor, who saw it (doubtless in an unfinished state) in 1600 and spoke of it as a work of great erudition and great length (pereruditum et prolixum).[31] The style of the Persian translation, according to Dr. Lee, is on the whole correct, though occasionally interspersed with Europeanisms; 'but it never makes,' he adds, 'the most distant approach to what may be termed elegance.'[32]

Its contents—the Prayer in the Preface

The book explains how twelve years previously the author had had the privilege of kissing the Imperial threshold, and how he now dedicated the work to Jahāngīr as a slight return for past favours and as a humble offering after his accession. The treatise is written in the form of a dialogue between a padre and a philosopher or freethinker whom he purports to have met at Court—a thinly-veiled personification of Akbar himself—while at times a mullā intervenes as a third interlocutor.[33] ' It is divided,' says Rieu, ' into five books (Bāb) subdivided into chapters (Fasl), a full table of which is given at the end of the Preface. The five books are as follows: (1) Necessity for a divine law. (2) What Christianity teaches regarding God, and proofs of its being conformable to wisdom. (3) Divinity of Jesus Christ, Our Lord. . . . (4) Commandments of the Gospel and their contrast with those of Muhammad. (5) The strength imparted by the Christian faith and its superiority to other religions.' Those who are curious in such matters will find a very full account of the contents of the *Ā'īna-i-Haqq Numā* in Father Desideri's Report and in Dr. Lee's Preface to Martyn's *Controversial Tracts* published at Cambridge in 1824. It will suffice to quote here the remarkable prayer contained in the introduction to Xavier's book:

' Pardon, O Lord, should I do what is unpleasing in Thy sight by obtruding myself into the things and properties that belong to Thee. Men plunge into the deep ocean, thence to fetch pearls and other precious things. Therefore, O Sea of Perfection, suffer me to sink deep in Thee and thence to enrich myself and my brethren, who are Thy servants ; and by describing Thy greatness and mercies, to help them. For although I am unworthy to speak to Thee, Thou art worthy that all should endeavour to praise Thee, since Thou art possessed of infinite goodness and beauty. . . . O Lord my God, this will be fruitless unless Thou assist both me and them with Thine infinite mercy. Give unto us, O Lord, the Key of the Knowledge of Thee. Grant to our understandings the power of comprehending Thy greatness, that Thy Majesty and Grace may not be to us an occasion of stumbling, and hence we remain unblessed by Thy many favours. Let not that come upon us which happens to the bat which is blinded by the light of the Sun and which in the midst of light, remains in darkness. Give us enlightened and far-discerning eyes, that we may believe in that greatness of which Thou art and which, for our sakes, Thou hast revealed. And, that by these words and actions, we may so follow Thee that in Paradise we may see Thy Godhead, in the mirror of Light, which, in this world, we can only contemplate by faith and (as in a glass) darkly. Amen.'[34]

An abridgement of the book was subsequently brought out by Father Xavier under the title of *Muntakhib-i Ā'īna-i-Haqq Numā* and a copy of this abridgement is among the British Museum manuscripts.[35] 'In a long preface addressed to Jahāngīr,' says Dr. Rieu, 'the author mentions his previous work, entitled *Ā'īna-i-Haqq Numā*, to which he had devoted so many years, and says that finding the Emperor's time taken up by the cares of government, he extracted its substance for his use and condensed it in the present "selection." This work, which is not like the original book, written in the form of a dialogue, contains the following four chapters (Fasl): (1) Knowledge of the Nature of God; (2) on Jesus Our Lord; (3) Commandments of the Gospel; (4) Divine assistance.'

The 'abridgement'

Father Xavier's work found its way in this form to Persia, and according to one authority it was sent by the Mogul himself to the Shah of Persia.[36] It was seen at Ispahān by the Carmelite Missionaries there; two of the priests at Ispahān showed it, in 1622–1623, to a devout Muslim called Sayyad Ahmad bin Zain-ul-'ābidīn, who had in 1621 written a treatise called *A book of divine rays in refutation of Christian Error.*[37] On seeing the *Muntakhib-i-Ā'īna-i-Haqq Numā*[38] (the authorship of which he ascribes to a great Christian divine bearing the enigmatic name of Pādrī Mīmīlād) Ahmad was inspired to reply to it in a work entitled *Misqal-i-Safā dar tahliya-i-Ā'īna-i-Haqq Numā*, or, 'The Clean Polisher for the Brightening of the Truth-Reflecting Mirror,' this work is referred to by European writers as the '*Politor Speculi*' and it was completed in 1623. The '*Politor Speculi*' was brought to the Congregation of the Propaganda in Rome by the Carmelites from Persia[39] and the Propaganda took a serious view of the effect which it would have on the spread of Christianity in the East. A rejoinder was issued at Rome in 1628 by a Franciscan, Father Malvasia, under the title of *Dilucidatio speculi veritatem Monstrantis,*[40] but this was considered inadequate by the Propaganda, and at their instance a further rejoinder was published in Rome in 1631 by another Franciscan, Father Philip Guadagnoli, under the designation of *Apologia pro Christiana Religione.* The first issue of the *Apologia* was in Latin, but the author was a well-known Arabic scholar and a printed Arabic version by the author was issued in 1637 and 1649.[41] The work was on a substantial scale covering 557 pages in the Latin and 1637 pages in the Arabic issue. Copies of the Arabic version were distributed in the East. We hear of its being used for propaganda at the Mogul Court in 1651, when Shāh Jahān's Wazīr Sa'dulla Khān declined

Consequent controversy

to take a copy from Dom Matheus.[42] And it was studied (in the Latin edition) by Father Strobl at Jaipur in 1743 as a help in religious controversy.[43] When first composed the book commenced with such imprecations against Muhammad that no one in the East would have read it, and Guadagnoli was induced to alter its tone—a task which he accomplished with such thoroughness that he incurred the censure of his ecclesiastical superiors for the excessive kindliness of the attitude taken in his revised work towards the Prophet.[44] It must, however, have been a satisfaction to the writer if, as one authority avers, the book as published had the effect of converting his opponent, Ahmad.[45] In any case it is matter for congratulation that the controversy was conducted, as we are assured it was, in an amicable spirit both by Ahmad and by Guadagnoli, and a contemporary writer contrasts the tone of these controversialists with the ferocity so often shown in the disputes of the day between Christians themselves on the subject of religion.[46]

The flame of the controversy set alight by Xavier's work seems, however, to have flickered up once more, for there is extant (in 260 pages) a still further refutation, said to have been written in India in 1654 by an anonymous Jesuit supporter of Xavier. We know nothing of the writer of the book, but his work was badly composed, its language ungrammatical, and its title vulgar.[47]

(III) *Dāstān-i Ahwāl-i Hawāriyān* (Lives of the Apostles).

Lives of the Apostles. Copies extant

There are two copies of this work in the Library of the Asiatic Society of Bengal in Calcutta :[48] one in the Jesuit ' Bibliothèque des Missions ' at Louvain (containing four lives only)[49] and one in the Serampur College Library.[50] The Bodleian Library has a copy,[51] and so have the Leyden Library[52] and the School of Oriental Studies in London,[53] and there are two copies in the Bibliothèque Nationale in Paris, one of which came from the library of Colonel Gentil and had been transcribed for Gaston Brouet, the biographer of Donna Juliana.[54]

History of its composition

The Apostles dealt with are SS. Peter, Paul, Andrew, James, John, Thomas, James the Less, Philip, Bartholomew, Matthew, Simon and Jude, and Matthias. The ' Lives ' seem to have been brought out by instalments. When Xavier in 1602 presented Akbar in Agra with a copy of his *Life of Christ*, Akbar bade him prepare another work which would deal with the Lives of the Apostles[55] and it is understood that Akbar received the first four of the Lives before he died in

1605.[56] Later on, in 1607, when Jahāngīr entered Lahore he was presented by the Fathers with 'a work of theirs, a book in Persian containing the Lives of the Apostles and interleaved with many pictures of their sufferings.'[57] This also must have been an incomplete or an advance copy, for the finished work was not issued till 1609. The copy in the School of Oriental Studies in London bears an inscription in Father Xavier's handwriting which says: 'Vida dos doze Apostolos do senhor Jesu—composta polo P. Jer° Xavier da compª de Jesu. Em Agra corte do graõ Mogol Rey Jahanguir, ano 1609.' That in the Bodleian was given to the Library by Archbishop Laud in 1640 and contains an inscription in Portuguese showing that it was presented by Father Joseph de Castro to William Methwold of the English East India Company (himself a proficient linguist) on September 8, 1638.

The preface of the book states that it was translated from Farangī into Persian with the help of Maulānā 'Abd-us-sattār (ba dastyārī Maulānā 'Abd-us-sattār), and the probability is that, as in the case of the *Life of Christ*, the book was originally written out in Portuguese.[58]

Translation into Hindustani

The work was translated into Urdū under the auspices of the Capuchin Fathers at Sardhāna and was printed there in 1894 with the title of 'Nuskha-i kitāb-i bāra Apostel.'[59]

Life of S. Peter. Its publication in Europe

One of the Lives—that of S. Peter—though no separate MS of it is known to exist,[60] was published also as a separate book, and a copy of this book was purchased in Agra in 1626 by one John Romanus of Rotterdam and passed at his death into the hands of John Eligman by whom it was shown to de Dieu.[61] By de Dieu it was, like the *Life of Christ*, printed at Leyden with a Latin translation and notes in 1639, and it was given the title of *Historia S. Petri sed contaminata*. 'Dāstān-i S. Pedro āmmā ālūda.' The production of the Life is ascribed by the writer to the forty-ninth year of the reign of Akbar, that is to 1604.[62] The work itself does not lay claim to Xavier as its author, but from a comparison with the *Life of Christ* there can be little doubt of his authorship. 'Egg is not more like egg,' says de Dieu, 'Non ovum ovo similius quam hic sibi Xaverius.' The earlier part of the book adheres fairly closely to the accounts given in the New Testament, but later on we get the story of Faustinus and Mathidiana, the legend of the chair of S. Peter, the magical contests with Simon Magus at Rome and the final crucifixion of the Saint. The incident of 'Tu es Petrus' is, moreover, recounted from the Catholic standpoint and S. Peter is represented as the Vicar of Christ on earth. This claim was dealt with by de Dieu in his controversial 'animadversions,' and the legends are there ridiculed and their origin set forth, with the result that de Dieu's book, like his *Life of Christ*, was placed upon the Index. Whatever may be thought of de Dieu's annotations, his translation of the Persian original was pronounced by the Italian traveller Pietro della Valle, himself a good linguist, to be with a few exceptions correct.[63]

(IV) *Zabūr* (The Psalter).

Translation of the Psalms. Copy possessed by Giambattista Vechiete

In dealing with translations of the Scriptures, real and alleged, by Jerome Xavier, we are introduced to an attractive character, the Florentine traveller Giambattista Vechiete, to whom brief allusions have already been made in this book. Vechiete was a cultured man, born in 1552, who in 1584 had been sent by the Pope on a mission, for the double purpose of conciliating the Patriarch of Alexandria and of enlisting the services of the Persians against the Turks. From this journey he returned by way of Ormuz and Goa; and he started again some years later on another journey, travelling through Persia and collecting texts of the Old Testament from the Persian Jews. In Ormuz in 1601 he commenced revising the Persian translations of the Psalms and other books of the Bible, and after reaching Tatta in 1603 he proceeded by Bhakkar to Lahore. There he was ill for three months, but he was consoled and helped by Father Pinheiro and by his fellow-Florentine, Father Corsi. From Lahore he travelled to Delhi and Agra and at the latter city was graciously welcomed by Akbar. At Agra also he was met on January 17, 1605, by his brother Girolamo, who had travelled from Egypt, and the two brothers started on April 3, 1605, to return by Tatta to Persia. Giambattista was subsequently captured by Tunisian pirates in the Mediterranean, and after being released from them he proceeded to Rome, where in later years he showed to the Pope two finely bound volumes, one containing the Psalms translated from the Hebrew into Persian and the other the Books of Solomon, Ruth and Esther. He failed, however, to get support from the Pope and died afterwards in poverty at Naples, on December 8, 1619.[64]

On his arrival in Agra in March 1604, Vechiete made friends with Fathers Xavier and Machado, and Xavier writes of him with much respect and affection. 'He has much friendship for us,' he says, 'in proof of which he gave us a book of the Holy Gospels in Arabic with the Latin at the foot, printed in the

Vatican, which we value very highly.[65] He had also with him the Psalter of David in Persian which he obtained with great pains and at great cost from a Jew who had it in Persian, but in Hebrew characters.[66] It was translated two hundred years ago by an eminent Jew of Persia. We gave ourselves to the transcribing of this book with much delight. While the Italian was here, he copied in Persian character the Books of Proverbs, Canticles, Ecclesiastes, Judith and Esther, which he had in Persian, but in the Hebrew character, and gave them to us freshly copied into the Persian tongue and character, but though the characters are new, the translation is more than two hundred years old : he obtained them from some Jews in Persia at a good price.'[67]

It is clear then that a Persian translation of the Psalms was in the possession of Vechiete. It was doubtless this version which was shown by him to the Pope and the same volume (dating from 1601) which we find later in the library of the scholar Renaudot.[68]

Xavier's version

The only manuscript of Xavier's translation known to us is in the School of Oriental Studies in London,[69] Xavier's version was evidently written after Vechiete left India and being from the Vulgate was different from that possessed by Vechiete. It has an inscription in Xavier's own handwriting ' Psalterio de David conforme a Edicaõ Vulgata traduzido polo P^{e} Jero^{o} Xavier da comp^{a} de Jesu, na cidade de Agra corte do graõ Mogol Rey Jahanguir,' and this is followed by a note showing that this copy was intended to be a present from Xavier to Vechiete.[70]

It has little vogue

When Bishop Walton's Polyglot Bible of 1657 was compiled, there were available a Persian translation of the Psalms composed by the Carmelites of Ispahān in Persian and another composed ' a Jesuitis quibusdam ' (not improbably Xavier and his colleagues) :[71] but neither of them were utilized for the Polyglot, because they were held to be inaccurate (plurimis erroribus et soloecismis utraque scatet) and because they were based on the Vulgate and not on the original Hebrew.[72]

It may be noted that a copy of the Psalms in Persian was presented to Oxford University by Sir Thomas Roe, but this was a copy not of Xavier's translation but of the translation made by the Carmelites at Ispahan in 1616.[73] Indeed, Xavier's version seems to have had very little vogue, as it is not mentioned among his works by Alcazar or Nieremberg or Alegambe, nor is it in the list of his works in the paper attached to the *Guide of Kings* in the School of Oriental Studies.

(V) *The Gospels*

Translation of the Gospels ascribed to Xavier

Father Xavier is credited with having made a translation of the Gospels into Persian. Father Maracci writing in 1649 states that in addition to composing several books he 'translated others, as the Gospels, into the Parthian tongue.'[74] Father Freyre writing from Goa in 1678 says that Aurangzeb had sent for 'the book of the Gospels which our Fathers had translated into Persian.'[75] The bibliographer Sommervogel ascribes to Father Xavier a translation of the Gospels dated 1607 which is said to be at Lisbon.[76] And there is in the library of the Capuchin Fathers at Agra a Persian translation of the Gospels which was transcribed about the year 1680 and which is believed by Father Hosten to be a copy of a translation by Xavier.[77]

On the other hand no such translation is included in the list of his Persian works in the paper attached to the *Guide of Kings* in the School of Oriental Studies, nor is it mentioned by Nieremberg, or Alegambe, or Alcazar in their lists of Xavier's works.

Translations already existing

We know from Indian sources that Akbar's minister Abu'-l-fazl was acquainted with the Pentateuch and the Gospels,[78] and that Abu'-l-fazl received instructions from Akbar to translate the 'Injīl,'[79] but whether this related to the Four Gospels or the Scriptures generally, and whether the order was ever carried out either directly or through the Fathers we do not know.[80]

The Fathers had in their possession more than one copy of the Gospels in Persian which they had not themselves translated. The facts regarding these various copies are somewhat difficult to unravel, but our information regarding them is briefly as follows.

Existing copies known to have been in the hands of the Jesuits

About the year 1597 the Christians of S. Thomas in Southern India wrote to their own Nestorian Patriarch at Mosul requesting him to appoint for them a new Archbishop. The Portuguese authorities being then engaged in a strong effort to substitute a Roman for a Nestorian hierarchy among the S. Thomas Christians, sent orders to Ormuz to prevent the embarkation of any such nominee. In view of these orders the prelate appointed by the Patriarch attempted to travel from Persia to India by land; but he died on the journey before reaching Lahore. The Jesuits, following a practice not uncommon at the time, speak of this priest as an Armenian, and tell us that part at any rate of his library came into the hands of Father Pinheiro at Lahore,[81] much against the wishes of the Armenians who desired to present it to the King. We subsequently find the Fathers disposing of five Persian translations of the Gospels : two of which certainly, and the others possibly, came from this library.

(i) In 1604 Xavier wrote : 'Last year (i.e. in 1603) we sent to Rome another book of the Gospels in Persian, the translation of which is more than 300 years old. God grant that it arrived safely.'[82] This copy would appear to be the same as one copied in 1388 from an older exemplar, which was sent from Agra to the College in Rome and was subsequently used by Cornelius a Lapide in his commentary on the Gospels.[83]

(ii) Then in 1604 when Giambattista Vechiete was at Agra, 'we gave him,' says Xavier, 'the book of the Four Gospels in Persian which he greatly desired, for he said they had the Gospel of S. Matthew in Persian at Rome but would like very much to have the other three.'[84]

(iii) Subsequently a Persian copy of the Gospels was despatched by Xavier with a view to its being presented to the Pope for the Vatican Library. This copy is now in the School of Oriental Studies, London,[85] and in it are notes written by Xavier and Pinheiro. That written by Xavier is in Spanish and is dated September 1605. It states that the book was written in Persian in 760 A.H. (A.D. 1359), that it was brought by Father Nicholas, brother of the Bishop of Jerusalem, that the Father died on the journey when near Lahore, and that his books reached the hands of the Jesuits with great difficulty owing to the opposition of the Armenians. The note by Pinheiro, written on August 7, 1609 (when he is believed to have been at Cambay), states that the book had been brought by an Armenian padre from Jerusalem for presentation to Akbar, that the padre died on the road and that the book had come into Pinheiro's hands. He then adds that it was originally intended that the book should be sent to Rome, but for certain reasons it seemed best to the Father Provincial that it should remain in the secretariat of the Province that afterwards such decision might be reached regarding it as should be best and most judicious. From the secretariat at Goa it would appear to have come with other books and papers into the hands of William Marsden who presented it to King's College from which it was transferred to the School of Oriental Studies. A duplicate copy of the same book was sent at the same time with a note by Xavier to the Professed House at Rome.[85a]

(iv) In 1610 a copy of the Gospels in Persian was received from the Fathers by the King of Spain and deposited in the Escurial. It bore a certificate by Father Xavier dated Lahore,

December 21, 1607, which states that the translation was written in A.D. 828 and was brought from Jerusalem by an Armenian padre who was travelling to India with Minuchihr Beg, the Georgian Ambassador of the King of Persia, and died upon the road.[86]

(v) In addition to the above we hear of a bi-lingual version which was under preparation by the Fathers in 1604. In that year Xavier, after mentioning the despatch of a copy of the Gospels to Rome in the previous year, adds: 'We are now arranging the same book of the Gospels in Persian with the corresponding Latin at foot, which, God willing, will be much esteemed in Europe.' Some two years later, when Jahāngīr was in Lahore in 1606, he spoke to the Fathers about the difficulties of printing the Persian characters, and to dissipate his doubts the Jesuits showed him their copy of the Arabic version of the Gospels which was printed at the Vatican in 1591. On his representing that he would like to see a copy of the Gospels in Persian, they took him a Persian copy, but he was not at leisure to see it at that time and they then decided to collate and amend the Persian 'in conformity with our Vulgate, which, to tell the truth, contains many copyists' errors.' This emended version they presented to the King when he set out for Kābul in March 1607.[87]

Whether the version prepared in 1606–1607 was that contemplated in 1604, and whether it was a fresh translation from the Vulgate or an adaptation of an old Persian version is not clear.

Uncertainty as to a translation having been made by Xavier

On our present information, therefore, we cannot say definitely that a translation of the Gospels was made by Father Xavier, but it is probable that a translation was made and that it was based largely on one of the existing Persian versions.[88]

(VI) *Ādāb-us-Saltanat* (The Guide of Kings)

The Guide of Kings

Of this work there is a well-written manuscript copy in the School of Oriental Studies in London.[89] It bears a Portuguese inscription by Xavier himself, saying that it was composed by Jerome Xavier at Agra in 1609 and dedicated to Jahāngīr. It has a further inscription: 'Ao Sr Joaõ baptista Vechiete ✠ Jero^o^ Xavier,' showing that this copy was intended by Father Xavier to be forwarded to Vechiete.[90] The book has four parts and was written, according to Father Alcazar, 'for the good Government of the Kingdom.'[91] Father Botelho in his *Relation* written some forty years later refers to a book by Father Xavier which was called *The Mirror of Princes*, but in view of the fact that this is described as a 'very big book ' and as dedicated to Akbar, the reference is probably not to the *Guide of Kings* but to the ' Mirror of Holiness ' (*Mirāt-ul-Quds*) or the ' Mirror of Truth ' (*Ā'īna-i-Haqq Numā*).[92]

(VII) *A History of the Martyrs and Saints*

History of the Martyrs and Saints

The Jesuit bibliographers mention a book of this name among Xavier's Persian works, but no copy of the work appears to be known.[93] It is not mentioned in the MS. list of Xavier's works included in the *Guide of Kings* at the School of Oriental Studies.

In the same way reference is made by Father Desideri to a *Life of the Blessed Virgin* and to books of prayer and pious exercises prepared by Xavier in Persian,[94] but of these there appears now to be no trace.

Other Persian works of the Jesuits at Agra

The list in the copy of the *Guide of Kings* in the School of Oriental Studies, while it does not credit Father Xavier with the translation of the Psalter and the Gospels or with the book on the Martyrs, does include among his works a *Compendium of Christian Doctrine*[95] and an expanded *Explanation of the Creed*, neither of which appears to have survived. On the other hand, the list includes a certain number of works which it does not ascribe to Father Xavier and which are apparently the production of someone else connected with the Mission. One of the Fathers writing in 1686 tells us that, apart from Jerome Xavier, there were other Fathers who had composed many other books not only in Arabic, Persian and Hīndustānī but also in Sanskrit. We have no record of any books so written in Arabic, or Hīndustānī, or Sanskrit, and the only books which we can reasonably ascribe to the Jesuit Fathers are those mentioned in our copy of the *Guide of Kings*, which all have Persian titles.[96] These works consist of ' The History of the Foundation of Rome and an account of her Kings ' (*Sharah bināi Rūma wa zikr-i pādshāhān*), a book of Philosophic Topics (*Sahāif-i muqaddamāt-i filāsafa*), ' A Summary of the Christian Faith ' (*Intakhāb-i Dīn-i 'Isāwiān*), ' Translations from Plutarch ' (*Tarjuma-i Plutārko*), Plutarch's ' Consolation in Death ' (*Kitāb-i Plutārko darbāb-i taskīnī marg sipr*), ' Plutarch on the advantage to be obtained from one's enemies ' (. . . *ki az dushmanān tawān ba dast āward*), ' Maxims from Plutarch ' (*Maqūlāt Plutārko*) and ' Selections from Cicero ' (*Ba'ze muqaddamāt-i Mārko Tulio*).[97]

The bibliographer Sommervogel includes among Xavier's works a *Rudimenta Linguae Persicae*[98] or Persian Grammar. There is a book with this title in the School of Oriental Studies which consists of a grammar in Latin of the Persian language and a vocabulary in Persian, Latin and Portuguese,[99] but the name of the author which was entered at the end of the grammar has at some time been carefully cut out. It may, however, be noted that the traveller Thevenot's library included a Persian MS. described as 'Vocabulaire Persan et Italien des mots contenus dans un Catechisme Persan composé par les Pères Jésuites de la Mission de Lahore.'[100]

NOTES

[1] *J.U.P.H.S.*, III, 1922 (Hosten), Part I, p. 181; *J.P.H.S.*, 1916 (Felix), p. 111.

[2] Scott O'Connor, *An Eastern Library*, 1920, p. 59; 'Abdul-Muqtadir, *Catal. of Arabic and Persian MSS. in the Oriental Public Library at Bankipur*, 1925, Vol. VIII, p. 1.

[3] Ivanow, *Catal. Pers. MSS.* in *A.S.B.*, 1924, p. 755, No. 1635, and *Catal. of Curzon Collection, A.S.B.*, p. 447, No. 665. A copy was exhibited at the A.S.B. in 1870 by Blochmann. See *Proc. A.S.B.*, May 1870, p. 140.

[4] See in Bulletin S.O.S., II, 1922, p. 533, and III, 1923, p. 138.

[5] Harl. 5455 and Addl. 16878 of the Yule Collection. Rieu, *Catal. Pers. MSS.*, I, p. 3.

[6] Sachau and Ethé, *Catal. Pers. MSS.*, No. 364. Cf. Fraser 256 of Catalogue in *Fraser's Nadir Shah*, 1742, p. 39. The copy presented to Prince Salīm had also an illuminated cross at the beginning and Salīm had a Christ Crucified painted on to it. On another page where there was the Name of Jesus surrounded by rays, he made the painter put in a Virgin and Child. Guerreiro, *Relaçam*, II, p. 61; Payne, *Akbar and the Jesuits*, 1926, pp. 190–191.

[7] *Bibl. Lindseiana*, 1898, p. 177.

[8] Ethé, *Catal. Pers. MSS.*, I, 1903, No. 619. This copy is merely a replica of the printed edition of de Dieu.

[9] Blochet, *Catal. Persian MSS.*, 1905, No. 13. *Cataloghi dei Codici Orientali di alcune Biblioteche d'Italia*, 1878, p. 436.

[10] *Pertsch. Catal.*, 1859, p. 57. There are two notes by Xavier: one at the end of the Persian text is in Latin, 'Laus Deo, etc.': the other in Portuguese protests that there is nothing in the book contrary to the Gospel and offers to submit in this matter to any decision that may be given by the Pope.

[11] *J.A.S.B.*, X, 1914 (Hosten), p. 68; La Croze, *Histoire du Christianisme des Indes*, The Hague, 1724, p. 333; 1758, II, p. 78. A note by the Orientalist Gagnier (d. 1740) in one copy in the British Museum also states that the work was 'primum Lusitanice composita,' cf. Figanier *Catalogue of the Portuguese Manuscripts in the British Museum*, 1853, p. 39

[12] Blochmann in *Proc. A.S.B.*, May 1870, p. 146, where he gives a full translation of the Preface and an analysis of the work (pp. 140–146).

[13] There seems to be some mistake in the statement made in *J.I.H.*, I, 1922, p. 359, that the book was 'translated by Abul Rahman Qandhari in 1604.' A note in the Manchester copy of 'Abdu-s-sattār's own work states that he was the son of Muhammad Qāsim, Farishta, the historian.

[14] See for instance the remarks of Smallbrooke, quoted on p. 216 of *J.R.A.S.*, 1899.

[15] *Tūzuk-i-Jahāngīrī*, translated by Beveridge, I, 389, and II, p. 82.

[16] There is a copy of this book in the Lindsey Collection in the John Rylands Library at Manchester and a manuscript in the Victoria Library at Patiāla, of which a copy is in the British Museum (*Or.* 5893); *J.R.A.S.*, 1901 (Beveridge), p. 78; Rieu, *Catal. Pers. MSS.*, III, p. 1077; and Sprenger, *Catal. of Elliot MSS.*, *J.A.S.B.*, XXIII, No. 197 (1854), p. 259; Darbār-i-Akbarī (Muhammad Āzād), p. 68; *Bib. Lindseiana*, 1898, p. 177, No. 445. The copy in the British Museum contains an interesting note of the contents by Beveridge, who presented it to the Museum in 1900. At page 259 there is a reference to Xavier's *Mirror of Holiness*. King's College, Cambridge, has also a copy of the work. (See Palmer Catalogue in *J.R.A.S.*, new series, Vol. III, 1867, p. 126, No. 222, where it is wrongly classed as an Arabic book.)

[17] Pinheiro's letter of September 9, 1610.

[18] The presentation of the book to Akbar is described in Guerreiro, *Relaçam*, II, Part II, p. 52, and its presentation to Prince Salīm on p. 61. The latter ordered illustrations to be made of all the 'Mysteries' of the Life of Christ, and there were pictures in the copy presented to Akbar (Xavier's letter, September 25, 1606).

[19] The Lahore MS. has a miniature illustrating the incident.

[20] Alegambe, *Bibl. Scriptorum, S.J.*, 1676, *s.v.* Hieronymus Xavier.

[21] *Ib.* Alcazar, *Chrono-Historia* (1710), II, p. 216; *J.A.S.B.*, XXIII, 1927 (Hosten), p. 129.

[22] E.g., by A. Rogers in the *Asiatic Quarterly Review* for July 1890, and in a paper read before the Royal Asiatic Society on March 10, 1896. *J.R.A.S.*, 1896, p. 366. See also *Calcutta Review*, 1844, Vol. II, p. 73.

[23] *J.A.S.B.*, LVII, 1888, p. 35.

[24] Zenker, *Bibliotheca Orientalis* (Leipzig, 1846), pp. 207–208, treats of it as a printed book edited by de Dieu, but this must be an error.

[25] Rieu, *Catal. Persian MSS.*, p. 4. Harleian 5478. It is marked: 'Donum Alexandri Pope Armigeri, mense Aprilis A.D. 1723.'

[26] Dorn, *Cat. des MSS. et xylographes orientaux de la Bibl Imp. publique de S. Petersbourg*, 1852, p. 245.

[27] Lee, Preface to Martyn's *Controversial Tracts*, 1824, p. v.

[28] *Cataloghi dei Codici Orientali di alcune Biblioteche d'Italia*, 1878, p. 437. *Catal. Arab. and Pers. MSS. in the Edinburgh University Library*, by Ashraful Haqq, etc., 1925, p. 47, No. 68.

[29] Th. Duka, *Life and Works of Csoma de Körös*, London, 1885, p. 96. If, however, as Duka reports, the work bore the date 1678, some other explanation of its origin must probably be sought.

[30] De Dieu, *Hist. Christi*, Leyden, 1639, p. 13.

[31] Letter of December 1, 1600. *Exemplum Epistolae* (Mainz, 1602). *J.A.S.B.*, LXV, 1896, p. 82. Sommervogel (VIII, 1339) treats of the *Fons Vitae* and the *Speculum Veritatis* as two separate books, each of which had a 'compendium': but other authorities seem to refer to one book only.

[32] Preface to Martyn's *Controversial Tracts*, 1824, p. xli.

[33] Somewhat similar dialogues are utilized in the Dābistān (Shea and Troyer's translation, III, 65–69) which was written about sixty years after Akbar's death. In Lee's preface to Martyn's *Controversial Tracts*, p. xxxvii, a portion of the Dābistān is quoted, which is said to be probably copied from Xavier's *Ā'īna-i-Haqq Numā*.

[34] Lee's Preface, pp. vi–ix ; *Calc. Rev.*, LXXXII, 1886, p. 9.

[35] Addl. 23584, Rieu, *Catal. Pers. MSS.*, I, p. 4. It is also in the State Library at Leningrad. Dorn, *Catal. des MSS.*, etc., p. 243.

[36] Antonio de Leon Pinelo, *Epitome de la Biblioteca Oriental e Occidental*, Madrid, 1629, p. 42, where, however, there is some confusion between this work and the *Life of Christ.*

[37] The book contains 350 pages and a full abstract of its contents is given by Lee in his Preface to Martyn's *Controversial Tracts*, xlii–ci.

[38] From the quotations given in the *Refutation*, Rieu concludes that the book seen by Ahmad was the abridgement and not the original work.

[39] Antonio de Leon Pinelo, *Epitome de la Biblioteca Oriental e Occidental*, Madrid, 1629, p. 42. There is a copy of the book in the Bibliothèque Nationale at Paris (Blochet, *Catal.*, No 52) and in the British Museum (Addl. 25857, Rieu, *Catal. Pers. MSS.*, I, p. 28).

[40] Hottinger, *Promtuarium*, Heidelberg, 1659, p. 93. Another rejoinder was composed in Persian by the French missionary, Chefaud, and sent to Rome, but it apparently was never published. Kircher, *La Chine Illustrée*, 1670, p. 116.

[41] The book is not uncommon. *Vide* also Schnurrer, *Bibliotheca Arabica*, Halle, 1811, p. 244.

[42] Beccari, *Rerum Aethiopicarum Scriptores*, IX, p. 421.

[43] *Weltbott*, no. 645.

[44] Thévenot, *Relations*, Paris, 1663, Part I, ' Discours sur les Mémoires de Thomas Rhoe,' p. 12.

[45] Niceron, *Mémoires*, Paris, 1729, VII, p. 275.

[46] Pierre Bergeron, in *Recueil de divers Voyages curieux faits en Tartarie, en Perse et ailleurs*, Leyden, 1729, II (*Abrégé de l'Histoire des Sarasins*), p. 36.

[47] *Ordures dont on a soullé le Miroir véridique*, a work from Gentil's library, now in the Bibliothèque Nationale. Blochet, *Catal. des MSS. Persans de la Bibliothèque Nationale*, No. 23. The arguments of Ahmad bin Zain-ul-'ābidīn still continue to receive attention in the discussion of the Christian *versus* Muslim question ; see L. Levonian's *Muslim Mentality*, 1928, p. 190, and pamphlets on the Muslim controversy by the Rev. E. M. Wherry.

[48] Ivanow, *Catal. of Persian MSS. in the A.S.B.*, 1924, p. 755, No. 1636, and *Catal. of the Curzon Collection*, 1926, p. 447, No. 666.

[49] Formerly in the Goethals Indian Library, Calcutta. *Catholic Herald India*, June 22, 1921, pp. 479–481. Said by Ranking to have been from Akbar's own library. *J.A.S.B.*, X, 1914, pp. 71–72.

[50] *J.A.S.B.*, X, 1914 (Hosten), pp. 65–83, which includes a minute description of the MS.

[51] Sachau and Ethé, *Catal. Pers. MSS.*, 1889, I, p. 195, No. 365.

[52] De Goeje, *Cat. Or. MSS.*, 1873, Vol. V, p. 91.

[53] *Bulletin S.O.S.*, II, p. 533, and III, p. 138.

[54] Sommervogel, VIII, p. 1340. Blochet, *Catal. Persian MSS. in Bib. Nat.*, Nos. 14 and 15. As to Brouet see Chapter X.

[55] Guerreiro, *Relaçam*, II, Part II, p. 52.

[56] *J.A.S.B.*, X, 1914, p. 66. Cf. Gentil, *Mémoires sur l'Indoustan*, Paris, 1822, Introduction, p. 22.

[57] *J.P.H.S.*, VII, 1918, p. 54 ; Guerreiro, *Relaçam*, V, p. 6 ; Xavier's letter of September 24, 1608 : ' cõ muitos registros de seus passos antresachados nelle.' As noted in Chapter XV, some of the mural paintings in Jahāngīr's palace at Agra consisted of scenes from the Acts

of the Apostles taken from the Book of their Lives which the Fathers had given him. See also Payne, *Jahangir and the Jesuits*, 1930, p. 101.

[58] Sachau and Ethé, *Catal. Persian MSS. in Bodleian Library*, 1889, I, p. 195, No. 365 ; Hosten in *J.A.S.B.*, X, 1914, p. 68. The preface is published in full with a translation by Beveridge on pp. 74–84 *ib.*

[59] Some curious circumstances connected with the production of this publication are given by Hosten in *J.A.S.B.*, X, 1914, p. 73.

[60] The only separate MS. now known is one which was copied from the printed work of de Dieu (mentioned later in the text) for Richard Johnson of Calcutta and which is now in the India Office, Ethé, *Catal.*, No. 620.

[61] *Hist. S. Petri*, pp. 120–121.

[62] De Dieu, p. 94. The corresponding date is mistakenly given in the work as 1600 and this mistake misled de Dieu into holding that it was issued before the Dāstān-i Masīh. *J.A.S.B.*, X, 1914, p. 66.

[63] Nicolas Antonio, *Bibliotheca Hispana*, Rome, 1672, II, p. 326.

[64] Amat di S. Filippo, *Biografia dei viaggiatori Italiani*, Rome, 1882, second edition, p. 355 ; Morelli, *I Codici manoscritti volgari della Libraria Naniana*, Venice, 1776, pp. 105 and 159–191.

[65] Cf. p. 196 above.

[66] The regular custom among Persian Jews. See *Ind. Ant.*, XVII, p. 115.

[67] Letter of September 6, 1604 ; *J.A.S.B.*, LXV, 1896, p. 95.

[68] Transliterated ' cura Johannis Baptistae Vecchiete.' Le Long, *Bib. Sacra.*, Paris, 1723, I, pp. 132–133. Possibly the same as the copy of 1601 based on a version of 1316 which is now in the Bibliothèque Nationale at Paris (Blochet, *Catal.*, 1905, No. 1).

[69] *Bulletin S.O.S.*, II, 1922, p. 532, and III, 1923, p. 138.

[70] ' Para o Sr Joaõ baptista Vecchiete.'

[71] This was the translation of which there is a copy in the Bodleian Library (Laud 141. Sachau and Ethé, *Catal. Persian MSS.*, I, No. 1830). This copy has the inscription ' Psalmos de David cotejados con os Latinos pollos P[es] da Comp[a] de Jesus muito praticados na lingoa Partiana.'

[72] Walton, *Prolegomena*, in *Scripturae Sacrae Cursus Completus* (Paris, 1839), I, p. 467, and Le Long, *Bib. Sac.*, Paris, 1723, I, p. 133.

[73] Sachau and Ethé, *Catal. Persian MSS. at Bodleian Library*, I, p. 1050, No. 1828.

[74] *Relation*, p. 23.

[75] Annual Report of 1670–1678, December 27, 1678.

[76] s.v. Xavier, VIII, p. 1340. See also de Filippi's *Desideri*, p. 328.

[77] *Bulletin S.O.S.*, III, 1923, p. 137 ; *Mem. A.S.B.*, V, 1916, p. 163. On page 39 of the Catalogue attached to Fraser's *Nadir Shah*, 1742, mention is made of *The Gospel of Geronimo Xavier*, but this is clearly a mistake for the *Life of Christ*.

[78] Sujān Rai, Khulāsat ut Tawārīkh (1695–1696), quoted by Beveridge in *J.R.A.S.*, 1894, p. 754.

[79] Badāonī, *Bib. Ind.* (Lowe's translation), II, p. 267.

[80] One of the Persian versions of the Gospels in the Bibliothèque Nationale (Blochet, No. 6) was said by the scholar Reinaud to have been executed by the command of Akbar, but this is probably an error as the version is nearly identical with one which was known to have had another origin. (See *Cat. Bib. Nat. Supplt.*, No. 5.)

[81] Guerreiro, *Relaçam*, I, p. 23 ; du Jarric, III, p. 52.

[82] Letter of September 6, 1604 ; *J.A.S.B.*, LXV, 1896, p. 97.

[83] Le Long, *Bib. Sacr.*, Paris, 1723, I, p. 133. Cornel. a Lapide, *Commentarii in IV Evangelia*, 1732, p. 11.

[84] Letter of September 6, 1604; *J.A.S.B.*, LXV, 1896, p. 97. When in slavery in Africa a few years later he was allowed to retain his copy of the Persian Gospels. Morelli, *I Codici manoscritti volgari della Libreria Naniana*, Venice, 1776, p. 183.

[85] *Bulletin II*, 1922, p. 532, and III, 1923, pp. 135–138. It has hitherto been wrongly assumed that the translation was made by Xavier. The *Bibliotheca Marsdeniana*, published by Marsden in 1827, only says (p. 305) that the book ' seems to have been in the possession of Jeronymo Xavier.'

[85a] See *Cataloghi dei Codici Orientali di alcune Biblioteche d'Italia*, 1878, p. 434.

[86] Casiri, *Bib. Arabo-Hispana*, 1760, II, p. 343; Blumhardt, *Hist. Gén. de l'établissement du Christianisme*, 1838, I, p. 325. Minuchihr arrived in India in 1598: *Akbarnāma*, transl. Beveridge, III, p. 1112.

[87] See Xavier, letters of September 6, 1604, September 25, 1606, and August 28, 1607. The letter of 1606 says: ' Depois tomamos de proposito de cotejar (e) emendar o Parsio, conforme a nossa vulgata q' na verdade tinha muitos erros dos escrivãos.'

[88] Portions of the Gospel were no doubt from time to time translated even in the days of the first Mission. As noted by Monserrate, *Commentarius*, fol. 35 (a), ' Data occasione, quaedam ex Evangelio, in Persicum sermonem conversa, Sacerdotes tradiderunt.'

[89] *Bulletin S.O.S.*, II, 1922, p. 533, and III, 1923, p. 138. There is also a copy in the Casanatense Library in Rome; see *Cat. dei Codici Orientali di alcune Biblioteche d'Italia*, 1878, p. 438.

[90] *Re* Vechiete, see p. 211 above.

[91] *Chrono-Historia*, 1710, II, p. 216; *J.A.S.B.*, XXIII, 1927, p. 129; Sommervogel, VIII, p. 1339. Xavier's inscription mentions the titles of the four chapters.

[92] *Mem. A.S.B.*, V, 1916 (Hosten), p. 152.

[93] J. Eusebius Nieremberg, *Claros Varones*, Madrid, 1647, s.v. J. Xavier, IV, p. 246; Alcazar, *Chrono-Historia*, 1710, II, 216; *J.A.S.B.*, XXIII, 1927, p. 129; Sommervogel, VIII, p. 1339. Desideri mentions ' other books of other Lives of Saints.'

[94] See his *Relazione*, Book I.

[95] The actual word is indecipherable, but doubtless ' doctrine ' is meant. It is the only work of Xavier other than the Lives of Christ and S. Peter, mentioned in Stoeger's *Historiographi Societatis Jesu* (Ratisbon, 1851). A ' dottrina Christiana conforme al paese,' i.e., a catechism suitable for the country, was drawn up in 1611 in Persian and Portuguese by Xavier and the other Jesuits at Lahore; see Xavier's letter of April 11, 1611. Desideri in 1721 was acquainted with ' a big and a small catechism ' by Xavier (Report, Florence MS., fol. 15).

[96] Annual letter of September 7, 1686.

[97] It may possibly be one of these books to which Xavier refers in his letter of September 6, 1604, where he says that he gave to Akbar in Agra ' a book in Persian containing sayings of some of our philosophers and curious things, which he had asked me for. He and his chiefs enjoy it very much and it is in great request.' *J.A.S.B.*, LXV, 1896, p. 93.

[98] VIII, p. 1339. He gives Alcazar as his authority, but the book does not appear to be mentioned by Alcazar.

[99] *Bulletin S.O.S.*, II, 1922, 533, and III, 1923, p. 138.

[100] *Bibliotheca Thevenotiana*, Paris, 1694, p. 199.

CHAPTER XV

THE MISSIONS AND MOGUL PAINTING

Dona . . .
Miratur, rerumque ignarus imagine gaudet.
(Virg., *Aen.* viii, 729–730.)

THERE was a strain of artistic feeling which ran through the successive generations of the ruling Mogul house in India. Of its expression in certain departments of art—in architecture, for instance, or decorative inlay or landscape gardening or calligraphy—much of value might be, and has been, written. But it will be convenient to confine ourselves here to a consideration of the interest taken by Mogul sovereigns in the art of painting, and the extent to which their patronage and taste in this department were affected by contact with specimens of Western art and more particularly with Christian art as introduced into India under Jesuit influence.

Painting under the Moguls

The Muhammadan faith has been less favourable than Christianity to the development of this form of art. To the orthodox Muslim it is forbidden to represent the image of any living creature, and as painting has always been very largely devoted to such representations, it is rare to find the art of painting approved or patronized by the stricter type of Muslim rulers. When the rulers were frankly unorthodox, as was the case with Akbar and Jahāngīr, painting was in great demand : and where the ruler was, like Aurangzeb, a rigid Muslim, it gradually suffered an eclipse. The religious aspect of the question in its relation to Christianity was intensified in India by the fact that the arts of painting and sculpture were in peculiarly close alliance with the Christian religion as represented by the Portuguese and the Jesuits. Throughout the Middle Ages and before the invention of printing, pictures and images were the handmaids of religion in Europe, and the violence of Protestant prejudice against religious imagery in the sixteenth and seventeenth centuries served to accentuate its use by the supporters of the Counter-reformation. Christianity

The Muslim attitude and that of the Mogul rulers

To face page 222] [*From Jahangir's Album, Berlin*

AN INDIAN ARTIST DRAWING THE MADONNA

By Kesho

(See p. 251)

in Mogul India was identified with the prominent and constant use of pictures and images. In the time of Akbar we find the historian Badāonī mentioning the special indignity which pilgrims sailing to Mecca were compelled to endure at the hands of the Portuguese owing to their passports having pictures of Mary and of Jesus (peace be upon Him !) stamped upon them.[1] A Mogul sovereign who wished to conciliate Muslim opinion on the subject of the Portuguese or the Jesuits was always ready—for the moment at any rate—to proclaim an interdict against the images and pictures of the foreigners. During the brief outburst of enmity to the Portuguese which marked the year 1614, the property of the church at Lahore was attached by Jahāngīr, and when the Jesuits ultimately obtained orders for the release of their property, the images in the church were expressly excluded from the order of restitution.[2] When the troops of Shāh Jahān attacked the Portuguese at Hūglī in 1632 they seized the images of the Christian saints and hung them on trees :[3] and when the Portuguese prisoners from Hūglī were brought to Agra in 1633 their images were confiscated, such as were ' likenesses of the prophets ' being thrown into the Jamna and the rest broken in pieces.[4] In the following year the officials of Shāh Jahān broke the images and ripped up the pictures in the church at Agra.[5] When anticipating trouble in 1650 the Fathers at Agra at once took their pictures from the church and hid them in their house.[6] In view of possible interference the Fathers then arranged that the church at Agra should be furnished mainly with paintings rather than statuary, and this precaution was found useful when the church was searched in Aurangzeb's time. The servants of the Mission were able to remove the pictures while the Fathers kept the officials in conversation at the gates, and though the Fathers did not escape a fine of 150 rupees they succeeded in saving their pictures.[7] The influence of the Mullās was consistently exerted against the use of pictures and images by the Christians, and their attitude, though flouted by Akbar and Jahāngīr, became gradually the accepted policy of the Court. We are assured, nevertheless, that a ruler so late and so decadent as Muhammad Shāh (1719–1748) supported the Christian attitude towards images, pointing out that the Jesuits' veneration for images was merely an outward sign of the feeling inwardly prevailing among Muslims ;[8] and attacks by the authorities on such forms of art, though not unknown, were in fact unusual and spasmodic. Speaking generally it may be said that the Mogul rulers looked with a good deal of tolerance on the Christian use of images and paintings, and in the case of the earlier sovereigns,

Akbar and Jahāngīr, the feeling was one not merely of toleration but also of sympathy and admiration.

Akbar's interest

To Akbar the art of painting so far from seeming irreligious presented itself as a revelation of the Divine. He himself took lessons in painting and his attitude is shown by his oft-quoted declaration that it appeared to him 'as if a painter had quite peculiar means of recognizing God.' It was an age of fine painters in India and he made every effort to encourage them by weekly exhibitions of their work and by the distribution of rewards. A large album was formed to contain the likenesses of men about the Court and many volumes, both of prose and of poetry, were illustrated with exquisite paintings. The great painters of the day—'Abd-us-samad, Daswanth, Basāwan, Kesho, Maskīn, and the rest—are mentioned by name in the *Ā'īn* of Abu'-l-fazl and many of their works are still extant in modern collections.[9]

Jahāngīr

Jahāngīr too was a connoisseur of considerable talent, and in his Memoirs he especially mentions his two favourite painters, Abu'-l-hasan and Mansūr. He was very fond of studying pictures and clever at recognizing the authorship of any work before him—so much so that, to use his own words, he could 'declare without fail by whom the brow and by whom the eyelashes were drawn.'[10] His agents ransacked India and the neighbouring countries for curiosities and works of art, and few presents were more acceptable to him than a good picture.

Presents of pictures by the English

Europeans therefore who wished to secure the goodwill of Jahāngīr would commonly present him with pictures from Europe. Sir Thomas Roe, the English ambassador, for instance, during his long negotiations of 1615–1618 made considerable use of pictures as a form of present. He urged on the East India Company to send him pictures for this purpose : they should, he wrote, be large pictures on cloth,[11] 'the frames in peeces,' and should represent some story with a variety of figures—a 'Diana' recently received had, he observed, given much content.[12] Above all he insisted that they should be good pictures ; those previously sent by the Company were not worth a penny.[13] For a Provincial Governor like Muqarrib Khān he seems to have thought a cheap article sufficient and we find him presenting that official with a series of thirteen pictures representing Christ and the Apostles which had cost in England eightpence apiece.[14] An officer like Jamāl-ud-dīn Hasan is given a book with forty-eight sheets of pictures portraying the whole history of the Saviour, valued in

England at twenty-four shillings.[15] The powerful Chief Minister, Āsaf Khān, on the other hand, gets a picture worth £6 13s. 4d.'[16] and Āsaf Khān is also used as an intermediary for the presentation of pictures to the King.[17] To the King's relative, Mīrzā Beg, Roe gives three or four paper pictures together with an old pair of spurs,[18] and the King himself receives four pictures representing the Four Elements. At the Nau Roz darbar of 1616 the King exhibited pictures of the King and Queen of England, the Princess Elizabeth, Lady Somerset, Lady Salisbury, a London citizen's wife, and Sir Thomas Smythe, Governor of the East India Company—doubtless received by him from Roe's embassy —and at the corresponding darbar in the following year a similar exhibition was made.[19] The King also extracted from Roe a picture of a lady, about whom Roe wrote so mysteriously that it is supposed to have been a portrait of his wife ; and the King was greatly impressed by it.[20] On another occasion he took possession of portraits of Lady Montague and Lady Molyneux, together with a picture of Venus and a Satyr, which, as Roe pointed out to the Company, was an extraordinarily unsuitable subject.[21] Through Roe's embassy alone therefore the Court was supplied with a considerable number and variety of European pictures.

Presents of pictures by the Dutch

The Dutch were little behind the English in the importation of pictures. Their agent Pelsaert, writing in 1626 after several years' experience of Agra, tells how the English imported tapestries worked with stories from the Old Testament, and he himself urged his employers to send out 'two or three good battle pictures, painted by an artist with a pleasing style, for the Moslems want to see everything from close by : also some decorative pictures showing comic incidents or nude figures.'[22]

Presents of pictures by the Jesuits to Akbar and Jahāngīr

The Jesuit missionaries had since the commencement of their Mission introduced a number of European pictures into Mogul territory both as aids to evangelization and as objects of veneration in their churches. At the same time they had not been behindhand in the presentation of pictures as offerings to Akbar and Jahāngīr, and both of these rulers were possessed of many Christian paintings most of which they had received through the Jesuits. One of the first offerings by the Jesuits to Akbar in 1580 was, as we have seen, a copy of Plantyn's Polyglot Bible of 1569–1572. This contained illustrations engraved by Flemish artists of the school of Quentin Matsys (1466–1530) : and the pictures of galleys in Mogul landscapes are said to be traceable to examples in this book.[23] In the Kābul expedition of 1581 Father Monserrate tried to interest Akbar in Christianity by showing him illustrated sacred books.[24] In 1595 we find Father Jerome Xavier writing from Lahore to the General of the Society that he should send out 'a beautiful large picture of the Holy Virgin or of the Nativity' for the King and the Prince Salīm, together with some little pictures for the Christian converts. The King already had, he wrote, large pictures of Our Lord Christ and of the Blessed Virgin, which were of the best kind of those brought from Europe.[25] In 1598 Father Xavier presented Akbar at Lahore with two 'exquisite pictures made in Japan,' one of Christ and one of S. Ignatius Loyola, and he found the King in possession of a picture of Christ at the pillar, which he treated with much respect.[26] In 1601 Fathers Xavier and Pinheiro presented the King with a pen-and-ink sketch of the Virgin which he sent away at once. The next day thinking that he was discontented with the picture because it was uncoloured they brought him a representation of Our Lady of Loretto on gilded metal, which he treated most reverently, joining his hands, and explaining that he had sent away the other picture merely because it seemed disrespectful for him to be sitting on a throne above the level of the picture.[27] In the following year the Fathers, no longer confining themselves to sacred objects, presented Akbar with a portrait—'retrato ao natural'—of the great Albuquerque and another of the Portuguese Viceroy Ayres de Saldanha.[28]

The same spirit that inspired Akbar displayed itself also in his son, the Prince Salīm, the future Emperor Jahāngīr. In 1595, for instance, he saw with the Fathers a picture of the Virgin and bade the Portuguese painter make him a copy.[29] He had pictures made of the life and death of Christ and ordered the insertion in a book of a picture of Christ crucified and of Our Lady with her infant Son with His arms about her neck.[30] We learn that the Prince was seriously angry with those who conducted the Fathers of the third Mission for failing to bring any picture of Our Lady for him from Goa, and when he found a traveller about to set out for Goa he impressed upon him his desire above all things to possess a beautiful picture of the Virgin.[31] This he apparently obtained, for in 1598 the Jesuits reported that he had pictures of Christ and the Lady Mary in his bed-chamber.[32] The Englishman Hawkins speaks of his praying in the morning at Agra upon a goodly jet stone at the upper end of which 'the pictures of Our Lady and Christ are placed': [33] and another Englishman, Coverte, found in 1610 that Jahāngīr had a picture of Our Lady 'in the place of his praier or Religious proceedings.'[34] In 1598 Father Jerome Xavier once found the Prince superintending the painting or copying of two small pictures, one of which represented the angels appearing to the Shepherds and the other the Descent from the Cross.[35] We hear too (as will be noted later) of his showing his collection of small pictures to the Fathers, and the display of these pictures led to long and curious arguments.[36] Jahāngīr's son, Prince Khurram, afterwards the Emperor Shāh Jahān, showed during his younger days the enthusiasm of his father for pictures, and like his father was anxious to receive presents in this form : but this attitude was not maintained in his later years.[37]

Enthusiasm for Christian pictures

The interest shown by the Mogul sovereigns in examples of European art is in itself remarkable. But still more remarkable is the extraordinary enthusiasm evinced by the Court and by the people at large for certain European pictures introduced by the Jesuits into Mogul territories. It will be of interest to refer to three outstanding instances of this enthusiasm which are recounted by the Jesuit authorities.

The Borghese Madonna, 1580

One of the earliest presentations by the first Mission—that of Father Rudolf Aquaviva—in 1580 was a fine copy of the Byzantine Virgin which is still to be seen in the Borghese Chapel of the Church of Santa Maria Maggiore at Rome. Some experts treat the picture at Rome as a copy of an older original, while others, who treat it as itself an original, ascribe it to the eighth or even to the fifth century. Like other similar pictures it was believed to be the work of S. Luke, and it still commands the greatest veneration for its age and its miraculous properties.[38] The copy brought by Father Rudolf Aquaviva had been made by the orders of S. Francis Borgia with the express permission of the Pope Pius V and sent to Goa in 1578. There is among the illustrations to the copy of Jerome Xavier's *Life of Christ* at the Lahore Museum, a picture which portrays the presentation of this painting by a priest and possibly represents the transfer of the painting by the Provincial to the Jesuit missionaries. There can be no doubt that the painting which is shown in the background of the picture is intended to represent the Borghese Madonna as it closely follows the form of the picture at Rome. The painting is shown behind an altar and under a baldacchino, while in the foreground are some nine or ten figures, several of whom are in the habit of priests and in attitudes of adoration : and at the foot there is a Persian inscription to the effect that 'after reciting a blessing on it the chief Pādre gave it into his hands.' The illustration, however, is so defaced that it is impossible to recognize more of its purport than the fact that it portrays the presentation of a copy of the Borghese painting by some high ecclesiastic to some unknown person.

The copy of the Borghese Madonna was greatly esteemed and is always spoken of by the Jesuit Fathers as a work of exquisite beauty. The accounts regarding it are not altogether clear, but it seems to have rested for a time in the Fathers' chapel at Fatehpur Sīkrī and while there to have attracted much attention and respect from large crowds both of Hindus and of Muslims—whose attitude, as Father Monserrate sadly remarks, was so different from that of the iconoclastic Protestants of Europe.[39] Akbar himself, when he came to see it, removed both his turban and his shoes and bade others do the same.[40] It seems to have been presented to Akbar together with a picture of Christ, and when he returned from Kābul to Fatehpur at the end of 1581 one of his relatives thinking to please him had ' a most beautiful picture of the Virgin ' which Akbar possessed (doubtless this same picture) removed and placed ' in the pillared hall opposite the royal balcony,' framed with rich and elegant decorations of gold cloth.[41] In 1590 when there were no Fathers at his Court, Akbar on his own initiative celebrated the feast of the Assumption by placing the same picture of the Virgin—that given to him by Father Rudolf Aquaviva—in an elevated place and calling on his courtiers to kiss it with due reverence.[42] When the third Mission reached Lahore in 1595 he seems to have had the picture with him and to have taken great pleasure in showing it to his friends, often holding it in his arms till he was weary.[43] We do not know what ultimately became of the picture, but there is a tradition current that it is now to be found in one of the churches in Cochin or elsewhere in Southern India.[44]

The Madonna del Popolo, 1602

Just as the Jesuits had in 1580 introduced at Fatehpur a copy of the Madonna of S. Maria Maggiore, so in 1602 they brought forward in Agra a copy of another prominent picture in Rome, the Madonna on the high altar of S. Maria del Popolo, another of the pictures ascribed to S. Luke. The enthusiasm caused by this picture both among the people and at the Court was one of the most extraordinary features of the Mission, and to any who have not had experience of the emotions of an Indian crowd the account of its reception would appear almost incredible.[45] For a parallel to this enthusiasm one has to go back to Vasari's account of the days when the Florentines carried Cimabue's Madonna from his house to the church ' in a stately procession with great rejoicing and blowing of trumpets ' and ' all the men and women of Florence flocked thither in a crowd with the greatest rejoicings.' The whole incident is remarkable, and in order that it may be fully appreciated it is worth while to quote as it stands the description of it given by the chronicler Guerreiro :[46]

'The Fathers had had the picture,' he says, 'for two years, but they had not dared to expose it for fear that the King would take it. Now, on the feast of Christmas and Circumcision of this year 602 [1602] they determined to place it in the church, which they decorated in their best style for the purpose. They had, however, no other intention than that of helping their own devotion and that of the Christians. But it happened one day during the octave, that some poor women in the Fathers' neighbourhood asked their permission to come and see the church in the evening. They were allowed, and were so enchanted at the sight of the sacred picture that, on going home, they went, like so many Samaritan women, praising it so highly and giving such glowing accounts of it to all whom they met and talked to, that from mouth to mouth the news spread all round and set the whole city astir. The people began to flock to the church, and they returned marvelling still more at what they had seen than they had been eager to come. They left their shops and their occupations to hasten to the church, and curiosity ran so high that more than two thousand persons came that evening alone from the adjoining streets.

The next day in the morning, the Fathers were obliged to say an early Mass, because the people were already waiting at the door to enter. Seeing the great concourse, which went on increasing, and fearing some disorder, the Fathers were obliged to see to the things of the house and guard the chief doors, so as to avoid a tumult. Then, they stationed themselves at the more convenient entrances to receive the people and speak to them. The sacred picture was exposed on the altar of the chapel, with candles burning round it. It was covered with two veils : one thin and transparent, the other a curtain of taffety, which remained always drawn until the church was full of people. It was then pulled aside, and besides two small boys always standing near the altar, there was always someone knowing the language of the country who, each time the picture was unveiled to the people, spoke to them of Our Lady and her Blessed Son, who had come down to earth to reveal and teach to the world the true way of salvation. To make the people enter in greater order, the Fathers saw that the women entered separately, and the men separately, a thing which gave great edification and no more were allowed in at a time than the church could hold. When these had gone out, others were let in, and at the unveiling of the picture they would all stand gazing and lost in admiration.

The feelings which the sight produced in them were something marvellous and evidently beyond the natural. They were feelings of admiration, emotion and consolation. Truly, even to those infidels, the Virgin showed herself a mother of consolation, seeing how consoled, contrite and touched by the sight they left her presence. Such was the impression of the Fathers, when they heard them speak after they had seen Our Lady. It was the case with many distinguished and noble personages ; for the Fathers took occasion of this to preach to them and speak of Christ Our Lord and that sovereign Lady, His Mother, and to discover to them at the same time the impostures and misdeeds of Mahomet. They listened with much compunction and confusion, and without protesting, to all the evil that was said of Mahomet ; and it is all the more astonishing if one knows how badly Moors bear to hear their false prophet spoken ill of, or how greatly they hold all kinds of pictures in abhorrence. Even so, all left with feelings of love and affection for the Holy Virgin.

Those who came the first days belonged generally to the lower class ; but, from the third and fourth day there came Moulas or men of letters, noblemen and lords, who before that deemed it dishonourable to come to the church. Their example increased still more the excitement in town, so that the number of those who went in and out of the church—which is small—was computed at ten thousand a day. They came not only from the town, but even from places outside, to which the fame of the sacred picture had spread. Except in the evening, the Fathers had not a quarter of an hour to themselves during the whole day, even to eat a morsel. Such was the concourse they had to attend to, and so wonderfully did the Mother of God wish to make herself and her Blessed Son known to those infidels, so that on the Day of Judgement they might have no excuse.

Among the lords and nobles who came, there was a great Captain with an escort of more than sixty persons on horseback, and many men on foot, altogether a man of great respectability. On seeing Our Lady, he stood as if spell-bound. After these, there began to come others and others, and they returned so much moved that, on reaching home, they brought all their people, and, what is more, their wives, ladies of the first nobility. The Fathers welcomed them with much courtesy ; and when they came, the other people were kept back and were refused admittance.

A Moor of the highest rank, one of the King's officers, could not on account of his many occupations come at any other time than one day very early in the morning. The Fathers took him to the chapel and unveiled the holy picture. Casting his eyes on it, he looked at it for a good while, lost in wonder and speechless, tears rolling from his eyes all the while. The Father asked him to sit down, and profited by the opportunity to speak to him of God, but he did nothing but weep, unable to detach his eyes from the picture. " Sir," asked the Father, " what harm did Mahomet find, or what harm do your people see, in the use and veneration of such a picture, since it excites in the heart such consolation and emotion ? " He answered that the Moors do not understand these things, and he went on to speak so plainly in disparagement of Mahomet and in honour of Christ and of Our Lady that a devout Christian could not have done better. He remained there until the concourse of people obliged him to leave, and he went his way much consoled and saying to all a thousand things in honour and praise of our holy Faith.

A brother and a nephew, and cousins and relatives of the King of Xhander (Khāndesh), and a son of the King of Candaar came also two or three times, with a large retinue and many nobles and lords of the court, and they said to the Fathers that the King would not be pleased if they did not mention to him something so much worth seeing. Hence they resolved to do so at once ; and, repairing to the palace, they gave an account of what was going on, to which the King answered that he knew it already, and that he also would like to see the picture of the Lady Mary. He wished them to bring it for his inspection. The Fathers said it was a pity that His Highness did not come to see it where it was, on the altar. " I shall go," he said. But his courtiers objected that he could not, because the house of the Fathers was very far. (In fact the house, though within the city, was half a league from the palaces.) It would, therefore be better if the Fathers brought the picture.

They did so the next day, but at night. When the King knew it was there, he was much pleased, and ordered that they should bring it to his room. Father Manoel Pinheyro went to fetch it. Meanwhile the King called for a black raincloak,[47] which he had kept for some days for the Fathers, and he asked Father Xavier if he found it good. " Yes, Sire," answered the Father. " Do you wish us to wear it ? It would do, Sire, against the rain, and to follow you in your service, but these cords and tassels of silk will not do for us." " Then there is no harm in cutting them off," he said, and descending four or five steps from the throne where he was seated, he vested the Father with it himself. Father Manoel Pinheyro arrived just then with the picture. It was as high as a man, and had been brought covered and very neatly framed.

The King had again seated himself ; but, when the Fathers uncovered the picture, he immediately came down again, approached quite close, took off his turban half to show it his deep reverence, and expressed himself extremely pleased to see it. Out of respect for the King, the grandees kept behind him and dared not approach ; but, he called them one by one to have a look at it, and they vied with one another in showing the astonishment and wonder it caused them. What they said and confessed all of them redounded greatly to God's glory and gave much satisfaction to the Fathers.

The King, who was very keen on getting the picture, said, " My father esteemed much things like this ; and, if anyone had given it him, he would have granted him any boon he might have asked." The Fathers understood perfectly his clever way of disguising his request, but they did as if they had not, and warded him off with some compliments. " For the moment," returned the King, " leave the picture in the room where I shall sleep to-night." And he entered the apartment with the Fathers, and told them to put it anywhere they liked and preferred. When it was hung up, he made a great reverence before it, taking off his turban almost completely, a thing he never does.

The Fathers had understood at once that his reason for wishing to keep the picture was to show it to his wives and daughters. He showed it to them the next day, and descanted himself on the excellence of the Queen of Angels and great was the respect and honour shown her by all these Moorish ladies. One of them, who until then had been very hostile to the Fathers and the law of Christ, was much changed after that, her opinion of us being very different now from what it had been. The next day, the Fathers returned, fearing not a little that the King would like to retain the picture ; but God was pleased that he should return it, and they took it back greatly consoled as he who " reducebat arcam domini in locum suum " (who brought back the ark of the Lord to its place).

The people had been very sad to hear the picture was in the King's palace ; for they thought they would never see it again ; but, on learning that it had been brought back to its place, they came to visit it once more.

Ere long, however, their devotion was again interrupted. The King's mother, who was very old, hearing what was going on, and not having seen the picture when it was in the palace, was anxious to see it. She begged her son to ask the Fathers again for it, which he did ; and, when the Fathers arrived with it, he excused himself saying that old as his mother was, she liked, however, to be still fondled as a mother. Without allowing anyone to help him, he took the picture in his arms and carried it inside, where he placed it high and conveniently. Not only his mother, but his wives and daughters, who had seen it already, came to view it, the sight giving them as much pleasure as it excited admiration. The King stood near the picture, and said that none of the women should touch it. When it had been shown, he had it carried by a eunuch to the Fathers, who were standing outside.

In the square before the palaces there were many people who were also eager to have a look at it. Captains and noblemen pressed the Fathers to show it to them, a request which could not be refused. As the picture was to be shown to so many at a time, great was the noise going on around it ; but, no sooner was it uncovered, than a hush came over the crowd, and all marvelled greatly. After this, the Fathers went home with it, and wherever they passed in the streets, the people rejoiced and congratulated the Fathers on their bringing it back. On seeing it taken again to the palace, they had thought the King would lay hold of it.

The concourse to our church began anew, and then it was soon broken off again, because many advised the King to have a copy of it made by his painters. The King contended that they would not be able to imitate it to perfection ; still, to try what they could do, he got together the best painters of the city and sent someone to ask the Fathers to bring the picture back. They went and put it in a becoming place, where it could be seen by all, and it was the King himself who was most demonstrative in his reverence, telling young pages in his suite not to go near. And, as numbers of Moorish and Gentio nobles, and the King's nephews came to see it, the Fathers had an excellent opportunity to explain to them and declare with great freedom, the whole of that day, the mysteries of that Lady and of her Most Holy Son. The Moors listened to it all, and took it very well, and they showed they had a high opinion of the things of our Faith, a remarkable and quite novel phenomenon, seeing their general arrogance, and supreme disdain of us.

Meanwhile, the painters merely took their measurements and threw out some lines ; (não fazião senão lansar suas linhas e debuxar) ; but, though this time the picture remained many days in the palace, and they worked as hard as they could, they achieved very little in the end, and were obliged to confess that they could not come up to the perfection of the model or equal the Portuguese in the art of painting. Many, therefore, tried to persuade the Fathers to present the sacred picture to the King ; but the Fathers parried them off gently, and on the feast of Our Lord's Resurrection they went to ask it back.

They took it home and put it away altogether. Many lords still asked for it repeatedly, to let it be seen by their wives ; but in order to conciliate greater prestige and reverence for the holy Virgin, the Fathers refused it to all. There were two, however, against whom they were powerless.

One was Agiscoa ('Azīz Koka), the chief captain and lord at court, the King's foster-brother and great favourite, and his joint brother-in-law, a son and daughter of his having married one of the King's daughters and sons. The Fathers depended very much on his favour. When the Fathers came with the picture, Agiscoa had assembled in his house all his wives and daughters, his daughters-in-law and female relatives, who were many. Not only were the Fathers received with honour and courtesy, but Agiscoa himself and one of his eunuchs took the picture and carried it inside. They brought it back in the same way to the Fathers. The result of the Fathers' attention was that such a bigoted Moor as Agiscoa now showed the Fathers respect and affection, a great change on what he had been before. The next day, he sent a very distinguished personage of his household on a visit to the Fathers, to thank them for having brought the picture and say that he would do anything for them, and wished very much to hear the mysteries of that Lady explained to him. If the image could be given away, he would give for it whatever they wanted ; if not, could they give him a similar one, which would do and prove acceptable ?

The other one to whose house the Fathers could not help taking the picture, was the King of Candaçar. He had been many years residing at the court of King Hiquebar, having entrusted to him his kingdom, which he was unable to defend against Abduxam, the King of Husbec. When carrying it over, the Father had himself escorted ; and, while the King, who had welcomed him very politely, was examining it at leisure with his wives inside there, the King's son remained outside with the Father, asking him what he thought of their Mahomet. Great was his surprise to hear that people such as we did not believe him to be a Prophet. His father's kingdom being situated so far away to the east, he thought the whole world was full of Moors and followed the law of Mahomet. Just then the King sent back the picture with many thanks and some cruzados for the young men who accompanied the Father, as also a goodly sum for the Father ; but the Father and his servants declined the present, to the great astonishment of the Moors, who consider it quite a marvel to refuse money when it is offered. After this the Fathers put the picture away for good and all.'

The Adoration of the Magi, 1608

A somewhat similar interest was aroused in the early years of Jahāngīr's reign by the receipt from Rome of a picture (quadro) of the Adoration of the Magi. The picture reached Father Pinheiro at Cambay and he found it to be 'a work of superior excellence and perfection.' It was exhibited in the church at Cambay and attracted enormous crowds, no less than 13,000 persons collecting to see it during the thirteen days for which it was on view. The local Judge stood lost in amazement before it and the Envoy Muqarrib Khān was so impressed with the majesty visible in the figure that he declared it was better for a man not to have been born than to miss seeing the picture. On its arrival in Agra Jahāngīr sent for the Fathers to explain its purport to him, and holding the picture in his hands he discoursed to his courtiers on the story of the Nativity, 'like a preacher in the pulpit.' He bade the Fathers have it mounted on a board so that it might not be damaged by being constantly unrolled, and at his request the Fathers added a border with an ornamental design in black and white, adapted from their own books and pictures which was afterwards incorporated in gold embroidery (recamo d'ouro). So pleased was the King that he ordered his own portrait to be inserted in the border at a spot indicated by Father Corsi.[48] It is possible that this picture may have been on silk or some similar material, and if so it was probably that referred to by Jahāngīr in his Memoirs, where he says that on June 1, 1608, 'Muqarrib Khān sent from the port of Cambay a European curtain (parda) the like of which in beauty no other work of the Frank painters (musawwarān) had ever been seen.'[49]

The three examples above quoted will help to furnish an idea of the extraordinary enthusiasm evoked among all classes, and more especially at the Mogul court, by the exhibition of European pictures of a religious character.

Such pictures were almost exclusively imported from Europe. There were, it is true, European painters at the Mogul court, but they were few in number and doubtless of mediocre quality, and we know very little about them. In 1595, for instance, the Jesuits had with them at Lahore a Portuguese painter who was commissioned to copy the picture of the Virgin in the Fathers' chapel.[50] So too in Jahāngīr's court there were two English painters, both of a somewhat nondescript character. One, named Robert Hughes, was a merchant in Sir Thomas Roe's entourage, an amateur who 'did with a pen draw some figures, but very meanly, far from the arte of painting.'[51] Another, called Hatfield, was brought out by the adventurer Steele, in order to secure the good graces of the King, and the King sat to him inside the zanāna for his portrait.[52] He was nominally the engineer for Steele's projected waterworks at Agra, but his real profession was that of painting, and he was acknowledged by Roe, who was a good judge, to have been in his proper line 'a very good woorkeman both in lymming and oyle.'[53]

European painters in Mogul territory

There was later on at the court of Aurangzeb a painter who seems to have been a Christian. His name was Muhammad Zamān, and this man appears almost certainly to have been identical with a Persian of that name who was sent as a student by Shāh 'Abbās II to Rome and was there converted and changed his name to Paolo Zamān. In Persia although he concealed his religion he met with harassment and so left about the year 1646 for India. He was given a stipend by Shāh Jahān and lived at first in Kashmīr, but later on he was summoned by Aurangzeb to Delhi in connection with a general scrutiny of the stipends of Persian refugees. At Delhi his way of life did not differ from that of the Muslims, but he lived in friendship with the Christians and more especially with the Jesuit Father Busi. Busi assures us that he concealed his religion 'for good reasons' and that he in reality held very tenaciously to Christianity (Christiana instituta, occulte licet justas ob causas, mordicus tenet).[54] As already noted in Chapter XIV Paolo Zamān owned several Latin books and himself wrote a translation into Persian of part of Father Ricci's Latin work on China. In 1675–1676 he was employed to fill up with pictures three blank spaces in a copy of the Khamsah of the poet Nizāmī, and in these three distinctive pictures (now in the British Museum) 'the costumes of his figures are, in several instances, of a European type and the landscapes are copied from late Italian paintings.'[55] There are some further pictures by him, including an Allegory of Fame

Paolo Zamān

after a European engraving and a portrait of two European ladies;[56] and reproductions have been made of a Visitation and of the Flight into Egypt.[57] Between 1675 and 1678 he was engaged in illustrating another manuscript of the Khamsah now in the Morgan Library in New York, and an inscription on one of these illustrations states that he was then in Ispahān. It is not certain whether he retained his Christianity, and there is reason to believe that he relapsed into Muhammadanism and performed the pilgrimage to Mecca.

Taste for copying European pictures

In spite of the existence of an excellent and flourishing school of indigenous painting, the courts both of Akbar and of Jahāngīr looked on European art as equal, if not superior, to that of India. It was the fashion, in some quarters at any rate, to treat European painting as the ideal to which Indian talent should strive to attain. European artists were held to be specially adept at giving expression to the mental states of men.[58] Abu'-l-fazl, in describing the progress of painting under Akbar, alluded to the masterpieces recently produced in India and spoke of them as worthy to be compared with the 'wonderful works of European painters who have attained world-wide fame.'[59] As early as 1580 we find Akbar having copies made of the pictures of the Virgin and of Christ which the Fathers had with them,[60] and in 1597 the Prince Salīm is reported to have begged for the loan of the picture of S. Ignatius Loyola that he might have it copied.[61] When Father Jerome Xavier in 1597 found (as has above been mentioned) the Prince Salīm having pictures made of the Angels appearing to the Shepherds and the Descent from the Cross, these were being copied from European originals.[62] The Prince employed the most skilled painters of the realm in preparing—doubtless copying—pictures of Our Saviour and of the Virgin.[63] One of the well-known painters of the day, Kesho the elder, had an album of Christian pictures which had been copied.[64] Jahāngīr was immensely proud of the skill shown by his painters in copying, and when Sir Thomas Roe showed him his picture of the mysterious lady, he offered to have five copies made and to put Roe to the test of identifying the original among the copies.[65] On another occasion the test was actually applied in respect of another picture which in Roe's opinion could not be copied in India. Five copies were attached to a table or board along with the original, and Roe confesses that, although he ultimately identified the original owing to his knowledge of art, he was at first much put to it to distinguish the pictures, and adds that the King thereupon was 'very merry and joyful and craked (boasted) like a Northern man.'[66] Even in the last year of his life, we find Jahāngīr anxious for an illustration of the Jesuit church at Lahore for insertion in the Royal chronicles and his painters were sent to the church to copy the ornamentations for insertion in the contemplated picture.[67] Nor did the practice of copying European art cease with the death of Jahāngīr, and it is indeed alleged by some authorities that the rage for copying European pictures reached its height towards the end of the reign of his successor; the Emperor Shāh Jahān being, we are told, so desirous of these copies as to have every European painting which he could obtain copied by the artists of his court.[68]

Pictures of European subjects in buildings

Not only were such paintings copied, but pictures of a European type—either in original or as copies—were plentifully used by Akbar and Jahāngīr for the adornment of their palaces and other buildings, sometimes as easel pictures framed and hung, and sometimes as frescoes or wall-paintings. We have records telling of the existence of this class of picture at Fatehpur, at Sikandra, at Agra, at Lahore, at Ajmīr and at Delhi. In some cases sculptured images are also mentioned.

(i) At Fatehpur

At Fatehpur Akbar had Christian pictures in his palace at an early date even before the arrival of the first Jesuit Mission. The Fathers when they arrived were told that he had in his dining-room pictures hung up (ymagines suspensas) of Christ, Mary, Moses and Muhammad: and that he treated that of Muhammad with less respect than the rest.[69] There are also still extant in the Maryam kī Kothī at Fatehpur the well-known remnants of two wall-paintings, which may possibly be interpreted as representing the Annunciation and the Fall.[70]

(ii) At Sikandra

At Akbar's tomb at Sikandra it is clear that there were Christian pictures at one time to be seen, but what these pictures were it is difficult to say, as the accounts given of them by contemporary authorities are not a little confusing. When Fra Sebastian Manrique was at Agra in 1641, the interior of the portico was, he states, covered from the summit of the dome to the base with 'cunning paintings,' the most remarkable being one of the Virgin.[71] Father Botelho who was at Agra between 1648 and 1654 speaks of two large marble vestibules at the entrance of Akbar's tomb, where a thousand skilful hands had fashioned figures, among which he recognized the Fathers of the Society who had first introduced

Christianity in Akbar's reign.[72] According to Tavernier who saw the tomb in 1665 there was at the gate of the garden a painting representing the tomb covered by a black pall with many torches of wax and two Jesuit Fathers at the ends.[73] Manucci writing later states that the figures on the principal gateway of the garden were a Crucifix, the Virgin Mary, and S. Ignatius Loyola. There was, he says, a Crucifix delineated on the wall: on its right hand the image of Our Lady with the Infant Jesus in her arms, and on the left S. Ignatius—'the whole delineated'—while on the ceiling of the 'dome' were great Angels and Cherubim and many other painted figures.[74] According to Catrou the Crucifixion was by Aurangzeb's orders covered over with a hanging of gold brocade which Manucci had to lift in order to see the forbidden art below. In Catrou's story the representations of the Virgin and S. Ignatius were statues, and it is not clear what Manucci meant to convey by the phrase 'the whole delineated,' as the word in the Italian version of his work is 'sculpite' (sculptured) and in the Portuguese 'debuxada' (painted or drawn). If the representations were pictures—and the fact that according to Manucci's account they were about to be whitewashed seems to support this view—it is not impossible that they were copies of the pictures of Christ and S. Ignatius made in Japan which were presented to Akbar in 1598.[75] It is difficult to decide from these various accounts whether there was one Christian work of art at the tomb or more, and what was represented there; but we may be certain that there were Christian figures of some kind and that they included portraits of one or more Jesuits. Whatever they were, we may with Tavernier express our astonishment at their being allowed by Shāh Jahān to remain untouched. This attitude was, as above noted, somewhat modified under Aurangzeb, and subsequently these representations—whatever they were—were entirely removed, for there are now no traces of them left.

(iii) At Agra

We have no record of European wall-paintings at the palace at Agra having been made during Akbar's lifetime, but shortly after his death various portions of the palace were profusely decorated by the order of his successor, Jahāngīr, with pictures representing Christian or European subjects. An interesting account of them is given by Father Xavier in a letter of September 24, 1608, the substance of which is reproduced by the chronicler Guerreiro in the last volume of his *Relaçam*.[76] The passage in Xavier's letter is of sufficient interest to justify its being quoted in full:

'When he came from Lahore he found his palace very beautifully decorated and adorned with many paintings which had already been completed, and others which were yet to be completed both on the inside and on the outside of a verandah where he sits daily to be seen by the people. On the inner side where he goes at night and where he sits before he wishes to appear on the outer verandah he has a large verandah, on the middle of the ceiling of which there is a good picture of Our Saviour in glory surrounded by Angels, and on the walls of the hall are some Portuguese figures of large size, beautifully painted, and some small pictures of Saints, including S. John the Baptist, S. Antonio, S. Bernardino of Siena, and other Saints, male and female, also well painted. Of the janela or outer window what shall I say? On the sides of the palace where the King sits when he shows himself to the people there had been some excellent life-size portraits of some of his favourites, but some days later he had these obliterated and in place of these he had painted some very smart Portuguese soldiers, under arms, of life-size so that they could be seen from all parts of the maidan. There were three figures on each side of the window. Above them on the right was a painting of Christ Our Lord with the globe of the world in His left hand, and on the other side Our Lady very well painted: but when he had seen a picture of Our Lady by S. Luke which we have in our Church, he had it obliterated and a copy of our picture substituted in life-size.[77] On either side of Our Lord and of Our Lady were various Saints in a posture of prayer. In the oriel of the verandah or janela where the King sits, at the sides, on the same wall, were full-sized pictures of his two sons, very splendidly attired. Above one of these was a representation on a small scale of Christ Our Lord and next to Him a Father with a book in his hand: and above the other was Our Lady. In the same oriel recess (no mesmo vaõ da charola) were S. Paul, S. Gregory and S. Ambrose: they, being inside the oriel and on a small scale, are scarcely visible to the people standing below, but the rest can all be seen. Often when attending on the King has one told one's beads before the picture (imagem) of Our Lady and commended oneself to Christ Our Lord represented there. The Moors are astonished at this and God is to be thanked that the representations of Christ Our Lord and of Our Lady and of the Portuguese are so much in evidence. The verandah looks, in fact, as though it belonged, not to a Muslim King, but to a King of great devoutness. Then in the interior of the palace the King has had the walls and ceilings of various halls painted with pictures of the mysteries of Christ Our Lord and scenes from the Acts of the Apostles taken from the book of their Lives which we gave him, and the stories of S. Anna, Susanna and others. All this the King did of his own accord without a suggestion from anyone. He had ordered his artists to consult the Fathers as to the colour to be given to the costumes and to adhere strictly to what we told them. The figures to be painted were selected by the King himself from his collection of prints (registros) and he decided where they were to be placed. He got his painters to make large-size sketches on paper of all the prints which he wished to have painted and the Fathers then stated how the painting should be done. All this decoration is very offensive to the

Moors who will not tolerate portraits, even of those whom they consider Saints, much less of those who hold a contrary Faith, to which they are so much opposed. As the Moors deny all that pertains to the Passion of Our Lord, they especially resented a picture of Christ at the Pillar which the King had made at this time from a small print. It was a large picture well coloured and was to serve as the pattern for a picture with the same figure woven in silk like arras (como pano de raz) and he had the title in Persian woven in the same fashion in the silk picture. On the wall of one of his halls he had life-size pictures painted of the Pope, the Emperor, King Philip and the Duke of Savoy, all on their knees adoring the Holy Cross which was in their midst—a copy of a print which he had of this subject.[78]

Of all this there appears to be now no trace. There is, however, against the wall of the old Catholic Cathedral at Agra a marble statue of a female figure with the hands joined, wearing a veil and shoes of European pattern, which has always been presumed to be a statue of the Virgin. It is said to have been originally in the ancient Palace in the Fort and to be of the same quality and kind of stone as many of the old works in the Fort. From the Fort it was taken to the Bank of Agra before 1871 ; and it was obtained from the Bank for the Cathedral by Monseigneur Van den Bosch who was Archbishop of Agra in 1892–1898.[79]

(iv) At Lahore

In the Fort at Lahore there was not the same profusion of Christian painting as at Agra, but Christian emblems were not wanting. The English traveller Finch, who was at Lahore in 1611, gives a minute account of a picture to be seen on the walls of the Diwān-khāna (which was apparently a building occupying the site now known as the Barī Khwāb-gāh). The picture represented a Darbār of Jahāngīr, with portraits of many of his nobles ; but there was also, apparently in the same room, a picture of Our Saviour over the door on the right of the King's picture as you entered and a picture of the Virgin Mary opposite it on the left hand.[80]

Father Andrade writing in 1623 tells us that Jahāngīr adorned his principal hall (sua sala principale) with a copy of a picture—apparently of the Virgin—which the Provincial had given to Andrade ; and he also relates how Jahāngīr had a picture of Christ copied on the roof of a handsome verandah in his palace at Lahore. In the sketch of the latter picture a dove was represented over the head of the Christ and the painter who copied the sketch had, either by design or by accident, substituted an owl in the place of the dove, an offence for which Jahāngīr had him thrashed, saying that he would have had him executed if he had not been satisfied that the substitution had been made by inadvertence.'[81]

The practice of utilizing Christian subjects for the adornment of buildings in Lahore was not confined to the King's palace, and similar pictures were to be seen in the mansion of the great Minister Āsaf Khān. When Fra Sebastian Manrique visited Āsaf Khān in 1641 he saw in the garden of the house a building used as a bath, and on the walls of this building were appropriately depicted the Ark of Noah and the life of John the Baptist.[82]

There was also an example of Christian influence in Lahore, which survived into the eighteenth century, namely a fine representation cut in alabaster of Our Saviour surrounded by Angels. This was seen in a gallery of the Parī Mahal Palace inside the town of Lahore by the Dutch ambassador Ketelaar on January 29, 1712.[83] The Parī Mahal was afterwards stripped bare by the Sikhs and there is now apparently no trace of this work of art.

(v) At Ājmīr

Even at Ājmīr, though no religious pictures are mentioned, there were examples of European art. The palace at Chashma-i-nūr behind the Tārāgarh hill had European portraits in some of the smaller rooms, and Sir Thomas Roe who was there in 1616 saw in several panels in the walls portraits of the French Kings and other Christian Princes.[84]

(vi) At Delhi

At Delhi, which was inaugurated as the capital in 1648, the practice was not altogether discontinued, for, as is well known, there was behind the throne in the Diwān-i-'ām a representation in mosaic of Orpheus, executed in all probability by European artists. But as was natural the reproduction of sacred subjects seems to have gradually died out in all the Mogul palaces under Shāh Jahān and Aurangzeb.

Pictures of such pictures

Most of the wall-paintings have in the nature of things disappeared, but the fact of their having previously existed is in some instances confirmed by their representation in portfolio pictures which reproduce the architectural features of the Mogul palaces. The prevalence of these Christian wall-paintings is indicated in one of the beautiful illustrations to the copy of Nizāmī's Khamsa prepared for Akbar in 1593. The illustration, which is by the painter Maskīn, depicts an incident in an Oriental building on the walls of which there are three paintings of a European type; one showing four children in some form of bath, the second a personage writing at the dictation of another, and the third a man (probably S. Matthew) writing under the supervision of an angel.[85] There is another interesting picture of this character now in the Wantage Collection at the India Museum in London which confirms still more closely the accounts given by the Jesuits. It represents the Empress Nūr Jahān entertaining Jahāngīr and one of the Princes in the year 1617, and in the background is a portion of a pavilion, on two panels of which are shown a Madonna and an Ecce Homo.[86] In a further picture, now at Boston, representing a darbār of Jahāngīr, the Emperor sits on a terrace in front of a wall on which there is a small painting of the Virgin Mary, with possibly a corresponding Ecce Homo out of sight.[87] So also in a picture in the Bodleian Library at Oxford which represents the reception of a Persian embassy by Shāh Jahān, the wall behind the Emperor's throne has a frieze of Europeanized cherubs, and in the background of the throne itself can be dimly discerned a part of the lower edges of two painted panels sufficient to enable us to identify the subjects as Christ and the Virgin.[88]

Portfolio pictures

Turning now to the class of pictures spoken of as ' miniatures ' or portfolio pictures—as contrasted with frescoes or wall-paintings —it may be noted in the first place that the Mogul painters did not produce easel pictures with the oil medium. Jahāngīr saw some European oil-paintings and did not like them,[89] and such paintings do not seem to have been copied in oils. The so-called miniatures of the Moguls were painted for the most part on prepared paper by means of successive layers of water-colour. The paintings are in some cases illustrations inserted in one or other of the sumptuous editions of the Persian and other classics which were in vogue at the time ; in others they were isolated paintings, mounted on paper and preserved indiscriminately in *muraqqas* or portfolios. The miniatures of Mogul times have come down to us in one or other of these two forms ; the illustrative pictures being often preserved after extraction from the books to which they originally belonged. Specimens of Mogul miniatures are as a rule somewhat difficult to find, being kept in public or private collections not always easy of access, and only a small proportion have been reproduced in the excellent but expensive volumes illustrative of Oriental art which have been published of late years.[90] There are public collections of value in the Bibliothèque Nationale at Paris, the Museum für Völkerkunde in Berlin, and the Museum of Fine Arts at Boston. For our present purposes, however, the bulk of the Mogul miniatures in question can be examined in four great public collections in England ; the Wantage Bequest in the India Museum in Kensington ; the Johnson Collection (put together by Johnson, the banker of Warren Hastings) in the India Office ;[91] the Oriental Collection in the British Museum ; and the Ouseley and Douce Collections in the Bodleian at Oxford. There is also a remarkable series of pictures in the Album of Jahāngīr, a collection of miscellaneous pictures mostly dating from 1608–1618, which was not improbably a gift from Jahāngīr to the Persian Shāh and which, after being obtained by Brugsch Pasha in Persia in 1860–1861, was finally deposited in the Prussian State Library in Berlin.[92] Many such pictures, of Indian origin, are to be found also in an album from the Teheran Museum which was sent to England for the Persian Exhibition of 1931.[92a] The private collections which help us are fairly numerous and among them that of Mr. Chester Beatty, in London, deserves special mention. In these collections, public and private, we find the chief examples illustrative of the influence of Christianity and European art on Mogul painting. It is not always easy to ascribe a date to such isolated paintings, but a general distinction can be made between the paintings of the true Mogul period—say, down to the early part of the eighteenth century—and the later productions of the Mogul school which came mostly from the debased surroundings of Lucknow, and in the present chapter reference is intended to the former class alone.

Reproductions of European costume

One form of curiosity affected by the collectors of the time consisted of portraits, prepared in India, of European types or of individuals dressed in European costume. Some of these may have been taken from life, others were no doubt copies of engravings or of coloured pictures imported from Europe. In the Album of Jahāngīr, for instance, there are marginal pictures of European huntsmen and of European peasants copied from a calendar composed by Hans Sebald Beham (1500–1550) and from an engraving by Egidius Sadeler (1575–1629) after R. Savery (1576–1639).[93] One similar sheet with exquisite marginal sketches of European origin, both secular and sacred, is to be found in the Album of the Teheran Museum to which allusion has been made above. The Album of Dārā Shikoh at the India Office contains a pretty picture, obviously painted in India, of a lady and gentleman in Elizabethan costume.[94] In the India Museum there are at least ten Indian pictures of persons in European dress. Two of them are portraits of some European of distinction, possibly Sir Thomas Roe; one is a vignette of a woman with light curled hair, a feather on her head, and a red gown opened square at the front, who is said by tradition to be Lady Shirley; another represents two women, one wearing a ruff and a feather, and the other holding a book and candle, both standing in front of an Indian landscape; in another we find a man and a woman seated at a table in European costume and hats, the woman wearing ear-rings and anklets; in another there is a woman in European costume with a feather in her hair seated on a European seat, wearing anklets and reading a book, while another woman somewhat similarly dressed presents her with a dish and vase of flowers ; and in four others there are portraits of Europeans.[95] An early full-length portrait of two Europeans finds a place in one of the Paris collections.[96] The pictures of Mr. Imre Schwaiger exhibited at the Coronation Durbar in Delhi in 1911 contained an Indian-made portrait of a Portuguese lady and gentleman.[97] The British Museum has a picture by Muhammad Zamān of a European woman with a man drinking, in a night scene of European character.[98] The Bodleian Library has a small oval miniature of an Elizabethan lady, possibly Elizabeth herself, set in a window panel in a wall,[99] and there is in Paris another portrait on somewhat similar lines dating from the early seventeenth century.[100] The Johnson Collection in the India Office has several pictures of Europeans accompanied by dogs, and a curious piece showing a European presenting a book to another who is seated on a chair, with two further Europeans pouring out liquor in the foreground.[101] So too there was on sale in London in 1929, a strange picture of four men in black European costume, including at least one ecclesiastic, arresting an old Muslim on the bank of a sea or river.[102] In some of the pictures of Mogul Darbārs one or two European figures are introduced, and there is one picture showing the reception by Shāh Jahān of some European deputation not hitherto identified.[103] From these examples, which are by no means exhaustive, it will be realized to what an extent the human subject in its European form entered into the indigenous art of the Mogul period.

European influence in Mogul miniatures

Even in their portraiture of Indian subjects in which they so markedly excelled, the Mogul painters would sometimes employ a European technique.[104] It has been urged that during the Mogul period the works of Indian painters relating to Biblical and other European subjects were undertaken merely to satisfy their patrons and that in copying or imitating European works they did not lose sight of their own tradition.[105] This is no doubt true, but it must at the same time be recognized that the Indian thought fit in certain instances to adopt for better or worse some definite aspects of the technique of the European pictures with which he had become acquainted.[106] It has been suggested that the idea of equestrian portraits is itself an importation from Europe, and in any case the fine equestrian study of Shāh Jahān now at Leningrad has a background of ships and clouds which at once betokens a European origin. 'The painting with its stormy sky,' writes one of our foremost authorities, 'reminds one of a Greco. Has some unknown picture by Titian, Clouet or Van Dyck given the artist the idea of this portrait, or is it simply the copy of such a one that has found its way to India, or merely an engraving of one? It is certainly not of Indian origin.'[107] The practice too which sprang up about the end of Jahāngīr's reign of finishing the head of a portrait while leaving the body in the form of a sketch is looked on by some authorities as an imitation of the methods of Holbein or of Dumoustier or his school.[108] It became customary to supply Indian pictures with a background of a European type,[109] and it was common to introduce a dark background of foliage corresponding to the dark backgrounds prevailing in the oil-paintings of Europe. But apart from special peculiarities of this character there is much to indicate the general influence of European examples on the whole Mogul art of the period. The exact determination of the spheres in which Hindu, Persian and European conceptions entered into Mogul painting is a question for experts, but the latest examination of the subject has led to a more ample recognition, than has hitherto been afforded, of the share attributable to European influence. The subject has been studied with the greatest minuteness in M. Stchoukine's recent work on the Indian Painting of the Mogul period, and there is much of extraordinary interest, from the historical as well as from the artistic standpoint, in the observations of so well-recognized an authority on such aspects of Mogul art as the treatment of backgrounds, the introduction of atmosphere and 'plein-air,' the attitudes of human subjects, the arrangement of draperies, the rounding and solidifying of the figures, the indications of personality and mentality in the portraits, the use of relief and shading, the alteration in ideas of perspective, the development of composition and the harmonizing of colour. In his well-documented treatise M. Stchoukine has set out his views as to the degree of influence exercised by European examples in each of these spheres, and whatever may be the ultimate verdict of expert opinion on his individual conclusions, there can be little doubt that the study of European pictures by the court painters of the Moguls introduced some modifications of technique which affected substantially the characteristics of their work.[110]

Mogul pictures illustrating the Christian religion

How far the taste for pictures of European costume and how far the introduction of European technique or European backgrounds in Mogul art was directly due to the influence of the Jesuits it is difficult to say. The same characteristics prevailed, though in a different degree, in Persia and in Turkey, and the importation of pictures of a secular character in India, as in those countries, was doubtless to a large extent the work of merchants and travellers rather than of missionaries. In India the taste for copying and collecting such pictures may possibly have originated from, and it must certainly have been encouraged by, the Jesuits; but a large proportion of the pictures themselves must have filtered into the country through other agencies.

When we turn, however, to pictures illustrative of the Christian religion, a more direct part must be ascribed to the Fathers. They were not indeed the sole purveyors of Christian examples. Sir Thomas Roe, for instance, as we have seen, made presents of pictures of Christ and the Apostles. But from what we know of the status and proclivities of the Jesuits and from the character of the matters delineated, it is obvious that the Jesuits were almost exclusively responsible for the remarkable vogue which Christian subjects enjoyed among the Mogul painters of the seventeenth century. A considerable number of Mogul pictures portraying Christian subjects have survived. In some of them the subject is treated in a purely Oriental manner; in others the method of treatment is in a greater or lesser degree European. In neither class of picture is it always easy to determine how far the result which we have before us is a pure copy or is a reminiscence or adaptation of a European original, and in detailing below some instances of this kind of picture no attempt has been made to determine the degree of conscious imitation which they exemplify. The fact that they deal in each case with a subject connected with the Christian religion is the common point of interest which they present in connection with the history of Jesuit Missions. It may also be noted that when pictures of this class are based on European originals, the originals in question were those in vogue among ordinary people in Europe at the time. The Jesuits were not art critics. They themselves admitted that they valued a picture according to its subject rather than in consideration of its artistic merits, and we must not expect to find among the pictures popularized by them copies of the masterpieces best known to those who visit the art galleries of Europe at the present day.

It was not indeed from European oil pictures that the Indian artist ordinarily took his ideas for Christian subjects. In some cases, no doubt, the large coloured pictures presented by the Jesuits or placed by them in their churches were utilized as guides, but the bulk of the Mogul sacred pictures received their inspiration from small engravings introduced from Europe. At the end of the sixteenth and the beginning of the seventeenth century there was an

Engravings from Europe, the chief influence

immense export of such engravings, proceeding for the most part from the Port of Antwerp and representing the work of artists connected with that city. The researches of Messrs. Kühnel and Goetz enable us to trace a number of the European subjects in Jahāngīr's Album to particular engravers of the Antwerp and other cognate schools. Allusion has already been made to the huntsmen and peasants adapted from engravings by Hans Sebald Beham and Egidius Sadeler, and we find traces in the Album of the work of other Flemish artists also, such as Theodor Galle (1571–1633) and of John and Raphael Sadeler (1550–1600 and 1555–1618). Some of the Flemish engravers, like John Wierix (b. 1549) and his brothers, were known to be strong supporters of the Jesuits in Europe and made a speciality of the production of small engraved pictures of sacred subjects, suitable for use as bookmarkers in works of devotion. It is to this class of picture more than to any other that we seem to be indebted for the bulk of the Christian subjects dealt with in Mogul art.

Original engravings

In the art albums of Mogul India it is not uncommon to find these European engravings inserted as they stand in their original form. Occasionally an engraving thus utilized was of a secular type. The Johnson Collection in the India Office, for instance, has an engraving, touched with gold, portraying Edward, Lord Sheffield, first Earl of Mulgrave, a Parliamentarian nobleman who died in 1646;[111] a portrait which was doubtless brought to India by the English. Of the religious prints some were introduced from Italy. Dr. Sarre of Berlin, for example, writing in 1904, speaks of an Album of Indian Miniatures in his possession into which an Italian engraving of the Magdalen had found its way.[112] The precious Album of Prince Dārā Shikoh, which is now at the India Office and which contains a dedication, dated 1641, from the Prince to his wife, his ' nearest and dearest friend the Lady Nādira Begam,' includes among a number of beautiful Indian pictures two small prints of Italian origin. One of them shows S. Catherine of Siena on her knees before a Crucifix and underneath, the words : ' S. Caterina di Siena. Ant. Carenzanus for. 1585.' The other is a picture of S. Margaret sitting with hands joined and below appears the curiously inaccurate inscription : ' S. Margarita, liberastia rugentibus praparastis ad escaeul.'[113] The same book has also a print of the Virgin and Child, possibly representing a rest during the Flight to Egypt.[114] We know that Jahāngīr held a large collection of European prints, and we have already seen how a number of them were utilized as the basis of the large wall-pictures with which Jahāngīr adorned his palace at Agra. In detailing his experiences of the summer of 1608 Father Xavier describes how at his evening meetings Jahāngīr would send his librarian to fetch his collection of prints, and how he would night by night go through them and obtain from the Fathers explanations of their meaning. Among those which he produced in this way were pictures of Sardanapalus, of the Circumcision, of God the Father, of the Crucifixion, of David kneeling before Nathan, and so forth.[115] We still have extant a remarkable collection of original engravings in the Berlin Album of Jahāngīr, which contains no less then eleven specimens. These appear to be in almost all cases of the Flemish school. Some are known prints by known artists ; such as a Massacre of the Innocents and a Holy Family on the way to Nazareth, both by John Sadeler after Marten de Vos (1531–1603), and a Flaying of Marsyas (possibly introduced as a Martyrdom of S. Bartholomew) by Theodor Galle after John Stradanus (1523–1605). There are also a Resurrection, a Descent into Hell and a vignette of S. John the Baptist, which are probably the work of Raphael Sadeler. Others which cannot be definitely attributed, include prints of the Four Evangelists, the Day of Pentecost, Noli me tangere, and the Adoration of the Magi, as well as an adaptation by some unknown engraver of the Ape in Dürer's well-known 'Madonna with the Ape.'[116]

Original European prints of this kind were kept in the Mogul portfolios, partly on account of their artistic merit and partly as curiosities. They serve also as an indication of the extent to which European prints were the basis of the Christian pictures, some of them very beautiful, which the Mogul painters produced in colour. There is a minute coloured Head of Christ imbedded in an illuminated border which was exhibited by Mr. Imre Schwaiger at the Coronation Darbār in 1911 and which appears to have been cut out of some missal ;[117] but as a rule coloured European pictures do not seem to have found their way into the Mogul collections. The coloured Mogul picture of a Christian subject was not, as a rule, a copy of a coloured European picture, but was based on some uncoloured European print. In some few cases it is possible that colour was imposed by the Indian artist on the print itself ; for Father Jerome Xavier tells us how he once saw one of the King's painters 'illustrating some small pictures by putting on colours and pigments.'[118] In one of the pictures in the British Museum—a small picture which portrays three subjects—(Christ disembarking from a boat with his disciples, Christ casting out a devil and the swine running down to the sea, and Christ asleep in a boat which is foundering on the shore)—

Coloured pictures based on European engravings

To face page 249] [*From Jahangir's Album, Berlin*

FIGURES FROM DÜRER

(See p. 249)

the colouring appears to have been imposed on an actual European woodcut or on a close imitation thereof,[119] and there are other pictures in which the characteristics of a woodcut have been preserved, wholly or partly, in conjunction with the colouring.[120] The general rule, however, was for the Indian artist to be provided with one of the small European prints—known to the Portuguese as ‘ registros ’—and to draw then in outline a copy or modification of the picture, adding thereafter such colouring as was thought advisable.

In Jerome Xavier's letter of 1608, already quoted, he tells us how Jahāngīr, when employing his artists to paint a picture from an engraving, required them to consult the Fathers as to the colours to be used for the costumes.[121] A painting by Manohar Dās in Mr. Chester Beatty's collection represents a woman addressing an attenuated figure in a jungle, and although it seems to illustrate the Persian story of Majnūn, there are some indications in the draperies and other details of its having been adapted from some uncoloured woodcut of Italian or German origin. Two similar pictures, executed by the same painter and exhibiting the same characteristics, find a place in the Album of the Teheran Museum. There is in the Berlin Album of Jahāngīr, a Holy Family copied from a known engraving of Raphael Sadeler after J. Rottenhammer (1564–1623) in which the colouring is said by the experts to be almost exactly what a European artist would have adopted for a coloured copy of the engraving.[122] Among the coloured pictures in which we are able to point to the original sources, the most remarkable are those in which the subjects have been copied or adapted from the productions of Albert Dürer—not necessarily from original engravings by that master, but in all probability from European copies of those engravings. Coloured figures based on various prints by Dürer have been inserted with much taste in the beautiful borders surrounding the specimens of calligraphy in Jahāngīr's Album. On one page there are four such figures which can be traced to known productions of the master : One of the Magi from an Adoration, a S. Peter from The Healing of the Cripple (1513), a S. John from a Crucifixion (1511), and the Virgin under a Tree from a print by John Wierix after Dürer.[123] On a similar page of the same Album, now in the Marteau Bequest at the Louvre in Paris, is a variation of Dürer's Burgundian Standard-bearer ;[124] and there was also a strange seventeenth-century picture exhibited at Paris in 1912 which shows several figures in European costume before a man who occupies a chair or throne—this man being curiously enough an almost exact replica of the Caiaphas in Dürer's engraving of 1512 which portrays the trial of Christ before Caiaphas.[125]

In order to give some idea of the enormous vogue enjoyed by Christian subjects in Mogul art during the period in which the Jesuits exercised an influence at the Mogul court, it is worth while to note briefly the classes of subjects treated and some of the examples which have survived. But before mentioning the undoubted examples of Christian pictures in Mogul art it may be well to allude to one series of pictures which have in the past been incorrectly considered to portray a Christian subject. In the collection exhibited by Colonel Hanna in London in 1890 and in the Johnson Collection at the India Office and in a considerable number of Albums elsewhere there are pictures of a holy man to whom angels are ministering. These were considered to be representations of the Angels ministering to Christ after the Temptation in the Wilderness, but it has been pointed out by Mr. Beveridge that the picture in Colonel Hanna's Collection—and the same may be said of similar pictures elsewhere—represents an incident in the history of Ībrāhīm bin Ādham, a Muslim saint, whose name is familiar to most English readers through a well-known poem of Leigh Hunt,[126] and the pictures in question, though at times incorporating clear reminiscences of Christian art, do not portray a Christian subject. The saint, according to the Muslim story, was provided by angels with ten plates of food and so caused discontent to a neighbouring dervish who was supplied with one only. The scowling figure, which appears in the corner of many of these pictures, was formerly considered to represent the foiled Tempter of the Christian story, but is in reality the discontented dervish of the Muslim legend.

Ībrāhīm bin Ādham

Among the genuine examples of Christian subjects dealt with in Mogul art, the most common, as might be expected, are the Virgin or Virgin and Child.

Pictures of the Virgin

It has been suggested by an eminent Sanskritist that the traditional treatment of the Virgin and Child in European art has, through these representations, influenced the type adopted by convention in modern Indian pictures of Devakī and the infant Krishna ;[127] and whether this be the case or not, the subject of the Virgin or Virgin and Child must have been very familiar to the Indian painters in Mogul times. Examples are still to be found in considerable numbers in different art collections. The State Library at Leningrad, for instance, is said to have a picture of the Virgin and Child accompanied by a minute inscription containing the words 'Yā Sāhib-ul-zamān' (O Lord of the Age) ;[128] and in the State Library at Berlin there is a Madonna and Child with the subscription 'Tasvīr Hazrat

'Īsā bin Maryam' (Picture of the Lord Jesus, son of Mary).[129] The Berlin Museum of Ethnology has a Madonna painted by the artist Bālchand,[130] and the Sarre Collection in Berlin has a seventeenth-century Mogul picture, based probably on a Flemish engraving of about the year 1520, which represents the Virgin attending the Child in a cradle, with a female servant standing by.[131] The Album of Jahāngīr at Berlin contains not only the adaptation of Dürer's 'Virgin under a Tree' of 1513, to which allusion has already been made, but also a picture of the Virgin, almost European in its conception, which is stated to be the work of the painter Kesho Dās, and an interesting study of an Indian painter who is occupied in drawing a picture of the Madonna.[132] A Mogul Madonna was among the Oriental pictures shown at the Munich Exhibition of 1910, and a Nativity, almost entirely European in style, which is probably a copy of an Italian print, is to be seen in the Goloubew Collection in Boston.[133] The British Museum contains an unusual representation of the Virgin and Child, attributed to Muhammad Afzal,[134] and the Johnson Collection at the India Office has several pictures of the Virgin. One of these is a second-rate orientalized painting of the Madonna and Child, in which the Child wears gold bangles and bracelets ; in another the Virgin and Child are standing on a crescent and snake after the manner familiar in European art ; in another the Virgin is of dark complexion and the Child holds a book ; and in a further picture two angels are represented as adoring a woman who is probably intended to be the Virgin.[135] The Bodleian Library has a small miniature of a Virgin with a mantle of Sassoferrato blue, set in a panel of Indian design.[136] There is also in this Library a curious monochrome Madonna of an Oriental type of countenance holding her Child, with three Cherubs hovering in the sky and three European women (in colour) in attendance, one wearing a hat and holding a yak's tail and the other two carrying books ; an animal like a cat sitting meanwhile in the corner.[137] Another strange Virgin and Child is in the same Library : the Virgin is enthroned and there are angels in the sky and other personages in the foreground, with the back view of a remarkable figure in a costume of grey and brown which apparently represents a religious of some Catholic order.[138] A Madonna descending near a Hindu Temple was the subject of one of the pictures exhibited in London by Colonel Hanna in 1890 ;[139] a Virgin with angels was included in Mr. Imre Schwaiger's loan to the Coronation Darbār Exhibition at Delhi in 1911 ;[140] and a portrait of the Virgin and her Son was exhibited to the Indian Historical

Records Commission in 1922 by L. Bulāqī Dās of Delhi.[141] The Government Art Gallery at Calcutta has a small and pretty oval miniature of a Madonna and Child, in which the Virgin is of a European type but her costume is Oriental.[142] At the Lahore Museum there is a seventeenth-century Madonna (with an attendant angel) holding an open book inscribed with Persian characters ;[143] and in one of the illustrations for the copy of Father Jerome Xavier's *Life of Christ* in the same Museum there is a happy representation of the youthful Virgin ascending the steps of the Temple.

Mention may also be made of two mysterious cases in which the introduction of incongruous features in such pictures has led critics to suspect that Indian artists employed on pictures of the Virgin have displayed anti-Christian leanings. In the State Museum at Berlin there is a curious seventeenth-century picture in which a woman with an Indian type of face and wearing a cross on her necklace is seated on a chair with a child. A man who resembles a Saint from an Italian picture is standing by with a book in his hand, but in the foreground are two Europeans, one pouring out wine and one lying back in a helpless attitude. The seat on which the woman is sitting is tilted back at an unsteady angle, and it has been suggested that the whole picture is a parody connecting the Christian religion with the drinking of wine.[144] The probability is that the picture merely represents some contemporary Christian woman and the ironical element, if contemplated, does not extend to anything in the shape of an insult to the Mother of Christ. So too in a picture included in the Jahāngīr Album there is a woman sitting with a child unclothed before her and minute examination discloses the figure of a small pig in part of the ornamentation of the chair. This also has been thought by some to be an inimical feature introduced by some anti-Christian painter : but here again it is by no means certain that the picture is intended to represent a Madonna, and in any case the practice of parodying such subjects is so alien to the spirit ordinarily shown by Indian artists that one would hesitate, without further evidence, to suggest that these pictures indicate disrespect to the Christian Madonna.[145]

Pictures of the Life of Christ

In addition to representations of the Virgin, the Mogul painters executed numerous pictures to illustrate incidents in the story of the Life of Christ. Among the miniatures at Leningrad there is said to be one which depicts the Annunciation ;[146] and the collection of Mr. A. P Charles in London contains an attractive illustration, detached from some copy of Father Jerome Xavier's *Life of Christ*, which shows the room at Bethlehem being swept and prepared by the

Virgin before the birth of her Son.[147] At the India Office there are two pictures in grisaille and gold of the Virgin and Angels adoring the Christ-Child outside the stable, and another in monochrome of the Child adored by a beautiful group of winged angels ;[148] while another study of the same subject, based probably on some European woodcut, is to be seen in Mr. Chester Beatty's Collection. Among the Douce pictures in the Bodleian Library is a representation of Christ enthroned with a globe in his hand:[149] and a remarkable item among the coloured pictures in Jahāngīr's Album is the Holy Family previously mentioned, which is based upon a known engraving of Raphael Sadeler.[150] One of the borders in the same Album portrays the Moorish King copied from Dürer's Adoration of the Magi,[151] and an Adoration of the Magi was among the pictures exhibited by Colonel Hanna in London in 1890.[152] The Circumcision is depicted in a slightly coloured picture in the British Museum,[153] and there is an outline sketch tinted with pink at the India Office which possibly represents the same subject.[154] Underneath a portrait of Jahāngīr at a window, by Nādir-ul-zamān, in Mr. Chester Beatty's Collection, there is a picture of a young Christ with a Cross, which is taken from some European original. Another picture in the same Collection shows Christ standing upon a raised platform, surrounded by a halo, and addressing a body of men and women, among whom both Indians and Europeans are depicted ; a representation possibly of Christ among the Doctors in the Temple. The illustrations in Father Jerome Xavier's book at Lahore include one of Christ raising his hands in prayer after being baptized in Jordan. The British Museum has a coloured picture, based upon a European woodcut, of a stormy sea with two boats struggling against the tempest, in one of which are four men in European hats and in the other one such passenger accompanied by a haloed figure, perhaps representing Christ, in an attitude of prayer.[155] A further illustration in the Lahore Museum copy of Father Jerome Xavier's *Life of Christ* is a picture of Christ healing the man with the withered hand, and although the greater part of the picture has been defaced by time, enough of the central figure still remains to show the tenderness and insight with which the subject had been treated. The India Office has a curious picture in monochrome, representing possibly the Marriage in Cana or the Last Supper, with two dogs in the foreground and nine disciples or guests, several of whom are in European costume and wearing European hats.[156] In one of the American collections is an Agony in the Garden in gold and colours,[157] and in an album of the Stow Collection in the British Museum is a Christ with a Crown of Thorns dating from about 1625. The latter picture is Italian in conception, and the two figures in front of the Christ are in Raffaelesque attitudes, but the expression on the face of the Saviour is unpleasing.[158]

Of the Crucifixion itself—a subject so common in Europe—there seems to be no example among the Mogul miniatures ; an omission which is probably due to the repulsion with which the incident was always regarded by Muslims. There is, however, a wonderful Descent from the Cross in the British Museum which exhibits a curious combination of Oriental and European conceptions ;[159] and the Album of Jahāngīr at Berlin contains a picture, which is purely European in its treatment, of the Women at the Tomb.[160]

In addition to these Mogul pictures which deal with the Madonna and the Life of Christ, there are not a few which deal with other Christian conceptions and characters. In the Johnson Collection at the India Office, for instance, two figures of a Persian type are represented in a mountainous landscape, one sitting with both hands upraised and the other looking up in prayer to the Christ who appears among the clouds in the sky.[161] In the same collection are two paintings which have hitherto been looked upon as unconventional representations of Christ as the Good Shepherd,[162] and there is a similar picture among the Oriental decorations at Schönbrunn ;[163] but the shepherd, carrying the sheep in his arms, is in these paintings a somewhat squat and ludicrous figure with a beard and an Indian head-dress, and there is nothing to show that they are intended to represent the Good Shepherd of the Gospel. On the other hand, there is a further picture in the Johnson Collection attributed to the painter Maskīn, in which the shepherd though provided with a European hat is a dignified figure, carrying a lamb upon his shoulders, and may quite possibly be accepted as an emblem of Christ.[164] Another Gospel type may possibly be recognized in a mysterious drawing in the John Rylands Library at Manchester, in which three female figures of a Renaissance pattern watch over a half-recumbent emaciated man in the foreground, upon whose arm a bearded figure—possibly the Good Samaritan—is carefully pouring some liquid.[165]

Other Christian subjects

Subjects from the Old Testament and the Apocrypha are not wanting. Mr. Chester Beatty, for example, has a monochrome picture of a well-modelled male figure, sitting unclothed with a hoe in his hand, which possibly represents Adam, and seems to be a copy of some sixteenth-century Italian drawing. The Lahore copy of Father Jerome Xavier's *Life of Christ* has an illustration depicting Gehazi in the presence of Elisha ; and there is in the Louvre a picture of the Angel of Tobias, dating from the end of the sixteenth or beginning of the seventeenth century.[166]

The Saints of the Church also find a place among the Mogul paintings. In the decorative borders of Jahāngīr's Album in Berlin there are adaptations above referred to of Dürer's S. Peter and S. John; and in the Bodleian Library at Oxford there is a beautifully coloured miniature of S. Matthew and an Angel by the painter Kesho Dās, which is almost entirely European in character.[167] In the John Rylands Library at Manchester there is a small round picture signed ''Alī Qulī,' which treats in European style a saint who is probably intended to represent a Magdalen;[168] and there is also in the collection of the Gaikwar of Baroda a miniature in which the Magdalen appears to be portrayed. In this latter picture the types and setting are entirely Indian; a woman kneels on a carpet between a piece of water and a grove of trees, while six winged figures bearing vessels, apparently of food, are waiting on her and two others are stooping from the clouds.[169] There is, too, in Mr. Coomeraswamy's private collection a beautiful Magdalen with ministering Angels—a seventeenth-century tracing or pouncing for a study of a night picture with a lovely landscape and a fine use of light from a lamp. The Magdalen is clearly of European origin, but the technique of the picture is Indian.[170] The India Museum at Kensington has also an admirable Magdalen, received from the executors of the late Sir Robert Nathan; a figure with remarkable features and long hair, sitting with hands clasped and having an alabaster cup and an open book before her and an Oriental city in the background.[171] The Wantage Bequest in the same Museum had an interesting S. Cecilia, which is a copy in colour of a print by Jerome Wierix.[172] The picture, which is the work of a painter called Nīnī, represents the Saint lying in the foreground tended by two women; a cherub with a palm branch is behind her and Christ is in the clouds with arms outstretched to welcome the Saint to Heaven. The exhumation of S. Cecilia's body at Rome at the end of the sixteenth century had doubtless lent additional vogue to representations of her martyrdom, and the attitude of the Saint in this picture is strongly reminiscent of, though not identical with, that adopted in the well-known statue executed by Stephano Maderno in 1599 for the Church of S. Cecilia in Rome. So too in the Album of the Teheran Museum there is a direct copy of a print by Sadeler of a S. Jerome painted by Petro Candido (Pieter de Witte, 1548–1628) and the picture contains an inscription in Persian which shows that it was executed by a lady called Nādira Bāno. If, as is just possible, the artist in this case was the Nādira who was the wife of Dārā Shikon, the picture is of special interest in view of the close intercourse between that Prince and the Jesuit Fathers.[172a]

The above enumeration of specific instances—though not exhaustive—will serve to show better than any general pronouncement how markedly a Christian atmosphere entered into the art of the Mogul period. Apart too from the portrayal of Christian incidents and characters there are certain characteristics in Mogul art—such as the use of the nimbus and the introduction of the Renaissance Cherub—which present features of interest in connection with this Christian influence.

The Nimbus and the Renaissance Cherub

The nimbus in some form or other was a recognized emblem in earlier forms of Indian art, and it is held by experts that this symbol after being popularized in the East emigrated in the fifth century of our era to the Byzantine art of Europe, and gradually fell into disuse in all countries where Muslim influence prevailed.[173] In India, however, the use of the circular nimbus round the head of exalted or holy personages was revived in the reign of Jahāngīr, and the increased use of the nimbus from the time of Jahāngīr onwards may reasonably be held to be due to growing acquaintance with Christian art acquired through the Jesuits. To the same influence we may possibly ascribe the gradual change after the time of the earlier Moguls, under which the solid-looking disc-nimbus gave way to the form of halo or aureole quite separated from the head.[174]

Another formality in Mogul art, which may be ascribed to a Jesuit origin, is the decorative use of the Cherub. The introduction of winged Angels in pictorial art is an Oriental feature and has a history of its own: but the employment of Cherubs of the Renaissance type for decorative purposes—even when the faces and figures are somewhat orientalized—is a characteristic for which the Jesuit influence may reasonably be held responsible. Reference has already been made to the picture in the Bodleian Library of the reception of a Persian Embassy by Shāh Jahān in which the wall behind the throne is decorated by a frieze of such Cherubs.[175] Angels or Cherubs, with varying proportions of Oriental or European elements in their composition, were also utilized to finish off the portraits of sovereigns and high dignitaries and were placed sometimes inside and sometimes outside the painted framework of the portrait. We find adornments of this type in pictures of Bābur,[176] of Humāyun, of Akbar, of Jahāngīr, of Shāh Jahān,[177] of Āsaf Khān, and of Farrukhsiyar,[178] all executed in the seventeenth or eighteenth centuries. We even find a picture of the Shāh Jahān period in which a bevy of purely European Cherubs hover benignly over a purely Indian love-scene.[179] And there is still more remarkable combination in a picture by Bichitr portraying a conversation between Shāh Jahān and an old courtier. In this picture there are two angels in the clouds, one of whom plays a musical instrument and the other pours rose leaves or some similar emblem of blessing on the head of the Emperor ; while alongside of them are displayed not only the Holy Dove but also the 'Padre Eterno' Himself with both hands raised in benediction, just as in an Italian canvas.[180]

Pictures of the Jesuit Fathers

It is interesting, in conclusion, to consider whether there is in the range of Mogul portraiture any record of the Fathers themselves or of their labours. There is nothing impossible in the idea that their portraits were in some cases taken either individually or in groups. We are told that shortly before 1650 the Rājā of Srīnagar in Garhwāl (where, it may be noted, a local school of painting was shortly to develop) wrote to the Fathers at Agra expressing his desire to see them and saying that if that were not possible he would wish 'to have their portraits.'[181] But in dealing with possible portraits of the Jesuits we are as a rule in the realm of conjecture only. There are, for instance, three interesting Mogul pictures belonging to the Bhārata Itihāsa Sanshodhaka Mandala at Poona representing religious conferences ; in two of them Akbar and Prince Salīm appear, and in the third, where these are not portrayed, there is a figure of European aspect which Father Heras, S.J., considers to be a portrait of Aquaviva, but the identification is by no means free from doubt.[182] In one of the illustrations in the copy of Jerome Xavier's *Life of Christ* at Lahore an ecclesiastic with three laymen is represented as offering a picture on a cloth to a king seated on a throne ;[183] but here again it is much more likely that the picture portrays the presentation of Christ's likeness to King Abgarus of Edessa than a scene before Akbar, and in any case the condition of the picture is such that nothing can be made of the face of the ecclesiastic. There is also a picture in the Johnson Collection at the India Office exhibiting a Prince surrounded by the apparatus of hunting—hawks, chītas, arrows, etc., and among the crowd in front of him there are two European figures, one of a young man in a ruff, and the other of an elderly clean-shaven man in a dark blue dress falling down to the heels with a black cloak and a black cap ornamented with minute crosses ; but we have nothing to show who the Prince was or which, if any, of the Fathers the latter figure may represent.[184] And there is a picture at Udaipur of Jahāngīr at the 'Jharokhā'-window of his palace, with a crowd of courtiers below, among whom there stands a man with European features and a thin white beard, wearing a black gown and a head-dress resembling a biretta, who might well stand for Father Jerome Xavier.[185] But here also we must speak from conjecture only.

We are on firmer ground with three other miniatures. One is a beautiful picture in Mr. Chester Beatty's Collection showing two Jesuits disputing with the Muslim doctors before Akbar in a courtyard at night. The picture was originally an illustration prepared by the painter Narsingh for a copy of the Akbarnāma which is believed to have belonged to Akbar himself, and it shows the two Fathers sitting on the ground at Akbar's right, clothed in black or very dark blue soutanes and cloaks, and wearing black flat-topped headgear similar to the lambskin cap affected in Persia. One of the Fathers is a young man with a clean-shaven face, the other is older and wears a beard. Above the picture is the sentence in the Akbarnāma describing the presence at the 'Ibādat-khāna, or hall of worship, of 'Pādrī Rodolf, one of the Nazarene sages.' One of the two Fathers in the picture is therefore undoubtedly Rudolf Aquaviva and the other must represent Monserrate or Henriques.[186]

Another picture is at Boston and illustrates the Darbār of a Mogul Sovereign. Among the numerous courtiers who throng the Darbār is a thin figure with a keen, clean-shaven face, attired in black. On many of the figures in the picture there are minute letters (possibly later additions but indicating probably an early tradition) which set forth the identity of the various portraits, and on the white lappet above the black coat of this particular figure can be dimly traced the letters of the word 'Pādrī.' The experts were at one time unable to agree whether the Darbār was of Akbar's time or of Jahāngīr's, but from such identifications as can be made of the figures in the assembly, it would seem now to be acknowledged that the Darbār was one held towards the latter part of Jahāngīr's reign (probably about 1620); and if this is so the 'padre' may reasonably be identified with Father Corsi.[187]

The third picture, which is in the Victoria Memorial at Calcutta, represents Jahāngīr sitting on his throne with his courtiers before him. Among these is a figure attired in much the same costume as that worn by the padre in the picture above described and standing with both hands open in an attitude of respect. The figure undoubtedly represents a Jesuit Father, and although the features are more rounded and placid than those of the padre in the Boston miniature they resemble them sufficiently to justify us in concluding that they represent the same individual, who probably is Father Corsi.[188]

NOTES

[1] Translation in *Bibliotheca Indica,* II, p. 206. Cf. Translation of the *Dābistān,* by Shea and Troyer, 1843, III, p. 87.

[2] Letter of Machado dated April 9, 1615; see *The Examiner*, Bombay (Hosten), August 16, 1919.

[3] Letter of Cabral dated November 14, 1633; see *Catholic Herald,* Calcutta (Besse), January 30, etc., 1918.

[4] Bādshāh-nāma, Elliot, *Hist. Ind.*, VII, p. 43. The 'Amal-i-sālih quoted in the *Catholic Herald,* Calcutta (Hosten), January 30-April 10, 1918, states that the rest after being broken were also thrown into the river.

[5] *Memoirs A.S.B.*, V, 1916 (Hosten), p. 145.

[6] Annual Report for 1650.

[7] Annual Report of September 7, 1686.

[8] Letter of Strobl dated October 27, 1746, *Weltbott*, No. 647.

[9] *Ā'īn-i-Akbarī,* transl. by Blochmann, I, pp. 107–109.

[10] Elliot, *Hist. Ind.*, VI, p. 360. In Rogers and Beveridge's translation this runs: 'whose work the original face is and who has painted the eye and eyebrows.' (*Tūzuk*, II, p. 21.)

[11] In 1614 Muqarrib Khān supplied the English with a list of his requirements for the King, and this included 'Pictures in cloth' (presumably canvas) 'not in wood' (*Letters Received,* II, pp. 173–174). Muqarrib Khān himself received from the English a curious assortment of pictures, including one of Mars and Venus, one of the Judgement of Paris, and one of Moses (Rawlinson, *British Beginnings in Western India*, 1920, p. 58).

[12] Foster, *The Embassy of Sir Thomas Roe to India*, 1926, p. 99.

[13] *Ib.*, p. 459.

[14] *Ib.*, p. 167.

[15] *Ib.*, p. 215.

[16] *Ib.*, p. 415.

[17] *Ib.*, p. 189.

[18] *Ib.*, p. 143.

[19] *Ib.*, pp. 125 and 357. There is in the Rāmpur State Library a picture showing Jahāngīr celebrating the feast of the Gulāb-pāshī, in the background of which are two European portraits which Percy Brown thinks were two of the portraits mentioned by Roe. Percy Brown, *Indian Painting under the Mughals*, 1924, p. 126.

[20] Foster, *The Embassy of Sir Thomas Roe to India*, 1926, p. 223. The original, or a copy of this very picture, a miniature by Isaac Oliver (d. 1617), is said to be extant (Percy Brown, *Indian Painting under the Mughals*, 1924, p. 146).

[21] Foster, *ib.*, pp. 349 and 350.

[22] Pelsaert's *Remonstrantie* (*Jahangir's India,* by Moreland and Geyl, 1925), pp. 25–26.

[23] *J.A.S.B.*, LXV, 1896, p. 50. Percy Brown, *Indian Painting under the Mughals*, 1924, pp. 166–167; See Martin, *The Miniature Painting and Painters of Persia, India and Turkey*, 1912, II, Plate 203.

[24] Commentarius in *Mem. A.S.B.*, III, 1914, fol. 78(a).

[25] Letter of August 20, 1595, *J.A.S.B.*, LXV, 1896, p. 66.

[26] Letter of July 26, 1598. *Ib.*, pp. 76 and 77.

[27] Guerreiro, *Relaçam*, I, p. 9; du Jarric, III, p. 36; Payne, *Akbar and the Jesuits*, 1926, pp. 110–111; *J.A.S.B.*, LXV, 1896, p. 85.

[28] Guerreiro, *Relaçam*, II, Part II, p. 50; du Jarric, III, p. 63; Payne, *Akbar and the Jesuits*, 1926, p. 153; *J.A.S.B.*, LXV, 1896, p. 86.

[29] Du Jarric, II, p. 473; Payne, *Akbar and the Jesuits*, 1926, p. 67.

[30] Guerreiro, *Relaçam*, II, Part II, p. 61; du Jarric, III, p. 85; Payne, *Akbar and the Jesuits*, 1926, p. 190.

[31] Du Jarric, II, p. 473; Payne, *Akbar and the Jesuits*, 1926, p. 66.

[32] Xavier's letter of July 26, 1598; *J.A.S.B.*, LXV, 1896, p. 73.

[33] *The Hawkins Voyages*, Hakluyt Society, 1878, p. 436; Foster, *Early Travels in India*, 1921, p. 115. He adds 'graven in stone': if this is accepted as accurate a statue must be referred to.

[34] Coverte, *A true and almost incredible report*, London, 1612, p. 40.

[35] Letter of July 26, 1598; *J.A.S.B.*, LXV, 1896, p. 74.

[36] Guerreiro, *Relaçam*, V, pp. 9, 11, 15; du Jarric, III, pp. 121 and 126.

[37] Foster, *The Embassy of Sir Thomas Roe to India*, 1926, p. 227.

[38] Full details regarding the picture are given in a pamphlet published in Rome in 1925 by Pinchetti-Sanmarchi, called 'Il più grande santuario e la più ricca cappella del mondo a gloria di Maria.'

[39] Commentarius, *Mem. A.S.B.*, III, 1914, fol. 37(a).

[40] De Souza, *Oriente Conquistado*, 1710, Vol. II, p. 166.

[41] Monserrate, Commentarius, *Mem. A.S.B.*, III, 1914, fol. 98(a).

[42] Letter of Provincial dated November 1590; *J.A.S.B.*, LXV, 1896, p. 62.

[43] Xavier's letter of August 20, 1595; *J.A.S.B.*, LXV, 1896, p. 66; Payne, *Akbar and the Jesuits*, 1926, p. 66.

[44] Footnote 36 to Hosten's transl. of de Souza in *The Examiner*, Bombay, June 19, 1920.

[45] A long and enthusiastic account of the beauty of this picture, the miracles performed by it, and the crowds that visited it at Rome will be found in Jacopo Alberici's *Compendio delle Grandezze dell' Illustre et Devotissima Chiesa di Santa Maria del Populo di Roma*, Rome, 1600.

[46] *Relaçam*, II, Part II, pp. 52–56; the translation adopted is that given by Hosten in *The Examiner*, Bombay, November 22, 29, 1919. Du Jarric's version will be found in Payne, *Akbar and the Jesuits*, 1926, pp. 160–172.

[47] Regarding the practice of giving a *bārānī* outfit for the rains, see Manucci, II, p. 464, and Irvine's note thereon.

[48] Guerreiro, *Relaçam*, V, pp. 14–15; J. Xavier in Zannetti's *Raguagli*, 1615, p. 26, and Letter of September 24, 1608; *J.P.H.S.*, VII, 1918 (Hosten), pp. 60–62.

[49] The suggestion is made in Payne, *Jahangir and the Jesuits*, 1930, p. 108. See *Tūzuk-i-Jahāngīrī*, Syad Ahmad's edition, 1864, p. 68, and Beveridge's translation, I, p. 144; Elliot, *Hist. India*, VI, p. 317.

[50] Xavier's letter of August 20, 1595; *J.A.S.B.*, LXV, 1896, p. 67. A painter was similarly deputed for the Tibetan Mission in 1626 (*J.A.S.B.*, VII, 1911, p. 20), but died before he could proceed to Tibet. (Wessels, *Early Jesuit Travellers in Central Asia*, 1924, p. 123.)

[51] Foster, *The Embassy of Sir Thomas Roe to India* (1926), p. 187. Two small specimens of Hughes' work, including a portrait apparently of himself, can be seen in a Persian glossary put together by him at Ajmīr in 1616 and now in the Bodleian Library. (Or. 492 Sachau and Ethé, *Catal. Persian MSS.*, No. 1915, p. 1099.)

[52] *Ib.*, pp. 427 and 468.

[53] *Ib.*, p. 447.

[54] Letter of September 20, 1649; cf. Report for 1648–9.

[55] Brit. Mus. Or. 2265, fol. 203 b, 213 a, 221 b. Arnold, *Painting in Islam*, 1928, pp. 148–149. The information available regarding this painter is collected by N. N. Markovitch in the *Journal of the American Oriental Society*, XLV, 1925, pp. 106–109. See also Manucci, *Storia do Mogor*, II, p. 17, and Irvine's note thereon; V. A. Smith, *A History of Fine Art in India and Ceylon* (1930), p. 217; Percy Brown, *Indian Painting under the Mughals* (1924), p. 177; F. R. Martin, *The Miniature Painting and Painters of Persia, India and Turkey* (1912), I, p. 76. In the Annual Relation of 1648–1649, published by Hosten in *J.I.H.*, I, 1922, p. 230, it is stated that Paolo Zamān was baptized in Persia by the Carmelites when a child. He was also known as Farangī Khān, see Ivanow, *Catal. Curzon Coll.*, *A.S.B.*, 1926, p. 96.

[56] Ph. Walter Schulz, *Die persisch-islamische Miniaturmalerei*, 1914, I, p. 195.

[57] Martin, op. cit., Plate 173. The Visitation is dated A.D. 1678, and both pictures, though tinged with Orientalism, are Italian in feeling.

[58] *Ā'īn-i-Akbarī* (Blochmann), I, p. 96.

[59] *Ib.*, I, p. 107.

[60] *J.A.S.B.*, LXV, 1896, p. 50.

[61] Xavier's letter of July 26, 1598; *J.A.S.B.*, LXV, 1896, p. 76.

[62] Xavier's letter of July 26, 1598; *J.A.S.B.*, LXV, 1896, p. 74.

[63] Guerreiro, *Relaçam*, II, Part II, p. 61.

[64] Percy Brown, *Indian Painting under the Mughals* (1924), p. 167; V. Smith, *A History of Fine Art in India and Ceylon* (1930), p. 220; *Indian Antiquary*, VI, p. 354.

[65] Foster, *Embassy of Sir Thomas Roe to India*, 1926, p. 224.

[66] *Ib.*, p. 199.

[67] Letter of de Castro dated July 26, 1627; *J.A.S.B.*, XXI, 1925 (Hosten), p. 56, and XXIII, 1927 (do), p. 152.

[68] F. R. Martin, *The Miniature Painting and Painters of Persia, India and Turkey*, 1912, p. 85.

[69] Monserrate, Commentarius in *Mem. A.S.B.*, III, 1914, fol. 21(a); Hoyland and Banerjee's translation, 1922, p. 29.

[70] They are reproduced in Edmund Smith's *Moghal Architecture of Fathpur Sikri*, Part I, Plate cix; see also pp. 33–34 (*Archæological Survey of India*, Vol. XVIII, 1894). Cf. Heras in *S. Xavier's College Magazine*, Bombay, October 1923.

[71] *Itinerario*, 1649, p. 350; Hakluyt edn. (Luard and Hosten), 1927, II, p. 168. Azevedo, who saw the tomb in 1632 and describes it at some length, does not mention the pictures.

[72] *J.A.S.B.*, VI, 1910 (Beveridge), p. 457. The Portuguese version uses the word ' pinturas ' : the Latin ' figuras.'

[73] Tavernier (Crooke, 1925), I, p. 91.

[74] *Storia do Mogor* (Irvine, 1907), I, p. 141, and IV, p. 419.

[75] See p. 226 above. *Vide* Heras in the *Catholic Herald*, Calcutta, June 6, 1923. It may be noted that some of the illustrations in Xavier's *Life of Christ* in the Lahore Museum are believed by Hosten to show Chinese or Japanese influence; *J.U.P.H.S.*, III, 1922, Part I, p. 181.

[76] *Relaçam*, V, pp. 13–14; which is translated in C. H. Payne, *Jahangir and the Jesuits*, 1930, pp. 63–65. There is another translation by Father Hosten in *J.P.H.S.*, VII, 1918, p. 58, and *J.U.P.H.S.*, III, 1922, Part I, p. 177. As, however, there are points in Xavier's letter which

have been omitted or misunderstood in Guerreiro's abstract it is best to read the account as given in the original letter.

[77] The English traveller Finch describing the King's chamber of audience in 1610 says, 'on the right hand of the King on the wall behind him is the picture of Our Saviour : on the left, of the Virgin.' (Foster, *Early Travels in India*, 1921, p. 184.) See also the quotations from Hawkins and Coverte made on p. 226 above. The picture by S. Luke was doubtless the S. Maria del Popolo referred to on pp. 228 *et seqq*. above.

[78] These pictures were noticed by Azevedo in 1631. 'Among various pictures,' he says, 'are those of Our Saviour, of Our Lady and of the Magdalene, as well as others of famous Captains in the world, but none of Muhammad for whom the King had no devotion.' Letter of 1632, fol. 19 ; Wessels, *Early Jesuit Travellers in Central Asia*, p. 284.

[79] *Agra Diocesan Calendar*, 1907 (Felix), p. 206, which quotes Rocco da Cesinale, *Storia delle Missioni dei Cappucini*, III, p. 285. See also *Transactions of the Archæological Society of Agra*, 1874, p. 7.

[80] Finch in Foster's *Early Travels in India*, 1921, p. 163. The information is repeated in De Laet, *India Vera* (1631), p. 59 ; Herbert's *Travels* (1677), p. 69 ; Thévenot, *Travels* (London, 1686), Part III, p. 60 ; Vogel, 'Mosaics of the Lahore Fort' (*Arch. Sur. India*, N.S., XLI, 1920), pp. 50–53.

[81] Andrade letter of August 14, 1623.

[82] Manrique, *Itinerario*, 1649, p. 369 ; Hakluyt edn. (Luard and Hosten), 1927, II, p. 207 ; see also *J.P.H.S.*, 1911, I, p. 99.

[83] Valentyn, *Oud- en Nieuw Oost Indiën*, IV, Part II (Amsterdam, 1726), p. 289 ; *J.P.H.S.*, VII, 1918, p. 47, and X, 1929, p. 19 ; Irvine, *Later Moguls*, I, p. 153. Desideri, who was in Lahore in 1714, also alludes in his 'Relation' to some statuary—possibly the same as that referred to in the text. 'I was shown,' he says, 'a number of fine white marble statues of Jesus Christ, the Blessed Virgin, Angels, Apostles and Divine Saints. They had formerly been set up in good array, but in the reign of Oranzeb, a violent iconoclast as I have already said, they were taken down and hidden away in a room.'

[84] Foster, *The Embassy of Sir Thomas Roe to India* (1926), p. 211.

[85] G. Warner, *Descriptive Catalogue of the Illuminated MSS. in the Library of C. W. Dyson Perrin*, 1920, I, p. 315, and II, Plate CXXII.

[86] No. 107 in Catalogue of Indian pictures (Dowdeswell) exhibited in London by Col. Hanna in May 1890 ; India Museum, Wantage Bequest, No. 7—115, 1921 I.M. ; C. Stanley Clarke, *Mogul Paintings, Period of the Emperors Jahangir and Shah Jahan*, 1922, Plate 9.

[87] This is the same picture as that in which a Jesuit padre has been portrayed : see page 258 and the references quoted in note 187. The coloured reproduction of the picture shows the Virgin to have been painted with a red robe with a mantle over her head of very dark purple.

[88] Ouseley, Addl. 173–13. The picture is reproduced in Binyon and Arnold's *Court Painters of the Grand Moguls*, 1921, Plate XXXVI, and in Percy Brown, *Indian Painting under the Mughals*, 1924, Plate XXIV. An English inscription on the original picture erroneously attributes the Darbār to Jahāngīr : so also Sachau and Ethé, *Catal. Persian MSS. Bodl. Lib.*, I, No. 1897.

[89] Foster, *The Embassy of Sir Thomas Roe to India*, 1926, p. 224.

[90] Special reference may be made to the paintings reproduced in F. R. Martin's *The Miniature Painting and Painters of Persia, India and Turkey* (1912) ; Binyon and Arnold's *The Court Painters of the Grand*

Moguls (1921); Coomeraswamy's *Indian Drawings* (1910–1912); Percy Brown's *Indian Painting under the Mughals* (1924); V. A. Smith's *History of Fine Art in India and Ceylon* (1911, revised by Codrington, 1930); Kühnel and Goetz, *Indian Book Painting from Jahāngīr's Album* (1926) and *Miniaturmalerei im islamischen Orient* (1922); and Blochet, *Mussalman Painting* (1929).

[91] An interesting account of this collection by Sir T. Arnold will be found in *Rupam*, April 1921, p. 10. For a comprehensive list of collections of Mogul miniatures see Appx. B of Percy Brown's work above cited. The Wantage Collection is sumptuously represented in C. Stanley Clarke's *Mogul Paintings, Period of the Emperors Jahangir and Shah Jahan*, 1605–1658, *and Persian Calligraphy, formerly in the Imperial Collection at Delhi, lent by Lady Wantage to the Victoria and Albert Museum* 1917. London, 1922.

[92] Kühnel and Goetz, *Indian Book Painting*, 1926. See also Weber in *Indian Antiq.*, VI, 1877, p. 353.

[92a] Photographs of a certain number of these pictures have been shown to me by Mr. J. V. S. Wilkinson and references are made later, in the text, to those which show European influence.

[93] Kühnel and Goetz, *Indian Book Painting*, 1926, Plates 27 and 29, and pp. 47–48.

[94] Fol. 74.

[95] India Museum, I.M. 386–1914; I.M. 9–1913; I.M. 8–1913; I.M. 293–1913; D. 354–1908; I.M. 7–1913.

[96] Cabinet des Estampes, O D 49. fol. 34; Stchoukine, *La peinture indienne à l'époque des Grands Moghols*, 1929, Plate XIX and p. 204.

[97] *Coronation Darbār Catalogue* (Archæological Survey of India). Plate LXXII.

[98] Or. 2265, p. 221b. Vincent Smith, *A History of Fine Art in India and Ceylon* (1911), p. 467, Plate CXVI; edn. 1930, p. 217. Other pictures of Europeans in the Museum are in *Indian Drawings*, Book XV, 1920–6–11–010 and Book X 1920–9–17–013(7).

[99] MSS. Ousely, Add., 171 b., 17 v. The same portfolio contains other pictures of a European type but they are probably of late date. Sachau and Ethé, *Catal. Pers. MSS. in Bodl.*, I, No. 1894.

[100] Cabinet des Estampes, O D 44 rés, fol. 11; Stchoukine, *La Peinture Indienne à l'époque des Grands Moghols*, 1929, Plate XXIV and p. 204.

[101] Books 14 and 16. See especially Book 16, No. 6.

[102] Sotheby, December 1929.

[103] Darbār of Sa'dulla Khān, Bodleian, Douce, Or. b. 3, fol. 21; Ethé, *Catal. Pers. MSS. Bodl.*, II (2068), 2383; Stchoukine, op. cit., Plate LV. Also *ib.*, p. 120, and N. C. Mehta, *Studies in Indian Painting*, Plate 39.

[104] The contrary influence—that of Mogul miniatures on European art—raises some interesting considerations. See, for instance, the papers by Sarre in *Jahrbuch der königlich-preussischen Kunstsammlungen, Berlin*, XXV, 1904, pp. 143–158, and XXX, 1909, pp. 283–290, on Rembrandt's sketches made under this influence. The latter paper reproduces a sketch by Rembrandt (exhibited in London in 1929), which almost certainly portrays Akbar and Jahāngīr. O. C. Ganguli in *Rupam*, No. 21, January 1925, p. 19, refers in this connection both to Rembrandt and to Delacroix.

[105] See e.g., Samarendra Nath Gupta in *Rupam*, No. 5, January 1921, pp. 20–23.

[106] In 1624 Jahāngīr sent one of his own painters to Goa where he was well received. *Lettere Annue d'Etiopia, etc.*, Rome, 1627, p. 330.

[107] F. R. Martin, *The Miniature Painting and Painters of Persia, India and Turkey*, 1912, I, p. 87, and II, Plate 203.

[108] F. R. Martin, op. cit., p. 83 ; cf. the same writer in *Meisterwerker Muhammadanischer Kunst in München*, 1910 (Munich, 1912), I, Plate 37.

[109] Such European or Europeanized backgrounds are by no means uncommon. A striking example is found in *Dārā's Album*, fol. 28, when an entirely Indian portrait is set against an entirely European background.

[110] Stchoukine, *La Peinture Indienne à l'époque des Grands Moghols*, 1929. Another, though less detailed, examination of the question of European influence will be found in Goetz's article in *Der Cicerone*, Leipzig, 1923, pp. 419–426. Cf. Heath's *Examples of Indian Art at the British Empire Exhibition of* 1924, Plate V. An interesting discussion regarding European influences on the technique of the treatment of landscape and architecture in Mogul painters will be found in Dr. Stella Kramisch's article in the *Journal of the Department of Letters of the Calcutta University*, Vol. X, 1923, pp. 107–110. O. C. Ganguli in *Rupam*, No. 21, January 1925, writes that although the Mogul painters were not substantially influenced by European art they were in some degree so influenced, more especially in the use of shadow, in night effects and in aerial perspective. Glück and Diez draw attention to the gradual introduction of shadow and of foreshortening and perspective in landscape ; *Die Kunst des Islam*, Berlin, 1925, p. 99.

[111] Book No. 22, No. 2.

[112] *Jahrbuch der königlich-preussischen Kunstsammlungen*, Berlin, 1904, Vol. XXV, p. 157.

[113] Caranzani was an obscure engraver of the period, ignored by most of the books of reference. Through the kindness of my publishers I find that the second inscription represents the words, 'Liberasti me a rugientibus praeparatis ad escam' which occur in Ecclus. li, 4, and form part of the Epistle of the Mass *Loquebar* of the Common of a Virgin Martyr.

[114] Fol. 42. Vincent Smith, *A History of Fine Art in India and Ceylon* (1911), p. 458 ; (1930), p. 212.

[115] Letter of September 24, 1608.

[116] Reproductions of some of those are given in Kühnel and Goetz's book : the Resurrection and Descent into Hell in Plate 42 and the Ape in Plate 43.

[117] *Coronation Darbār Catal.*, 1911, Plate LXVII.

[118] Letter of July 26, 1598, *J.A.S.B.*, LXV, 1896, p. 74 : 'inductis coloribus et pigmentis parvas quasdam imagines illustrabat.'

[119] Indian Drawings, Book XI, 1920–9–17–031.

[120] See e.g., Book XI, 1920–9–17–032 referred to in note 155 below.

[121] Guerreiro, *Relaçam*, V, p. 14.

[122] Kühnel and Goetz, *Indian Book Painting*, 1926, Plate 41, p. 5.

[123] Kühnel and Goetz, *Indian Book Painting*, p. 47, Plate 30.

[124] Op. cit., p. 39. Marteau and Vever *Miniatures Persanes*, Paris, 1913, Plate clxviii ; Stchoukine, *Miniatures Indiennes du Musée du Louvre*, 1929, Plate V, and p. 35.

[125] Marteau and Vever, *Miniatures persanes*, 1913, II, Plate CLXXIX.

[126] 'Abou Ben Adhem (may his tribe increase !)'

[127] Weber in *Indian Antiquary*, VI, December 1877, p. 353.

[128] *Catalogue des Manuscrits et xylographes orientaux de la Biblio-*

thèque Impériale Publique de St. Petersbourg, 1852, p. 424. Ouseley, *Biographical Notes on Persian Poets*, London, 1846, p. ccxxiv. Weber in *Indian Antiquary*, VI, December 1877, pp. 352-353.

[129] Library pictures, A. 100 ; Weber, loc. cit. In the original the word *bin* is written twice over.

[130] Kühnel and Goetz, *Indian Book Painting*, 1926, p. 12 ; *Mus. Ethnol.*, I, C 24338, p. 12 b.

[131] Kühnel, *Miniaturmalerei im Islamischen Orient*, 1922, p. 67, Plate 141.

[132] Kühnel and Goetz, *Indian Book Painting*, 1926, p. 47, Plates 30, 42 and 39.

[133] *Ars Asiatica*, XIII (1929), p. 83, Plate LXXVII, and Coomerswamy, *Catalogue of the Indian Collections*, Part VI (1930), p. 50, Plate LXXXIII.

[134] Indian Drawings, Book XVIII, No. 9-17-0208.

[135] Book 14, No. 2 ; Book 14, Nos. 9 and 10 ; and Book 6, Nos. 3 and 4.

[136] Ouseley, Addl. 171 b., 16 v. Sachau and Ethé, *Catalogue of Persian MSS.*, I, No. 1894.

[137] MS. Douce, Or. b, 2, 36. Ethé, *Catal. Pers. MSS.*, II, No. (2065), 2380.

[138] MS. Douce, Or. C. 4. Ethé, *lib. cit.*, No. (2064) 2379. For further specimens of Madonnas see Douce, Or. a. 1, fol. 43 and Douce, Or. b. 1, fol. 1, in the same Library.

[139] Catalogue (Dowdeswell), No. 22.

[140] Catalogue, Plate lxix.

[141] Record of the 4th meeting of the Commission, 1922, p. 104.

[142] *Rupam*, January 1930, pp. 23-24, where the writer suggests that the picture reflects some Flemish painting of the school of Quintin Matsys.

[143] S. N. Gupta, *Catalogue of Paintings in the Central Museum*, Lahore, 1922, Plate VI.

[144] Kühnel, *Miniaturmalerei im Islamischen Orient*, 1922, p. 67, Plate 142.

[145] Kühnel and Goetz, *Indian Book Painting*, 1926, Plate 29 and p. 48. I may note that the view put forward by me in the text was that held by the late Sir Thomas Arnold.

[146] Weber in *Indian Antiquary*, VI, December 1877, p. 353.

[147] See de Dieu's *Historia Christi*, Leyden, 1639, p. 61. A reproduction of this picture forms one of the illustrations of this volume.

[148] *Johnson Collection*, Book 6, Nos. 1 and 2, and Book 1, No. 1.

[149] MSS. Douce, Or. a. 1. Ethé, *Catal. Pers. MSS.*, II (2069) 2384.

[150] Kühnel and Goetz, *Indian Book Painting*, 1926, Plate 41.

[151] Kühnel and Goetz, *Indian Book Painting*, 1926, Plate 30.

[152] Catalogue (Dowdeswell), No. 124.

[153] *Indian Drawings*, Book XIII, 1920-9-7-0276A.

[154] *Johnson Collection*, Book 14, No. 3.

[155] *Indian Drawings*, Book XI, 1920-9-17-032.

[156] *Johnson Collection*, Book 6, No. 6.

[157] It was for sale at Messrs. Maggs in London a few years ago.

[158] Stow, Or. 16, fol. 18. Percy Brown, *Indian Paintings under the Mughals*, 1924, p. 168. The background contains a wonderful blue cloud of the Chinese pattern.

[159] *Indian Drawings*, Book XIII, 1920-9-17-0276B. Another version of this picture with some slight variations was shown by Mrs. Jopling Rowe in the Festival of Empire Exhibition in 1911.

[160] Kühnel and Goetz, *Indian Book Paintings*, 1926, Plate 41 and p. 4.

[161] Book 1, No. 1.

[162] Book 6, Nos. 7 and 8. One of these pictures is reproduced in Vincent Smith's *A History of Fine Art in India and Ceylon* (1911), p. 465, Plate CXV; edn. 1930, p. 216.

[163] Strzygowski and Glück, *Die indischen Miniaturen im Schlosse Schönbrunn*, 1923, Plate 54.

[164] Book 16. See the reproduction which forms an illustration to this volume.

[165] *Indian MSS. Drawings*, Vol. 12. Similar female figures in a similar setting appear in another drawing in Vol. 7, but without any men in the foreground.

[166] Stchoukine, *Les Miniatures Indiennes de l'époque des Grands Moghols au Musée du Louvre*, 1929, p. 18.

[167] Douce, Or. a.l., fol. 41. Ethé, *Catal. Pers. MSS.*, II (2066) 2381–26. Stchoukine, *La Peinture Indienne à l'époque des Grands Moghols*, 1929, Plate XIX and p. 204. A picture with wonderful execution and colouring, but marked by the unconventional way in which the Angel who is holding the book leans his knee against the Evangelist's leg.

[168] *Indian MSS. Drawings*, Vol. 6.

[169] A similar, but not identical picture was in October 1929 in the possession of Mr. Imre Schwaiger.

[170] Coomeraswamy, *Indian Drawings*, India Society, 1910, Plate XVII. A similar but inferior scene is to be found in D. 1188–1903 in the Green Volume in the E.I.D. Department of the Victoria and Albert Museum.

[171] I.M. 235–1901. Reproduced opposite to p. 190 of Payne, *Akbar and the Jesuits*, 1927.

[172] I.M. 30–139 (1921). Reproduced in this volume. See also C. Stanley Clarke, *Mogul Paintings, the Period of the Emperors Jahangir and Shah Jahan*, 1922, Plate 33. The print by Wierix is in Album No. III of the *Collection of Wierix Prints* in the British Museum (1859–7–9–3192). The picture in the India Museum is let into a specimen of the work of Sultān 'Alī Mashhadī, a well-known calligraphist of the fifteenth century.

[172a] The picture reproduces faithfully not only the Saint and his lion but also the Latin couplet appended by the European artist. The Persian inscription (which is inserted in the book which the Saint is reading) is in four lines, which run, commencing at the top: 'Banda Bādshāh Salīm|'amal Nādira Bāno|Shāhgird Razā|dukhtar Mīr Takī.' This should probably be interpreted: 'The work of Nādira Bāno, daughter of Mīr Takī and pupil of Razā, the slave of Bādshāh Salīm.' The difficulty in connecting the artist with Dārā's 'nearest and dearest friend the Lady Nādīra Begam' lies in the fact that the latter is known to have been the daughter of Prince Parwīz.

[173] See Percy Browne, *Indian Painting under the Mughals*, 1924, pp. 172–173.

[174] See Taverner-Perry, *Burlington Magazine*, XII, 1907, pp. 20–23 and 95–96; and Stchoukine, *La Peinture Indienne à l'époque des Grands Moghols*, 1929, p. 121.

[175] Ouseley, Addl. 173–13, see p. 242 above.

[176] Stchoukine, *Les Miniatures Indiennes de l'époque des Grands Moghols*, Plate XIV.

[177] Martin, *The Miniature Painting and Painters of Persia, India and Turkey*, II, Plates 211, 212 and 213, and I, p. 79. The cherubs appear

in pictures of Akbar, of Jahāngīr (by Nādirulzamān) and of Shāh Jahān (by Bālchand) in Mr. Chester Beatty's Collection.

[178] Stchoukine, *La Peinture Indienne à l'époque des Grands Moghols*, 1929, Plates XXXVIII and LXVII. See also the picture, p. 167 of Vol. IX of the *J.P.H.S.*, believed by Mr. Kanwar Sen to represent Rājā Mān Singh of Amber.

[179] Berlin Museum für Völkerkunde, I, C 24343, fol. 13 a, reproduced in Plate 25 of Vol. I of *Jahrbuch der asiatischen Kunst*, Leipzig, 1924.

[180] From the Collection H. Vever in Paris ; Stchoukine, *La Peinture Indienne à l'époque des Grands Moghols*, 1929, Plate XXXIX.

[181] *Relation* of 1650 ; quoted in Hazart, *Kerckelycke Historie*, Antwerp, 1682, I, p. 278.

[182] 'Three Mogul Paintings on Akbar's Religious Discussions,' *Journal*, Bombay Branch, Royal Asiatic Society, Vol. III, 1928, pp. 191–202.

[183] *J.U.P.H.S.*, III, 1922 (Hosten), Part I, p. 181.

[184] Book 8, No. 6.

[185] *Coronation Darbār Exhibition Catalogue*, 1911 (Archaeological Survey of India), Plate XXXVIII. Enquiries made on my behalf at Udaipur have unfortunately failed to trace the picture itself or to ascertain any further particulars regarding it.

[186] A reproduction of it is given in Blochet's *Musalman Painting*, 1929, Plate CLXXX. See also the Frontispiece to this Volume.

[187] Kühnel, *Miniaturmalerei im islamischen Orient*, 1922, Plate 109 and p. 65 ; Coomeraswamy, Museum of Fine Arts, Boston, *Portfolio of Indian Art*, Plate LXXXVI, and *Catalogue of Indian Collections*, Part VI (1930), p. 44 and Plate XXXIV ; Sarre and Martin, *Meisterwerker Muhammadanischer Kunst in München*, 1910, Plate 38 ; F. R. Martin, *The Miniature Painting and Painters of Persia, India, and Turkey*, 1912, II, Plate 216 ; Schulz, *Die persisch-islamische Miniaturmalerei*, 1914, Plate 193 ; Marteau and Vever, *Miniatures Persanes*, 1913, II, Plate CLXV ; *Ars Asiatica*, XIII, 1929, *Les Miniatures Orientales de la Collection Goloubew*, p. 76, Plate LXXII ; Glück and Diez, *Die Kunst des Islam*, Berlin, 1925, Plate on p. 518, and Stchoukine, 'Portraits Moghols,' in *Revue des Arts Asiatiques*, 1929–1930, VI, p. 235. The picture is reproduced in colour in *Zeitschrift für bildende Kunst*, Leipzig, Vol. XIX, 1908, p. 17, and in this reproduction the padre's coat is coloured a very dark purple difficult to distinguish from black. In *Les Arts*, Paris, No. 145, January 1914, p. 15, the picture is again reproduced with a note from Goloubew. Speaking of the padre he says : ' Quant au visage on dirait un portrait de Jean Fouquet mais légèrement amolli par le pinceau caressant du peintre hindou.' There is a small painting of the Madonna on the palace wall in the background of this picture ; see p. 242 above.

[188] See Percy Brown, *Indian Painting under the Mughals*, 1924, p. 146.

CHAPTER XVI

THE CONGREGATIONS

Nolite timere, pusillus grex.
(Luc., xii, 32.)

AT many of the larger towns of the Mogul Empire there were a certain number of Europeans, most of whom, in the earlier days at least, were by origin Catholics. In the coastward towns of Bengal and Gujarāt there were, of course, considerable numbers of Catholic Europeans engaged in trade—in Cambay, for instance, there were as early as 1598 several hundreds of Portuguese ;[1] but elsewhere also in the kingdom of the Mogul there were European Catholics to be found. They were merchants, lapidaries, enamellers, goldsmiths, physicians, surgeons, and artizans of all descriptions,[2] and also very commonly artillerymen in the Mogul Army. On their first arrival at Fatehpur Sīkrī in 1580 the Jesuits found Portuguese already resident there, who had arrived in the following of the Portuguese captain, Tavares. There were Christians, apparently Europeans, in the army which Akbar took to Kābul in 1581.[3] There were 200 Portuguese in the army with which Shāh Jahān rebelled against his father in 1624.[4] The nobleman, Mīr Jumla, who died in 1653, had eighty European gunners in his army,[5] and Dārā Shikoh, when fighting his brother Aurangzeb in 1658, had over 200 European artillerymen in his camp.[6] The number was much reduced in the reign of Aurangzeb, and Manucci assures us that when he visited Lahore in 1670 there were no Europeans there.[7] But European soldiers, especially artillerymen, continued to be employed to some extent in the Mogul armies. Manucci asserts that Akbar invited the Jesuits to his capital merely in order to provide spiritual supervision for his European employees,[8] and Thévenot seems to suggest that they were invited in order to furnish education for the children of European merchants at headquarters.[9] These statements do not represent the real origin of the Missions, but they indicate one important aspect of their functions, and the Fathers, though primarily devoted to the conversion of non-Christians,

European Christians in Mogor

were also much occupied in the service of European Catholics scattered through Mogor. Even in Kashmīr, Father de Castro when working with the King's Court in 1627 had two Venetians in his congregation and several Portuguese and Frenchmen.[10] When the Fathers visited a station where there was no resident priest, a number of the European Catholics would find their way to the chapel, and would, after long intermission, make their confession and attend Mass.[11]

The European element was not, indeed, at all times a credit to its religion. It was a Portuguese Christian who, about the year 1603, fomented a movement in the Agra congregation against the Fathers.[12] A few years later two Europeans, named Mesquita and Lobo, at the Mogul Court went so far as to threaten to pervert all the Fathers' congregations and cause them to renounce Christianity; with the result that orders were received in Goa, from the King of Spain, to effect their capture and repatriate them to Europe.[13] The Farangī gunmen in Dārā's army are described as having been Christian in name only: polygamous in habit, gamblers, cheats, and constantly drunk.[14] The progress of conversion was sadly impeded by the bad lives of so many of the Europeans, and the Fathers had many strange characters to deal with. In 1628 a somewhat disreputable trio of Italians sued a Portuguese for certain property and the Jesuit Superior, Father Leam, in taking up the case of the Portuguese was injudicious enough to petition the powerful Āsaf Khān against one of the Italians, alleging that he had surreptitiously married a Muslim girl with Muslim rites and requesting permission to have him excommunicated and banished. The petition led to the Italian's arrest and nearly to his execution, with the result that on his release he displayed such animosity against the Fathers that he threatened to become a Muslim himself with all his household, and was only dissuaded by the representations of his companions, who pointed out the disgrace which would ensue.[15] Father Strobl writing from Delhi in 1747 mentions several instances of troublesome Europeans, including the extraordinary case of a monk who had escaped from a cloister in Europe and had settled down in India as an interpreter and teacher of the Qur'ān.[16] Another strange case was that of Mansūr Khān, an officer in the army of Jahāngīr, who is described as ' a mulatto from Coimbra ' ; though apparently living as a Muslim, he stated that he had never been a Muslim at heart, and he promised the Fathers to conform to Christianity on his return from the war of 1623, but he was killed in a skirmish before he could redeem his promise.[17] Most of the Europeans were united to Indian women, and their half-caste children came in some degree under the care of the Fathers. The number of lapses to Islām—whether these were caused by allowances given by Muslim rulers, or by the desire to marry Muslim women, or by other reasons—was not inconsiderable, and every effort was made by the Fathers to reclaim the renegades. Manucci tells us a long story of a struggle which took place in 1666 between a French surgeon called St. Jacques and his wife's aunt, the renegade Portuguese wife of the powerful nobleman 'Alī Mardān Khān; and we learn from the Jesuits how they saved one of the Frenchman's sons from forcible conversion by sending him post-haste to the College at Hūglī, and how St. Jacques himself was arrested by the Qāzī and refused to secure his release by abandoning his faith.[18] Another curious story is that of a Portuguese soldier who arrived in India in 1672 and gave himself out to be Don Luis da Sylveira, Count of Sarzedas and Viceroy-elect of Portuguese India. After receiving every attention in this capacity in Malacca and Southern India he suddenly appeared in Delhi under the name of Don João de Souza Montenegro and there married a Portuguese lady whose mother, Maria Toscana, had been converted from Islām and baptized at the age of forty. Montenegro himself then embraced Islām, assuming the name of Dīn Muhammad, and had the baseness to accuse his mother-in-law before the Qāzī of the crime of adopting Christianity, though born of Muslim parents. He also included in his accusation, as accessories, his wife and her brother, and for some time these three Christians went in great fear of their lives. They presented a spirited defence, however, resisting all the attempts made to seduce them from their faith, and ultimately they were acquitted by the Qāzī. Montenegro, we are told, was subsequently seized with contrition and once more became a Christian.[19] He was tended by the Fathers during a long illness and died after confessing and receiving the Sacrament.[20]

Many of the renegades were slaves or captives, and the Fathers were able in several cases to liberate and re-convert them. It will be remembered how in 1583 Father Rudolph Aquaviva secured from Akbar the free release of a family of Russian slaves who were in the household of the Queen-Mother, and how, after the Deccan War of 1601, a number of half-castes and others, including a Portuguese Jew who was ninety years of age, were freed and baptized. A French renegade who was skilled in the casting of cannon is recorded in 1608–1609 to have been re-converted by the Fathers and to have received the Sacrament on his deathbed.[21] In 1606 we read of two Christian negroes who deserted the service of their Muslim master because he wished to marry them to Muslim women and of the Fathers doing their best to conceal and protect them.[22] A Hungarian from Buda Pesth, who 'knew Christian doctrine and prayers in Latin,' was in the same manner reclaimed in 1602 from a Turkish deputation which he had accompanied to India ;[23] and a Polish slave who had adhered to his faith was in 1648 concealed by the Fathers and smuggled back to Europe. As a rule the Fathers endeavoured to purchase the liberty of European slaves, but, failing that, they resorted to other means, and in 1648 we are told that some twelve slaves were reclaimed, 'some of them by means of money, and others whom the masters refused to sell we saved from their tyranny by stratagem.'[24]

The Armenians in Mogor

Another class of foreigners commonly resident in the towns of Mogul India was that of the Armenians, an enterprising race, mainly engaged in trade, but found also in possession of land and of posts under the Government. It was not uncommon for Europeans to class all Asiatic Christians, including Greeks, Chaldeans, Syrians and Nestorians as Armenians, just as the Orientals classed all Europeans, whether Portuguese, Spanish, Germans or Italians, as Franks.[25] The Armenians, properly so-called, had a form of Christianity which differed in ceremonial from that of the Jesuit Fathers, but approached it in many respects more nearly than that of the Protestants from Europe. They still, like the Protestants, observed the old style of calendar, which the Catholics abandoned in 1582, but at Ahmadābād in 1595 the Fathers, who were travelling to the Court with some Armenians, were able to induce their Armenian fellow-travellers—with the exception of an 'obstinate old doctor'—to join with them in celebrating Easter according to the new Gregorian date, 'whether through fear (because they had to return through Portuguese territory), or because they were convinced of the truth.'[26] The Armenians appear at the time to have been ecclesiastically somewhat demoralized ; they are said to have had a church in Agra in 1562,[27] but we hear nothing of this church from the Jesuits ; and cases were known in which Armenians concealed their Christianity and lived among the non-Christians as though belonging to them.[28] The professed Christians among the Armenians in Mogor were at first much opposed to the Jesuits, but later on a certain number consented to join the Catholic congregations, and the Jesuits throughout their Mission in Northern India paid special attention to the conversion of Armenians to the Catholic Church.[29] Among the converts so made there were several men of remarkable personality. One of them, for instance, an Armenian called Isaac, accompanied the Jesuit Brother Goes from Lahore on his long and adventurous journey to Cathay in 1603, and adhered to him with great heroism until he died. Another, a rich and pious Armenian called Khwāja Martinus or Martyros, travelled from India to Rome and evidently considered himself to be one of the Fathers' congregation, insomuch that he desired Father Xavier to compose the inscription for his tomb in the Catholic cemetery at Agra.[30] Another and still more remarkable convert was Mīrzā Zū'lqarnain, who held high official appointments under Jahāngīr and Shāh Jahān and not only helped the Jesuits in every possible way, but himself also conformed very completely to the Catholic ideal of a devout life.[31] The Fathers adopted the practice of looking on all scattered members of the Armenian community as forming part of their charge, whether Catholics or not. In a letter written by Father Jerome Xavier in 1604 we hear of an Armenian landholder near Agra who died suddenly 'without so much time as to cry "Jesus!"' and how, on learning of his death, the Father forthwith set out to comfort his relations and help in settling his affairs.[32] When the poorer Armenians in Lahore were threatened by the Viceroy in 1604 for making wine, Father Pinheiro intervened and induced them to desist from this calling.[33] When an Armenian in the same city was condemned to lose his arm for having committed a murder and declined to escape the penalty by recanting his faith, the Fathers tended him in prison and provided for his family.[34] The Armenians had indeed on more than one occasion given cause for anxiety to the Jesuit Fathers. When the Christian community in Agra expressed dissatisfaction with Father Jerome Xavier in 1604, the Armenian element was especially mutinous.[35] When the Governor of Lahore in the same year threatened to arrest all the Christians in the city, some twenty-three Armenian merchants fled with haste, escaping through different gates. 'It seems,' wrote Father Pinheiro, 'they have no mind to be martyrs, may God make them good confessors. I met three or four of them, but they would not be seen speaking to me, as they did not wish to be known as Christians—God help them.'[36] The Fathers, however, were still looked on as the natural protectors of the community, and when Lahore was in a turmoil in 1606 owing to the revolt of Prince Khusrū, Armenian merchants stowed their goods for safety at the Fathers' house.[37] In dealing with the maintenance of the captives of the Deccan War of 1601 the Fathers obtained valuable aid from an Armenian.[38] And in their intercourse with the Mogul Court the Fathers in the early stages of the Mission made free use of Armenian interpreters. One of these, Domingo Pires, was, it is true, distrusted by Father Rudolf Aquaviva and involved the Fathers in 1582 in some sort of trouble, but in September of the same year we find Father Rudolf conducting the ceremony of his marriage in the presence of the King.[39] Later on, in 1604, we hear of an Armenian merchant being near to death and calling in the Fathers, confessing to them, and begging with much feeling that the Passion of Christ should be read to him. ' He was buried,' says Father Xavier, ' very differently from other Armenians, to show how the Roman Church honours even after death those who have been obedient to her in life.'[40] In Agra alone there were in Father Botelho's time (1648–1654) some fifty or sixty Armenian merchants,[41] and the old Catholic cemeteries in Northern India contain many Armenian tombs. In the Padres Santos Chapel at Agra the oldest tomb is that of Khwāja Martinus, the Armenian merchant above mentioned, and a number of Armenians were buried in other parts of the Lashkarpur cemetery at Agra during the seventeenth and eighteenth centuries and in the D'Eremao cemetery at Delhi during the latter part of the eighteenth century. There is nothing to show whether these interments were ever made without Latin rites, but the cemeteries seem to have been open for the use of Armenians of all classes, although the later Jesuits held somewhat aloof from those Armenians who declined to conform to Catholicism.[42] In after times there was a dispute between the Catholic Fathers and the Armenians as to the claim of the latter to have the use of the Lashkarpur cemetery at Agra if they had become Muslims, and some years after the close of the Jesuit Mission the matter was brought to an issue in the Civil Courts.[43] Speaking generally, however, the Armenian community appears to have lived on good terms with the Catholics, and, as above noted, there were some notable cases of Armenians who not only conformed to Catholic practice, but were also ardent devotees of the Catholic form of faith.

Other Eastern Christians

As regards the members of such other Eastern Churches as were represented among the Christians living in the Mogul Empire, the attitude of the Fathers was similar to that adopted by them towards the Armenians. We hear of the Fathers having intervened in 1597 to obtain from the Governor of Lahore the release of a ' Chaldæan Christian '—probably a Nestorian is meant—who had been condemned to death.[44] And in 1602 the Fathers baptized the two sons of a Georgian Christian called Manuchihr Beg, an ambassador from the Shāh of Persia, who had resided for four years in India and who presumably belonged to the Orthodox Greek Church.[45] It appears that even when they did not definitely adopt them as

Catholics, the Fathers, as Bernier asserts, acted in the capacity of advisers and helpers to the Eastern Christians of all kinds in Northern India—Greeks, Armenians, Nestorians, Jacobites, and others.[46]

Indian converts: Few of the higher classes

The bulk of the Fathers' congregations, however, consisted, as was to be expected, of natives of India, and it is they who are specially referred to by them under the collective title of the 'Christiandade of Mogor.' In the early days of the Mission the Fathers concentrated their efforts largely on the conversion of the King, and even after the death of Akbar much time was devoted to attendance on the King and on Princes of the Royal Family. So long as these royal personages looked favourably on the Jesuits, there were also nobles and high officials who would from time to time make advances towards the acceptance of the Christian faith. In the initial stages of the Mission the sons of some of the nobles came to the Fathers' school to learn Portuguese, and with them were the three sons of the Chief of Badakhshān.[47] Among Father Pinheiro's converts was a Sayad, a descendant of the Prophet; a Shaikh of some position who had been to Mecca and who after conversion was sent from Lahore to Agra to join the Fathers there as an assistant; and two ladies—a mother and a daughter—who belonged to the royal tribe of the Chaghatai.[48] In 1611 mention is made of the baptism at Agra of the daughter of some unnamed Rājā.[49] The physician of Prince Salīm was induced to accept the Faith and to be baptized, but he was allowed at his own request to keep his conversion secret.[50] Allusion has been made in Chapter V to Muqarrib Khān, another physician, who rose to high honour under Jahāngīr as Governor successively of Gujarāt and Bihār, and was in 1610 actually baptized, but kept his conversion secret for fear of losing his post and remained so far outside the fold that he maintained a plurality of wives and was for this reason excluded from the Sacraments. There were almost to the end of the Mission friends and sympathisers among the aristocracy, but actual conversions from the higher classes were rare. The bulk of the Jesuits' converts were persons of comparatively humble birth. The Italian traveller Vechiete, who was in Agra in 1604, reports that a number of converts had been made, but from the lower classes—'vero è che della gente bassa.'[51] Father Xavier in speaking to Jahāngīr in 1606–1607 acknowledged that the converts at Lahore came from a low grade of society (gente comũ e baixa).[52] Father Botelho, fifty years later, found them to be mostly servants to Armenians or Europeans, or else embroiderers, surgeons (nāis), and the like.[53] In the eyes of the

Fathers, however, these also were ' souls redeemed by the precious blood of the Lamb as assuredly as if they had been of the highest rank,' and they seem to have been guided and protected by the Jesuit priests of Mogul times with the same paternal care as that shown by the Catholic pastors of our day.

Inducements to conversion

The Fathers of the first Mission to Akbar did little in the way of direct proselytizing. Father Rudolf Aquaviva was more of a recluse than an evangelist, and Father Monserrate seems seldom to have discoursed on religion outside Court circles. The initiation of a real pastoral Mission was due in the main to Father Pinheiro of the Third Mission. Allusion has been already made in dealing with that Mission to the official obstacles placed in the way of evangelization, and the successful efforts made by Pinheiro and Xavier to have these obstacles, nominally at least, removed. A good deal of latitude was, in fact, permitted in the Mogul dominions to expressions of religious opinion. The eccentric English traveller Coryate is reported to have ascended a minaret at the time of prayer and to have proclaimed an ' āzān ' of his own to the effect that there was no god but God and that Hazrat 'Īsā was the Son of God ;[54] and he tells us himself of a disputation he had in Multān with a Muslim renegade, adding, in his half-witted but shrewd manner, that if he had spoken as much in Turkey or Persia against Muhammad he would have been ' rosted upon a spitt.'[55] His immunity in the latter incident was due largely to the fact that his diatribe was in the Italian language, but he was doubtless right in holding that the danger attached to public disputations was ordinarily less in India than in other Muslim countries. The local authorities, it is true, were not always complacent, and Father Pinheiro, for instance, was on one occasion instructed by the Viceroy in Lahore to confine his evangelizing activities to his own house ; but he had royal support behind him and was able to answer on behalf of the Jesuits, ' that not only in their house with closed doors, but in the centre of the city, in its streets and open places, nay, on every side, far and near, would they preach the truth of the Christian law.'[56] We hear of the Fathers penetrating even to the mosque on a Friday and obtaining a hearing there, so long as they did not speak against the law of Muhammad.[57] As regards what would now be called street preaching, however, there seems, as a matter of fact, to have been little or nothing done by the Jesuits, and the practice is only very rarely referred to.[58] Most of the converts who were drawn to the Christian law were attracted not by street addresses, but by the ceremonial activities of the Mission. It was the Jesuits' policy to make these ceremonies as public as possible and non-Christians were encouraged to attend and take part in them. The churches were decorated as richly as circumstances permitted; the services were performed with a due amount of ritual and of music; and processions were from time to time organized with palm branches, crucifixes, bands of music, priests in their vestments, and so forth, to march through the city. In the early days of the Mission it was not uncommon for a Muslim or a Hindu to show a personal interest in the ceremonial connected with a baptism or a burial or the inauguration of a church; many would prostrate themselves before the images, and others would attend the services to listen to the sermon. So great was the curiosity of some to acquaint themselves with the Christian forms of worship that in one case a Muslim sympathizer, when asked to withdraw from the church during the celebration of Mass, consented with all courtesy, but returned surreptitiously to witness the service.[59] The acquisition of a new picture on the altar would attract large crowds, and the Christmas representations of the Child in the Manger would always be devoutly admired by throngs of non-Christians. On such occasions the Fathers would be present, spending long hours with the crowd in readiness to answer questions and to explain the Gospel story. It was in such ways that the Jesuits got most easily in touch with all classes of the people. They attended, as we have seen, with considerable regularity at Court; they mixed to some extent in general society, and they not infrequently invited officials to their residence. Both in regular disputations at the Court and in ordinary discussions at private houses they were always ready to argue for their Faith, and though some of their arguments may seem strange to us they appear not infrequently to have been effectual. But they evidently felt throughout that it was less by street preaching or by discussion in public or private than by the appeal of ceremonial or scenic display, that the conscience of the people could most successfully be reached.

As indicated above attractions of this character were, as a rule, accompanied by explanatory discourses leading on to an exposition of the Christian faith, accompanied not infrequently by attacks on other forms of belief. We are given, by Father Xavier, an example of the form of discourse employed on such occasions.[60] The discourse in question was delivered in connection with the exhibition of a representation of the Manger at Agra during the Christmas-tide of 1610. The spectators, seeing that one of the Magi in the representation was shown as weeping, asked the reason.

A specimen of the Fathers' preaching

'I replied,' says Xavier, 'that it was for joy at seeing the great compassion of the Lord God, who for love of him and of mankind took this lowly guise; and who (I asked) would not weep, with wonder and devotion to behold God in that state for His love of us? I reproduced to them the words he might have said and the passion with which he spoke. "My God, I see you in this world so poor for my sake. What need have I of a kingdom, of greatness, of wives, of children? I will leave all and follow you." Many were moved and some wept, while all listened attentively. Afterwards I told them how that Child grew to be a man and gave His life for our sins, how rising from the dead He had ascended into heaven, and how He had many times told those who believed in Him that He would give them the water of life "which that font which you see represents," and then I told them that the water of life was the salvation of the soul, at which they were filled with amazement; much more when I told them how much they ought to do to save it, for they had but one and it was our treasure, etc. Also I told them that Christ Our Lord had said that until the day of judgement no other Law would come, and that they should not give credit to anyone who claimed to be the Prophet or Ambassador of God, and that Muhammad was not a prophet of God but of falsehood, etc. It was remarkable to see the different feelings which this aroused: some received it with approval, others *stridebant dentibus in me* (ground their teeth at me) and went away, and others waited and dissembled. To prove to them that Muhammad was not a prophet, I brought forward a stock argument, which, as it had stood me in good stead in the beginning, I have always made use of. "Behold," I said, "your Muhammad has slain neither my father nor my mother, nor has he done me any injury: but I give you the message which this Lord orders me to give. Hear me; this Lord commanded in His Holy Gospel that no man should have more than one wife, and in no circumstances should have two: by this, confidence, love and peace, etc., reign in the house. Now, behold, your Muhammad took to himself nine wives and permitted others to have three or four and as many negresses as they desired and could get. Is it this man you call a prophet? Is it this man you would follow?" . . .

Many, both men and women, on entering and approaching the Crib, asked me "Where is God?" having heard others speak of the little Child, Jesus, God incarnate. I used to say to them, "That little Child is He," and I explained to them that what their eyes beheld was a human child, but that God was within the child. I made use of a comparison which they understood very well: "When a woman walks in the street covered by a veil (which they call a *burqa'*) so that she is hidden from view, if you ask some stranger who the woman is, he will say, 'I do not know: I can see only the cloth which covers her,' but he who is of her house will say, 'This is my mistress' or 'This is my mother,' for he has other means of recognizing her. So when God comes into the world clad with humanity, as with a *burqa'*, so that His divinity is hidden from sight, if you ask a Moor or a Gentile,

'Who is this 'Īsā (i.e. Jesus)?' he will say, 'He is a holy man, a man of purity, a prophet.' He does not know more than that, because he does not see more. But that Angel (pointing to the Angel of glory), I see him crying out and saying: 'This is our Lord God,' and Christians who have been taught the Holy Gospel will give the same answer." This appealed to them strongly.'

'All this,' adds Father Xavier, 'was, as it were, a downpour of rain, which is very heavy whilst it lasts, but does not penetrate deeply. None the less that which took place cannot but have been of great service to the Lord.'

Maintenance of converts

For the poorer converts—and most of the Christians were very poor—economic help had to be provided, and they were maintained by the Fathers from funds placed at their disposal, such funds being supplemented in the early days by grants from the King. Cases of hardship were taken up and pressed before the authorities; and provision was made for housing poor Christians in distress. Assistance of this character gave rise to the criticism made by Protestant writers such as Withington, Roe, Terry and others, to the effect that the Jesuits' converts were not real Christians but were baptized 'for money's sake'[61]—that they 'for want of means were content to wear crucifixes.' And the criticism had no doubt in some cases a foundation of fact. The Jesuits' report of 1619, for instance, reports naïvely enough that the largesses of their protégé, Mīrzā Zū'lqarnain, were 'the bait with which he concealed his hook' whereby he was enabled to fish up many Gentoos and Muhammadans into the Church of Jesus Christ.[62] And in 1613 when a convert had been cross-examined by Jahāngīr about the Christian religion and had answered him stoutly, the Jesuits seem to have considered it only natural to express their appreciation of his conduct by increasing his 'rozīna' or daily allowance.[63] It is difficult without a greater knowledge of individual cases than we possess to say how far money so spent was a bribe to conversion and how far it represented the relief of destitution. And in any case, it must be remembered that there was much undisguised persuasion of this kind on the other side and that poor Christians were not infrequently tempted to accept allowances (rozīna) from the Muslims if they abandoned their faith.[64] The taunt that the converts accepted baptism in return for subsistence was made also by Muslims in the presence of Jahāngīr, and we are told how, in order to test the accuracy of this charge, the King ordered his servants to go out and bring to him the first Christian whom they might meet. This happened to be a household servant belonging to the Fathers, and Jahāngīr offered to give him far higher pay if he would abandon Christianity, but he refused with firmness to change his faith, and received the approbation of the King for his constancy.[65]

We have, as a matter of fact, no specific instances of the grant or promise of money to non-Christians with the object of securing their conversion, and cases of such action, if they occurred, seem to have been very rare. As indicated above, however, a great deal of time and trouble was taken by the Jesuits to alleviate distress among those who had been converted. The bulk of the converts—including not a few orphans, old men and widows—were in the most abject poverty, earning a bare living by such occupations as the making of bangles or lace-work, and always on the verge of famine.[66] When the capital was removed from Agra, many of the more prosperous Christians left the town, and the converts who remained were faced by a considerable amount of unemployment and a marked fall in the prices obtained for the articles they produced. When Aurangzeb left Delhi for the Deccan a similar effect was produced on the Christian community at Delhi.[67] There were no private agencies in Mogor on whom claims could be made for the relief of destitute Christians, and the whole charge for their support fell on the funds of the Jesuit Mission.[68] After the death of Jahāngīr those funds received little or no assistance from the Mogul Government, and the resources available for the poorer converts became more and more exiguous. From an inspection note of the Mission accounts which has been preserved, it appears that in the years 1675-1681 the amount expended by the Fathers on the poor in Agra did not exceed an average of 850 rupees a year.[69] A few years later we hear of 1500 rupees being available from the College at Agra.[70] The money earned by the Fathers in saying Masses and the stock of medicines sent up by the Jesuits from Goa were in constant demand for relieving destitution and sickness among the poor converts.[71] During the last days of the Mission there were occasional gifts of money from some of the richer European military commanders in Northern India, but the congregation itself had become even more helpless than before. Practically all the adult male population was away on military service, and the Christians in Agra were represented by wives and widows who endeavoured to eke out a living by spinning and weaving, but who also looked, not infrequently, for the Fathers' assistance.[72] There were no doubt cases during the history of the Mission of men who took the Fathers' alms and refused to work. There were even cases of men who clamoured for alms and threatened to become Muslims if they did not receive them.[73] But the bulk of the small funds available seem to have been distributed with care and the administration of relief took up a large portion of the time and attention of the Fathers.

As regards conversions, the bulk of these seem to have been genuine enough. They were doubtless due to circumstances of a very various character, but one may be pardoned if one concludes that the human agency most potently at work was the influence and example of the Fathers themselves. It is likely that in most cases it was the spectacle of the Fathers' lives of unselfishness, purity and devotion that led men and women to enquire about the religion they professed. To those who enquired, the tenets of that religion were presented in clear-cut decisive terms by men of education and special training, who had no hesitation as to their own beliefs, and whose one earnest preoccupation in life was to save souls for Christ.

In various ways the Fathers attracted enquirers, and when an enquirer definitely demanded baptism he or she was received on to the list of 'catechumens': and the instruction of these catechumens was a serious part of the Fathers' duties. The Protestant minister Terry speaks regretfully of the Jesuit converts who were content to wear crucifixes, but who for want of instruction were Christian only in name;[74] but his ideals of instruction were of a different character to those of the Jesuits. It is true that the methods of instruction differed in some ways from those of modern days, and for many years the Catechism seems to have been taught in Portuguese, the converts looking on that language as the language of the Gospels, very much as Arabic was of the Qur'ān; and although we hear of the women and children in 1607 being taught in the vernacular, it was not till 1611 that the Fathers decided to instruct the converts generally in the catechism in Persian and Hindustani.[75] Even then the teaching was verbal only, the converts being nearly all illiterate: a system of teaching the children to read and write, or to learn industrial work, was indeed introduced in 1650 at the instance of Father Botelho, but with an educational rather than a religious object in view.[76] In one way or another the catechumens received a good deal of elementary doctrinal instruction on Catholic lines, and as a rule they served a long time of probation before being baptized. In view of the opposition which the enquirer was liable to encounter from friends and relatives it was thought prudent that he should be fully established in the faith before proceeding to baptism.[77] In the Tibetan Mission the Fathers were so embarrassed by the clamour for baptism that they purposely withheld the rite in order to increase the esteem for it.[78] In exceptional cases only

Teaching of catechumens

was due preparation dispensed with. There was, for instance, a case at Lahore in Father Pinheiro's time in which a resolute young girl, some fifteen years of age, insisted on being baptized along with a body of catechumens who were undergoing the rite, and the Father, after a summary examination of her knowledge of the Catechism, thought it wise to accede to her request.[79] The preliminary preparation was also necessarily dispensed with or curtailed in the case of persons at the point of death who evinced a desire to be baptized.[80] It was also, of course, omitted in the case of very young children.

Baptism of Infants

The baptism of young children requires special notice, because the Fathers had a sincere faith in the efficacy of infant baptism for the salvation of souls, and took frequent occasion to administer the rite to dying infants whose parents were not Christians. A notable occasion for this practice was the famine in Kashmīr in 1597. During that visitation the priests would collect and baptize children whom their mothers had put out on the streets to die, and sometimes the mothers themselves would call in the priests to baptize their children at the point of death.[81] In one case, we are told, Father Xavier declined, as the child did not seem *in extremis* and would probably grow up in error, but when it afterwards was at the point of death he agreed, with the father's assent, to baptize it.[82] It was the ordinary practice of the Fathers not to baptize infants except when death was at hand because of the danger of their afterwards renouncing their faith.[83] During the Deccan campaign of 1601 a servant of Father Xavier found an infant on a dung-heap and brought it to the Father, who baptized it. 'The child,' says the chronicler, 'survived for one day and then went to join the company of the blessed in Paradise': and the verse of the Psalmist at once suggested itself, when he says, 'He lifteth the needy from the dung-hill that he may set him with princes'—'De stercore erigens pauperem ut collocet eum cum principibus.'[84] Even when the parents were consenting parties the baptism of infants sometimes entailed unexpected results. We are told, for instance, of a Muslim mother at Lahore in 1599 who had her child baptized, but was so taunted by her relations that she put poison in the infant's milk. 'The poor child,' says Pimenta, 'after seventeen hours of terrible torture bore testimony to Christ not by words but by death'—Christum non loquendo sed moriendo confessus;—and expired before the altar in the church forty days after its birth and eighteen days after its baptism. Father Pinheiro writes that after the child had surrendered its soul to Christ its face still shone with so unwonted a grace, that the glory of its blessed soul which it had attained on rising to Christ appeared to be reflected on its features below.[85] In 1602 an infant found by the wayside was brought to the Fathers at Lahore. It was baptized and died : and the Fathers gave it 'a very beautiful funeral,' leaving it with its face exposed in the church and then taking it on a bier covered with flowers through the middle of the city.[86] In his report of 1649 Father Maracci tells us of an infant baptized within a few moments of its death, who 'in the space of a Credo flew to Heaven.'[87] In the same year the Annual Letter from Agra tells of several infant children of pagan parents who 'insured the Fathers' gain by being enrolled in Heaven after baptism.'[88] In some cases the Fathers went so far as to purchase little children from poverty-stricken parents for small sums in order to baptize them.[89] The rite could, in emergency, be performed by laymen, and the imaginative adventurer Manucci, who in his character as physician had much access to the infants of the country, gravely assures us that, apart from those whom he found moribund on the roadsides, he himself had in the space of eight years baptized more than 15,000 infants.[90] He says that he was often asked by parents to sprinkle a child, but only did so when he thought it was bound to die. 'With the profession of doctor,' he complacently adds, 'it is possible to do some service for God,' and he makes the strange recommendation that missionaries should be trained to bleed patients and to cure ulcers so that they might be called into houses where they would get opportunities of baptizing infants. Whatever we may think of his statistics, the attitude of mind which underlies his remarks was one which was shared by the Catholic missionaries of his time, not only in Mogor, but also in Southern India, Persia, China and elsewhere.

The practice of infant baptism, under such circumstances, makes it a little difficult to appraise the significance of such few data as we possess to show the extent to which the Jesuits were successful in their efforts at conversion. In 1599 Father Pinheiro wrote from Lahore that in the period of five or six months since Father Xavier had left for Agra there had been 39 persons baptized by the Mission in Lahore.[91] In 1600 we are told that in the course of the year the Fathers at Lahore had baptized on one occasion 39 persons, on another 20 and on another 47.[92] After the Deccan War of 1601 more than 70 persons (in addition to half-castes and Portuguese) were baptized, 'many of whom were straightway received into the glory of Heaven.'[93] In 1604–1605 there were troublous times in Lahore, and Father Pinheiro who was in charge in that

The number of Baptisms

city confesses that no conversions were then made.[94] In 1606, when Jahāngīr was strongly pro-Muslim in his policy, the number of conversions in Agra was about 20 only,[95] and even in 1608, when his attitude had changed, the number of neophytes there is described as very small—numero paucissimos.[96] In 1618–1619 40 adults were baptized at Sāmbhar.[97] Father de Castro, who was in the Mission from 1610 to 1646, was reported to have effected a large number of conversions from among the heathen.[98] In 1620 the number of conversions in the newly-established Mission at Patna was four.[99] In 1623 the number of conversions in Mogor for the previous year was reported to be 100.[100] In writing from Kashmīr in 1627 Father de Castro alludes enigmatically to a case of whole villages (apparently in Kashmīr) which were desirous of conversion, and of a mysterious people (possibly those of the villages in question) who wished to become Christians and were neither Hindus nor Muslims, but immigrants who observed the law of Abraham.[101] In the Agra Mission a number of persons were baptized during the plague of 1619,[102] and between May 1648 and August 1649, 49 pagans were baptized in the same Mission—' Those who are aware,' says the Annual Report, ' of the immense difficulties of this Mission will not think lightly of the number.'[103] Father Morando at Sāmbhar about the same period ' brought ten heathen into the Catholic Church.'[104] In September of the same year, 1649, Father Ceschi, writing from Agra, says, ' This year I have baptized many heathen, and I hope that many will come to the Faith,'[105] and the Report of 1650 says that in the current year 21 persons were baptized at Agra, including nine who were baptized on their death-beds. In 1653 Ceschi writes again from Agra, ' I have baptized many infidels this year,'[106] but the Annual Report states that in 1653 only 30 baptisms were effected in the whole Mogul Mission.[107] The next year Ceschi writes from Delhi : ' Thirty-two infidels were baptized this year in this Mission.'[108] Father Botelho reported that during the years when he was Superior of the Mission at Agra (1648–1654) he himself baptized 21 pagans,[109] and Father Malpica was in 1654 reported to have baptized five persons in the State of Srīnagar in Garhwāl.[110] This rate of progress was too slow for the full-blooded Father Busi, who was in the Mission from 1648 to 1667 and he was accustomed to say that the only way to preach in Hindustān was with a well-sharpened sword.[111] But the number of conversions showed little tendency to increase as the time went on. In the ten years ending 1675 the baptisms of all kinds at Agra averaged 25 only for the year and in 'the years immediately preceding ' 1678 there were 80 conversions from Islām and Hinduism. In those preceding 1686 there were 90, of which 16 were of adults.[112] In the six years ending in 1693 there were 220 baptisms, of which 115 represented children of Christians and 105 outsiders : 15 of the latter being death-bed baptisms.[113] In 1735 Father Figueredo speaks indeed of conversions in Delhi, but they were apparently conversions of dying persons or infants,[114] and in 1747 Father Strobl, writing from the same centre, intimates that the Mission had enough to do to tend the existing congregation and that there was little or no chance of fresh conversions.[115] Thenceforward, until the disappearance of the Jesuits in 1803, the number of converts in Mogor seems to have been insignificant.

Ill success among Muslims

Father Trigault, writing in 1607 about the Mogor Missions, refers to the smallness of their success in conversions, 'which,' he says, ' is nothing new among Mahommedans.'[116] The difficulty was throughout with Islām rather than with Hinduism. The chronicles speak at an early stage of the Muslims being ' as hard as diamonds to work upon,' and Terry in his sententious way writes of ' that most acceptable but hard labour of washing Moors.'[117] As early as 1597 Father Xavier had in sowing the Word distinguished between the thorns of Hinduism and the stony ground of Islām—spinas Gentilium, petrosa Maurorum,[118] and he noted later the great difficulty caused by the fact that while the Muslims agreed with the Jesuits in all that concerned the nature of God, they came into conflict with them ' about that which we cannot prove with reason but only with miracles which the Lord will work by whom and when it will please Him.'[119] According to a later dictum the Muslim was ' easy to convince but difficult to convert.'[120] Even when a convert had been made from Islām the Muslim atmosphere around him rendered his life intolerable, and the Fathers often hesitated to baptize such converts because, it was said, they ' could place so little reliance on the people of this Moor-ridden land that to convert them was like building with worm-eaten timber.'[121] Bernier, in his discourse on Christian missions in India, warns his readers against the impression that converts can be expected from Islām. ' La secte est trop libertine,' he says, ' et trop attrayante pour la quitter.'[122] We are repeatedly told by the Fathers how great a stumbling-block, especially at the Court, they found in the practice of polygamy and its attendant evils. The Protestant chaplain Terry, who was in India with Sir Thomas Roe, tells us that he would gladly have attempted to evangelize but was discouraged, partly by the bad lives of many professing Christians and partly by the 'Mahumatane libertie for women,' that is to say, the attractions offered by polygamy.[123] According to Pyrard de Laval, it was a common saying among the Jesuits in the Indies 'that it was more easy to convert fifty—nay, a hundred—Gentiles or idolators than one Mahometan.'[124] The Fathers, wrote Bernier, might by their instruction, coupled with their alms and charity, make some progress among the Hindus, but their instruction and reasoning would not in ten years bring a single Muslim to Christianity.[125] On some occasions we find that conversions from among Hindus were permitted by the authorities, while conversions from Muslims were prohibited: not only was an order of this kind issued by the Muslim ruler, Shā'ista Khān, in Dacca, but even in a powerful Hindu State like Jaipur the Fathers were precluded by the Rājā, Jai Singh Sawāī, from extending their evangelization to his Muslim subjects.[126] Father Botelho, in speaking of Shāh Jahān's order prohibiting proselytizing among Muslims, describes it as a superfluous injunction as 'no Moor becomes a Christian in those parts, however much the Fathers may speak to them.'[127] We know from the extant reports that these statements would not be applicable as they stand to the circumstances of the earlier days of the Mission, but they indicate the general obduracy of the Muslim attitude. Father Pinheiro in the days of Akbar and Jahāngīr, though at times harassed by particular Hindus, made a large proportion of his converts at Lahore from the Hindu population, and Father de Castro at the same place had, later on, more success with the Hindus than with the Muslims.[128] The Fathers were from the beginning trained to study the contents of the Qur'ān and to speak in Persian, as these qualifications enabled them to deal with the ruling classes, and it was not till the time of Father Roth (1653–1668) that a serious effort was made to study Sanskrit and to understand the Hindu point of view. One of the attractions of the Tibetan Mission, both to Father Roth and to some of his predecessors, was the fact that it would take them to a country where there were no Muslims.[129] The difficulty in the case of the higher class Hindus lay in their ceremonial abhorrence of Europeans as barbarous and unclean, but they raised fewer objections than the Muslims to the doctrines put forward by the Fathers.[130] It is clear that, at any rate after the days of Akbar and Jahāngīr, the Hindus offered a better field for conversion than the Muslims, and it is probable that from the beginning the bulk of the Jesuits' converts were of Hindu origin.

It is not easy to get a clear idea of the size of the congregations dealt with at various periods by the Fathers. They were for the most part mixed congregations of Europeans and Indians. The origin of a real congregation at Agra is ascribed by Father Botelho to the fusion of the Portuguese captives of the Deccan War of 1601 and the local Indian converts ;[131] but we are given no indication of the number of Christians at Agra in the earliest days of the Mission. In 1604 there were more than forty converts from Islām who received Holy Communion in the Agra church ;[132] in 1607 the number of believers of all ages in Agra was put at seventy.[133] The numbers, however, depended largely on the presence or absence of the Court, and during the years 1606–1608 when the Court was away from Agra the Jesuits found it unnecessary to leave a priest in charge of the Agra congregation. In 1614 we are told that the Jesuits decided not to abandon the Mogor Mission because there were 500 Christians at stake, but it is not clear whether this figure refers to Agra alone or to the whole Mission.[134] In 1623 the number of Christians scattered in various places in Mogor, excluding Armenians, etc., was estimated at 1000.[135] In 1632 Father Azevedo put the number of the congregation of Agra at about 400, including Armenians and Europeans.[136] In 1649 the Agra congregation is described as ' a tiny fire in the midst of the blasts of the North Wind,'[137] and in 1654 as a tiny flock—' pusillus grex '—although at the latter date it contained 700 Christians who went to confession and received the Holy Communion.[138] Father Roth, ten years later, put his congregation at Agra at 1000 souls,[139] and this seems to represent the normal size of the congregation in the middle of the seventeenth century as near as we can get it. The Report of 1675 puts the number of Christians (native and foreign) connected with the Court at Agra and in Delhi at about 600. The Report of 1678, in a somewhat rhetorical passage, says that the Mission began with ten and ended with 1000, thus carrying out the ' hundredfold ' of the Parable of the Sower. Other figures have been recorded which seem clearly erroneous. Bernier, for instance, writing a few years later than Roth, speaks of the Fathers as teaching the children of twenty-five to thirty Christian families only,[140] while on the other hand an estimate mentioned, but not supported, by Thévenot a few years subsequently puts the number of Christian families at Agra at 25,000. This latter statement was an absurd exaggeration, but as Col. Sleeman pointed out such a figure could scarcely have been put forward if there had not in reality been quite a considerable congregation.[141] Towards the

Size of the congregations

end of the seventeenth century the numbers decreased. The figures quoted by the Jesuits for 1686 is 300; for 1693 it is 400, including foreigners of all kinds;[142] and the Italian Legrenzi, speaking of the period immediately following, puts the total number of Christians in Agra, including Armenians, at 300 only.[143] When the Jesuits abandoned their Mission at Agra in 1784 the Carmelite Fathers who succeeded them estimated that in Agra and its neighbourhood there were some 300 Christian families, aggregating about 1000 souls.[144]

When Jahāngīr was in Lahore in 1606–1607 and wished to make a grant of money to the Fathers, he asked them how many Christians there were there, and they replied that there were forty or fifty, but one gathers that in making this reply Father Xavier felt that he was understating the number and that he had feared to exaggerate because Jahāngīr was quite capable of requiring him to produce his converts before him.[145] Although there was a fair Christian population in Lahore during the presence of the Court, the permanent part of it cannot have been very large because, when the troubles of 1614 broke out, it was found possible to transfer the whole Indian Christian congregation of Lahore to Agra:[146] and thereafter the Christian element in Lahore was of a very transient character, being mainly connected with the army. A special journey was taken in 1648 by the Rector of Agra to Lahore to instruct and recall those in the army who had fallen from Christian practices.[147] When the Father Desideri was about to visit the town in 1714 he expected to find only five or six Christians there,[148] but later on we are told that the kern of the army at Lahore was Christian, observing Christian practices and marching under banners which bore the emblem of the Cross; and in 1735 there were 'numerous Christians at Lahore apart from the army.'[149]

At Sāmbhar there was a temporary influx of Christians in the middle of the seventeenth century, when the high official, Mīrzā Zū'lqarnain, was established there with a following of 400, most of whom were Christians.[150] At Delhi the congregation in 1650 numbered 120;[151] in 1654 the zealous Father Ceschi tells us that the number of Christians was 'by no means small,' and implies that they were more numerous than he by himself could cope with.[152] In 1686 when the capital was at Delhi, but the Court was in the Deccan, the number was 300.[153] Father Desideri puts the Christian population of Delhi in 1714 at 300;[154] in 1740, after the massacre by Nādir Shāh, the surviving Christian population was said to be 700;[155] and in 1748 Father Strobl writes from Delhi of the 'little handful' of Christians there—the 'kleines

Häuflein der Christen.'[156] Father Figueredo in 1735 speaks of the Rājā of Jaipur as having 600 Christian servants,[157] but in 1742 Father Strobl found there a 'kleine Christenheit' of some forty souls only.[158] At Narwar, Patna and elsewhere there were similar small communities, but their numbers are not indicated.

The various figures given above are as a rule modest enough, and I can find nothing in the reports of the Jesuits to show that they intentionally exaggerated the numbers of their congregations. The enthusiasm of some of their earlier letters led the Protestant Roe to charge them with having sung in Europe 'loud prayses and glorious successes' of the growth of their Church on a very slender basis. He looked on the results of their work as 'a leane and barren harvest,' and described them as having obtained in some few cities of Northern India a building rather than a congregation—'templum' rather than 'ecclesiam.'[159] We have seen what their difficulties were, and the smallness of the results compared with the output of many other Jesuit Missions must at times have depressed the spirits even of the most ardent of the missionaries. Father de Castro, for instance, bewails in 1626 the smallness of his success, saying, 'God alone knows why it is so small,' and suggests that it might be due partly to his own unworthiness and partly to the evil disposition and the carnal appetites of both Hindus and Muslims.[160] Others, like Andrade, found cause for contentment in a contemplation of the delay with which results had been achieved in Japan and the continuing want of success in China and in Abyssinia.[161] And there were still others who, while admitting the smallness of the flock, found compensation in its standard of character and discipline.

Religious ceremonies and spectacles.—Sermons

The flock which the Fathers endeavoured so zealously to train and to inspire was almost entirely illiterate. Explanations of the Gospel and instruction in the Catechism to which much time was devoted were ordinarily conducted in the vernacular. Sermons in the churches were delivered both in the vernacular and in Portuguese. In 1604 we are told that at Agra there was a sermon on Sundays and on all ordinary feast days. The sermon to the Indians was in the vernacular, but when there were Portuguese prisoners at Agra after the Deccan War of 1601 there were two sermons, including one in Portuguese for the prisoners.[162] In 1607 we are told that the Sunday sermon was in Persian.[163] Later on, Portuguese sermons would at times be preached to mixed congregations of Indians and Portuguese and, strange as it may seem, such sermons appear at times to have been extraordinarily effective. We hear, for instance, that at Agra a Good

Friday sermon on the Descent from the Cross, although in Portuguese, so moved the Christians to tears that the Muslims in the neighbourhood came running to learn the cause of the sobbing and weeping which they heard.[164]

Music

The services in the churches during the earlier days of the Mission were accompanied by music and the Fathers were at considerable pains to elaborate this phase of their ceremonial. Their churches were usually provided with organs of some description. An organ was imported to Akbar's Court from Goa, about the working of which the historian Badāonī gives an amusing and sarcastic account.[165] We hear also at the commencement of Jahāngīr's reign of two negroes who were said to be able to play upon the organs and sing Portuguese music;[166] at the baptism of Jahāngīr's nephews in 1610 there is mention of organs accompanied by flutes—tubis organisque concinientibus[167]—and in the accounts of the services at Agra in 1611 there is mention both of the organ and of organs (plural).[168] But the character of the instruments referred to is not explained, and in the absence of any more specific mention it may be surmised that the organ used in the Jesuit churches in Mogor was of the small portable type exemplified in contemporary Indian art.[169] The other instruments employed for services were ordinarily hautboys and flutes (charamellas, frautas), and on occasions of rejoicing, as at Christmas, recourse was had to tom-toms and drums (atambores, atabeles) played outside the building.[170] For the conduct of the musical part of the church services a special training of an expensive character was held necessary. In 1599 several young converts were sent from Lahore to Bāndra in Bombay 'in order that they might be taught by the best masters every kind of musical instruments for the new church.'[171] In 1606 we find pipers playing in the Lahore church who had been sent to Goa for instruction,[172] in 1611 the Agra services were improved by singers freshly imported from Goa,[173] and when a new Superior came to Mogor in 1626 he brought with him from Goa new instruments and players for the church services.[174] In 1607 four negroes for the Lahore church were conducted from Goa by a Venetian, and when Jahāngīr expressed a wish to entertain these men in his own service the Jesuits seem to have acceded to his desire on the understanding that these musicians would also be at their disposal for employment in the church.[175] In Agra in 1623 we are told that on Sundays after Mass the Litanies of the Virgin and some sacred songs were sung, the priest commencing and the whole body of Christians then joining in, and we are assured that Moors passing in the street would stop and listen to the heavenly harmony.[176] In later days, however, owing to the troubles of 1633–5 and the increasing poverty of the Mission, the use of music in the churches appears to have fallen into desuetude.[177]

Pictures and images

The churches appear to have been well ornamented and to have been provided as far as possible with sacred pictures and images. The extent to which the Jesuits interested themselves in pictures of a sacred character and the extraordinary effect which such pictures had on the emotions of those who saw them have been dealt with in Chapter XV of this work ; they formed a special feature of the churches and exerted a powerful influence over the converts. Among the pictures and statues in the churches those of the Virgin Mary were prominent, and, as in Europe, the special cult of the Virgin attracted the reprehension of Protestant critics. The English traveller Coryate notes that as beggars in India would beg from a Christian in the name not of Hazrat 'Īsā, but of Bībī Mariam, it was clear that the Jesuits preached ' Mary more than Jesus.'[178] The Virgin, however, was not the only subject represented, and the figures of Christ and of the Prophets and Saints were also at all times available for devotion in the churches ; before them both Christians and non-Christians would often be found kneeling in prayer.

The representations of the Manger

Another matter to which the Fathers gave special attention was the Christmas representation of the Manger at Bethlehem, which served to bring vividly to the senses of the converts the circumstances relating to the Birth of Christ. These ' Cribs '—the ' Kunābalān ' which attracted the scornful attention of the historian Badāonī[179]—were prepared, as a rule, by trained workmen under the special superintendence of one of the missionaries. In 1597 the explorer Goes prepared one in Lahore ' as exquisite as those of Goa itself ' ; midnight and morning Mass were said with great ceremony and a pastoral eclogue on the subject of the Nativity was enacted by some youths in the Persian tongue, with some vernacular sentences added—' adjunctis aliquot Industani sententiis.' At the conclusion of the sacred office the gates were opened to admit the non-Christian crowd, and so great was the number of visitors that the spectacle was kept open for twenty days.[180] In the following year there was so great a crowd of all ages and classes that for twenty days continuously some three or four thousand persons were admitted to worship the image of the Child.[181] In 1600 the representation included images of the three wise Kings and figures of certain Prophets, with copies in Persian of their prophecies of the birth of Christ. It was followed by a 'pastorale' in which Simeon offered consolation to Adam, a philosopher was convinced of the Sonship of Christ, Mercy and Justice disputed regarding Adam's trangression, and the shepherds announced to some Brahmins the Birth at Bethlehem.[182] Immense pains were often taken in elaborating these exhibitions, special experts being deputed from Goa for their preparation, and the scenic apparatus at times included 'hydraulic inventions.'[183] There were artificial birds which sang, images of apes which spouted water from their eyes and mouths, figures of Magi which wept tears and so forth.[184]

After the Christmas of 1610 the Crib at Agra was open to the public for forty days and Father Xavier tells us that on one day (and that not the most crowded) he had the curiosity to count the number of visitors and found it amounted to 14,000. It fell to Father Xavier to stand all day in the church expounding the story of the Nativity, and although the old man's limbs grew very weary his heart was consoled by the extraordinary devotion shown by Muslims and Hindus, men and women alike. Numbers of the latter would embrace his feet and some would take away straws from the Manger as relics.[185]

The popularity of the Cribs was maintained for many years, and in 1626 we still hear of their being kept open for a fortnight. No jubilee or feast in Europe, we are told, was ever so frequented.[186]

Religious processions

The Fathers would also often organize processions to celebrate the great festivals of the Church and the great occasions in the Christian life of their converts. There was, in the early days at least, a fine procession every Christmas, which moved the Christians to great devotion;[187] and in Agra a small procession would march devoutly on Fridays in Lent with a crucifix round the little quadrangle adjoining the Jesuit church.[188] The baptism of converts was generally performed at one of the great festivals; as many as were ready for the rite were brought forward together and conducted through the city with palms in their hands. At Pentecost in 1599 the candidates for baptism in Lahore marched through streets strewn with leaves, with trees planted on either side. They were received at the church by Father Pinheiro in his cope, and there amidst the uproar of a crowding multitude the sacred service was with difficulty performed.[189] We read of a procession on Thursday in Holy Week in Lahore which made a circuit of the city to the church, headed by a crucifix and children singing litanies, and accompanied by a band of disciplinants whose penances excited the horror and admiration of the Hindu onlookers. On Easter Eve of the same year the Fathers utilized the roof of the church for illuminations and fireworks, and on Easter Day a procession of Christians in holiday attire, with candles in their hands, set forth at dawn, working their way through an immense crowd ; at their head was a Cross adorned with flowers, and this was followed by the musicians of the church and by the Fathers in their surplices 'chanting their best' (cantando como podiam) and carrying with them an image of the infant Christ which had come from Portugal. On the following feast of Corpus Christi one of the Fathers carried the Sacred Host through the streets to the church, enclosed in a monstrance covered by a canopy ; a band of Christians surrounded him bearing torches and candles, while others followed playing on hautboys and singing, and at the places where the Father halted a Christian boy prostrated himself and confessed the Real Presence of the Redeemer.[190] At the Christmas of 1607 all the Christians in Lahore went to confession and attended midnight Mass which was celebrated with singing and the music of hautboys. Before the ceremony there was a great display of different kinds of lights in the compound of the church ; these were visible from a great distance and were accompanied by an immense din (grande estrondo) from the playing of tom-toms and drums.[191] In 1608 there was a Maundy Thursday procession at Agra which was attended by a Mogul officer of justice who provided it with a guard to clear the way. It passed a great 'captain' sitting on an elephant, who waited to watch it go by, 'marvelling to see the good order which the Christians kept and the multitude of lights which they carried.' One of the Fathers held aloft a crucifix, while another, 'wearing his Capa de Asperges,' chanted litanies, to which the children under instruction responded. Amongst those who followed were twelve disciplinants whose scourgings roused astonishment among the Muslim crowd.[192] In their letters the Fathers are fond of giving details which show that the chief Feasts of the year were celebrated with much ceremony : the church was ornamented and illuminated, drums were beaten, trumpets were sounded, muskets were fired, the bells were rung and much stir was created.[193]

Christian funerals

When a Christian died, all the other Christians in the place accompanied him to the grave. He was carried in a coffin as in Europe ; before him went a procession of small boys in white surplices singing the prayers, and a copper crucifix on a small staff and covered with a black veil headed the cortège. It was a source of harmless delight to the Fathers to find outsiders recognizing the superiority of their Christian funerals to those of the Muslims and Hindus.[194]

On such occasions, especially if the deceased had endeared himself by his ministrations, Muslims would sometimes join and even help to carry the coffin. The style of grave and the type of gravestone adopted by the Christians conformed largely to prevalent Muslim usage. On All Souls' Day the Fathers of the Agra Mission would go with the Christians to the Padres Santos Chapel and there after celebrating Mass would preach a sermon on the souls in Purgatory. They would then proceed among the graves in their copes, sprinkling water and reciting prayers, and the Christians would lay food on napkins on the graves, which the Fathers at once distributed to the faqīrs and jogīs there assembled.[195]

Rarity of non-Christian practices

This practice has its analogue in Muslim custom, but we have no means of determining how far the Fathers in adopting it were influenced by non-Christian ideas. There were no doubt certain non-Christian practices maintained among the converts. The Fathers, writing in 1649, had to admit that there were some rites among the converts which savoured of paganism and Saracenism ; but we are assured the priests had in a published sermon insisted very strongly on such rites being abolished, and that this abolition in Agra had served as an example elsewhere.[196] The adventurer Manucci tells us of Christian women who when unwell would send their children to touch the graves in the cemeteries in order to secure their recovery, but he tells us also that the Fathers preached against such abuses.[197] In the Bengal villages between Hūglī and Dacca the Hindu converts of the end of the seventeenth century evinced the greatest distaste for any action inconsistent with the retention of caste and the services of Brahmins, but the Jesuit Father Santucci, in reporting this attitude to his superiors, opposed the adoption of any concession to it.[198] There seems indeed to have been in the Mogul Mission little if anything of that wholesale adoption of non-Christian methods and practices which so markedly characterized the Jesuit activities in Southern India and which led there to so great an amount of controversy. The tendency seems rather to have been in the direction of preserving European practices which primâ facie were unsuitable to the country, and we find the Fathers going so far as to persuade their young converts to leap through fires on S. John's day—an occupation little suited to an evening in June in the temperature of Agra.[199]

Miracles and exorcisms

Among the occurrences mentioned by the Fathers in connection with their converts there are several of an unusual and even of a miraculous character. Father Xavier, for instance, writing in 1598, tells us of cases where persons were cured of illness by the mere receipt of baptism or by hearing the Gospel read to them, and Father Pimenta, the Provincial, heard of the case of an unbeliever who was felled by a brick from an unseen hand in the middle of an argument with a catechumen.[200] A few years later we learn of a great lady at Lahore who obtained a son in clear response to her prayer to the Virgin, and of a Muslim who was similarly blessed by Christ who appeared to him in a dream and gave him a portion of some fruit to eat.[201] Later on we have the case of the wife of Mīrzā Zū'lqarnain who was relieved in childbirth by the imposition of a cross with relics ;[202] and that of a boy who was rescued from death by drinking water in which a relic of the Blessed Margarida of Chaves had been placed.[203] In the Report of 1648–1649 we are told of a young Muslim servant of an Englishman in Agra who blasphemed against the Virgin and suffered the loss of his appointment until he confessed his sin ; and of a woman relieved in childbirth by the application of some holy water blessed by prayer to S. Ignatius of Loyola.[204] S. Francis Xavier was the object of special devotion among converts and his medals were much used in cases of sickness.[205] In 1653 Ceschi tells us of a sick girl who was cured by baptism received in obedience to a vision of the Virgin, and of a woman who saw the Infant Jesus at Mass 'all glorious and resplendent in the Sacred Host.'[206]

The treatment of evil spirits—which entered so largely into the feelings of the time in contemporary Europe[207]—formed also an issue of considerable interest to the Fathers. For the expulsion of devils the presence of a Father or the making of the sign of the Cross would sometimes suffice : but another common remedy was the reading of the Gospel, or the placing of the Gospel in the hands of the energumen. A Christian whose house was pelted with stones by diabolic agency laid the evil spirit by walking round the house reading from the Gospel.[208] A devil who appeared by the well in the Jesuits' house at Agra under the form of a small Ethiop encircled by flames and entered into the body of a Christian boy, was forced by the touch of a Father's hand on the chest of the boy to confess his presence with loud groans and to leave his victim in peace.[209] Such was the fame of the Jesuits in this direction that their services were employed on one occasion by one of the great noblemen at the Court, whose brother was attempting to compass his death by sorcery. The Fathers recited the exorcisms of the Roman ritual, applied a medal of S. Ignatius and administered water taken from the holy Chalice, with the result that after three days the distinguished sufferer was cured and the reputation of the Fathers at the Court was greatly enhanced.[210] In later times it was noted that the residences of Christians were free from devils, but the Fathers were frequently called in by non-Christians to exorcize devils from non-Christian houses. Father Figueredo tells us how the Devil used to serve at the house of a sorcerer, but ceased to do so if a Christian came to dine. He tells us, too, how there would be a dance held in the streets of Delhi by 'heathen of both sexes' in which the Devil would join, and how he refused to appear when a Christian woman looked on the dance from afar off.[211]

Manucci, who is full of curious information, asserts that Christians, and especially Christian women, often dealt definitely in magic. The examples he gives are mostly from Southern India, but some of his instances are from the north. He has a strange tale to the effect that a Bengal woman called Anna Vas, who lived in Lahore, had by praying naked in an oratory ascertained that a certain deceased renegade was not in purgatory but in hell; and another which tells how Susanna Borges of Agra was made by a sorcerer to go through certain formalities with a magic doll in order to secure long life to her daughter-in-law. He also tells how Pero Gomes de Oliveira at Agra was taken by a sorcerer to a tree on which a corpse was hanging and how the corpse uttered a piercing shriek when the sorcerer applied a lighted candle to its feet.[212] The existence of such beliefs and practices among certain of the half-castes and converts may be accepted as a fact, and considering the class from which they mostly came and the prevalence of similar beliefs among all classes both in Asia and in Europe at the time, the fact is one at which we need not be surprised.

Religious life of the Mogor Church

Of the general religious life of the Christians we can judge from a sketch given to us by Father Xavier of the conditions prevailing in the infant church at Agra in 1604.

'We endeavour,' he says,[213] 'to confirm our converts in the faith which they have adopted and in a fitting way of life. To this end on Sundays and on ordinary feasts there is always a sermon. . . . At the principal feasts numbers both of men and women come to confession and receive communion, which you will learn to your consolation and ours. At Christmas there was a fine procession, as is customary every year. . . . Our Christians keep Lent well, with the full rigour of fasting and abstinence from all milk food. We gave them leave to eat butter, but many did not avail themselves of it. All through Lent nothing is conceded, even to those under age. We do not extend to them the usual dispensations, because it is well that being new Christians they should, from devotion, imitate in something the austerity of the early Christians. There will be no lack of opportunity hereafter for their availing themselves of the concessions which will be made to them in the course of time. Also we have regard to the Muhammadans who hold our fasting in great contempt, seeing we eat twice a day; and to those Christians who were formerly Muhammadans it would seem as if they did not fast at all, so that "sicut exhibuerunt membra sua servire in iniquitate ad iniquitatem," having observed the Muhammadan fast with such rigour "ita exhibeant illa servire justitiae in sanctificationem." (As they presented their members as servants to iniquity unto iniquity, even so now they may present their members as servants to righteousness unto sanctification. Rom. vi, 19.) Every Friday evening in Lent we have a sermon to the Christians; at the end we show them the Crucifix which is placed covered on the altar, after which the Litany is recited and then as many men as the church will hold (for here in Agra it is very small) take the discipline while the Father recites the "Miserere." When they have finished others take their place and so on until all have taken their turn. They take the discipline across the back, according to our custom; so do nearly all the Christians, old and new. When we have a larger church there will be more room to conduct these exercises with greater ceremony. The offices for Holy Week are simply recited, but the other ceremonies are carried out with all solemnity. The washing of the feet is performed fully with great devotion and consolation. All go to confession during Lent; and on Maundy Thursday more than forty persons of both sexes who a few years ago were followers of Muhammad received the Holy Communion. The mystery of the Supreme Sacrament is preached to them individually and in general, and the privilege of approaching it is highly prized whenever we give them leave. May God keep and advance them in perfection every day. Amen.'

Some twenty years later we find a similar description of the observances of the Indian Christians:

'Here in Agra,' says the Report of 1623,[214] 'they have a very fine and well-made church, and in that church, apart from sermons on Sundays and Saints' days, they have doctrinal sermons every evening in Lent, after which they say together the Rosary of Our Lady. The Friday sermons are on the Passion and after them they take the discipline with great fervour. Every night in the year the Litanies of the Virgin are recited, followed by a short prayer for the health and conversion of the King and his sons. On Sundays Mass is celebrated with much ceremony, at which many boys attend clothed in white surplices with tapers in their hands; the altar and chapel are decorated with many leaves and flowers which are plentiful in this land. After Mass is the Catechism, and after that they sing Litanies of the Virgin and some sacred songs in excellent tune, the Father commencing and the whole body of Christians then joining in.'

A high standard maintained

Twenty-five years later the same congregation still maintained its reputation for devotion, and its practice is described as follows:[215]

'The more violent the storm of Muhammadan aversion grows the more favourably do the followers of Christ pursue the Christian practice, faithfully keeping the feasts, frequenting with profit the Sacraments of Confession and the Eucharist, so much that hardly could one dare to approach the Holy Table without going to those whom he may have offended and receiving their pardon. That most praiseworthy practice is in force among them. You will find many who keep their consciences free of mortal sin for a whole year.'

Father Botelho, speaking of the same period, adds:

'Rare is the Christian who misses Mass on days of obligation. Many hear it even on week-days; and besides going to confession annually, they confess and communicate many times; chiefly on the feasts of Christ, Our Lady and the Apostles and other chief Saints of the year.'

The same Father points out how the Christians of Mogor, being few, were well taught, and gave it as his considered opinion that 'the Christians of the Christianity of Mogol are the best and most solidly grounded in our Faith of the whole of this East.'[216] This grounding was especially successful in Agra where the Christians lived together in the immediate neighbourhood of the church and under the eye of the Fathers.[217]

We have the independent testimony of two Franciscans who visited Sāmbhar in 1624 and reported that the Christian community under Corsi in that place were so well instructed that one could desire nothing better.[218] And in 1735 the Christians at Agra were said to be as punctilious in their observances as Catholics in Europe; coming to prayer, reverencing images, attending funerals, and abstaining from manual labour on Sundays and feast days.[219]

There is every reason, therefore, to believe that the Mogor congregations, though small, had attained a high standard of discipline and devotion.

Behaviour of converts under persecution

The life of the Christian convert was not at any time an easy one, and on occasion the converts were in great danger of imprisonment or death. The Church underwent in Mogor three main crises which may be spoken of as persecutions. There was a troublous time in Lahore in 1604—lasting for about a month—when the Governor, Qulīj Khān, a strong Muslim, laid hands on some of the Christians and had fixed a day for the wholesale seizure of the Christians' wives and children. In 1614 again, dissensions between the Moguls and the Portuguese on the west coast led to the forcible closure of the churches at Agra and Lahore, and the Father in charge at Lahore was so terrified that he brought his whole congregation to Agra for protection. And again, in

1633–1635, after the capture of Hūglī from the Portuguese, the position of the Christians in Agra, both of the prisoners from Hūglī and of the local converts, was most precarious. It will be noted that except in the case of the trouble of 1604, these exacerbations of feeling against the Christians were due primarily to political causes connected with the high-handed action of the Portuguese and not to considerations of religious rivalry. There was, even on these occasions, little of sustained or systematic repression, but at these crises the fear of maltreatment prevailing in ordinary times became greatly accentuated. The Christians were at all times despised and maligned by the more fanatical Muslims. 'In the proud eyes of the Muhametans,' says one report, 'they are looked on as if they were like the dirt and the cess-pool of the world.'[220] There were occasions on which they would be pelted with stones or filth in the bazaars: there were constant efforts made, especially in the case of reconverted renegades, to seduce the converts by money and other means back to Islām; and when there was a conversion from Islām or Hinduism there was generally someone to complain that it had been obtained by force. The converts were far away from the protecting arm of the Portuguese civil power; and whatever may have been the case at the Court in the days of Akbar and Jahāngīr, the whole atmosphere in which the poorer Christians lived was as a rule strongly antipathetic. There were from time to time regrettable lapses, but on the whole the attitude of the Christian community, acting under the inspiration of the Fathers, was most praise-worthy and even, on occasion, heroic. During the Lahore persecution of 1604, the Indian Christians showed great courage, even the catechumens refusing to seek safety in concealment;[221] and in the troubles of 1614 and 1633 the Christian community, though subject to much ill-treatment, displayed great patience and constancy. In the missionary reports we are given many stories of their devotion to the Faith. We are told at great length of the harassment of a young Brahmin pandit of Lahore, called Prahlād, in 1602; how his wife was spirited away by her parents; how the young convert was drugged by his mother, and how four times she tried to poison him; how he struggled against a band of men whom his parents brought to seize him; how, in his enthusiasm, he broke asunder his Brahminical thread and cut off his scalp lock; how he was dragged before the Governor and sent on by him to the 'Cateris' (shāstrīs?); how he was accompanied by a howling mob to the house of the 'Coxi' (who was 'as it were the Provisor of the Gentiles'); how he declined a bribe of two thousand rupees to bathe in the Ganges, was threatened with death, and ultimately, on the failure of all efforts to shake his faith, was released and restored to the Fathers.[222] In the Agra Report of 1648–1649, we read of several instances of fortitude.[223] Among them is that of a young woman of respectable family, harassed firstly by the cruelties of her so-called Christian husband, and then by the importunities of her Muslim parents at Lahore, but remaining constant and coming to the Father Rector for confession when he visited that town. There was also the case of a female convert accused of having converted her Muslim slave to Christianity, who confessed before the Governor her devotion to the Faith, and when the Qāzī tried to persuade the Governor to have her thrown from a high tower close by 'was overjoyed, as if invited to her reward.' In some cases the profession of Christianity involved the punishment of death, even in the case of Europeans. In 1667 when the Prince Shāh 'Ālam was campaigning in the Deccan he came across a strange being called Frey Jacinto, a fugitive friar, who having become a Muslim reverted to Christianity and refused in spite of all persuasion and force to recant his faith ; finding him obdurate, the Prince ordered his execution. 'If he caused some scandal,' says Manucci, 'by his evil life and apostasy, he gave equal edification by confirming the truth, weeping over his sins and dying for the love of Christ.'[224] As the years went on the special animus against Christians seems to have abated, and while the poorer Christians suffered with the rest of the population the ordinary tyrannies of the time, they seem to have been tolerated as Christians. For the first century, however, after the arrival of the Jesuits they were, notwithstanding the easy attitude of the Court, in constant apprehension of harassment or mishandling on account of their faith.

Converts and Holy Orders

Of the converts some appear to have been specially trained for a religious life. There was never any difficulty about Indians being ordained as secular priests and they were freely admitted to the Church in that capacity. It has been stated by Protestant writers, however, that Indian converts could not become members of an Order, the Jesuits admitting pure-bred Europeans only and the other Orders none but Europeans and half-castes :[225] and although the history of Missions in Southern India shows that this was not an absolute rule, it is evident that in practice Indians seldom became members of the Society of Jesus and we have no record of any convert from Northern India having joined the Society. Father Garcia, from Bengal, of whom mention has been made in the account of the troubles of 1633, was a secular, and Dom Mattheus, the Brahmin Bishop of Chrysopolis who gave the Jesuits so much trouble in 1652, although brought up by the

Jesuits, was himself an Oratorian and was ordained at Rome. It was one of Dom Mattheus's complaints that the Jesuits did not admit Brahmins to their schools because they were too clever, but we have no information to support or refute the correctness of this statement. We know that a fair number of Indians from Mogor received special training. It was one of Father Aquaviva's dreams that a school should be started at Goa to teach the converts each in his own tongue ; and though we hear nothing more of this particular scheme we know that a considerable number of Indians, including some from Mogor, were trained by the Jesuits at Goa. As early as 1600 two young Indians, of whom one at least came from Lahore, were entered at Goa in the College of Santa Fé to be trained for the priesthood :[226] and (as noted earlier in this chapter) a Shaikh, who had been converted after being a most earnest Muslim, was sent after baptism from Lahore to Father Xavier at Agra 'that he might be of service to him in the conversion of others,'[227] probably in some clerical capacity. Even as late as 1698 we have a glimpse of four Punjab converts being educated by the Jesuits at Bāndra in Bombay.[228] But we have no indication as to the extent, if any, to which the Mogor converts were trained for, or admitted to, Holy Orders.

The costume of the Jesuits in Mogor

We have a few details on record as to the costume worn by the Jesuit Fathers in Mogor. Father Monserrate tells us of the astonishment which their appearance created on their first arrival in Fatehpur in 1580 : 'When they entered,' he writes, 'their outlandish appearance created a stir. All eyes were turned on them. People stopped, agape in wonderment, rooted to the ground and forgetting to get out of the way betimes, for who were those men coming along, unarmed, dressed in long black robes, with their faces shaven, and their close-cropped heads stuck in hats ?'—atrati, inermes, togati, petasati, tonsi rasique.[229] In the contemporary picture of Father Rudolf Aquaviva and a companion at the Court of Akbar, which forms the frontispiece to this book, the two priests are shown as wearing black soutanes and above them black or very dark blue capes, such as are still worn on ceremonial occasions ; the priests are, however, represented as having each on his head a kind of black lambskin fez. In the Boston picture of Jahāngīr's Court, which is also mentioned in the last chapter, the Jesuit padre, who may probably be identified as Corsi, is shown as clean shaven and bareheaded, wearing a robe of very dark blue—(so dark as almost to be black)—with a white collar of some soft material. The most marked feature of the Jesuits' apparel was the black dress, and in Father Aquaviva's time the Jesuit Fathers were spoken of by their enemies as 'black devils.'[230] The Jesuits in the Mogul dominions went by the name of 'siāh-posh' or 'black-clothed,'[231] and the Englishman Fryer, writing in 1698, tells us that the Jesuits at Goa in his time wore black gowns with a collar and rings, and high round caps flat at the top, and shoes but no stockings.[232] On the other hand, Father Figueredo, in a letter of 1735, gives us the somewhat curious information that the priests in Mogor wore the usual Muslim dress, but instead of red wore white.[233] It is also of interest to observe that in Jahāngīr's time Father de Castro when marching with the King displayed a flag with a cross upon it both above his tent and on the camels which carried the ornaments for the Holy Mass and the clothes of the Fathers.[234]

The costume of the converts in Mogor

The Jesuits made no attempt to vary in any substantial degree the costume of their converts. The Christians wore the ordinary clothes of the country, adopting the style rather of the Muslim than of the Hindu. The women appear to have worn loose trousers after the Muslim fashion.[235] The men wore a 'cabaya' or qabā (a long tunic, narrow at the top and wide below the waist) 'reaching down to the knees, trousers reaching down to the heels, and a turban.'[236] That there was, however, some distinction between the Christian costume and that of the Muslims, is plain from the fact that Akbar allowed a converted renegade to reside in Mogor in Christian dress—vestu à la mode des Chrestiens,[237]—and that Jahāngīr recognized the religion of the servant of a European from his being in Christian costume—en trajo de christão.[238] Jahāngīr is reported to have rebuked an Armenian for omitting to wear a cross on his head or on his breast.[239] Converts seem to have been expected to wear about them a cross in some form or other, and many carried the sign of the cross on their foreheads 'as a royal diadem.'[240] It was common also for them to wear beads round their necks.[241] They ate in Indian fashion, and although they were allowed to drink wine, they were supposed to abstain from pork.[242] They sat in the ordinary Indian way, and in their churches also sat upon the ground.[243]

At the church services the feelings of the country were so far respected that the men and women, while both enjoying a full view of the altar, were divided from each other by a curtain.[244] In some congregations the sermon and the celebration of the Sacrament took place at different hours for men and women[245]; and out of deference to Indian custom women did not attend the funerals of Christians.[246]

During the period of more than two hundred years in which the Jesuit missionaries worked in Mogor, the Jesuit Society in Europe, in Goa, and in Southern India was subjected to much criticism. It was accused of paltering with heathen customs, forging records, mismanaging institutions, persecuting the religious of other Orders, active trading, corruption, luxurious living and other evils. But in Mogor we have little or no echo of these criticisms. The Jesuits in Mogor were no doubt openly anxious to exert such political influence as they had in favour of the great Catholic European power in India, the Portuguese; but they seem to have been free from the serious faults imputed to the Jesuits elsewhere. We have occasional references to the execution of disciplinary measures within the Society itself. In one case, for instance, a Superior in Agra was superseded because of his unwise and intemperate interposition in a judicial case,[247] and in another certain missionaries are mentioned who left Tibet without permission.[248] But such cases constituted no flagrant scandal and were dealt with as matters of internal discipline by the Fathers themselves. There were no doubt some weaker members, but speaking generally the Fathers of the Mission were men of piety and zeal, and their relations with their converts and with the outer world were free from any suspicion of the offences ascribed to the members of the Society in other parts of India.

Freedom of the Mogor Mission from scandal

NOTES

[1] Du Jarric, II, p. 463.

[2] A number of them are specified by name in Hosten's article on 'European Art at the Mogul Court' in *J.U.P.H.S.*, III, Part I, 1922.

[3] Monserrate, Commentarius, *Mem. A.S.B.*, III, 1914, fol. 60(a).

[4] Annual Letter from Goa, 1924; *The Examiner*, Bombay (Hosten), April 6, 1912.

[5] Manucci, *Storia do Mogor,* I, p. 226.

[6] *Ib.*, I, p. 265.

[7] *Ib.*, II, p. 176.

[8] *Ib.*, I, p. 140.

[9] Thévenot, *Voyages contenant la relation de l'Indostan*, Paris, 1684, p. 96.

[10] Letter of August 15, 1627; *J.A.S.B.*, XXIII, 1927, p. 165.

[11] As e.g., at Cambay when Father Corsi passed through in 1600. Pimenta's Report of December 1, 1600; Payne, *Akbar and the Jesuits,* 1926, p. 99; *J.A.S.B.*, XXIII, 1927, p. 72.

[12] Jerome Xavier's letter of September 6, 1604; *J.A.S.B.*, LXV, 1896, p. 93.

[13] *Collecção de Monumentos Ineditos*, published by the Academy of Sciences at Lisbon, 1884, VIII, p. 56; Letter of the King of Spain, dated February 22, 1611.

[14] Manucci, *Storia do Mogor*, II, p. 7.

[15] The story is told at length in Corsi's and Leam's letters of June 13 and October 6, 1628. The leading Italian was Angelo Gradenigo, and his companions were Bernardino Maffei, a physician, and Jeronimo Veroneo, the jeweller.

[16] Letter of October 26, 1747 ; *Weltbott*, No. 648.

[17] Letter of Andrade dated August 14, 1623 ; Marsden MSS., Brit. Mus., Addl. 9854, fol. 92. A mulatto was a man of mixed Portuguese and negro blood. Mansūr Khān is spoken of in Jahāngīr's *Memoirs* as Mansūr Khān Farangī, and Jahāngīr tells how he was killed in a solitary charge made by him on the enemy when he was drunk. *Tūzuk* (Rogers and Beveridge), II, pp. 258 and 271.

[18] Manucci, *Storia do Mogor*, IV, p. 200, and Irvine's note thereon ; Annual Report of December 27, 1678.

[19] Annual Report of December 27, 1678, and 'Appontamentos' taken from a letter of Leitão dated December 12, 1677, in the Marsden MSS.

[20] Annual Report of September 7, 1686.

[21] Guerreiro, *Relaçam*, V, p. 18.

[22] Guerreiro, *Relaçam*, IV, p. 156.

[23] *J.A.S.B.*, LXV, 1896, p. 88 ; Guerreiro, II, Part I, p. 58. Payne, *Akbar and the Jesuits*, 1926, p. 178.

[24] Annual Letter of 1648–1649 ; *J.I.H.*, I, 1922, pp. 233–234.

[25] See Monserrate, Commentarius, fol. 77 b.

[26] Pinheiro, Letter of September 3, 1595 ; *J.A.S.B.*, LXV, 1896, p. 68.

[27] Seth, *History of the Armenians in India*, 1895, p. 24. The authority of this statement is weak, see *J.U.P.H.S.*, II, Part I, 1919, p. 46.

[28] Guerreiro, *Relaçam*, IV, p. 155. It was sometimes asserted that this was the general practice, but Andrade denies this strongly. Letter of August 14, 1623.

[29] Legrenzi, *Il Pellegrino nell' Asia*, 1705, II, p. 239.

[30] Letter of João de Velasco of December 25, 1612 ; *Mem. A.S.B.*, V, 1916 (Hosten), p. 183 ; *Journal Asiatique*, 11e. série, XIX, 1922 (Seth), pp. 276–282.

[31] His history has been given in Chapter XI.

[32] Xavier's letter of September 6, 1604 ; *J.A.S.B.*, LXV, 1896, p. 91.

[33] Xavier's letter of September 6, 1604 ; *J.A.S.B.*, LXV, 1896, p. 96.

[34] Guerreiro's *Relaçam*, V, p. 17 ; du Jarric, III, p. 135 ; Jer. Xavier in Zannetti, *Raguagli*, 1615, p. 27.

[35] Xavier's letter of September 6, 1604 ; *J.A.S.B.*, LXV, 1896, p. 93.

[36] Letter of August 12, 1605 ; *J.A.S.B.*, LXV, 1896, p. 102.

[37] Letter of Xavier, dated September 25, 1606, quoted by Payne, *Jahangir and the Jesuits*, 1930, p. 91.

[38] Guerreiro, *Relaçam*, II, Part II, p. 59 ; Payne, *Akbar and the Jesuits*, 1926, p. 175.

[39] Letter of Aquaviva, September 27, 1582 ; *J.A.S.B.*, LXV, 1896, p. 56.

[40] Letter of September 6, 1604 ; *J.A.S.B.*, LXV, 1896, p. 98.

[41] *Mem. A.S.B.*, V, 1916 (Hosten), p. 155.

[42] See Figueredo, Letter of 1735 in *Weltbott*, No. 595, and Strobl (1751), in *Weltbott*, No. 650.

[43] *Agra Catholic Diocesan Calendar*, 1907 (Felix), pp. 207–210.

[44] *Literae Annuae* for 1597 (Naples, 1607), p. 571.

[45] Guerreiro, *Relaçam*, II, Part II, p. 56 ; Payne, *Akbar and the Jesuits*, 1926, p. 177 ; Akbarnāma, *Bib. Ind.*, transl. Beveridge, III, p. 1112.

[46] Constable's edn., p. 289 ; Amsterdam edn., 1724, II, p. 84.

[47] Letter of Sept. 3, 1595, from Pinheiro ; *J.A.S.B.*, LXV, 1896, p. 70.

[48] Guerreiro, *Relaçam*, I, p. 21 ; *J.A.S.B.*, LXV, 1896, p. 85 ; Payne, *Akbar and the Jesuits*, 1926, pp. 131–132.

[49] Xavier's letter of September 24, 1611.

[50] Guerreiro, *Relaçam*, IV, p. 140 ; du Jarric, III, p. 87 ; Payne, *Akbar and the Jesuits*, 1926, p. 194. A case is related of a man who declined to give any indication of his Christianity beyond binding a friend by oath to bury him according to Christian rites. Guerreiro, IV, p. 155 ; du Jarric, III, p. 113. These instances of secrecy seem in Mogor to have occurred chiefly among Muslim officials.

[51] Morelli, *I codici manoscritti volgari della Libreria Naniana*, Venice, 1776, p. 187.

[52] Letter of August 28, 1607.

[53] *Mem. A.S.B.*, V, 1916 (Hosten), p. 153. The anti-Jesuit Bishop Dom Matheus accused the Jesuits of neglecting the poor—' omnia magna tonant, sapiunt : nec illis ulla est pauperum curatio.' (Beccari, *Rer. Aeth. Script*, p. IX, p. 423) ; but whatever may have been the case elsewhere, the charge has nothing to support it in Mogor.

[54] Foster, *Early Travels in India*, 1921, p. 315.

[55] *Ib.*, p. 271.

[56] Guerreiro, *Relaçam*, IV, p. 141 ; du Jarric, III, p. 89 ; Payne, *Akbar and the Jesuits*, 1926, p. 196.

[57] Guerreiro, *Relaçam*, IV, pp. 161–162 ; du Jarric, III, p. 118 ; J. Xavier in Zannetti, *Raguagli*, 1615, pp. 24–25, and his letter of August 28, 1607.

[58] Du Jarric, II, p. 476.

[59] Du Jarric, III, p. 119.

[60] Letter of 1611 in the Marsden MSS. of the British Museum. The extract quoted from a translation kindly furnished by Mr. C. H. Payne.

[61] Foster, *Early Travels in India*, 1921, p. 223 ; Foster's *Roe*, p. 275 ; Terry in *Purchas* (MacLehose, 1905), IX, p. 52.

[62] *Lettere Annue dal Giappone*, etc., Naples, 1621, p. 121 ; *The Examiner*, Bombay (Hosten), February 10, 1912.

[63] Xavier's letter of September 23, 1613.

[64] Manucci, *Storia do Mogor*, II, p. 452 ; Botelho's *Relation* in *Mem, A.S.B.*, V, 1916 (Hosten), p. 154. When a European ' turned Moor ' it was the regular practice to give him a handsome allowance : cf. Foster, *Early Travels in India*, 1921, p. 204. An Indian Christian. Sikandar, who was one of Aurangzeb's doctors, refused large sums which were offered to him on condition of his abandoning Christianity : Annual Report of 1668. In Shāh Jahān's time any Christian who embraced Islām was sure to get an allowance, see Botelho's *Relation*.

[65] Andrade, Letter of August 14, 1623.

[66] See e.g., the Annual Report of 1675.

[67] Annual Report of September 7, 1686.

[68] See Xavier's letter of 1611.

[69] Marsden MSS., British Museum, Addl. 9854, fol. 150.

[70] Annual Report of September 7, 1686. The report for 1693 says that most of the expenditure on alms was met by the income of the College.

[71] Annual Report of 1675.

[72] Letter of Father Angelino, 1785 (Propaganda Archives, Indie Orientali e Cina, Relazioni, *Scritture riferite nei Congressi*, CC, RR, Vol. No. 40).

[73] Annual Report of September 7, 1686.

[74] *Purchas* (MacLehose, 1905), IX, p. 52 ; Foster, *Early Travels in India*, 1921, p. 331.

[75] Xavier's letter of 1611 in Marsden MSS., Addl. 9854, fol. 170, and his letter of April 11, 1611, in Zannetti's *Raguagli*, 1615, p. 38 ; see also his letter of August 28, 1607.

[76] Annual Report of 1650.

[77] Guerreiro, *Relaçam*, I, p. 21 ; du Jarric, III, p. 50 ; Payne, *Akbar and the Jesuits*, 1926, p. 133 ; cf. *Lit. Ann.* 1597 (Naples, 1607), p. 568.

[78] Godinho, Letter of August 16, 1626 ; *J.A.S.B.*, XXI, 1925 (Hosten), p. 69.

[79] Pinheiro, Letter of 1599 ; *J.A.S.B.*, LXV, 1896, p. 79.

[80] Guerreiro, *Relaçam*, I, p. 20 ; Payne, *Akbar and the Jesuits*, 1926, pp. 130–131. Many such persons were baptized during the plague at Lahore in 1597. *Lit. Ann.*, 1597 (Naples, 1607), p. 567.

[81] Xavier's letter of July 26, 1598 ; *J.A.S.B.*, LXV, 1896, p. 72.

[82] Payne, *Akbar and the Jesuits*, 1926, p. 78.

[83] Payne, *Akbar and the Jesuits*, 1926, p. 87.

[84] Ps. cxii, 7–8. Guerreiro, *Relaçam*, I, p. 9 ; Payne, *Akbar and the Jesuits*, 1926, p. 109.

[85] Pimenta's Report of December 1599 ; *J.A.S.B.*, LXV, 1896, p. 81, and XXIII, 1927, p. 65.

[86] Guerreiro, *Relaçam*, II, p. 57 ; Payne, *Akbar and the Jesuits*, 1926, p. 177.

[87] Maracci, *Relation*, p. 18.

[88] *J.I.H.*, I, 1922 (Hosten), p. 233.

[89] Guerreiro, IV, p. 161 ; du Jarric, III, p. 117.

[90] *Storia do Mogor*, III, p. 198. For similar stories see *Calcutta Review*, 1844, II, pp. 95–96 ; Guerreiro, IV, p. 161 ; du Jarric, III, p. 117.

[91] Letter of 1599, *J.A.S.B.*, LXV, 1896, p. 79.

[92] Guerreiro, *Relaçam*, I, p. 20 ; Payne, *Akbar and the Jesuits*, 1926, p. 130.

[93] *Ib.*, p. 9. *Ib.*, p. 109.

[94] Letter of August 12, 1605 ; *J.A.S.B.*, LXV, 1896, p. 105.

[95] Guerreiro, *Relaçam*, IV, p. 155 ; Xavier's letter of September 25, 1606.

[96] Du Jarric, *Thesaurus*, III, p. 170.

[97] Corsi, Letter of October 28, 1619.

[98] Maracci, *Relation*, p. 21.

[99] *Histoire de ce qui s'est passé*, Paris, 1628, p. 109.

[100] Andrade, Letter of August 14, 1623. This report mentions the case of a woman who was married to a respectable Christian, but who for a long time refused to be baptized because she had been told by the Hindus that at a baptism all present spat into the mouth of the convert.

[101] Letters of July 26 and August 15, 1627 ; *J.A.S.B.*, XXIII, 1927 (Hosten), pp. 157 and 164, and XXI, 1925, p. 73.

[102] Corsi, Letter of October 28, 1619.

[103] *J.I.H.*, I, 1922 (Hosten), p. 233.

[104] *Ib.*, p. 244.

[105] Letter of September 15, 1649; *The Examiner*, Bombay (Hosten), September 1, 1917.

[106] Letter of September 1, 1653; *The Examiner*, Bombay (Hosten), September 8, 1917.

[107] *Lit. Ann.*, 1653, p. 219, quoted by Müllbauer, *Geschichte der Katholischen Missionen in Ostindien*, 1852, p. 285.

[108] Letter of August 24, 1654; *The Examiner*, Bombay (Hosten), September 8, 1917.

[109] *Mem. A.S.B.*, V, 1916, p. 152.

[110] Ceschi, Letter of August 24, 1654; *The Examiner*, Bombay (Hosten), September 8, 1917.

[111] Manucci, *Storia do Mogor*, II, p. 238. The author of the Report of 1675 propounds a similar view and holds that Islām which grew by the sword can only be exterminated by the sword.

[112] Reports of 1675, 1678 and 1686.

[113] Annual Report for 1688–1693.

[114] *Weltbott*, No. 595.

[115] *Weltbott*, No. 648.

[116] *J.A.S.B.*, XXIII, 1927 (Hosten), p. 137.

[117] *A Voyage to East India* (edn. of 1777), p. 427.

[118] Letter of September 1, 1597; *J.A.S.B.*, XXIII, 1927 (Hosten), p. 119.

[119] Letter of September 14, 1609; *J.A.S.B.*, XXIII, 1927 (Hosten), p. 120.

[120] Annual Report of 1668.

[121] Guerreiro, *Relaçam*, IV, p. 155 (Payne's translation); Xavier's letter of September 25, 1606.

[122] Constable's edn., 1914, pp. 290–292; Amsterdam edn., 1724, II, pp. 85–86; cf. Pyrard de Laval, Hakluyt edn., 1888, II, Part I, p. 252.

[123] *Purchas* (MacLehose, 1905), IX, p. 52.

[124] Hakluyt edn., 1887, II, Part I, p. 252.

[125] Constable's edn., 1914, p. 290; Amsterdam edn., 1724, II, p. 85.

[126] Figueredo in *Weltbott*, No. 595.

[127] *Mem. A.S.B.*, V, 1916 (Hosten), p. 157. Manucci tells us that in forty-eight years he had never seen a Muslim become a Christian. *Storia*, II, p. 452.

[128] Maracci, *Relation*, 1651, p. 21.

[129] *Weltbott*, No. 35.

[130] Du Jarric, III, p. 41.

[131] *Mem. A.S.B.*, V, 1916 (Hosten), p. 152.

[132] Xavier's letter of September 6, 1604; *J.A.S.B.*, LXV, 1896, p. 90.

[133] *Drei Newe Relationes*, 1611, p. 166.

[134] Cordara, *Hist. Soc. Jesu*, Part VI, I, p. 60.

[135] Andrade, Letter of August 14, 1623.

[136] Wessels, *Early Jesuit Travellers in Central Asia*, 1924, p. 283.

[137] Annual Letter of 1648; *J.I.H.*, I, 1922 (Hosten), p. 234.

[138] Botelho in *Mem. A.S.B.*, V, 1916 (Hosten), p. 152.

[139] Letter of 1664 in *Weltbott*, No. 35.

[140] Bernier, Constable's edn., 1914, p. 286; Amsterdam edn., 1714, II, p. 80.

[141] Thévenot, *Voyages, contenant la relation de l'Indostan*, Paris, 1684, p. 102; Crooke's *Tavernier*, 1925, II, p. 137 (note); Col. Sleeman

Rambles and Recollections (Vincent Smith, 1915), p. 335. Another huge number (172,000) is given in Rhay's notes on Roth, 1664, but this figure is apparently for the Mogul dominions generally.

[142] Annual Report of September 7, 1686, and Report for 1688–1693.

[143] *Il Pellegrino nell' Asia*, 1705, II, p. 239.

[144] Letter of Father Angelino, 1785 (Propaganda Archives, Indie Orientali e Cina, Relazioni, *Scritture riferite nei Congressi*, Vol. No. 40).

[145] Letter of August 26, 1607.

[146] De Castro, Letter of April 10, 1615, to the General of the Society; *The Examiner*, Bombay (Hosten), August 16, 1919.

[147] Report of 1648–1649 ; *J.I.H.*, I, 1922 (Hosten), p. 243.

[148] Letter of August 21, 1714 ; *The Examiner*, Bombay (Hosten), October 5, 1918.

[149] Figueredo in 595 *Weltbott*.

[150] Maracci, *Relation*, 1651, p. 23. In 1619 the number of Christians was 200 : Corsi, Letter of October 28, 1619.

[151] Annual Letter 1650.

[152] Letter of August 24, 1654 ; *The Examiner*, Bombay (Hosten), September 8, 1917.

[153] Annual Letter of September 7, 1686.

[154] Letter of August 21, 1714 ; *The Examiner*, Bombay (Hosten), October 5, 1918.

[155] Saignes, Letter of February 9, 1740 ; *Lettres Édif. et Cur.*, 1780, IV, pp. 260–261.

[156] *Weltbott*, No. 649.

[157] *Weltbott*, No. 595.

[158] *Weltbott*, No. 643.

[159] Letter of October 30, 1616, to the Archb. of Canterbury. (Foster's *Roe*, pp. 271–275.)

[160] Letter of August 24, 1626 ; *J.A.S.B.*, XXIII, 1927 (Hosten), p. 146.

[161] Letter of August 14, 1623.

[162] Xavier's letter of September 6, 1604 ; *J.A.S.B.*, LXV, 1896, p. 89.

[163] Xavier's letter of August 28, 1607.

[164] Botelho's *Relation* (1648–1654), *Mem. A.S.B.*, V, 1916 (Hosten), p. 153.

[165] *Bib. Ind.*, transl., II, p. 299, and Rehatsek, *The Emperor Akbar's Renunciation of Esllām*, Bombay, 1866, p. 45 ; Akbarnāma, transl. Beveridge, *Bib. Ind.*, III, p. 322. The organ was supposed to have been invented by Plato, and a picture of a European organ can be seen in an illustration by Mādho Khānazād in the copy of Nizāmīs Khamsa in the possession of Mr. Dyson Perrin ; F. R. Martin, *The Miniature Painting and Painters of Persia, India and Turkey*, 1912, II, Plate 181.

[166] Xavier, letter of September 25, 1606. In 1612 the English at Surat contemplated sending ' a small pair of organs ' to the Mogul. *Lett. Rec.*, I, p. 239.

[167] Jouvency, *Hist. Soc. Jesu*, Part V, II, p. 468. ' Con musica organa.' Xavier in Zannetti, *Raguagli*, 1615, p. 33.

[168] Xavier, Letter of 1611. Marsden MSS., Addl. 9854, fol. 165.

[169] See e.g., Kühnel and Goetz, *Indian Book Painting*, 1926, Plate 28, and Martin, loc. cit. (note 165 above).

[170] Guerreiro, *Relaçam*, IV, p. 158, and V, p. 7.

[171] Pimenta's Report of December 1, 1600 ; *J.A.S.B.*, XXIII, 1927 (Hosten), p. 68.

[172] Guerreiro, *Relaçam*, IV, p. 158.

[173] Xavier's letter of April 11, 1611, in Zannetti's *Raguagli*, 1615, p. 35.

[174] De Castro, Letter of July 26, 1627; *J.A.S.B.*, XXIII, 1927 (Hosten), p. 153.

[175] Guerreiro, *Relaçam*, IV, p. 159.

[176] Andrade, Letter of August 14, 1623.

[177] Annual Letter of 1675.

[178] *Purchas* (MacLehose), IV, p. 488; Foster, *Early Travels in India*, 1921, p. 276.

[179] See p. 36 in Chapter II.

[180] Letter from Xavier, July 26, 1598; *J.A.S.B.*, LXV, 1896, pp. 72–73.

[181] Provincial Report of December, 1599; *J.A.S.B.*, LXV, 1896, p. 81, and XXIII, 1927, p. 64.

[182] Guerreiro, *Relaçam*, I, p. 17; du Jarric, III, p. 46; Payne, *Akbar and the Jesuits*, 1926, pp. 127–129.

[183] Botelho, *Relation; Mem. A.S.B.*, V, 1916 (Hosten), p. 158.

[184] Xavier's letter of 1611 in Marsden MSS., Addl. 9854, fol. 165.

[185] Zannetti, *Raguagli*, 1615, pp. 36–37; letter of April 11, 1611.

[186] De Castro, Letter of July 26, 1627; *J.A.S.B.*, XXIII, 1927, p. 152.

[187] Xavier, Letter of September 6, 1604; *J.A.S.B.*, LXV, 1896, p. 89.

[188] Botelho, *Relation; Mem. A.S.B.*, V, 1916 (Hosten), p. 153.

[189] *J.A.S.B.*, LXV, 1896, p. 79; du Jarric, II, p. 490.

[190] Xavier's letter of August 26, 1607; Guerreiro, *Relaçam*, IV, p. 158; du Jarric, III, p. 114. At the Corpus Christi processions in Agra a boy would halt before each altar on the route to describe a miracle of the Host, and the members of the procession would sing sacred songs and even dance—'cantando suas cantigas novas e dançando algũas mudanças.' Xavier's letter of 1611; Marsden MSS., Addl. 9854, fol. 165.

[191] Guerreiro, *Relaçam*, V, p. 7; du Jarric, III, p. 119.

[192] Guerreiro, *Relaçam*, V, p. 18.

[193] Andrade, Letter of August 14, 1623, ; and Xavier's letter of 1611 above cited.

[194] Guerreiro, *Relaçam*, IV, p. 161; du Jarric, III, p. 117.

[195] Bothelho, *Relation; Mem. A.S.B.*, V, 1916 (Hosten), pp. 154–155. Pyrard de Laval, the French traveller, says that a similar practice was prevalent among the Portuguese in Goa. There, however, the priest took the viands and in return prayed to God for the souls of the deceased.

[196] Annual Report, 1648–1649; *J.I.H.*, I, 1922 (Hosten), p. 234.

[197] *Storia do Mogor*, II, p. 16. He goes so far as to say: 'The Christian women in India are more inclined to heathendom and superstition than to the true Faith or the recognized aids of Holy Mother Church.' There is a curious picture in the *Album of Jahāngīr* at Berlin which represents an Indian ascetic being requested by a Portuguese woman to bless her son. Kühnel and Goetz, *Indian Book Painting*, 1926, Plate 40, p. 32.

[198] Letter of January 3, 1683; *Catholic Herald of India*, 1917 (Hosten), between pp. 752 and 844.

[199] Letter from Xavier dated September 6, 1604; *J.A.S.B.*, LXV, 1896, p. 94.

[200] Pimenta, Letter of December 1, 1600.

[201] Guerreiro, *Relaçam*, IV, 140; du Jarric, III, p. 86; Payne, *Akbar and the Jesuits*, 1926, p. 193.

[202] Annual Relation, 1619; *The Examiner*, Bombay (Hosten), February 17, 1912.

[203] Guerreiro, *Relaçam*, IV, p. 161; du Jarric, III, p. 117; Payne, *Jahangir and the Jesuits*, 1930, p. 41. Similar cases are instanced in Andrade's letter of August 14, 1623.

[204] Report of 1648–1649; *J.I.H.*, I, 1922 (Hosten), pp. 242, 246.

[205] Annual Report of 1668.

[206] Letter of September 1, 1653; *The Examiner*, Bombay (Hosten), September 8, 1917.

[207] Those who have had the curiosity to read the wonderful adventures of Mr. J. Campbell and his Protestant friends will recollect the 'greate Devell' that appeared to them when they were digging for treasure in Old Delhi in 1668, and the use of the Bible as a means for exorcizing him. *Ind. Ant.*, XXXV, 1906 (Temple), pp. 137–142.

[208] Report of 1648–1649; *J.I.H.*, I, 1922, pp. 239–240.

[209] Annual Report of December 27, 1678.

[210] Report for 1688–1693.

[211] *Weltbott*, No. 595.

[212] *Storia do Mogor*, III, pp. 209–220.

[213] Letter of September 6, 1604; *J.A.S.B.*, LXV, 1896, p. 89. A somewhat similar description for 1611 is given in Xavier's letter in Brit. Mus., Marsden MSS., Addl. 9854, fols. 165–167.

[214] Andrade, Letter of August 14, 1623.

[215] Annual Letter for 1648–1649; *J.I.H.*, I, 1922 (Hosten), p. 234.

[216] Relation for 1648–1654; *Mem. A.S.B.*, V, 1916 (Hosten), p. 153.

[217] Annual Report of September 7, 1686; also Report for 1688–1693.

[218] *Lettere Annue d'Etiopia*, etc., 1627, p. 337.

[219] Figueredo, in *Weltbott*, No. 595.

[220] Annual Letter, Mogor, 1648–1649; *J.I.H.*, I, 1922 (Hosten), p. 247.

[221] Pinheiro, Letter of August 12, 1605; *J.A.S.B.*, LXV, 1896, p. 103; Payne, *Akbar and the Jesuits*, 1926, p. 199.

[222] Guerreiro, *Relaçam*, I, pp. 24–33; Payne, *Akbar and the Jesuits*, 1926, Chapter XIV.

[223] *J.I.H.*, I, 1922 (Hosten), pp. 236–237.

[224] *Storia do Mogor*, II, pp. 159–161.

[225] See the French traveller, Pyrard de Laval, describing the novitiate at S. Roch in Goa in 1608. Hakl. Soc., edn. II, Part I, pp. 61 and 96; cf. La Croze, *Hist. du Christianisme des Indes*, 1724, p. 524; 1748, II, p. 366.

[226] Provincial's Report of December 1, 1600; *J.A.S.B.*, LXV, 1896, p. 82, and XXIII, 1927, p. 68.

[227] Du Jarric, III, p. 3; Pimenta, *Exemplum Epistolae*, p. 4, says 'Societati nostrae nomen dedit.'

[228] J. Gerson da Cunha, *The Origin of Bombay*, *J. Bo, Bch. R.A.S.*, extra number, 1900, p. 213. In the middle of the seventeenth century Father Balthasar de Loyola, a converted son of the King of Fez in N. Africa, was among the Jesuit missionaries to be deputed to Mogor. (Hazart, I, p. 278; Blunt, p. 37.)

[229] *Commentarius*, fol. 19(*b*), Hosten's translation.

[230] Bartoli, *Missione* (Piacenza edn.), p. 60.

[231] Hosten, note in *Manrique* (Hakl. Soc.), I, p. 30.

[232] *A New Account of East-India and Persia*. London, 1698, p. 150; Hakl., 1912, II, p. 12. Tavernier says that the Jesuits at Goa did

'not wear hats or three-cornered caps as in Europe, but a kind of cap which resembles, in form, a hat from which the brim has been removed,' Crooke's. *Tavernier*, 1925, I, p. 159.

When watching the ceremonial departure of Shāh Jahān from Agra, the Fathers so far conformed to the festive character of the occasion as to adopt Persian headgear and to throw coloured silks over their shoulders. Botelho's *Relation*.

[233] *Weltbott*, No. 595.

[234] Letter of August 15, 1627; *J.A.S.B.*, XXIII, 1927 (Hosten), p. 163.

[235] Manucci, *Storia do Mogor*, II, p. 13.

[236] Botelho, *Relation; Mem. A.S.B.*, V, 1916 (Hosten), p. 153.

[237] Du Jarric, II, p. 447.

[238] Guerreiro, *Relaçam*, II, Part II, p. 60.

[239] Andrade, Letter of August 14, 1623.

[240] Report of 1648–1649; *J.I.H.*, I, 1922 (Hosten), p. 237; Guerreiro, *Relaçam*, I, p. 33. Hosten notes that it was an Armenian custom to have the cross branded or tattooed on the forehead.

[241] Botelho, *Relation; Mem. A.S.B.*, V, 1916, pp. 153–154. In Goa the Indians wore beads round the neck while Portuguese and half-castes carried them in the hand. Pyrard de Laval, Hakl. edn., II, p. 99.

[242] Mīrzā Zū'lqarnain and his brother, as boys, insisted that they were Christians, but in spite of much cruel treatment refused to substantiate their statement by eating pork. Xavier's letter of September 25, 1606. The Fathers themselves (in later days at least) abstained from pork out of consideration for Muslim feeling. Figueredo, *Weltbott*, No. 595.

[243] Figueredo, *Weltbott*, No. 595 (1735).

[244] Xavier's letter of August 26, 1607.

[245] Corsi's letter of October 28, 1619.

[246] Report of 1675.

[247] Letter of Corsi, June 13, 1628; *J.A.S.B.*, XXI, 1925, p. 57. Allusion has already been made to the action of the Superior (Leam) in this case, and it may be noted that his conduct created disgust among his subordinates.

[248] Letter of Antonio Mendez, 1636; *J.A.S.B.*, XXI, 1925, p. 58.

CHAPTER XVII

CHURCHES AND RESIDENCES

Zelus domus tuae comedit me.
(Ps. lxviii, 10.)

WE learn from Badāonī that in 1594 Akbar issued a decree that if any of the infidels wished to build a church or synagogue or idol temple or fire temple, none were to prevent them.[1] In Akbar's time, therefore, there was little or no difficulty about the construction and maintenance of churches and houses by the Jesuits. And with rare intermissions the same liberty was enjoyed under subsequent Mogul rulers.

Liberty to build

Fatehpur Sīkrī

It cannot be said with certainty where the Fathers resided and where they had their chapel during their stay at Fatehpur Sīkrī between 1580 and 1583, but the subject has been investigated with much care by Father H. Heras of S. Xavier's College, Bombay, and his views which are noted below are of considerable interest.[2]

We are told by Father Monserrate that when the Fathers first arrived, in the Lenten season of 1580, they were in an inn (hospitium), where apparently they lodged with their predecessor, Father Pereira; but they were inconvenienced by the number of other lodgers 'ob celebritatem commorantium,' and on the day before Easter the King went with them to show them the part of the Palace where he wished them to stay, in order to be nearer to him. After Easter they moved into the new quarters and the King forthwith visited them and went into their chapel (sacellum). The new quarters, however, were in their turn open to objection owing, it would seem, to the difficulty which their situation involved in the way of frequent converse with the King, and shortly before Christmas the Fathers suggested that they might change them for quarters in the Khushboi-khāna or House of Perfumes. The proposed

Three sets of quarters occupied

quarters were immediately adjacent to the King's 'Palace' and from them there could, by the construction of a door in the wall, be unrestricted communication with the King. Akbar agreed to the change and had the place cleared out for the Fathers and certain repairs executed in accordance with their wishes. The building was then occupied; the chapel was adorned with rich curtains and a Crib was constructed in honour of the Christmas season. Even here, however, the Fathers failed at first to get peace owing to the vicinity of the petition writers (scribae)—and the crowds that come to do business with them; but fortunately Akbar, hearing of this inconvenience, took steps of his own initiative to remove the writers, and the Fathers appear to have occupied these quarters during the remaining two years of their stay in Fatehpur.[3] Proposals made by Akbar for the building of a regular church were under consideration when the Mission left Fatehpur in 1583,[4] and the town was practically abandoned by Akbar two years later.

Identification of these by Father Heras

The Fathers had then three different places of residence at Fatehpur. The first—the hospitium—Father Heras would locate in the village below the main buildings of the Palace, perhaps near the road to Agra; and the second—the room in the Palace—he would put in the vicinity of Bīrbal's house towards the Hāthī Pol. As regards the third we have no outside evidence as to the position of the 'House of Perfumes'; but Father Heras assumes that the 'Palace' or Regia of Father Monserrate to which it was adjacent, was the building known as the Palace of Jodh Bai and identifies the house and chapel of the Fathers with the adjoining 'Bībī Miriam kī Kothī.' This building has long been held by the Capuchins in Agra to have been the house occupied by the Jesuit Fathers. It contains the remains of mural paintings which are not improbably of a Christian character, including one which may portray the Virgin Mary.[5] The main room in the building may well have been a chapel; there is an apse in a suitable place, an alteration in the paving where an altar would have been, an iron ring in the ceiling from which the Lamp of the Blessed Sacrament may have been hung, the remains of lime or gypsum in the transom of a window which may indicate the attachment of an organ, and a lobby on the second floor which could have served as a choir overlooking the chapel. It is difficult to imagine that Akbar would have appropriated so striking and beautiful a building to the use of foreign priests, but without claiming any certainty for Father Heras' identification, we may accept it as by no means impossible.

Agra

The first and second chapels

The Catholic archives at Agra contain a copy of a farmān from Akbar granting permission to the Fathers to build a church; and on the strength of this farmān, a small church was built about the year 1599.[6] It was apparently in or adjacent to the building occupied by the Fathers at that time, which was in the city a half-league from the palace (mea legoa dos paços com estar dentro da cidade).[7] We know nothing more of this church except that it was soon found to be far too small for the congregation.[8] In view of the crowding entailed, permission was obtained for the construction of a new church and the building of the new edifice was commenced in or before the year 1604. The church was liberally supported by Prince Salīm, but it may have been completed during the reign of Akbar, and the 'Native Chapel' of to-day, which is the successor of the church of those times, is still spoken of as the 'Akbar Bādshāh kā girjā.'[9] It was situated 'within our walls and precincts,' it was entirely vaulted and it cost 11,000 or 12,000 rupees, most of which had been given by the pious Armenian, Khwāja Martinus.[10] The first stone was laid with much ceremony, and Father Xavier wrote shortly afterwards: 'Many Muhammadans were present and were greatly edified by the rites which Christians use on such occasions. These works are not as expensive here as with you, being made of bricks, and large use being made at the same time of chunam and of clay made from earth taken from the foundations. The chapel will be well finished though perfect workmanship may be wanting.'[11] The owner of the site was believed to be dead, but during the absence of the Jesuits from Agra in 1606–1608, he reappeared and settled some of his relations in part of the area intended for the main body of the church. The Jesuits on their return had for a time to make shift with the chapel of the church as their place of worship, an arrangement which caused inconvenience as there was room for the men only and not for the women.[12] From an account which we have of the Christmas celebrations of 1610 it would appear that the nave of the church, though then in the possession of the Jesuits and under lock and key, was without a roof, for it was found necessary to protect the Christmas Crib which was in part of the nave by building a thatched roof over it.[13] The nave, however, was completed in 1613, and the church was then described by Xavier as 'very spacious.'[14] In 1614, we find Withington, a factor of the English East India Company, describing the church of the Jesuits as 'a verye fayer church, buylte them by the Kinge.'[15] Father Azevedo writing in 1632 describes it as a pretty church, not very large but handsome—não muito grande mas linda igreja,[16] and Father Botelho speaks of it as a 'very fine' building.[17] We know from one of Jerome Xavier's letters that there was on the roof of the church a cross which could be seen from a considerable distance.[18] According to Bernier it was a beautiful and large church over which there was a tower with a bell which could be heard throughout the city—fort belle et grande église . . . sur laquelle il y avoit une haute tour avec une cloche qui se faisoit entendre de toute la ville.[19]

Incidents of 1614 and 1616

When there was a breach between the Moguls and the Portuguese in 1614, Jahāngīr ordered the church to be walled up, and the Jesuits had to say Mass in their own residence, using, however, the house of Sir Robert Shirley also during his short stay in Agra in the summer of 1614.[20] The closure was of a very short duration, but not long afterwards, in 1616, there was a fire at the church and house of the Jesuits which must have done considerable damage, as much wonder was occasioned by the fact that the crucifix which stood outside the house remained unharmed.[21] The damage in this case also was only temporary and the church with its bell-tower was again in full use before the accession of Shāh Jahān.

Experiences of 1632–5

It has been recounted in Chapter VI how Shāh Jahān, in 1632, took Hūglī, and how in the following year the Portuguese captives from Hūglī were maltreated in Agra. The anger of the King against the Portuguese had its reactions on the Agra Jesuits and their church. It is somewhat difficult to piece together the sequence of events from the scattered notices in the records, but apparently what happened was as follows.

The first part of the building to suffer was the bell-tower to which Bernier refers. The tower with its three bells, one of which was a gift from Jahāngīr, was dismantled in January 1633.[22] In order not to be outdone by the Muslim calls to prayer, the Fathers had made a practice of ringing the big bell (o sino grande) at four o'clock every morning.[23] The traveller Tavernier tells us that when Shāh Jahān was visiting the sick-bed of an Armenian friend in the neighbourhood, the church bell began to ring, and out of consideration for the sick man the King became so enraged as to order its immediate removal. The bell was then hung round the neck of an elephant, but being found too heavy it was subsequently transferred to the Kotwālī, where it still remained when Tavernier was in Agra in 1665.[24] One of the bells, bearing the date of 1624 and covered with Portuguese and Persian inscriptions, came afterwards into the possession of the neighbouring Jāts and was recovered from them by the French adventurer, René Madec (1736–1784), but was subsequently melted down to make a gun.[25] If, as seems certain, the Armenian referred to by Tavernier was Mīrzā Zū'lqarnain, the Jesuits' friend, the cause assigned for Shāh Jahān's action seems an unlikely one: but the bells being the most prominent and most characteristic feature of the Christian edifice would doubtless be the first item in the building to invite destruction at such a time. The church itself was left untouched, but unfortunately the Christian prisoners from Bengal crowding to the church on Sundays and holidays, created so much stir and noise as to provoke further action, and at the end of 1634 the church was forcibly entered by the officials. The altar was broken down with crowbars and the sacred images after being smashed to atoms were spat upon and trampled under foot.[26] In December 1635 a farmān was issued under which the church was demolished, but in the same farmān every care was taken to confine the damage to the demolition of the church itself: the materials were to be handed over to the Fathers for the construction of a 'havelī' or mansion, access to the Fathers was not to be obstructed, and the rites of sepulture were to be allowed as before.[27] Without allowing the church to be re-erected, these orders (for which the Jesuits were indebted to their old friend Āsaf Khān) went as near as possible to retaining the *status quo*, and allowed the Jesuits to construct in their own premises a house in which they could teach and expound the Faith. This they proceeded to do and within a short time they had prepared on the site of the old church, or immediately adjoining it, a building consisting of a ground floor with a terrace above it. The building was 'something quite big enough to have in it the Divine Offices, Mass, etc.,' and though it was not equipped like the old church with a tower and bell, it was for all practical purposes a chapel and used as such. It was within the College enclosure and had a special door near the sanctuary (capella mor) by which the women would separately enter and Mass could be celebrated in such a way that the men on one side and the women on the other would hear the service without being seen by one another. The first Mass was said in this new edifice on September 8, 1636, but the views of the authorities were still uncertain, and care had to be taken to keep the matter as secret as possible by removing the vestments and other sacred articles after the services.[28] It was here—'in a chapel belonging to the Jesuit Fathers which stood in their house'—that Fra Manrique spent the eve of

Christmas 1640 in prayer,[29] and as time went on and no interference was experienced from the authorities the building took on more completely the appearance of a church.

Subsequent structure

We are given a description of the church as it was in 1675, and are told that whereas the previous church had three altars the existing church had one only. The walls were of kaccha brick, and owing to the damage done by damp and rain it had been found necessary to supply a dado of white stone on the side adjoining the garden (a quella parte que fica pera o quintal) and a higher and more ornamental dado of the same stone in the chapel. The altar was of stone and the chapel had a stone pavement. There was no retable, but there was a half-face picture of the Saviour and one of the Virgin by S. Luke (probably the S. Maria del Popolo already mentioned). There were other pictures (pajnel) :—S. Peter, S. Paul, and S. Mary Magdalene on the Gospel side and the Eleven Thousand Virgins on the Epistle side : also S. Ignatius, S. Francis Xavier and S. John the Baptist, and others of the Saviour and Our Lady. The greater part of the plate had been sold in view of possible robberies, but the chapel seems to have been sumptuously furnished with damask, brocade and carpets so that on festal days it appeared ' like the Paradise of the Lord '—' sicut Paradisus Domini.'[30]

By the middle of the eighteenth century the church was practically in ruins, and it was only saved from extinction by the liberality of two of the European military commanders of the time. One of them was a Prussian whose name has not been recorded, and the other was the notorious Walter Reinhardt or Sombre. A brief inscription still extant over a door of the church —consisting merely of the words :—' I H S. Anno MDCCLXIX ' —indicates the date of the earlier repairs, and another inscription in greater detail shows that a later renovation was carried out by Father Wendel in 1772 at the expense of Reinhardt. The church was completely rebuilt and the resulting edifice was considered to possess a proper degree of strength and beauty—' a fundamentis erectum satis venuste et solide constructum fuit.'[31]

A further inscription shows that the church was restored and enlarged—restaurata et amplificata—in 1835 under Bishop Pezzoni by Colonel John Baptist Filose of the Mahratta army—trib. mil. in exercitu Regis Maratorum.[32]

The house of the Fathers. The College

The house occupied by the Fathers in the earliest days of the Mission was adjacent to the church of those days and is described in 1604 as being ' a canto alla Chiesa.'[33] When the new church was built about 1605–1606, Jahāngīr allowed the Fathers to occupy a house of which the owner was supposed to be dead, but during the absence of the Fathers in 1606–1608, the owner (as has been already noted) reappeared and occupied the house, compelling the Fathers on their return to content themselves for a time with a place near by which they had bought for their servants.[34] The house occupied by them in 1611 was, as before, in immediate proximity to the church, and during the Easter festivities of that year an acrobat passed on a tight-rope from the house to the roof of the chapel.[35] It was doubtless a poor edifice, but about the year 1617 the Fathers were enabled by the liberality of Mīrzā Zū'lqarnain to arrange for the construction of a superior kind of Mission house, which is spoken of as the 'Collegium inchoatum,' 'une maison,' as Bernier says, 'qu'ils y appellent College.'[36] The actual construction was carried out by Father Antonio Andrade in, or soon after, the year 1621. The College had eight rooms and two stories with verandahs and was shaped like the letter Z—'ao modo de z,' 'in litterae Z specimen.' Father Botelho when Visitor (1648–1654) added two small bedrooms and a hall for guests, and it is pleasant to learn that for these additions he received a contribution of six or seven hundred rupees from the Dutch and English at Agra. We can gain, too, from Father Botelho's memoranda some stray facts regarding the internal conditions of the College building. It was intended to provide accommodation for a normal strength of four Fathers and the outhouses provided for a maximum staff of twelve to sixteen servants drawing three to four rupees *per mensem* apiece. In the room at the gateway the staff kept a few birds whose songs the Fathers would hear in the night season ; on the roof there would be a tame pigeon or two : and in the house there were two cats and a dog. There was a courtyard or garden attached to the house, with a verandah adjoining it which the Jesuits spoke of as their 'cloisters,' and somewhere in the enclosure there was a well. In the hot weather the Fathers would sleep in an open verandah : their bedrooms had windows which were filled by some kind of lattice (adufa) made of white waxed cloth (pano encerado branco).[37]

On the death of Zū'lqarnain the officials seized the College as being part of his estate, but were obliged shortly afterwards to restore it.[38] The Tibetan traveller, Father Desideri, resided at the College during his halt at Agra in 1714,[39] and from a deed preserved in the Mission archives it appears that on July 22, 1757, the College acquired a small house in 'Daulatābād Mallatad Faringī Tol,' but whether this adjoined the College building or not is not known.[40] That the College was a fine building is clear from Father Strobl's description of it in 1743 as a spacious and imposing and well-arranged residence—weitschichtig, ansehnlich und wohl zugerichtete Wohnung.[41] Father Tieffenthaler, too, writing about 1770, speaks of it as an edifice not to be despised and an ornament to the town.[42]

Dangers experienced

Although the building survived so long, it was more than once near to destruction. We learn that it was raided by turbulent Muslims some time before 1735.[43] A few years later, in 1741, when Agra was occupied on behalf of the Moguls by Rājā Jai Singh, the ruler of Jaipur, and a number of buildings near the city walls were levelled to the ground in accordance with a scheme introduced by him for the defence of the town, the church and College were found to be within the zone so dealt with, and it was only through the intercession of the Rājā's Christian doctor that the Rājā (who was already well disposed towards the Jesuits) agreed to spare these buildings from demolition. This concession, however, left the buildings in an isolated position away from the town walls and other buildings, 'a muro civitatis caeterisque aedibus separata.' When the troops of Ahmad Shāh Abdālī besieged Agra in 1757, the buildings were found to be just out of the range of gunfire from the Fort and the Afghāns accordingly took up a position adjoining the College. They tried to batter in the outer gates of the enclosure, but failed in their attempt, and this happy issue was ascribed by the Fathers to the protection of the Blessed Virgin to whom the building was dedicated.[44]

Situation of building

The church and College at Agra were in one enclosure and their position seems capable of identification. The 'Church of Our Lady' is described by Father Roth in 1664 as being 'a stone's throw from the city,'[45] whereas Father Botelho speaks of the College as being 'in the city itself, not much in the centre of it but towards the western third of it.'[46] In the eighteenth century the town had two walls, an inner and an outer wall built by Shā'ista Khān and Jai Singh respectively, and Father Tieffenthaler writing of the College in the middle of the century speaks of it as being 'in the northern part of the city between the new and old walls.' The reconciliation of these various indications presents difficulties, but these will mostly disappear when it is borne in mind that owing to the terrible misrule of the eighteenth century, a site which had been in the centre of the city in Botelho's time was outside the city in the days of Tieffenthaler. By 1785 the church and the quarters of the Jesuits were outside the city 'in a desert place'; and in a description of some repairs executed about that date we are informed not only that the house was large and commodious, but also that it was 'adequately fortified to repel the attack of robbers.'[47] There seems in any case no reason to question the conclusion arrived at by Father Hosten that the church was on the site occupied by the Old Cathedral which is now the 'Native Chapel,' and that the old College is embedded in the present residence of the Capuchin Fathers. The fact that the Old Cathedral and its enclosure were occupied by the Jesuit Mission is borne out by the discovery in 1913 of an inscription of 1646, commemorating Father Joseph de Castro, in the enclosure of the Old Cathedral.[48] If this is so we may look on the Agra church as having passed through three main stages. There was first the small church commenced about the year 1599. Then the larger church begun in 1604, neglected during 1606–1608, completed in 1613, damaged by fire in 1616, and destroyed in 1635. And lastly the chapel opened in 1636, reconstructed in 1769–1772, extended in 1835 and subsequently known as the 'Old Cathedral' and the 'Native Chapel.'

LAHORE

Our information regarding the Jesuit properties in Lahore is less definite than it is in respect of Agra. When the Third Mission reached Lahore in May 1595 they had at first to be contented with a chapel, situated probably in their own house; but the chapel was well furnished, for we hear of Akbar sending costly gold and silk cloths for its adornment.[49] On August 15, 1596, a Christian in his service, probably Mīrzā Sikandar, obtained some precious cloths for the same purpose, and on the same day the King presented the Fathers with pictures of Our Saviour and the Blessed Virgin to be deposited in the Chapel.[50]

Temporary arrangements 1595–1597

Meanwhile steps were being taken for the construction of a separate church. Soon after the arrival of the Mission, both Akbar and Prince Salīm had suggested the building of a church, but the usual delays occurred. The Jesuits reminded the Prince, but nothing further was done until August 5, 1595, when Akbar remembered the matter and bade the Fathers proceed. When, however, they asked for a written authorization he demurred. The Prince, none the less, interested himself in the matter and promised all that was necessary for the building. A site was ultimately obtained which was 'extremely convenient and near to the Palace.' When Akbar

The new church 1597–1633

was in Kashmīr in the summer of 1597, Father Pinheiro remained in Lahore to superintend the building of the church, and during that summer no building operations were allowed in Lahore except the restoration of the Palace, which had recently been gutted by a great fire, and the construction of the Jesuits' church. The church was opened on September 7, 1597, with great ceremony, the Governor of Lahore being himself present.[51] It is described by the writer of the Annual Letter for 1597 as elegant and commodious—neque incommodum neque inconcinnum.[52] The Italian Vechiete who saw it in 1604, speaks of it as a 'magnifica chiesa,' 'grande chiesa,'[53] and Father Azevedo in 1632 describes it as a handsome church, 'fermoza igreja.'[54] It had a large flat roof or terrace (eirado) which was used for the Easter illuminations.[55] The chronicler, du Jarric, tells us that it was a large building and so beautiful that the pagans and Saracens from other localities visited it as one of the marvels of the time—'une chose des plus rares qu'il y ait.'[56] It was, however, built on ground escheated by Akbar to the Crown, and one of the first boons conferred on the people by Jahāngīr after his accession was the cancellation of all escheats made by his predecessor. An effort was therefore made by the previous owners to oust the Fathers from their church and residence and certain other properties in Lahore on the strength of this concession, but the Fathers represented that the land had been confiscated to meet debts due by the owners to the Crown, and Jahāngīr decided to leave the property in the possession of the Jesuits.[57] A few years later there was more serious trouble, for in 1614 when Jahāngīr was irritated by the Portuguese activities on the Bombay coast, the resident priest, Father Machado, received orders to quit the church,[58] and the Lahore Mission was abandoned for ten years, an old Venetian being left in charge of the church as caretaker.[59] The church was reoccupied in 1624, and we hear of new instruments and players for the church music at Lahore being brought from Goa in 1627. But when Shāh Jahān fell out with the Portuguese of Hūglī in 1632, he ordered the destruction of the Lahore church, and we have no definite information after this as to the existence of a church building at Lahore. All we know is that by the middle of the seventeenth century Mass was being celebrated on the ground-floor of the Fathers' residence,[60] and in 1832 we find the Bishop of Agra writing that the churches in Lahore and certain other places had been levelled to the ground and abandoned, 'uguagliate al suolo o abbandonate.'[61]

The Fathers of the Second Mission (1590–1591) occupied an apartment in the King's palace at Lahore.[62] Those of the Third

Mission were in 1595–1596 also living in a part of Akbar's Palace within the Fort. Their house was only fifteen spans from the river, which then flowed past the walls of the Fort, and when the King went to his pleasure boat, he would sometimes pass that way and hold converse with them. The Fathers were even permitted to pass in a boat under the walls of the zanāna and sometimes, we are told, the King's daughter would cry out to them, 'Eh ! Pādrī, Pādrī ! By the sign of the Holy Cross, God deliver us !' The house was indeed so near the zanāna that in spite of the sultriness of their rooms, the Fathers forbore to sleep on the roof, and the King hearing of this, arranged to have a boat moored in front of their house for them to sleep in.[63] When the new church was built in 1597 a residence was built along with it, and it is spoken of by one of the Chroniclers as 'the rest of the building,' so that it may have been actually attached to the church.[64] When Brother Goes passed through Lahore on his way to Tibet in 1603, he lodged with a Venetian merchant in the town, as he thought it inadvisable to attract attention by staying 'at the church,' by which is doubtless meant 'at the Fathers' residence';[65] and his action is further explained by the fact that a number of Christians were lodged in or in close proximity to the Fathers' house.[66] We do not know where the house—and church—were, but from the fact that during the disturbances of 1606 the Armenians outside the city stored their goods with the Fathers, it may be presumed that these buildings were inside the city walls.[67] The Fathers received visits from Jahāngīr at their residence during the early part of his reign, and the house in his time is described as 'a two-storied house made on the plan of a College with large commodious rooms below and upstairs surrounded with verandahs.'[68] Father Xavier tells us how it contained fine verandahs and cubicles in the upper story for winter use and in the lower for the summer. It enclosed a garden to refresh the eye and was provided with separate offices and a porter's lodge with a bell. 'Thus,' as Guerreiro writes, 'in the heart of a Moorish Kingdom there is a company established as though it were in a Christian land.'[69] In 1614 when the Fathers were expelled from their church, the Imperial seals were at the same time placed on the doors of their house, but the house was doubtless reoccupied in 1624 when the church was reopened, and some years later we find it described as 'a very large house containing two small halls, a bedroom and a very fine verandah.' It was under this verandah on the ground-floor that Mass was celebrated when opportunity occurred after the disappearance of the church.[70]

The Fathers' residences

The Fathers had some house property in Lahore in addition to their residence and church. Akbar's grant included some houses in mohalla Talwāra belonging to a rich Hindu named Panna Surī, which had defaulted to the Crown, and the Fathers used this property partly for a church and partly for a shelter for married Christians. The houses were claimed by the Hindu in Akbar's time and the Governor of the city expropriated the Fathers, but after some prevarication on the part of the officials they were reinstated by the King's command.[71] On Jahāngīr's succession a further claim was, as noted above, put forward by the heirs of the old owners in respect both of the church and the 'College,' but it was disallowed by the king.[72] A still further effort was made in 1611 on the plea that Akbar in giving the site had been deceived as to its real value, but this attempt also was foiled and Jahāngīr sought to solve the question by expressly dedicating and granting the property 'to the Lord Jesus.'[73] Some further difficulties seem to have occurred in Shāh Jahān's reign, for we find Father Oliveira in Lahore in 1635 selling some houses which Shāh Jahān had ordered to be restored to the Fathers.[74] In 1637 Father Morando was still struggling to get back the houses which were lost after the demolition of the church, and with the help of Āsaf Khān he appears to have been successful.[75] Father de Castro in 1641 was again selling house-property, with a view to the closing of the Lahore Mission, but on his own responsibility he retained 'one rather commodious house' for the use of any of the Fathers who might in future come to Lahore. This may have been the so-called 'College,' or it may have been one of the outlying properties.[76] Indeed both may have been retained, for in 1652 we find Father Botelho speaking of 'our houses'—in the plural—in Lahore.[77]

Other house property

Delhi

The Jesuits started a Mission in Delhi shortly after it became the headquarters of Government in 1648. In 1650 and for some years afterwards a Father was deputed from Agra each year for the season of Lent. Later on a Father was permanently stationed at Delhi, and ultimately the Jesuits had two Fathers and two churches there.

The two Churches of the Jesuits

When Father Desideri came to Delhi in 1722, however, only one church was in use, namely one which adjoined the house used as the Fathers' residence and lay in the area where most of the Christians lived. There were other Christians scattered through the town, and owing to their distance from the church these Christians would attend the services three or four times only in the year : the women especially being kept away by the cost of the palanquins required to bring them to the church. The church in the city, which used to serve the needs of these scattered Christians, had fallen into ruin and was in any case very small, but Desideri had it extended and rebuilt so as to provide the congregation with a building which he describes as 'a new and sumptuous church.' This was dedicated to the Virgin and the first Mass was said in it on All Saints' Day 1723.[78] It enjoyed, however, a very brief existence, for in 1739 both the Christian churches in Delhi were destroyed by the soldiery of Nādir Shah during the great massacre of that year.[79]

In 1746 there were again two churches in existence ; one at the Fathers' residence in the city and one serving the bulk of the Christian population in the suburbs. The city church was a chapel in the Fathers' house, where ordinary services were held and where the Christians' gatherings served, we are told, for the edification of outsiders. The other or suburban church was a spacious building, entirely new, which is described by Father Strobl as being in the suburb in which most of the Christians lived. The building cost 3,000 rupees, which had to be raised locally as the Goa authorities were unable to afford a subscription. It was a finer building than its predecessor which had been destroyed by Nādir ; its vaulting was much admired ; it had nine large windows let in according to European taste ; the music-loft was over the portal in the inside ; and there was ample room on either side of the altar for the women to assemble and see the Mass without being visible to the congregation in the nave. The first Mass in this church was held by Father Strobl on Christmas Eve in 1746, and the church, though not apparently employed for the daily office, was thenceforward open for Christian services on Sundays and on Saints' days.[80]

Their two houses

For some time after the Jesuits came to Delhi, the Fathers at the Court used to live in some part of the older Delhi outside the walls of the new city of Shāh-Jahānābād.[81] In the eighteenth century the Fathers had two houses, doubtless in proximity in each case to one of the two churches. Father Tieffenthaler, writing before 1770, tells us that one of these was near the slaughter-house (macellum), apparently in the city. The other was, he says, in the farthest corner of the town (im aüssersten Winkel der Stadt) where the heavy artillery was kept and where the Christians had their cemetery.[82] The terms used by Tienffenthaler would seem to indicate that the bulk of the Christian population lived at a distance from the Fort; but there was also an enclosed area close to the Fort (muris cinctum, arci regiae contiguum) occupied by Indian and Armenian Christians, which according to the same authority was saved from pillage in the invasion of Ahmad Shāh Abdālī in 1757 by the intervention of the Armenian and Georgian soldiers of the invading army.[83] The immunity thus enjoyed by the Jesuit buildings inside the city was unfortunately not shared by those outside the walls. Father Strobl, who was in charge at the time, failed to secure a similar guard for these buildings and they were looted. The Afghāns took away part of the scanty furniture of the Fathers' house, but the clock, we are told, was left by them lying on the ground as an article for which they had no use. The church was at the same time pillaged, the sacred images were thrown on the floor and the altar despoiled of its ornaments.[84] When the Afghāns were again in Delhi in November 1759 the few movables possessed by the churches and by the Fathers were hidden in a private house, but none the less were discovered and looted by the invaders.[85] By 1781 both the churches and the houses would seem to have been destroyed or deserted, for in that year Father Tieffenthaler wrote that there was in Delhi 'no house and no church and no money to build one.'[86]

Other Places

Churches elsewhere

Regarding Jesuit places of worship and residence in Bengal and Gujarāt there are a number of scattered references of considerable interest, but as regards the churches and residences in the more central provinces of Mogor we have little information beyond what has been given above regarding Fatehpur, Agra, Lahore and Delhi. We know that a church was built for the Jesuits at Patna by Muqarrib Khān about the year 1620, but the Jesuit settlement at Patna did not last long and we have no traces of their church.[87] At Sāmbhar in Rājputāna the piety of Mīrzā Zū'lqarnain had provided a church as early as 1648:[88] and at Jaipur a church was built for the Jesuits by the generosity of Rājā Jai Singh (1699–1743).[89] At Narwar the Fathers maintained a church which was erected in 1743 by the local head of the Bourbon family,[90] and it is said to be still extant in the Fort at that place.[91]

When travelling with the camp of the Mogul in the Deccan War of 1601, the Jesuits officiated in what is termed a 'portable church,'[92] the nature of which is not indicated but which was doubtless copied from the portable mosque which Akbar is said to have possessed.[93] In Aurangzeb's time we hear of a chapel at the camp of Galgala in the Deccan with mud walls, in which two Canarese priests officiated.[94]

NOTES

[1] Badāonī (*Bib. Ind.*, transl.), II, p. 406 ; cf. Foster's *Roe*, p. 275.

[2] 'The Jesuit dwellings at Fatehpur Sīkrī' (*The Examiner*, Bombay, July 28, 1923), 'The Palace of Akbar at Fatehpur Sīkrī' (*J.I.H.*, IV, pp. 53–68), and 'A Catholic Chapel in the Court of Akbar' (*S. Xavier's College Magazine*, Bombay, October 1923).

[3] Monserrate, Commentarius, fols. 20a, 31a, and 35b.

[4] Letter of Aquaviva dated September 27, 1582 ; *J.A.S.B.*, LXV, 1896, p. 57 ; Goldie, *The First Christian Mission to the Great Mogul*, 1897, p. 101.

[5] Führer in his *List of Monumental Antiquities and Inscriptions in the N.W. Provinces*, 1891, p. 72, states that these are ascribed by tradition to scenes in the poems of the Persian poet Firdausī.

[6] Father Felix in *Agra Diocesan Calendar*, 1907, p. 204.

[7] Guerreiro, *Relaçam*, II, Part II, p. 54.

[8] Guerreiro, *Relaçam*, II, Part II, p. 53 ; *The Examiner*, Bombay, November 29, 1919 ; Xavier, Letter of September 6, 1604 ; *J.A.S.B.*, LXV, 1896, p. 90.

[9] Felix, *Agra Diocesan Calendar*, 1907, p. 201 ; Payne, *Akbar and the Jesuits*, 1926, p. 191. A translation of Akbar's farmān of 1599 allowing the building of the church is given by Felix (op. cit., p. 204). A similar farmān by Jahāngīr is said by him to be among the Mission archives at Agra.

[10] Botelho, *Relation ; Mem. A.S.B.*, V, 1916 (Hosten), p. 156.

[11] Letter of September 6, 1604 ; *J.A.S.B.*, LXV, 1896, p. 93.

[12] Letter of September 24, 1608.

[13] Xavier in Marsden MSS., Addl. 9854, p. 164. The enemies of the Jesuits set fire to the thatched roof and Xavier gives a graphic account of the way in which the fire was extinguished.

[14] Letter of September 23, 1613.

[15] Foster, *Early Travels in India*, 1921, p. 222.

[16] Wessels, *Early Jesuit Travellers in Central Asia*, 1924, pp. 282–283.

[17] *Mem. A.S.B.*, V, 1916 (Hosten), p. 156.

[18] Letter of 1611 ; Marsden MSS., Addl. 9854, fol. 171.

[19] Amsterdam, edn. 1724, I, p. 236.

[20] *Lett. Rec.*, II, p. 141 ; *Cal. State Papers*, Colonial Series, East Indies, 1513–1616 (1862), pp. 331 and 334, Nos. 781 and 788 ; Foster, *Early Travels in India*, 1921, p. 223.

[21] Botelho, *Mem. A.S.B.*, V, 1916 (Hosten), p. 156.

[22] Peter Mundy, Hakl. Edition (Temple), II, p. 380 ; Jer. Xavier in Zannetti, *Raguagli*, 1615, p. 28.

[23] Andrade, Letter of August 24, 1623.

[24] Tavernier (Crooke's edn., 1925), I, p. 92.

[25] Modave, *Voyage du Bengale à Delhi ;* a manuscript account quoted by Barbé, *Le Nabab René Madec*, 1894, p. 124, referred to in *The Examiner*, Bombay (Hosten), April 20, 1918. The writer says the bell was given to the Jāts by Jahāngīr, which is an evident error.

[26] Botelho's *Relation ; Mem. A.S.B.*, V, 1916 (Hosten), pp. 156–157 ; de Castro's letter of September 5, 1635.

[27] *J.P.H.S.*, V, 1916 (Felix), p. 25, where a copy of the order is given. See also de Castro's letter of September 17, 1636.

[28] De Castro, Letter of April 16, 1637, quoted by Hosten in *Mem. A.S.B.*, V, 1916, p. 157, and Botelho, *Relation* (*ib.*).

[29] *Itinerario*, Rome, 1649, p. 344 ; Hakl. edn. (Luard and Hosten), II, p. 152.

[30] Annual Report of 1675.

[31] Letter of Angelino di San Guiseppe, O.D.C., 1785, in the Archives of the Propaganda, Indie Orientali—Relazioni, *Scritture riferite nei Congressi*, CC, RR, Vol. No. 40. According to Thomas Twining (W. Twining's *Travels in India a Hundred Years Ago*, London, 1893, p. 204), the Capuchin priest who succeeded the Jesuits in Agra was living in 1794 in rooms above the church. The difficulties arising from this statement are discussed by Hosten in the *Catholic Herald of India*, February 17, 1917.

[32] *Agra Diocesan Calendar*, 1907 (Felix), p. 205.

[33] Girolamo Vechiete in letter of March 26, 1620 ; Morelli, *Codici manoscritti volgari della Libreria Naniana*, Venice, 1776, p. 172.

[34] Xavier, Letter of September 24, 1608,

[35] Xavier in Marsden MSS., Addl. 9854, fol. 168.

[36] Amsterdam edn., 1724, II, p. 80.

[37] Botelho's *Summa ; J.A.S.B.*, VI, 1910, p. 458 ; *Mem. A.S.B.*, V, 1916, p. 185. See also (regarding the well) the Annual Letter of December 27, 1678.

[38] Figueredo, Letter of 1735, *Weltbott*, No. 595. Figueredo states that the restoration was made in obedience to a vision of the Virgin.

[39] Letter of August 21, 1714 ; *The Examiner*, Bombay (Hosten), October 5, 1918.

[40] *Agra Diocesan Calendar*, 1907 (Felix), p. 239.

[41] Letter of October 13, 1743 ; *Weltbott*, No. 645.

[42] Bernoulli, *Description de l'Inde*, 1791, I, p. 162.

[43] Figueredo in *Weltbott*, No. 595.

[44] Strobl, Letter of October 13, 1743, *Weltbott*, No. 645 ; Bernoulli, *Beschreibung von Hindustan*, II, Part II, p. 177.

[45] *Weltbott*, No. 35. As noted in Chapter VI, note 28, it is not altogether certain that the church here referred to was at Agra and not in Delhi.

[46] If this is indeed the meaning of Botelho's 'naõ muito no mayo della senaõ pera ạ terceira parte que cae pera o Occidente.'

[47] 'In loco deserto extra urbis moenia,' Tieffenthaler, Letter of November 19, 1781. 'Extra muros civitatis prope portam ejusdam qui locus quondam quasi medius erat celebris hujus metropolis quando triplici murorum ductu circumdabatur.' Letter from Angelino, 1785 ; Propaganda Archives, Indie Orientali, Relazione, *Scritture referite nei Congressi*, CC, RR, Vol. No. 40.

[48] *Mem. A.S.B.*, V, 1916 (Hosten), pp. 153, 155, and 185.

[49] Xavier, Letter of August 20, 1595 ; *J.A.S.B.*, LXV, 1896, p. 66.

[50] Xavier, Letter of September 8, 1596; *Mem. A.S.B.*, V, 1916 (Hosten), p. 174.

[51] The Annual Letter for 1597 gives the date wrongly and with some misgiving as September 7, 1593. The facts are recounted in Guzman, *Historia*, I, p. 268. Pinheiro, Letter of September 3, 1595; *J.A.S.B.*, LXV, 1896, p. 69; Payne, *Akbar and the Jesuits*, 1926, p. 75.

[52] Annual Letter for 1597 (Naples, 1607), p. 573.

[53] Morelli, *I Codici manoscritti volgari della Libreria Naniana*, Venice, 1776, pp. 171 and 187.

[54] Wessels, *Early Jesuit Travellers in Central Asia*, 1924, p. 283.

[55] Xavier, Letter of August 28, 1607.

[56] Du Jarric, III, p. 105; cf. Guerreiro, IV, p. 152; Hazart, I, p. 272; *J.A.S.B.*, LXV, 1896, p. 96.

[57] Guerreiro, IV, 151; du Jarric, III, p. 105.

[58] Felix in *J.P.H.S.*, V, 1916, pp. 90–93. The Englishman Kerridge writing on September 20, 1614, says: 'The King hath caused the Jesuits' churches to be shut up, debarring them from the public exercise of their religion and hath taken their allowances from them, yet their goods untouched.' *Letters Received*, II, p. 107.

[59] Von Poser, the German traveller, saw him in November 1621, and speaks of him as an old Venetian 'welcher schon bey zwanzig Jahren von den Jesuiten von Agra der Kirchen allhier fürzustehen gelassen worden.'

[60] Botelho, *Relation; Mem. A.S.B.*, V, 1916 (Hosten), p. 158.

[61] Wolff, *Researches and Missionary Labours*, London, 1835, p. 306. De Castro in his letter of April 16, 1637, states positively that the Lahore church had then been destroyed.

[62] Guzman, I, p. 256.

[63] Xavier, Letter of September 8, 1596; *Mem. A.S.B.*, V, 1916 (Hosten), pp. 173–174; Payne, *Akbar and the Jesuits*, 1926, p. 62.

[64] Guerreiro, *Relaçam*, IV, p. 152; du Jarric, III, p. 105. Akbar's parwāna of 1604, quoted in Pinheiro's letter of August 12, 1605, speaks of the property as being in Talwāra, which Pinheiro describes as a ward or mohalla (bairro) of Lahore.

[65] Yule-Cordier, *Cathay and the Way Thither*, IV, p. 203; Guerreiro, *Relaçam*, II, p. 63.

[66] Du Jarric, III, p. 90.

[67] Xavier's letter of September 25, 1606.

[68] Hazart, I, p. 272. See Felix in *J.P.H.S.*, V, 1916, p. 91, and du Jarric, III, p. 105.

[69] *Relaçam*, IV, p. 151.

[70] Botelho, *Relation; Mem. A.S.B.*, V, 1916 (Hosten), p. 158.

[71] Pinheiro, Letter of August 12, 1605; *J.A.S.B.*, LXV, 1896, p. 101. A translation of Akbar's order accompanies Pinheiro's letter.

[72] A claim was also made as regards 'the house of the neophytes.'

[73] Xavier's letter of 1611. Marsden MSS., Addl. No. 9854, fol. 171.

[74] Coresma, Letter of December 14, 1635; *J.A.S.B.*, XXI, 1925, p. 58.

[75] *J.P.H.S.*, V, 1916 (Felix), pp. 94–95.

[76] Letter of January 1, 1642, quoted by Felix in *J.P.H.S.*, V, 1916, p. 95. When Fra Manrique arrived in 1641 he was proceeding in Indian garb to the Sarāi of the Farangīs (wherever that was) when he met de Castro and addressed him in Latin. *J.P.H.S.*, I, 1911, p. 91; *Itinerario*, 1649, p. 359; Hakl. edn. (Luard and Hosten), II, p. 190.

[77] Letter of January 20, 1652.

[78] Desideri's *Relation*, Florence MS., fol. 224–227.

[79] *Lettres Édif. et Cur.*, Paris, 1780, IV, p. 260; Letter from de Saignes dated February 9, 1740. The writer erroneously states that the churches were built by the liberality of Jahāngīr. Cf. Figueredo in *Weltbott*, No. 595, and Felix in *J.P.H.S.*, V, 1916, p. 50.

[80] Strobl, Letter of October 26, 1747, *Weltbott*, No. 648.

[81] *Tavernier*, Crooke's edn., 1925, I, p. 78.

[82] Bernoulli, *Description de l'Inde*, 1791, I, p. 128; *Beschreibung von Hindostan*, I, p. 88, and II, Part II, p. 175. According to Manucci, all Christians, except physicians and surgeons, were removed by Aurangzeb to a site 'near the park of artillery, which was beyond the suburbs at one league's distance from the city.' *Storia do Mogor*, II, p. 6. Early in Aurangzeb's reign (in April 1668) one of the sites occupied by the Christians was seriously threatened by a great fire in the city, but miraculously escaped; see Annual Report for 1668.

[83] The incident relates to Delhi, not Lahore as assumed in *J.P.H.S.*, V, 1916, p. 99.

[84] Bernoulli, *Beschreibung von Hindostan*, II, Part II, p. 175.

[85] *Ib.*, II, Part II, p. 179.

[86] 'Nec domus est neque fabrica templi, ad quod construendum pecuniae desunt.' Letter of November 29, 1781.

[87] O'Malley, *Patna Gazetteer*, 1924, p. 73; *Catholic Herald of India*, August 22, 1906, and Annual Letter from Cochin, December 20, 1620, there quoted. The Jesuits' church and house were on the river bank. The house afterwards occupied by the Capuchins was in the middle of the city. *Lettres Édif. et Cur.*, 1780, XV, p. 350.

[88] Annual Report of 1648–1649; *J.I.H.*, I, 1922 (Hosten), p. 244.

[89] Noti, *Land und Volk des königlichen Astronomen Dschaisingh*, II, Berlin, 1911, p. 92. Strobl, writing from Lisbon in April 1737, speaks of three churches having been built, but he seems to have been misinformed (*Weltbott*, No. 641).

[90] Strobl in *Weltbott*, No. 645; Bernoulli, *Description de l'Inde*, 1780, I, p. 176; *Beschreibung von Hindostan*, I, p. 126.

[91] *Gwalior Gazetteer* (Luard), 1908, p. 273.

[92] Pimenta, Letter of December 1, 1600; *J.A.S.B.*, XXIII, 1927, p. 71; du Jarric, III, p. 28.

[93] Monserrate, Comment., fol. 88b; Blochm., *Ā'īn*, I, p. 46.

[94] Gemelli Carrieri, Giro del Mondo, Naples, 1700, III, p. 152; Macmillan, *The Globe Trotter in India 200 years ago*, 1895, p. 40.

CHAPTER XVIII

CEMETERIES

Et sunt quorum non est memoria.
(Ecclus. xliv, 9.)

REFERENCE has been made already to the ceremonial adopted at the burial of a Christian in Mogor and to the observances at the cemeteries on All Souls' Day. Wherever there were Christians in any considerable number, they had a separate burial-ground of their own; and it is of interest to try and locate some of these from such data as are available.

Cemeteries at Narwar and Delhi

At Narwar, for instance, there is a cemetery still extant in the Fort in which the tombs date back to 1747,[1] and there can be little doubt that this was the burying-ground of the congregation at that place, over which the Jesuits presided between 1743 and 1765. In Delhi, according to Father Tieffenthaler, the Christians had a cemetery in the furthest corner of the town, near the place where the heavy artillery was kept :[2] but we have no closer indication of its position. The oldest cemetery now existing at Delhi is that known as the D'Eremao Cemetery (towards Rohilla Sarāi), and this may be that referred to, but the oldest tomb in that cemetery does not date from earlier than 1784. The tomb in question is that of an Indian Christian called Masīh, and it has a touching inscription in Persian which runs: 'In the memory of Masīh. Lo, like Christ (Masīh) he left this painful world friendless on Sunday the 10th January. May God send him to heaven.'[3]

Cemetery at Lahore

Our information regarding the cemetery or cemeteries at Lahore is fuller, but is still incomplete. The first mention of a cemetery at that place is in du Jarric's account of the Christmas celebrations of 1606 in which he says that various kinds of fireworks or artificial lights were displayed in the cemetery of the church and were visible for some distance—diverses sortes de feux artificiels au cimitière de l'Eglise qui se voyoient de bien loing.[4] His authority, Guerreiro, speaks of 'muitas maneiras de fogos no adro da igreja,'[5] and it seems to have been the case that the cemetery in 1606 was in immediate proximity to the church which was built in 1597. In 1613, Mīrzā Sikandar, the father of Mīrzā Zū'lqarnain, left 600 rupees by will for maintaining a cemetery (pera concertar hum adro) for the deceased Christians of Lahore.[6] The money appears to have been applied by Father Joseph de Castro and the other European Fathers to the purchase of twelve bīghas of land with a masonry well in the village of Jumā'h Muzang Harī Phulwārī immediately adjoining the south of Lahore city.[7] Their hold over this land was doubtless lost while the Mission remained closed during the years 1614 to 1624, but we have a copy of a farmān of Jahāngīr, dated 1626, confirming the Fathers once more in the possession of this area, as 'in'ām,' free of land revenue, for use as a cemetery or garden, and there is a further parwāna of Aurangzeb dated 1671, again confirming the grant of the land as a gift to the cemetery, etc. (muqābira waghaira).[8] The wife of Mīrzā Zū'lqarnain was buried in 1638 in a very fine tomb in a garden at Lahore which was said to be owned by the Mīrzā—possibly the cemetery above mentioned, and the tomb was seen by Father Botelho some time between 1648 and 1654.[9] There is, however, nothing now to show the site on which this tomb or the cemetery was situated.

Special position of Agra—as a place of burial

Among the Christian cemeteries in Mogor those of Agra held a pre-eminent place. In the seventeenth and eighteenth centuries, Europeans dying in India attached great importance to sepulture in blessed ground, and the bodies of those who died in Mogor were often transferred long distances to secure a sanctified burying-place. Not only so, but a special sanctity was attached to the cemeteries in Agra, and men like the English Catholic, Mildenhall, who died at Ājmīr in 1614, were buried in Agra.[10] Even when there was a Christian cemetery available locally, the bodies of deceased Christians would often be taken to Agra for final burial; the Italian Veroneo who died in Lahore in 1640 and Father Joseph de Castro who died in Lahore in 1646 were both transferred to Agra, although there was, as we have seen, a cemetery available in Lahore, and in the latter case the transfer was made a year after interment.[11] Among the Jesuits buried in Agra are Fathers Busi (1667), Magalhaens (1702), and da Cruz (1742), who all died in Delhi, De Paiva (1706), who died apparently in Peshāwar, Gabelsperger (1741), who died in Jaipur, Rodriguez (1742), who died at Narwar, and F. Xavier (1767), who died probably in Faizābād. Fathers Tieffenthaler and Wendel in the same way, though they died in Lucknow—in 1785 and 1803 respectively—were buried in Agra. A special interest, therefore, attaches to the burial-grounds in that city.

The three cemeteries in Agra

The Christian cemeteries at Agra were three in number and may be described briefly as (i) the old Catholic cemetery, (ii) the Pādrītolla cemetery and (iii) the cemetery on the Pūya Ghāt road.

(i) The old Catholic cemetery at Lashkarpur

The first of these adjoins the present civil courts and dates from 1610 or 1611, but Christians were buried in Agra previous to that year. It is not known where they were buried before that date, but from certain old European gravestones discovered in 1875 or 1876 near the present convent, it seems possible that the original burying-place was in the vicinity of the convent.[12] The discovery in 1917 of an Armenian memorial tablet of 1656 in the adjacent jail compound and the fact that a window-sill in the 'Native Chapel' in the Catholic Cathedral compound consists of an Armenian tombstone of 1671, may point to the existence near the Cathedral (probably in the convent garden) of a burial-place once used by members of the Armenian community.[13] Whatever may have been the site of the earlier Christian burials, the remains of the Christians there buried were transferred[14] with much ceremony on All Souls' Day in 1610 or 1611 to a new cemetery lying in the north part of the town and mainly within the village limits of Lashkarpur.[15] This cemetery is still in use, though curiously enough only half full. In the course of certain litigation in 1821 it was alleged that the Catholic community held a sanad for this land, dating from Akbar's time, but the land appears to have been granted by Jahāngīr and we have a copy of the farmān of 1609 given by him which confers upon the Farangīs a cemetery and garden of six bīghās of which three bīghās were in the 'mauzah' of Agra.[16] This is the oldest Christian cemetery in Northern India and was in use continuously till 1728; but between that date and 1771 it seems to have been unused. In 1775 we find Father Wendel, S.J., obtaining a parwāna confirming him in possession of two groves of trees in Mauza Lashkarpur, forming the cemetery of the Christians, which (according to one reading of the document) had been granted by an unknown lady of the name of Maryam.[17] The property seems to have been further confirmed by Mādhojī Sindhia during his supremacy in 1785 and the revenues of Lashkarpur assigned in addition. The assignment and the land were resumed shortly after British annexation, but a claim to the cemetery by the Armenians was dismissed by the Courts in 1812, and a further order was issued in November 1824 by which the cemetery was allotted to the Catholics on condition that it was made available for the interment of Christians of all denominations.[18] Such of the land originally held by the Jesuits as lay outside the cemetery does not seem to have been restored, but the right to the cemetery itself, which even in the time of Tieffenthaler was surrounded by a masonry wall, was secured for the Catholics.[19]

This cemetery contains the oldest European tomb in Northern India, that of John Mildenhall, the self-styled envoy of Queen Elizabeth, who died in 1614. It also contains the tomb of Jeronimo Veroneo (1640) who is credited by some with the designing of the Tāj, of Bronzoni the Venetian lapidary (1677), of Marie, the daughter of the adventurer, René Madec (1771), of Walter Reinhard, the celebrated Sombre (1778), of the four children of General Perron (1793), of Colonel Hessing of Sindhia's service (1803) and of several members of the Bourbon and Derridon families.[20]

Remarkable tombs in the cemetery

In the south part of the cemetery stands an edifice described by Father Tieffenthaler about the year 1770 as a ' a spacious, vaulted building, decorated inside with flowers and looking like a chapel.'[21] It is a handsome, octagonal building surmounted by a dome and cross and still in good repair. It is spoken of as ' the Padres Santos Chapel ' or ' the Martyrs' Chapel ' : but the origin of those names is not certain.[22] It has been held by some that the chapel is a memorial of the ' Holy Fathers ' who were martyred in Agra during the persecutions of 1633, and by others that it commemorates the name of Father Santucci, a saintly Italian priest who came to India in 1668 and died in 1689. The word ' Martyrs,' however, probably originated in the name (Martyros or Martinus) of the pious Armenian buried in the chapel (of whom mention is made below), and the words ' Padres Santos ' doubtless represent the Portuguese expression ' cemiterio dos Padres Santos ' or ' Cemetery of the Priests.'[23] The building dates from the earliest days of the cemetery and was erected in honour of Khwāja Martinus, a rich and pious Armenian who had been to Rome and who died in 1611.[24] It contains a marvellous collection of interesting epitaphs commencing from the year 1611. The floor is made up of tombstones and some twenty-five of the Mogor missionaries are interred there, including Joseph de Castro (1646), D'Orville (1662), Busi (1667), Santucci (1686) and Strobl (1758). The chapel was little used for interments between 1706 and 1767 and only six inscriptions belonging to this period have been found.[25] The building is now under the care of the Government.

The Padres Santos chapel

The second cemetery in Agra is that in Pādrītolla, at the back of the Old Cathedral and close to the New Cathedral. This contains tombs dating from 1785 to 1851, including inscriptions commemorating Fathers Tieffenthaler (1785) and Wendel (1803), both of whom died in Lucknow.[26]

(ii) The Pādrītolla cemetery

The third cemetery—if it can be so called—consists of a few tombs on the Pūya Ghāt road about a mile north of Lashkarpur. This little cemetery, which was in use from about 1730 to 1770 and includes the tomb of at least one descendant of Mīrzā Zū'lqarnain, is said to have been at one time covered by a dome.[27] It immediately adjoins a Muslim burial-ground and the tomb of a Muslim saint; and it was apparently resumed by the British Government in 1824.[28]

(iii) The tombs on the Pūya Ghāt road

NOTES

[1] *Gwalior Gazetteer*, 1908 (Luard), p. 273. Cunningham in *Arch. Survey India*, II, 1871.

[2] Bernoulli, *Description de l'Inde*, 1791, I, p. 128; *Beschreibung von Hindostan*, I, p. 88.

[3] Irving, *A list of Inscriptions on Christian Tombs and Monuments in the Punjab*, 1910, p. 5.

[4] III, p. 119.

[5] *Relaçam*, V, p. 7.

[6] Corsi's report in *Mem. A.S.B.*, V, 1916 (Hosten), p. 134; cf. *J.P.H.S.*, V, 1916 (Felix), p. 20.

[7] See the farmān in *J.P.H.S.*, V, 1916 (Felix), p. 20. Muzang is a well-known suburb of Lahore. Hari Phulwārī may stand for 'Abdulla Wārī, a suburb adjoining Muzang. Latīf, *Lahore*, 1892, p. 93.

[8] *J.P.H.S.*, V, 1916 (Felix), pp. 19–24.

[9] Botelho, *Relation*; *Mem. A.S.B.*, V, 1916 (Hosten), p. 164.

[10] So also Lord Bellamont who died near Hodal in 1656. Manucci, *Storia do Mogor*, I, p. 71.

[11] Annual Letter of 1648–1649; *J.I.H.*, February 1921 (Hosten), p. 247.

[12] *Mem. A.S.B.*, V, 1916 (Hosten), p. 184; *The Examiner*, Bombay (Heras), 1923, p. 168. Xavier reports (Zannetti, *Raguagli*, 1615, p. 28) that about 1610 Jahāngīr gave a plot of 120 cubits 'per ingrandire il cimiterio,' but it is difficult to draw conclusions from this statement.

[13] *J.U.P.H.S.*, II, 1919, Part I, pp. 40–55, and III, 1922, Part I, p. 129.

[14] Letter of Father João de Velasco, dated December 25, 1612, in *Mem. A.S.B.*, V, 1916 (Hosten), p. 183.

[15] It was spoken of by the Fathers as lying 'near the town.' See Annual Letter of 1650.

[16] The farmān is given in full by Felix in *J.P.H.S.*, V, 1916, p. 12. The parwāna from Akbar quoted by Felix at p. 210 of the *Agra Diocesan Calendar* for 1907 as relating to Agra is the grant of land at Muzang in Lahore to which allusion is made in note 7 above. A letter of Father de

Castro dated 1637 which is quoted by Blunt at p. 39 of his *Christian Tombs and Monuments of the United Provinces,* ascribes the grant of the Agra cemetery to the father of Shāh Jahān, i.e., to Jahāngīr.

[17] *Agra Diocesan Calendar,* 1907, p. 208. See also p. 159 above and *J.P.H.S.*, V, 1916 (Felix), pp. 45 and 47.

[18] *Agra Diocesan Calendar,* 1907, pp. 209–210.

[19] Bernoulli, *Beschreibung von Hindostan,* I, p. 116; *Description de l'Inde* (1791), I, p. 162.

[20] A list of the more interesting inscriptions is given in Blunt's *Christian Tombs and Monuments of the United Provinces,* 1911, pp. 39–51; and a list of the Armenian inscriptions in the cemetery was published by Felix on pp. 228–231 of the *Agra Diocesan Calendar,* 1907. There are also MS. notes on the cemetery inscriptions among the Agra Catholic Records.

[21] Bernoulli, *Beschreibung von Hindostan,* I, p. 116; *Description de l'Inde* (1791), I, p. 162.

[22] In his letter of September 23, 1613, Xavier speaks of it merely as 'the chapel in our garden where the Christians are buried.' He tells how on one occasion a drunken servant shot at birds on the roof and then with many blasphemies threw a brick at the stone cross on the dome.

[23] See Hosten in *Mem. A.S.B.*, V, p. 183; Bernoulli, *Description de l'Inde* (1791), I, p. 162.

[24] See Mesrovb J. Seth, 'La plus ancienne tombe chrétienne de l'Inde septentrionale,' *Journal Asiatique,* 11e série, XIX, 1922, pp. 276–282.

[25] Lists of the inscriptions in this chapel have been published by (i) Colonel A. S. Allan in the *Bengal Catholic Herald,* of September 1849; (ii) A. C. (Dr. Christian) in the *Transactions of the Agra Archæological Society,* 1876, Appx., pp. x–xi; (iii) Father Symphorien in the same *Transactions,* 1878, Appx., pp. v–xv; (iv) Mr. Fanthome in his *Reminiscences of Agra,* 1894; (v) Dr. Führer in his *Christian Tombs and Monuments of the North West Provinces,* 1896, pp. 174–175; (vi) Father Felix, O.C., in the *Agra Diocesan Calendar,* 1907; and (vii) Mr. Blunt in his *Christian Tombs and Monuments of the United Provinces,* 1911.

[26] Blunt, op. cit., pp. 51–53; *Agra Diocesan Calendar,* 1907, pp. 232–233.

[27] Blunt, op. cit., p. 31, and Appendix; Father Hosten in *Mem. A.S.B.*, V, 1916, I, pp. 85–89; *Transactions of the Agra Archæological Society,* 1875, appx., p. xvi. The Archæological Society decided on March 15, 1876, to remove the stones to the Museum, but this does not appear to have been done. (*Transactions,* 1876, p. 33, and appx., pp. vii–x.)

[28] Blunt, op. cit.

To face page 335] [*From the Lisbon Academia das Sciencias*

FATHER ANTONIO DE ANDRADE, S.J.

(See p. 351)

CHAPTER XIX

THE TIBETAN MISSION—TSAPARANG

Quam pulchri super montes pedes annunciantis et praedicantis pacem.
(Is. lii, 7.)

In itineribus saepe, periculis fluminum, periculis latronum, periculis ex genere, periculis ex Gentibus, periculis in civitate, periculis in solitudine, periculis in falsis fratribus, in labore et aerumna, in vigiliis multis, in fame et siti, in jejuniis multis, in frigore et nuditate.
(2 Cor. xi, 26–27.)

IT was through the Mogor Mission that the Jesuits first came into contact with Tibet, and their relations with that country form one of the most remarkable among the many remarkable episodes in the history of the Society. No history of the Jesuits in Mogor would be complete without mentioning the extension of their activities to Tibet, and a sketch is therefore given in this chapter of the Jesuit enterprise in Western Tibet which was conducted under the auspices of the Mogor Mission, together with a reference to cognate expeditions, previous and subsequent, which were accomplished by members of the Society in the trans-Himalayan areas.[1]

Tibet reached through Mogor

It must be borne in mind that at the end of the sixteenth century the country beyond the Himalayas was an absolutely unknown land. Very few Europeans had heard of Tibet and none knew what relation it bore to the Cathay of medieval travellers or where Cathay itself was situated. It was vaguely surmised from the medieval records that there had at one time been considerable numbers of Christians in the lands beyond the mountains, but no one knew how much, if any, of this Christianity had survived. For men of enterprise and enthusiasm like the Jesuits of that age there were therefore two main interests involved. On the one hand there was the geographical problem of the situation of Cathay ; and on the other there was the possibility of rediscovering and resuscitating a forgotten and neglected Christianity.

A double problem to be solved

The geographical problem was an old one. For some two

centuries before the conquests of Chingīz Khān a Manchu tribe called Khitan from the areas north-west of China had dominated Northern China and the adjacent tracts. The country which they occupied was overrun at the end of the twelfth century by the Mongols under Chingīz Khan, but to the nations of Western Asia and of Europe that country still went by the name of Khitai or Cathay. In the thirteenth and fourteenth centuries a few European travellers, including the famous Marco Polo, had penetrated by the land route to Cathay, but with the fall of the Mongols in the fourteenth century, the establishment of a policy of exclusion in China and the consolidation of the Muslim powers of Western Asia, the contact between China and Europe gradually ceased; and in the absence of contemporary information Western geographers came to look on Cathay as something distinct from China—a mysterious and inaccessible country situated somewhere in the east or centre of Asia. The problem of Cathay excited the curiosity of the West, and it was largely to find a new route to the Cathay of Marco Polo that Columbus crossed the Atlantic in 1492. When the Western nations reached the shores of China by sea in the sixteenth century, they found nothing in the names of the towns which they saw to remind them of Marco Polo's Cathay. The Christian missionaries, however, as they penetrated into the interior of China, began to suspect that the China of their day was the Cathay of the former travellers, and by the end of the sixteenth century the Jesuit missionary, Matthew Ricci, had convinced himself that the identification was correct. Ricci was a man of powerful character and great learning, but his views were by no means widely accepted and the geographical problem was still unsolved when the seventeenth century began. It exercised the minds of the Jesuits at Goa who still suspected that Cathay was a kingdom separate from China, and their forceful Provincial, Father Nicolas Pimenta, determined that a journey of exploration was necessary to lay the question at rest.

A geographical problem

In coming to this decision he was, however, swayed also by other and more potent considerations of a religious character. It was supposed that in the countries north of the Himalayas there had at one time been an appreciable number of Christians, and it was further supposed that Christianity in some form survived in those tracts. The former supposition was correct; the latter was based on erroneous information. The Nestorian form of Christianity had in the sixth and seventh centuries spread from the West to Merv, Samarkand, Tangut, and even China itself. The number of Christians in those

A question of religion

areas subsequently died down; but in the eleventh century rumours began to reach Europe of these Christian communities and of a mysterious Christian potentate in Cathay, known as Prester John.[2] A further wave of Christianity spread over these regions in the days of the Mongol supremacy and by the end of the thirteenth century a Nestorian Church was firmly established in China. There were Metropolitans in China even in the latter part of the fifteenth century, but before the Portuguese arrived on the Chinese coast all traces of Nestorian Christianity in that country had practically disappeared. For a time too—especially during the Mongol supremacy—there had been Catholics in Cathay, even bishops and an archbishop; but these also had long ago ceased to exist. Nevertheless the tradition persisted that there was a Christianity beyond the Himalayas, and to the Fathers at Goa this tradition seemed to be confirmed when they heard through the missionaries in Mogor of rites and ceremonies in Cathayan and Tibetan worship similar to their own, of sacred images in the temples, of lamps and wax lights on the altars, of priestly vestments like theirs, of processions similar to those of the Catholic Church, and of chants that might be mistaken for Gregorian. Like other Europeans before them, they might well suppose that by penetrating beyond the mountains they would not only solve the problem of Cathay, but might also find and revive a widespread though dormant Christian Church.

Recommendations by Father Rudolf Aquaviva

The idea of a mission beyond the Himalayas was first mooted by the Mogor missionaries in 1581. The proposal then made was to send a mission to Tibet. Father Monserrate, when he was with Akbar at Kalãnaur in the Punjab, obtained a number of interesting particulars regarding the Tibetans, whom he called Bothi or Bothantes. Among other things he stated that they never washed their faces or hands or feet. 'The reason they give for this is that it is sinful to sully the beautiful translucent element with which they slake their thirst.' He said nothing about their country being Cathay, but he gave a favourable account of the Tibetans as being a peaceful and pious people, and he heard rumours of there being Christians among them. In the map which he appended to his 'Commentarius' the country adjoining the Mansarovar Lake in Western Tibet is marked with the words: 'Hic dicũtur christiani habitare,' and he heard from wandering Jogis that there was in that tract a town where the people congregated at the temples every eighth day and at a solemn service received severally from the priest a small loaf and a draught of wine. These reports suggested to the Jesuit missionaries that it might be advisable to try to reach the Tibetan area in the guise of merchants, but the information which they received required further testing, and the termination of Father Aquaviva's mission in 1583 interrupted their enquiries.[3] Before the mission retired, however, Father Aquaviva pointed out to his uncle, the General of the Society, the piety of the Tibetans and the gratifying fact that no Muslims dwelt among them and urged that two earnest Fathers should be sent to their country.[4]

Proposals of Father Jerome Xavier

Owing to the disruption of the First Mogul Mission in 1583 nothing could be done at the time. And when the question was again raised after the arrival of the Third Mission, the proposal put forward was that a Mission should be sent, no longer to Tibet, but to the vague area known as Cathay with which Tibet was at that time often confused. The subject was one in which Father Jerome Xavier, especially after his visit to Kashmīr in 1597, took special interest and we have two letters from him regarding it, one despatched from Lahore in 1598 and the other written in 1599 from Agra.[5] He wrote in the former letter how he had been present at Lahore when an old Muslim merchant gave information to Prince Salīm about Cathay, telling him among others things how he had been thirty years in the capital, Kambalu, and how the main portion, though not all, of the people in Cathay were 'Isauites,' that is Christians. Father Xavier further ascertained from the merchant that the inhabitants of Cathay had temples and images, including figures of the crucified Saviour, how there were priests who were celibate and wore black frocks and caps like Xavier's ('only a little bigger'), and how the King went often to the church as he was a Christian. A Mission to Cathay, wrote Xavier, could best travel by way of Kashmīr and Tibet (by which he meant Ladāk), and he added, that when he was in Kashmīr in 1597 he heard that there were many Christians with churches and bishops in Tibet, and that he had despatched letters thither in Portuguese and Persian to ascertain the facts. When he wrote again from Agra in 1599 he stated that Cathay could be reached through Ghoraghāt in Bengal, but that a better road, and one that although longer was more frequented, was by Lahore and Kābul. He recommended the adoption of this latter route as it lay so largely in Akbar's dominions and in countries where Akbar had influence. He had asked Akbar if three or four priests could be sent to Cathay and Akbar had replied, 'Rahat met Xoda,'[6] that is 'May the blessing of God be on you,' adding, that he himself was sending an ambassador in that direction with whom they could go. Father Xavier further pointed out that Badakhshān, which was on the route which he recommended, was ruled by a king who had been at Akbar's Court and whose sons had been taught at Lahore by the Jesuits.[7] The proposal to send a Mission to Cathay was strongly supported by the Visitor, Father Pimenta, at Goa and was referred to the Pope and to the civil authorities in Europe. It received the approval of King Philip III of Spain, and in 1601 it was decided to despatch a mission of exploration. The mission was to combine the two objects in view, namely, the discovery of Cathay and the reclamation of the peoples lying between India and that country. 'Tum ad Cataium explorandum,' as a Jesuit writer puts it, 'tum ad incolas intermediorum Regnorum Christiana Lege imbuendos.'[8]

The Mission was entrusted to Bento or Benedict de Goes, a humble member of the Third Mogor Mission, who is now recognized as having been one of the bravest explorers that the world has known. He was born at Villa Franca do Campo in the Azores, a town which in 1907 erected a statue of him in commemoration of the tercentenary of his death.[9] Early in life he sailed to India, serving as a soldier, and in 1583 he experienced a sudden, and as it seemed to him a miraculous, conversion while kneeling before a picture of the Virgin in a church near Travancore.[10] In 1584 he was admitted as a novice into the Society of Jesus. Within two years he had broken loose and migrated to Ormuz; but early in 1588 he was again admitted as a novice, and in spite of his subsequent qualifications he humbly refused to advance to the higher stages of the Society. In 1594 he was chosen, as we have seen, to accompany Father Xavier on the Third Mission to the Mogul Court. He was a modest man and did not frequent Court circles as much as Father Xavier, but he attended on Father Xavier both in Lahore and Kashmīr, and in May 1601 he returned to Goa along with a mission sent thither by the King. He was in no sense a man of culture, but his acquaintance with the Mogul Court and Kashmīr, his skill in the Persian language, and above all his capacity and prudence marked him out for selection as the pioneer in the great enterprise now contemplated, and he was at Agra early in 1602 making preparations for the journey.

Benedict de Goes

In the following year there arrived at Goa from the north a mysterious Portuguese of whom the Jesuits make no mention. His name was Diogo de Almeida, and he informed the Archbishop of Goa that he had been two years in Tibet, that the King there was called Tammiguia (Namgyal) and his chief fortress Babgo (Basgo in Ladāk), and that the people had churches, priests and images of Christ. All

Diogo d'Almeida

this he confirmed by oath on the Gospels, but the Archbishop, knowing that Goes had started on his journey, decided to take no action until the results of Goes' expedition could be ascertained.[11]

Meanwhile Goes had commenced his long journey, travelling not through Ladāk or any portion of Tibet, but by the route recommended by Father Xavier. Garbed as an Oriental bearing the name of Banda 'Abdulla and fortified by money and letters delivered to him by Akbar, he travelled by way of Lahore and Attock to Kābul. With him were Leo Grimon (the Greek who had been sent by Akbar to Goa in 1590),[12] a Greek merchant called Demetrius and an Armenian from Lahore named Isaac. The first went with him no further than Kābul ; the second, after leaving him at Kābul and rejoining him at Yārkand, was unable to proceed further ; but the last-named—the Armenian—remained with him as his 'fidus Achates ' till the last, and it is to him that we owe such particulars as we have of his long and adventurous journey. Between Peshāwar and Kābul Goes obtained news of Kāfiristān, where the people were not Muslims, drank wine and wore black clothes,[13] and ' a suspicion arose that perhaps the country was inhabited by Christians.' He did not conceal his own Christianity, and when, later on, he was in Eastern Turkistan he argued the cause of his religion before the ruler of the country, a relative of the Chief of Kāshgar, until the latter announced that ' Christians were really Misermans or True Believers, adding that his own ancestors were professors of their faith.' Beyond these vague hints and tales of extant Christianity in Tibet and China, Goes found little or nothing of Christianity on his route. He travelled on, suffering many hardships, attacked by robbers, threatened by Muslim fanatics and vexed by many grievous delays, through Yārkand along the north of the Tarīm basin by Turfān and Hami, until at last at the end of the year 1605 be arrived at Su-cheu on the farther side of the Chinese wall.

The great journey of Goes, 1603–1607

News of his departure from India had been duly communicated to Father Ricci in Pekin, and the Father had for some time looked out for news of Goes, but none reached him. Before he reached Turfān Goes had seen merchants from Cathay who had met the Fathers at Pekin and he had thus solved the question of the identity of China and Cathay. On his arrival at Su-cheu he despatched a letter to Father Ricci, but it never reached its destination as Goes did not know Father Ricci's Chinese name. Another letter written at Easter in 1606 was more successful, and reached Ricci in November. The Father at once despatched a letter to Su-cheu by the hand of a

His death, 1607

young Chinese pupil called Juan Fernandez who, after many trials and misfortunes, reached Su-cheu at the end of March in the following year. It was almost too late. Goes had suffered much hardship and privation in Su-cheu and was now lying dangerously ill. On receiving Father Ricci's letter he wept and burst into the 'Nunc dimittis servum tuum.' In spite of the careful attentions of Fernandez he succumbed eleven days later and died on April 11, 1607. 'Seeking Cathay,' as one of his brethren has put it, 'he found Heaven.'[14]

His death was followed by further disaster. He had kept the most careful record of his travels, but unfortunately the same book which contained this record contained also his memoranda of the debts owed to him by his Muslim fellow-travellers. As soon as he was dead the diary was seized by his debtors and torn up, Isaac and Fernandez being able to retain some fragments only. Isaac was thrown into prison, and it was only after five months that he and Fernandez were able to set forth to lay before Father Ricci in Pekin such papers and information as they had. On this slender basis Father Ricci put together in 1608–1610 a brief record of Goes' journey, and this was incorporated by him in his own manuscript memoirs, of which a Latin translation was published in 1615 by a Belgian missionary named Nicolas Trigault. In 1911 the original manuscript of these memoirs in Italian was unearthed and published by Father Tacchi Venturi, and the memoirs in this Italian edition[15] are a better authority than the translation made by Trigault. The data provided by these memoirs can be supplemented from the passages in Guerreiro's *Relaçam* which deal with Cathay, and they in their turn are based partly on a brief advance report which was sent by Father Ricci to the General of the Society at Rome in a letter of March 8, 1608, and partly on the letters—not now available—which Goes despatched 'rather frequently' to his Superiors in India during the earlier part of his journey.[16]

The scanty records of the journey

Apart from his qualifications as an explorer, Goes was endowed with a devotion to his faith which he was able to maintain under the greatest difficulties. 'His piety,' says the chronicler Guerreiro, 'was such that amid all the confusion and turmoil of his interminable journey he never failed to observe the holy seasons of the Church, after withdrawing himself for many days beforehand to perform the religious exercises of our Company, so that there was none who did not marvel at his devotion.'[17] Whether we regard the adventure of Goes from a religious or from a geographical standpoint, it is difficult to read the scanty accounts which we have of him

Devout character of Goes

without emotion and reverence. With his devoted follower and admirer, Sir Aurel Stein, who searched in vain at Su-cheu for any trace of his grave, we may hope that means may be found in the Catholic Chapel now in use at Su-cheu to recall to those at worship the memory of this wonderful pioneer.[18]

So far as the experts were concerned, the problem of Cathay was now solved. In future the Jesuit missionaries aimed at the evangelization not of Cathay, but of Tibet—at one time in the west and at another in the south. Goes had met near Kāshgar a King of Tibet (presumably of Ladāk) from whom he obtained information confirming all that Xavier had heard regarding traces of Christian doctrine and worship in that country;[19] and some time during the twenty years following Goes' expedition an attempt was made by some unnamed Jesuit to reach Western Tibet from Kashmīr, but owing to the snow on the passes the expedition had to be abandoned.[20] In Europe, however, the distinction between Tibet and Cathay and the identification of Cathay with China was still very incompletely appreciated. To Europeans, moreover, the name Cathay was better known than that of Tibet. When the next explorer of the Himalayas returned from an expedition to the Upper Sutlej Valley on the western fringe of Tibet, he himself laid no claim to having approached the land of Cathay, but his experiences were published in Europe in a little book, now very rare, to which the publishers gave the title of *Novo descobrimento do Gram Cathayo, ou reinos de Tibet.* This book was the reproduction of a letter written from Agra on November 8, 1624, by Father Antony de Andrade of the Society of Jesus, and it was published in Lisbon in 1626.[21] The object of the journey which it records was not to solve questions of geography but to open up a new mission field, and the incentive for the expedition lay in the accounts constantly heard by the Fathers for many years past of Christian kingdoms in the mysterious North. It was a journey of hardship and peril but it was a comparatively brief one, and it must be looked on mainly as a reconnaissance made before the opening of a missionary campaign among the Tibetans.

Publication of the 'Descobrimento' of Father Andrade

The conductor of this reconnaissance, Father Antony de Andrade, was a Portuguese, a native of Oleyros, in the Province of Beira Baixa, where he was born in 1580.[22] He embarked for India in 1600 and after various services, including the Rectorship of the College at Goa, he was in 1621 made Superior of the Mogor Mission.

Andrade's journey of 1624 to Srīnagar in Garhwāl

On March 30, 1624, he left Agra with a lay brother, Manuel Marques, to follow the King, Jahāngīr, on his journey to Kashmīr. On reaching Delhi, however, he learnt of the projected departure of a band of Hindu pilgrims to Badrināth in the Himalayas, and with characteristic promptitude he decided to join them with a view to penetrating beyond the mountains. Wearing Indian clothes, Andrade and Marques with two servants[23] accompanied the pilgrims. Father Andrade in his description of their journey dilates on the beauties and the dangers of his journey through the hills, the fine trees and lovely flowers, the narrow paths, the yawning precipices, the foaming Ganges far below and the pilgrims' chant of 'Ye Badrinate, ye ye!' His first substantial halt was at Srīnagar, the capital of Garhwāl and the seat of a Rājā, a place of some importance which was to form the advanced base for future operations against Tibet. The fact that the town bears the same name as the capital of Kashmīr has led to no little trouble and confusion, and several writers have on this account ascribed to Andrade a journey to Kashmīr which was never undertaken. There is indeed no indication of any Mission station of the Jesuits having ever been established in the Kashmīr Valley.[24]

And thence to Tsaparang

At Srīnagar Father Andrade had to submit to interrogatories. He was obviously not a trader or a pilgrim, and his story was that he was Portuguese, travelling to see a sick brother in Tibet. The black soutane in his baggage was explained by him as a garment which he was taking with him in case his brother had died and he had to wear mourning. After some further vexatious delay he got leave to proceed towards Badrīnāth. The journey became more and more difficult as he ascended the higher mountains to Joshīmath, and he notes that the river had to be crossed and recrossed on bridges of snow. We have extant a letter written by him 'at five days' journey from Scrinagar on the way to Bardinara,'[25] and we have in his report of November 8, 1624, an account of Badrināth itself, its temples, its pilgrims, its hot springs and the difference in language and customs between its inhabitants and those of Srīnagar. From Badrināth the party moved on to Māna at the head of the pass into Tibet, and here they heard that the Rājā of Srīnagar had issued orders for their detention. With his usual energy Father Andrade decided that he must push on, and leaving Marques behind him he launched with his two Christian servants into the terrible snows of the Māna pass. After much suffering from snowstorms, frost bite, snow blindness, frozen feet and violent thirst, which are vividly described in his courageous narrative, he reached, he says, 'the summit of the mountain range where the

River Ganges takes its rise from a large pond (tanque) and from the same another river takes its rise which waters the territories of Tibet '—a cryptic pronouncement with which much geographical misunderstanding and controversy is connected.[26] Having reached this point, however, he was forced to return part of the way, and it was only after receiving the assistance of a party of Tibetans from Māna and of Marques who rejoined him, that he was able, as the snows abated, to make his way once again over the pass and then down to the town of Tsaparang in the valley of the Upper Sutlej.[27]

Reception at Tsaparang and return

Tsaparang is now an insignificant village in the Tibetan district known as Gūge, and although it is the head-quarters of Gūge under a Dzongpon, or district officer, it contains—besides the Dzongpon himself and one or more temple establishments—four families only. In former days, however, it was a considerable town. The Tibetan annals tell us of a powerful kingdom of Gūge where great saints of Buddhism flourished in the eleventh century and of its capital at Totling, some nine miles from Tsaparang. The kingdom continued for some centuries, but we have little or no knowledge of its history[28] for some time before Andrade's visit. When Andrade arrived in August 1624 it was under a local king of some note who lived at Tsaparang. The progress of Andrade's party in Gūge territory had been facilitated in every way by the King and on their arrival at Tsaparang, which was then the capital, they were greeted by large crowds and were watched by the Queen and her attendants as they climbed the street to the citadel. After some hesitation, due to the perfidy of a Muslim interpreter, the King (influenced largely by the Queen) adopted a favourable attitude towards them; had them well housed and fed, and started a series of daily religious discussions conducted through an interpreter of Hindu origin. The Father's time was short, as he had to return before the passes closed, but in a little over three weeks he had created a most favourable impression upon the King and had supplied him with relics and with an image of the Virgin and Child. The King would only allow him to go back to India with his companion on the clear understanding that they would revisit Tsaparang in the following year, and to this Andrade agreed upon certain conditions. His return journey was made easy, and though he was detained at Māna by a war between the forces of Tsaparang and those of the Rājā of Srīnagar, he was able to be back in Agra by the beginning of November 1624. On November 8 he wrote his report to the Provincial at Goa, and this report, as we have seen, was published as a small book in Lisbon two years afterwards.

The book had a great vogue in Europe and within a few years it had been reproduced in many European towns in Spanish, French, Italian, Flemish and even Polish.[29]

Andrade's second visit to Tsaparang 1625

The reconnaissance which excited such interest in Europe had been in every way successful. Father Andrade had brought back with him a document signed by the King of Gūge, asking for his return and embodying the conditions agreed upon with him. It ran as follows :

'We, the King of the kingdom of Potente (Tibet) rejoicing in the arrival in our lands of Padre Antonio Frangim to teach us the holy law, take him for our chief Lama, and give him full authority to teach the holy law to our people. We shall not allow that anyone molest him in this, and we shall issue orders that he shall be given a site and all the help needed to build a house of prayer. And should any Farangi merchants come to our country we are content that the Padre and his companions should abstain from any interference in matters concerned with their traffic, as being contrary to their profession. Moreover, we shall not give credence to any intrigues of the Moors against the Padres, because we know that as they have no law they oppose those who follow the truth. We earnestly desire the Great Padre (the Provincial) at Goa to send us at once the said Padre Antonio, that he may be of assistance to our peoples.'

When forwarding this application Father Andrade had at the same time reported most hopefully of the prospects in Tibet. He had pointed out the piety of the Tibetans, their distaste for Islām and for Hinduism, and the similarity of their doctrines, their religious constitution and their ceremonies to those of the Catholic Church ; and had urged strongly the initiation of a Mission in Tsaparang. On receipt of the King's letter, therefore, it was decided to take immediate action. Three men were detailed from Goa to accompany Father Andrade to Tsaparang in the summer of 1625 ; but they were unable to reach Agra in time for the opening of the passes, and Andrade—impatient as usual of delay—started in advance on June 17, accompanied only by his old companion, Brother Marques, and a Father Gonzales de Sousa. They had some troubles on the road, especially at Srīnagar, where no regard was paid to the rescripts from Jahāngīr and Āsaf Khān with which they had armed themselves ; but they crossed the Māna Pass successfully and at four days' distance from Tsaparang were met by the servants of the King, who escorted them with all honour to the capital.

This was reached on August 28, 1625, and from this date a

Mission was maintained in Tsaparang which was not finally closed until some twenty-five years later.

The Tsaparang Mission

The Mission was started by Andrade and Marques, but they were soon joined by others, and these again by others, a constant succession of arrivals and departures being henceforth maintained.[30] Father Hosten has calculated that between the years 1625 and 1650 there were twenty-six missionaries employed in the Mission, and a careful attempt has been made by him to trace the personnel of the Mogor and Tibet Missions in each year from 1625 to 1635.[31] We learn from his records the names of a number of the Fathers employed at Tsaparang, but it will be unnecessary in this sketch to notice more than a few of these.

Hopeful commencement

The Mission started with every hope of success. Full liberty was given to the Fathers and they began to study the language and the manners of the inhabitants. The impression they received was on the whole favourable to the Tibetans. They spoke of their 'strange and penetrating minds,' their 'good disposition and rare piety.' The Lamas came in for special reprobation, but even in their case there were qualifications—'Souls bred in laziness' and yet 'far from evil and very white, seeing that they are much given to vocal prayer.' Father Andrade gives us much information about their fastings, their prophecies, their incantations, their dress, their red and yellow caps, their monasteries. We are introduced by Father Andrade and Father Godinho to the well-known Buddhist prayer formula 'om mani padme hum,' which the former gives as 'om mani patmeonri' and the latter as 'om mañi pat mem ri.'[32] The Lamas, says Andrade, could not explain the meaning of the formula, but they were ready to accept his dictum that it must mean 'Lord God, forgive us our sins.' The Lamas were the great obstacle to the progress of Christianity and the ultimate cause of the downfall of the Mission. At first, however, the Fathers were triumphant. In their public disputes with the Lamas they poured scorn on the Lamas' pretensions and on their views on such subjects as the efficacy of prayer and the transmigration of souls. In their disputes the Fathers had the support of the King and imbued him with a strong repugnance to the local Lamas. The King's brother was the chief Lama and he was the first to suffer. The King complained that while the kingdom was in special need of soldiers, his brother was admitting an excessive number of men as Lamas, and he deprived his brother of sundry lands and revenues. He then proceeded to compel large numbers of the Lamas to return to secular life, and he expected soon to see them all succumb to his wishes. ‘When all this is settled,’ wrote Father Andrade in 1627, ‘and everything is quiet, we hope that the King will receive baptism, and he says he will, though he wishes first to know thoroughly the errors of their book in order to refute them in meetings which he intends having with the most learned of his ecclesiastics. He also wants the Queen and all her people to be baptized first, and he says he and the prince his son will at once do the like. Many of the other people have been converted and received the water of holy baptism.’[33] The fields seemed white already for harvest: ‘Respicite,’ quotes the Father, ‘quia albæ sunt jam ad messem.’

The church at Tsaparang

At an early date the King had granted a site for a church. It was one of the best sites in the town; the old occupants were evicted (with compensation), their houses were destroyed and a road was diverted to allow of the new building. All the expenditure on the church was met by the King, the people and even some of the Lamas giving at the same time willing contributions in kind or in labour. On Easter Day, 1626, the first stone was laid, the King and his Court assisting at the ceremony, and the church was appropriately dedicated to ‘Our Lady of Hope.’ The building was small, but Andrade pointed out that when the country was converted there would be plenty of temples that could be used as churches, and meantime the new church sufficed for the existing converts. It was ‘very pretty and very rich’ and the Fathers covered the interior with paintings of scenes from the New Testament and the life of Our Lady, adding also a crucifix and a statue of the Virgin and Child. The King often visited the church. He had the ceremony of the Mass explained to him, and he was allowed to eat some of the unconsecrated bread. Crosses were placed on the neighbouring hills, and the King arranged for the preparation of ‘high pyramids’ or chortens on which more crosses were to be erected.[34] The King and his grandees wore little crosses round their necks, and the King presented the Fathers with pearls, gold and wool, valued at 8000 rupees, which they despatched to India to serve as capital for the endowment of the Mission.[35]

Buddist resemblances to Christianity

The Fathers, as might be expected, were attracted by the resemblance between the Buddhist ideas and practices and those of their own Church. ‘The peoples of the Great Tibet,’ they wrote, ‘are not idolators, for we found they acknowledged the adorable Unity and Trinity of the true God; they know that there are three Hierarchies of the Angelic Spirits, divided into nine Choirs according to the differences in their excellencies and dignities; that there is a

Hell which awaits the wicked and a Paradise for the reward of the good.' Tibetans were heard reciting words which the Fathers understood to assert that the Word was made Flesh. There were traces of the use of confession, of baptism and of holy water; and the Tibetan priests wore long tunics and a closed form of mitre.[36] In a temple in the neighbourhood the Fathers saw a fresco of 'an angel depicted as a young man wearing a breast-plate and threatening the devil, whom he had beneath his feet, with a sword,' and the figure, which doubtless represented a Tibetan saint, was at once identified by them as that of the Archangel Michael. The old tradition of a pre-existing Christianity in Tibet had not yet died out of their minds.

Scope of the Mission

How far the Jesuits penetrated beyond Tsaparang, it is difficult to say. We hear at an early date of a Mission station with two missionaries at Rodoa (Rudok), and Father Kircher, writing forty years later on information supplied by Father Grueber, certifies the fact that Father Andrade visited this very cold district—frigidissimam regionem.[37] Whether this visit was actually paid by Father Andrade or not, we know from information supplied by Father Desideri that, when the Tsaparang Mission was broken up, two missionaries at Rudok were captured by the Lādakīs and taken to Leh, but afterwards released. It is possible that Andrade paid a visit to Mariūl or Ladāk, for when Father Azevedo described his stay in Mariūl in 1631 he wrote how the ex-king of that country had displayed his good-will in the hospitality which he had shown to Father Andrade (no gazalhado que fes ao Padre Antonio de Andrade).[38] On the other hand, Andrade had met a King of Ladāk near Tsaparang and the hospitality in question may have been displayed there.[39] As regards Leh, the capital of Ladāk, it was probably visited in 1627 by Father Godinho who proceeded that year (by what route we are not told) from Tsaparang to Kashmīr; and in 1631 Father Azevedo obtained leave from the ruler of Ladāk to maintain a Mission at Leh, but we have no information as to any Mission having been actually started there.[40] There may possibly have been a Mission even at Kāshgar, for the Catalogue of Manuscripts presented by William Marsden in 1835 to King's College, London, mentions certain letters said to have been sent 'from Antonio d'Andrade in Tibet to the Mission at Cashgar,'[41] but the manuscripts themselves are at present missing and we have no other indication of such a Mission having been founded. The indefatigable Andrade has been credited by later writers with extensive journeys which on our present information it seems most unlikely that he ever undertook. Father Grueber, for instance, forty years later, stated positively that in addition to Srīnagar, Tsaparang and Ladāk Father Andrade had traversed the region of Baramtola or Southern Tibet,[42] and Father Desideri, nearly ninety years after Andrade, wrote from Leh, 'it is said, but I am not sure, that ten or twelve years ago the King of the third Tibet [that is of the Provinces including Lhāsa and Shigatse] sent people to Mogor in search of Fathers of the Society of Jesus because they say that a dress, a biretta and other things of Father Andrade are there.'[43] In the French edition of Father Kircher's work on China it is even stated that Father Andrade travelled through the country of Maranga and Tanjut into China; but this is a mistranslation of the original Latin which merely says that he went to Rudok from which the kingdom of Cathay or China can be reached by way of Maranga and Tanjut in two months.[44] All that we can at present say is that there was a Mission station at Rudok, but that apart from this there are no substantial indications of any missionary activity in Tibet beyond Tsaparang itself and its immediate neighbourhood.[45]

Invasion and conquest of Tsaparang by Ladāk

In Tsaparang the bright hopes with which the Mission began were destined to fade away. The crusade against the Lamas which had been initiated by the King and fostered by the impetuous zeal of the missionaries led to a violent reaction. Before 1630, moreover, Father Andrade, who had been the driving force of the Mission, was promoted to be Provincial at Goa and had left Tsaparang. The King fell ill, and the Lamas' party rebelled and called in his inveterate enemy, the ruler of Ladāk. The invaders proved too powerful, and the King of Gūge was besieged in his fort at Tsaparang. After a month he offered to surrender and become a tributary of Ladāk, but he was entrapped and carried off to Leh. Gūge became a province of Ladāk, and the Christian population, numbering, according to Desideri, some four hundred, suffered much ill-treatment, many being carried off to Leh as slaves. The church was stripped of its plate and furnishings, and the Mission after some five years of success and hope came practically to a standstill.

Tibetan accounts of this event

The Ladākī invasion and conquest are historical events confirmed by the Ladākī chronicles. The name of the Ladākī ruler is known, but the Ladākī records do not give us the name of the Jesuits' friend who was the last King of Gūge. The Tibetan scholar Francke, who has specially studied the question of the identity of this King, tells us of two inscriptions, one in Spiti and one on the Spiti–Gūge border, which give a name to a king who reigned, he holds, some time between 1600 and 1630 at Tsaparang, and one of these may be read as alluding to his apostasy. The Ladākī chronicle merely speaks of him as 'Los-lang' or the 'truly blind.' Though the identification is not yet clearly made out, there seems from the Tibetan records to have been at this time a King of Gūge, who had made himself obnoxious to the Buddhists, and it may be that, as has been suggested, the Tibetan chroniclers have for this reason conspired to suppress his name. However this may be we have no cause, on our present information, to throw doubt on the Jesuit account of him, and he contributes an interesting and unique instance of a Tibetan potentate who was very near to receiving baptism and founding a Christian kingdom on the Upper Sutlej.[46]

The deputation of Father Azevedo to report on the Mission

There were five missionaries in Gūge when it was conquered by the Ladākīs. Their house and church were sacked, but they themselves do not appear to have been otherwise molested. Father Andrade had returned to Goa before the invasion to take up the post of Provincial and, while still unconscious of the catastrophe, despatched three further missionaries in February 1631; but when he obtained news of the disaster he appointed Father Francis de Azevedo as Visitor to report upon the situation. Father Azevedo ordered the three missionaries already deputed to stop in Agra and proceeded himself to Tsaparang.

Azevedo was a man of some distinction. He was born in Lisbon in 1578 and had been in the Society from the age of nineteen. After serving on the West Coast of India and in Mozambique, he joined the Mogor Mission in 1627 and was a man of fifty-two years of age when he started for Tsaparang. We owe to him a valuable account of his expedition set forth in a long letter written, probably in 1632, to the Procurator of Indian Missions in Portugal. This letter was for the first time brought to light by Father Wessels in 1924, and the portion of the letter which deals with the journey from Agra to Tibet and back is reprinted as an appendix to his *Early Jesuit Travellers in Central Asia.* It is of great geographical interest and a full resumé of it is given in Father Wessels' book.

Azevedo's journey, 1631

Father Azevedo marched from Agra through the Doab and reached Srīnagar in Garhwāl just after the death of the local Rājā, in time to witness the burning of sixty members of the Rājā's zanāna. Accompanied by the faithful Manuel Marques, he followed the ordinary route through Māna and on August 25, 1631, he reached Tsaparang.

Finding the situation there most unsatisfactory, he determined to proceed at once to the head-quarters of the Ladākī kingdom, to which Tsaparang now belonged, and after considerable difficulties succeeded in starting on October 6, 1631, with Father Oliveira as his interpreter, on the road to Leh. After a journey over very rough country by Hānle and Gya they reached Leh on October 25, and were received favourably by the King. Within a fortnight they had obtained from him an order authorizing the Fathers to continue their work as before, not only in Gūge but also in Rudok and even in Leh. They were given presents, including a horse 'very like that of Don Quixote,' and started immediately on their home journey to carry the news of their success to their superiors. It was now November, and to avoid the possibility of being shut up in Tsaparang for the winter they decided to take the Kulu trade route to the Punjab. They crossed the Bārālācha Pass into Lāhul, and then continued their journey under conditions of great hardship by the Rohtang Pass into Kulu. Travelling through Makarsa and Mandī, they abandoned their original idea of returning through Lahore, and striking the Imperial road further south they proceeded by that road through Sarhind and Delhi to Agra, reaching their destination on January 3, 1632.[47]

It was a fine journey and Azevedo had accomplished with success the duty imposed upon him. His connection with Tibet now ceased, but he worked for many years longer in other fields, and it was only in 1660 that he died at Goa at the age of eighty-two. The information conveyed by his report of 1632 roused again the enthusiasm of Father Andrade and incited him to revisit the scene of his former success.

Death of Andrade

As soon as he was relieved of his post at Goa, Father Andrade prepared to start for Tibet and had arranged to take with him no less than six companions, when—without warning—he suddenly died on March 19, 1634, not without suspicion of his having been poisoned by a local opponent.[48] The energy and earnestness of this great pioneer can be gauged from the accounts which we have of his missionary work, and fortunately we can realize the man still more fully from a portrait of him in the Lisbon Academia das Sciencias, of which a copy has been prefixed to this chapter.[49] The inscription on the portrait describes Andrade as '17th Provincial of the Province of Goa and first explorer and founder of the Tibet Mission'; and to those who have followed the story of his labours in this latter capacity the portrait cannot fail to be a source of increased appreciation.

From the date of Andrade's death the history of the Mission is one of increasing gloom. In spite of the order obtained from

Ladāk by Father Azevedo, the Fathers at Tsaparang were treated by the local commandant as prisoners in their own house. The six missionaries contemplated by Father Andrade started indeed from Goa in the year following his death, but ill-fortune attended them. We learn from the letters of their leader, a Spaniard called Nuño Coresma, how they travelled to Garhwāl through areas devastated by famine, how two died by the way, and how three had to be left behind in Srīnagar because of illness, so that Coresma on reaching Tsaparang had one companion only, a Father named Ambrosio Correa. Father Coresma was not long in making up his mind as to the prospects of the Mission. The remaining Christians were few and scattered; supplies were precarious and very expensive, and the Ladākī Governor was far from sympathetic. At the end of August, 1635, Father Coresma submitted his recommendation that the Mission should be closed, and Correa carried his report to India, leaving Coresma alone at Tsaparang with Marques. Within a short time these two remaining missionaries found themselves confined by a guard of soldiers to their house. Shortly afterwards they were banished from the country, and on December 11, 1635, these two forlorn relics of this once promising Mission were back again at Agra.

Withdrawal of the Mission from Tsaparang, 1635

Even this, however, was not quite the end. On receipt of Father Coresma's recommendation the Provincial at Goa decided to abandon the Tsaparang Mission, but to retain Srīnagar in Garhwāl as an advanced base from which a renewed attack could be made on Tibet if circumstances improved. Two Fathers—Pereira and Dos Anjos—were sent to Srīnagar in June 1636, and on the death of the latter his place was taken by Father Stanislas Malpica, the friend of Dārā Shikoh, in January 1637. The Fathers had not long to wait for the orders to advance. They had on the one hand received news of an encouraging, though vague, character from Tsaparang itself; and on the other hand they obtained fresh orders issued by the General of the Society, superseding those of the Provincial and requiring a fresh attempt to be made on Tsaparang. Three Fathers arrived from Goa in 1640 with Brother Manuel Marques to help in carrying out these instructions. Father Malpica then moved forward with the indispensable Marques to ascertain the position in Tsaparang. They were, however, almost immediately taken prisoners, and although Malpica escaped, his report on the position was very discouraging. Andrade's church was still standing, but the other buildings had been utterly destroyed, and both rulers and people were most hostile. Efforts to obtain the

The last effort, 1640

release of Brother Marques were entirely unsuccessful, although supported by 'the father of the Queen of Lahore.'[50] Marquez was still a prisoner in 1641, and from this time forward we have no information regarding the fate of this humble but valuable missionary.

The Mission at Srīnagar in Garhwāl

The Jesuit Father Maracci reporting to the Propaganda in 1649 stated that at that time no missionary was permanently maintained in Tibet owing to the cold,[51] but that one was occasionally sent there.[52] We have, however, no details of any expedition beyond the passes after 1640, and although summer visits may have been paid to Tsaparang, the attention of the Fathers was for the next few years mainly concentrated on the evangelization of Srīnagar. The ruler of that district, although he paid tribute to the Moguls, was in Andrade's time sufficiently independent to disregard the parwānas which the Jesuits brought from the Mogul Court, and in 1635–1636 an attempt on the part of the Moguls to effect a military occupation of the tract had been decisively repulsed.[53] Some years later, in 1658, Sulaimān Shikoh, the son of Dārā, found an asylum in Garhwāl from the powerful arm of Aurangzeb, until he was betrayed by the son of the local Rājā.[54] During the earlier days of the Tibetan Mission the authorities in Srīnagar had been on the whole unfriendly to the Jesuits, but when the Fathers settled down at Srīnagar the ruler of the day, Prithī Singh by name, treated them with much kindness, and it was mainly owing to his intervention that Father Malpica was extricated from Tsaparang. He permitted the Fathers to preach and allowed a church to be erected by the pupils of the Jesuits.[55] He himself had some leaning towards Christianity, but was, in the opinion of the Fathers, deterred from declaring himself owing to his dependence on the income of a celebrated shrine (doubtless Badrīnāth) in his territories. When, later on, his son betrayed Sulaimān Shikoh to Aurangzeb, the Rājā declined to be a party to the crime, and his conduct in this respect is ascribed by the historian Catrou (on what authority we are not told) to his having been imbued with Christian ideas.[56] Whether this be a purely gratuitous assumption or not, there can be little doubt that the Jesuits were in favour at the Rājā's Court. Unfortunately we have no connected report on the Mission at Srīnagar, and the stray references that we find regarding this Mission leave its history somewhat obscure. There appears to have been a period between 1644 and 1650 during which there were no Fathers in Srīnagar,[57] and we hear of the Rājā having written some time before 1650 to the Fathers at Agra expressing a wish to see them—a wish which it was found impossible at the time to meet.[58] The most prominent of the Fathers in the Mission was Malpica, and the Rājā was on intimate terms with him and with Father Ceschi. Father Malpica seems to have been at Srīnagar both before and after the interval of six years above mentioned; and we hear of his having—with the help of a crucifix which had belonged to his old comrade dos Anjos—exorcised a demon who had possessed a prominent captain of the State, and of his having succeeded in converting this captain as well as a secretary of the Rājā and the secretary's son.[59] Father Botelho, however, writing in 1652 reported that in seven years Malpica had secured five converts only, of whom one had already reverted to Hinduism.[60] Malpica returned to Agra about the year 1656, and the Mission seems to have come to an end not long after his departure.[61]

One curious relic of the Mission has been preserved in a copy of the Arabic Gospels printed in folio in Rome in 1592, which was in the library of the famous scholar Sir Henry Yule who died in 1889. The title-page of this copy bears an inscription stating that it was read in Mesopotamia in 1616 by one George Strachan of the Mearns, a Catholic traveller from Scotland, of whom we have glimpses in the records of that period; and underneath this inscription is written in another hand the two words: 'Missionis Xrinagarensis.' At what date and for what purpose the book was in the Mission, and how it came back to Europe are matters on which we can only speculate.[62]

A solitary relic of the Tsaparang Mission

Of the Tsaparang Mission there was nothing left. Gūge was annexed by Lhasa in 1650 and received a Governor from Southern Tibet. The very existence of the Mission in Tsaparang was soon forgotten, even by scholars and missionaries, and there is now no tradition of it among the people of the place. In 1909 Dr. Francke sent a Tibetan to investigate Tsaparang with a view to ascertaining if there were any indications of Christianity there, but none were forthcoming.[63] Tsaparang is off the present main routes and although Totling, a few miles distant, has been seen by several Europeans during the present century, Tsaparang has only twice been visited by Europeans since the Jesuits left it. In 1855 it was seen by the scientific explorer Adolf Schlagintweit, but this visitor was unaware of its previous connection with the Jesuits and paid it but scant attention.[64] The other visitor was a civil servant from the Punjab, Mr. Gerard Mackworth Young, who in 1912 was deputed to hold an official inquiry connected with the British Trade Agency at Gartok. This officer, at the instance of the ever-watchful Father Hosten, arranged to visit Tsaparang on his return journey and all that he saw there confirmed the story of the Fathers ;—the traces of a former town of large dimensions, the Fort built by the Ladākīs during the siege, the old palace of the King, and the Queen's room from which she saw the Jesuits climbing the main street in 1624. But of the Mission itself there was no trace, and nothing that can be called a tradition. The houses are all of mud and there is nothing to show where the Fathers lived and where the church of Our Lady of Hope once stood. One thing, indeed, he saw—a large chorten or pyramid of stone, some forty feet high, and on its summit, lying horizontally, a weatherbeaten cross of wood.[65] We may be pardoned if we look on this as a relic—possibly the only relic—of an enterprise once so fraught with energy and faith and hope.

Cacella and Cabral in Southern Tibet 1626–1632

While Father Andrade was establishing the Mission in Western Tibet, efforts were simultaneously being made to support his enterprise by the introduction of a Mission in the South. When he was at Tsaparang in 1625, Father Andrade learned of the existence of a great kingdom, known as U-Tsang,[66] which lay a month's or six weeks' journey from Tsaparang, and he suggested that efforts should be made to extend the Mission to that area and to approach the country from the side of Bengal. As a new Province had been constituted by the Jesuits in 1610 in Malabar with head-quarters at Cochin, and as Bengal was in the jurisdiction of the new Province, the proposal was not dealt with by the authorities at Goa but by those at Cochin. These authorities approved of the suggestion and a Mission was accordingly organized which had its basis at Hūglī. Of this Mission—more feebly manned and more short-lived than that of Tsaparang—we had till recently little knowledge. Two letters of the Mission were however published in 1924 by Father Wessels, and there are several other letters, as yet unpublished, in the possession of the Society of which Father Wessels has abstracted the contents in his book.[67] From these we learn that two Fathers, Stephen Cacella and John Cabral, left Hūglī on August 2, 1626, and travelled through Kūch Bihār to Paro in Bhūtān. Here they were well treated by the Dharmarājā, but were refused permission to depart. Lhāsa had not in those days attained its subsequent pre-eminence and the objective of the Fathers was Shigatze which was then the most prominent town of U-Tsang, or Southern Tibet. This they reached after considerable difficulties, and here they were well received by the King, who provided them with a house and a church. Father Cabral, after a short halt, returned to Hūglī in 1628 by the route through Nipāl and Patna, and Father Cacella also left at the beginning of the succeeding year. In September 1629 Father Cacella started again for Shigatze in the company of a Father Manuel Diaz ; but the journey was fatal to both of them, Diaz dying in November in the Tarai and Cacella in the following March in Shigatze itself. The King of Shigatze thereupon invited Father Cabral to his capital and, on his arrival in June 1631, accorded him a very kind reception.

Relations with Tsaparang : Withdrawal in 1632

The various journeys thus baldly summarized represented an immense amount of hardship, disappointment and ill-health, which was bravely borne by the missionaries. Their one source of consolation was the probability of establishing a junction with Father Andrade's Mission at Tsaparang. Even in Kūch Bihār Father Cacella, who had himself been in Tsaparang, had with him a man who had served as a guide to Andrade,[68] and in 1628 he found a lama from Tsaparang at the head-quarters of the Dharma-rājā in Bhūtān.[69] He studied Tibetan in Bhūtān with a teacher from Tsaparang.[70] Merchants were constantly travelling from Bhūtān to Kashmīr through Tsaparang,[71] and the missionaries made vain efforts in 1627 to obtain permission from the Dharma-rājā to proceed themselves to Tsaparang.[72] When Father Cacella returned in 1629 to Kūch Bihār from Shigatze, he did so because he was prevented by snow from going, as he had intended, to Tsaparang.[73] At Tashi Lumpo near Shigatze the Fathers found a monastery of lamas from Tsaparang and they state that on this account they got frequent tidings about the Fathers of the Tsaparang Mission.[74] In a letter of October 6, 1627, Father Cacella states that he had already written three times to Tsaparang, and he had even sent his reports for his Provincial to be forwarded from Tsaparang through Goa to Cochin.[75] It was to Tsaparang that the Fathers in Southern Tibet looked for help rather than to their own superiors in Cochin or Bengal. The King at Shigatze had in 1627 sent to Father Andrade a farmān and a letter of invitation to his Court.[76] In the summer of 1631 Father Cabral wrote to Father Azevedo in Tsaparang, suggesting that the latter should establish a permanent station at Shigatze, a plan to which, he said, the King would raise no objection. His own Provincial, he hinted, was not enthusiastic for the Tibetan Mission,[77] and on hearing of the deaths of Fathers Cacella and Diaz he would almost certainly bring it to a close. Father Cabral therefore urged that he himself should be transferred to the jurisdiction of the Fathers at Tsaparang and so ensure the continuance on a stable footing of the Mission in Tibet.[78] In forwarding these suggestions to Goa Father Azevedo urged their acceptance. The route from Shigatze through Tsaparang was, he argued, easier than through the Eastern Himalayas, and it was important to establish a Mission at the seats of Tibetan learning, as, if these were captured for the Faith, the whole country would follow.[79] Whether any of the Tsaparang Fathers attempted to reach Shigatze, as seems to be implied in one of the Jesuit reports,[80] is uncertain, but the authorities decided against the maintenance of the Shigatze Mission ; the Mission was closed and in 1632 Father Cabral was once more in Hūglī where further adventures awaited him.[81] When Father Coresma, in August 1635, reported against the continuance of the Tsaparang Mission he, at the same time, advised against the maintenance of a Mission at Shigatze owing to the attendant risks and the uncertainty of success.[82] A protest against the decision was made by a Father Mendez in 1636, and a last despairing appeal was made by Father Simon Figueredo in the Annual Report for 1643. He pointed out the sacrifices already made and the merits of the people. 'Ite angeli veloces,' he cried, 'ite ad gentem expectantem!'[83] But meanwhile the efforts at Tsaparang had also collapsed, and it was useless to expect, for the present at least, any resuscitation by the Jesuit authorities in India of the brave adventure started by the Fathers in Southern Tibet.

Grueber and D'Orville in Lhāsa, 1661

By 1661 there were Jesuits again in Southern Tibet, but the circumstances on this occasion were of an entirely different character. The expedition was not organized either from Goa or from Cochin, but from China. The explorers were no longer Portuguese or Spaniards : but a German and a Belgian. The journey was achieved by missionaries, but its object was not to found a Mission. Tibet, indeed, was not its objective, but was taken on the way as an incident in a fine piece of geographical enterprise. The scheme originated in the fact that owing to the Dutch command of the Eastern seas the Jesuits of Pekin were no longer able to communicate with Rome as easily by sea as in former times.[84] Fathers Grueber and D'Orville of the Society of Jesus were accordingly despatched in April 1661 from Pekin by land, and they travelled by the Koko Nor route to Lhāsa, which they succeeded in reaching in October of the same year. With the possible exception of Friar Odoric of Pordenone in 1328, they were the first Europeans to reach that city, and the fact is one of which the Society may justly be proud.[85] Their stay at Lhāsa was, however, short and they proceeded by way of Kātmandu to Patna and thence to Agra, where they met Fathers Roth and Busi. Here, on April 8, 1662, on the afternoon of Saturday in Holy Week, Father D'Orville died—' media Europam inter et Chinam via '—and he was buried in the Padres Santos Chapel, where we can still read on his grave: ' Aqui iazo Pe. Alberto Derville faleceo aos 8 d'Abril, 1662.'[86] His place was taken by Father Roth, and Grueber with his new companion reached Rome in 1664.

Projects of Father Roth

After a short stay in Rome the two Fathers received instructions to return to the East and proceeded by way of Central Europe and parts of Russia to Constantinople. Father Grueber here fell ill and Father Roth appears to have continued by himself the journey overland to India. For information regarding his further movements we have to depend largely on some rather elusive references in a ' Eulogium ' which was written after his death by Father Grueber.[87] What further journeys he may have carried out it is hard to say. In a letter written by him in 1664 he states that he had four times been invited by the ' King of Tibet ' to come and convert his Kingdom: and he indicated his anxiety to be sent to Tibet or Nipāl.[88] Father Grueber tells us that Roth had been destined for service in the Kingdoms of Lotak, Rotok and Gernaqui (which may represent Ladāk, Rudok and Srīnagar); and that before he died he actually attempted to proceed from Europe through the difficult ' Caucasian Mountains ' and to penetrate through Tartary to China.[89] He died at Agra in 1668 without leaving any record of such journeys, and all we can say is that previous to his death he may have made an experimental journey to Nipāl.[90] How far he attempted or contemplated explorations within Tibet remains undetermined.

The Capuchin Mission

Grueber's visit to Lhāsa led to no immediate extension of missionary effort to Tibet. The evangelization of Tibet was assigned by the Holy See to the Capuchin Order in 1703 or 1704, and the Capuchins then penetrated through Nipāl to Lhāsa, which they reached in 1708. They remained at Lhāsa on this occasion till August 1711 and then returned to obtain further assistance in men and money from Europe.[91]

Ippolito Desideri

Meanwhile the Jesuits at Goa, strange as this may seem, appear to have been in ignorance of the orders assigning Tibet to the Capuchins, and while the Capuchins were proposing to enter Tibet the Jesuits were once more taking up the question of re-establishing their own Mission in that country. The proposal seems to have been first mooted about the year 1704, and on more than one occasion after this date missionaries were nominated for the enterprise, but circumstances intervened to prevent their departure. The scheme received the approval of the General of the Society in 1709, and it became known to members of the Society in Europe. Among those who heard of it there was a young and enthusiastic Italian from Pistoja, called Ippolito Desideri, who had entered the novitiate of the Society in 1700 at the age of fifteen. Even before he was ordained priest in 1712 Desideri had conceived the idea that he should devote himself to this field of work. He was in due time despatched to India, and very soon after his arrival at Goa on September 27, 1713, he succeeded in being nominated to the duty which he so greatly coveted. There seems to have been some hesitation among the authorities as to the despatch of a Mission. It was by this time known that the Capuchins had occupied part of Tibet, but it was probably also known that they had, to all outward appearances, subsequently abandoned their Mission. In any case, the Mission to Tibet was approved by the Jesuit authorities at Goa. On or about November 17, 1713, Desideri started for the North, and after a halt at Delhi, went to visit the Fathers at Agra. His colleague—and superior—in this Mission was a Father Manuel Freyre, and the two Fathers after considerable delay succeeded in leaving Delhi on September 24, 1714.

Authorities for his journey

Until recently our information regarding the travels of Desideri was practically confined to the details given in a French translation, published in the *Lettres Édifiantes et Curieuses*, of a letter written by him on April 10, 1716.[92] A considerable amount of further original matter has, however, been examined of late years, and a detailed description will be found in Father Wessels' *Early Jesuit Travellers in Central Asia* of the documents written by Desideri which are known to be in existence. These include more than a dozen letters, certain controversial works, four manuscripts in the Tibetan language and a volume of Hints for the guidance of missionaries in Tibet: but the most important document from the point of view of this work is a long and elaborate *Relazione* by Desideri, which describes not only the country and religion of Tibet, but also his own personal experiences from the time when he embarked from Europe to the close of his 'Mission' at Lhasa.[93] The *Relazione* was published in 1904 by Puini, but his transcript omitted certain sections of the Report including the interesting chapters which deal with the history and existing circumstances of the Mogor Mission. These omissions have now to a large extent been made good in the valuable translation of Desideri's Report recently published by Sir Filippo de Filippi.[94]

If we bear in mind that the object of their journey was to revive the mission of Andrade, it appears at first sight difficult to explain satisfactorily the fact that Fathers Freyre and Desideri on leaving Delhi travelled, not to Srīnagar in Garhwāl and thence to Tsaparang, but by Lahore through the Pīr Panjāl Pass to Srīnagar in Kashmīr and thence to Leh. It was at one time thought that while aiming at the Garhwāl Srīnagar they travelled by mistake to the Srīnagar in Kashmīr, and that in searching for Tsaparang from the Kashmīr side they stumbled into Lhāsa. There is no doubt, as has been indicated earlier in this chapter, that several writers have confused the two places known as Srīnagar, but there is nothing to show that these two Fathers themselves were misled by the identity of the names. Desideri nowhere calls the Kashmīr Srīnagar by that name but speaks of it as 'Kascimir.' He and his comrade had very vague ideas as to the locality of Andrade's Mission, and Desideri does not anywhere allude to Tsaparang as the objective of their journey, nor indeed does he mention the name of Tsaparang in any of his published letters. Their desire was to evangelize the 'Tibet' which Andrade had visited, but—almost incredible as this may appear—they seem to have started with no clear notion where this 'Tibet' was situated.[95]

Journey to Kashmir 1714–1715

By the time they had reached Leh, they had obtained fresh information which affected the scope of their journey. They had been under the impression that there were two Tibets only; namely, Little Tibet, or Bāltistān, which was Muhammadan, and Greater Tibet, which included Ladāk, Rudok and Gūge and was Buddhist. But they were now told that there was a third Tibet, greater than either of the others, which lay beyond them and which was easily accessible from the Mogul dominions. This was the country known from its two main provinces as U-Tsang, with capitals at Shigatze and Lhāsa; and they thought—though not without hesitation—that this was the Tibet which Andrade had visited. On arrival at Leh the two Fathers disagreed as to the next step to be taken. Father Desideri wished to stay in the Second Tibet, while Father Freyre desired to proceed to the Third Tibet. Father Desideri pointed out that there were already Capuchins in the Third Tibet; that the people of the Second Tibet were well disposed to receive the Gospel; that the Second Tibet was difficult of access owing to the mountains and untouched by missionary enterprise, past or present—showing that he was unaware of its having been previously visited—and that consequently it had a better claim on the services of the

Decision to proceed to Southern Tibet

Fathers. Father Freyre, on the other hand, maintained that as the Third Tibet was the tract to which Father Andrade had gone in former times, they were required by their instructions to proceed to it. Father Desideri implies that Father Freyre was in reality anxious to return to India by the route which he considered the easiest, namely, by Lhāsa and Nipāl;[96] but Father Desideri did not contest the view that it was the Third Tibet that Andrade had visited. He states that this view was credible and he recounts the story above mentioned how some ten or twelve years previously the King of the Third Tibet had sent to Mogor to invite the Fathers of the Society to him, as he had in his Treasury the biretta, habit and other articles which had belonged to Andrade. He adds that the King's messengers went by mistake to Surat where the Capuchins resided and that the Capuchins had dealt with the invitation themselves. In view of these considerations and of the fact that Father Freyre was in any case his superior and entitled to his obedience, he ultimately submitted to Freyre's opinion and on August 17, 1715, the two Fathers set out together from Leh on the road to Lhāsa.[97]

Of their extraordinary winter journey from Leh by Gartok to Lhāsa it is unnecessary to speak here, nor need we be detained by the further experiences of the Fathers, interesting though these are. Father Freyre, on reaching Lhāsa, returned almost at once to Hindustān, but Father Desideri stayed for some five years in Lhāsa and its neighbourhood, studied the language and the sacred literature of the country with great diligence, and put together a wonderful description of the town of Lhāsa, of the religion and literature of the people and of their very turbulent contemporary history.[98] On his arrival in Lhāsa on March 18, 1716, he found no Capuchins in residence, but on October 1 a party of three Capuchins arrived from Bengal. He remained on excellent terms with them, but none the less contested that Tibet was both by prescriptive right and by actual possession a Jesuit station and that it was for the Capuchins to withdraw. The dispute had ultimately to be referred to Rome and the decision there was in favour of the Capuchins. On December 12, 1718, the Congregation of the Propaganda issued orders to the General of the Jesuits to withdraw all Jesuit Missions in Tibet as the field had been already assigned to the Capuchins, and on January 16, 1719, the General wrote direct to Father Desideri commenting as follows on the order of recall: 'When I allowed your Reverence,' he said, 'to move to the Kingdom of Tibet, I was unaware of the assignation of the Tibet Mission by the Propaganda to the Capuchins; indeed, I thought

Desideri at Lhāsa 1716–1721

that the said Mission, which was founded by our Fathers and maintained by them until 1650 when they had to leave owing to persecution, had never been reopened by others.'[99] Early in 1721 Desideri received these orders of recall and on April 28, 1721, he departed for India, leaving the Capuchins to maintain a precarious hold on the station at Lhāsa for another quarter of a century. His return journey was through Nipāl, Patna and Benares to Agra, which he reached on April 20, 1722. He was at Delhi in September of the same year, and left for Pondicherry in 1725. He was sent to Rome in 1727 with the process for the beatification of John de Britto, and died there on April 14, 1733. He had hoped to return to Tibet, but death intervened and transferred him, as the Chronicler puts it, 'from the Roman College to Heaven'—'Quod optabat maxime ut Thibetanum in Regnum rediret, obtinere non potuit, morte intercedente, quae illum ex Collegio Romano ad superos evocavit.'[100]

Desideri's inadequate information as to objective

His journey to Lhāsa, magnificent as it was, failed absolutely to carry out the object with which he was despatched from Goa, namely, the resuscitation of the Mission of Father Andrade, and the failure appears to have been due entirely to the neglect of the authorities to consult the records which must have been available regarding the locality of that Mission. It is true that after his return to Rome, Father Desideri consulted the Annual Reports and compiled from them a useful summary of the history of the Tsaparang Mission: but when he was starting on his journey in 1713 no one, either at Rome or at Goa, seems to have thought of looking up the information already on record. 'Freyre and Desideri,' writes Father Hosten, 'set out without discovering that some of de Andrade's fellow-labourers had been in Ladāk; they passed through Rudok without suspecting that de Andrade's party had had a Mission there; at Gartok, where they passed, they were within easy reach of Tsaparang, and yet they went on to Lhāsa. There the inevitable happened when the Capuchins reappeared upon the scene. What labour and what expense were thus thrown away because a few points of history and geography had not been cleared up at the start!'[101]

No further attempt to revive the Tsaparang Mission

So far as the Tsaparang Mission was concerned, this was the end. No further effort was made to revive the gallant enterprise of Father Andrade.

NOTES

[1] Much of the information in this chapter is based on Father Wessels' valuable work: *Early Jesuit Travellers in Central Asia*, 1603–1721, published at The Hague in 1924.

[2] As to the origin of these rumours see Yule-Cordier, *Cathay and the Way Thither*, III, p. 15. Subsequent research is summarized by Sir E. Denison Ross in Chapter IX of *Travel and Travellers in the Middle Ages*, 1926. For the history of the Christians of Central Asia in the Middle Ages reference may be made to the works of Prof. Paul Pelliot. That of the early Christians of China is fully dealt with by A. C. Moule in his *Christians in China before the year* 1530 (S.P.C.K., London, 1930).

[3] Monserrate, 'Commentarius,' *Mem. A.S.B.*, III, 1914, fol. 60 (b), 116 (b); Sven Hedin, *Southern Tibet*, 1922, VII, p. 26. Austin of Bordeaux, writing from Lahore in 1622, assumes the existence of Christianity in Tibet: 'lequel gran Tabet est Chrestien et duquel le Pape n'a nulle notice.' *J.P.H.S.*, IV, 1916, p. 8.

[4] Letter of April 15, 1582; *J.A.S.B.*, LXV, 1896, p. 55.

[5] *J.A.S.B.*, LXV, 1896, pp. 78–80, and XXIII, 1927, pp. 59–65; Yule-Cordier, *Cathay and the Way Thither*, IV, pp. 174–177; du Jarric, II, pp. 494–497.

[6] Rahmat-i Khudā.

[7] *Re* the Wālī of Badakhshān and his family; see Blochm., *Ā'īn*, I, pp. 311–312.

[8] Kircher, *China Illustrata*, 1667, p. 63.

[9] A picture of the statue is given in Ribeiro's centenary pamphlet of 1907 and in Wessels, *Early Jesuit Travellers in Central Asia*, 1924, showing him in the garb of a Persian. A portrait of Goes in the Jesuit College of Tortosa is reproduced in Tacchi Venturi's edition of Ricci's *Commentaries*, Macerate, 1911, I, p. 529.

[10] De Sousa, *Or. Conq.*, 1710, II, pp. 258–259; *J.A.S.B.*, XXIII, 1927, pp. 138–139.

[11] Antonio de Gouvea, *Jornada do Arcebispo de Goa*, Coimbra, 1606, fol. 3, and the same author's *Histoire Orientale* (translation in French by J. B. de Glen), Antwerp, 1609, pp. 10–13. See also Sven Hedin, *Southern Tibet*, 1927, VII, p. 52, and Esteves Pereira, *O Descobrimento do Tibet*, Coimbra, 1921, p. 34. It was intended to organize a Mission to Tibet from the staff in Mogor and at Cambay after Goes had made his preliminary journey.

[12] Grimon is described as a good Christian, acquainted with Persian and Turkī. By going on this journey he sacrificed a pension of a crown a day and the company of a newly-wedded wife. Du Jarric, III, p. 147.

[13] The Siāh-posh Kāfirs.

[14] Yule-Cordier, *Cathay and the Way Thither*, 1916, I, p. 182, and IV, p. 171.

[15] Vol. I, pp. 526–558, relate to Goes.

[16] A full bibliography is given in Yule-Cordier, *Cathay and the Way Thither*, 1916, IV, pp. 194–195. Tacchi Venturi's work, published at Macerate in 1911, is entitled *Opere Storiche del P. Mattheo Ricci*. See also *J.A.S.B.*, XXIII, 1927 (Hosten), p. 138. The authorities for Goes' journey are clearly set out in Payne, *Jahangir and the Jesuits*, 1930, pp. xxi–xxvi, and on pp. 119–162 of the same work. Guerreiro's interesting account of the journey is translated into English for the first time. There is also a 'necrology' of Goes in the Jesuit Annual Letter from

Goa, December 9, 1609 (*Bibliotheque Royale de Belgique*, Brussels, MS., 4156, pp. 182–186).

[17] *Relaçam*, V, p. 27. He took with him from India a list showing the dates of all the movable feasts down to the year 1620.

[18] See *Ruins of Desert Cathay*, 1912, II, p. 292.

[19] *Drei Newe Relationes*, 1611, pp. 166–170.

[20] Our only authority for this incident is Andrade's letter of August 15, 1626, mentioned below (Esteves Pereira, *O Descobrimento*, 1921, pp. 75–77).

[21] Wessels, op. cit., p. 45. A useful reprint of the book was published in 1921 at Coimbra by F. M. Esteves Pereira. Regarding the confused use of the term Cathay at the time see Wessels, pp. 71, 83–84, 125, 147 and 155–156. *J.A.S.B.*, XXI, 1925, pp. 62, 67 and 76.

[22] Wessels, p. 46 ; *J.A.S.B.*, VI, 1910, p. 458.

[23] One of these, an Indian Christian called Joseph, was alive and in vigorous health in Rome some forty years later, being then eighty-five years of age. He was brought to Rome by the missionary Roth in 1664 (Kircher, *China Illustrata*, p. 49 ; Wessels, pp. 59, 200), and accompanied Roth to Neuburg in Bavaria, where the Duke and Duchess of Pfalz Neuburg partook (timore deposito) of rice cooked by him after the Indian fashion. (*Rhay's Notes of* 1664.)

[24] Even Huc and Launay make the mistake ; and as Andrade went from Srīnagar to Tsaparang they place Tsaparang between Kashmīr and Ladāk. Huc, *Le Christianisme en Chine*, Paris, 1857, II, p. 279 ; Launay, *Histoire de la Mission du Thibet*, Paris, 1903, I, p. 23.

[25] Wessels, p. 50 ; *Lettere Annue d'Etiopia, Malabar, Bresil and Goa*, 1620–1624, Rome, 1627, p. 342, and the corresponding *Histoire*, Paris, 1628, p. 449.

[26] The question is carefully discussed by Wessels (pp. 56–62), who points out that Andrade makes no reference, as has been sometimes assumed, to the Mansarovar Lake. See also Wilford in *Asiatick Researches*, VIII, 1805, p. 324, and Sven Hedin, *Southern Tibet*, 1917, I, p. xxii.

[27] The sufferings of Andrade, a man of no great physique, in this journey are exemplified by the fact that owing to snow-blindness he was unable to read one word of his breviary for twenty-five days.

[28] Some details are given by Cunningham in *J.A.S.B.*, XIII, 1844, p. 231. The King of Gūge of Andrade's time possibly owed some sort of allegiance to the King of Ladāk. Sven Hedin, *Southern Tibet*, 1922, VII, p. 53.

[29] C. Cordier, *Bibliotheca Sinica*, p. 2899 *et seqq.* ; Sommervogel, I, p. 329 ; Esteves Pereira, *O Descobrimento do Tibet*, 1921, p. 40. A transcript of the letter was afterwards published in Franco's *Imagem da Virtude*, for Lisbon, at Coimbra in 1717.

[30] The route appears as a rule to have been by Srīnagar and the Māna Pass, but Hosten thinks that there are grounds for supposing that in 1626 the missionaries may have come by Chīnī and the Sutlej Valley. *J.A.S.B.*, XXI, 1925, p. 62.

[31] *J.A.S.B.*, XXI, 1925, pp. 59–61.

[32] See their letters of 1627, and *J.A.S.B.*, XXI, 1925 (Hosten), p. 68.

[33] *J.A.S.B.*, XXI, 1925 (Hosten), pp. 79–80. According to Desideri the Queen and her niece actually were baptized.

[34] *J.A.S.B.*, XXI, 1925 (Hosten), pp. 70–71.

[35] *J.A.S.B.*, XXI, 1925 (Hosten), pp. 53–55.

[36] A summary of the resemblances between Lamaism and Catholic ceremonial will be found in Sven Hedin, *Trans-Himalaya*, 1913, III, pp. 310–329.

[37] *China Illustrata*, 1667, p. 64 ; *La Chine Illustrée*, 1770, p. 88.

[38] Report of 1632 ; Wessels, p. 304.

[39] Esteves Pereira, *O Descobrimento*, 1921, p. 92 ; Sven Hedin, *Trans-Himalaya*, 1913, III, p. 307.

[40] As stated in note 14 to Chapter XIII, a printed copy of the Bible, which had almost certainly belonged to the Jesuits, was extant in Ladāk in 1822.

[41] See also *Bibliotheca Marsdeniana*, 1827, p. 306.

[42] *La Chine Illustrée*, by Kircher, 1670, p. 320.

[43] Letter of August 5, 1715 ; Wessels, p. 73.

[44] *La Chine Illustrée*, 1670, p. 88 ; *China Illustrata*, 1667, p. 64.

[45] Sven Hedin, *Southern Tibet*, 1917, I, p. 168, holds that Andrade never went anywhere beyond Tsaparang.

[46] Francke, *Tibet* (*Arch. Survey of India*, N.S., XXXVIII, Calcutta, 1914), I, p. 36, and (N.S.L. 1926) II, pp. 110 and 171 ; *Arch. Survey of India*, Report 1909–1910, p. 111 ; Wessels, op. cit., pp. 77–80 ; *Zeitschrift für Missionswissenschaft*, Berlin, XV (1925) ; *J.P.H.S.*, VII, 1919 (Mackworth Young), pp. 185–187. Francke's Spiti inscription runs : 'He who clears away all the apostacy and darkness at the great palace of Tsabarangrtse.' And the name of the king referred to was Khri-bkra-shis-grags-pa-lde. Francke conjectures that the King of Gūge was restored to his kingdom, but in the position of a vassal and of an upholder of Buddhism. An anonymous account of Tibet given in Vol. XXIV of the *Lettres Edifiantes* (1780) gives the name of Andrade's friend as Tsang-pa-han, and by a confusion of dates represents him as having been defeated and killed by an army from Koko Nor on the Chinese border.

[47] The route from Mandī to Sarhind is not clear. Azevedo talks of going through 'Mella' and 'Bayaora.'

[48] An engraving showing Andrade with the poisoned cup, receiving consolation from a vision of the Virgin, will be found in Tanner, *Societas Jesu . . . militans*, Prague, 1675, p. 372. His death is said to have been due to the rigour with which he supported the proceedings of the Inquisition in Goa. See Franco, *Imagem . . . Lisboa*, Coimbra, 1717, p. 416.

[49] As to the provenance of the portrait and other details see *J.A.S.B.*, XXI, 1925, pp. 92–93 ; and Esteves Pereira, *O Descobrimento do Tibet*, 1921, p. 137.

[50] Doubtless Āsaf Khān, the father of Mumtāz Mahal.

[51] In the winter months the wine for the Sacrament had to be heated before use—Andrade in Esteves Pereira, *O Descobrimento*, p. 91.

[52] *Relation*, Paris, 1651, p. 16.

[53] *J.P.H.S.*, II, 1913–1914 (Vogel), p. 147.

[54] Manucci, *Storia do Mogor*, I, pp. 215, 378–379.

[55] Bernoulli, *Description de l'Inde*, 1786, I, p. 148, and his *Beschreibung*, 1765, I, p. 105. The position of the church can no longer be identified, as the old town of Srīnagar was swept away by floods in 1894.

[56] *Hist. Gén. de l'Empire du Mogol*, 1705, p. 229.

[57] Maracci, Letter to Roth of June 16, 1650 ; Beccari, *Rerum Aethiopicarum Scriptores*, XIII, p. 348.

[58] Hazart, I, p. 278.

[59] Maracci, *Relation*, Paris, 1651, pp. 19–20.

[60] Letter of February 1, 1652, to the Provincial.

[61] Launay reports, on the strength of Capuchin documents, that the Tibetan Mission terminated in 1652, and the General of the Society in a letter of January 16, 1719, spoke of it as ending in 1650; but it is not clear whether they refer to Tsaparang or Srīnagar. Launay, *Histoire de la Mission du Thibet*, 1903, I, pp. 30 and 34.

[62] The existence of the inscription was reported by Yule in the *Asiatic Quarterly Review* for April 1888, pp. 321–322, and again by Hosten in some interesting articles published by him on April 1, 8 and 15, 1922, in *The Examiner*, Bombay, entitled 'Was George Strachan, the Oriental traveller, a Jesuit?' The book is now in the Tarradale Memorial Library in Scotland, founded by Yule's daughter. One issue of this translation was furnished with prints, but the Tarradale copy is unillustrated.

[63] Francke, *Tibet* (*Arch. Survey of India*, N.S., XXXVIII, Calcutta, 1914), I, p. 27.

[64] Schlagintweit, *Reisen in Indien*, Jena, 1872, III, p. 90.

[65] *J.P.H.S.*, VII, 1919, p. 198. Young's description of Tsaparang is full of interesting detail.

[66] The provinces of U and Tsang in which Shigatze and Lhāsa are situated.

[67] The published letters are of October 6, 1627, and June 17, 1628, which are printed in Appendices II and III of Wessels, *Early Jesuit Travellers in Central Asia*, 1924. Details of the unpublished letters and reports are given on p. 163, ditto. An extract from another letter is given in Azevedo's published letter of 1632 at p. 301, ditto.

[68] Wessels, p. 130.

[69] *Ib.*, p. 138.

[70] *Ib.*, p. 144.

[71] *Ib.*, pp. 150 and 331.

[72] *Ib.*, p. 148.

[73] *Ib.*, p. 158.

[74] *Ib.*, p. 155.

[75] *Ib.*, pp. 151 and 331.

[76] *Ib.*, p. 73.

[77] The Malabar Province was, moreover, 'muyto pobre' and the want of funds was much felt. F. de Qeyros, *Historia da Vida do Veneravel Irmão Pedro de Basto*, Lisbon, 1689, p. 222.

[78] Wessels, pp. 159 and 302.

[79] *Ib.*, pp. 159 and 302.

[80] De Castro, Letter of August 8, 1632; Wessels, p. 159.

[81] See Chapter VI. Esteves Pereira states (I do not know on what authority) that Cabral retired from Shigatze via Leh. *O Descobrimento do Tibet*, p 14.

[82] Wessels, p. 160.

[83] Ditto, p. 161.

[84] It was probably for the same reason that Busi, who in 1647 expected a transfer from Mogor to China, contemplated performing the journey by land. See his letter of November 12, 1647.

[85] The original documents relating to this journey are mentioned in Cordier, *Bibliographia Sinica*, p. 2903. A detailed study of the journey is given by Richard Tronnier in the *Zeitschrift der Gesellschaft für Erdkunde*, Berlin, 1904, No. 5, pp. 328 *seqq.*

[86] I adopt Blunt's reading, pp. 35, 36 of *List of Christian Tombs and Monuments in the United Provinces*, 1911. See also *Agra Diocesan Calendar*, 1907 (Felix), p. 219. In *The Examiner*, Bombay, April 28, 1923, pp. 168–169, an article entitled ' A valuable Inscription discovered at Agra ' (Heras) tells of the discovery on the terrace of the Agra convent of a duplicate tombstone which includes in the epitaph the words : ' Sancte vixit et sancte obiit.' The lower part of the tombstone is broken and it shows part of a Chinese inscription, provided doubtless by Grueber. A eulogy of D'Orville, written by Grueber at Rome in 1664, was published in Bosman's *Documents sur Albert Dorville*, Louvain, 1911, from copies in the Archives génerales du Royaume at Brussels.

[87] This Eulogium, dated January 30, 1670, is in the Munich State Archives (Jesuitica in genere, Fasc. 13, No. 215), and a copy supplied by Prof. Th. Zachariae to Hosten has been seen by me.

[88] See his letter in *Weltbott*, No. 35.

[89] The passage in the Eulogium runs as follows : ' Qua de causa etiam factum, quod cum singulari affectu et alacritate Missiones Tartaricas in Lotak, et Rotok, et Gernaqui regna, ad quae ex obedientia destinatus fuerat, adire solus voluerit, redire vero ex Europa in Indias ex voluntate admodum R. P. Generalis sine comite Caucasea juga difficillima pedestri itinere superare, ac per Tartariam desertam in vastissimum Sinarum regnum penetrare, laeto, resolutoque animo non tantum intenderit sed etiam eidem [*sic*] conatus immortuus fuerit.'

[90] In November 1677 the Catalogue of the Mogor Mission states that he was ' destinatus ad auspicandam missionem Napalensem.' Wessels, op. cit., p. 199.

[91] Puini, *Il Tibet*, 1904 (see note 93 below) ; Launay, *Histoire de la Mission du Tibet*, I, p. 32. The assignment of Tibet to the Capuchins is attributed by Wessels (p. 208) to the year 1702 and by Hosten to 1703.

[92] *Lett. Édifi.*, 1780, XII, pp. 430–445 ; *Weltbott*, No. 175. An English translation of the French was published in Markham's *Narrative, of the Mission of George Bogle to Tibet*, 1876, pp. 302–308, and a copy of this English translation was reproduced by Hosten in *The Examiners* Bombay, December 14, 1918.

[93] See ' Two letters of Fr. Ippolito Desideri,' in *The Examiner*, Bombay (Hosten), August 24, 1918 ; Puini, ' Il Tibet secondo la Relazione del Viaggio del P. Ippolito Desideri (1715–1721), in *Memorie della Società Geografica Italiana*, Rome, 1904, X, p. xlii ; Wessels, *Early Jesuit Travellers in Central Asia*, pp. 274–281. The last-named work gives photographic reproductions of two pages of the Tibetan Manuscripts and the opening page of the second book of the MS. of the ' Relation.'

[94] See also p. 181 above.

[95] Franco, *Imagem . . . Lisboa*, Coimbra, 1717, p. 417, seems to indicate that the route through Kashmīr was taken as being easier and safer, but the reference there is vague.

[96] Freyre was no enthusiast and appears later on to have left the Society. His object, when at Leh, was to return to India by the shortest and easiest route and he had contemplated going by Srīnagar in Garhwāl, but was deterred by the brigandage prevailing on this route. Puini, *Il Tibet*, 1904, p. 7.

[97] Desideri, Letter of August 5, 1715 ; Puini, *Il Tibet*, 1904, p. 32.

[98] He saw Lhāsa taken both by the Mongols and by the Chinese.

[99] Quando R.V. dedi licentiam se transferendi ad Regna Tibeti, assignatio haec Missionum Tibeti facta a Sacra Congregatione Capucinis nota mihi non erat ; imo a me fuit suppositum quod cum dicta Missio fuerit a nostris Patribus fundata et ab iis usque ad annum 1650, quo ob persecutionem fuerunt ejecti, culta, ab aliis non amplius fuerit reaperta.' Launay, *Histoire de la Mission du Thibet*, Paris, 1903, II, p. 378.

[100] Markham, *Narratives of the Mission of George Bogle to Tibet*, 1879, pp. lviii–lix ; Launay, *Histoire de la Mission du Thibet*, 1903, I, p. 34 ; Zacharia, *Bibliotheca Pistoriensis*, Turin, 1752, p. 186. The subsequent history of the Mission at Lhāsa and the correspondence regarding it between the Pope and the Dalai Lama contains much of great interest. The Mission terminated in 1745. Cf. Wolff, *Researches and Missionary Labours*, London, 1835, p. 310.

[101] *The Examiner*, Bombay, August 24, 1918.

MAPS TO ILLUSTRATE THE TIBETAN MISSIONS OF THE JESUITS

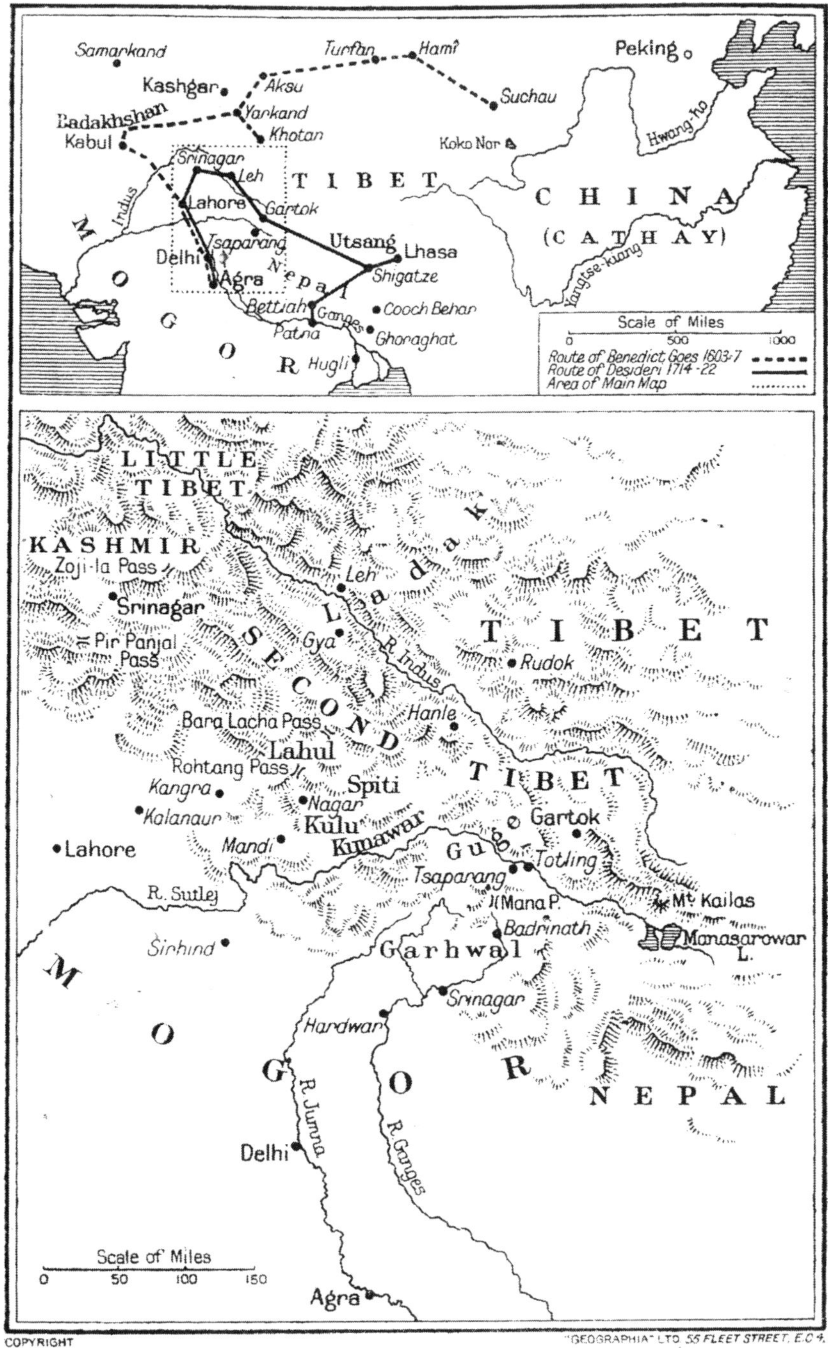

APPENDICES

I

TENTATIVE LISTS OF JESUIT LETTERS AND REPORTS FROM (*a*) MOGOR; (*b*) BENGAL, 1677–1685; AND (*c*) TSAPARANG

(A)

LIST OF LETTERS AND REPORTS RELATING TO THE MOGOR MISSION

1580–1605

1579. *November* 17: From Father Rudolf Aquaviva to his Uncle from Goa. An extract is given in Bartoli, *Missione* (Piacenza edition), p. 24.

Date unknown: From Father Rudolf Aquaviva to Laurence Petri. An extract is quoted at p. 80 of Father Goldie's *The First Christian Mission to the Great Mogul.*

1580. *July* 18: From Father Rudolf Aquaviva from Fatehpur to the General of the Society. The concluding paragraph is quoted on p. 59 of Bartoli's *Missione* (Piacenza edition), and p. 75 of Goldie's *The First Christian Mission to the Great Mogul.* A facsimile of the final part of the letter is given in Suau's *Les Bienheureux Martyrs de Salsette*, p. 108.

1580. *September* 10: From Father Rudolf Aquaviva to Father Nuñez Rodriguez, Rector at Goa. See Alegambe, *Mortes Illustres*, pp. 138–139; Bartoli, *Missione* (Piacenza edition), p. 131, and Goldie, *The First Christian Mission to the Great Mogul*, pp. 76–79. The letter is given in full by Goldie, the date ascribed to it being December 10, 1580. In Alegambe the date given is IV Id. Sept. 1580. See also *J.A.S.B.*, 1896, LXV, p. 51.

1581. *July* 28: From Father Rudolf Aquaviva to Father Michael Loretano at Rome. Quoted by Suau, *Les Bienheureux Martyrs de Salsette*, p. 114, and Goldie, *The First Christian Mission to the Great Mogul*, p. 88. See also *J.P.H.S.*, V, 1916 (Felix), p. 66.

1582. *April* 15 : From Father Rudolf Aquaviva from Fatehpur Sīkrī to his uncle, Claud Aquaviva, General of the Order. Quoted at p. 116 of Suau, *Les Bienheureux Martyrs de Salsette.* See also Bartoli, *Missione* (Piacenza edition), p. 48. An extract is given in *J.A.S.B.*, 1896, LXV, p. 55.

1582. *September* 27 : From Father Rudolf Aquaviva from Fatehpur Sīkrī to Father Ruy Vincente, Provincial at Goa. British Museum, Addl. MSS. (Marsden) 9854, fols. 1–3. A good copy of the letter is given in Goldie, *The First Christian Mission to the Great Mogul*, pp. 171–178, and a translation will be found on pp. 97–103 *ib.* and in *J.A.S.B.*, LXV, 1896, pp. 56–58. See also *J.P.H.S.*, V, 1916 (Felix), p. 68, where Goldie's translation is given in full. A copy of Goldie's transcript is given in Gracias *Una dona portugueza*, p. 189.

1582. *November* 26 : Report by Father Monserrate, written at Goa, in Portuguese, entitled *Relaçam do Equebar Rei dos Mogores.* In 1879–1880 three manuscript copies are known to have been in existence which have since disappeared (see Chapter VIII). A copy taken from a manuscript in the possession of the Society was published with an English translation by Hosten in *J.A.S.B.*, VIII, 1912, pp. 185–221. The substance of the report was reproduced in Italian in Peruschi's *Informatione* (1597), of which translations were published shortly after in French, German and Latin.

1590. *November :* From the Provincial at Goa to the General of the Order. An extract is given in Spitilli, *Ragguaglio* (1592), and subsequent translations of that book : and an extract in English will be found in *J.A.S.B.*, LXV, 1896, p. 62.

1591. *January* 6 : The work written by Father Monserrate at San'a in Arabia in Latin, entitled *Mongolicae Legationis Commentarius.* The MS. was discovered in 1909 in S. Paul's Cathedral, Calcutta, and published by Hosten in 1914. For details see Chapter VIII.

1591. *November :* From the Provincial at Goa to the General of the Order. An extract is given in Spitilli, *Ragguaglio* (1592), and subsequent translations of that book : and an extract in English will be found in *J.A.S.B.*, LXV, 1896, p. 63.

1593. *November* 12 : From Father Jerome Xavier from Goa to Father Francesco de Benavides. Published in *Chrono-Historia de la Compañia de Jesus en la Provincia de Toledo*, Madrid, 1710, Part II, p. 205. The original is there stated to be in the Jesuit archives at Alcala. Translated in English by Hosten in *J.A.S.B.*, XXIII, 1927, pp. 111–115. The letter has a few words about the failure of the Second Mission.

APPENDIX I

1594. *October* 28: From Father Jerome Xavier from Goa to Don Bernardo de Ezpeleta, his brother. In the archives of the Marquis del Ampara, and published on p. 464 of L.-J.-M. Cros' *Saint François de Xavier*, Toulouse, 1894: a fac-simile of the last page of the original being given on p. 465, *ib.* A translation in English is available in *J.A.S.B.*, XXIII, 1927, pp. 133–134 (Hosten). The date in Cros' book is given as October 18, but in the letter itself as October 28. It was written after Father Xavier had received orders to go to Mogor.

1595. *November*: From Father Nicolas Pimenta, Provincial at Goa, to the General of the Society: containing three enclosures: (*a*) from Father Pinheiro from Cambay; (*b*) from Father Jerome Xavier from Lahore, dated August 20, 1595; and (*c*) from Father Pinheiro from Lahore to Father J. Alvarez, Assistant of Portugal at Rome, dated September 3, 1595. Published in Peruschi, *Historica Relatio*, pp. 16–28. Extract translations are given in English in *J.A.S.B.*, LXV, 1896, pp. 65–70.

1596. *September* 8: From Father Jerome Xavier from Lahore. MS. in the possession of the Society. An extract in English is given in *Mem. A.S.B.*, V, 1916, p. 174.

1597. *September* 1: From Father Jerome Xavier from Kashmīr to Father Thomas de Ituren. Published in *Chrono-Historia de la Compañia de Jesus en la Provincia de Toledo*, Madrid, 1710, Part II, pp. 207–209, the original being there stated to be in the Archives of the Imperial College, Madrid. A translation by Hosten is in *J.A.S.B.*, XXIII, 1927, pp. 115–118.

1598. *July* 26: From Father Jerome Xavier from Lahore to the General of the Society. Published in *Oranus* (1601) and in the Mainz *Recentissima* (1601). Also in Hay and de Dieu (*Historia S. Petri*). An abstract in English is given in *J.A.S.B.*, 1888 (Beveridge), and more fully, with extracts, in *J.A.S.B.*, LXV, 1896, pp. 71–78.

1598. *August* 1: From Father Jerome Xavier from Lahore to the General of the Society. An unpublished letter in the possession of the Society, from which a sentence is quoted by Hosten in *J.A.S.B.*, X, 1914, p. 68.

1598. *August* 2: From Father Jerome Xavier from Lahore to Father Thomas de Ituren. Published in *Chrono-Historia de la Compañia de Jesus en la Provincia de Toledo*, Madrid, 1710, Part II, pp. 209–210, the original being there stated to be in the Archives of the Imperial College, Madrid. Translated by Hosten into English in *J.A.S.B.*, XXIII, 1927, pp. 118–120.

1598. *August* 13: From Father Jerome Xavier from Lahore. MS. in the possession of the Society. Mentioned by Hosten in *J.A.S.B.*, VI, 1910, p. 542.

1598. *August* 26: From Father Jerome Xavier from Lahore. MS.

in the possession of the Society. Mentioned by Hosten in *J.A.S.B.*, VI, 1910, p. 542.

1599. *After Whitsuntide:* From Father Pinheiro from Lahore. Published in *Oranus* (1601) and in the Mainz *Recentissima* (1601). Also in Hay and de Dieu (*Historia S. Petri*). Briefly abstracted in English in *J.A.S.B.*, LXV, 1896, p. 79.

1599. *December* 21 : From Father Nicolas Pimenta, Visitor, from Goa, to the General of the Society. Has quotations from Father Jerome Xavier's letters of July 26, 1598, and August 1, 1599, and also from a letter of Father Pinheiro. Published in *Nova Relatio*, Mainz, 1601 ; in the *Cartas que o P. Pimenta escreveo*, Lisbon, 1602 ; and in Hay, *De Rebus Japonicis*, 1605. The MS. of the Latin translation is in the possession of the Society (*Goan. Hist.*, 1539–1599, II, Goa, 32) and an English translation of the portion relating to Mogor is given by Hosten in *J.A.S.B.*, XXIII, 1927, pp. 57–65. The date is given by Sommervogel and in the Cartas as November 26, 1599, and the question of date is discussed in *J.A.S.B.*, XXIII, 1927, p. 57 (Hosten).

1600. *December* 1 : From Father Nicolas Pimenta, Provincial, from Goa to the General of the Society. Published in Italian at Venice and Rome in 1602 : but best known in the Latin translation, *Exemplum Epistolae*, Mainz, 1602. There are other copies published in Latin, French, German and Portuguese. Abstracted in English in *J.A.S.B.*, LXV, 1896, pp. 81–83, and a full translation (Hosten) available in the *Examiner*, Bombay, October 11, 1919, pp. 407–409, and in *J.A.S.B.*, XXIII, 1927, pp. 67–82. The letter includes extracts from letters of Father Corsi, dated May 12, 1600, and August 4, 1600.

1601. *December* 1 : From Father Nicolas Pimenta, Visitor, from Margão to the General of the Society. MS. in the possession of the Society. The original Portuguese and an English translation were published by Hosten in *J.A.S.B.*, XXIII, 1927, pp. 83–107.

1602. *August* 14 : From Father Jerome Xavier from Agra to Don Miguel de Ezpeleta, his nephew. MS. in the Archives of the Marquis del Ampara. Extract published on p. 466 of L.-J.-M. Cros' *Saint François de Xavier*, Toulouse, 1894, and translated into English by Hosten in *J.A.S.B.*, XXIII, 1927, p. 135.

1602. *September* 9 : From Father Pinheiro from Lahore. MS. in the possession of the Society. Mentioned by Hosten in *J.A.S.B.*, VI, 1910, p. 542.

1602. *December* 30 : From Brother Benedict Goes from Lahore to the Provincial at Goa. Referred to by Guerreiro in *Relacam*, II, Part II, p. 62.

1603. *February* 14 : From Bro. Goes to Father Jerome Xavier. This letter is referred to in Guerreiro's *Relaçam*, II, Part II, pp. 63–65, but its whereabouts is not known. As to the date see Payne, '*Jahangir and the Jesuits*,' p. 167.

1603. *September* 18: From Father Pinheiro from Lahore. MS. in the possession of the Society. Mentioned by Hosten in *J.A.S.B.*, VI, 1910, p. 542.

1603. *October* 21: From Father Jerome Xavier from Agra. MS. in the possession of the Society. Mentioned by Hosten in *J.A.S.B.*, VI, 1910, p. 542.

1604. *August* 10: From Father Corsi from Agra. MS. in the possession of the Society. Mentioned by Hosten in *J.A.S.B.*, VI, 1910, p. 542.

1604. *September* 6: From Father Jerome Xavier from Agra, to Father Manoel da Veiga, Provincial at Goa. Marsden MSS., British Museum, Addl. 9854, fol. 7–19. A very long letter in Portuguese; extracts in English are given in *J.A.S.B.*, LXV, 1896, pp. 89–98.

1605. *August* 12: From Father Pinheiro from Lahore to Father Manoel da Veiga, Provincial at Goa. Marsden MSS., British Museum, Addl. 9854, fols. 21–29 and 30–37. Fairly full extracts are given in *J.A.S.B.*, LXV, 1896, pp. 98–106.

1605–1627

1606. *September* 25: From Father Jerome Xavier from Lahore. In the Marsden MSS., British Museum, Addl. 9854, fol. 38–52. A long neatly-written report in Portuguese, the substance of which is given in Guerreiro, IV, pp. 148–157. See also under December 20, 1607, below. Extracts are given in Payne's *Jahangir and the Jesuits*, pp. 89–95.

1607. *June* 18: From Father Corsi from Lahore. MS. in the possession of the Society. Mentioned by Hosten in *J.A.S.B.*, VI, 1910, p. 542.

1607. *August* 28 (S. Augustine's day): From Father Jerome Xavier from Lahore. In the Marsden MSS., British Museum, Addl. 9854, fol. 53–63. A long Annual Report in Portuguese, the substance of which is given in Guerreiro, IV, pp. 157–162. See also under December 20, 1607, below. Extracts are given in Payne's *Jahangir and the Jesuits*, pp. 97–100.

1607. *September* 27: From Father Pinheiro. MS. in the possession of the Society. Mentioned by Hosten in *J.A.S.B.*, VI, 1910, p. 542.

1607. *December* 18: From Father Jerome Xavier from Lahore. MS. in the possession of the Society. Mentioned by Hosten in *J.A.S.B.*, VI, 1910, p. 542.

1607. *December* 20: From the Provincial from Goa. Published in *Drei Newe Relations* (1611), pp. 139–170. Incorporates abstracts of two reports from Mogor (i), pp. 139–159. Report of 1606 and (ii), pp. 159–170, Report of August 1607: viz.:—the letters of September 25, 1606, and August 28, 1607, mentioned above.

1607. *December* 21 : From Father Jerome Xavier from Lahore. MS. in the possession of the Society. Mentioned by Hosten in *J.A.S.B.*, VI, 1910, p. 542.

1608. *July* 30 : From Father Jerome Xavier from Fremona (?). MS. in the possession of the Society. Mentioned by Hosten in *J.A.S.B.*, VI, 1910, p. 542.

1608. *September* 24 : From Father Jerome Xavier from Agra. In the Marsden MSS., British Museum, Addl. 9854, fol. 64-75. A long letter in Portuguese, the substance of which is reproduced in Guerreiro, V, fol. 6a *et seqq.* Extracts are given in Payne's *Jahangir and the Jesuits*, pp. 101–109.

1609. *September* 14 : From Father Jerome Xavier from Agra to Father Thomas de Ituren. Reported in 1710 to be in the Archives of the Imperial College at Madrid. Published in *Chrono-Historia de la Compañia de Jesus en la Provincia de Toledo*, Part II, pp. 210–212, Madrid, 1710, and translated into English by Hosten in *J.A.S.B.*, XXIII, 1927, pp. 120-123.

1609. *October* 20 : From Father Jerome Xavier from Agra to Father Juan Ximenez de Occo. A short extract is given by Father Occo in a note of January 1, 1621, quoted on pp. 461–462 of L.-J.-M. Cros' *Sant François de Xavier*, Toulouse, 1894. See *J.A.S.B.*, XXIII, 1927, pp. 131–132.

1610. *September* 4 : From Father Jerome Xavier from Agra. MS. in the possession of the Society. Mentioned by Hosten in *J.A.S.B.*, VI, 1910, p. 542. Possibly the same as the undated letter from Xavier to the Provincial reproduced at pp. 14–33 of Zannetti's *Raguagli* of 1615.

1610. *September* 9 : From Father Pinheiro from Agra. Copy in *Bibliothèque Royale de Belgique*, Brussels, MS. 4156, pp. 217–230. Copies of this and other letters from the same library are in the possession of Father Hosten.

1610. *September* 15 : From Father Pinheiro from 'Talacoso.' Copy in *Bibliothèque Royale de Belgique*, Brussels, MS. 4156, pp. 230–231.

1610. *September* 2 (20?) : From Father Pinheiro from 'Sicungi' Copy in *Bibliothèque Royale de Belgique*, Brussels, MS. 4156, pp. 231–232.

1610. *October* 19 : From Father Jerome Xavier from Agra, MS. in *Bibliothèque Royale de Belgique*, Brussels, MS. 4156, pp. 232–233.

1611. *April* 11 : From Father Jerome Xavier from Agra to the General of the Society. Published in Italian in Zannetti's *Raguagli*, 1615, pp. 34–38.

1611. *July* 11 : From Father Antony Laubegeois from Coimbra to his Brethren in Belgium. *Bibliothèque Royale de Belgique*, Brussels, MS. 4156, pp. 177–179. Has two paragraphs on happenings in Mogor.

1611. *After July* 31 : From Father Jerome Xavier from Agra. A copy (not in Xavier's handwriting) is in the Marsden MSS., British Museum, Addl., No. 9854, fol. 162–171. The copy is imperfect, having lost the first page and the concluding portion of the letter. It refers to incidents which took place on S. Ignatius' Day, July 31.

1611. *September* 20 : From Father Jerome Xavier from Agra. MS. in the possession of the Society. Mentioned by Hosten in *J.A.S.B.*, VI, 1910, p. 542.

1612. *January* 23 : From Father Antony Laubegeois from Coimbra to the Provincial of the Gallo-Belgic Province. Contains extracts from an overland letter from Father Antony Figueredo, dated Goa, March 6, 1611. *Bibliothèque Royale de Belgique*, Brussels, MS. 4156, pp. 277–282.

1612. *October* 15 : From Father Jerome Xavier from Goa to Father Juan Ximenes de Occo. MS. in the Archives of the Marquis del Ampara. Published on p. 466 of L.-J.-M. Cros' *Saint François de Xavier*, Toulouse, 1894, and translated into English by Hosten in *J.A.S.B.*, XXIII, 1927, p. 135.

1612. *December* 25 : From Father João de Velasco. MS. in the possession of the Society (*Goana Hist.*, 1600–1624, Goa 33, fol. 388, V—389 R. Litt. Ann.) A part of the letter is quoted in English by Hosten in *Mem. A.S.B.*, V, 1916, p. 183.

1613. *September* 23 : From Father Jerome Xavier from Agra. MS. in Marsden MSS., British Museum, Addl. 9854, fol. 82–86.

1613. *September* 25 : From Father Jerome Xavier from Agra. MS. in the possession of the Society. Mentioned by Hosten in *J.A.S.B.*, VI, 1910, p. 542.

1613. *December* 24 : Annual Letter by Father Pinheiro. MS. in the possession of the Society. Mentioned by Hosten in *J.A S.B.*, VI, 1910, p. 542.

1615. *February* 26 : From Father Corsi from Ājmīr to the General of the Society. A MS. giving a contemporary translation into English is in British Museum, Cottonian MSS., Titus B., VIII, 231 (221), and this translation was published by Hosten in *The Examiner*, Bombay, August 9, 1919.

1615. *March* 6 : From Father Corsi from Ājmīr to Rafael Corsi, the writer's father at Florence. A MS. giving a contemporary translation into English is in British Museum, Cottonian MSS., Titus B., VIII, 233 (223), and this translation was published by Hosten in *The Examiner*, Bombay, August 16, 1919.

1615. *April* 9 : From Father Antony Machado from Agra to the General of the Society. The original MS. in Portuguese and a contemporary translation into English are in British Museum, Cottonian MSS., Titus B., VII, 117 (118), and Vespasian, F. XII, 141 respectively. The latter was published by Hosten in *The Examiner*, Bombay, August 16, 1919.

1615. *April* 10: From Father Joseph de Castro from Agra. The original Italian MS. and a contemporary translation into English are in British Museum, Cottonian MSS., Titus B., VII, 111 (112), and Vespasian, F. XII, 143 respectively. The latter was published by Hosten in *The Examiner*, Bombay, August 23, 1919.

1615. *April* 10: From Father Joseph de Castro from Agra to Brother Joseph Baudo at Milan. The original Italian MS. and a contemporary translation into English are in British Museum, Cottonian MSS., Titus B., VII, 132 and VIII, 249 (239). The latter was published by Hosten in *The Examiner*, Bombay, August 23, 1919.

1615. *December* 4: From Father Jerome Xavier from Chaul to Father Thomas de Ituren. Reported in 1710 to be in the Archives of the Imperial College at Madrid. Published in *Chrono-Historia de la Compañia de Jesus en la Provincia de Toledo*, Part II, pp. 212–214, Madrid, 1710, and translated into English by Hosten in *J.A.S.B.*, XXIII, 1927, pp. 123–126.

1616. *October* 18: From Father Corsi from the Emperor's Court and Camp. MS. in the possession of the Society. Mentioned by Hosten in *J.A.S.B.*, VI, 1910, p. 542.

1617. *January* 5: From Father Jerome Xavier from Goa to Father Thomas de Ituren. Reported in 1710 to be in the Archives of the Imperial College, Madrid. Published in *Chrono-Historia de la Compañia de Jesus en la Provincia de Toledo*, Part II, p. 214, Madrid, 1710; and translated into English by Hosten in *J.A.S.B.*, XXIII, 1927, pp. 127–128.

1619. *February* 1: From Father Gasparo Luis from Goa to the General of the Society. In *Lettere Annue del Giapone negli anni, 1615–1619*, Naples, 1621. The portions relating to Mogor are translated by Hosten in *The Examiner*, Bombay, February 3, 1912.

1619. *April* 3: From Father Corsi from Fatehpur. MS. in the possession of the Society. Mentioned by Hosten in *J.A.S.B.*, VI, 1910, p. 542, and *Mem. A.S.B.*. V, 1916, p. 136.

1619. *October* 28: From Father Corsi from Agra to the Provincial at Goa. *Carta Annua da Missao do Mogol.* In Marsden MSS., British Museum, Addl. 9854, fol. 87–91. The gist of the letter is reproduced in the Goa letter of February 1, 1620, published at Naples in 1621 in *Lettere Annue del Giapone etc. negli anni, 1615–1619*; and translated by Hosten in *The Examiner*, Bombay, February 10 and 17, 1912. The Latin version is to be found in *Archives générales du Royaume de Belgique*, Brussels, *Archives Jésuitiques*, Province Flandro-Belgique, Registre, cahier relié, No. 1427, fol. 239–241.

1620. From Father Gironimo Maiorica from Goa. In *Lettere Annue d'Étiopia*, etc., 1620–1624, Rome, 1627, pp. 137–176, and *Histoire de ce qui s'est passé en Éthiopie*, etc., 1620–1624, Paris, 1628, pp. 171–216. The portions relating to Mogor were translated by Hosten in *The Examiner*, Bombay, March 9, 1912. The Latin version is to be found in *Archives générales du Royaume de Belgique*, Brussels, *Archives Jésuitiques*, Province Flandro-Belgique, Registre, cahier relié, No. 1427, fol. 281–282.

1620. *September* 28: From Father Corsi from Kashmīr. MS. in the possession of the Society. Mentioned by Hosten in *J.A.S.B.*, VI, 1910, p. 542.

1620. *September* 27: From Father I. Pereira from Cochin (*Literae Annuae*). Contains letter of December 20, 1620, from Father Simon Figueredo. See O'Malley's *Patna Gazetteer*, 1924, p. 73, and *Histoire de ce qui s'est passé en Éthiopie*, etc. (1628), pp. 108–118. A long extract is translated by Father Besse, S.J., in the *Catholic Herald of India*, August 22, 1906 (Hosten), p. 804.

1621. *December* 2: From Father Gironimo Maiorica from Goa. In *Lettere Annue d'Ethiopia*, etc., 1620–1624, Rome, 1627, pp. 177–242, and *Histoire de ce qui s'est passé en Éthiopie*, etc., 1620–1624, Paris, 1628, pp. 217–303. The portions relating to Mogor are translated by Hosten in *The Examiner*, Bombay, March 16, 1912.

1623. *August* 14: From Father Antonio de Andrade from Agra. In Marsden MSS., British Museum, Addl. 9854, fol. 92–107. *Annua do Mogor*.

1623. *December* 11: From Father Juan de Sylva from Goa. In *Lettere Annue d'Etiopia*, etc., 1620–1624, Rome, 1627, pp. 243–282, and *Histoire de ce qui s'est passé en Éthiopie*, etc., 1620–1624, Paris, 1628, pp. 304–359. The portions relating to Mogor are translated by Hosten in *The Examiner*, Bombay, March 30, 1912.

1624. *September* 17: From Father Corsi from Sāmbhar to Father Virgilio Cepario. MS. in the possession of the Society. Mentioned by Hosten in *J.A.S.B.*, VI, 1910, p. 542.

1624. *November* 24: From Father Joseph de Castro from Agra to Brother Joseph Baudo in Turin. MS. in the possession of the Society. Mentioned by Hosten in footnote 11 to letter 5 in *The Examiner*, Bombay, August 23, 1919. (Possibly the letter quoted in *Histoire de ce qui s'est passé en Éthiopie*, etc., Paris, 1628, pp. 442–449.)

1624. *December* 15: From Father Sebastiano Barreto, from Goa. In *Lettere Annue d'Etiopia*, etc., 1620–1624, Rome, 1627, pp. 283–343, and *Histoire de ce qui s'est passé en Éthiopie*, etc., 1620–1624, Paris, 1628, pp. 360–451. The portions relating to

Mogor are translated by Hosten in *The Examiner*, Bombay, April 6, 1912.

1626. *August* 24 : From Father Joseph de Castro from the Kingdom of Kābul to Brother Joseph Baudo in Turin. MS. in the possession of the Society. Published in Italian and in an English translation by Hosten in *J.A.S.B.*, XXIII, 1927, pp. 144–149. (Three other letters of this year from Father de Castro are mentioned in *J.A.S.B.*, XXIII, 1927, p. 141, but they seem to have disappeared.)

1626. *October* 15 : From Father Corsi from Dinduāna (in the Jodhpur State, 40 miles north-west of Sāmbhar)—' terra do Governo do Mirza '—to the Assistant of Portugal, Rome. MS. in the possession of the Society. Mentioned by Hosten in *J.A.S.B.*, VI, 1910, p. 542, and XXI, 1925, p. 52.

1627. *April* 3 : From Father Corsi from Ājmīr to the Provincial at Goa. In the Marsden MSS., British Museum, Addl. 9854, fol. 108–115. The main letter is from Agra dated January 22, 1627, but is followed by a postscript forwarding it from Ājmīr on April 3 after it had been seen by the new Superior, Father Leam.

1627. *July* 26 : From Father Joseph de Castro from the Kingdom of Kashmīr to Father Nuño Mascarenas, Assistant of Portugal, at Rome. MS. in the possession of the Society. Briefly abstracted by Hosten in *J.A.S.B.*, XXI, 1925, p. 56. Published by him in Portuguese and in an English translation in *J.A.S.B.*, XXIII, 1927, pp. 149–158.

1627. *August* 15 : From Father Joseph de Castro from the Kingdom of Kashmīr to Father Claudio Septalio at Como. MS. in the possession of the Society. Mentioned by Hosten in *J.A.S.B.*, XXI, 1925, p. 56. Published by him in Italian and in an English translation in *J.A.S.B.*, XXIII, 1927, pp. 158–166.

1627. *September* 8 : From Father Corsi from Ājmīr to the General of the Society. MS. in the possession of the Society. Mentioned by Hosten in *J.A.S.B.*, XXI, 1925, p. 56.

1627. (*Probably*) : An account of two periods in Jahāngīr's reign, (i) the events of 1620–1623 and (ii) the *coup d'état* of 1626. Apparently attributed to Father de Souza. Both accounts are incomplete and, by some mistake in copying, one runs into the other. Marsden MSS., British Museum, Addl. 9855, fol. 46–51 ; unsigned and undated.

1627–1658

1628. *May :* From Father Corsi from Agra to the General of the Society. MS. in possession of the Society. (*Goana Hist.*, 1600–1624, Goa, 33, fol. 671R–678, V.) A Portuguese report which commences : *Da Origem da Fundação do Collegio incoato na Cidade de Agra feita por Mirza Zulcarné, e aceitada polo N.R.P. Geral Mutio Vitellesqi o anno* 1621, which is translated by Hosten in *Mem. A.S.B.*, V, 1916, pp. 132–141.

1628. *June* 13 : An unsigned document in Father Corsi's handwriting. In the Marsden MSS., British Museum, Addl. No. 9854, fol. 116–129. Is a report by Fathers Corsi and de Payva and de Castro on the conduct of the Superior, Father Leam.

1628. *October* 6 : From Father Leam from Agra to the Provincial at Goa. A copy in Father Corsi's handwriting is in Marsden MSS., British Museum, Addl. 9854, fol. 116–132. See Hosten in *J.A.S.B.*, XXI, 1925, pp. 56–57.

1631. *November* 20 : From Father Joseph de Castro from the Kingdom of Bengala, probably Patna. MS. in the possession of the Society. Mentioned by Hosten in *J.A.S.B.*, VI, 1910, pp. 531 and 542, and XXIII, 1927, p. 142 ; by Wessels, p. 93 ; and by Josson, *La mission du Bengale Occidental*, 1921, I, p. 70.

1632. *Early month :* From Father Azevedo from Agra. MS. in the possession of the Society. Mentioned by Hosten in *Mem. A.S.B.*, V, 1916, p. 143.

1632. *August* 8 : From Father Joseph de Castro from Mogol to Brother Joseph Baudo in Turin. Alluded to by Wessels, pp. 81 and 93, and by Hosten in *J.A.S.B.*, VI, 1910, pp. 531 and 542, and XXIII, 1927, p. 142 ; also in footnote 11 to letter 5 in *The Examiner*, Bombay, August 23, 1919. Wessels, p. 159, quotes a sentence regarding the Tibet Mission.

1632. *August* 28 : From Father Joseph de Castro from Bengala. MS. in the possession of the Society. Mentioned by Hosten in *J.A.S.B.*, VI, 1910, p. 542, and XXIII, 1927, p. 142 ; by Wessels, pp. 81 and 93 ; and by Josson, *La Mission du Bengale Occidental*, p. 70.

1632. *November* 24 : From Father Joseph de Castro from Agra to the General. MS. in the possession of the Society. Mentioned by Hosten in *J.A.S.B.*, VI, 1910, pp. 531 and 542, and XXIII, 1927, p. 142.

1633. *February* 6 : From Father Joseph de Castro from Agra. MS. in the possession of the Society. Mentioned by Hosten in *J.A.S.B.*, VI, 1910, pp. 531 and 542, and XXIII, 1927, p. 142 ; also in *Mem. A.S.B.*, V, 1916, p. 143 ; and by Wessels, p. 93.

1633. *September* 17 : From Father Joseph de Castro from Agra. MS. in the possession of the Society. Mentioned by Hosten in *J.A.S.B.*, VI, 1910, p. 542.

1633. *October* 5 : From Father Corsi from Agra to the General of the Society. MS. in the possession of the Society. Mentioned by Hosten in *Mem. A.S.B.*, V, 1916, p. 143, and *J.A.S.B.*, VI, 1910, pp. 458, 531 and 542. See also *J.P.H.S.*, V, 1916 (Felix), p. 25, and *Peter Mundy* (Hakl. Soc ; Temple), II, p. 380.

1633. *October* 8: From Father Joseph de Castro from Agra to Father Nuño Mascarenas, Assistant of Portugal, Rome. MS. in the possession of the Society. Mentioned by Hosten in *J.A.S.B.*, VI, 1910, pp. 531 and 542, and XXIII, 1927, p. 142; and *Mem. A.S.B.*, V, 1916, p. 144. Also by Tanner, *Societas Jesu . . . militans* (Prague, 1675), p. 341, where a long quotation from the letter is given. The letter is referred to in *Peter Mundy* (Hakl. Soc; Temple), II, p. 380.

1633. *October* 15: From Father Joseph de Castro. Stated—erroneously—in note on p. 25, *J.P.H.S.*, V, 1916, to be in the Marsden MSS., British Museum.

1633. *October* 15: From Father Francesco Morando from Agra. MS. in the possession of the Society. Mentioned by Hosten in *J.A.S.B.*, VI, 1910, pp. 531 and 542; and by Felix in *J.P.H.S.*, V, 1916, p. 25.

1633. *November* 14: From Father John Cabral. MS. in the possession of the Society. His account of the siege of Hūglī. A translation into English by L. Besse, was published by Hosten in the *Catholic Herald of India*, Calcutta, on January 30, etc., 1918.

1635. *September* 5: From Father Joseph de Castro from Agra. MS. in the possession of the Society. Mentioned by Hosten in *J.A.S.B.*, XXIII, 1927, p. 142. He has shown me a transcript in MS. of an Italian copy of this letter.

1636. *September* 17: From Father Joseph de Castro from Agra. MS. in the possession of the Society. Mentioned by Hosten in *J.A.S.B.*, XXIII, 1927, p. 142, and by Wessels, p. 93. The former has let me see a MS. transcript of this letter.

1637. *April* 16: From Father Joseph de Castro from Agra. MS. in the possession of the Society. Mentioned by Hosten in *J.A.S.B.*, VI, 1910, p. 542, and XXIII, 1927, p. 142, and by Wessels, p. 93. The former has let me see a MS. transcript of this letter.

1637. *October* 7: From Father Morando from Lahore. An extract is given by Felix in *J.P.H.S.*, V, 1916, p. 94.

1637. *October* 29: From Father Joseph de Castro from Agra. MS. in the possession of the Society. Mentioned by Hosten in *J.A.S.B.*, VI, 1910, p. 542, and XXIII, 1927, p. 142.

1637. An unpublished letter from Father de Castro of this year is alluded to by Blunt, in *Christian Tombs and Monuments in the United Provinces*, 1911, p. 39.

1638. From Father Morando from Agra to the Provincial at Goa. An extract is given by Felix in *J.P.H.S.*, V, 1916, p. 95.

1638. *August* 20: From Father Joseph de Castro from Agra. MS. in the possession of the Society. Mentioned by Hosten in *J.A.S.B.*, VI, 1910, p. 542, and XXIII, 1927, p. 142, and by Wessels, p. 93.

1638. *September* 15: From Father Morando from Agra to Father Nuño Mascarenas, Rome. MS. in the possession of the Society.

1640. *September* 1: From Father Joseph de Castro from Agra to the General of the Society. MS. in the possession of the Society. Mentioned by Hosten in *Mem. A.S.B.*, V, 1916, p. 146, and in *J.A.S.B.*, VI, 1910, p. 542, and XXIII, 1927, p. 142, and by Wessels, p. 93.

1640. *October* 3: From Father Joseph de Castro from Agra. MS. in the possession of the Society. Mentioned by Hosten in *J.A.S.B.*, VI, 1910, p. 542, and XXIII, 1927, p. 142, and by Wessels, p. 93.

1641. *August* 3: From Father Joseph de Castro from Agra. MS. in the possession of the Society. Mentioned by Hosten in *J.A.S.B.*, XXIII, 1927, p. 142.

1641. *August* 15: From Father Joseph de Castro from Agra. MS. in the possession of the Society. Mentioned by Hosten in *J.A.S.B.*, VI, 1910, p. 542.

1641. *August* 25: From Father Joseph de Castro from Agra. MS. in the possession of the Society. Mentioned by Hosten in *J.A.S.B.*, VI, 1910, p. 542, and XXIII, 1927, p. 142; by Wessels, p. 93; by Felix in *J.P.H.S.*, V, 1916, p. 95; and by Josson, *La Mission du Bengale Occidental*, I, p. 82.

1642. *January* 1: From Father Joseph de Castro from Agra to the General of the Order. MS. in the possession of the Society. Mentioned by Hosten in *Mem. A.S.B.*, V, 1916, p. 146; and in *J.A.S.B.*, VI, 1910, p. 542, and XXIII, 1927, p. 142, and by Wessels, p. 93. An extract is given by Felix in *J.P.H.S.*, V, 1916, p. 95.

1645. *July* 20: From Father Joseph de Castro from Sāmbhar. MS. in the possession of the Society. Mentioned by Hosten in *Mem. A.S.B.*, V, 1916, p. 146.

1647. *November* 12: From Father Busi from Goa to Father J. B. Engelgrave, S.J., Provincial of the Gallo-Belgian Province. The autograph MS. is in the *Archives du Royaume de Belgique*, Brussels, *Archives Jésuitiques*, Province Flandro-Belgique, Registre, cahier relié, No. 872–915, fol. 147. Announces his impending departure for Mogor.

1649. *September* 15: From Father A. Ceschi from Agra to his parents and friends. Published in *Estratto e Registro di lettere spirituali . . . del P. Antonio Ceschi* (Trent, *circa* 1683). An abstract by Morizzo, translated by Hosten, is given in *The Examiner*, Bombay, August 11, 1917. Very little in this report relates to Mogor.

1649. A Latin report (incomplete) in the handwriting of Father Ceschi, in Marsden MSS., British Museum, Addl. 9854, fol. 133–136; also two copies (complete) in the possession of the Society. It is entitled *Annuae Literae Collegii Agrensis et Missionis Mogorensis collectae ex parte anni* 1648 *et ex parte anni* 1649. An English translation from the Latin of one of the Society's copies by Father L. De Vos was published by Hosten in the *Journal of Indian History*, I, 1922.

1649. *September* 20 : From Father Busi from Agra to Father J. B. Engelgrave, S.J., Provincial of the Flandro-Belgian Province, Antwerp. The autograph MS. is in the *Archives du Royaume de Belgique*, Brussels, *Archives Jésuitiques*, Province Flandro-Belgique, Registre, cahier relié, No. 873–915, fol. 148–151. This letter is a repetition with small changes of parts of the Annual Report mentioned above.

1650. *June* 16 : From Father Maracci from Rome to Father Roth. Printed in Beccari, *Rerum Aethiopicarum Scriptores*, XII, pp. 347–349.

1650. Annual Report for Mogor. In Portuguese. Marsden MSS., British Museum, Addl. 9855, fol. 52–76. An abstract of the contents is given in Hazart, I, p. 277. The Latin version of the first part of the Report (pp. 52–60 in Marsden MSS.) is in the possession of the Society and has been copied by Hosten.

1650. *Annuae Literae*, 1650 ; contains a section (pp. 339–350) about Mogor. In Latin : embodying, in different language, part of the information given in the above. A copy from a printed volume of the *Literae* is in the possession of Father Hosten, together with a translation by Father L. De Vos.

1650. *November* 1 : From Father Ceschi to Father Maracci from Agra. In the possession of the Society.

1650. From Father Ceschi to his family from 'the Great Mogol.' Published in '*Estratto e Registro di lettere spirituali . . . del P. Antonio Ceschi*' (Trent, *circa* 1683). An extract by Morizzo, translated by Hosten, is in *The Examiner*, Bombay, September 1, 1917.

1651. *September* 5 : From Father Ceschi from Agra to his parents. Published in *Estratto e Registro di lettere spirituali . . . del P. Antonio Ceschi* (Trent, *circa* 1683). An extract by Morizzo, translated by Hosten, is given in *The Examiner*, Bombay, September 8, 1917.

1651. *December* 17 : From Father Busi from Lahore to the General of the Society, referred to by Felix in *J.P.H.S.*, V, 1916, p. 97.

1652. *January* 20 : From Father Botelho from Agra to Father Bento Ferreira in Goa. In Marsden MSS., British Museum, Addl. 9854, fol. 137–140. Referred to by Felix in *J.P.H.S.*, V, 1916, p. 97.

1652. *January* 28 : From Father Ceschi from Agra. Contains a letter from Mīrzā Zū'lqarnain to the Pope. Referred to by Felix in *J.P.H.S.*, V, 1916, p. 96.

1652. *February* 1 : From Father Botelho from Agra to the Provincial. In Marsden MSS., British Museum, Addl. 9854, fol. 141–142.

1652. *February* 1 : From Father Botelho from Agra to Father Bento in Goa. In Marsden MSS., British Museum, Addl. 9854, fol. 143–144.

1652. *February* 19 : From Father Ceschi from Agra to Father Joseph Fürstein and the writer's parents. Published in *Estratto e Registro di lettere spirituali . . . del Padre Antonio Ceschi* (Trent, *circa* 1683). An extract by Morizzo, translated by Hosten, is given in *The Examiner*, Bombay, September 8, 1917.

1653. *February* 10 : From Father Ceschi from Agra to his family. Published in *Estratto e Registro di lettere spirituali . . . del Padre Antonio Ceschi* (Trent, *circa* 1683). A short extract by Morizzo, translated by Hosten, is given in *The Examiner*, Bombay, September 8, 1917.

1653. *September* 1 : From Father Ceschi from Agra to his family. Published in *Estratto e Registro di lettere spirituali . . . del Padre Antonio Ceschi* (Trent, *circa* 1683). An extract by Morizzo, translated by Hosten, is given in *The Examiner*, Bombay, September 8, 1917.

1654. *August* 24 : From Father Ceschi from Delhi to the Rector of the House at Trent. Published in *Estratto e Registro di lettere spirituali . . . del Padre Antonio Ceschi* (Trent, *circa* 1683). Extracts by Morizzo, translated from the Latin by Hosten, are given in *The Examiner*, Bombay, September 8, 1917. See also Felix in *J.P.H.S.*, V, 1916, p. 98.

1658–1803

1664. From Father Roth from Rome to a Jesuit priest in Germany. Published in *Weltbott*, No. 35. A letter to encourage recruits for the East, dating from 'shortly before the Battle of S. Gothard.' (August 1, 1664.)

1664. Notes by Father Theodore Rhay, S.J., a verbal narrative given by Father Roth to the Duke of Pfalz Neuburg. In the *Bibliothèque de Bourgogne*, Brussels ; N 6838 ||29 for 145.

1668. From Father Manoel de Valle. *Carta annua da Missão de Mogol*, 1668. In Marsden MSS., British Museum, Addl. 9855, fol. 77–82.

1670. *January* 18 : From Father Botelho. A beautifully written MS. (pp. 1–16 in Latin and pp. 17–45 in Portuguese) in Marsden MSS., British Museum, Addl. 9855, fol. 1–45 ; comprising (*a*) a report on the state of the Mogul Empire during Botelho's ministry in Agra 1648–1654, *Summa memorandarum rerum in Mogor*, and (*b*) a note on Christianity in Mogor, *De Christiana apud Mogorem Religione*. An abstract by Beveridge is given at pp. 453–460 of *J.A.S.B.*, VI, 1910, and a translation of (*b*) was published by Hosten in *Mem. A.S.B.*, V, 1916, pp. 149–165. The Report was known to the scholar (Wilford ?) who wrote marginal comments on Monserrate's Commentarius (*Mem. A.S.B.*, III, 1914, p. 529). A note by J. B. Van Meurs, S.J.

(*ib.*, p. 530), says that Botelho wrote his *De Moribus et natura religionis Mogorensis* when he was Provincial at Goa in 1670. There is a copy of the Latin text of both parts of the Report in the possession of the Society: and the date (VIII Kal, February 1670) is given in this copy. The Latin is an abbreviation of the first part of the Portuguese Report, but contains variations.

1674. *June* 26: From Father Gregorio Roiz from Agra to the Provincial at Goa. In Marsden MSS., British Museum, Addl. 9855, fol. 119–120.

1675. *A Relation of the Mogor Mission*, 1666–1675; Annua Carta for 1675. In Marsden MSS., British Museum, Addl. 9854, 145–148.

1675. *July* 5: From Father Gregorio Roiz from Mogor to the Provincial at Goa. In Marsden MSS., British Museum, Addl. 9855, fol. 121–122.

1676. *February* 29: From Father Gregorio Roiz from Mogor to Father Bento at Goa. In Marsden MSS., British Museum, Addl. 9855, fol. 123–124.

1677. *December* 12: From Father John Leytam from Agra. In Marsden MSS., British Museum, Addl. 9855, fol. 125–126. Docketed 'Appontamentos da Missão de Mogol, p[a] a Carta Annua.' The MS. contains the 'appontamentos' or Notes on a case of edification, but not the letter of December 12, 1667, with which they were forwarded.

1678. *December* 27: From Father José Freyre from Goa to the General of the Society. In Marsden MSS., British Museum, Addl. 9855, fol. 83–103. *Carta Annua da Missão do Imperio do Gran Mogol*, 1670–1678—contains an account, dated Agra, August 2, 1678, and sent by Antonio de Magelhaens to Fernando de Queyros, Provincial at Goa, of the Mission in Bengal: a translation of fol. 96–101 including this account is given by Hosten at pp. 615 *et seqq.* of the *Catholic Herald of India*, Calcutta, September 12, 1917. A copy of this Carta Annua was owned by Mr. H. Tolbort and afterwards by Father Goldie (*J.A.S.B.*, VI, 1910, p. 449), and a copy (possibly the same) has appeared in booksellers' catalogues. (See Maggs, *Bib. Asiatica*, 455, 1924, No. 1242.) The Carta was seen by Mr. Irvine, who quotes information from it in Manucci, IV, 200 note.

1681. *February* 28: From Father Magalhaens from Agra. In Marsden MSS., British Museum, Addl. 9854, fol. 149–150. Two notes on the Mission accounts.

1681. *March* 20: From Father de Faria to Father Magalhaens from Chapra, Patna. In Marsden MSS., British Museum, Addl. 9855, fol. 135 (*re* Nāgpur Mission).

1683. *September* 8 *and* 15: From Father J. Leitam to Father de Faria from Patna. In Marsden MSS., British Museum, Addl. 9855, fols. 145–148 (*re* Nāgpur Mission).

1684. *July* 16: From Father J. Leytam from Agra. In Marsden MSS., British Museum, Addl. 9855, fol. 157.

1684. *July* 20: From Father J. Leytam from Agra to Provincial at Goa. In Marsden MSS., British Museum, Addl. 9855, fol. 151. Merely forwards a translation of a petition against the jazia tax.

1686. *September* 7: From Father Ignatio Gomez from Agra to Provincial at Goa. In Marsden MSS., British Museum, Addl. 9854, fol. 151–158. Is Carta Annua of the Mogor Mission.

1693. Carta Annua of the Mogor Mission, 1688–1693, unsigned. In Marsden MSS., British Museum, Addl. 9854, fol. 159–172. In the middle (fol. 161) is an undated note in Italian.

1701. *January* 28: From Father Diusse from Surat to the Director of French Jesuit Missions in India and China. Published in *Lettres Édifiantes et Curieuses* (1780), X, p. 231; and Stöcklein's *Weltbott*, No. 74.

1706. From Father Francis Borgia Koch from Goa to Father Mordax in Vienna. Published in Stöcklein, *Weltbott*, No. 117. As Franco gives 1709 as the date of Koch's departure from Lisbon for India, Hosten suggests that the date of this letter may be wrongly recorded by Stöcklein (*Jesuit Missionaries in N. India*, 1907, p. 35).

1714. *August* 21: From Father Desideri from Agra to Father Piccolomini. The original is in Stonyhurst College Library. Published by Wessels in *Atti e Memorie del Convegno di Geografi-Orientalisti i Macerata*, 1911. A translation was published by Hosten in *The Examiner*, Bombay, October 5, 1918.

1714. *September* 20. From Father Desideri from Delhi to the General of the Society. MS. in the possession of the Society.

1733. From Father Calmette. In *Lettres Édifiantes et Curieuses* (1780), XIII, p. 390. On the Mission to Jaipur.

1735. From Father Emmanuel Figueredo from Mogor to Queen Anna Maria of Portugal. In Stöcklein, *Weltbott*, No. 595. Part is translated by Hosten in *Mem. A.S.B.*, V, 1916, p. 169.

1738. *March*: From Father Strobl, said by Sommervogel to be in Stöcklein's *Weltbott*, No. 806.

1740. *February* 10: From Father Saignes from Chandernagore to Madame Hyacinthe of Sauveterre. Published in *Lettres Édifiantes et Curieuses* (1780), IV, p. 230; and Stöcklein's *Weltbott*, No. 631. Has a passing reference to the Mission in Delhi.

1740. *October*: From Father Strobl, said by Sommervogel to be in Stöcklein's *Weltbott*, No. 807.

1742. *October* 6: From Father Strobl from Jaipur to his brother. Stöcklein, *Weltbott*, No. 643.

1743. *October* 18: From Father Strobl from Jaipur to his brother. Stöcklein, *Weltbott*, No. 644.

1743. *October* 13: From Father Strobl from Jaipur to Father Leonard Tschiderer, S.J., in Rome; Stöcklein, *Weltbott*, No. 645. Described in *Weltbott* as two letters combined in one.

1744. *October* 13: From Father Strobl from Jaipur to Queen Anna Maria of Portugal: Stöcklein's *Weltbott*, No. 646. The original is said to have been in Latin.

1746. *October* 27: From Father Strobl from Delhi to Father Joseph Ritter, Confessor of Queen Anna Maria of Portugal. Stöcklein, *Weltbott*, No. 647.

1747. *October* 26: From Father Strobl from Delhi to Queen Anna Maria of Portugal. Stöcklein, *Weltbott*, No. 648. Contains a translation of Akbar's letter of 1582.

1748. *September* 26: From Father Tieffenthaler to Pope Benedict XIV from Narwar. *Archivium Propagandae, Indie Orientali e Cina dal* 1746 *al* 1748. Not published. Copy with Father Hosten.

1748. *October* 5: From Father Strobl from Delhi to Father Joseph Ritter, S.J., Confessor to the Queen of Portugal. Stöcklein, *Weltbott*, No. 649. The original is said to have been in Latin.

1750. *October* 22: From Father Tieffenthaler from Goa to Father Joseph Ritter, S.J., Confessor to the Queen of Portugal. Stöcklein, *Weltbott*, No. 651.

1751. *September* 19: From Father Strobl from Narwar to Father Joseph Ritter, S.J., Confessor to the Queen of Portugal. Stöcklein's *Weltbott*, No. 650.

1759. *May* 17: From Father Tieffenthaler to Anquetil Duperron: Bernoulli, *Description de l'Inde*, 1786, II, p. 419; *Beschreibung*, II, p. 128.

1781. *November* 29: From Father Tieffenthaler from Agra to Father Angelino in the same station. Forms an enclosure to a letter dated Bombay April 12, 1782, from Friar Clemente, Discalced Carmelite, Administrator and Vicar-General of the Great Mogul, to the Cardinal-Prefect of the Propaganda. (*Archivium Propagandae, Indie Orientali e Cina dal* 1782 *al* 1784. *Scritture riferite nei Congressi*, Vol. No. 37.) MS. copy with Father Hosten.

(B)

LIST OF LETTERS AND REPORTS RELATING TO THE BENGAL MISSION

1677–1685.

1678. *August* 2: From Father Anthony Magalhaens. From Agra to the Provincial at Goa. In the Marsden MSS., British Museum,

Addl. 9855, fol. 99–101. Forms an enclosure to the Annual Letter from Mogor 1670–1678: see below. A translation was published by Hosten in the *Catholic Herald of India*, September 12, 1917.

1678. *October* 7: From the Provincial of the Jesuits at Goa to the Provincial of the Augustinians. In the Marsden MSS., British Museum, Addl. 9855, fol. 127.

1678. *December* 27: From Father Freyre from Goa to the General of the Society. *Carta Annua da Missão do Imperio do Grão Mogol*, 1670–1678. In the Marsden MSS., British Museum, Addl. 9855, fol. 83–101. A translation of fol. 96–101 was published by Hosten in the *Catholic Herald of India*, September 12, 1917. See also entry above under August 2, 1678.

1679. *August* 29: From Father Santucci from Patna to the Provincial at Goa. In the Marsden MSS., British Museum, Addl. 9855, fol. 129.

1680. *April* 29: From Father de Queyros, Provincial at Goa. Instructions for the missionaries in Nepal, Patna and Bengala. In the Marsden MSS., British Museum, Addl. 9855, fol. 130–1.

1680. *November* 26: From Father Santucci from Hūglī to the Provincial at Goa. In the Marsden MSS., British Museum, Addl. 9855, fol. 132–4.

1683. *June* 21: From Father Santucci from Noluacot to the Provincial at Goa. In the Marsden MSS., British Museum, Addl. 9855, fol. 143–4.

1683. *January* 3: From Father Santucci from Noluacot to the Provincial at Goa. Forms an enclosure to the letter of January 15, 1685, from the Viceroy at Goa to the King of Portugal. *Livro das Monções*, No. 49, fol. 147: reprinted in *O Chronista de Tissuary*, Nova Goa, Vol. I, 1866, pp. 316–319, and Vol. II, 1867, pp. 8–13: and translated by Hosten in the *Catholic Herald of India*, 1917, pp. 752–844.

1683. *December* 17: From Father Ignatios Gomez from Busna to the Provincial at Goa. In the Marsden MSS., British Museum, Addl. 9855, fol. 141.

1683. *December* 18: From Father Manoel Sarayva from Basna to the Provincial at Goa. In the Marsden MSS., British Museum, Addl. 9855, fol. 139.

1684. *January* 26: From Father Santucci from Patna to the Provincial at Goa. In the Marsden MSS., British Museum, Addl. 9855, fol. 149.

1684. *August* 20: From Father Santucci from Hūglī to the Provincial at Goa. There are two copies in the Marsden MSS., British Museum, Addl. 9855, fol. 160 and 164.

1684. *December* 20: From Father Santucci from Hūglī to the Provincial at Goa. In the Marsden MSS., British Museum, Addl. 9855, fol. 169.

(C)

LIST OF LETTERS AND REPORTS RELATING TO THE TSAPARANG MISSION

1624. *May* 16: From Father Andrade. From a spot five days' journey from Srīnagar on the way to Badrinath. Published in Italian—*Lettere Annue d'Etiopia*, etc., Rome, 1627, pp. 342–343; and in French in *Histoire de ce qui s'est passé en Ethiopie*, etc., Paris, 1628, pp. 449–452. Translated by Hosten in *The Examiner*, Bombay, April 6, 1912.

1624. *November* 8: From Father Andrade to the Provincial at Goa, from Agra. Published in Lisbon in 1626 as *Novo Descobrimento do Gram Cathayo, ou reinos de Tibet*, and translated into several languages (see Esteves Pereira, *O Descobrimento do Tibet*, Coimbra, 1921, pp. 39–40). Reprinted with some modifications in Franco, *Imagem . . . Lisboa*, Coimbra, 1717, pp. 376–399, and a full translation is given in Nieremberg, *Varones Illustres*, Madrid, 1643, I, pp. 412–426. Republished in 1921 by Esteves Pereira, op. cit., pp. 45–74. A manuscript copy of this letter is extant in the Library of Ajuda.

1625. *September* 10: From Father Andrade to the Provincial at Goa. From Tsaparang. Forwarded to Europe with the Annual Letter from Goa, dated February 20, 1616. Manoel de Veiga, *Relaçam geral do estado da Christiandade da Ethiopia*, etc., Lisbon, 1628, pp. 105–107; Franco, *Imagem . . . Lisboa*, Coimbra, 1717, pp. 400–402; Esteves Pereira, *O Descobrimento do Tibet*, Coimbra, 1921, pp. 123–126. An extract is given in *J.A.S.B.*, XXI, 1925 (Hosten), pp. 51–52. See also Wessels, p. 92.

1626. *August* 15: From Father Andrade to the General of the Society, from Tsaparang. Partially reproduced in Manoel de Veiga's *Relaçam geral*, Lisbon, 1628, pp. 103–124; and Franco, *Imagem . . . Lisboa*, Coimbra, 1717, pp. 403–415. Fully given in Esteves Pereira, *O Descobrimento do Tibet*, Coimbra, 1921, pp. 75–120. Translations were published in Spanish—*Segunda Carta*, Segovia, 1628; in Italian, *Lettere Annue del Tibet del* 1626, Rome, 1628; and in French, *Histoire de ce qui s'est passé au Royaume du Tibet*, Paris, 1629. See also Wessels, p. 92, and *J.A.S.B.*, XXI, 1925 (Hosten), p. 53.

1626. *August* 16: From Father Godinho from Tsaparang. Translations in French were published in *Advis certain d'une plus ample descouverte du Royaume de Catai*, Paris (and with some modifications of title, Bordeaux), 1628; and in *Extrait des lettres . . . contenant ce qui s'est passé . . . au Royaume de Tibet . . .*;

Pont-à-Mousson, 1628, pp. 232–234. The *Advis certain* version was reprinted with an English translation and notes by Hosten in *J.A.S.B.*, XXI, 1925, pp. 62–73.

1627. *August* 29: From Fathers Andrade, Oliveira and Alano dos Anjos from Tibet to the Provincial at Goa. MS. in the possession of the Society. Mentioned in *J.A.S.B.*, XXI, 1925 (Hosten), p. 53. Published in Spanish (copy in British Museum) without date or provenance, probably in 1629, but apparently not in its entirety. The Spanish copy was reprinted with an English translation and considerable quotations from the original Portuguese MS. in *J.A.S.B.*, XXI, 1925 (Hosten), pp. 75–81.

1627. *September* 2: From Father Andrade, from Tibet to the General of the Society. MS. in the possession of the Society. Mentioned in *J.A.S.B.*, XXI, 1925 (Hosten), p. 53, and Wessels, p. 92.

1631. *December* 20: From Father Andrade from Goa to the General of the Society, enclosing three letters:

(1) *November* 10, 1627, from Alano dos Anjos from Tibet to the Provincial at Goa.

(2) *November* 12, 1627, from Antonio Pereira from Tibet to the same.

(3) *November* 16, 1627, from Oliveira from Tsaparang to the same.

The MSS. of these letters are in the possession of the Society. Mentioned in *J.A.S.B.*, XXI, 1925 (Hosten), pp. 54–55.

1632. Report by Father Azevedo, probably in 1632, to Father Antony Freyre, Procurator of Indian Missions in Portugal. The second part of the Report, relating to Azevedo's journey in Tibet, is reprinted in Wessels, op. cit., pp. 282–313. A copy of the entire MS. is with Father Hosten.

1633. *February* 4: From Father Andrade from Goa. The first part deals with the Tibet Mission. MS. in the possession of the Society. Mentioned by Wessels, p. 92.

1635. *August* 30: From Father Coresma from Tsaparang to the Provincial at Goa, also signed by Correa and Marques. MS. in possession of the Society. Mentioned by Wessels, p. 92. Two letters of the same date.

1635. *December* 14: From Father Coresma from Agra to the Provincial at Goa. A report on the Tsaparang Mission, mentioned by Hosten in *J.A.S.B.*, XXI, 1925, p. 58, and by Wessels, p. 93. MS. in the possession of the Society.

1636. From Father Mendez, undated, to the General of the Society.

MS. in the possession of the Society. Mentioned in *J.A.S.B.*, XXI, 1925 (Hosten), p. 58, and Wessels, p. 92.

Wessels, pp. 81–82 and p. 93, also refers to twelve letters of Father de Castro, dating from 1631 to 1642, and written from Bengal, Agra and Lahore, which contain allusions to the Tibet Mission. These are included in the general list of letters on the Mogor Mission, as they do not deal primarily with Tsaparang.

II

THE CHIEF CONTRIBUTIONS BY FATHER H. HOSTEN, S.J., TO THE HISTORY OF THE JESUITS AT THE MOGUL COURT

The Catholic Herald of India (Calcutta).

1906. Foundation of the Jesuit Mission at Patna (1620), by L. Besse, S.J., notes by H. Hosten, pp. 804–805.

1907. Father Henry Roth, S.J., 1650–1651, translated from the German, by J. Bosk, S.J., introduction, notes and conclusion by H. Hosten, pp. 171–172.

1910. The List of Jesuit Missionaries in Mogor, July 13 ; November 2 (p. 698).

1911. On Father Monserrate's *Mongolicae Legationis Commentarius*, December 10, pp. 815–816.

1913. Mīrzā Zū'lqarnain, the founder of the Agra College, pp. 478–479 (also in *Statesman*, Calcutta, of July 6, 1913).

1914. *Western Art at the Mogul Court*, pp. 670–672 ; part of this is reproduced in *J.U.P.H.S.*, Vol. III, 1922, Part I, pp. 110–114.

1916. Summary of a paper by Fr. Felix, O.M.C., on Moghul Farmāns, Parwānas and Sanads, August 30, and September 6, 13, 1916, pp. 584–585.

1916. Akbar's Christian wife ; August 23, September 27 (p. 634).

1917. Catholic Antiquities in North India, according to Rev. Fr. J. Treffenthaler, S.J., January 17, 31 ; March 7.

1918. The Fall of Hūglī : at various places between pp. 91 and 671 of 1918.

1918. The Pathans in 1581 : a Query, p. 888.

1920. Father Antony Monserrate's Commentary on the Mongol Mission to Akbar's Court. Translated from the Latin. At numerous places between p. 636 of 1920 and p. 920 of 1921.

1921. Persian Lives of the Apostles : from Akbar's Agra Library, June 22, pp. 479–481.

1924. Father Matthew Ricci, S.J., of Pekin, November 19, pp. 737–738.

The Examiner (Bombay).

1912. Jesuit Annual Letters from Goa and Cochin (1618–1624). At various places between p. 47 and p. 139, February 3 to April 6.

1916. Akbar's Christian wife, p. 372.

1917. Father Henry Uwens *alias* Henry Busi, S.J., a missionary in Mogor (1648–1667), October 13 and 20, pp. 407–409 and 418–420.

1917. The Spiritual Letters of Father Antonio Ceschi di Santa Croce, . . . a Jesuit missionary in the Moghul Mission (1647–1656). On various dates between July 7 and September 8, pp. 267–358.

1918. René Madec, or a French Catholic Nawab in the N.W. Provinces (b. 1736, d. 1784); April 20, pp. 158–160.

1918. Father Francis Xavier Wendel, S.J., the last Jesuit in Mogor (d. 1803), May 4, pp. 178–179.

1918. Two Letters of Fr. Ippolito Desideri, S.J. a missionary in Tibet (1715–1721); August 24; October 5, 12; December 14, pp. 338–340, 399–400, 409–410, 498–500.

1918. The Rishi and Jerome Xavier, November 9, p. 446.

1919. The Jesuit Post from Mogor for 1615, gone to England, August 9–23, pp. 318–320, 329–330 and 338–340.

1919. Letter of Fr. N. Pimenta, S.J., on Mogor (December 1, 1600), translated from the Latin, October 11, pp. 407–409.

1919. Fr. Fernão Guerreiro's Annual *Relation* of 1602–1603 on the Mogor Mission, November 22, 29, pp. 469–470, 478–480.

1920. The First Jesuit Mission to Akbar's Court (1579–1583) according to Father de Souza, S.J. On various dates between March 13 and July 3, between pp. 107 and 270.

1922. Was George Strachan, the Oriental traveller, a Jesuit? On April 1, 8 and 15, between pp. 128 and 149.

The Journal of the Asiatic Society of Bengal.

1910. The Marsden MSS. in the British Museum, VI, pp. 437–461.

1910. List of Jesuit missionaries in Mogor, VI, pp. 527–542.

1911. A list of Portuguese Jesuit missionaries in Bengal and Burma (1576–1742), VII, pp. 15–23. (With Father Besse, S.J.)

1911. Father A. Monserrate's *Mongolicae Legationis Commentarius*, VII, pp. cxxxvi-cxli. (Same as in *Catholic Herald of India*, December 10, 1911.)

1912. Father A. Monserrate's Account of Akbar (November 26, 1582), VIII, pp. 185–221.

1914. Father Jerome Xavier's *Lives of the Apostles*, X, pp. 65–84.

1915. Notes on Father Monserrate's *Mongolicae Legationis Commentarius*, by H. Beveridge; edited and annotated by H. Hosten, XI, pp. 187–204.

1922. Father A. Montserrate, S.J., and Captain F. Wilford, XVIII, pp. 371–374.

1925. A letter from Father A. de Andrade, S.J. (Tibet, August 25, 1627), XXI, pp. 75–93.

1925. A letter of Father Francisco Godinho, S.J., from Western Tibet (Tsaparang, August 16, 1626), XXI, pp. 49–73.

1927. Father N. Pimenta's Annual Letter on Mogor (Goa, December 21, 1599), XXIII, pp. 57–65).

1927. Father N. Pimenta, S.J., on Mogor (Goa, December 1, 1600), XXIII, pp. 67–82.

1927. Father N. Pimenta's Annual of Margão, December 1, 1601, XXIII, pp. 83–107.

1927. Eulogy of Father Jerome Xavier, S.J., a missionary in Mogor, XXIII, pp. 108–130.

1927. Some letters of Father Jerome Xavier, S.J., to his family (1593–1612), XXIII, pp. 131–136.

1927. Some notes on Brother Bento de Goes, S.J. (1583–1607), XXIII, pp. 137–140.

1927. Three letters of Father Joseph de Castro, S.J., and the Last Year of Jahāngīr, XXIII, pp. 141–166.

Memoirs of the Asiatic Society of Bengal.

1914. Jesuit Letters and Allied Papers on Mogor, Tibet, Bengal and Burma. *Mongolicae Legationis Commentarius, or First Jesuit Mission to Akbar*, by Father Antony Monserrate, S.J. (Latin Text), III, No. 9, pp. 513–704.

1916. Jesuit Letters and Allied Papers on Mogor, Tibet, Bengal and Burma. Mīrzā Zū'lqarnain, a Christian Grandee of three Great Moghuls, with notes on Akbar's Christian wife and the Indian Bourbons, V, No. 4, pp. 115–194.

Bengal, Past and Present (Calcutta).

1915–1916. Padre Maestro Fray Seb. Manrique in Bengal (1628—September 11, 1629), 1916, Vol. XII, pp. 272–315; 1916, Vol. XIII, pp. 1–43.

1925. Jesuit letters from Bengal, Arakan and Burma (1599–1660). A new version of the Annual Letter from Goa (December 1, 1600), dated September 8, 1602, Vol. XXX, No. 59, pp. 52–76.

1927. Akbar's Queen Mary, Vol. XXXIV, No. 68, pp. 97–105.

Journal of the Punjab Historical Society.

1911. Travels of Fra Sebastian Manrique in the Punjab. (Assistance given by Hosten), I, pp. 83–106 and 151–166.
1918. The family of Lady Juliana Diaz da Costa, VII, pp. 39–49.
1918. The Annual *Relation* of Father Fernão Guerreiro, S.J., for 1607–1608, VII, pp. 50–73.

Journal of the United Provinces Historical Society.

1918. Fra Sebastian Manrique's description of Agra (December 24, 1640—January 1641), I, Part II, pp. 109–136.
1919. The Armenian Inscription of the Central Jail Compound, Agra, II, Part I, pp. 40–50.
1919. Armenian Inscription from the Native Chapel, Catholic Cathedral Compound of Agra, II, Part I, pp. 51–55. (With Mesrovb J. Seth.)
1922. European Art at the Mogul Court, III, Part I, pp. 110–184.

Journal of Indian History.

1922. Jesuit Annual Letter from Mogor (March 1648–August 1649), I, pp. 226–248. (With Father L. De Vos.)

Bulletin of the School of Oriental Studies

1923. The Marsden MSS. and Indian Mission Bibliography, III, pp. 129–150.

The Englishman (Calcutta).

1926. Akbar's Christian wife, August 19 and September 10.

The Statesman (Calcutta).

1916. Akbar's Christian wife, September 16 and November 14.

Separately Published.

1907. Jesuit Missionaries in Northern India and Inscriptions on their Tombs, Agra (1580–1803). Catholic Orphan Press, Calcutta.
1927. Travels of Fra Sebastien Manrique, 1629–1643 (Hakluyt Soc.). By Col. C. Eckford Luard, C.I.E., assisted by Father H. Hosten, S.J. 2 Vols.

III

CHRONOLOGY
OF THE CHIEF EVENTS CONNECTED WITH THE JESUIT MISSION IN MOGOR

1510. Establishment of the Portuguese at Goa.
1526. Arrival of the Moguls in India.
1539. Establishment of the Society of Jesus in Europe.

1556. *Akbar.*
1573. Akbar's first meeting with the Portuguese.
1578. Arrival of Julian Pereira at Akbar's Court.
1579. November 17. The first Mission under Father Aquaviva, S.J., leaves Goa.
1580. February 27 or 28. The Mission reaches Fatehpur Sīkrī.
1581. February 8. Akbar starts on his expedition to Kābul: taking Father Monserrate, S.J., with him.
1581. December 1. Akbar returns to Fatehpur Sīkrī.
1582. April. An embassy from Akbar, accompanied by Father Monserrate, S.J., starts for Goa.
1583. February. Father Aquaviva leaves Fatehpur.
1583. July 27. Father Aquaviva martyred near Goa.
1590. Akbar invites a further Mission.
1591. Second Mission reaches Lahore, and returns shortly afterwards to Portuguese India.
1594. December 3. The Third Mission under Father Jerome Xavier, S.J., starts from Goa.
1595. May 5. The Mission reaches Lahore.
1597. May 15–November 13. Father Xavier and Brother Goes accompany Akbar to Kashmīr.
1598. Towards the end of this year Father Xavier goes with Akbar to Agra.
1599. July. Father Xavier accompanies Akbar to the Deccan.
1600. March 5. Death of Father Monserrate near Goa.

1601. May. Father Xavier returns with Akbar to Agra.
1602. Completion of Father Xavier's Persian *Life of Christ.*
1603. February 24. Brother Goes leaves Lahore for Cathay.
1605. October 17. Death of Akbar.

1605. *Jahāngīr.*
1606. May 9. Jahāngīr enters Lahore after crushing the revolt of Prince Khusrū.
1607. April 11. Death of Brother Goes at Su-cheu in China.
1607. Father Pinheiro leaves Lahore for Goa.
1608. March. Jahāngīr returns to Agra.
1609. April. Arrival of William Hawkins at Agra.
1609. Completion of Father Xavier's Persian work, *The Truth-showing Mirror.*
1610. September 5. Baptism of the sons of Prince Dāniāl at Agra.
1610. Baptism of Muqarrib Khān at Goa.
1613. Autumn. Jahāngīr leaves Agra for the South.
1614. Hostilities between the Moguls and the Portuguese. Father Xavier leaves Mogor.
1615. September. Sir Thomas Roe arrives in India.
1617. June 17. Death of Father Xavier at Goa.
1619. April. Jahāngīr returns to Agra.
1621. Building of the 'College' at Agra.
1624. March 30. Father Andrade leaves Agra on his journey to Tsaparang.
1625. August 25. Mission established at Tsaparang.
1627. October 28. Death of Jahāngīr.

1627. *Shāh Jahān.*
1631. October 25. Father Azevedo reaches Leh.
1632. June 26–September 24. Siege and capture of Hūglī by the Moguls.
1633. Sufferings of the Christians in Agra and elsewhere.
1634. March 9. Death of Father Andrade in Goa.
1640. Conclusion of the Mission in Tsaparang.
1640. December. Arrival of Fra Manrique at Agra.
1650. A Jesuit Father posted to Delhi.
1651. February 1. Arrival of Dom Mattheus at Agra.
1656. (About). Death of Mīrzā Zū'lqarnain.
(1656. Or later). End of the Mission at Srīnagar in Garhwāl.

APPENDIX III

1658. *Aurangzeb* assumes the Government.
1659. Prince Dārā Shikoh put to death.
1667. Publication of Sanskrit characters in Europe by Father Roth, S.J., of Agra.
1677–1685. Attempted Jesuit Mission in Eastern Bengal.

1707. *Bahādur Shāh.* (Shāh 'Ālam).
1711. Reception of the Dutch Embassy at Lahore by Donna Juliana.

1712. *Jahāndār Shāh.*

1713. *Farrukh-siyar.*
1714. September 24. Father Desideri, S.J., leaves Delhi for Tibet.
1716. March 18. Father Desideri's arrival at Lhāsa.

1719. *Muhammad Shāh.*
1721. April 28. Father Desideri leaves Lhāsa.
1734. Death of Donna Juliana.
1739. Massacre at Delhi by Nādir Shāh.
1740. Fathers Strobl and Gabelsperger, S.J., reach Jaipur.

1748. *Ahmad Shāh.*

1754. *'Ālamgīr II.*
1756. Ahmad Shāh Abdālī takes Delhi.

1759. *Shāh 'Ālam.*
1759. The Jesuits are banished from Portuguese territory.
1765. The Mission at Narwar abandoned by the Jesuits.
1773. The Pope abolishes the Society of Jesus.
1705. Death of Father Tieffenthaler, ex-Jesuit, at Lucknow.
1803. Death of Father Wendel, ex-Jesuit, at Lucknow.

IV

OUTLINE OF THE GENEALOGY OF THE MOGUL KINGS OF INDIA

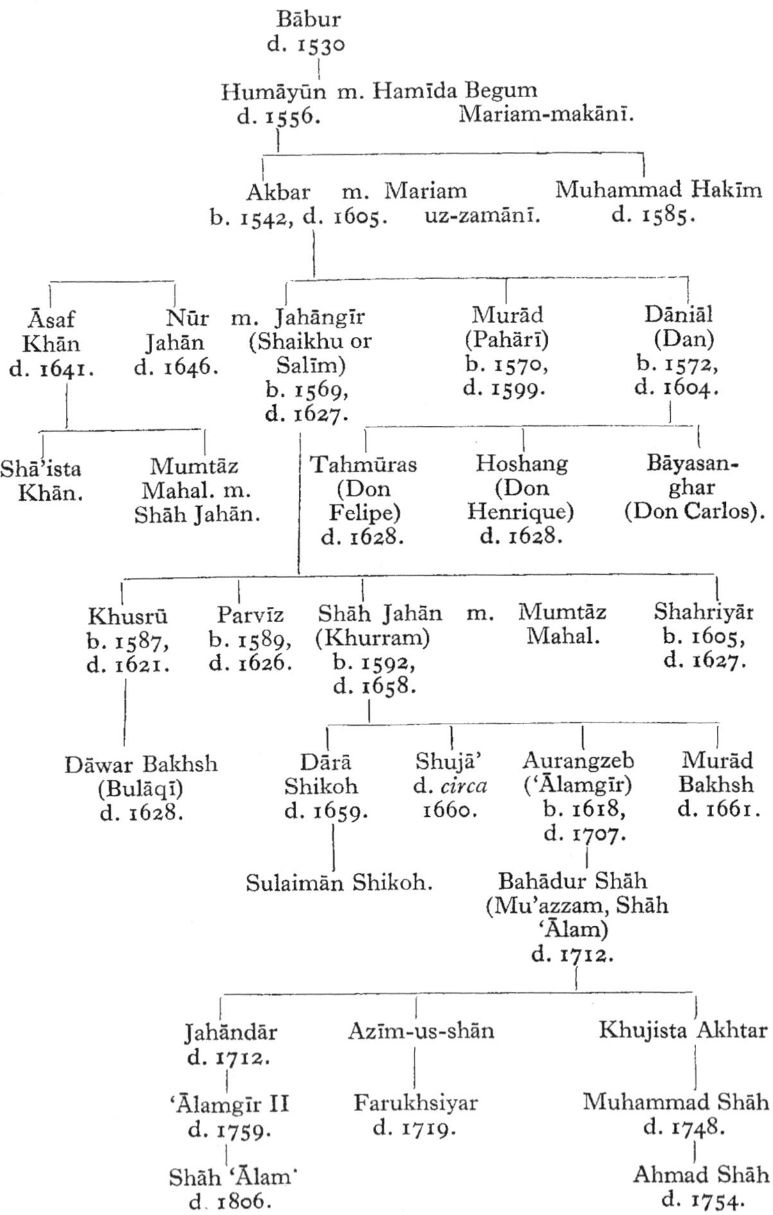

V

ABBREVIATIONS

Letters Received.	*Letters received by the East India Company from its servants in the East.* Edited by Sir W. Foster (London, 1896, etc.).
English Factories.	*The English Factories in India.* By Sir W. Foster (Oxford, 1906, etc.).
J.I.H.	*Journal of Indian History* (Diocesan Press, Vepery, Madras).
J.P.H.S.	*Journal of the Punjab Historical Society* (Lahore).
J.U.P.H.S.	*Journal of the United Provinces Historical Society* (Longmans, Green, Calcutta).
B.P. and P.	*Bengal Past and Present* (G. B. Das, Dharmtolla St., Calcutta).
J.R.A.S.	*Journal of the Royal Asiatic Society* (London).
J.Bo.R.A.S.	*Journal of the Bombay Branch of the Royal Asiatic Society* (Bombay).
J.A.S.B.	*Journal of the Asiatic Society of Bengal* (Calcutta).
Mem. A.S.B.	*Memoirs of the Asiatic Society of Bengal* (Calcutta).
Bib. Ind.	*Bibliotheca Indica* (Asiatic Society of Bengal, Calcutta).
Bulletin S.O.S.	*Bulletin of the School of Oriental Studies, London Institution* (London).
Ind. Ant.	*The Indian Antiquary* (Bombay).

INDEX

D

E

K

M

N

S

U

V

W

X

Y

Z